American Negro Slavery

American Negro Slavery

• A MODERN READER

SECOND EDITION

EDITED BY

ALLEN WEINSTEIN AND FRANK OTTO GATELL

NEW YORK

OXFORD UNIVERSITY PRESS

LONDON TORONTO 1973

To the memory of David Potter

Preface to the Second Edition

"America is catching hell," observed a speaker at Yale's 1968 conference on black studies in the university, "and that's why white folks are interested in black studies."[1] Whatever the merits of that statement as an explanation, a substantial amount of new research on the black experience, much of it dealing with slavery, *has* been published since this collection first appeared in 1968. Although Negro slavery has remained of interest largely to scholars, it did become a subject of more general concern to Americans several times in recent years. Perhaps the best known of these instances involved the controversy over William Styron's portrait of America's most important slave-rebel in *The Confessions of Nat Turner*.[2] Many blacks particularly were angered by Styron's attempt to characterize this major Negro folk hero as a brooding and sexually disturbed personality. For a long period after the book's publication in the mid-1960's, arguments over its literary and historical merits filled the popular press and scholarly journals.[3] Yet even his severest critics acknowledge that Styron's novel stimulated keen public interest in the entire question of Negro slavery. The critics complained, however, that the average American's view of slavery's impact on Negro character was likely to draw heavily in future upon Styron's best seller.

The recent development of Afro-American Studies programs in universities, colleges, and high schools throughout the United States has contributed to the revival of scholarly interest in slavery. Only a handful of such programs existed at the time this collection was first published in 1968. Scholars today can hardly complain, as we did in the introduction to that edition (which we have reprinted substantially unchanged), about the lack of adequate teaching or research materials on the black experience. During the past half-decade, monographs and primary sources that help provide a more balanced picture of the Afro-American past have been published generally as soon as they have become available or were rediscovered. This has allowed scholars to revise earlier anti-Negro biases in the writing of American history in favor of what C. Vann Woodward has termed a more fair-minded "Clio With Soul."[4] The black American's own written record of oppression and survival, those narratives by ex-slaves that Woodward called the "hidden sources of Negro history," have now become easily accessible in reprint editions.[5] Moreover, a number of scholars—historians, anthropologists, and folklorists among them—have turned increasingly toward an imaginative use of oral and folk traditions to shed light on American slave society through *nonliterary, black* sources.[6]

It is still too early to tell what this revival of scholarly attention may produce in the way of important new insights into the patterns of American slavery. "It is remarkable," observed Orlando Patterson, himself a first-rank scholar of New World slavery, "that in spite of the many scholarly works produced on the period of slavery in the United States, no major attempt has yet been made at interpreting the nature of the social and cultural response of the Blacks to their enslavement."[7] Patterson's point remains essentially valid, but several new selections added to the current edition of this collection do attest to the increased historical attention to the slaves themselves.[8]

Renewed concern for other aspects of slavery has already begun to produce an impressive new body of insights. Debate among scholars studying North American bondage, for one thing, has shifted markedly away from its preoccupation during the 1960's with the "Elkins thesis" on slave "infantalization," a thesis discussed extensively in our 1968 Introduction and in the collection itself. Elkins's central theories have been attacked, often persuasively, by a variety of critics, notably on two questions of special interest to historians of the ante-bellum South: first, how reasonable is his analogy between the experience of Southern slavery and that of the concentration camps, and second, how credible is his (and Frank Tannenbaum's) key distinction between the supposedly quite different impact of North American and Latin American slavery upon Negro personality? The present collection includes a selection from Elkins's work and also adds several important essays attacking his major premises.[9]

Elkins himself has pointed to "the phenomenon of ideology" as a topic of renewed interest among recent scholars of American slavery.[10] Both Eugene D. Genovese and George M. Frederickson have contributed impressively to an understanding of the world view shared by slaveholders and their apologists in the ante-bellum South.[11] At the same time, scholars such as Eric Foner and Aileen Kraditor have performed a similar function for the belief patterns of antislavery Republicans and abolitionists.[12] The problem of ideology also received masterful treatment in Winthrop D. Jordan's *White Over Black*, which traced in sobering detail the unflagging sense of hostility among successive generations of English-speaking whites toward Negroes, a racial animus brought from England to the early settlements and nurtured throughout the colonial and revolutionary eras.[13] Each of the above-mentioned works, stressing in its own manner the persistence of racist ideology in the national past from colonization to Civil War, has sharpened our awareness of the way such beliefs helped shape the response toward North American slaves of planters and nonplanters, Northerners and Southerners, alike.

Several of the new essays in the second edition deal with the social history of black slaves in the ante-bellum South. These articles, along with other recent books like Gerald W. Mullin's *Flight and Rebellion: Slave Resistance in Eighteenth-Century Virginia*, build on earlier contributions by scholars such as Ulrich B. Phillips and Kenneth M. Stampp in attempting the difficult task of recreating the inner world of American bondsmen.[14] Additional studies on "the social and cultural response of the Blacks to their enslavement" will undoubtedly appear in the near future, weaving from both oral and written primary sources a much fuller tapestry than we now possess of Negro family, religious, and cultural life under Southern slavery.

Work on the comparative analysis of slave systems also continues, following in the wake of such important and provocative recent books as Carl N. Degler's *Neither Black Nor White*, Herbert S. Klein's *Slavery in the Americas*, and Eugene D. Genovese's *The World the Slaveholders Made*.[15] Genovese and other Marxist scholars have shown the importance, in this connection, of treating different New World slaveholding societies—including our own—as a series of colonial cultures located "within the process of world-wide capitalist development itself."[16] The comparative study of New World master classes and the problem of ante-bellum Southern bondage's economic viability are questions that will continue to attract considerable attention from historians.[17]

The second edition of *American Negro Slavery* incorporates major examples of new research in all of the preceding areas. Linking these new selections with those retained from the first edition, we have tried to provide a balanced, one-volume coverage of North American slavery's 240 year history. Half the readings have been included for the first time in the second edition. Furthermore, certain subjects, notably the socio-cultural history of Afro-Americans under slavery and the ideology of slaveholders, receive much fuller treatment in the present edition, because of the greater availability of first-rate research in these areas. Beyond these specific changes, however, we have tried to reinforce the collection's over-all theme. "Slavery and the position of the Negro," the late, talented young historian, Robert Starobin, wrote, "seemed to determine important political decisions and party formations from the framing of the Constitution until the Civil War [while] racism was characteristic of American society from its early beginnings. . . . In short, the Negro is becoming recognized as a key to American history and one of its distinctive themes."[18] Slavery's central importance to the national experience from Jamestown to Appomatox (and beyond) remains the essential thread linking together the two dozen selections that follow.

NOTES

1. Armstead L. Robinson *et al.*, ed., *Black Studies in the University* (New Haven, 1969), p. 70.

2. William Styron, *The Confessions of Nat Turner* (New York, 1966).

3. See, for example, John Henrik Clarke, *William Styron's Nat Turner: Ten Black Writers Respond* (Boston, 1968); Eugene D. Genovese, "The Nat Turner Case," *New York Review of Books*, XI (September 12, 1968), pp. 34-37; Herbert Aptheker and William Styron, "Truth and Nat Turner: An Exchange," *The Nation*, CCVI (April 22, 1968), pp. 543-47; John B. Duff and Peter M. Mitchell, eds., *The Nat Turner Rebellion: The Historical Event and the Modern Controversy* (New York, 1971); and Henry Irving Tragle, ed., *The Southampton Slave Revolt of 1831* (Amherst, Mass., 1971). See especially Seymour L. Gross and Eileen Bender, "History, Politics and Literature: The Myth of Nat Turner," *American Quarterly*, XXIII (October 1971), pp. 487-518.

4. C. Vann Woodward, "Clio With Soul," *Journal of American History*, LVI (June 1969), pp. 5-20.

5. See, for example, William Loren Katz, gen. ed., *The American Negro: His History and Literature* (New York, 1969), 141 volumes reprinted; George P. Rawick, ed., *The American Slave, A Composite Autobiography* (Westport, Conn., 1972), 18 volumes of reprinted W. P. A. Federal Writers' Project slave narratives and interviews with ex-slaves.

6. Some of the more interesting recent contributions in this vein include Sterling Stuckey, "Through the Prism of Folklore: The Black Ethos in Slavery," *Massachusetts Review*, IX (Summer 1968), pp. 417-37; Lawrence W. Levine, "Slave Songs and Slave Consciousness: An Exploration in Neglected Sources," from Tamara K. Hareven, ed., *Anonymous Americans: Explorations in Nineteenth-Century Social History* (Englewood Cliffs, N. J., 1971), pp. 99-130; Vincent Harding, "Religion and Resistance Among Antebellum Negroes, 1800–1860," from August Meier and Elliott Rudwick, eds., *The Making of*

Black America, I (New York, 1969), pp. 179-97; Jan Vansina, "The Use of Ethnographic Data as Sources for History," from T. O. Ranger, ed., *Emerging Themes of African History* (Boston, 1968); and George P. Rawick, *From Sundown to Sunup: The Making of the Black Community* (Westport, Conn., 1972).

7. Orlando Patterson, "Rethinking Black History," *Harvard Educational Review*, 41 (August 1971), pp. 297-315.

8. See particularly the articles in "Part II: The Slave" by George M. Frederickson and Christopher Lasch, Sterling Stuckey, Lawrence L. Levine, and Eugene D. Genovese. John W. Blassingame's book, *The Slave Community*, a major study of American bondage from the slave's perspective, appeared after this preface was written just as the present collection went to press. Blassingame's admirable volume represents the most ambitious and successful scholarly work thus far which is addressed to Orlando Patterson's call for studies of "the social and political response of the Blacks to their enslavement" in the United States. John W. Blassingame, *The Slave Community: Plantation Life in the Ante-Bellum South* (New York, 1972).

9. See the articles mentioned in footnote 8 and Carl N. Degler's article in "Part IV: The System." A systematic compendium of essays generally critical of Elkins's work—and Elkins's rebuttal to these—has been collected by Ann J. Lane under the title *The Debate Over Slavery: Stanley Elkins and His Critics* (Urbana, Ill., 1971). See also Kenneth M. Stampp's rigorous assault on Elkins's ideas in his recent article, "Rebels and Sambos: The Search for the Negro's Personality in Slavery," *Journal of Southern History*, XXXVII (August 1971), pp. 367-92.

10. Lane, ed., *The Debate Over Slavery*, p. 328.

11. Eugene D. Genovese, *The World the Slaveholders Made* (New York, 1969); George M. Frederickson, *The Black Image in the White Mind* (New York, 1971).

12. Eric Foner, *Free Soil, Free Labor, Free Men: The Ideology of the Republican Party before the Civil War* (New York, 1970); Aileen S. Kraditor, *Means And Ends in American Abolitionism* (New York, 1967).

13. Winthrop D. Jordan, *White Over Black: American Attitudes Toward the Negro, 1550–1812* (Chapel Hill, 1968).

14. Gerald W. Mullin, *Flight and Rebellion: Slave Resistance in Eighteenth-Century Virginia* (New York, 1972).

15. Genovese, *op. cit.*; Carl N. Degler, *Neither Black Nor White: Slavery and Race Relations in Brazil and the United States* (New York, 1971); Herbert S. Klein, *Slavery in the Americas, A Comparative Study of Cuba and Virginia* (Chicago, 1967).

16. Genovese, *op. cit.*, p. 95.

17. *Ibid.* See also Robert W. Fogel and Stanley L. Engerman, eds., *The Reinterpretation of American Economic History* (New York, 1971), Part VII, "Slavery and The Civil War," pp. 310-79.

18. Robert S. Starobin, "The Negro: A Central Theme in American History," *Journal of Contemporary History* (April 1969), pp. 37-53.

Table of Contents

American Negro Slavery

Introduction

Historians writing on American Negro slavery have usually begun with some general moral judgment of the institution. Over the past century, slavery in the United States has found its share of apologists and detractors among scholars. Just as James Ford Rhodes and other late nineteenth-century writers indicted the system as evil and intrinsically corrupt, a number of Progressive era historians, most notably Ulrich B. Phillips, viewed the institution instead through the eyes of white Southerners and created the image of a benign and patriarchal system of bondage. Phillip's sympathetic portrait of slavery in the ante-bellum South dominated historical response to the subject up to World War II, partly because it embodied prevailing American beliefs in Negro inferiority and in the black man's subordinate place within the society.[1] The work of anthropologists like Franz Boas earlier in the century had undermined the intellectual respectability of racist ideas among social scientists but had failed to affect significantly the ordinary white American's stereotypes of the Negro—those alternately cheerful and buffonish Mammies and Sambos. Public rejection of overt racism in the United States, as Eugene D. Genovese noted, "probably had more to do with [Adolph Hitler] than Franz Boas." Some Americans, in other words, finally recognized the discomfiting analogy between their own assumptions about the Negro and the Nazi's attitudes toward the Jews.

Confronted with the genocidal handiwork of German racists, American scholars began reassessing their own perspectives on slavery. Even before the end of World War II, some historians, Herbert Aptheker for one, had challenged sharply the mythology of the ante-bellum South, but a critical appraisal of Phillip's work in 1944 by Richard Hofstadter served as a starting point in the re-examination of slavery among liberal scholars.[2] "Let the study of the Old South be undertaken by other scholars," Hofstadter wrote, "who have absorbed the viewpoint of modern cultural anthropology, who have a feeling for social psychology. . .who will concentrate upon the neglected rural (i.e. non-slaveholding) elements that formed the great majority of the

Southern population, who will not rule out the testimony of more critical observers, and who will realize that any history of slavery must be written in large measure from the standpoint of the slave. . . ." [8] Subsequent research on American slavery has reflected these concerns.

The process of reassessment remains in its earliest stage, and historians still disagree about the nature of the system itself. Passionate neo-abolitionist scholars like Kenneth B. Stampp and Herbert Aptheker have attempted to refute, point by point, the milder picture of plantation bondage, drawn earlier by Phillips, of submissive, carefree slaves who endured their servitude with little protest. Phillips's use of evidence as well as his racism have undergone critical scrutiny by Hofstadter, Stampp, and other post-World War II commentators. Stanley Elkins has pointed out, however, that Stampp's own synthesis of Southern slavery, *The Peculiar Institution*, remained bound by the older moral argument with historians like Phillips over the question of whether slavery was good or evil, whether it had been harsh or gentle for those black men who lived under it. "The coercions of a century-old debate remain irresistible," Elkins noted. Stampp "has joined the debate; he may even have won it, but it is still very much the same debate. In spite of its outcome, the strategy of *The Peculiar Institution* was still dictated by Ulrich Phillips." [4] A similar observation can be made of Eugene D. Genovese's recent efforts to restore both Ulrich B. Phillips's declining reputation among historians and Phillips's concept of a patriarchal slave society. No more fervent and thoughtful historical defense of ante-bellum Southern society has appeared in the past two decades than Genovese's. This Northern Marxist views slavery as "a social system within which whites and blacks lived in harmony as well as antagonism with little evidence of massive organized Negro opposition to the regime. . . ." [5] Where Stampp, along with other liberal and radical historians, found most bondsmen hating both their masters and slavery itself, Genovese—like Phillips—has discerned instead a smoothly functioning, semifeudal social order, distinct in many essentials from the rest of American society during the ante-bellum period. On this disputed problem of slavery as a social system, most historians have taken their stand somewhere between the Aptheker-Stampp and Phillips-Genovese models of "the peculiar institution."

Profound disagreements among historians also remain on the question of how the slaves behaved in bondage. Only a few scholars, however, have attempted to analyze carefully the impact of American slavery upon Negro personality, the most controversial work in this area being Stanley M. Elkins's *Slavery, A Problem in American Institutional and Intellectual Life*, probably the most influential study of slavery in the United States to be published since World War II.[6] Elkins's book remains, a decade after its publication, the baseline for present historical work in the field, and students should be familiar with the entire volume. The excerpts contained in this collection discuss some but not all of Elkins's most subtle and challenging concepts: his belief in the slave's acceptance of his own inferiority or "Sambo-ness" through the deliberate efforts of slaveholders to encourage Negro infantilism; the absence in the United States of an adequate institutional framework in the areas of law, religion, and political authority to protect the slave's status as a human being, especially when compared with the institutional buffers of Latin America's slave cultures; the vulnerability of Negro slaves in the English mainland colonies to total manipulation by the master caste because of the absence of institutional controls on the system of "unopposed capitalist" agriculture; finally, the author's controversial analogy suggesting that the master's absolute power over his bondsmen in the United States had destructive effects on slave personality comparable to the impact of Nazi concentration camps on their inmates. Many of these ideas are examined, criticized, or defended by other authors in this collection. Elkins's over-all impact on the modern study of American slavery remains singular. Applying concepts of social psychology and Frank Tannenbaum's comparative analysis of English and Latin American slave societies, he opened up lines of investigation into the study of master and slave personalities that few other recent historians have shown sufficient daring to exploit.

The comparative study of slave societies, unlike the question of slave personality, has become a popular and productive field of inquiry among recent scholars. In the first volume of his projected history of antislavery movements, *The Problem of Slavery in Western Culture*, David Brion Davis traced the evolution of beliefs and social patterns on the subject from antiquity to colonial North and South America in a careful comparative discussion of ideologies and institutions.[7] Davis and other writers have challenged the Tannenbaum-Elkins hypothesis on the basis of research into existing Spanish and Portuguese scholarship. Hopefully, other such studies will follow, which will allow for more confident assessment of the argument.

Certain older questions regarding slavery in the United States continue to receive fresh treatment from scholars. Controversy over slavery's profitability in the ante-bellum South has been "a historical perennial" among American writers. In this collection, Harold Woodman reviews the relevant literature on slavery as an economic institution; works such as Eugene D. Genovese's *The Political Economy of Slavery* and Alfred H. Conrad and J. H. Meyer's *The Economics of Slavery* are important recent contributions to more precise understanding of Southern economic development under slavery.[8] Race relations under the slave system have also attracted recent attention from writers such at Kenneth Stampp and Richard Wade. A selection from Wade's *Slavery in the Cities: The South, 1820–1860* traces the patterns of racial accommodation in the urban South.[9] Despite previous studies, the extent to which racial segregation existed in the ante-bellum South and the forms which it took remain important questions for future investigators. In time, a work similar to Leon Litwack's *North of Slavery: The Negro in the Free States, 1790–1860* may detail the complexities of social adjustment between the races in the slaveholding South.[10] Recent historians have also disputed the origins of American slavery, debating whether race prejudice, economic necessity, or some combination of these and other factors led to the enslavement of Negroes in the English mainland colonies. In this collection, David Brion Davis compares the factors which conditioned slavery's emergence in various parts of the Western Hemisphere during the era of colonization.

The discussion above suggests only some of the major questions dealing with American Negro slavery which have preoccupied scholars. Most of the readings in this book concern slavery in the South, even though the institution existed in every English mainland colony until after the American Revolution. The editors chose not to focus on the problem of slavery in the North, but not because it lacks either importance or a growing body of literature. On the contrary, recent works such as Arthur Zilversmit's *The First Emancipation: The Abolition of Negro Slavery in the North* and Edgar J. McManus's *A History of Negro Slavery in New York* reveal the continuing interest of scholars in the evolution of slavery north of the Mason-Dixon line.[11] Yet within a few decades after the Revolution, the North had abandoned the institution, leaving to the South alone the dilemma which slavery posed. For the next century and a half, the problem of white over black in America would be centered in the states of the Old South.

The question of race, which Ulrich B. Phillips called the "central theme of Southern history," re-emerged in the 1960's from its regional base to become again the central theme of our national experience. No collection of readings on American slavery can do more than suggest some of the historical background of present racial conflict, but the road from Samboism to Black Power began within the confines of ante-bellum Southern slavery. If many slaveholders viewed their Negro chattels as child-like, shiftless, and content, others were tormented by images of less accommodating bondsmen. South Carolinians during the Nullification Crisis of the 1830's knew, for example, as William W. Freehling has shown, that for every Sambo there might also exist a Spartacus. Freehling's recent study of South Carolinian society, *Prelude to Civil War: The Nullification Crisis in South Carolina, 1816–1836*, showed that fear of Negro revolts played a major role in causing the Southern shift from apologetic embarrassment for slavery to aggressive defense of it against antislavery advocates.[12] Although in the United States the incidence of slave uprisings remained remarkably low compared with Latin American and West Indian slave societies, Southerners believed in their possibility and prepared systematically to prevent their occurrence. As many Northerners, who for generations have had little concern for the black ghettoes in their midst, have now come to realize, those to whom evil is done, in W. H. Auden's phrase, do evil in return (or at least might be expected to).

Modern historical reassessment of American Negro slavery remains far from complete. Much more has been promised than has been fulfilled, even by writers included in this collection. In some important instances, their major works on the subject remain in progress, and the selections printed here often suggest new directions that scholars are taking rather than offer an individual historian's final or conclusive ideas on a topic. For example, students of American slavery eagerly await Eugene D. Genovese's forthcoming elaboration and synthesis of his theories on Southern ante-bellum society and David Brion Davis's future volumes on antislavery movements. Comparative studies of Latin American, West Indian, and North American slave cultures currently in progress should help to clarify the patterns which slavery *in practice* took in each culture—the degree of similarity and the precise quality of the differences. Scholars are also re-examining the influence of the Negro's varied African tribal origins on his behavior under American slavery, continuing the work of Melville Herskovits and other anthropologists who pioneered in this area. No doubt other historians will extend and reshape Elkins's theories on slave personality after careful and imaginative use of available primary source materials in Southern archives, materials which Elkins himself did not exploit in his book.

Hopefully, scholars will also begin to abandon the self-imposed insularity of many previous writers on American slavery and begin studying the institution within the context of broader developments in American life. This would involve supplementing single-minded concern for how the system functioned with more curiosity about the impact of events on the course of Southern slave society. William W. Freehling's superb *Prelude to Civil War: The Nullification Crisis in South Carolina, 1816–1836* contributed notably to such a re-assessment. This approach would view slavery not as an unchanging or relatively fixed set of institutional patterns, but as an unstable regional culture, subject to shock waves both from outside and within, whether in the form of abolitionist propaganda, Andrew Jackson's tariff messages, or Nat Turner's calls for slave rebellion. More monographs like Freehling's, combining hard political and economic research with skillful social psychological analysis, are needed in order to appraise the shifting moods and habits of slave society. Historians might examine more carefully the impact on the South of such important cultural developments and events as Northern industrial growth, the Compromise of 1850, the rise of political antislavery groups, and John Brown's raid. Parallel studies concerning the changing patterns of slave life wrought by Southern or national developments are also needed. Earlier syntheses of American Negro slavery such as Phillips's and Stampp's have presented different versions of the institution's operation by studying its *intact* structure. Any future synthesizer faces the even more complex task of piecing together the changing patterns of Southern slave society *in process*.

The reader should be sufficiently aware by this time that, on most questions concerning American slavery, a century of historical research has left more to be undertaken and explored than to be catalogued and filed away. Until the paperback revolution, recent literature on slavery in the United States often remained hidden in scholarly journals, largely inaccessible to most students of American history. Even today, only a few leading historians of the subject, notably Phillips, Stampp, and Elkins, have become familiar to students. The present collection offers a sampling of their work and of many other recent contributors to the re-assessment of American slavery. It also contains a bibliographic guide to further reading. Although slavery no longer exists in this country, Americans continue to confront the problems it left unresolved, not the smallest of which was its long duration. Slavery lasted for 240 years in the South and for almost 180 years in the North. In the South, the institution did not die out or collapse ultimately from inner weakness: it was crushed by superior force. The residual effects of slavery on both black and white people in America today remain profound. The ordeal of black men in the United States spans our entire colonial and national past, two-thirds of which time they spent as slaves. In the readings which follow, historians treat the major dimensions of this experience—its origins, the slave, the master, and the system itself.

NOTES

1. See, for example, Ulrich Bonnell Phillips, *American Negro Slavery* (New York, 1918, reprinted 1967 by Louisiana State University Press).

2. Herbert Aptheker, *American Negro Slave Revolts* (New York, 1943); see also Joseph C. Carroll, *Slave Insurrections in the United States, 1800–1865* (Boston, 1938).

3. Richard Hofstadter, "U.B. Phillips and the Plantation Legend," *Journal of Negro History*, XXIX (April 1944).

4. Stanley M. Elkins, *Slavery, A Problem in American Institutional and Intellectual Life* (Chicago, 1959); Kenneth M. Stampp, *The Peculiar Institution: Slavery in the Ante-bellum South* (New York, 1956).

5. Eugene D. Genovese, "The Legacy of Slavery and the Roots of Black Nationalism," *Studies on the Left*, Vol. 6, No. 6 (November-December 1966), p. 3. See also Eugene D. Genovese, *The Political Economy of Slavery: Studies in the Economy and Society of the Slave South* (New York, 1965).

6. Elkins, *Slavery, passim.*

7. David Brion Davis, *The Problem of Slavery in Western Culture* (Ithaca, 1966).

8. Alfred H. Conrad and J. R. Meyers, *The Economics of Slavery and Other Studies in Economic History* (Chicago, 1964).

9. Richard C. Wade, *Slavery in the Cities, The South, 1820–1860* (New York, 1964.

10. Leon Litwack, *North of Slavery: The Negro in the Free States, 1790–1860* (Chicago, 1961).

11. Arthur Zilversmit, *The First Emancipation: The Abolition of Negro Slavery in the North* (Chicago, 1967); Edgar J. McManus, *A History of Negro Slavery in New York* (Syracuse, 1966).

12. William W. Freehling, *Prelude to Civil War: The Nullification Crisis in South Carolina, 1816–1836* (New York, 1966).

I: THE ORIGINS

• For the first time in 1619, twenty Negro slaves were brought to Jamestown. The English who settled the American colonies were predisposed toward a negative set of attitudes regarding Negroes, in part because of cultural and religious images inherited from the mother country and in part because of the experiences of earlier European-African contacts. Yet the English who settled the mainland colonies had not held slaves in the Old World. How then did the institution of slavery emerge in the New World setting? What factors led to the differences in treatment accorded European indentured servants and African slaves with Negroes relegated automatically to slave status in every mainland colony by the end of the seventeenth century? Were economic necessities more important in triggering this process than the race prejudice of white settlers, or did pre-Jamestown English racism foreclose the long-range prospects for Negro freedom? Winthrop D. Jordan, in his book on American attitudes toward the Negro from the seventeenth-century settlements to the early national period, examines thoroughly the colonial development of slavery and concludes, "Rather than slavery causing 'prejudice,' or vice versa, they seem rather to have generated each other. Both were, after all, twin aspects of a general debasement of the Negro." In the following selection, Jordan discusses the reasons for the emergence of slavery in the American colonies.

"Unthinking Decision": The Enslavement of Negroes in America to 1700

WINTHROP D. JORDAN

At the start of English settlement in America, no one had in mind to establish the institution of Negro slavery. Yet in less than a century the foundations of a peculiar institution had been laid. The first Negroes landed in Virginia in 1619, though very, very little is known about their precise status during the next twenty years. Between 1640 and 1660 there is evidence of enslavement, and after 1660 slavery crystallized on the statute books of Maryland, Virginia, and other colonies. By 1700 when African Negroes began flooding into English America they were treated as somehow deserving a life and status radically different from English and other European settlers. The Negro had been debased to a condition of chattel slavery; at some point, Englishmen in America had created a legal status which ran counter to English law.

Unfortunately the details of this process can never be completely reconstructed; there is simply not enough evidence (and very little chance of more to come) to show precisely when and how and why Negroes came to be treated so differently from white men, though there is just enough to make historians differ as to its meaning. Concerning the first years of contact especially we have very little information as to what impression Negroes made upon English settlers: accordingly, we are left knowing less about the formative years than about later periods of American slavery. That those early years were crucial ones is obvious, for it was then that the cycle of Negro debasement began; once the Negro became fully the slave it is not hard to see why men looked down upon him. Yet precisely because understanding the dynamics of these early years is so important to understanding the centuries which followed, it is necessary to bear with the

From Winthrop D. Jordan, *White Over Black: American Attitudes Toward the Negro, 1550–1812* (Chapel Hill: University of North Carolina Press, 1968), pp. 44-52, 66-82, 85-86, 88-98. Published for the Institute of Early American History and Culture at Williamsburg, Virginia. Reprinted by permission of the University of North Carolina Press.

less than satisfactory data and to attempt to reconstruct the course of debasement undergone by Negroes in seventeenth-century America. In order to comprehend it, we need first of all to examine certain social pressures generated by the American environment and how these pressures interacted with certain qualities of English social thought and law that existed on the eve of settlement, qualities that even then were being modified by examples set by England's rivals for empire in the New World.

THE NECESSITIES OF A NEW WORLD

When Englishmen crossed the Atlantic to settle in America, they were immediately subject to novel strains. In some settlements, notably Jamestown and Plymouth, the survival of the community was in question. An appalling proportion of people were dead within a year, from malnutrition, starvation, unconquerable diseases, bitter cold, oppressive heat, Indian attacks, murder, and suicide. The survivors were isolated from the world as they had known it, cut off from friends and family and the familiar sights and sounds and smells which have always told men who and where they are. A similar sense of isolation and disorientation was inevitable even in the settlements that did not suffer through a starving time. English settlers were surrounded by savages. They had to perform a round of daily tasks to which most were unaccustomed. They had undergone the shock of detachment from home in order to set forth upon a dangerous voyage of from ten to thirteen weeks that ranged from unpleasant to fatal and that seared into every passenger's memory the ceaselessly tossing distance that separated him from his old way of life.[1]

Life in America put great pressure upon the traditional social and economic controls that Englishmen assumed were to be exercised by civil and often ecclesiastical authority. Somehow the empty woods seemed to lead much more toward license than restraint. At the same time, by reaction, this unfettering resulted in an almost pathetic social conservatism, a yearning for the forms and symbols of the old familiar social order. When in 1618, for example, the Virginia Company wangled a knighthood for a newly appointed governor of the colony the objection from the settlers was not that this artificial elevation was inappropriate to wilderness conditions but that it did not go far enough to meet them; several planters petitioned that a governor of higher rank be sent, since some settlers had "only Reverence of the Comanders Eminence, or Nobillitye (whereunto by Nature everye man subordinate is ready to yeild a willing submission without contempt, or repyning)."[2] English social forms were transplanted to America not simply because they were nice to have around but because without them the new settlements would have fallen apart and English settlers would have become men of the forest, savage men devoid of civilization.

For the same reason, the communal goals that animated the settlement of the colonies acquired great functional importance in the wilderness; they served as antidotes to social and individual disintegration. The physical hardships of settlement could never have been surmounted without the stiffened nerve and will engendered by commonly recognized if sometimes unarticulated purposes. In New England lack of articulation was no problem. The Puritans knew precisely who they were (the chosen of God, many of them) and that they were seeking to erect a Godly community. Though that community (eventually) eluded them, they retained their conviction that they manned a significant outpost of English civilization. As Cotton Mather grandly told the Massachusetts governor and General Court in 1700, "It is no Little Blessing of God, that we are a part of the *English nation*."[3] A similar deep sense of self-transplantation buttressed the settlements in Virginia and Maryland. While there was less talk than in New England about God's special endorsement, virtually every settler knew that Englishmen were serving His greater glory by removing to Virginia and by making a prosperous success of the project. They recognized also that their efforts at western planting aggrandized English wealth and power and the cause of reformed Christianity. As Richard Hakluyt summarized these purposes, "This enterprise may staye the spanishe kinge ["the supporter of the greate Antechriste of Rome"] from flowinge over all the face of that waste firme of America, yf wee seate and plante there in time."[4] For Englishmen planting in America, then, it was of the utmost importance to know that they were Englishmen, which was to say that they were educated (to a degree suitable to their station), Christian (of an appropriate Protestant variety), civilized, and (again to an appropriate degree) free men.

It was with personal freedom, of course, that wilderness conditions most suddenly reshaped English laws, assumptions, and practices. In America land was plentiful, labor scarce, and, as in all new colonies, a cash crop desperately needed. These economic conditions were to remain important for centuries; in general they tended to encourage greater geographical mobility, less specialization, higher rewards, and fewer restraints on the processes and products of labor. Supporting traditional assumptions and practices, however, was the need to retain them simply because they were familiar and because they served the vital function of maintaining and advancing orderly settlement. Throughout the seventeenth century there were pressures on traditional practices which similarly told in opposite directions.

In general men who invested capital in agriculture in America came under fewer customary and legal restraints than in England concerning what they did with their land and with the people who worked on it. On the other hand their activities were constrained by the economic necessity of producing cash crops for export, which narrowed their choice of how they could treat it. Men without capital could obtain land relatively easily: hence the shortage of labor and the notably blurred line between men who had capital and men who did not. Men and women in England faced a different situation. A significant amount of capital was required in order to get to America, and the greatest barrier to material advancement in America was the Atlantic Ocean.

Three major systems of labor emerged amid the interplay of these social and economic conditions in America. One, which was present from the beginning, was free wage labor, in which contractual arrangements rested upon a monetary nexus. Another, which was the last to appear, was chattel slavery, in which there were no contractual arrangements (except among owners). The third, which virtually coincided with first settlement in America, was temporary servitude, in which complex contractual arrangements gave shape to the entire system. It was this third system, indentured servitude, which permitted so many English settlers to cross the Atlantic barrier. Indentured servitude was linked to the development of chattel slavery in America, and its operation deserves closer examination.

A very sizable proportion of settlers in the English colonies came as indentured servants bound by contract to serve a master for a specified number of years, usually from four to seven or until age twenty-one, as repayment for their ocean passage. The time of service to which the servant bound himself was negotiable property, and he might be sold or conveyed from one master to another at any time up to the expiration of his indenture, at which point he became a free man. (Actually it was his *labor* which was owned and sold, not his *person*, though this distinction was neither important nor obvious at the time.) Custom and statute law regulated the relationship between servant and master. Obligation was reciprocal: the master undertook to feed and clothe and sometimes to educate his servant and to refrain from abusing him, while the servant was obliged to perform such work as his master set him and to obey his master in all things. This typical pattern, with a multitude of variations, was firmly established by mid-seventeenth century. In Virginia and Maryland, both the legal and actual conditions of servants seem to have improved considerably from the early years when servants had often been outrageously abused and sometimes forced to serve long terms. Beginning about 1640 the legislative assemblies of the two colonies passed numerous acts prescribing maximum terms of service and requiring masters to pay the customary "freedom dues" (clothing, provisions, and so forth) at the end of the servant's time.[5] This legislation may have been actuated partly by the need to attract more immigrants with guarantees of good treatment, in which case underpopulation in relation to level of technology and to natural resources in the English colonies may be said to have made for greater personal freedom. On the other hand, it may also have been a matter of protecting traditional freedoms threatened by this same fact of underpopulation which generated so powerful a need for labor which would not be transient and temporary. In this instance, very clearly, the imperatives enjoined by settlement in the wilderness interacted with previously acquired ideas concerning personal freedom. Indeed without some inquiry into Elizabethan thinking on that subject, it will remain impossible to comprehend why Englishmen became servants in the plantations, and Negroes slaves.

FREEDOM AND BONDAGE IN THE ENGLISH TRADITION

Thinking about freedom and bondage in Tudor England was confused and self-contradictory. In a period of social dislocation there was considerable disagreement among contemporary observers as to what actually was going on and even as to what ought to be. Ideas about personal freedom tended to run both ahead of and behind actual social conditions. Both statute and common law were sometimes considerably more than a century out of phase with actual practice and with commonly held notions about servitude. Finally, ideas and practices were changing rapidly. It is possible, however, to identify certain important tenets of social thought that served as anchor points amid this chaos.

Englishmen lacked accurate methods of ascertaining what actually was happening to their social institutions, but they were not wrong in supposing that villenage, or "bondage" as they more often called it, had virtually disappeared in England. William Harrison put the matter most strenuously in 1577: "As for slaves and bondmen we have none, naie such is the privilege of our countrie by the especiall grace of God, and bountie of our princes, that if anie come hither from other realms, so soone as they set foot on land they become so free of condition as their masters, whereby all note of servile bondage is utterlie remooved from them."[6] Other observers were of the (correct) opinion that a few lingering vestiges—bondmen whom the progress of freedom had passed by—might still be found in the crannies of the decayed manorial system, but everyone agreed that such vestiges were anachronistic. In fact there were English men and women who were still "bond" in the mid-sixteenth century, but they were few in number and their status was much more a technicality than a condition. In the middle ages, being a villein had meant dependence upon the will of a feudal lord but by no means deprivation of all social and legal rights. In the thirteenth and fourteenth centuries villenage had decayed markedly, and it may be said not to have existed as a viable social institution in the second half of the sixteenth century.[7] Personal freedom had become the normal status of Englishmen. Most contemporaries welcomed this fact; indeed it was after about 1550 that there began to develop in England that preening consciousness of the peculiar glories of English liberties.

How had it all happened? Among those observers who tried to explain, there was agreement that Christianity was primarily responsible. They thought of villenage as a mitigation of ancient bond slavery and that the continuing trend to liberty was animated, as Sir Thomas Smith said in a famous passage, by the "perswasion . . . of Christians not to make nor keepe his brother in Christ, servile, bond and underling for ever unto him, as a beast rather than as a man."[8] They agreed also that the trend had been forwarded by the common law, in which the disposition was always, as the phrase went, *in favorem libertatis,* "in favor of liberty." Probably they were correct in both these suppositions, but the common law harbored certain inconsistencies as to freedom which may have had an important though imponderable effect upon the reappearance of slavery in English communities in the seventeenth century.

The accreted structure of the common law sometimes resulted in imperviousness to changing conditions. The first book of Lord Coke's great *Institutes of the Laws of England* (1628), for example, was an extended gloss upon Littleton's fifteenth-century treatise on *Tenures* and it repeatedly quoted the opinions of such famous authorities as Bracton, who had died in 1268. When Bracton had described villenage, English law had not yet fully diverged from the civil or Roman law, and villenage actually existed. Almost four hundred years later some legal authorities were still citing Bracton on villenage without even alluding to the fact that villenage no longer existed. The widely used legal dictionary, Cowell's *Interpreter* (1607 and later editions), quoted Bracton at length and declared that his words "expresse the nature of our villenage something aptly."[9] Anyone replying solely on Cowell's *Interpreter* would suppose that some Englishmen in the early seventeenth century were hereditary serfs. Thus while villenage was actually extinct, it lay unmistakably fossilized in the common law. Its survival in that rigid form must have reminded Englishmen that there existed a sharply differing alternative to personal liberty. It was in this vague way that villenage seems to have been related to the development of chattel slavery in America. Certainly villenage was not the forerunner of slavery, but its survival in the law books meant that a possibility which might have been foreclosed was not. Later, after Negro slavery had clearly emerged, English lawyers were inclined to think of slavery as being a New World version of the ancient tenure described by Bracton and Cowell and Coke.

That the common law was running centuries behind social practice was only one of several important factors complicating Tudor thought about the proper status of individuals in society. The social ferment of the sixteenth century resulted not only in the impalpable mood of control and subordination which seems to have affected English perception of Africans but also in the well-known strenuous efforts of Tudor governments to lay restrictions on elements in English society which seemed badly out of control. From at least the 1530's the countryside swarmed with vagrants, sturdy beggars, rogues, and vagabonds, with men who could but would not work. They committed all manner of crimes, the worst of which was remaining idle. It was an article of faith among Tudor commentators (before there were "Puritans" to help propound it) that idleness was the mother of all vice and the chief danger to a well-ordered state. Tudor statesmen valiantly attempted to suppress idleness by means of the famous vagrancy laws which provided for houses of correction and (finally) for whipping the vagrant from constable to constable until he reached his home parish.

They assumed that everyone belonged in a specific social niche and that anyone failing to labor in the niche assigned to him by Providence must be compelled to do so by authority.

Some experiments in compulsion ran counter to the trend toward personal liberty. In 1547, shortly after the death of Henry VIII, a parliamentary statute provided that any able-bodied person adjudged a vagabond upon presentment to two justices of the peace should be branded with a "V" on the chest and made a "slave" for two years to the presenter who was urged to give "the saide Slave breade and water or small dryncke and such refuse of meate as he shall thincke mete [and] cause the said Slave to worke by beating cheyninge or otherwise in such worke and Labor how vyle so ever it be." Masters could "putt a rynge of Iron about his Necke Arme or his Legge for a more knowledge and suretie of the keepinge of him." A runaway "slave" convicted by a court was to be branded on the cheek or forehead and adjudged "to be the saide Masters Slave for ever." These provisions reflected desperation. Fully as significant as their passage was their repeal three years later by a statute which frankly asserted in the preamble that their "extremitie" had "byn occation that they have not ben putt in ure [use]."[10]

Englishmen generally were unwilling to submit or subscribe to such debasement. Despite a brief statutory experiment with banishment "beyond the Seas" and with judgment "perpetually to the Gallyes of the Realme" in 1598,[11] Tudor authorities gradually hammered out the legal framework of a labor system which permitted compulsion but which did not permit so total a loss of freedom as lifetime hereditary slavery. Apprenticeship seemed to them the ideal status, for apprenticeship provided a means of regulating the economy and of guiding youth into acceptable paths of honest industry. By 1600, many writers had come to think of other kinds of bound labor as inferior forms of apprenticeship, involving less of an educative function, less permanence, and a less rigidly contractual basis. This tendency to reason from apprenticeship downward, rather than from penal service up, had the important effect of imparting some of the very strong contractualism in the master-apprentice relationship to less formal varieties of servitude. There were "indentured" servants in England prior to English settlement in America. Their written "indentures" gave visible evidence of the strong element of mutual obligation between master and servant: each retained a copy of the contract which was "indented" at the top so as to match the other.

As things turned out, it was indentured servitude which best met the requirements for settling in America. Of course there were other forms of bound labor which contributed to the process of settlement: many convicts were sent and many children abducted.[12] Yet among all the numerous varieties and degrees of non-freedom which existed in England, there was none which could have served as a well-formed model for the chattel slavery which developed in America. This is not to say, though, that slavery was an unheard-of novelty in Tudor England. On the contrary, "bond slavery" was a memory trace of long standing. Vague and confused as the concept of slavery was in the minds of Englishmen, it possessed certain fairly consistent connotations which were to help shape English perceptions of the way Europeans should properly treat the newly discovered peoples overseas.

. . .

ENSLAVEMENT: NEW ENGLAND

Negro slavery never really flourished in New England. It never became so important or so rigorous as in the plantation colonies to the southwards. There were relatively few Negroes, only a few hundred in 1680 and not more than 3 per cent of the population in the eighteenth century; no one thought that Negroes were about to rise and overwhelm the white community.[13] Treatment of slaves in New England was milder even than the laws allowed: Negroes were not employed in gangs except occasionally in the Narragansett region of Rhode Island, and the established codes of family, congregation, and community mitigated the condition of servitude generally. Negroes were not treated very differently from white servants—except that somehow they and their children served for life.

The question with New England slavery is not why it was weakly rooted, but why it existed at all. No staple crop demanded regiments of raw labor. That there was no compelling economic demand for Negroes is evident in the numbers actually imported: economic exigencies scarcely required establishment of a distinct status for only 3 per cent of the labor force. Indentured servitude was adequate to New England's needs, and in fact some Negroes became free servants rather than slaves. Why, then, did New Englanders enslave Negroes, probably as early as 1638? Why was it that the Puritans rather mindlessly (which was not their way) accepted slavery for Negroes and Indians but not for white men?

The early appearance of slavery in New England may in part be explained by the provenance of the first Negroes imported. They were brought by Captain William Pierce of the Salem ship *Desire* in 1638 from the Providence Island colony where Negroes were already being kept as perpetual servants.[14] A minor traffic in Negroes and other products developed between the two Puritan colonies, though evidently some of the Negroes proved less than satisfactory, for Governor Butler was cautioned by the Providence Company to take special care of "the cannibal negroes brought from New England."[15] After 1640 a brisk trade got under way between New England and the other English islands, and Massachusetts vessels sometimes touched upon the West African coast before heading for the Caribbean. Trade with Barbados was particularly lively, and Massachusetts vessels carried Negroes to that bustling colony from Africa and the Cape Verde Islands. As John Winthrop gratefully described the salvation of New England's economy, "it pleased the Lord to open to us a trade with Barbados and other Islands in the West Indies."[16] These strange Negroes from the West Indies must surely have been accompanied by prevailing notions about their usual status. Ship masters who purchased perpetual service in Barbados would not have been likely to sell service for term in Boston. Then too, white settlers from the crowded islands migrated to New England, 1,200 from Barbados alone in the years 1643–47.[17]

No amount of contact with the West Indies could have by itself created Negro slavery in New England; settlers there had to be willing to accept the proposition. Because they were Englishmen, they were so prepared—and at the same time they were not. Characteristically, as Puritans, they officially codified this ambivalence in 1641 as follows:

> there shall never be any bond-slavery, villenage or captivitie amongst us; unlesse it be lawfull captives taken in just warrs, and such strangers as willingly sell themselves, or are solde to us: and such shall have the libertyes and christian usages which the law of God established in Israell concerning such persons doth morally require, provided, this exempts none from servitude who shall be judged thereto by Authoritie.[18]

Here were the wishes of the General Court as expressed in the Massachusetts Body of Liberties, which is to say that as early as 1641 the Puritan settlers were seeking to guarantee in writing their own liberty without closing off the opportunity of taking it from others whom they identified with the Biblical term, "strangers." It was under the aegis of this concept that Theophilus Eaton, one of the founders of New Haven, seems to have owned Negroes before 1658 who were "servants forever or during his pleasure, according to Leviticus, 25:45

and 46."[19] ("Of the children of the strangers that do sojourn among you, of them shall ye buy, and of their families . . . : and they shall be your possession. And ye shall take them as an inheritance for your children . . . ; they shall be your bondmen for ever: but over your brethren the children of Israel, ye shall not rule one over another with rigor.") Apart from this implication that bond slavery was reserved to those not partaking of true religion nor possessing proper nationality, the Body of Liberties expressly reserved the colony's right to enslave convicted criminals. For reasons not clear, this endorsement of an existing practice was followed almost immediately by discontinuance of its application to white men. The first instance of penal "slavery" in Massachusetts came in 1636, when an Indian was sentenced to "bee kept as a slave for life to worke, unless wee see further cause." Then in December 1638, ten months after the first Negroes arrived, the Quarter Court for the first time sentenced three white offenders to be "slaves" —a suggestive but perhaps meaningless coincidence. Having by June 1642 sentenced altogether some half dozen white men to "slavery" (and explicitly releasing several after less than a year) the Court stopped.[20] Slavery, as had been announced in the Body of Liberties, was to be only for "strangers."

The Body of Liberties made equally clear that captivity in a just war constituted legitimate grounds for slavery. The practice had begun during the first major conflict with the Indians, the Pequot War of 1637. Some of the Pequot captives had been shipped aboard the *Desire*, to Providence Island; accordingly, the first Negroes in New England arrived in exchange for men taken captive in a just war! That this provenance played an important role in shaping views about Negroes is suggested by the first recorded plea by an Englishman on the North American continent for the establishment of an African slave trade. Emanuel Downing, in a letter to his brother-in-law John Winthrop in 1645, described the advantages:

> If upon a Just warre [with the Narragansett Indians] the Lord should deliver them into our hands, wee might easily have men woemen and children enough to exchange for Moores, which wilbe more gaynefull pilladge for us then wee conceive, for I doe not see how wee can thrive untill wee get into a stock of slaves sufficient to doe all our business, for our children's children will hardly see this great Continent filled with people, soe that our servants will still desire freedome to plant for themselves, and not stay but for verie great wages. And I suppose you know verie well

how wee shall mayneteyne 20 Moores cheaper than one Englishe servant.[21]

These two facets of justifiable enslavement—punishment for crime and captivity in war—were closely related. Slavery as punishment probably derived from analogy with captivity, since presumably a king or magistrates could mercifully spare and enslave a man whose crime had forfeited his right to life. The analogy had not been worked out by commentators in England, but a fearly clear linkage between crime and captivity seems to have existed in the minds of New Englanders concerning Indian slavery. In 1644 the commissioners of the United Colonies meeting at New Haven decided, in light of the Indians' "proud affronts," "hostile practices," and "protectinge or rescuinge of offenders," that magistrates might "send some convenient strength of English and, . . . seise and bring away" Indians from any "plantation of Indians" which persisted in this practice, and if no satisfaction was forthcoming, could deliver the "Indians seased . . . either to serve or be shipped out and exchanged for Negroes."[22] Captivity and criminal justice seemed to mean the same thing, slavery.

It would be wrong to suppose that all the Puritans' preconceived ideas about freedom and bondage worked in the same direction. While the concepts of difference in religion and of captivity worked against Indians and Negroes, certain Scriptural injunctions and English pride in liberty told in the opposite direction. In Massachusetts the magistrates demonstrated that they were not about to tolerate glaring breaches of "the law of God established in Israel" even when the victims were Negroes. In 1646 the authorities arrested two mariners, James Smith and Thomas Keyser, who had carried two Negroes directly from Africa and sold them in Massachusetts. What distressed the General Court was that the Negroes had been obtained during a raid on an African village and that this "haynos and crying sinn of man stealing" had transpired on the Lord's Day. The General Court decided to free the unfortunate victims and ship them back to Africa, though the death penalty for the crime (clearly mandatory in Scripture) was not imposed.[23] More quietly than in this dramatic incident, Puritan authorities extended the same protections against maltreatment to Negroes and Indians as to white servants.

Only once before the eighteenth century was New England slavery challenged directly, and in that instance the tone was as much bafflement as indignation. This famous Rhode Island protest perhaps derived from a diffuse Christian equalitarianism which operated to extend the English presumption of liberty to non-Englishmen. The Rhode Island law of 1652 actually forbade enslavement.

> Whereas, there is a common course practised amongst English men to buy negers, to that end they may have them for service or slaves forever; for the preventigge of such practices among us, let it be ordered, that no blacke mankind or white being forced by covenent bond, or otherwise, to serve any man or his assighnes longer than ten yeares, or untill they come to bee twentie four years of age, if they bee taken in under fourteen, from the time of thier cominge within the liberties of this Collonie. And at the end or terme of ten yeares to sett them free, as the manner is with the English servants. And that man that will not let them goe free, or shall sell them away elsewhere, to that end that they may bee enslaved to others for a long time, hee or they shall forfeit to the Collonie forty pounds.

Perhaps it was Rhode Island's tolerance of religious diversity and relatively high standard of justice for the Indian which led to this attempt to prevent Englishmen from taking advantage of a different people.[24]

The law remained a dead letter. The need for labor, the example set in the West Indies, the condition of Negroes as "strangers," and their initial connection with captive Indians combined to override any hesitation about introducing Negro bond slavery into New England. Laws regulating the conduct of Negroes specifically did not appear until the 1690's.[25] From the first, however, there were scattered signs that Negroes were regarded as different from English people not merely in their status as slaves. In 1639 Samuel Maverick of Noddles Island attempted, apparently rather clumsily, to breed two of his Negroes, or so an English visitor reported: "Mr. Maverick was desirous to have a breed of Negroes, and therefore seeing [that his "Negro woman"] would not yield by persuasions to company with a Negro young man he had in his house; he commanded him will'd she to go to bed to her which was no sooner done but she kickt him out again, this she took in high disdain beyond her slavery." In 1652 the Massachusetts General Court ordered that Scotsmen, Indians, and Negroes should train with the English in the militia, but four years later abruptly excluded Negroes, as did Connecticut in 1660.[26] Evidently Negroes, even free Negroes, were regarded as distinct from the English. They were, in New England where economic necessities were not sufficiently pressing to determine the decision, treated differently from other men.

ENSLAVEMENT: VIRGINIA AND MARYLAND

In Virginia and Maryland the development of Negro slavery followed a very different course, for several reasons. Most obviously, geographic conditions and the intentions of the settlers quickly combined to produce a successful agricultural staple. The deep tidal rivers, the long growing season, the fertile soil, and the absence of strong communal spirit among the settlers opened the way. Ten years after settlers first landed at Jamestown they were on the way to proving, in the face of assertions to the contrary, that is was possible "to found an empire upon smoke." More than the miscellaneous production of New England, tobacco required labor which was cheap but not temporary, mobile but not independent, and tireless rather than skilled. In the Chesapeake area more than anywhere to the northward, the shortage of labor and the abundance of land—the "frontier"—placed a premium on involuntary labor.

This need for labor played more directly upon these settlers' ideas about freedom and bondage than it did either in the West Indies or in New England. Perhaps it would be more accurate to say that settlers in Virginia (and in Maryland after settlement in 1634) made their decisions concerning Negroes while relatively virginal, relatively free from external influences and from firm preconceptions. Of all the important early English settlements, Virgina had the least contact with the Spanish, Portuguese, Dutch, and other English colonies. At the same time, the settlers of Virginia did not possess either the legal or Scriptural learning of the New England Puritans whose conception of the just war had opened the way to the enslavement of Indians. Slavery in the tobacco colonies did not begin as an adjunct of captivity; in marked contrast to the Puritan response to the Pequot War the settlers of Virginia did *not* generally react to the Indian massacre of 1622 with propositions for taking captives and selling them as "slaves." It was perhaps a correct measure of the conceptual atmosphere in Virginia that there was only one such proposition after the 1622 disaster and that that one was defective in precision as to how exactly one treated captive Indians.[27]

In the absence, then, of these influences which obtained in other English colonies, slavery as it developed in Virginia and Maryland assumes a special interest and importance over and above the fact that Negro slavery was to become a vitally important institution there and, later, to the southwards. In the tobacco colonies it is possible to watch Negro slavery *develop*, not pop up full-grown overnight, and it is therefore possible to trace, very imperfectly, the development of the shadowy, unexamined rationale which supported it. The concept of Negro slavery there was neither borrowed from foreigners, nor extracted from books, nor invented out of whole cloth, nor extrapolated from servitude, nor generated by English reaction to Negroes as such, nor necessitated by the exigencies of the New World. Not any one of these made the Negro a slave, but all.

In rough outline, slavery's development in the tobacco colonies seems to have undergone three stages. Negroes first arrived in 1619, only a few days late for the meeting of the first representative assembly in America. John Rolfe described the event with the utmost unconcern: "About the last of August came in a dutch man of warre that sold us twenty Negars."[28] Negroes continued to trickle in slowly for the next half century; one report in 1649 estimated that there were three hundred among Virginia's population of fifteen thousand—about 2 per cent.[29] Long before there were more appreciable numbers, the development of slavery had, so far as we can tell, shifted gears. Prior to about 1640, there is very little evidence to show how Negroes were treated—though we will need to return to those first twenty years in a moment. After 1640 there is mounting evidence that some Negroes were in fact being treated as slaves, at least that they were being held in hereditary lifetime service. This is to say that the twin essences of slavery—the two kinds of perpetuity—first become evident during the twenty years prior to the beginning of legal formulation. After 1660 slavery was written into statute law. Negroes began to flood into the two colonies at the end of the seventeenth century. In 1705 Virginia produced a codification of laws applying to slaves.

Concerning the first of these stages, there is only one major historical certainty, and unfortunately it is the sort which historians find hardest to bear. There simply is not enough evidence to indicate with any certainty whether Negroes were treated like white servants or not. At least we can be confident, therefore, that the two most common assertions about the first Negroes—that they were slaves and that they were servants—are *unfounded*, though not necessarily incorrect. And what of the positive evidence?

Some of the first group bore Spanish names and presumably had been baptized, which would mean they were at least nominally Christian, though of the Papist sort. They had been "sold" to the English; so had other Englishmen but not by the Dutch. Certainly these Negroes were not fully free, but many Englishmen were not. It can be said, though, that from the first in Virginia Negroes were set apart from white men by the word *Negroes*. The earliest Virginia census reports plainly distinguished Negroes from white men, often giving Negroes no personal name; in 1629 every commander of the several plantations was ordered to "take a generall muster of all the inhabitants men woemen and Children as well *Englishe* as Negroes."[30] A distinct name is not attached to a group unless it is regarded as distinct. It seems logical to suppose that this perception of the Negro as being distinct from the Englishman must have operated to debase his status rather than to raise it, for in the absence of countervailing social factors, the need for labor in the colonies usually told in the direction of non-freedom. There were few countervailing factors present, surely, in such instances as in 1629 when a group of Negroes were brought to Virginia freshly captured from a Portuguese vessel which had snatched them from Angola a few weeks earlier.[31] Given the context of English thought and experience sketched in this chapter, it seems probable that the Negro's status was not ever the same as that accorded the white servant. But we do not know for sure.

When the first fragmentary evidence appears about 1640 it becomes clear that *some* Negroes in both Virginia and Maryland were serving for life and some Negro children inheriting the same obligation.[32] Not all Negroes, certainly, for Nathaniel Littleton had released a Negro named Anthony Longoe from all service whatsoever in 1635, and after the mid-1640's the court records show that other Negroes were incontestably free and were accumulating property of their own. At least one Negro freeman, Anthony Johnson, himself owned a Negro. Some Negroes served only terms of usual length, but others were held for terms far longer than custom and statute permitted with white servants.[33] The first fairly clear indication that slavery was practiced in the tobacco colonies appears in 1639, when a Maryland statute declared that "all the Inhabitants of this Province being Christians (Slaves excepted) Shall have and enjoy all such rights liberties immunities priviledges and free customs within this Province as any natural born subject of England." Another Maryland law passed the same year provided that "all persons being Christians (Slaves excepted)" over eighteen who were imported without indentures would serve for four years.[34] These laws make very little sense unless the term *slaves* meant Negroes and perhaps Indians.

The next year, 1640, the first definite indication of outright enslavement appears in Virginia. The General Court pronounced sentence on three servants who had been retaken after absconding to Maryland. Two of them, a Dutchman and a Scot, were ordered to serve their masters for one additional year and then the colony for three more, but "the third being a negro named John Punch shall serve his said master or his assigns for the time of his natural life here or elsewhere." No white servant in any English colony, so far as is known, ever received a like sentence. Later the same month a Negro (possibly the same enterprising fellow) was again singled out from a group of recaptured runaways; six of the seven culprits were assigned additional time while the Negro was given none, presumably because he was already serving for life.[35]

After 1640, when surviving Virginia county court records began to mention Negroes, sales for life, often including any future progeny, were recorded in unmistakably language. In 1646 Francis Pott sold a Negro woman and boy to Stephen Charlton "to the use of him . . . forever." Similarly, six years later William Whittington sold to John Pott "one Negro girle named Jowan; aged about Ten yeares and with her Issue and produce duringe her (or either of them) for their Life tyme. And their Successors forever"; and a Maryland man in 1649 deeded two Negro men and a woman "and all their issue both male and Female." The executors of a York County estate in 1647 disposed of eight Negroes—four men, two women, and two children—to Captain John Chisman "to have hold occupy posesse and injoy and every one of the afforementioned Negroes forever."[36] The will of Rowland Burnham of "Rapahanocke," made in 1657, dispensed his considerable number of Negroes and white servants in language which clearly differentiated between the two by specifying that the whites were to serve for their "full terme of tyme" and the Negroes "for ever."[37] Nothing in the will indicated that this distinction was exceptional or novel.

Further evidence that some Negroes were serving for life in this period lies in the prices paid for them. In many instances the valuations placed on Negroes (in estate inventories and bills of sale) were far higher than for white servants, even those servants with full terms yet to serve. Higher prices must have meant that Negroes were more highly valued because of their greater length of service. Negro women may have been especially prized, moreover, because their progeny could also be held perpetually. In 1643, for example, William Burdett's inventory listed eight servants, with the time each had still to serve, at valuations ranging from 400 to 1,100 pounds of tobacco, while a "very anntient" Negro was valued at 3,000 and an eight-year-old Negro girl at 2,000 pounds, with no time remaining indicated for either. In the late 1650's an inventory of Thomas Ludlow's estate evaluated a white servant with six years to serve at less than an elderly Negro man and only one half of a Negro woman.[38] Similarly, the labor owned by James Stone in 1648 was evaluated as follows:

	1b tobo
Thomas Groves, 4 yeares to serve	1300
Francis Bomley for 6 yeares	1500
John Thackstone for 3 yeares	1300
Susan Davis for 3 yeares	1000
Emaniell a Negro man	2000
Roger Stone 3 yeares	1300
Mingo a Negro man	2000[39]

The 1655 inventory of Argoll Yeardley's estate provides clear evidence of a distinction between perpetual and limited service for Negroes. Under the heading "Servants" were listed "Towe Negro men, towe Negro women (their wifes) one Negro girle aged 15 yeares, Item One Negro girle aged about teen yeares and one Negro child aged about sixe moneths," valued at 12,000 pounds, and under the heading "Corne" were "Servants, towe men their tyme three months," valued at 300 pounds, and "one Negro boye ["about three yeares old"] (which by witness of his godfather) is to bee free att twenty foure yeares of age and then to have towe cowes given him," valued at 600 pounds.[40] Besides setting a higher value on Negroes, these inventories failed to indicate the number of years they had still to serve, presumably because their service was for an unlimited time.

Where Negro women were involved, higher valuations probably reflected the facts that their issue were valuable and that they could be used for field work while white women generally were not. This latter discrimination between Negro and white women did not necessarily involve perpetual service, but it meant that Negroes were set apart in a way clearly not to their advantage. This was not the only instance in which Negroes were subjected to degrading distinctions not immediately and necessarily attached to the concept of slavery. Negroes were singled out for special treatment in several ways which suggest a generalized debasement of Negroes as a group. Significantly, the first indications of this debasement appeared at about the same time as the first indications of actual enslavement.

The distinction concerning field work is a case in point. It first appears on the written record in 1643, when Virginia almost pointedly endorsed it in a tax law. Previously, in 1629, tithable persons had been defined as "all those that worke in the ground of what qualitie or condition soever." The new law provided that *all* adult men were tithable and, in addition, *Negro* women. The same distinction was made twice again before 1660. Maryland adopted a similar policy beginning in 1654.[41] This official discrimination between Negro and other women was made by men who were accustomed to thinking of field work as being ordinarily the work of men rather than women. As John Hammond wrote in a 1656 tract defending the tobacco colonies, servant women were not put to work in the fields but in domestic employments, "yet som wenches that are nasty, and beastly and not fit to be so employed are put into the ground."[42] The essentially racial character of this discrimination stood out clearly in a law passed in 1668 at the time slavery was taking shape in the statute books:

> Whereas some doubts, have arisen whether negro women set free were still to be accompted tithable according to a former act, *It is declared by this grand assembly* that negro women, though permitted to enjoy their Freedome yet ought not in all respects to be admitted to a full fruition of the exemptions and impunities of the English, and are still lyable to payment of taxes.[43]

Virginia law set Negroes apart from all other groups in a second way by denying them the important right and obligation to bear arms. Few restraints could indicate more clearly the denial to Negroes of membership in the white community. This first foreshadowing of the slave codes came in 1640, at just the time when other indications first appeared that Negroes were subject to special treatment.[44]

Finally, an even more compelling sense of the separateness of Negroes was revealed in early reactions to sexual union between the races. Prior to 1660 the evidence concerning these reactions is equivocal, and it is not possible to tell whether repugnance for intermixture preceded legislative enactment of slavery. In 1630 an angry Virginia court sentenced "Hugh Davis to be soundly whipped, before an assembly of Negroes and others for abusing himself to the dishonor of God and shame of Christians, by defiling his body in lying with a negro," but it is possible that the "negro" may not have been female. With other instances of punishment for interracial union in the ensuing years, fornication rather than miscegenation may well have been the primary offense, though in 1651 a Maryland man sued someone who he claimed had said "that he had a black bastard in Virginia." (The court recognized the legitimacy of his complaint, but thought his claim for £20,000 sterling somewhat overvalued his reputation and awarded him 1500 pounds "of Tobacco and Cask.")[45] There may have been no racial feeling involved when in 1640 Robert Sweet, a gentleman, was compelled "to do penance in church according to laws of England for getting a negroe woman with child and the woman whipt."[46] About 1650 a white man and a Negro woman were required to stand clad in white sheets before a congregation in lower Norfolk County for having had relations, but this punishment was sometimes used in cases of fornication between two whites.[47] A quarter century later in 1676, however, the emergence of distaste for racial intermixture was unmistakable. A contemporary account of Bacon's Rebellion caustically described one of the ringleaders, Richard Lawrence, as a person who had eclipsed his learning and abilities "in the darke imbraces of a Blackamoore, his slave: And that in so fond a Maner, . . . to the noe meane Scandle and affrunt of all the Vottrisses in or about towne."[48]

Such condemnation was not confined to polemics. In the early 1660's when slavery was gaining statutory recognition, the assemblies acted with full-throated indignation against miscegenation. These acts aimed at more than merely avoiding confusion of status. In 1662 Virginia declared that "if any christian shall committ Fornication with a negro man or woman, hee or shee soe offending" should pay double the usual fine. (The next year Bermuda prohibited all sexual relations between whites and Negroes.) Two years later Maryland banned interracial marriages: "forasmuch as divers freeborne English women forgettfull of their free Condicion and to the disgrace of our Nation doe intermarry with Negro Slaves by which alsoe divers suites may arise touching the Issue of such woemen and a great damage doth befall the Masters of such Negroes for prevention whereof for deterring such freeborne women from such shamefull Matches," strong language indeed if "divers suites" had been the only problem. A Maryland act of 1681 described marriages of white women with Negroes as, among other things, "always to the Satisfaccion of theire Lascivious and Lustfull desires, and to the disgrace not only of the English butt allso of many other Christian Nations." When Virginia finally prohibited all interracial liaisons in 1691, the Assembly vigorously denounced miscegenation and its fruits as "that abominable mixture and spurious issue."[49]

From the surviving evidence, it appears that outright enslavement and these other forms of debasement appeared at about the same time in Maryland and Virginia. Indications of perpetual service, the very nub of slavery, coincided with indications that English settlers discriminated against Negro women, withheld arms from Negroes, and—though the timing is far less certain—reacted unfavorably to interracial sexual union. The coincidence suggests a mutual relationship between slavery and unfavorable assessment of Negroes. Rather than slavery causing "prejudice," or vice versa, they seem rather to have generated each other. Both were, after all, twin aspects of a general debasement of the Negro. Slavery and "prejudice" may have been equally cause and effect, continuously reacting upon each other, dynamically joining hands to hustle the Negro down the road to complete degradation. Much more than with the other English colonies, where the enslavement of Negroes was to some extent a borrowed practice, the available evidence for Maryland and Virginia points to less borrowing and to this kind of process: a mutually interactive growth of slavery and unfavorable assessment, with no cause for either which did not cause the other as well. If slavery caused prejudice, then invidious distinctions concerning working in the fields, bearing arms, and sexual union should have appeared *after* slavery's firm establishment. If prejudice caused slavery, then one would expect to find these lesser discriminations preceding the greater discrimination of outright enslavement. Taken as a whole, the evidence reveals a process of debasement of which hereditary lifetime service was an important but not the only part.

White servants did not suffer this debasement. Rather, their position improved, partly for the reason that they were not Negroes. By the early 1660's white men were loudly protesting against being made "slaves" in terms which strongly suggest that they considered slavery not as wrong but as inapplicable to themselves. The father of a Maryland apprentice petitioned in 1663 that "he Craves that his daughter may not be made a Slave a tearme soe Scandalous that if admitted to be the Condicion or tytle of the Apprentices in this Province will be soe distructive as noe free borne Christians will ever be induced to come over servants."[50] An Irish youth complained to a Maryland court in 1661 that he had been kidnapped and forced to sign for fifteen years, that he had already served six and a half years and was now twenty-one, and that eight and a half more years of service was "contrary to the lawes of God and man that a Christian Subject should be made a Slave." (The jury blandly compromised the dispute by deciding that he should serve only until age twenty-one, but that he was now only nineteen.) Free Negro servants were generally increasingly less able to defend themselves against this insidious kind of encroachment.[51] Increasingly, white men were more clearly free because Negroes had become so clearly slave.

Certainly it was the case in Maryland and Virginia that the legal enactment of Negro slavery followed social practice, rather than vice versa, and also that the assemblies were slower than in other English colonies to declare how Negroes could or should be treated. These two patterns in themselves suggest that slavery was less a matter of previous conception or external example in Maryland and Virginia than elsewhere.

The Virginia Assembly first showed itself incontrovertibly aware that Negroes were not serving in the same manner as English servants in 1660 when it declared "that for the future no servant comeing into the country without indentures, of what christian nation soever, shall serve longer then those of our own country, of the like age." In 1661 the Assembly indirectly provided statutory recognition that some Negroes served for life: "That in case any English servant shall run away in company with any negroes who are incapable of makeing satisfaction by addition of time," he must serve for the Negroes' lost time as well as his own. Maryland enacted a closely similar law in 1663 (possibly modeled on Virginia's) and in the following year, on the initiative of the lower house, came out with the categorical declaration that Negroes were to serve "Durante Vita."[52] During the next twenty-odd years a succession of acts in both colonies defined with increasing precision what sorts of persons might be treated as slaves.[53] Other acts dealt with the growing problem of slave control, and especially after 1690 slavery began to assume its now familiar character as a complete deprivation of all rights.[54] As early as 1669 the Virginia Assembly unabashedly enacted a brutal law which showed where the logic of perpetual servitude was inevitably tending. Unruly servants could be chastened by sentences to additional terms, but "WHEREAS the only law in force for the punishment of refractory servants resisting their master, mistris or overseer cannot be inflicted upon negroes, nor the obstinacy of many of them by other than violent meanes supprest," if a slave "by the extremity of the correction should chance to die" his master was not to be adjudged guilty of felony "since it cannot be presumed that prepensed malice (which alone makes murther Felony) should induce any man to destroy his owne estate."[55] Virginia planters felt they acted out of mounting necessity: there were disturbances among slaves in several areas in the early 1670's.[56]

By about 1700 the slave ships began spilling forth their black cargoes in greater and greater numbers. By that time, racial slavery and the necessary police powers had been written into law. By that time, too, slavery had lost all resemblance to a perpetual and heredi- tary version of English servitude, though service for life still seemed to contemporaries its most essential feature.[57] In the last quarter of the seventeenth century the trend was to treat Negroes more like property and less like men, to send them to the fields at younger ages, to deny them automatic existence as inherent members of the community; to tighten the bonds on their personal and civil freedom, and correspondingly to loosen the traditional restraints on the master's freedom to deal with his human property as he saw fit.[58] In 1705 Vir- ginia gathered up the random statutes of a whole generation and baled them into a "slave code" which would not have been out of place in the nineteenth century.[59]

.   .   .

THE UN-ENGLISH: SCOTS, IRISH, AND INDIANS

In the minds of overseas Englishmen, slavery, the new tyranny, did not apply to any Europeans. Something about Negroes, and to lesser extent Indians, set them apart for drastic exploitation, oppression, and degradation. In order to discover why, it is useful to turn the problem inside out, to inquire why Englishmen in America did not treat any other peoples like Negroes. It is especially revealing to see how Eng- lish settlers looked upon the Scotch (as they frequently called them) and the Irish, whom they often had opportunity and "reason" to en- slave, and upon the Indians, whom they enslaved, though only, as it were, casually.

In the early years Englishmen treated the increasingly numerous settlers from other European countries, especially Scottish and Irish servants, with condescension and frequently with exploitive brutality. Englishmen seemed to regard their colonies as exclusively *English* preserves and to wish to protect English persons especially from the exploitation which inevitably accompanied settlement in the New World. . . .

The necessity of peopling the colonies transformed the long-standing urge to discriminate among non-English peoples into a necessity. Which of the non-English were sufficiently different and foreign to warrant treating as "perpetual servants"? The need to answer this question did not mean, of course, that upon arrival in America the colonists immediately jettisoned their sense of distance from those persons they did not actually enslave. They discriminated against Welshmen and Scotsmen who, while admittedly "the best servants," were typically the servants of Englishmen. There was a considerably stronger tendency to discriminate against Papist Irishmen, those "worst" servants, but never to make slaves of them.[60] And here lay the crucial difference. Even the Scottish prisoners taken by Cromwell at Worcester and Dunbar—captives in a just war!—were never treated as slaves in England or the colonies. Certainly the lot of those sent to Barbados was miserable, but it was a different lot from the African slave's. In New England they were quickly accommodated to the prevailing labor system, which was servitude. As the Reverend Mr. Cotton of the Massachusetts Bay described the situation to Oliver Cromwell in 1651,

> The Scots, whom God delivered into you hand at Dunbarre, and whereof sundry were sent hither, we have been desirous (as we could) to make their yoke easy. Such as were sick of the scurvy or other diseases have not wanted physick and chyrurgery. They have not been sold for slaves to perpetuall servitude, but for 6 or 7 or 8 yeares, as we do our owne; and he that bought the most of them (I heare) buildeth houses for them, for every 4 an house, layeth some acres of ground thereto, which he giveth them as their owne, requiring 3 dayes in the weeke to worke for him (by turnes) and 4 dayes for themselves, and promisteth, as soone as they can repay him the money he layed out for them, he will set them at liberty.[61]

Here was the nub: captive Scots were men "as our owne." Negroes were not. They were almost hopelessly far from being of the English nation. As the Bermuda legislature proclaimed in 1663, even such Negroes "as count themselves Free because no p.ticler masters claymeth their servies, in our judgments are not Free to all nationall priviledges."[62]

Indians too seemed radically different from Englishmen, far more so than any Europeans. They were enslaved, like Negroes, and so fell on the losing side of a crucial dividing line. It is easy to see why: whether considered in terms of complexion, religion, nationality, savagery, bestiality, or geographical location, Indians were more like Negroes than like Englishmen. Given this resemblance the essential problem becomes why Indian slavery never became an important institution in the colonies. Why did Indian slavery remain numerically insignificant and typically incidental in character? Why were Indian slaves valued at much lower prices than Negroes? Why were Indians, as a kind of people, treated like Negroes and yet at the same time very differently?

Certain obvious factors made for important differentiations in the minds of the English colonists. As was the case with first confrontations in America and Africa, the different contexts of confrontation made Englishmen more interested in converting and civilizing Indians than Negroes. That this campaign in America too frequently degenerated into military campaigns of extermination did nothing to eradicate the initial distinction. Entirely apart from English intentions, the culture of the American Indians probably meant that they were less readily enslavable than Africans. By comparison, they were less used to settled agriculture, and their own variety of slavery was probably even less similar to the chattel slavery which Englishmen practiced in America than was the domestic and political slavery of the West African cultures. But it was the transformation of English intentions in the wilderness which counted most heavily in the long run. The Bible and the treaty so often gave way to the clash of flintlock and tomahawk. The colonists' perceptions of the Indians came to be organized not only in pulpits and printshops but at the bloody cutting edge of the English thrust into the Indians' lands. Thus the most pressing and mundane circumstances worked to make Indians seem very different from Negroes. In the early years especially, Indians were in a position to mount murderous reprisals upon the English settlers, while the few scattered Negroes were not. When English-Indian relations did not turn upon sheer power they rested on diplomacy. In many instances the colonists took assiduous precautions to prevent abuse of Indians belonging to friendly tribes. Most of the Indians enslaved by the English had their own tribal enemies to thank. It became a common practice to ship Indian slaves to the West Indies where they could be exchanged for slaves who had no compatriots lurking on the outskirts of English settlements.[63] In contrast, Negroes presented much less of a threat—at first.

Equally important, Negroes had to be dealt with as individuals— with supremely impartial anonymity, to be sure—rather than as nations. Englishmen wanted and had to live with their Negroes, as it were, side by side. Accordingly their impressions of Negroes were forged in the heat of continual, inescapable personal contacts. There were few pressures urging Englishmen to treat Indians as integral constituents in their society, which Negroes were whether Englishmen liked or not. At a distance the Indian could be viewed with greater detachment and his characteristics acknowledged and approached more coolly and more rationally. At a distance too, Indians could retain the quality of nationality, a quality which Englishmen admired in themselves and expected in other peoples. Under contrasting circumstances in America, the Negro nations tended to become Negro people.

Here lay the rudiments of certain shadowy but persistent themes in what turned out to be a multi-racial nation. Americans came to impute to the braves of the Indian "nations" an ungovernable individuality (which was perhaps not merited in such exaggerated degree) and at the same time to impart to Negroes all the qualities of an eminently governable sub-nation, in which African tribal distinctions were assumed to be of no consequence and individuality unaspired to. More immediately, the two more primitive peoples rapidly came to serve as two fixed points from which English settlers could triangulate their own position in America; the separate meanings of *Indian* and *Negro* helped define the meaning of living in America. The Indian became for Americans a symbol of their American experience; it was no mere luck of the toss that placed the profile of an American Indian rather than an American Negro on the famous old five-cent piece. Confronting the Indian in America was a testing experience, common to all the colonies. Conquering the Indian symbolized and personified the conquest of the American difficulties, the surmounting of the wilderness. To push back the Indian was to prove the worth of one's own mission, to make straight in the desert a highway for civilization. With the Negro it was utterly different.

RACIAL SLAVERY: FROM REASONS TO RATIONALE

And *difference*, surely, was the indispensable key to the degradation of Negroes in English America. In scanning the problem of *why* Negroes were enslaved in America, certain constant elements in a complex situation can be readily, if roughly, identified. It may be taken as given that there would have been no enslavement without economic need, that is, without persistent demand for labor in underpopulated colonies. Of crucial importance, too, was the fact that for cultural reasons Negroes were relatively helpless in the face of European aggressiveness and technology. In themselves, however, these two elements will not explain the enslavement of Indians and Negroes. The pressing exigency in America was labor, and Irish and English servants were available. Most of them would have been helpless to ward off outright enslavement if their masters had thought themselves privileged and able to enslave them. As a group, though, masters did not think themselves so empowered. Only with Indians and Negroes did Englishmen attempt so radical a deprivation of liberty—which brings the matter abruptly to the most difficult and imponderable question of all: what was it about Indians and Negroes which set them apart, which rendered them *different* from Englishmen, which made them special candidates for degradation?

To ask such questions is to inquire into the *content* of English attitudes, and unfortunately there is little evidence with which to build an answer. It may be said, however, that the heathen condition of the Negroes seemed of considerable importance to English settlers in America—more so than to English voyagers upon the coasts of Africa—and that heathenism was associated in some settlers' minds with the condition of slavery.[64] This is not to say that the colonists enslaved Negroes because they were heathens. The most clear-cut positive trace of such reasoning was probably unique and certainly far from being a forceful statement: in 1660 John Hathorne declared, before a Massachusetts court in partial support of his contention that an Indian girl should not be compelled to return to her master, that "first the law is undeniable that the indian may have the same distribusion of Justice with our selves: ther is as I humbly conceive not the same argument as amongst the negroes[,] for the light of the gospell is a begineing to appear amongst them—that is the indians."[65]

The importance and persistence of the tradition which attached slavery to heathenism did not become evident in any positive assertions that heathens might be enslaved. It was not until the period of legal establishment of slavery after 1660 that the tradition became manifest at all, and even then there was no effort to place heathenism and slavery on a one-for-one relationship. Virginia's second statutory definition of a slave (1682), for example, awkwardly attempted to rest enslavement on religious difference while excluding from possible enslavement all heathens who were not Indian or Negro.[66] Despite such logical difficulties, the old European equation of slavery and religious difference did not rapidly vanish in America, for it cropped up repeatedly after 1660 in assertions that slaves by becoming Christian did not automatically become free. By about the end of the seventeenth century, Maryland, New York, Virginia, North and South Carolina, and New Jersey had all passed laws reassuring masters that conversion of their slaves did not necessitate manumission.[67] These acts were passed in response to occasional pleas that Christianity created a claim to freedom and to much more frequent assertions by men interested in converting Negroes that nothing could be accomplished if masters thought their slaves were about to be snatched from them by meddling missionaries.[68] This decision that the slave's religious condition had no relevance to his status as a slave (the only one possible if an already valuable economic institution was to be retained) strongly suggests that heathenism was an important component in the colonists' initial reaction to Negroes early in the century.

Yet its importance can easily be overstressed. For one thing, some of the first Negroes in Virginia had been baptized before arrival. In the early years others were baptized in various colonies and became more than nominally Christian; a Negro woman joined the church in Dorchester, Massachusetts, as a full member in 1641.[69] With some Negroes becoming Christian and others not, there might have developed a caste differentiation along religious lines, yet there is no evidence to suggest that the colonists distinguished consistently between the Negroes they converted and those they did not. It was racial, not religious, slavery which developed in America.

Still, in the early years, the English settlers most frequently contrasted themselves with Negroes by the term *Christian*, though they also sometimes described themselves as *English*;[70] here the explicit religious distinction would seem to have lain at the core of English reaction. Yet the concept embodied by the term *Christian* embraced so much more meaning than was contained in specific doctrinal affirmations that it is scarcely possible to assume on the basis of this linguistic contrast that the colonists set Negroes apart because they were heathen. The historical experience of the English people in the sixteenth century had made for fusion of religion and nationality; the qualities of being English and Christian had become so inseparably blended that it seemed perfectly consistent to the Virginia Assembly in 1670 to declare that "noe negroe or Indian though baptised and enjoyned their owne Freedome shall be capable of any such purchase of christians, but yet not debarred from buying any of their owne nation." Similarly, an order of the Virginia Assembly in 1662 revealed a well-knit sense of self-identity of which Englishness and Christianity were interrelated parts: "METAPPIN a Powhatan Indian being sold for life time to one Elizabeth Short by the king of Wainoake Indians who had no power to sell him being of another nation, *it is ordered* that the said Indian be free, he speaking perfectly the English tongue and desiring baptism."[71]

From the first, then, vis-à-vis the Negro the concept embedded in the term *Christian* seems to have conveyed much of the idea and feeling of *we* as against *they*: to be Christian was to be civilized rather than barbarous, English rather than African, white rather than black. The term *Christian* itself proved to have remarkable elasticity, for by the end of the seventeenth century it was being used to define a species of slavery which had altogether lost any connection with explicit religious difference. In the Virginia code of 1705, for example, the term sounded much more like a definition of race than of religion: "And for a further christian care and usage of all christian servants, *Be it also enacted, by the authority aforesaid, and it is hereby enacted,* That no negroes, mulattos, or Indians, although christians, or Jews, Moors, Mahometans, or other infidels, shall, at any time, purchase any christian servant, nor any other, except of their own complexion, or such as are declared slaves by this act." By this time "Christianity" had somehow become intimately and explicitly linked with "complexion." The 1705 statute declared "That all servants imported and brought into this country, by sea or land, who were not christians in their native country, (except Turks and Moors in amity with her majesty, and others that can make due proof of their being free in England, or any other christian country, before they were shipped, in order to transportation hither) shall be accounted and be slaves, and as such be here bought and sold notwithstanding a conversion to christianity afterwards."[72] As late as 1753 the Virginia slave code anachronistically defined slavery in terms of religion when everyone knew that slavery had for generations been based on the racial and not the religious difference.[73]

It is worth making still closer scrutiny of the terminology which Englishmen employed when referring both to themselves and to the two peoples they enslaved, for this terminology affords the best single means of probing the content of their sense of difference. The terms *Indian* and *Negro* were both borrowed from the Hispanic languages, the one originally deriving from (mistaken) geographical locality and the other from human complexion. When referring to the Indians the English colonists either used that proper name or called them *savages*, a term which reflected primarily their view of Indians as uncivilized, or occasionally (in Maryland especially) *pagans*, which gave more explicit expression to the missionary urge. When they had reference to

Indians the colonists occasionally spoke of themselves as *Christians* but after the early years almost always as *English*.

In significant contrast, the colonists referred to *Negroes* and by the eighteenth century to *blacks* and to *Africans*, but almost never to Negro *heathens* or *pagans* or *savages*. Most suggestive of all, there seems to have been something of a shift during the seventeenth century in the terminology which Englishmen in the colonies applied to themselves. From the initially most common term *Christian*, at mid-century there was a marked drift toward *English* and *free*. After about 1680, taking the colonies as a whole, a new term appeared—*white*.

So far as the weight of analysis may be imposed upon such terms, diminishing reliance upon *Christian* suggests a gradual muting of the specifically religious element in the Christian-Negro disjunction in favor of secular nationality: Negroes were, in 1667, "not in all respects to be admitted to a full fruition of the exemptions and impunities of the English."[74] As time went on, as some Negroes became assimilated to the English colonial culture, as more "raw Africans" arrived, and as increasing numbers of non-English Europeans were attracted to the colonies, the colonists turned increasingly to the striking physiognomic difference. By 1676 it was possible in Virginia to assail a man for "eclipsing" himself in the "darke imbraces of a Blackamoore" as if "Buty consisted all together in the Antiphety of Complections." In Maryland a revised law prohibiting miscegenation (1692) retained *white* and *English* but dropped the term *Christian*—a symptomatic modification. As early as 1664 a Bermuda statute (aimed, ironically, at protecting Negroes from brutal abandonment) required that the "last Master" of senile Negroes "provide for them such accommodations as shall be convenient for Creatures of that hue and colour untill their death." By the end of the seventeenth century dark complexion had become an independent rationale for enslavement: in 1709 Samuel Sewall noted in his diary that a "Spaniard" had petitioned the Massachusetts Council for freedom but that "Capt. Teat alledg'd that all of that Color were Slaves."[75] Here was a barrier between "we" and "they" which was visible and permanent: the Negro could not become a white man. Not, at least, as yet.

What had occurred was not a change in the justification of slavery from religion to race. No such justifications were made. There seems to have been, within the unarticulated concept of the Negro as a different sort of person, a subtle but highly significant shift in emphasis. Consciousness of the Negro's heathenism remained through the eighteenth and into the nineteenth and even the twentieth century, and an awareness, at very least, of his different appearance was present from the beginning. The shift was an alteration in emphasis within a single concept of difference rather than a development of a novel conceptualization. The amorphousness and subtlety of such a change is evident, for instance, in the famous tract, *The Negro's and Indians Advocate*, published in 1680 by the Reverend Morgan Godwyn. Baffled and frustrated by the disinterest of planters in converting their slaves, Godwyn declared at one point that "their *Complexion*, which being most obvious to the sight, by which the *Notion* of things doth seem to be most certainly conveyed to the Understanding, is apt to make no *slight* impressions upon rude Minds, already prepared to admit of any thing for *Truth* which shall make for Interest." Altering his emphasis a few pages later, Godwyn complained that "these two words, *Negro* and *Slave*" are "by custom grown Homogeneous and Convertible; even as *Negro* and *Christian*, *Englishman* and *Heathen*, are by the like corrupt Custom and Partiality made Opposites."[76] Most arresting of all, throughout the colonies the terms *Christian*, *free*, *English*, and *white* were for many years employed indiscriminately as metonyms. A Maryland law of 1681 used all four terms in one short paragraph![77]

Whatever the limitations of terminology as an index to thought and feeling, it seems likely that the colonists' initial sense of difference from the Negro was founded not on a single characteristic but on a congeries of qualities which, taken as a whole, seemed to set the Negro apart. Virtually every quality in the Negro invited pejorative feelings. What may have been his two most striking characteristics, his heathenism and his appearance, were probably prerequisite to his complete debasement. His heathenism alone could never have led to permanent enslavement since conversion easily wiped out that failing. If his appearance, his racial characteristics, meant nothing to the English settlers, it is difficult to see how slavery based on race ever emerged, how the concept of complexion as the mark of slavery ever entered the colonists' minds. Even if the colonists were most unfavorably struck by the Negro's color, though, blackness itself did not urge the complete debasement of slavery. Other qualities—the utter strangeness of his language, gestures, eating habits, and so on—certainly must have contributed to the colonists' sense that he was very different, perhaps disturbingly so. In Africa these qualities had for Englishmen added up to *savagery*; they were major components in that sense of *difference* which provided the mental margin absolutely requisite for placing the European on the deck of the slave ship and the Negro in the hold.

The available evidence (what little there is) suggests that for Englishmen settling in America, the specific religious difference was initially of greater importance than color, certainly of much greater relative importance than for the Englishmen who confronted Negroes in their African homeland. Perhaps Englishmen in Virginia, living uncomfortably close to nature under a hot sun and in almost daily contact with tawny Indians, found the Negro's color less arresting than they might have in other circumstances. Perhaps, too, these first Virginians sensed how inadequately they had reconstructed the institutions and practices of Christian piety in the wilderness; they would perhaps appear less as failures to themselves in this respect if compared to persons who as Christians were *totally* defective. In this connection they may be compared to their brethren in New England, where godliness appeared (at first) triumphantly to hold full sway; in New England there was distinctly less contrasting of Negroes on the basis of the religious disjunction and much more militant discussion of just wars. Perhaps, though, the Jamestown settlers were told in 1619 by the Dutch shipmaster that these "negars" were heathens and could be treated as such. We do not know. The available data will not bear all the weight that the really crucial questions impose.

Of course once the cycle of degradation was fully under way, once slavery and racial discrimination were completely linked together, once the engine of oppression was in full operation, then there is no need to plead *ignoramus*. By the end of the seventeenth century in all the colonies of the English empire there was chattel racial slavery of a kind which would have seemed familiar to men living in the nineteenth century. No Elizabethan Englishman would have found it familiar, though certain strands of thought and feeling in Elizabethan England had intertwined with reports about the Spanish and Portuguese to engender a willingness on the part of English settlers in the New World to treat some men as suitable for private exploitation. During the seventeenth century New World conditions had exploited this predisposition and vastly enlarged it, so much so that English colonials of the eighteenth century were faced with full-blown slavery—something they thought of not as an institution but as a host of ever present problems, dangers, and opportunities.

NOTES

1. There is an eloquent revivification by William Bradford, *Of Plymouth Plantation, 1620–1647*, ed. Samuel Eliot Morison (N. Y., 1952), 61-63.

2. Susan M. Kingsbury, ed., *Records of the Virginia Company of London*, 4 vols. (Washington, D.C., 1906–35), III, 216-19, 231-32.

3. Cotton Mather, *A Pillar of Gratitude* . . . (Boston, 1700), 32-33.

4. From his own "Discourse on Western Planting" (1584), in E. G. R. Taylor, ed., *The Original Writings and Correspondence of the Two Richard Hakluyts (Works Issued by the Hakluyt Soc.*, 2d Ser., 76-77 [1935]), II, 314-15. See Perry Miller, "Religion and Society in the Early Literature of Virginia," in his *Errand into the Wilderness* (Cambridge, Mass., 1956), 99-140.

5. William Waller Hening, ed., *The Statutes at Large Being a Collection of All the Laws of Virginia*, 13 vols. (Richmond, N.Y., and Phila., 1809–23), I, 257, 435, 439-42, II, 113-14, 240, 388, III, 447-62; *Archives of Maryland*, 69 vols. (Baltimore, 1833–), I, 53, 80, 352-53, 409-10, 428, 443-44, 453-54, 464, 469, II, 147-48, 335-36, 527.

6. [Harrison], *Historical Description of Britaine*, in *Holinshed's Chronicles*, I, 175.

7. The best place to start on this complicated subject is Paul Vinagradof, *Villainage in England: Essays in English Mediaeval History* (Oxford, 1892). The least unsatisfactory studies of vestiges seem to be Alexander Savine, "Bondmen under the Tudors," *Royal Historical Society, Transactions*, 2d Ser., 17 (1903), 235-89; I. S. Leadman, "The Last Days of Bondage in England," *Law Quarterly Review*, 9 (1893), 348-65. William S. Holdsworth, *A History of English Law*, 3d ed., 12 vols. (Boston, 1923), III, 491-510, explodes the supposed distinction between villeins *regardant* and *gross*.

8. Thomas Smith, *De Republica Anglorum: A Discourse on the Commonwealth of England*, ed. L. Alston (Cambridge, Eng., 1906), 133.

9. Coke's section on villenage is Lib. II, cap. XI; see John Cowell, *The Interpreter: Or Booke Containing the Signification of Words* . . . (Cambridge, Eng., 1607), "villein."

10. *The Statutes of the Realm*, 11 vols. ([London], 1810–28), 1 Edw. VI. c. 3; 3and 4 Edw. VI. c. 16. A standard treatment is Frank Aydelotte, *Elizabethan Rogues and Vagabonds* (Oxford, 1913).

11. *Statutes of the Realm*, 39 Eliz. c. 4.

12. The "standard" work on this subject unfortunately does not address itself to the problem of origins: Abbot Emerson Smith, *Colonists in Bondage: White Servitude and Convict Labor in America, 1607–1776* (Chapel Hill, 1947).

13. Lorenzo J. Greene, *The Negro in Colonial New England, 1620–1776* (N. Y., 1942); report by the Massachusetts governor, Box 4, bundle: The Royal African Co. of England, MS. relating to the Company's trade in Negroes (1672–1734/35). 13, Parish Transcripts, N.-Y. Hist. Soc.

14. John Winthrop, *Winthrop's Journal: "History of New England," 1634–1649*, ed. James K. Hosmer, 2 vols. (N. Y., 1908), I, 260.

15. Newton, *Colonising Activities of the English Puritans*, 260-61.

16. Winthrop, *Journal*, ed. Hosmer, II, 73-74, 328; Donnan, ed., *Documents of the Slave Trade*, III, 4-5, 6, 9, 10, 11-14.

17. Harlow, *Barbados*, 340.
18. Max Farrand, ed., *The Laws and Liberties of Massachusetts* (Cambridge, Mass., 1929), 4. See the very good discussion in George H. Moore, *Notes on the History of Slavery in Massachusetts* (N. Y., 1866).
19. Simeon E. Baldwin, "Theophilus Eaton, First Governor of the Colony of New Haven," New Haven Colony Historical Society, *Papers*, 7 (1908), 31.
20. Nathaniel B. Shurtleff, ed., *Records of the Governor and Company of the Massachusetts Bay in New England*, 5 vols. in 6 (Boston, 1853–54), I, 181, 246; John Noble and John F. Cronin, eds., *Records of the Court of Assistants of the Colony of the Massachusetts Bay, 1630–1692*, 3 vols. (Boston, 1901–28), II, 78-79, 86, 90, 94, 97, 118.
21. Donnan, ed., *Documents of the Slave Trade*, III, 8.
22. Nathaniel B. Shurtleff and David Pulsifer, eds., *Records of the Colony of New Plymouth in New England*, 12 vols. (Boston, 1855–61), IX, 70-71. See also Ebenezer Hazard, comp., *Historical Collections; Consisting of State Papers, and Other Authentic Documents . . .* , 2 vols. ((Phila., 1792–94), II, 63-64.
23. Donnan, ed., *Documents of the Slave Trade*, III, 6-9. Exodus 21:16: "And he that stealeth a man, and selleth him, or if he be found in his hand, he shall surely be put to death." Compare with Deuteronomy 24:7: "If a man be found stealing any of his brethren of the children of Israel, and maketh merchandise of him, or selleth him; then that thief shall die; and thou shalt put evil away from among you."
24. John R. Bartlett, ed., *Records of the Colony of Rhode Island and Providence Plantations, in New England*, 10 vols. (Providence, 1856–65), I, 243. The act passed during the Coddington secession; only two of the four towns, Providence and Warwick, were represented. Roger Williams was in England, and it seems likely Samuel Gorton pressed passage. The absence of the two southern towns (where trading in Negroes must have centered) suggests a strangely prophetic division of opinion. See Charles M. Andrews, *The Colonial Period of American History*, 4 vols. (New Haven, 1934–38), II, 29-30.
25. *The Acts and Resolves, Public and Private, of the Province of the Massachusetts Bay . . .* , 21 vols. (Boston, 1869–1922), I, 130, 154, 156, 325, 327; J. Hammond Trumbull and Charles J. Hoadly, eds., *The Public Records of the Colony of Connecticut*, 15 vols. (Hartford, 1850–90), IV, 40. For treatment of servants see Lawrence W. Towner, " 'A Fondness for Freedom': Servant Protest in Puritan Society," *Wm. and Mary Qtly.*, 3d Ser., 19 (1962), 201-19.
26. John Josselyn, *An Account of Two Voyages to New-England . . .* , 2d ed. (London, 1675), reprinted in Massachusetts Historical Society, *Collections*, 3d Ser., 3 (1833), 231; Shurtleff, ed., *Records of Massachusetts Bay*, III, 268, 397, IV, Pt. i, 86, 257; *Acts and Resolves Mass.*, I, 130; Trumbull and Hoadly, eds., *Recs. Col. Conn.*, I, 349.
27. Kingsbury, ed., *Recs. Virginia Company*, III, 672-73, 704-7.
28. Arber, ed., *Travels of John Smith*, II, 541.
29. *A Perfect Description of Virginia . . .* (London, 1649), reprinted in Peter Force, ed., *Tracts . . .* , 4 vols. (N. Y., 1947), II, no. 8.
30. Henry R. McIlwaine, ed., *Minutes of the Council and General Court of Colonial Virginia, 1622–1632, 1670–1676* (Richmond, 1924), 196. Lists and musters of 1624 and 1625 are in John C. Hotten, ed., *The Original Lists of Persons of Quality . . .* (N. Y., 1880), 169-265.

31. Philip A. Bruce, *Economic History of Virginia in the Seventeenth Century* . . . , 2 vols. (N. Y., 1896), II, 73.

32. Further details are in Winthrop D. Jordan, "Modern Tensions and the Origins of American Slavery," *Journal of Southern History*, 28 (1962), 18-30.

33. Susie M. Ames, *Studies of the Virginia Eastern Shore in the Seventeenth Century* (Richmond, 1940), 99; John H. Russell, *The Free Negro in Virginia, 1619–1865* (Baltimore, 1913), 23-39; and his "Colored Freemen As Slave Owners in Virginia," *Journal of Negro History*, 1 (1916), 234-37.

34. *Archives Md.*, I, 41, 80, also 409, 453-54.

35. "Decisions of the General Court," *Virginia Magazine of History and Biography*, 5 (1898), 236-37.

36. For these four cases, Northampton County Deeds, Wills, etc., no. 4 (1651–54), 28 (misnumbered 29), 124, Virginia State Library, Richmond; *Archives Md.*, XLI, 261-62; York County Records, no. 2 (transcribed Wills and Deeds, 1645–49), 256–57, Va. State Lib.

37. Lancaster County Loose Papers, Box of Wills, 1650–1719, Folder 1656–1659, Va. State Lib.

38. Northampton County Orders, Deeds, Wills, etc., no. 2 (1640–45), 224; York County Deeds, Orders, Wills, etc. (1657–62), 108-9; in 1645 two Negro women and a boy sold for 5,500 lbs. of tobacco, York County Records, no. 2, 63; all Va. State Lib.

39. York County Records, no. 2, 390, Va. State Lib.

40. Nora Miller Turman and Mark C. Lewis, eds., "Inventory of the Estate of Argoll Yeardley of Northampton County, Virginia, in 1655," *Va. Mag. of Hist. and Biog.*, 70 (1962), 410-19.

41. Hening, ed., *Statutes Va.*, I, 144, 242, 292, 454; *Archives Md.*, I, 342, II, 136, 399, 538-39, XIII, 538-39.

42. John Hammond, *Leah and Rachel, or, the Two Fruitfull Sisters Virginia, and Mary-land: Their Present Condition, Impartially Stated and Related* . . . (London, 1656), 9.

43. Hening, ed., *Statutes Va.*, II, 267.

44. *Ibid.*, I, 226; for the same act in more detail, "Acts of General Assembly, Jan. 6, 1639–40," *Wm. and Mary Qtly.*, 2d Ser., 4 (1924), 147. In Bermuda, always closely connected with Virginia, the first prohibition of weapons to Negroes came in 1623, only seven years after the first Negro landed. The 1623 law was the first law anywhere in English specifically dealing with Negroes. After stressing the insolence of Negroes secretly carrying "cudgells and other weapons and working tools, very dangerous and not meete to be suffered to be carried by such vassalls," it prohibited (in addition to arms) Negroes going abroad at night, trespassing on other people's lands, and trading in tobacco without permission of their masters. Unfortunately the evidence concerning lifetime service for Negroes is much less definite in the scanty Bermuda sources than in those for Maryland and Virginia; the first known incident suggestive of the practice might reasonably be placed anywhere from 1631 to 1656. Later evidence shows Bermuda's slavery and proportion of Negroes similar to Virginia's, and it seems unlikely that the two colonies' early experience was radically different. Henry C. Wilkinson, *The Adventurers of Bermuda; A History of the Island from Its Discovery until the Dissolution of the Somers Island Company in 1684* (London,

1933), 114; J. H. Lefroy, comp., *Memorials of the Discovery and Early Settlement of the Bermudas or Somers Islands, 1515–1685* . . . , 2 vols. (London, 1877–79), I, 308-9, 505, 526-27, 633, 645, II, 34-35, 70. But Negroes were to be armed at times of alarm (*ibid.*, II, 242, 366, 380 [1666–73]) : Bermuda was exposed to foreign attack.

45. Hening, ed., *Statutes Va.*, I, 146. (The term "negro woman" was in very common use.) *Archives Md.*, X, 114-15.

46. Hening, ed., *Statutes Va.*, I, 552; McIlwaine, ed., *Minutes Council Va.*, 477.

47. Bruce, *Economic History of Va.*, II, 110.

48. "The History of Bacon's and Ingram's Rebellion, 1676," in Charles M. Andrews, ed., *Narratives of the Insurrections, 1675–1690* (N. Y., 1915), 96. Cf. the will of John Fenwick (1683), *Documents Relating to the Colonial, Revolutionary and Post-Revolutionary History of the State of New Jersey* . . . [New Jersey Archives], 1st Ser. (Newark, etc., 1880–1949), XXIII, 162.

49. Hening, ed., *Statutes Va.*, II, 170, III, 86-87; *Archives Md.*, I, 533-34, VII, 204; Lefroy, comp., *Memorials Bermudas*, II, 190 (a resolution, not a statute). Some evidence suggests miscegenation was not taken as seriously in 17th-century Bermuda as on the mainland: *ibid.*, I, 550, II, 30, 103, 141, 161, 228, 314.

50. *Archives Md.*, I, 464.

51. *Ibid.*, XLI, 476-78, XLIX, 123-24. Compare the contemporary difficulties of a Negro servant: William P. Palmer *et al.*, eds., *Calendar of Virginia State Papers* . . . , 11 vols. (Richmond, 1875–93), I, 9-10.

52. Hening, ed., *Statutes Va.*, I, 539, II, 26; *Archives Md.*, I, 449, 489, 526, 533-34. The "any negroes who are incapable" suggests explicit recognition that some were free, but in several sources the law as re-enacted the next year included a comma between "negroes" and "who," as did the Maryland act of 1663. See *The Lawes of Virginia Now in Force: Collected out of the Assembly Records* . . . (London, 1662), 59.

53. Hening, ed., *Statutes Va.*, II, 170, 270, 283, 490-91, III, 137-40, 447-48; *Archives Md.*, VII, 203-5, XIII, 546-49, XXII, 551-52.

54. Especially Hening, ed., *Statutes Va.*, II, 270-71, 481-82, 493, III, 86, 102-3; *Archives Md.*, XIII, 451-53, XIX, 167, 193, XXII, 546-48, XXVI, 254-56.

55. Hening, ed., *Statutes Va.*, II, 270; compare law for servants, I, 538, II, 118.

56. *Ibid.*, II, 299.

57. Robert Beverley, *The History and Present State of Virginia*, ed. Louis B. Wright (Chapel Hill, 1947), 271-72.

58. For illustration, Hening, ed., *Statutes Va.*, II, 288, 479-80 (Negro *children* taxed from age 12, white *boys* from 14), III, 102-3; *Archives Md.*, VII, 76 (county courts required to register births, marriages, burials of all "Except Negroes Indians and Molottos").

59. Hening, ed., *Statutes Va.*, III, 447-62.

60. The designations are a prominent planter's, quoted in Higham, *Development of the Leeward Islands*, 169, also 170n.

61. Boston, July 28, 1651, W. H. Whitmore and W. S. Appleton, eds.

Hutchinson Papers, 2 vols. (Prince Society, *Publications* [Albany, 1865], I, 264-65. For prisoners to Barbados see Smith, *Colonists in Bondage*, 152-59.

62. Lefroy, comp., *Memorials Bermudas*, II, 190-91.

63. Hening, ed., *Statutes Va.*, II, 299. A good study of Indian slavery is needed, but see Almon Wheeler Lauber, *Indian Slavery in Colonial Times within the Present Limits of the United States* (N. Y., 1913). In 1627 some imported Carib Indians proved unsalable in Virginia and were turned over to the colony; the General Court decided that, since the Caribs had stolen goods, attempted murder, tried to run away to the Virginia Indians, and might prove the downfall of the whole colony, the best way to dispose of the problem was to hang them: McIlwaine, ed., *Minutes Council Va.*, 155.

64. See above, chap. 1, sec. 3. Also John C. Hurd, *The Law of Freedom and Bondage in the United States*, 2 vols. (Boston, 1858–62), I, 159-60; Horne, *The Mirror of Justices*, ed. Robinson, 124; Marcus W. Jernegan, *Laboring and Dependent Classes in Colonial America, 1607–1783; Studies of the Economic, Educational, and Social Significance of Slaves, Servants, Apprentices, and Poor Folk* (Chicago, 1931), 24-26; Helen T. Catterall, ed., *Judicial Cases Concerning American Slavery and the Negro*, 5 vols. (Washington, 1926–37), I, 55n. Data in the following pages suggest this. The implication that slavery could last only during the heathen state is in Providence Company to Gov. Philip Bell, London, Apr. 20, 1635, Box 9, bundle: List no. 7, 2d portion, MS. relating to the Royal African Co. and Slavery matters, 43, Parish Transcripts, N.-Y. Hist. Soc.: ". . . a Groundless opinion that Christians may not lawfully keepe such persons in a state of Servitude during their strangeness from Christianity." In 1695 Gov. John Archdale of South Carolina prohibited sale of some Indians, captured by his own Indian allies, as slaves to the West Indies and freed them because they were Christians: John Archdale, *A New Description of That Fertile and Pleasant Province of Carolina* . . . (London, 1707), in Alexander S. Salley, Jr., ed., *Narratives of Early Carolina, 1650–1708* (N. Y., 1911), 300.

65. *Records and Files of the Quarterly Courts of Essex County Massachusetts, 1636–1683*, 8 vols. (Salem, 1911–21), II, 240-42.

66. Hening, ed., *Statutes Va.*, II, 490-92.

67. *Archives Md.*, I, 526, 533 (1664), II, 272; "Duke's Laws," C. O. 5/1142, f. 33v., P. R. O., a portion of the section of "Bondslavery" omitted from the standard New York printed sources which reads "And also provided that This Law shall not extend to sett at Liberty Any Negroe or Indian Servant who shall turne Christian after he shall have been bought by Any Person." (This unpublished Crown Copyright material is reproduced by permission of the Controller of H. M. Stationery Office.) *The Colonial Laws of New York from the Year 1664 to the Revolution* . . . , 5 vols. (Albany, 1894–96), I, 597-98 (1706); Hening, ed., *Statutes Va.*, II, 260 (1667); Saunders, ed., *Col. Recs. N. C.*, I, 204 (1670), II, 837; Cooper and McCord, eds., *Statutes S. C.*, VII, 343 (1691), 364-65; *Anno Regni Reginae Annae* . . . *Tertio;* [*The Acts Passed by the Second Assembly of New Jersey in December, 1704*] ([N. Y., 1704]), 20, an act which was disallowed for other reasons.

68. For example, in 1652 a mulatto girl pleaded Christianity as the reason why she should not be "a perpetuall slave" (Lefroy, comp., *Memorials Bermudas*, II, 34-35, also 293-94), and in 1694 some Massachusetts ministers asked

the governor and legislature to remove that "wel-knowne Discouragement" to conversion of slaves with a law denying that baptism necessitated freedom (*Acts and Resolves Mass.*, VII, 537).

69. Winthrop, *Journal*, ed. Hosmer, II, 26.

70. These statements on prevailing word usage are based on a wide variety of sources, many of them cited in this chapter; some passages already quoted may serve to amplify the illustrations in the following paragraphs.

71. Hening, ed., *Statutes Va.*, II, 281 (1670), 155 (1662).

72. *Ibid.*, III, 447-48 (1705), also 283, V, 547-48, VI, 356-57. Lingering aftereffects of the old concept cropped up as late as 1791, when *Negro* was still contradistinguished by *Christian*: Certificate of character of Negro Phill, Feb. 20, 1791, Character Certificates of Negroes, Papers of the Pennsylvania Abolition Society, Historical Society of Pennsylvania, Philadelphia.

73. Hening, ed., *Statutes Va.*, VI, 356-57.

74. *Ibid.*, II, 267.

75. "History of Bacon's and Ingram's Rebellion," Andrews, ed., *Narratives of the Insurrections*, 96; *Archives Md.*, XIII, 546-49; Lefroy, comp., *Memorials Bermudas*, II, 216; *Diary of Samuel Sewall, 1674-1729* (Mass. Hist. Soc., *Collections*, 5th Ser. 5-7 [1878-82]), II, 248. In 1698 Gov. Francis Nicholson informed the Board of Trade that the "major part" of Negroes in Maryland spoke English: *Archives Md.*, XXIII, 499. For first use of "white" in statutes of various colonies, Bartlett, ed., *Recs. Col. R. I.*, I, 243 (1652); *Archives Md.*, VII, 204-5 (1681); Aaron Leaming and Jacob Spicer, eds., *The Grants, Concessions, and Original Constitutions of the Province of New Jersey . . .* , 2d ed. (Somerville, N. J., 1881), 236 (1683); *Col. Laws N. Y.*, I, 148 (1684); Cooper and McCord, eds., *Statutes S. C.*, VII, 343 (1691); Hening, ed., *Statutes Va.*, III, 86-87 (1691); *Acts of Assembly, Made and Enacted in the Bermuda or Summer-Islands, from 1690, to 1713-14* (London, 1719), 12-13 (1690 or 1691). West Indian assemblies used the term in the 1680's and 1690's, possibly earlier. Officials in England were using "whites" and "blacks" as early as 1670 in questionnaires to colonial governors: Hening, ed., *Statutes Va.*, II, 515; Trumbull and Hoadly, eds., *Recs. Col. Conn.*, III, 293.

76. Godwyn, *The Negro's and Indians Advocate*, 20, 36.

77. *Archives Md.*, VII, 204.

• Negro slavery quickly became established not only in North America but in the British West Indies and in the Spanish, Portugese, and French colonies of the Western Hemisphere. David Brion Davis compares the evolution of slavery and the special characteristics of the institution in British America with slavery in Latin America.

The Evolution of Slavery in British America and Latin America: A Comparison

DAVID BRION DAVIS

The slave trade itself was a powerful agent of acculturation—one might say, of Americanization—which tended to blur distinctions in custom and give a more uniform character to Negro slavery than would have been found among earlier forms of European serfdom and villenage. With the acquisition of important Caribbean islands by Holland, Britain, and France, and with the development of sugar planting in the 1640's, the mounting demand for slaves made it impossible for mercantilist governments to prevent the growth of a vast system of smuggling and illicit trade. The same slave ships brought cargoes to mainland and island colonies, and competed with one another in supplying the Spanish. Planters of various nationalities bought slaves at reduced prices at the great Dutch entrepôts at Saint Eustatius and Curaçao. From their forts on the African coast to their colonies in America, the Dutch, French, English, Danes, and Portuguese were thrown together in a common enterprise that doubtless produced some blending of customs and attitudes toward the Negro slave.[1] Barbadians not only studied and imitated Brazilian methods of sugar cultivation, but possessed slaves by the 1650's who knew the language and customs of Brazil. In Guadeloupe and Martinque, Dutch émigrés from Brazil introduced the Portuguese practice of allowing slaves to grow their own provisions. During the seventeenth century there were close ties between Barbados and the mainland colonies of North America; and many of the Negroes in the continental colonies had lived for a time in the West Indies. Some of them spoke French, Dutch, or Spanish.[2]

Much is yet to be learned about this process of cultural exchange and its possible influence on the evolution of systems of slavery in the various colonies. Few questions in American history have been so controversial or so charged with moral significance as the origin of chattel slavery and its relation to racial prejudice. The most convincing recent studies suggest that the mainland colonists adopted from Barbados the view that Negroes were especially suited for perpetual slavery; and that while the early status of some Negroes was close to that of white servants, an increasingly degraded position was both a source and result of racial prejudice.[3] But however unfamiliar perpetual servitude may have been to most Elizabethan Englishmen, as early as 1617 a noted Puritan writer could assume that "slavish" servants were "perpetually put under the power of the master, as blackamores with us." [4] The problem is considerably complicated by the ambiguity of seventeenth-century terms. Some historians have assumed that a "servant" was not a slave, and yet Samuel Purchas and Thomas Hobbes, to mention only two writers of that century, used the word "servant" to refer to the most absolute slaves.[5] In the French and Spanish colonies, as well as in the English, the word for "Negro" was frequently used as a synonym for "slave." But Richard Ligon considered the condition of white servants in Barbados worse than that of the Negroes. Although white men were not subject to perpetual and inheritable servitude, it would be a mistake to think they were free from all burdens of slavery. In many colonies white servants could be sold, inherited, wagered, or recovered for a debt; Gabriel Towerson, an eminent English divine, complained that too many servants confused service with a profession and thought they needed to obey only when assigned a specific task.[6]

There were two historical circumstances, however, which differentiated the white from the Negro servant. As Oscar and Mary Handlin have observed, the emigration of white laborers was in large part voluntary, and the demand for their services was great enough to induce colonial legislators to offer them various protections and rewards: this was not only true on the mainland, but also in the West Indies, where there was the additional incentive of increasing public safety and avoiding a rebellious union of Negroes and lowly whites. We should also remember that white servitude was based on the customs and laws of particular countries. The English servant was not ordinarily an article of international commerce, nor was he subject to the ancient laws of slavery, as incorporated in the *jus gentium*.[7] Yet it was a general belief that Christianity permitted the enslavement of men "of infidel origin," and that Negroes purchased on the African coast had either been convicted of crime or captured, hopefully in a just war, and were therefore slaves by virtue of the law of nations. Hence Sir Edward Coke could affirm, in *Calvin's Case*, that infidels could either be put to death or enslaved; and Cotton Mather, doubtless drawing on Aristotle, could tell Massachusetts Negroes that they were "the *Animate, Separate, Active Instruments* of other men." [8]

Even if colonists were inclined to apply ancient concepts of slavery to the Negro, there was nothing, of course, to prevent individual masters from evolving their own rules and practices. First in Barbados and the Leeward Islands, then in Virginia and Maryland, and finally in Pennsylvania, New York, New England, and French Canada, societies accepted the perpetual slavery of Indians and Negroes without specific legislative sanction. In some areas the actual status of Negroes differed little from that of white servants; in New England, where the Confederation of 1643 recognized the slavery of captives, bondsmen were considered for a time to be under the protective regulations of the Old Testament. But the fact that stands out from all the variations in temporary custom is the cumulative debasement of the Negro in every British and French colony. Whether he served the Puritans of Old Providence Island or the French of Martinique, the Jamaica overseer or the Virginia farmer, the Pennsylvania Quaker or the Canadian convent, his person was the property of his owner, and he and his progeny, if they were born of a slave woman, were condemned to eternal bondage.[9]

From 1680 to 1710 virtually every English and French colony from the Saint Lawrence to South America acquired laws that attempted to define the slave's peculiar position as conveyable property, subject to rules respecting debt, descent, and taxation; and as a man who might be protected, punished, or prevented from exercising human capacities. Given the wide range of differences in colonial societies, the surprising fact about these laws is their underlying similarity. Everywhere they embodied ambiguities and compromises that arose from the impossibility of acting consistently on the premise that men were things. The basic contradiction was elucidated much later by a Virginia court, which echoed the doctrine of Seneca: "Slaves are not only property, but they are rational beings, and entitled to the humanity of the Court, when it can be exercised without invading the rights of property; and as regards the owner, their value is much enhanced by the mutual attachment of master and slave; a value which cannot enter into the calculation of damages by a jury." [10]

Both French and English colonial law assumed that the slave had essentially the attributes of personal property, and like a horse or cow could be moved, sold, or rented out at the will of his owner. In several colonies, however, there was doubt whether for purposes of taxation slaves should be rated as persons, personal property, or real estate. And while no colony presumed to infringe upon the slaveholder's right to move or sell his property, it was widely recognized that, in the interests of both the slave and society, there should be special rules regarding debt and inheritance.[11]

As early as the 1660's planters in the Leeward Islands were disturbed by the fact that merchant creditors could force the sale of Negroes and other chattels at auction, and thus deprive an estate of its productive capacity. In addition, the death of a planter sometimes resulted in the ruin of his estate when executors or minor heirs needlessly disposed of slaves. To prevent these evils, colonial legislators tried to invest bondsmen with some of the attributes of real estate, and thus provided lawyers with a subject for endless debate and confused litigation. In 1669 an Antigua law ruled that if a debtor's chattels, including white servants, were insufficient to satisfy a claim, the creditor must accept slaves as "estates of inheritance," attached to the freehold, and assume management of the plantation. In the previous year Barbados had defined slaves as freehold property, although in 1672 they were deemed chattels for the payment of an owner's debts. For more than a century, legislators in Jamaica and the Leeward Islands sought to make the descent of slaves conform to the law for freehold property, and to prevent Negroes from being seized for debt when claims could be satisfied by other means. But in all other respects, as a Nevis statute of 1705 made clear, there was no question that slaves were chattels.[12]

The French islands, Virginia, and South Carolina all experienced the same difficulties in trying to reconcile the notion of a slave as personal property with the desire to protect the integrity of estates. Under the *Code Noir* the slave was unmistakably a chattel; but a royal decree of 1721 prohibited heirs under the age of twenty-five from selling slaves from their estates.[13] After 1705 bondsmen in Virginia were accounted real estate for purposes of descent, but chattels, by an act of

1727, with respect to gifts and devises. Three years later a court decided that, regardless of previous statutes, executors were to consider slave property as no different from horses or cattle, a view which the assembly endorsed in 1748, when it was decided that confusion could be lessened by reducing bondsmen to their "natural condition" as personal goods. This new law was nullified, however, by the crown. There is evidence that Negroes in Virginia were sometimes annexed to the land and entailed, and were considered by courts as in some sense bound to the soil in inheritance. But in 1794 it was held, in Walden v. Payne, that though the law had protected bondsmen from unnecessary sale for the payment of debts and levies, they were chattels by nature. We might note that the confusion was carried across the mountains into Kentucky, which adopted the Virginia law of 1705 defining slaves as real estate for certain purposes. In colonial South Carolina bondsmen were regarded as chattels personal, notwithstanding an attempt in 1690 to class them as real estate; and yet as late as 1837 a court upheld an action of trespass against the captain of a patrol who had whipped a slave belonging to the plaintiff, but hired out to another man, on the ground that a slave was more analogous to land than to personal property. In addition to appealing to the analogy of an easement, the court maintained that a master possessed all the legal means of protecting his slave that the slave himself would have, had he been a freeman.[14]

It is not quite accurate, then, to think of chattel slavery as a well-defined status which put the Negro on precisely the same footing as other personal property. In no American colony was he attached to the soil in the sense of the *colonus*, or in a way that limited the freedom of his owner. But for both economic and humanitarian reasons, judges and lawmakers recognized that the slave was something more than a private and expendable possession.

The ambiguity was more pronounced when it came to regulating the bondsman's daily life and defining his relations with other people. If we think of freedom as a power to act or cause others to act, then it is clear that even the most authoritarian master, supported by the most oppressive laws, was to some extent limited by the will of his slaves, who had the power to appeal, flatter, humiliate, disobey, sabotage, or rebel. Richard Ligon reported that Barbadian Negroes not only persuaded planters to improve their diet, but complained so long about a shortage of women that their owners felt obliged to purchase more, the coveted females being apportioned by the slaves themselves in accordance with their own social hierarchies.[15] Courts and legislatures were farther removed from the direct influence of slaves, and had, besides, the mission of maintaining the standards and morale of slaveholders; yet in few instances could the law ignore the human capacities of slaves.

We have already seen that there were formidable obstacles to the religious conversion of slaves. By and large, Catholics showed far more concern for the souls of Negroes than did Protestants; and yet a number of British colonies, including New York, Jamaica, and South Carolina, gave official encouragement to such missionary work. If this amounted to little more than pious lip-service, the same could be said of the religious provisions in the *Code Noir*. The Spanish and Portuguese were more successful in winning converts, but it is doubtful whether the mass of slaves in any colony enjoyed a meaningful religious life.[16]

Whether a Negro worked on Sunday or had an opportunity to marry were largely matters of local custom and circumstance. An article in the *Code Noir* forbidding Sunday work was apparently no better enforced than similar laws in colonial Georgia and South Carolina. But in many British colonies it was customary to reserve Sundays for leisure and marketing, and to grant days of respite at Christmas, Easter, and Whitsuntide.[17] Since even Pennsylvania prohibited the marriage of white servants without their masters' consent, it is not surprising that this was a minimal restriction for slaves under both English and French law. A Massachusetts statute said that so long as servants were of the same "nation," their marriage should not be unreasonably denied. But in French Canada, where slave marriages were legally valid when permitted by a master, infants were disposed of at the will of the mother's owner, and when they died, were listed only as the property of a master, with no indication of their parentage. In the British West Indies and Southern mainland colonies, slave marriages were no more legal than under Roman law. But as in Roman law, nineteenth-century Louisiana courts acknowledged that such a *contubernium* had legal consequences, and could become valid as a contract after manumission. In 1871 a judge of the supreme court of Tennessee delivered the opinion that slave marriages had always been valid in that state, though not followed by all the legal consequences of a marriage between freemen. This somewhat questionable view simply underlines the essential point: it was impossible to ignore the fact that slaves could and did marry; but even where given legal sanction, such marriages were radically altered by the effects of bondage.[18]

NOTES

1. Evidence of the mixing of nationalities in the slave trade, and of the frequent contact between Dutch, English, French, Spanish, Portuguese, Danes, and Swedes, can be found throughout Elizabeth Donnan's *Documents Illustrative of the History of the Slave Trade to America* (Washington, 1930–35). Fernando Romero stresses that the entire slave trade was a single process divided into various branches. (Romero, "The Slave Trade and the Negro in South America," *Hispanic American Historical Review*, XXIV [Aug., 1944], 371. See also, Scelle, *Traite négrière*, I, 707; Basil Davidson, *Black Mother: The Years of the African Slave Trade* [Boston, 1961], *passim*; Daniel P. Mannix and Malcolm Cowley, *Black Cargoes: A History of the Atlantic Slave Trade, 1518–1865* [New York, 1962], *passim*).

2. Richard Ligon, *A True & Exact History of the Island of Barbados* (London, 1757), pp. 52, 85; Vincent T. Harlow, *A History of Barbados, 1625–1685* (Oxford, 1926), pp. 268-91; Jean-Baptiste Du Tertre, *Histoire générale des Antilles habitées par les François* (Paris, 1667–71), II, 515; Frank Wesley Pitman, *The Development of the British West Indies, 1700–1763* (New Haven, 1917), pp. 6-15; Frank Wesley Craven, *The Southern Colonies in the Seventeenth Century, 1607–1689* (Baton Rouge, 1949), pp. 18, 25; "Eighteenth-Century Slaves as Advertised by Their Masters," *Journal of Negro History*, I (Apr., 1916), 163-216; Pierre-François-Xavier de Charlevoix, *Histoire de l'Isle Espagnole ou de Saint-Domingue . . .* (Amsterdam, 1733), III, 162-63; Winthrop D. Jordan, "The Influence of the West Indies on the Origins of New England Slavery," *William and Mary Quarterly*, 3rd ser., XVIII (Apr., 1961), 248-49.

3. See especially the following articles: Winthrop Jordan, "Influence of West Indies," pp. 243-50; Jordan, "American Chiaroscuro: The Status and Definition of Mulattoes in the British Colonies," *William and Mary Quarterly*, 2nd ser., XIX (Apr., 1962), 183-200; Jordan, "Modern Tensions and the Origins of American Slavery," *Journal of Southern History*, XXVIII (Feb., 1962), 18-30; M. Eugene Sirmans, "The Legal Status of the Slave in South Carolina, 1670–1740," *Journal of Southern History*, XXVIII (Nov., 1962), 462-73; Carl N. Degler, "Slavery and the Genesis of American Race Prejudice," *Comparative Studies in Society and History*, II (Oct., 1959), 49-67. The seminal study which raised issues that have not yet been resolved is Oscar and Mary Handlin, "Origins of the Southern Labor System," *William and Mary Quarterly*, 3rd ser., VII (Apr., 1950), 199-222.

4. Paul Baynes, *An Entire Commentary upon the Whole Epistle of the Apostle Paul to the Ephesians*, reprinted in *Nichol's Series of Commentaries*, XI (Edinburgh, 1865), pp. 365-69. Although this work was not published until 1643, Baynes died in 1617. I am indebted to Lawrence W. Towner for supplying me with a copy of this document.

5. Thomas Hobbes, *De Cive, or the Citizen* (ed. and with introd. by Sterling P. Lamprecht, New York, 1949), ii, viii; Samuel Purchas, *Purchas His Pilgrimes in Five Bookes* (London, 1625), III, 419 (Purchas refers to the "cholopey" of Novograde both as "bondslaves" and "servants").

6. Ligon, *True & Exact History*, pp. 43-44; Abbot Emerson Smith, *Colonists*

in Bondage: White Servitude and Convict Labor in America, 1607–1776 (Chapel Hill, 1947), pp. 224, 233; Richard B. Schlatter, *The Social Ideas of Religious Leaders, 1660–1688* (Oxford, 1940), p. 66.

7. Oscar and Mary Handlin, "Origins of the Southern Labor System," pp. 210-21; *Acts of Assembly . . . Charibbee Leeward Islands*, pp. 159-63; Harlow, *History of Barbados*, pp. 303-5; *Journals of the Assembly of Jamaica*, I (Jamaica, 1811), 120-21, 125; Smith, *Colonists in Bondage*, pp. 227-38. The servitude of English and Irish convicts and prisoners was not, of course, contractual in character; it was mitigated only by the traditional belief that "Christians," meaning men who were not of "infidel" origin, should not be held in perpetual slavery. My interpretation differs from that of the Handlins with respect to the origins of chattel slavery and the degree of similarity between West Indian and mainland colonies.

8. W. S. Holdsworth, *A History of English Law*, VII (London, n.d.), 484; Lawrence W. Towner, " 'A Fondness for Freedom': Servant Protest in Puritan Society," *William and Mary Quarterly*, 2nd ser., XIX (Apr., 1962), 210.

9. J. H. Lefroy, *Memorials of the Discovery and Early Settlement of the Bermudas or Somers Islands, 1515–1685, Compiled from the Colonial Records and Other Original Sources* (n.p., 1932 reprint ed.), I, 526-27; II, 70, 166; Degler, "Slavery and the Genesis of American Race Prejudice," pp. 49-67; Ligon, *True & Exact History*, pp. 22-37; Lucien Peytraud, *L'Esclavage aux Antilles françaises avant 1789* (Paris, 1897), pp. 144-45; Ulrich Bonnell Phillips, *American Negro Slavery: A Survey of the Supply, Employment and Control of Negro Labor as Determined by the Plantation Regime* (reprint ed., Gloucester, Mass., 1959), pp. 46, 52, 98-99; Trudel, *L'Esclavage au Canada français*, pp. 99-100; Almon W. Lauber, *Indian Slavery in Colonial Times Within the Present Limits of the United States* (New York, 1913), pp. 214-16; Susie M. Ames, *Studies of the Virginia Eastern Shore in the Seventeenth Century* (Richmond, 1940), pp. 101-6; Towner, "Fondness for Freedom," pp. 201-19; Lorenzo J. Greene, *The Negro in Colonial New England, 1620–1776* (New York, 1942), pp. 124-26, 167-90; Edward R. Turner, *The Negro in Pennsylvania: Slavery, Servitude, Freedom, 1639–1861* (Washington, 1911), pp. 18-26; Jordan, "Influence of West Indies," pp. 243-50; Jordan, "Modern Tensions," pp. 23-30. For interpretations which place more emphasis on local conditions and differences, see Handlin, "Origins of Southern Labor System," pp. 199-22; John M. Mecklin. "The Evolution of the Slave Status in American Democracy," *Journal of Negro History*, II (Apr., 1917), 105-25; (July, 1917), 229-51; James C. Ballagh, *History of Slavery in Virginia* (Baltimore, 1902), *passim*. Stanley Elkins provides an excellent summary and discussion of the entire question in *Slavery*, pp. 37-52.

10. Helen T. Catterall (ed.), *Judicial Cases Concerning American Slavery and the Negro* (Washington, 1926-1937), I, 142, 144.

11. Peytraud, *L'Esclavage aux Antilles français*, pp. 144-45; 213-41, 253-65; Trudel, *L'Esclavage au Canada français*, pp. 99-102; Lauber, *Indian Slavery*, pp. 216-17, 226-29; Greene, *Negro in Colonial New England*, p. 126; George H. Moore, *Notes on the History of Slavery in Massachusetts* (New York, 1866), pp. 62-65.

12. *Acts of Assembly . . . Charibbee Leeward Islands*, pp. 18-19, 82; *The Laws of the Island of Saint Vincent, and Its Dependencies, from the First Establishment of a Legislature to the End of the Year, 1809* (Bridgnorth, Eng-

land, 1811), pp. 24-49; C. S. S. Higham, *The Development of the Leeward Islands Under the Restoration, 1660–1688: A Study of the Foundations of the Old Colonial System* (Cambridge, England, 1921), pp. 157-59; *Journals of the Assembly of Jamaica*, II (London, 1824), 16-17, 30-31; *The Statutes and Laws of the Island of Jamaica* (rev. ed., Jamaica, 1889), pp. 115-16; Lawrence Henry Gipson, *The Triumphant Empire: New Responsibilities Within the Enlarged Empire, 1763–1766* (New York, 1956), p. 259. There was considerable conflict between British and colonial governments on the precise legal character of slave property. This was especially true after 1732, when Parliament enacted a law to facilitate the recovery of colonial debts. Although British law defined slaves as real estate, and the government disallowed a Virginia statute classing them as personal goods, the dispute involved the interests of debtors and creditors and had nothing to do with the general status of slaves as conveyable property. For this reason I think that M. Eugene Sirmans exaggerates the moral significance of slaves being defined as freehold property for purposes of descent in Barbados and South Carolina ("The Legal Status of the Slave in South Carolina, 1670–1740," *Journal of Negro History*, XXVIII [Nov., 1962], 462-73). Even in Louisiana, where slaves were long classed as real estate, they retained most of the characteristics of chattels personal (Kenneth M. Stampp, *The Peculiar Institution: Slavery in the Ante-Bellum South* [New York, 1956], p. 197). I have seen no evidence to show that a definition of slaves as freehold property implied that an owner had a right only to the services of his slave and not to the slave himself. Regardless of rules on descent and seizure for debt, slaves in both British and French colonies could be sold or otherwise conveyed apart from the land on which they worked.

13. *Le Code Noir, ou recueil des reglemens rendus jusqu'à présent. Concernant le gouvernement, l'administration de la justice, la police, la discipline & le commerce des negres dans les colonies françoises* (Paris, 1742), pp. 308-9; Peytraud, *L'Esclavage aux Antilles français*, pp. 247-65. Article 44 of the Code Noir classed slaves as *meubles*, but the law prohibited seizure and separate sale of husbands and wives, or of children under the age of puberty.

14. John Codman Hurd, *The Law of Freedom and Bondage in the United States* (Boston, 1858–62), I, 239, 242-43, 297, 303; II, 15-16; Sirmans, "Legal Status of the Slave in South Carolina," pp. 462-73; Catterall (ed.), *Judicial Cases*, I, 83-86, 93, 99-103, 269, 312, 318; II, 365, 393-96.

15. Ligon, *True & Exact History*, pp. 43, 47-48. A thoughtful dicussion of the meanings and complexities of liberty is Oscar and Mary Handlin, *The Dimensions of Liberty* (Cambridge, Mass., 1961), pp. 18-20.

16. Hurd, *Law of Freedom*, I, 232, 281, 297, 300; *Journals of the Assembly of Jamaica*, I, 120-25; Peytraud, *L'Esclavage aux Antilles français*, pp. 243-45; Martin, "Slavery and Abolition in Brazil," p. 168; Stein, *Vassouras*, pp. 196-99. In some English colonies, such as Pennsylvania, the proportion of converted Negroes may have been as high as that in any of the Spanish and Portuguese colonies (Turner, *Negro in Pennsylvania*, pp. 43-45).

17. Peytraud, *L'Esclavage aux Antilles français*, pp. 213-41; Hurd, *Law of Freedom*, I, 306-7; Ruth Scarborough, *The Opposition to Slavery in Georgia Prior to 1860* (Nashville, Tenn., 1933), p. 84; *Laws of Island of Saint Vincent*, p. 46; [Long], *History of Jamaica*, II, 491. Unlike the *Code Noir*, the laws of many of the British colonies, both on the mainland and in the West Indies, attempted to limit the number of hours a slave could work each day.

18. Smith, *Colonists in Bondage*, p. 271; Peytraud, *L'Esclavage aux Antilles français*, pp. 244-45; Turner, *Negro in Pennsylvania*, pp. 45-46; Hurd, *Law of Freedom*, I, 263; Trudel, *L'Esclavage au Canada français*, pp. 267-73; Cobb, *Law of Negro Slavery*, p. 243; Catterall (ed.), *Judicial Cases*, II, 479, 592. Although the Catholic Church had long accepted the right of slaves to marry even without their masters' permission, this measure was still being demanded by Brazilian reformers of the nineteenth century (José Bonifácio, *Memoir Addressed to the General, Constituent and Legislative Assembly*, pp. 45-46). There is considerable evidence to suggest that slaves benefited very little from having their marriages recognized by law. In Brazil, Saint Domingue, Québec, and Massachusetts such legal sanction did not prevent the separation of families or the independent sale of small children (Williams, "Treatment of Negro Slaves in Brazilian Empire," p. 325; Greene, *Negro in Colonial New England*, p. 211). William Huskisson, as Secretary of State for the British Colonial Office, pointed out that a Jamaican law of 1826 permitting slave marriages was largely meaningless because it required baptism and permission from masters, and because, in any event, the integrity of slave families was unprotected. And yet in certain regions of the South, Christian marriages of slaves were widely sanctioned by public opinion even if not by law (*Slave Law of Jamaica*, pp. 62, 145-58; Edward W. Phifer, "Slavery in Microcosm: Burke County, North Carolina," *Journal of Southern History*, XXVIII [May, 1962], p. 148).

II: THE SLAVE

• Ulrich B. Phillips produced the classic historical defense of American Negro slavery. His research uncovered a wealth of important material concerning the institution and, although more recent scholars have challenged his racist beliefs and his sympathetic attitude toward slavery, Phillips's writings remain extremely important for any student of slavery. The following selection offers a good summary of his perspectives on slavery as a social system and on the character of the Negro slave.

Southern Negro Slavery: A Benign View

ULRICH BONNELL PHILLIPS

The simplicity of the social structure on the plantations facilitated Negro adjustment, the master taking the place of the accustomed chief.[1] And yet these black voyagers experienced a greater change by far than befell white immigrants. In their home lands they had lived naked, observed fetish, been bound by tribal law, and practiced primitive crafts. In America none of these things were of service or sanction. The Africans were thralls, wanted only for their brawn, required to take things as they found them and to do as they were told, coerced into self-obliterating humility, and encouraged to respond only to the teachings and preachings of their masters, and adapt themselves to the white men's ways.

In some cases transported talent embraced the new opportunity in extraordinary degree. . . . But in general, as always, the common middle course was passive acquiescence.

To make adaptation the more certain, it was argued that "no Negro should be bought old; such are always sullen and unteachable, and frequently put an end to their lives." [2] And indeed planters who could afford an unproductive period were advised to select young children from the ships, "for their juvenile minds entertain no regrets for the loss of their connections. They acquire the English language with great ease, and improve daily in size, understanding and capacity for labour." [3] The proportion of children in the cargoes was great enough to permit such a policy by those who might adopt it.[4] But the fact that prices for imported Negroes, even after seasoning, ranged lower than for those to the American manner born is an evidence that the new habituation as a rule never completely superseded the old. Thanks, however, to plantation discipline and to the necessity of learning the master's language if merely to converse with fellow slaves of different linguistic stocks, African mental furnishings faded even among adult arrivals.

To the second and later generations folklore was transmitted, but for the sake of comprehension by the children an American Brer Rabbit replaced his jungle prototype. If lullabies were crooned in African phrase their memory soon lapsed, along with nearly all other African terms except a few personal names, Quash, Cuffee, Cudjoe and the like.[5] And even these may have owed such perpetuation as they had to the persistence of the maritime slave trade which long continued to bring new Quashes and Cuffees from the mother country. In short, Foulahs and Fantyns, Eboes and Angolas begat American plantation Negroes to whom a spear would be strange but a "languid hoe" familiar, the tomtom forgotten but the banjo inviting to the fingers and the thumb. Eventually it could be said that the Negroes had no memories of Africa as a home.[6] Eventually, indeed, a Virginia freedman wrote after thirteen years of residence in Liberia, "I, being a Virginian," rejoice that "the good people of my old state are about to settle a colony on the coast of Africa"; and went on to say of himself and his compatriots, "there is some of us that would not be satisfied in no other colony while ever there was one called New Virginia." [7] His very name, William Draper, is an index of his Anglo-Americanization; and a pride which he expresses that Virginia Negroes have been the founders and the chief rulers "of almost all the settlements" in Liberia proves him a true son of the Old Dominion, "the mother of states and of statesmen." But William Draper was an exceptional specimen. In the main the American Negroes ruled not even themselves. They were more or less contentedly slaves, with grievances from time to time but not ambition. With "hazy pasts and reckless futures," they lived in each moment as it flew, and left "Old Massa" to take such thought as the morrow might need.

*   *   *

The plantation force was a conscript army, living in barracks and on constant "fatigue." Husbands and wives were comrades in service under an authority as complete as the commanding personnel could wish. The master was captain and quartermaster combined, issuing orders and distributing rations. The overseer and the foreman, where there were such, were lieutenant and sergeant to see that orders were executed. The field hands were privates with no choice but to obey unless, like other seasoned soldiers, they could dodge the duties assigned.

But the plantation was also a homestead, isolated, permanent and peopled by a social group with a common interest in achieving and maintaining social order. Its régime was shaped by the customary human forces, interchange of ideas and coadaptation of conduct. The intermingling of white and black children in their pastimes was no more continuous or influential than the adult interplay of command and response, of protest and concession. In so far as harmony was attained—and in this the plantation mistress was a great if quiet factor —a common tradition was evolved embodying reciprocal patterns of conventional conduct.

The plantation was of course a factory, in which robust laborers were essential to profits. Its mere maintenance as a going concern required the proprietor to sustain the strength and safeguard the health of his operatives and of their children, who were also his, destined in time to take their parents' places. The basic food allowance came to be somewhat standardized at a quart of corn meal and half a pound of salt pork per day for each adult and proportionably for children, commuted or supplemented with sweet potatoes, field peas, sirup, rice, fruit and "garden sass" as locality and season might suggest. The clothing was coarse, and shoes were furnished only for winter. The housing was in huts of one or two rooms per family, commonly crude but weathertight. Fuel was abundant. The sanitation of the clustered cabins was usually a matter of systematic attention; and medical service was at least commensurate with the groping science of the time and the sparse population of the country. Many of the larger plantations had central kitchens, day nurseries, infirmaries and physicians on contract for periodic visits.[8] The aged and infirm must be cared for along with the young and able-bodied, to maintain the good will of their kinsmen among the workers, if for no other reason. Morale was no less needed than muscle if performance were to be kept above a barely tolerable minimum.

*   *   *

The plantation was a school. An intelligent master would consult his own interest by affording every talented slave special instruction and by inculcating into the commoner sort as much routine efficieny, regularity and responsibility as they would accept. Not only were many youths given training in the crafts, and many taught to read and write, even though the laws forbade it, but a goodly number of planters devised and applied plans to give their whole corps spontaneous incentive to relieve the need of detailed supervision. . . .

The civilizing of the Negroes was not merely a consequence of definite schooling but a fruit of plantation life itself. The white household taught perhaps less by precept than by example. It had much the effect of a "social settlement" in a modern city slum, furnishing models of speech and conduct, along with advice on occasion, which the vicinage is invited to accept. . . . The bulk of the black personnel was notoriously primitive, uncouth, improvident and inconstant, merely because they were Negroes of the time; and by their slave status they were relieved from the pressure of want and debarred from any full-force incentive of gain.

Many planters, however, sought to promote contentment, loyalty and zeal by gifts and rewards, and by sanctioning the keeping of poultry and pigs and the cultivation of little fields in off times with the privilege of selling any produce. In the cotton belt the growing of nankeen cotton was particularly encouraged, for its brownish color would betray any surreptitious addition from the master's own fields. Some indeed had definite bonus systems. A. H. Bernard of Virginia determined at the close of 1836 to replace his overseer with a slave foreman, and announced to his Negroes that in case of good service by the corps he would thereafter distribute premiums to the amount of what had been the overseer's wages. . . .

But any copious resort to profit-sharing schemes was avoided at large as being likely to cost more than it would yield in increment to the planter's own crop. The generality of planters, it would seem, considered it hopeless to make their field hands into thorough workmen or full-fledged men, and contented themselves with very moderate achievement. Tiring of endless correction and unfruitful exhortation, they relied somewhat supinely upon authority with a tone of kindly patronage and a baffled acquiescence in slack service. . . .

It has been said by a critic of the twentieth century South: "In some ways the negro is shamefully mistreated—mistreated through leniency," which permits him as a tenant or employee to lean upon the whites in a continuous mental siesta and sponge upon them habitually, instead of requiring him to stand upon his own moral and economic legs.[9] The same censure would apply as truly in any preceding generation. The slave plantation, like other schools, was conditioned by the nature and habituations of its teachers and pupils. Its instruction was inevitably slow; and the effect of its discipline was restricted by the fact that even its aptest pupils had no diploma in prospect which would send them forth to fend for themselves.

* * *

The plantation was a parish, or perhaps a chapel of ease. Some planters assumed the functions of lay readers when ordained ministers were not available, or joined the congregation even when Negro preachers preached.[10] Bishop Leonidas Polk was chief chaplain on his own estate, and is said to have suffered none of his slaves to be other than Episcopalian; [11] but the generality of masters gave full freedom as to church connection.

The legislature of Barbados, when urged by the governor in 1681 to promote the Christianization of slaves on that island, replied, "their savage brutishness renders them wholly incapable. Many have endeavored it without success." [12] But on the continent such sentiments had small echo; and as decades passed masters and churches concerned themselves increasingly in the premises. A black preacher might meet rebuke and even run a risk of being lynched if he harped too loudly upon the liberation of the Hebrews from Egyptian bondage; [13] but a moderate supervision would prevent such indiscretions. The Sermon on the Mount would be harmless despite its suggestion of an earthly inheritance for the meek; the Decalogue was utterly sound; and "servants obey your masters," "render unto Caesar the things that are Caesar's," and "well done, thou good and faithful servant" were invaluable texts for homilies. The Methodists and Baptists were inclined to invite ecstasy from free and slave alike. Episcopalians and Presbyterians, and the Catholics likewise, deprecating exuberance, dealt rather in quiet precept than in fervid exhortation—with far smaller statistical results.[14]

The plantation was a pageant and a variety show in alternation. The procession of plowmen at evening, slouched crosswise on their mules; the dance in the new sugarhouse, preceded by prayer; the bonfire in the quarter with contests in clogs, cakewalks and Charlestons whose fascinations were as yet undiscovered by the great world; the work songs in solo and refrain, with not too fast a rhythm; the baptizing in the creek, with lively demonstrations from the "sisters" as they came dripping out; the torchlight pursuit of 'possum and 'coon, with full-voiced halloo to baying houn' dawg and yelping cur; the rabbit hunt, the log-rolling, the house-raising, the husking bee, the quilting party, the wedding, the cock fight, the crap game, the children's play, all punctuated plantation life—and most of them were highly vocal.[15] A funeral now and then of some prominent slave would bring festive sorrowing, or the death of a beloved master an outburst of emotion.[16]

*　　*　　*

The plantation was a matrimonial bureau, something of a harem perhaps, a copious nursery, and a divorce court. John Brickell wrote of colonial North Carolina: "It frequently happens, when these women have no Children by the first Husband, after being a year or two co-habiting together, the Planters oblige them to take a second, third, fourth, fifth, or more Husbands or Bedfellows; a fruitful Woman amongst them being very much valued by the Planters, and a numer-ous Issue esteemed the greatest Riches in this Country." [17] By run-ning on to five or more husbands for a constantly barren woman Brickell discredits his own statement. Yet it may have had a kernel of truth, and it is quite possible that something of such a policy persisted throughout the generations. These things do not readily get into the records. I have myself heard a stalwart Negro express a humorous re-gret that he was free, for said he in substance: "If I had lived in slavery times my master would have given me half a dozen wives and taken care of all the children." This may perhaps voice a tradition among slave descendants, and the tradition may in turn derive from an actual sanction of polygamy by some of the masters. A planter doubtless described a practice not unique when he said "that he in-terfered as little as possible with their domestic habits except in mat-ters of police. 'We don't care what they do when their tasks are over— we lose sight of them till next day. Their morals and manners are in their own keeping. The men may have, for instance, as many wives as they please, so long as they do not quarrel about such matters.' " [18] But another was surely no less representative when he instructed his overseer: "Marriages shall be performed in every instance of a nuptial contract, and the parties settled off to themselves without encumber-ing other houses to give discontent. No slave shall be allowed to co-habit with two or more wives or husbands at the same time; doing so shall subject them to a strict trial and severe punishment." [19]

Life was without doubt monogamous in general; and some of the matings were by order,[20] though the generality were pretty surely spontaneous. . . .

In the number of their children the Negro women rivaled the remarkable fecundity of their mistresses. One phenomenal slave mother bore forty-one children, mostly of course as twins;[21] and the records of many others ran well above a dozen each. As a rule, perhaps, babies were even more welcome to slave women than to free; for childbearing brought lightened work during pregnancy and suckling, and a lack of ambition conspired with a freedom from economic anxiety to clear the path of maternal impulse.

Concubinage of Negro women to planters and their sons and overseers is evidenced by the census enumeration of mulattoes and by other data.[22] It was flagrantly prevalent in the Creole section of Louisiana, and was at least sporadic from New England to Texas. The régime of slavery facilitated concubinage not merely by making black women subject to white men's wills but by promoting intimacy and weakening racial antipathy. The children, of whatever shade or paternity, were alike the property of the mother's owner and were nourished on the plantation. Not a few mulattoes, however, were manumitted by their fathers and vested with property.

Slave marriages, not being legal contracts, might be dissolved without recourse to public tribunals. Only the master's consent was required, and this was doubtless not hard to get. On one plantation systematic provision was made in the standing regulations: "When sufficient cause can be shewn on either side, a marriage may be annulled; but the offending party must be severely punished. Where both are in the wrong, both must be punished, and if they insist on separating must have a hundred lashes apiece. After such a separation, neither can marry again for three years."[23] If such a system were in general effect in our time it would lessen the volume of divorce in American society. But it may be presumed that most plantation rules were not so stringent.

The home of a planter or of a well-to-do townsman was likely to be a "magnificent negro boarding-house," at which and from which an indefinite number of servants and their dependents and friends were fed.[24] In town the tribe might increase to the point of embarrassment. . . .

Each plantation had a hierarchy. Not only were the master and his family exalted to a degree beyond the reach of slave aspiration, but among the Negroes themselves there were pronounced gradations of rank, privilege and esteem. An absent master wrote: "I wish to be remembered to all the servants, distinguishing Andrew as the head man and Katy as the mother of the tribe. Not forgetting Charlotte as the head of the culinary department nor Marcus as the Tubal Cain of the community, hoping that they will continue to set a good example and that the young ones will walk in their footsteps." [25] The foreman, the miller and the smith were men of position and pride. The butler, the maid and the children's nurse were in continuous contact with the white household, enjoying the best opportunity to acquire its manners along with its discarded clothing. The field hands were at the foot of the scale, with a minimum of white contact and privileged only to plod, so to say, as brethren to the ox.

At all times in the South as a whole perhaps half of the slaves were owned or hired in units of twenty or less, which were too small for the full plantation order, and perhaps half of this half were on mere farms or in town employment, rather as "help" than as a distinct laboring force. Many small planters' sons and virtually all the farmers in person worked alongside any field hands they might possess; and indoor tasks were parceled among the women and girls white and black. . . .

However the case may have been as to relative severity on farms and plantations, there can be no doubt that the farmers' slaves of all sorts were likely to share somewhat intimately such lives as their masters led [26] and to appropriate a considerable part of such culture as they possessed—to be more or less genteel with their gentility or crude with their crudity, to think similar thoughts and speak much the same language. On the other hand, the one instance of wide divergence in dialect between the whites and the Negroes prevailed in the single district in which the scheme of life was that of large plantations from the time when Africans were copiously imported. On the seaboard of South Carolina and Georgia most of the blacks (and they were very black) still speak Gullah, a dialect so distinct that unfamiliar visitors may barely understand it. And dialect, there as elsewhere, is an index to culture in general.

*　　*　　*

The life of slaves, whether in large groups or small, was not without grievous episodes. A planter's son wrote to his father upon a discovery of mislaid equipment: "The bridle and martingal which you whipped Amy so much for stealing was by some inattention of Robert's left in Mr. Clark's stable." Again, an overseer, exasperated by the sluggishness of his cook, set her to field work as discipline, only to have her demonstrate by dying that her protestations of illness had been true.

Grievances reinforced ennui to promote slacking, absence without leave, desertion and mutiny. The advertising columns of the newspapers bristled with notices of runaways; and no detailed plantation record which has come to my hand is without mention of them. . . .

Certain slaves were persistent absconders, and the chronic discontent of others created special problems for their masters. . . .

By one means or another good will and affection were often evoked. When his crop was beset with grass and the work strenuous, a Mississippian wrote of his corps as being "true as steel." [27] A Georgian after escaping shipwreck on his way to Congress in 1794 wrote: "I have ever since been thinking of an expression of Old Qua's in Savannah a few days before I sailed. The rascal had the impudence to tell me to stay at home & not fret myself about Publick—'What Publick care for you, Massa? God! ye get drowned bye & bye, Qua tell you so, and what going come of he Family den?' " [28] An Alabama preacher while defending slavery as divinely ordained said of the Negro: "He is of all races the most gentle and kind. The *man*, the most submissive; the *woman*, the most affectionate. What other slaves would love their masters better than themselves?" [29] And a British traveler wrote from his observation of slaves and masters: "There is an hereditary regard and often attachment on both sides, more like that formerly existing between lords and their retainers in the old feudal times of Europe, than anything now to be found in America." [30]

On some estates the whip was as regularly in evidence as the spur on a horseman's heel.[31] That cruelties occurred is never to be denied. Mrs. Stowe exploited them in *Uncle Tom's Cabin* and validated her implications to her own satisfaction in its *Key*. Theodore D. Weld had already assembled a thousand more or less authentic instances of whippings and fetters, of croppings and brandings, of bloodhound pursuits and the break-up of families.[32] Manuscript discoveries continue to swell the record. . . .

Most of the travelers who sought evidence of asperity in the plantation realm found it as a rule not before their eyes but beyond the horizon. Charles Eliot Norton while at Charleston in 1855 wrote home to Boston: "The slaves do not go about looking unhappy, and are with difficulty, I fancy, persuaded to feel so. Whips and chains, oaths and brutality, are as common, for all that one sees, in the free as the slave states. We have come thus far, and might have gone ten times as far, I dare say, without seeing the first sign of Negro misery or white tyranny." [33] Andrew P. Peabody wrote of the slaves of his host at Savannah: "They were well lodged and fed, and could have been worked no harder than was necessary for exercise and digestion." [34] Louis F. Tasistro remarked of the slaves on a plantation at the old battle field below New Orleans: "To say that they are underworked and overfed, and far happier than the labourers of Great Britain would hardly convey a sufficiently clear notion of their actual condition. They put me much more in mind of a community of grown-up children, spoiled by too much kindness, than a body of dependants, much less a company of slaves." [35] Frederika Bremer had virtually nothing but praise for the slave quarters which she visited or their savory food which she tasted.[36] Welby, Faux, Lyell, Basil Hall, Marshall Hall, Robert Russell, William Russell, Olmsted [37] and sundry others concur in their surprise at finding slavery unsevere, though some of them kept seeking evidence to the contrary without avail.

The surprise was justified, for tradition in the outer world ran squarely opposite. And the tradition was reasonable. Slavery had been erected as a crass exploitation, and the laws were as stringent as ever. No prophet in early times could have told that kindliness would grow as a flower from a soil so foul, that slaves would come to be cherished not only as property of high value but as loving if lowly friends.[38] But this unexpected change occurred in so many cases as to make benignity somewhat a matter of course. To those habituated it became no longer surprising for a planter to say that no man deserved a Coromantee who would not treat him rather as a friend than as a slave; [39] for another to give his "people" a holiday out of season because "the drouth seems to have afflicted them, and a play day may raise their spirits"; [40] or for a third to give one of his hands an occasional week-end with a dollar or two each time to visit his wife in another county,[41] and send two others away for some weeks at hot springs for the relief of their rheumatism.[42]

The esteem in epitaphs, whether inscribed in diaries or on stone, was without doubt earned by their subjects and genuinely felt by their composers. . . .

On the other hand slaves in large numbers were detached from their masters, whether by sale, by lease to employers or by hire to themselves. The personal equation was often a factor in such transactions. Some slaves were sold as punishment, for effect upon the morale of their fellows. On the other hand some whose sales were impelled by financial stress were commissioned by their masters to find buyers of their own choice; some purchases were prompted by a belief that the new management would prove more congenial and fruitful than the old; [43] and still more transfers were made to unite in ownership couples who desired union in marriage.

In the hiring of slaves likewise the personal equation often bulked large, for the owner's desire for a maximum wage was modified by his concern for assured maintenance of physique and morale, and the lessee on his part wanted assurance from the slave of willing service or of acquiescence at least.[44] The hiring of slaves to the slaves themselves was a grant of industrial freedom at a wage. It was an admission that the slave concerned could produce more in self-direction than when under routine control, a virtual admission that for him slavery had no industrial justification. In many cases it was a probationary period, ended by self-purchase with earnings accumulated above the wages he had currently paid his owner.

Slave hiring and self-hire were more characteristic of town than of country. Indeed urban conditions merely tolerated slavery, never promoted it. And urban slaveholders were not complete masters, for slavery in full form required a segregation to make the master in effect a magistrate. A townsman's human chattels could not be his subjects, for he had no domain for them to inhabit. When a slave ran an errand upon the street he came under the eye of public rather than private authority; and if he were embroiled by chance in altercation with another slave the two masters were likely to find themselves champions of opposing causes in court, or partisans even against the constables, with no power in themselves either to make or apply the law.[45]

Town slaves in a sense rubbed elbows with every one, high and low, competed with free labor, white and black, and took tone more or less from all and sundry. The social hierarchy was more elaborate than on the plantations, the scheme of life more complex, and the variety wider in attainment and attitude. The obsequious grandiloquence of a barber contrasted with the caustic fluency of a fishwife. But even the city chain gang was likely to be melodious, for its members were Negroes at one or two removes from the plantation. All in all, the slave régime was a curious blend of force and concession, of arbitrary disposal by the master and self-direction by the slave, of tyranny and benevolence, of antipathy and affection.

NOTES

1. *Cf.* N. S. Shaler, "The Nature of the Negro", in the *Arena*, III, 28.
2. *Gentleman's Magazine*, XXXIV, 487 (London, 1764).
3. *Practical Rules*, reprinted in *Plantation and Frontier Documents*, II, 133.
4. For example there were 102 below ten years of age among the 704 slaves brought by five ships to South Carolina between July and October, 1724.— British transcripts in the South Carolina archives, XI, 243.
5. A table of the names most common among imported Negroes, which were derived from the days of the week, is printed in Long's *Jamaica*, II, 427.
6. Charleston *Courier*, July 8, 1855.
7. Letter of William Draper, Bassa Cove, Liberia, August 17, 1837, to

William Maxwell, Norfolk, Va. T. C. Thornton, *An Inquiry into the History of Slavery* (Washington, 1841), 272.

8. For example, James Hamilton, Jr., while Congressman from South Carolina, engaged Dr. Furth of Savannah to make visits on schedule to his plantation a few miles away. In 1828 he wrote from Washington to his factor at Savannah: "I have just received a letter from Mr Prioleau, informing me that the eyes of my old and faithful Servant Peter were in a perilous condition. I will [thank] you to request Dr Furth to attend to them promptly and effectually. . . . I will thank you to supply for my Hospital on his requisition all that may be necessary *in his opinion* to make my negroes comfortable when they are sick. I will thank you to request him to drop me a line occasionally of the health of my people and the success of the reform I propose thro him to institute in attention to the sick. . . . Be so good as to give to Peter the value of a couple of Dollars monthly for comforts to his family." Manuscript in private possession.

On rations, quarters, work schedules and the like see [Ebenezer Starnes] *The Slave-holder Abroad* (Philadephia, 1860), appendix; *DeBow's Review*, VIII, 381, X, 621, XI, 369; *Southern Literary Messenger*, VII, 775; and travelers' accounts at large.

9. Howard Snyder in the *Atlantic Monthly*, CXXVII, 171.

10. E.g., Rev. I. E. Lowery, *Life on the Old Plantation in Ante-bellum Days* (Columbia, S. C., 1911), 71, 72. The author was an ex-slave.

11. Olmsted, *Back Country*, 107 note.

12. *Calendar of State Papers, Colonial*, 1681-1685, p. 25.

13. E.g., letter of James Habersham, May 11, 1775, to Robert Kean in London, in the *Georgia Historical Society Collections*, VI, 243, 244.

14. Surveys of religious endeavor among the slaves: Rev. Charles C. Jones, *The Religious Instruction of the Negroes in the United States* (Savannah, 1842): C. F. Deems, ed., *Annals of Southern Methodism for 1856* (Nashville [1857]); W. P. Harrison, ed., *The Gospel among the Slaves* (Nashville, 1893).

15. Doubtless many a plantation was blessed, or cursed as the case might be, with a practical joker such as Jack Baker, who kept himself and his whole neighborhood in Richmond entertained by his talent in mimicry. "Jack's performances furnished rare fun in the dog-days, when business was dull, and his pocket was furnished by the same process." One of his private amusements was to call some other slave in the tone of his master, and vanish before the summons was answered. "His most frequent dupe was a next door neighbor, whose master, a Scotchman, took frequent trips to the country on horseback. During his absence Jack would, before retiring to bed, rap on the gate and call 'Jasper! come and take my horse.' Jasper, aroused from his nap, came, but found neither master nor horse, and well knew who quizzed him. One night the veritable master made the call, some time after Jack had given a false alarm. Jasper was out of patience, and replied in a loud voice, 'D—n you, old fellow, if you call me again I'll come out and thrash you!' After that, poor Jasper was at Jack's mercy, unless he resorted to 'thrashing.' "—*DeBow's Review*, XXVIII, 197.

16. *Cf.* Catherine Bremer, *Homes of the New World*, I, 374.

17. John Brickell, *The Natural History of North Carolina* (Dublin, 1737), 275.

18. Basil Hall, *Travels*, III, 191.

19. *Southern Agriculturist*, III, 329. These instructions continued: "All my slaves are to be supplied with sufficient land, on which I encourage and even compel them to plant and cultivate a crop, all of which I will, as I have hitherto done, purchase at a fair price from them."

20. An instance of coercive breeding is reported by Frederick Douglass, in *Narrative* (Boston, 1849), 62. For this item I am indebted to Mr. Theodore Whitfield of Johns Hopkins University.

21. Phillips, *American Negro Slavery*, 298, 299.

22. It is hinted, for example, by the exclamation point in this Virginian letter of 1831: "P. P. Burton has quit his wife, sent her to her father's and gone off with Sandy Burton to Texas and taken a female slave along!" Manuscript in private possession.

23. Plantation manual of James H. Hammond. Manuscript in the Library of Congress.

24. A. P. Peabody, in the *Andover Review*, XVI, 156.

25. P. Carson, *Life of James Louis Petigru* (Washington, 1920), 431. In another letter Petigru conjured his sister: "Do not allow the little nigs to forget that their hands were given them principally for the purpose of pulling weeds." —*Ibid.*, 23.

26. *Cf.* Basil Hall, *Travels*, III, 279.

27. *Mississippi Historical Society Publications*, X, 354.

28. T. U. P. Charlton, *Life of James Jackson* (Augusta, 1809, reprint Atlanta, n. d.), 154 of the reprint.

29. Fred A. Ross, *Slavery Ordained of God* (Philadephia, 1859), 26.

30. Sir Charles Lyell, *Second Visit*, 2d ed., I, 352.

31. E.g., J. W. Monette in [J. H. Ingraham] *The South-West*, II, 286-288.

32. *American Slavery as it is: Testimony of a Thousand Witnesses* (New York, 1839).

33. *Letters of Charles Eliot Norton* (Boston, 1913), I, 121.

34. *Andover Review*, XVI, 157.

35. *Random Shots and Southern Breezes* (New York, 1842), II, 13.

36. *Homes of the New World*, I, 293 *et passim*.

37. Some of these are quoted in Phillips, *American Negro Slavery*, 306-308.

38. A Virginia woman, talking in 1842 with a visiting preacher from the North, said that her superannuated cook was "as pious a woman, and a lady of as delicate sensibilities as I ever saw; she is one of the very best friends I have in the world." The visitor wrote on his own score: "I am more and more convinced of the injustice we do the slaveholders. Of their feelings toward their negroes I can form a better notion than formerly, by examining my own toward the slaves who wait on my wife and mind my children. It is a feeling most like that we have to near relations." And again as to the slaves: "They are unspeakably superior to our Northern free blacks, retaining a thousand African traits of kindliness and hilarity, from being together in masses. I may say with Abram [Venable, a planter whom he visited], 'I love a nigger, they are better than we.' So they are: grateful, devoted, self-sacrificing for their masters." —John Hall ed., *Forty Years' Familiar Letters of James W. Alexander, D. D.* (New York, 1860), I, 351-353.

39. Christopher Codrington, in *Calendar of State Papers, Colonial*, 1701, p. 721.

40. Diary of Landon Carter, in the *William and Mary College Quarterly*,

XIII, 162.

41. "The Westover Journal of John A. Seldon," in *Smith College Studies*, VI, 289 *et passim*.

42. *Ibid.*, 308.

43. For a striking example see *Plantation and Frontier*, I, 337, 338.

44. For a vivid account of a tripartite negotiation see Robert Russell, *North America* (Edinburgh, 1857), 151.

45. *E.g.*, Carson, *Petigru*, 348; Phillips, *American Negro Slavery*, 414, 415.

• The most important recent synthesis of American slavery is Kenneth M. Stampp's The Peculiar Institution. Stampp has criticized severely both Phillips's handling of evidence connected with Southern slave society and his tolerant moral outlook regarding its practices. The historical issues which divide Stampp and Phillips reflect, to a great extent, American assumptions concerning the Negro at the time of their writing. Phillips, a benign Southern racist, believed that, despite excesses on the part of some slaveholders, the institution had served a useful civilizing purpose for the Negro. Stampp, on the other hand, viewed the institution as a thoroughly cruel and brutal system of social control. The following selection from the chapter entitled "To Make Them Stand in Fear" discusses some aspects of slavery which helped produce Stampp's moral outrage over Phillips's gentle apology for slaveholding.

Southern Negro Slavery:
"To Make Them Stand in Fear"

KENNETH M. STAMPP

A realistic Arkansas slaveholder once addressed himself to the great problem of his class, "the management of Negroes," and bluntly concluded: "Now, I speak what I know, when I say it is like 'casting pearls before swine' to try to *persuade* a negro to work. He must be *made* to work, and should always be given to understand that if he fails to perform his duty he will be punished for it." Having tested the "*persuasion* doctrine" when he began planting, he warned all beginners that if they tried it they would surely fail.[1]

Most masters preferred the "persuasion doctrine" nevertheless. They would have been gratified if their slaves had willingly shown proper subordination and wholeheartedly responded to the incentives offered for efficient labor. They found, however, that some did not respond at all, and that others responded only intermittently. As a result, slaveholders were obliged to supplement the lure of rewards for good behavior with the threat of punishment for bad. One Virginian always assumed that slaves would "not labor at all except to avoid punishment," and would "never do more than just enough to save themselves from being punished." Fortunately, said a Georgian, punishment did not make the Negro revengeful as it did members of other races. Rather, it tended "to win his attachment and promote his happiness and well being." [2]

Without the power to punish, which the state conferred upon the master, bondage could not have existed. By comparison, all other techniques of control were of secondary importance. Jefferson Davis and a few others gave their bondsmen a hand in the chastisement of culprits. On Davis's Mississippi estate trusted slaves tried, convicted, and punished the violators of plantation law.[3] But this was an eccentric arrangement. Normally the master alone judged the seriousness of an offense and fixed the kind and amount of punishment to be administered.

Slaveholders devised a great variety of penalties. They demoted unfaithful domestics, foremen, and drivers to field labor. They denied passes to incorrigibles, or excluded them from participating in Saturday night dances. An Arkansas planter gave his bondsmen a dinner every Sunday and required those on the "punishment list" to wait on the others without getting any of the food themselves. Masters forced malingerers to work on Sundays and holidays and at night after the others had finished. They penalized them by confiscating the crops in their "truck patches," or by reducing the sums due them. They put them on short rations for a period of time, usually depriving them of their meat allowances. And they sold them away from their families and friends.

Some of the penalties were ingenious. A Maryland tobacco grower forced a hand to eat the worms he failed to pick off the tobacco leaves. A Mississippian gave a runaway a wretched time by requiring him to sit at the table and eat his evening meal with the white family. A Louisiana planter humiliated disobedient male field-hands by giving them "women's work" such as washing clothes, by dressing them in women's clothing, and by exhibiting them on a scaffold wearing a red flannel cap.[4]

A few slaveholders built private jails on their premises. They knew that close confinement during a working day was a punishment of dubious value, but they believed that it was effective during leisure hours. "Negroes are gregarious," explained a small planter, "they dread solitariness, and to be deprived from the little weekly dances and chitchat. They will work to death rather than be shut up." Accordingly, a Louisianian locked runaways in his jail from Saturday night until Monday morning. When he caught a cotton picker with a ten pound rock in his basket, he jailed him every night and holiday for five months.[5]

Others made use of public jails, paying the jailer a fee for the service. One South Carolinian put a runaway in solitary confinement in the Charleston workhouse; another had a slave "shut in a darkcell" in the same institution. A Georgia Planter advised his overseer to take a disobedient slave "down to the Savannah jail, and give him prison discipline and by all means solitary confinement for 3 weeks, when he will be glad to get home again." [6]

The stocks were still a familiar piece of equipment on the plantations of the ante-bellum South. . . .

"Chains and irons," James H. Hammond correctly explained, were used chiefly to control and discipline runaways. "You will admit," he argued logically enough, "that if we pretend to own slaves, they must not be permitted to abscond whenever they see fit; and that if nothing else will prevent it these means must be resorted to." [7] Three entries in Hammond's diary, in 1844, indicated that he practiced what he preached. July 17: "Alonzo runaway with his irons on." July 30: "Alonzo came in with his irons off." July 31: ". . . re-ironed Alonzo."

Hammond was but one of many masters who gave critics of the peculiar institution a poignant symbol—the fettered slave. A Mississippian had his runaway Maria "Ironed with a shackle on each leg connected with a chain." When he caught Albert he "had an iron collar put on his neck"; on Woodson, a habitual runaway, he "put the ball and chain." A Kentuckian recalled seeing slaves in his state wearing iron collars, some of them with bells attached. The fetters, however, did not always accomplish their purpose, for numerous advertisements stated that fugitives wore these encumbrances when they escaped. For example, Peter, a Louisiana runaway, "Had on each foot when leaving, an iron ring, with a small chain attached to it." [8]

But the whip was the most common instrument of punishment—

indeed, it was the emblem of the master's authority. Nearly every slaveholder used it, and few grown slaves escaped it entirely. Defenders of the institution conceded that corporal punishment was essential in certain situations; some were convinced that it was better than any other remedy. If slavery were right, argued an Arkansas planter, means had to be found to keep slaves in subjugation, "and my opinion is, the lash—not used murderously, as would-be philanthropists assert, is the most effectual." A Virginian agreed: "A great deal of whipping is not necessary; *some* is." [9]

The majority seemed to think that the certainty, and not the severity, of physical "correction" was what made it effective. While no offense could go unpunished, the number of lashes should be in proportion to the nature of the offense and the character of the offender. The master should control his temper. "Never inflict punishment when in a passion," advised a Louisiana slaveholder, "but wait until perfectly cool, and until it can be done rather in sorrow than in anger." Many urged, therefore, that time be permitted to elapse between the misdeed and the flogging. A Georgian required his driver to do the whipping so that his bondsmen would not think that it was "for the pleasure of punishing, rather than for the purpose of enforcing obedience." [10]

Planters who employed overseers often fixed the number of stripes they could inflict for each specific offense, or a maximum number whatever the offense. On Pierce Butler's Georgia plantation each driver could administer twelve lashes, the head driver thirty-six, and the overseer fifty. A South Carolinian instructed his overseer to ask permission before going beyond fifteen. "The highest punishment must not exceed 100 lashes in one day and to that extent only in extreme cases," wrote James H. Hammond. "In general 15 to 20 lashes will be a sufficient flogging." [11]

The significance of these numbers depended in part upon the kind of whip that was used. The "rawhide," or "cowskin," was a savage instrument requiring only a few strokes to provide a chastisement that a slave would not soon forget. A former bondsman remembered that it was made of about three feet of untanned ox hide, an inch thick at the butt end, and tapering to a point which made it "quite elastic and springy." [12]

Many slaveholders would not use the rawhide because it lacerated the skin. One recommended, instead, a leather strap, eighteen inches long and two and a half inches wide, fastened to a wooden handle. In Mississippi, according to a visitor, the whip in general use consisted of a "stout flexible stalk" covered with a tapering leather plait, about three and a half feet in length, which formed the lash. "To the end of the lash is attached a soft, dry, buckskin cracker, about three eights of an inch wide and ten or twelve inches long, which is the only part allowed to strike, in whipping on the bare skin. . . . When it is used by an experienced hand it makes a very loud report, and stings, or 'burns' the skin smartly, but does not bruise it." [13]

How frequently a master resorted to the whip depended upon his temperament and his methods of management. On some establishments long periods of time elapsed with relatively few whippings—until, as a rice planter explained, it seemed "as if the devil had got into" the hands, and for a time there was "a good deal of it." Or, occasionally, a normally amiable slave got out of hand and had to be flogged. "Had to whip my Man Willis for insolence to the overseer," wrote a Tennesseean. "This I done with much regret as he was never whipped before." [14]

On other establishments the whip was in constant use. The size of the estate may have had some relationship to the amount of whipping, but the disposition of the proprietor was decidedly more crucial. Small farmers, as well as large planters, often relied upon corporal punishment as their chief method of enforcing discipline. Southern women were sometimes equally prone to use the lash upon errant domestics.

Some overseers, upon assuming control, thought it wise to whip every hand on the plantation to let them know who was in command. Some masters used the lash as a form of incentive by flogging the last slave out of his cabin in the morning.[15] Many used it to "break in" a young slave and to "break the spirit" of an insubordinate older one. "If the negro is humble and appears duly sensible of the impropriety of his conduct, a very moderate chastisement will answer better than a severe one," advised a planter. "If however, he is stubborn . . . a slight punishment will only make bad worse." Slaves had to be flogged, explained an Alabamian, until they manifested "submission and penitence." [16]

In short, the infliction of stripes curbed many a bondsman who could not be influenced by any other technique. Whipping had a dispiriting effect upon most of them. "Had to administer a little rod to Bob this morning," reported a Virginian. "Have seen for more than 3 months I should have to humble him some, hope it may benefit him." [17]

"To manage *negroes* without the exercise of too much passion, is next to an impossibility. . . . I would therefore put you on your guard, lest their provocations should on some occasions transport you beyond the limits of decency and christian morality." The Reverend Charles Pettigrew, of North Carolina, gave this advice to his sons when he willed them his estate. John H. Cocke, of Virginia, cautioned the overseer on his Bremo Plantation: "Most persons are liable to be thrown into a passion by the improper conduct of those they have to govern." After traveling through the South, Olmsted wondered "whether humanity and the accumulation of wealth, the prosperity of the master and the happiness and improvement of the subject, are not in some degree incompatible." [18] Physical cruelty, as these observations suggest, was always a possible consequence of the master's power to punish. Place an intemperate master over an ill-disposed slave, and the possibility became a reality.

Not that a substantial number of slaveholders deliberately adopted a policy of brutality. The great majority, in fact, preferred to use as little violence as possible. Many small slaveholders, urban and rural, who had close personal contacts with their bondsmen and knew them as human beings, found it highly disagreeable to treat them unkindly. Large planters, in their instructions to overseers, frequently prohibited barbarous punishments. Thomas Affleck's plantation record book advised overseers that the "indiscriminate, constant and excessive use of the whip" was "altogether unnecessary and inexcusable." A Louisiana proprietor was very explicit on this point. In whipping a slave the overseer was never to be "cruel or severe," though he could repeat the whipping at intervals "until the most entire submission" was achieved. "I object to having the skin cut, or my negroes marked in any way by the lash. . . . I will most certainly discharge any overseer for striking any of my negroes with a club or the butt of his whip." [19]

A master who gave some thought to his standing in the community certainly wished to avoid a reputation for inordinate cruelty. To be counted a true Southern Gentleman one had to be humane to his bondsmen, to exercise self-control in dealing with them, to know how to give commands without raising his voice. Plenty of masters possessed these qualities. A European visitor marveled at the patience, the "mild forbearance," some of them exhibited. It seemed that every slaveholder's temper was subjected to a discipline which either ruined or perfected it. And more than a few met the test with remarkable success. [20]

Many openly censured those who were guilty of inhumanity. A Georgian told a Northerner that the government of slaves was necessarily despotic, but that Southerners despised ruthless masters. A South

Carolinian wrote in a published letter, "The overseer whose constant and only resort is to the lash . . . is a brute, and deserves the penitentiary." And a North Carolinian denounced a neighbor as a *"moral miasma"* because of the way he treated his slaves.[21]

Those who were destitute of humane instincts might still be restrained by the slave's economic worth. To injure by harsh punishment a prime field-hand valued at a thousand dollars or more was a costly indulgence. It may be, therefore, that rising slave prices encouraged a decline in the incidence of brutality.

But these restraints were not always enough. Some masters, made irascible by the endless irritations which were an inevitable part of owning slaves, were unmerciful in exercising their almost unlimited powers. Some were indifferent about their reputations among neighbors, or hoped to conceal the conditions that existed on their isolated estates. Some were as prodigal in the use of human chattels as they were in the use of other property. Neither law, nor social pressure, nor economic self-interest made Southern Gentlemen out of all slaveholders. As long as the peculiar institution survived, the master class contained a group of unfeeling men.

Few who knew southern slavery intimately denied that there existed within it an element of savagery. No apologist disputed the evidence published by Theodore Dwight Weld, the abolitionist, for he gathered it from southern newspapers and public records.[22] It is unnecessary, however, to turn to the abolitionists—or to former slaves—for proof. Daniel R. Hundley, a Southerner who admired and defended his section's institutions, agreed that the South was "no second paradise." He knew that slaves were "badly treated" on some estates, and that masters were sometimes unconcerned about it. Moreover, "he must be a very bold man who will deny that the overseers on many southern plantations, are cruel and unmercifully severe." [23]. . .

Southerners themselves having established the fact of cruelty, it only remains to estimate its extent and to examine its nature. Proslavery writers asserted that cases of cruelty were the rare exceptions to the general rule of humanity by which slaves were governed. Travelers in the South gave conflicting testimony. Abolitionists and ex-slaves insisted that cruelty was far more common than defenders of the institution would admit.

The exact truth will never be known, because surviving records are fragmentary and sometimes hint only vaguely at conditions. There is no way to discover what went on in the "voiceless solitudes" where no records were kept, or on hundreds of plantations where visitors were unwelcome and the proprietors were in residence only part of the year. (In 1860, several large planters in Rapides Parish, Louisiana, would not even permit the census takers to trespass upon their estates.) Even so, the public and private records that do survive suggest that, although the average slaveholder was not the inhuman brute described by the abolitionists, acts of cruelty were not as exceptional as pro-slavery writers claimed.

As a South Carolina judge sadly confessed, there were "men and women on earth who deserved no other name than *fiends*," for they seemed to delight in brutality.[24] No southern state required masters to be tested for their competence to rule slaves. Instead, they permitted slaves to fall willy-nilly into the hands of whoever inherited them or had the cash or credit to buy them. As a result, bondsmen were owned by persons of unsound minds, such as the South Carolinian who had his chattels "throw dirt upon [his] roof . . . to drive off witches." They were owned by a woman "unable to read or write, . . . scarcely able to count ten," legally incompetent to contract marriage.[25] They were owned by drunkards, such as Lilburne Lewis, of Livingston County, Kentucky, who once chopped a slave to bits with an ax; and by sadists, such as Madame Lalourie, of New Orleans, who tortured her slaves for her own amusement. It would be pointless to catalogue the atrocities committed by psychopaths.

Cruelty, unfortunately, was not limited to the mentally unbalanced. Men and women, otherwise "normal," were sometimes corrupted by the extraordinary power that slavery conferred upon them. Some made bondsmen the victims of their petulance. (The repentant wife of a Louisiana planter once wrote in her diary: "I feel badly got very angry and whipped Lavinia. O! for government over my temper." [26]) Others who were reasonably humane to most of their slaves made the ones who annoyed them beyond endurance the targets of their animosity. Still others who were merely irresponsible, rather than inherently brutal, made slaves the objects of their whims. In other words, masters were seldom consistent; they were apt to be indulgent or harsh depending upon their changing moods, or their feelings toward individual slaves. In truth, said one Southerner, "men of the right stamp to manage negroes are like Angels visits few and far between." [27]

Kindness was not a universal trait among small slaveholders, especially among those who were ambitious to climb the economic ladder. Both a shoemaker and a carpenter, each of whom owned a single slave, were guilty of atrocities.[28] Southern farmers with modest holdings were also, on occasion, capable of extreme cruelty toward slaves.

But brutality was more common on the large plantations. Overseers, almost all of whom were native-born Southerners, seldom felt any personal affection for the bondsmen they governed. Their inclination in most cases was to punish severely; if their employers prohibited severity, they ignored such instructions as often as not. Planters complained that it was difficult to find an overseer who would "condescend to take orders from his employer, and manage according to the system of another man." The typical overseer seemed to have little confidence in the use of incentives as a method of governing slaves; he had a decided preference for physical force.[29]

Illustrations of this problem sometimes found their way into the records of southern courts. Overseers sued masters for their wages when discharged for cruelty; masters sued overseers for injuring slave property; occasionally the state intervened to prosecute an overseer for killing or maiming a bondsman.[30] Most of these cases never reached the courts, as the planter dealt with the problem himself. An Alabamian discovered that he had found no solution even when he employed a relative to oversee. "I want you to distinctly understand me," he scolded, "withhold your rushing whipping and lashing—for I will not stand it any longer." A Louisiana planter, returning to his estate after a year's absence, related in his journal the "most terrible account of the severity [and] cruelty" of his overseer. At least twelve slaves had died from "negligence and ill treatment." Discharging this overseer and employing another, he was dismayed to find that the new one also "punished severely without discretion." [31]

A planter was often in a quandary when his overseer was both brutal and efficient. "I do not know whether I will keep Harris another year or not," a Mississippian told his wife. "He is a first rate manager except he is too cruel. I have had my feelings greatly shocked at some of his conduct." But he re-employed Harris after exacting from him a promise to be less harsh. Harris, he explained, made big crops, and he did not wish "to break it all up by getting a new manager."

A few years later this same planter, having transferred his operations to Arkansas, viewed the problem of slave management in a different light. While Harris was away on a month's leave of absence, the proprietor ran the estate himself. He found governing slaves to be a "pretty rough business" and waited impatiently for his overseer to return.[32]

Ordinarily the owner of a large plantation was realistic enough to know that controlling a gang of field-hands was at best a wretched business, and that a certain amount of savagery was inevitable. There seemed to be no other way to keep certain bondsmen under control. "Experience and observation have taught me that some negroes require a vast deal more punishment than others to be brought to a performance of their duties," wrote an Arkansas planter. And a Louisiana sugar planter assured his distressed wife that he would not sanction the admitted cruelty of his overseer unless there was "a *great* necessity for it." Indeed, he found the management of slaves "exceedingly disagreeable . . . under any and all circumstances." [33]

Although cruelty was endemic in all slaveholding communities, it was always most common in newly settled regions. Along the rough southern frontier thousands of ambitious men were trying swiftly to make their fortunes. They operated in a frantically competitive society which provided few rewards for the virtues of gentility and almost put a premium upon ruthlessness. In the eastern tobacco and rice districts brutality was unquestionably less prevalent in the nineteenth century than it had been during the colonial period. But in the Southwest only limited areas had developed a mellowed gentry as late as 1860. In the Alabama-Mississippi Black Belt, in the cotton and sugar parishes of Louisiana, along the Arkansas River, and in eastern Texas the master class included the "parvenus," the "cotton snobs," and the "Southern Yankees." If these planters failed to observe the code of the patrician, they apparently thought none the less of each other for it.

The hired slave stood the greatest chance of subjection to cruel punishments as well as to overwork. His employer, a Kentucky judge confessed, had no incentive to treat him kindly "except the mere feelings of humanity, which we have too much reason to believe in many instances . . . are too weak to stimulate the active virtue." [34] This was no exaggeration.

Southerners who were concerned about the welfare of slaves found it difficult to draw a sharp line between acts of cruelty and such measures of physical force as were an inextricable part of slavery. Since the line was necessarily arbitrary, slaveholders themselves disagreed about where it should be drawn. Was it barbarous to "correct" a slave by putting him in the stocks, or by forcing him to wear chains or an iron collar? How severely might a slave be flogged before the punishment became brutal? These were matters of personal taste.

But no master denied the propriety of giving a moderate whipping to a disobedient bondsman. During the seventeenth and eighteenth centuries the lash was used to punish free men as well as slaves. By mid-nineteenth century, however, it was seldom used upon any but slaves, because public opinion now considered it to be cruel. Why it was less cruel to whip a bondsman was a problem that troubled many sensitive masters. That they often had no choice as long as they owned slaves made their problem no easier to resolve. . . .

Beyond this were cases of pure brutality—cases of flogging that resulted in the crippling, maiming, or killing of slaves. An early nineteenth-century Charleston grand jury presented "as a serious evil the many instances of Negro Homicide" and condemned those who indulged their passions "in the barbarous treatment of slaves.[35] "Salting"—washing the cuts received from the whip with brine—was a harsh punishment inflicted upon the most obstinate bondsmen. Though all but a few deplored such brutality, slaveholders found themselves in a dilemma when nothing else could subdue a rebel.

If a master was too squeamish to undertake the rugged task of humbling a refractory bondsman, he might send him to a more calloused neighbor or to a professional "slave breaker." John Nevitt, a Mississippi planter not averse to the application of heroic remedies, received from another master a young chattel "for the purpose of punishing him for bad conduct." Frederick Douglass remembered a ruthless man in Maryland who had a reputation for being "a first rate hand at breaking young negroes"; some slaveholders found it beneficial to send their beginning hands to him for training.[36]

The branding of slaves was a widespread custom in colonial days; it was less common in the nineteenth century. But as late as 1838, a North Carolinian advertised that Betty, a fugitive, was recently "burnt . . . with a hot iron on the left side of her face; I tried to make the letter M." In 1848, a Kentuckian identified his runaway Jane by a brand mark "on the breast something like L blotched."[37] Mutilation as a form of punishment also declined without disappearing entirely. A Louisiana jailer, in 1831, gave notice that he had a runaway in his custody: "He has been lately gelded, and is not yet well." Another Louisianian recorded his disgust for a neighbor who had "castrated 3 men of his."[38]

Some masters who were otherwise as humane as the peculiar institution would permit tolerated almost anything that might "cure" habitual runaways. Andrew Jackson once offered fifty dollars reward for the capture of a fugitive, "and ten dollars extra for every hundred lashes any person will give him to the amount of three hundred.". . . The tracking of runaways with dogs was no figment of abolitionist imaginations; it was a common practice in all slave states, defended and justified in the courts. Groups of slaveholders sometimes rode through the swamps with their dogs and made the search for fugitives a sport comparable to fox hunting. Others preferred to hire professional slave catchers who provided their own "Negro dogs.". . .

The dogs could give a fugitive a severe mauling if the owner was willing to permit it. After a Mississippi master caught an escaped slave he allowed his dogs to "bite him very severely." A Louisiana planter "treed" a runaway and then "made the dogs pull him out of the tree, Bit him very badly, think he will stay home awhile." On another occasion his dogs tore a slave naked; he then "took him Home Before the other negro[es] . . . and made the dogs give him another over hauling." [39]

The angry mobs who dealt extra-legal justice to slaves accused of serious crimes committed barbarities seldom matched by the most brutal masters. . . .

Mobs all too frequently dealt with slaves accused of murder or rape. They conducted their own trials or broke into jails or court rooms to seize prisoners for summary execution. Their more fortunate victims were hanged; the others were burned to death, sometimes in the presence of hundreds of bondsmen who were forced to attend the ceremony. . . .

The abolition of slavery, of course, did not bring to a close the record of brutality in the South any more than it did elsewhere. But it did make less tenable the argument that brutality was sometimes in the public interest. And it did rescue many a master from the dilemma he faced when his desire to be humane was compromised by the demands of proper discipline.

NOTES

1. *Southern Cultivator*, XVIII (1860), pp. 130-31, 239-40.
2. Olmsted, *Seaboard*, pp. 104-105; *Southern Cultivator*, XII (1854), p. 206.
3. Walter L. Fleming, "Jefferson Davis, the Negroes and the Negro Problem," *Sewanee Review*, XVI (1908), pp. 410-11.
4. John Thompson, *The Life of John Thompson, A Fugitive Slave* (Worcester, Mass., 1856), p. 18; Sydnor, *Slavery in Mississippi*, p. 89; Davis (ed.), *Diary of Bennet H. Barrow*, pp. 112, 154, 175.
5. *De Bow's Review*, XI (1851), p. 371; Davis (ed.), *Diary of Bennet H. Barrows*, pp. 165, 269.
6. Gaillard Plantation Journal, entry for May 22, 1849; Gavin Diary, entry for March 26, 1856; Phillips (ed.), *Plantation and Frontier*, II, pp. 31-32.
7. *De Bow's Review*, VII (1849), p. 500.
8. Nevitt Plantation Journal, entries for November 9, 1827; March 28, 1831; July 18, 1832; Coleman, *Slavery Times in Kentucky*, pp. 248-49; New Orleans *Picayune*, December 26, 1847.
9. *Southern Cultivator*, XVIII (1860), p. 239-40; *Southern Planter*, XII (1852), p. 107.
10. *De Bow's Review*, XXII (1857), pp. 376-79; *Southern Agriculturist*, IV (1831), p. 350.

11. Kemble, *Journal*, pp. 42-43; Phillips (ed.), *Plantation and Frontier*, I, pp. 116-22; Plantation Manual in Hammond Papers.

12. Douglass, *My Bondage*, p. 103.

13. *Southern Cultivator*, VII (1849), p. 135; [Ingraham], *South-West*, II, pp. 287-88.

14. Olmsted, *Seaboard*, pp. 438-39; Bills Diary, entry for March 30, 1860.

15. *Southern Cultivator*, II (1844), pp. 169-70; Davis, *Cotton Kingdom in Alabama*, pp. 54-55.

16. *Southern Cultivator*, VIII (1850), p. 164; William P. Gould Ms. Plantation Rules.

17. Adams Diary, entry for July 2, 1860.

18. Johnson, *Ante-Bellum North Carolina*, p. 496; John H. Cocke Ms. Plantation Rules, in N. F. Cabell Collection of Agricultural Papers; Olmsted, *Seaboard*, pp. 367-68.

19. *De Bow's Review*, XXII (1857), pp. 376-79.

20. Martineau, *Society in America*, II, pp. 109-10.

21. Lester B. Shippee (ed.), *Bishop Whipple's Southern Diary 1843–1844* (Minneapolis, 1937), pp. 31-32; *Southern Cultivator*, II (1844), p. 107; William S. Pettigrew to James C. Johnston, September 24, 1846, Pettigrew Family Papers.

22. Theodore Dwight Weld, *American Slavery As It Is: Testimony of a Thousand Witnesses* (New York, 1839).

23. Hundley, *Social Relations*, pp. 63-64, 187-88, 203-205.

24. Charleston *Courier*, May 14, 1847.

25. Catterall (ed.), *Judicial Cases*, II, pp. 336, 427.

26. Quoted in Taylor, "Negro Slavery in Louisiana," p. 254.

27. Moore Rawls to Lewis Thompson (n.d.), Lewis Thompson Papers.

28. New Orleans *Picayune*, March 16, 1858; Northup, *Twelve Years a Slave*, pp. 105-16.

29. *Southern Cultivator*, II (1844), p. 107; Bassett, *Plantation Overseer*, pp. 3-5.

30. Catterall (ed.), *Judicial Cases, passim*.

31. James P. Tarry to Samuel O. Wood, November 27, 1853; July 1, 1854, Samuel O. Wood Papers; Haller Nutt Ms. Journal of Araby Plantation, entries for November 1, 1843, *et seq.*

32. Gustavus A. Henry to his wife, December 12, 17, 1848; December 7, 1857, Henry Papers.

33. *Southern Cultivator*, XVIII (1860), p. 287; Sitterson, *Sugar Country*, p. 105.

34. Catterall (ed.), *Judicial Cases*, I, p. 284.

35. Henry, *Police Control*, pp. 67-68.

36. Nevitt Plantation Journal, entry for June 5, 1828; Douglas, *My Bondage*, p. 203; Sydnor, *Slavery in Mississippi*, pp. 69-70.

37. Johnson, *Ante-Bellum North Carolina*, pp. 493-94; Coleman, *Slavery Times in Kentucky*, pp. 248-49.

38. Taylor, "Slavery in Louisiana," p. 236; Davis (ed.), *Diary of Bennet H. Barrow*, pp. 173-74.

39. William Read to Samuel S. Downey, August 8, 1848, Downey Papers; Davis (ed.), *Diary of Bennet H. Barrow*, pp. 369-70, 376.

● The following selection presents Stanley M. Elkins's influential analysis of the mechanisms used by American slave-holders to produce infantile behavior among their Negro bondsmen. It also discusses his controversial concentration-camp analogy. The student should remember that Elkins is attempting only to describe the "Sambo"-like characteristics which he associates with role-playing expected of American Negro slaves; he is not in any sense expressing his approval of the concept, whatever its validity as an explanation of slave personality.

Slavery and Negro Personality

STANLEY M. ELKINS

PERSONALITY TYPES AND STEREOTYPES

. . . It will be assumed that there were elements in the very structure of the plantation system—its "closed" character—that could sustain infantilism as a normal feature of behavior. These elements, having less to do with "cruelty" per se than simply with the sanctions of authority, were effective and pervasive enough to require that such infantilism be characterized as something much more basic than mere "accommodations." It will be assumed that the sanctions of the system were in themselves sufficient to produce a recognizable personality type.[1]

It should be understood that to identify a social type in this sense is still to generalize on a fairly crude level—and to insist for a limited purpose on the legitimacy of such generalizing is by no means to deny that, on more refined levels, a great profusion of individual types might have been observed in slave society. Nor need it be claimed that the "Sambo" type, even in the relatively crude sense employed here, was a

From Stanley M. Elkins, *Slavery, A Problem in American Institutional and Intellectual Life* (Chicago: University of Chicago Press, 1968), pp. 86-9, 115-39. Reprinted by permission of the University of Chicago Press. Copyright © 1968 by The University of Chicago Press.

universal type. It was, however, a plantation type, and a plantation existence embraced well over half the slave population.[2] Two kinds of material will be used in the effort to picture the mechanisms whereby this adjustment to absolute power—an adjustment whose end product included infantile features of behavior—may have been effected. One is drawn from the theoretical knowledge presently available in social psychology, and the other, in the form of an analogy, is derived from some of the data that have come out of the German concentration camps. It is recognized in most theory that social behavior is regulated in some general way by adjustment to symbols of authority—however diversely "authority" may be defined either in theory or in culture itself—and that such adjustment is closely related to the very formation of personality. A corollary would be, of course, that the more diverse those symbols of authority may be, the greater is the permissible variety of adjustment to them—and the wider the margin of individuality, consequently, in the development of the self. The question here has to do with the wideness or narrowness of that margin on the antebellum plantation.

The other body of material, involving an experience undergone by several million men and women in the concentration camps of our own time, contains certain items of relevance to the problem here being considered. The experience was analogous to that of slavery and was one in which wide-scale instances of infantilization were observed. The material is sufficiently detailed, and sufficiently documented by men who not only took part in the experience itself but who were versed in the use of psychological theory for analyzing it, that the advantages of drawing upon such data for purposes of analogy seem to outweigh the possible risks.

The introduction of this second body of material must to a certain extent govern the theoretical strategy itself. It has been recognized both implicitly and explicitly that the psychic impact and effects of the concentraion-camp exprience were not anticipated in existing theory and that consequently such theory would require some major supplementation.[3] It might be added, parenthetically, that almost any published discussion of this modern Inferno, no matter how learned, demonstrates how "theory," operating at such a level of shared human experience, tends to shed much of its technical trappings and to take on an almost literary quality. The experience showed, in any event, that infantile personality features could be induced in a relatively short time among large numbers of adult human beings coming from very diverse backgrounds. The particular strain which was thus placed upon prior theory consisted in the need to make room not only for the cultural and environmental sanctions that sustain personality (which in a sense Freudian theory already had) but also for a virtually unanticipated problem: actual change in the personality of masses of adults. It forced a reappraisal and new appreciation of how completely and effectively prior cultural sanctions for behavior and personality could be detached to make way for new and different sanctions, and of how adjustments could be made by individuals to a species of authority vastly different from any previously known. The revelation for theory was the process of detachment.

These cues, accordingly, will guide the argument on Negro slavery. Several million people were detached with a peculiar effectiveness from a great variety of cultural backgrounds in Africa—a detachment operating with infinitely more effectiveness upon those brought to North America than upon those who came to Latin America. It was achieved partly by the shock experience inherent in the very mode of procurement but more specifically by the type of authority-system to which they were introduced and to which they had to adjust for physical and psychic survival. The new adjustment, to absolute power in a closed system, involved infantilization, and the detachment was so complete that little trace of prior (and thus alternative) cultural sanctions for behavior and personality remained for the descendants of the first generation. For them, adjustment to clear and omnipresent authority could be more or less automatic—as much so, or as little, as it is for anyone whose adjustment to a social system begins at birth and to whom that system represents normality. We do not know how generally a full adjustment was made by the first generation of fresh slaves from Africa. But we do know—from a modern experience—that such an adjustment is possible, not only within the same generation but within two or three years. This proved possible for people in a full state of complex civilization, for men and women who were not black and not savages. . . .

THREE THEORIES OF PERSONALITY

The immense revelation for psychology in the concentration-camp literature has been the discovery of how elements of dramatic personality change could be brought about in masses of individuals. And yet it is not proper that the crude fact of "change" alone should dominate the conceptual image with which one emerges from this problem. "Change" per se, change that does not go beyond itself, is productive of nothing; it leaves only destruction, shock, and howling bedlam behind it unless some future basis of stability and order lies waiting to guarantee it and give it reality. So it is with the human psyche, which is apparently capable of making terms with a state other than liberty as we know it. The very dramatic features of the process just described may upset the nicety of this point. There is the related danger, moreover, of unduly stressing the individual psychology of the problem at the expense of its social psychology.

These hazards might be minimized by maintaining a conceptual distinction between two phases of the group experience. The process of detachment from prior standards of behavior and value is one of them, and is doubtless the more striking, but there must be another one. That such detachment can, by extension, involve the whole scope of an individual's culture is an implication for which the vocabulary of individual psychology was caught somewhat unawares. Fluctuations in the state of the individual psyche could formerly be dealt with, or so it seemed, while taking for granted the more or less static nature of social organization, and with a minimum of reference to its features. That such organization might itself become an important variable was therefore a possibility not highly developed in theory, focused as theory was upon individual case histories to the invariable minimization of social and cultural setting. The other phase of the experience should be considered as the "stability" side of the problem, that phase which stabilized what the "shock" phase only opened the way for. This was essentially a process of adjustment to a standard of social normality, though in this case a drastic readjustment and compressed within a very short time—a process which under typical conditions of individual and group existence is supposed to begin at birth and last a lifetime and be transmitted in many and diffuse ways from generation to generation. The adjustment is assumed to be slow and organic, and it normally is. Its numerous aspects extend much beyond psychology; those aspects have in the past been treated at great leisure within the rich provinces not only of psychology but of history, sociology, and literature as well. What rearrangement and compression of those provinces may be needed to accommodate a mass experience that not only involved profound individual shock but also required rapid assimilation to a drastically different form of social organization, can hardly be known. But perhaps the most conservative beginning may be made with existing psychological theory.

The theoretical system whose terminology was orthodox for most of the Europeans who have written about the camps was that of Freud. It was necessary for them to do a certain amount of improvising, since the scheme's existing framework provided only the narrowest leeway for dealing with such radical concepts as out-and-out change in personality. This was due to two kinds of limitations which the Freudian vocabulary places upon the notion of the "self." One is that the superego—that part of the self involved in social relationships, social values, expectations of others, and so on—is conceived as only a small and highly refined part of the "total" self. The other is the assumption that the content and character of the superego is laid down in childhood and undergoes relatively little basic alteration thereafter.[4] Yet a Freudian diagnosis of the concentration-camp inmate—whose social self, or superego, did appear to change and who seemed basically changed thereby—is, given these limitations, still possible. Elie Cohen, whose analysis is the most thorough of these, specifically states that "the superego acquired new values in a concentration camp." [5] The old values, according to Dr. Cohen, were first silenced by the shocks which produced "acute depersonalization" (the subject-object split: "It is not the real 'me' who is undergoing this"), and by the powerful drives of hunger and survival. Old values, thus set aside, could be replaced by new ones. It was a process made possible by "infantile regression"—regression to a previous condition of childlike dependency in which parental prohibitions once more became all-powerful and in which parental judgments might once more be internalized. In this way a new "father-image," personified in the SS guard, came into being. That the prisoner's identification with the SS could be so positive is explained by still another mechanism: the principle of "identification with the aggressor." "A child," as Anna Freud writes, "interjects some characteristic of an anxiety-object and so assimilates an anxiety-experience which he has just undergone. . . . By impersonating the aggressor, assuming his attributes or imitating his aggression, the child transforms himself from the person threatened into the person who makes the threat." [6] In short, the child's only "defense" in the presence of a cruel, all-powerful father is the psychic defense of identification.

Now one could, still retaining the Freudian language, represent all this in somewhat less cumbersome terms by a slight modification of the metaphor. It could simply be said that under great stress the superego, like a bucket, is violently emptied of content and acquires, in a radically changed setting, new content. It would thus not be necessary to postulate a literal "regression" to childhood in order for this to occur. Something of the sort is suggested by Leo Alexander. "The psychiatrist stands in amazement," he writes, "before the thorough-ness and completeness with which this perversion of essential superego values was accomplished in adults . . . [and] it may be that the decisive importance of childhood and youth in the formation of [these] values may have been overrated by psychiatrists in a society in which allegiance to these values in normal adult life was taken too much for granted because of the stability, religiousness, legality, and security of the 19th Century and early 20th Century society." [7]

A second theoretical scheme is better prepared for crisis and more closely geared to social environment than the Freudian adaptation in-dicated above, and it may consequently be more suitable for accommo-dating not only the concentration-camp experience but also the more general problem of plantation slave personality. This is the "interper-sonal theory" developed by the late Harry Stack Sullivan. One may view this body of work as the response to a peculiarly American set of needs. The system of Freud, so aptly designed for a European society the stability of whose institutional and status relationships could al-ways to a large extent be taken for granted, turns out to be less clearly adapted to the culture of the United States. The American psychiatrist has had to deal with individuals in a culture where the diffuse, shift-ing, and often uncertain quality of such relationships has always been more pronounced than in Europe. He has come to appreciate the ex-tent to which these relationships actually support the individual's psychic balance—the full extent, that is, to which the self is "social" in its nature. Thus a psychology whose terms are flexible enough to permit altering social relationships to make actual differences in char-acter structure would be a psychology especially promising for dealing with the present problem.[8]

Sullivan's great contribution was to offer a concept whereby the really critical determinants of personality might be isolated for pur-poses of observation. Out of the hopelessly immense totality of "in-fluences" which in one way or another go to make up the personality, or "self," Sullivan designated one—the estimations and expectations of others—as the one promising to unlock the most secrets. He then made a second elimination: the *majority* of "others" in one's existence may for theoretical purposes be neglected; what counts is who the *significant* others are. Here, "significant others" [9] may be understood very crudely to mean those individuals who hold, or seem to hold, the keys to security in one's own personal situation, whatever its nature. Now as to the psychic processes whereby these "significant others" become an actual part of the personality, it may be said that the very

sense of "self" first emerges in connection with anxiety about the attitudes of the most important persons in one's life (initially, the mother,
father, and their surrogates—persons of more or less absolute authority), and automatic attempts are set in motion to adjust to these
attitudes. In this way their approval, their disapproval, their estimates
and appraisals, and indeed a whole range of their expectations become
as it were internalized, and are reflected in one's very character. Of
course as one "grows up," one acquires more and more significant
others whose attitudes are diffuse and may indeed compete, and thus
"significance," in Sullivan's sense, becomes subtler and less easy to
define. The personality exfoliates; it takes on traits of distinction and,
as we say, "individuality." The impact of particular significant others
is less dramatic than in early life. But the pattern is a continuing one;
new significant others do still appear, and theoretically it is conceivable
that even in mature life the personality might be visibly affected by
the arrival of such a one—supposing that this new significant other
were vested with sufficient authority and power. In any event there are
possibilities for fluidity and actual change inherent in this concept
which earlier schemes have lacked.

The purest form of the process is to be observed in the development of children, not so much because of their "immaturity" as such
(though their plasticity is great and the imprint of early experience
goes deep), but rather because for them there are fewer significant
others. For this reason—because the pattern is simpler and more
easily controlled—much of Sullivan's attention was devoted to what
happens in childhood. In any case let us say that unlike the adult, the
child, being drastically limited in the selection of significant others,
must operate in a "closed system."

Such are the elements which make for order and balance in the
normal self: "significant others" plus "anxiety" in a special sense—
conceived with not simply disruptive but also guiding, warning functions.[10] The structure of "interpersonal" theory thus has considerable
room in it for conceptions of guided change—change for either bene-
ficent or malevolent ends. One technique for managing such change
would of course be the orthodox one of psychoanalysis; another, the
actual changing of significant others.[11] Patrick Mullahy, a leading ex-
ponent of Sullivan, believes that in group therapy much is possible
along these lines.[12] A demonic test of the whole hypothesis is available in the concentration camp.

Consider the camp prisoner—not the one who fell by the wayside
but the one who was eventually to survive; consider the ways in which

he was forced to adjust to the one significant other which he now had —the SS guard, who held absolute dominion over every aspect of his life. The very shock of his introduction was perfectly designed to dramatize this fact; he was brutally maltreated ("as by a cruel father"); the shadow of resistance would bring instant death. Daily life in the camp, with its fear and tensions, taught over and over the lesson of absolute power. It prepared the personality for a drastic shift in standards. It crushed whatever anxieties might have been drawn from prior standards; such standards had become meaningless. It focused the prisoner's attention constantly on the moods, attitudes, and standards of the only man who mattered. A truly childlike situation was thus created: utter and abject dependency on one, or on a rigidly limited few, significant others. All the conditions which in normal life would give the individual leeway—which allowed him to defend himself against a new and hostile significant other, no matter how powerful—were absent in the camp. No competition of significant others was possible; the prisoner's comrades for practical purposes were helpless to assist him.[13] He had no degree of independence, no lines to the outside, in any matter. Everything, every vital concern, focused on the SS: food, warmth, security, freedom from pain, all depended on the omnipotent significant other, all had to be worked out within the closed system. Nowhere was there a shred of privacy; everything one did was subject to SS supervision. The pressure was never absent. It is thus no wonder that the prisoners should become "as children." It is no wonder that their obedience became unquestioning, that they did not revolt, that they could not "hate" their masters. Their masters' attitudes had become *internalized* as a part of their very selves; those attitudes and standards now dominated all others that they had. They had, indeed, been "changed."

There still exists a third conceptual framework within which these phenomena may be considered. It is to be found in the growing field of "role psychology." This psychology is not at all incompatible with interpersonal theory; the two might easily be fitted into the same system.[14] But it might be strategically desirable, for several reasons, to segregate them for purposes of discussion. One such reason is the extraordinary degree to which role psychology shifts the focus of attention upon the individual's cultural and institutional environment rather than upon his "self." At the same time it gives us a manageable concept—that of "role"—for mediating between the two. As a mechanism, the role enables us to isolate the unique contribution of culture and institutions toward maintaining the psychic balance of the individual. In it, we see formalized for the individual a range of choices in models of behavior and expression, each with its particular style, quality, and attributes. The relationship between the "role" and the "self," though not yet clear, is intimate; it is at least possible at certain levels of inquiry to look upon the individual as the variable and upon the roles extended him as the stable factor.[15] We thus have a potentially durable link between individual psychology and the study of culture. It might even be said, inasmuch as its key term is directly borrowed from the theater, that role psychology offers in workable form the long-awaited connection—apparently missed by Ernest Jones in his *Hamlet* study—between the insights of the classical dramatists and those of the contemporary social theorist.[16] But be that as it may, for our present problem, the concentration camp, it suggests the most flexible account of how the ex-prisoners may have succeeded in resuming their places in normal life.

Let us note certain of the leading terms.[17] A "social role" is definable in its simplest sense as the behavior expected of persons specifically located in specific social groups.[18] A distinction is kept between "expectations" and "behavior;" the expectations of a role (embodied in the "script") theoretically exist in advance and are defined by the organization, the institution, or by society at large. Behavior (the "performance") refers to the manner in which the role is played. Another distinction involves roles which are "pervasive" and those which are "limited." A pervasive role is extensive in scope ("female citizen") and not only influences but also sets bounds upon the other sorts of roles available to the individual ("mother," "nurse," but not "husband," "soldier"); a limited role ("purchaser," "patient") is transitory and intermittent. A further concept is that of "role clarity." Some roles are more specifically defined than others; their impact upon performance (and, indeed, upon the personality of the performer) depends on the clarity of their definition. Finally, it is asserted that those roles which carry with them the clearest and most automatic rewards and punishments are those which will be (as it were) most "artistically" played.

What sorts of things might this explain? It might illuminate the process whereby the child develops his personality in terms not only of the roles which his parents offer him but of those which he "picks up" elsewhere and tries on. It could show how society, in its coercive character, lays down patterns of behavior with which it expects the individual to comply. It suggests the way in which society, now turning its benevolent face to the individual, tenders him alternatives and defines for him the style appropriate to their fulfilment. It provides us with a further term for the definition of personality itself: there appears an extent to which we can say that personality is actually made up of the roles which the individual plays.[19] And here, once more assuming "change" to be possible, we have in certain ways the least cumbersome terms for plotting its course.

The application of the model to the concentration camp should be simple and obvious. What was expected of the man entering the role of camp prisoner was laid down for him upon arrival:

> Here you are not in a penitentiary or prison but in a place of instruction. Order and discipline are here the highest law. If you ever want to see freedom again, you must submit to a severe training. . . . But woe to those who do not obey our iron discipline. Our methods are thorough! Here there is no compromise and no mercy. The slightest resistance will be ruthlessly suppressed. Here we sweep with an iron broom! [20]

Expectation and performance must coincide exactly; the lines were to be read literally; the missing of a single cue meant extinction. The role was pervasive; it vetoed any other role and smashed all prior ones. "Role clarity"—the clarity here was blinding; its definition was burned into the prisoner by every detail of his existence:

> In normal life the adult enjoys a certain measure of independence; within the limits set by society he has a considerable measure of liberty. Nobody orders him when and what to eat, where to take up his residence or what to wear, neither to take his rest on Sunday nor when to have his bath, nor when to go to bed. He is not beaten during his work, he need not ask permission to go to the W.C., he is not continually kept on the run, he does not feel that the work he is doing is silly or childish, he is not confined behind barbed wire, he is not counted twice a day or more, he is not left unprotected against the actions of his fellow citizens, he looks after his family and the education of his children.
>
> How altogether different was the life of the concentration-camp prisoner! What to do during each part of the day was arranged for him, and decisions were made about him from which there was no appeal. He was impotent and suffered from bedwetting, and because of his chronic diarrhea he soiled his underwear. . . . The dependence of the prisoner on the SS . . . may be compared to the dependence of children on their parents. . . .[21]

The impact of this role, coinciding as it does in a hundred ways with that of the child, has already been observed. Its rewards were brutally simple—life rather than death; its punishments were automatic. By the survivors it was—it had to be—a role *well played*.

Nor was it simple, upon liberation, to shed the role. Many of the inmates, to be sure, did have prior roles which they could resume, former significant others to whom they might reorient themselves, a repressed superego which might once more be resurrected. To this extent they were not "lost souls." But to the extent that their entire personalities, their total selves, had been involved in this experience, to the extent that old arrangements had been disrupted, that society itself had been overturned while they had been away, a "return" was fraught with innumerable obstacles.[22]

It is hoped that the very hideousness of a special example of slavery has not disqualified it as a test for certain features of a far milder and more benevolent form of slavery. But it should still be possible to say, with regard to the individuals who lived as slaves within the respective systems, that just as on one level there is every difference between a wretched childhood and a carefree one, there are, for other purposes, limited features which the one may be said to have shared with the other.

Both were closed systems from which all standards based on prior connections had been effectively detached. A working adjustment to either system required a childlike conformity, a limited choice of "significant others." Cruelty per se cannot be considered the primary key to this; of far greater importance was the simple "closedness" of the system, in which all lines of authority descended from the master and in which alternative social bases that might have supported alternative standards were systematically suppressed.[23] The individual, consequently, for his very psychic security, had to picture his master in some way as the "good father," [24] even when, as in the concentration camp, it made no sense at all.[25] But why should it not have made sense for many a simple plantation Negro whose master did exhibit, in all the ways that could be expected, the features of the good father who was really "good"? If the concentration camp could produce in two or three years the results that it did, one wonders how much more pervasive must have been those attitudes, expectations, and values which had, certainly, their benovolent side and which were accepted and transmitted over generations.

For the Negro child, in particular, the plantation offered no really satisfactory father-image other than the master. The "real" father was virtually without authority over his child, since discipline, parental responsibility, and control of rewards and punishments all rested in other hands; the slave father could not even protect the mother of his children except by appealing directly to the master. Indeed, the mother's own role loomed far larger for the slave child than did that of the father. She controlled those few activities—household care, preparation of food, and rearing of children—that were left to the slave family. For that matter, the very etiquette of plantation life removed even the honorific attributes of fatherhood from the Negro male, who was addressed as "boy"—until, when the vigorous years of his prime were past, he was allowed to assume the title of "uncle."

From the master's viewpoint, slaves had been defined in law as property, and the master's power over his property must be absolute. But then this property was still human property. These slaves might never be quite as human as *he* was, but still there were certain standards that could be laid down for their behavior: obedience, fidelity, humility, docility, cheerfulness, and so on. Industry and diligence would of course be demanded, but a final element in the master's situation would undoubtedly qualify that expectation. Absolute power for him meant absolute dependency for the slave—the dependency not of the developing child but of the perpetual child. For the master, the role most aptly fitting such a relationship would naturally be that of the father. As a father he could be either harsh or kind, as he chose, but as a *wise* father he would have, we may suspect, a sense of the limits of his situation. He must be ready to cope with *all* the qualities of the child, exasperating as well as ingratiating. He might conceivably have to expect in this child—besides his loyalty, docility, humility, cheerfulness, and (under supervision) his diligence—such additional qualities as irresponsibility, playfulness, silliness, laziness, and quite possibly) tendencies to lying and stealing. Should the entire prediction prove accurate, the result would be something resembling "Sambo."

The social and psychological sanctions of role-playing may in the last analysis prove to be the most satisfactory of the several approaches to Sambo, for, without doubt, of all the roles in American life that of Sambo was by far the most pervasive. The outlines of the role might be sketched in by crude necessity, but what of the finer shades? The sanctions against overstepping it were bleak enough,[26] but the rewards —the sweet applause, as it were, for performing it with sincerity and feeling—were something to be appreciated on quite another level. The law, untuned to the deeper harmonies, could command the player to be present for the occasion, and the whip might even warn against his missing the grosser cues, but could those things really insure the performance that melted all hearts? Yet there was many and many a performance, and the audiences (whose standards were high) appear to have been for the most part well pleased. They were actually viewing their own masterpiece. Much labor had been lavished upon this chef d'oeuvre, the most genial resources of Southern society had been available for the work; touch after touch had been applied throughout the years, and the result—embodied not in the unfeeling law but in the richest layers of Southern lore—had been the product of an exquisitely rounded collective creativity. And indeed, in a sense that somehow transcended the merely ironic, it was a labor of love. "I love the simple and unadulterated slave, with his geniality, his mirth, his swagger, and his nonsense," wrote Edward Pollard. "I love to look upon his countenance shining with content and grease; I love to study his affectionate heart; I love to mark that peculiarity in him, which beneath all his buffoonery exhibits him as a creature of the tenderest sensibilities, mingling his joys and his sorrows with those of his master's home."[27] Love, even on those terms, was surely no inconsequential reward.

But what were the terms? The Negro was to be a child forever. "The Negro . . . in his true nature, is always a boy, let him be ever so old. . . ." [28] "He is . . . a dependent upon the white race; dependent for guidance and direction even to the procurement of his most indispensable necessaries. Apart from this protection he has the helplessness of a child—without foresight, without faculty of contrivance, without thrift of any kind." [29] Not only was he a child; he was a happy child. Few Southern writers failed to describe with obvious fondness the bubbling gaiety of a plantation holiday or the perpetual good humor that seemed to mark the Negro character, the good humor of an everlasting childhood.

The role, of course, must have been rather harder for the earliest generations of slaves to learn. "Accommodation," according to John Dollard, "involves the renunciation of protest or aggression against undesirable conditions of life and the organization of the character so that protest does not appear, but acceptance does. It may come to pass in the end that the unwelcome force is idealized, that one identifies with it and takes it into the personality; it sometimes even happens that what is at first resented and feared is finally loved." [30]

Might the process, on the other hand, be reversed? It is hard to imagine its being reversed overnight. The same role might still be played in the years after slavery—we are told that it was [31]—and yet it was played to more vulgar audiences with cruder standards, who paid much less for what they saw. The lines might be repeated more and more mechanically, with less and less conviction; the incentives to perfection could become hazy and blurred, and the excellent old piece could degenerate over time into low farce. There could come a point, conceivably, with the old zest gone, that it was no longer worth the candle. The day might come at last when it dawned on a man's full waking consciousness that he had really grown up, that he was, after all, only playing a part.

MECHANISMS OF RESISTANCE TO ABSOLUTE POWER

One might say a great deal more than has been said here about mass behavior and mass manifestations of personality, and the picture would still amount to little more than a grotesque cartoon of humanity were not some recognition given to the ineffable difference made in any social system by men and women possessing what is recognized, any-where and at any time, simply as character. With that, one arrives at something too qualitatively fine to come very much within the crude categories of the present discussion; but although it is impossible to generalize with any proper justice about the incidence of "character" in its moral, irreducible, individual sense, it may still be possible to con-clude with a note or two on the social conditions, the breadth or narrow-ness of their compass, within which character can find expression.

Why should it be, turning once more to Latin America, that there one finds no Sambo, no social tradition, that is, in which slaves were defined by virtually complete consensus as children incapable of being trusted with the full privileges of freedom and adulthood? There, the system surely had its brutalities. The slaves arriving there from Africa had also undergone the capture, the sale, the Middle Passage. They too had been uprooted from a prior culture, from a life very different from the one in which they now found themselves. There, however, the system was not closed.

Here again the concentration camp, paradoxically enough, can be instructive. There were in the camps a very small minority of the sur-vivors who had undergone an experience different in crucial ways from that of the others, an experience which protected them from the full impact of the closed system. These people, mainly by virtue of wretched little jobs in the camp administration which offered them a minute measure of privilege, were able to carry on "underground" activities. In a practical sense the actual operations of such "under-grounds" as were possible may seem to us unheroic and limited; stealing blankets; "organizing" a few bandages, a little medicine, from the camp hospital; black market arrangements with a guard for a bit of extra food and protection for oneself and one's comrades; the circulation of news; and other such apparently trifling activities. But for the psychological balance of those involved, such activities were vital; they made possible a fundamentally different adjustment to the camp. To a prisoner so engaged, there were others who mattered, who gave real point to his existence—the SS was no longer the *only* one. Conversely, the role of the child was not the only one he played. He could take initiative; he could give as well as receive protection; he did things which had meaning in adult terms. He had, in short, alternative roles; this was a fact which made such a prisoner's transition from his old life to that of the camp less agonizing and destructive; those very prisoners, moreover, appear to have been the ones who could, upon liberation, resume normal lives most easily. It is, in fact, these people—not those of the ranks—who have described the camps to us.[32]

It was just such a difference—indeed, a much greater one—that separated the typical slave in Latin America from the typical slave in the United States. Though he too had experienced the Middle Passage, he was entering a society where alternatives were significantly more diverse than those awaiting his kinsman in North America. Concerned in some sense with his status were distinct and at certain points competing institutions. This involved multiple and often competing "significant others." His master was, of course, clearly the chief one—but not the only one. There could, in fact, be a considerable number: the friar who boarded his ship to examine his conscience, the confessor; the priest who made the rounds and who might report irregularities in treatment to the *procurador*; the zealous Jesuit quick to resent a master's intrusion upon such sacred matters as marriage and worship (a resentment of no small consequence to the master); the local magistrate, with his eye on the king's official protector of slaves, who would find himself in trouble were the laws too widely evaded; the king's informer who received one-third of the fines. For the slave the result was a certain latitude; the lines did not all converge on one man; the slave's personality, accordingly, did not have to focus on a single role. He was, true enough primarily a slave. Yet he might in fact perform multiple roles. He could be a husband and a father (for the American slave these roles had virtually no meaning); open to him also were such activities as artisan, peddler, petty merchant, truck gardener (the law reserved to him the necessary time and a share of the proceeds, but such arrangements were against the law for Sambo); he could be a communicant in the church, a member of a religious fraternity [33] (roles guaranteed by the most powerful institution in Latin America—comparable privileges in the American South depended on a master's pleasure). These roles were all legitimized and protected *outside* the plantation; they offered a diversity of channels for the development of personality. Not only did the individual have multiple roles open to him as a slave, but the very nature of these roles made possible a certain range of aspirations should he some day become free. He could have a fantasy-life not limited to catfish and watermelons; it was within his conception to become a priest, an independent farmer, a successful merchant, a military officer.[34] The slave could actually—to an extent quite unthinkable in the United States—conceive of himself *as a rebel*. Bloody slave revolts, actual wars, took place in Latin America; nothing on this order occurred in the United States.[35] But even without a rebellion, society here had a network of customary arrangements, rooted in antiquity, which made possible at many points a smooth transition of status from slave to free and which provided much social space for the exfoliation of individual character.

To the typical slave on the ante-bellum plantation in the United States, society of course offered no such alternatives. But that is hardly to say that something of an "underground"—something rather more, indeed, than an underground—could not exist in Southern slave society. And there were those in it who hardly fitted the picture of "Sambo."

The American slave system, compared with that of Latin America, was closed and circumscribed, but, like all social systems, its arrangements were less perfect in practice than they appeared to be in theory. It was possible for significant numbers of slaves, in varying degrees, to escape the full impact of the system and its coercions upon personality. The house servant, the urban mechanic, the slave who arranged his own employment and paid his master a stipulated sum each week, were all figuratively members of the "underground." Even among those working on large plantations, the skilled craftsman or the responsible slave foreman had a measure of independence not shared by his simpler brethren. Even the single slave family owned by a small farmer had a status much closer to that of house servants than to that of plantation labor gang. For all such people there was a margin of space denied to the majority; the system's authority-structure claimed their bodies but not quite their souls.

Out of such groups an individual as complex and as highly developed as William Johnson, the Natchez barber, might emerge. Johnson's diary reveals a personality that one recognizes instantly as a type—but a type whose values came from a sector of society very different from that which formed Sambo. Johnson is the young man on the make, the ambitious free-enterpriser of American legend. He began life as a slave, was manumitted at the age of eleven, and rose from a poor apprentice barber to become one of the wealthiest and most influential Negroes in ante-bellum Mississippi. He was respected by white and black alike, and counted among his friends some of the leading public men of the state.[36]

It is of great interest to note that although the danger of slave revolts (like Communist conspiracies in our own day) was much overrated by touchy Southerners; the revolts that actually did occur were in no instance planned by plantation laborers but rather by Negroes whose qualities of leadership were developed well outside the full coercions of the plantation authority-system. Gabriel, who led the revolt of 1800, was a blacksmith who lived a few miles outside Richmond; Denmark Vesey, leading spirit of the 1822 plot at Charleston, was a freed Negro artisan who had been born in Africa and served several years aboard a slavetrading vessel; and Nat Turner, the Virginia slave who fomented the massacre of 1831, was a literate preacher of recognized intelligence. Of the plots that have been convincingly substantiated (whether they came to anything or not), the majority originated in urban centers.[37]

For a time during Reconstruction, a Negro elite of sorts did emerge in the South. Many of its members were Northern Negroes, but the Southern ex-slaves who also comprised it seem in general to have emerged from the categories just indicated. Vernon Wharton, writing of Mississippi, says:

> A large portion of the minor Negro leaders were preachers, lawyers, or teachers from the free states or from Canada. Their education and their independent attitude gained for them immediate favor and leadership. Of the natives who became their rivals, the majority had been urban slaves, blacksmiths, carpenters, clerks, or waiters in hotels and boarding houses; a few of them had been favored body-servants of affluent whites.[38]

The William Johnsons and Denmark Veseys have been accorded, though belatedly, their due honor. They are, indeed, all too easily identified, thanks to the system that enabled them as individuals to be so conspicuous and so exceptional and, as members of a group, so few.

NOTES

1. The line between "accommodation" (as conscious hypocrisy) and behavior inextricable from basic personality, though the line certainly exists, is

anything but a clear and simple matter of choice. There is reason to think that the one grades into the other, and vice versa, with considerable subtlety. In this connection, the most satisfactory theoretical mediating term between deliberate role-playing and "natural" role-playing might be found in role-psychology.

2. Although the majority of Southern slaveholders were not planters, the majority of slaves were owned by a planter minority. "Considerably more than half of them lived on plantation units of more than twenty slaves, and one-fourth lived on units of more than fifty. That the majority of slaves belonged to members of the planter class, and not to those who operated small farms with a single slave family, is a fact of crucial importance concerning the nature of bondage in the ante-bellum South." Stampp, *Peculiar Institution*, p. 31.

3. See esp. below, . . . n. 7.

4. "For just as the ego is a modified portion of the id as a result of contact with the outer world, the super-ego represents a modified portion of the ego, formed through experiences absorbed from the parents, especially from the father. The super-ego is the highest evolution attainable by man, and consists of a precipitate of all prohibitions and inhibitions, all the rules of conduct which are impressed on the child by his parents and by parental substitutes. The feeling of *conscience* depends altogether on the development of the super-ego." A. A. Brill, Introduction to *The Basic Writings of Sigmund Freud* (New York: Modern Library, 1938), pp. 12-13. "Its relation to the ego is not exhausted by the precept: 'You *ought to be* such and such (like your father); it also comprises the prohibition: 'You *must not be* such and such (like your father); that is, you may not do all that he does; many things are his prerogative.'" Sigmund Freud, *The Ego and the Id* (London: Hogarth Press, 1947), pp. 44-45. ". . . and here we have that higher nature, in this ego-ideal or super-ego, the representative of our relation to our parents. When we were little children we knew these higher natures, we admired them and feared them; and later we took them into ourselves." *Ibid.*, p. 47. "As a child grows up, the office of father is carried on by masters and by others in authority; the power of their injunctions and prohibitions remains vested in the ego-ideal and continues, in the form of conscience, to exercise the censorship of morals. The tension between the demands of conscience and the actual attainments of the ego is experienced as a sense of guilt. Social feelings rest on the foundation of identification with others, on the basis of an ego-ideal in common with them." *Ibid.*, p. 49.

5. *Human Behavior*, p. 136.

6. Anna Freud, *The Ego and the Mechanisms of Defence* (London: Hogarth Press, 1948), p. 121. "In some illustrative case reports, Clara Thompson stresses the vicious circle put in motion by this defense-mechanism. The stronger the need for identification, the more a person loses himself in his omnipotent enemy—the more helpless he becomes. The more helpless he feels, the stronger the identification, and—we may add—the more likely it is that he tries even to surpass the aggressiveness of his aggressor. This may explain the almost unbelievable phenomenon that prisoner-superiors sometimes acted more brutally than did members of the SS. . . Identification with the aggressor represented the final stage of passive adaptation. It was a means of defense of a rather paradoxical nature: survival through surrender; protection against the fear of the enemy—by becoming part of him; overcoming helplessness—by re-

gressing to childish dependence." Bluhm, "How Did They Survive?" pp. 24-25.

7. Leo Alexander, "War Crimes: Their Social-Psychological Aspects," *American Journal of Psychiatry*, CV (September, 1948), 173. "The super-ego structure is . . . in peril whenever these established guiding forces weaken or are in the process of being undermined, shifted, or perverted, and becomes itself open to undermining, shifting, or perversion even in adult life—a fact which is probably more important than we have been aware of heretofore." *Ibid.*, p. 175.

8. My use of Sullivan here does not imply a willingness to regard his work as a "refutation" to that of Freud, or even as an adequate substitute for it in all other situations. It lacks the imaginative scope which in Freud makes possible so great a range of cultural connections; in it we miss Freud's effort to deal as scientifically as possible with an infinite array of psychological and cultural phenomena; the fragmentary nature of Sullivan's work, its limited scope, its cloudy presentation, all present us with obstacles not to be surmounted overnight. This might well change as his ideas are elaborated and refined. But meanwhile it would be too much to ask that all connections be broken with the staggering amount of work already done on Freudian models.

9. Sullivan refined this concept from the earlier notion of the "generalized other" formulated by George Herbert Mead. "The organized community or social group [Mead wrote] which gives to the individual his unity of self may be called 'the generalized other.' The attitude of the generalized other is the attitude of the whole community. Thus, for example, in the case of such a social group as a ball team, the team is the generalized other in so far as it enters—as an organized process or social activity—into the experience of any one of the individual members of it." George H. Mead, *Mind, Self and Society: From the Standpoint of a Social Behaviorist* (Chicago: University of Chicago Press, 1934), p. 154.

10. The technical term, in Sullivan's terminology, for the mechanism represented by these two elements functioning in combination, is the individual's "self-dynamism." David Riesman has refined this concept; he has, with his "inner-directed, other-directed" polarity, considered the possibility of different kinds of "self-dynamisms." The self-dynamism which functions with reference to specific aims and which is formed and set early in life is characterized as the "gyroscope." On the other hand the self-dynamism which must function in a cultural situation of constantly shifting significant others and which must constantly adjust to them is pictured as the "radar." See *The Lonely Crowd*, *passim*. The principles summarized in this and the preceding paragraphs are to be found most clearly set forth in Harry Stack Sullivan, *Conceptions of Modern Psychiatry* (Washington: William Alanson White Psychiatric Foundation, 1945). Sullivan's relationship to the general development of theory is assessed in Patrick Mullahy, *Oedipus Myth and Complex: A Review of Psychoanalytic Theory* (New York: Hermitage House, 1948).

11. Actually, one of the chief functions of psychoanalysis as it has been practiced from the beginning is simply given more explicit recognition here. The psychiatrist who helps the patient exhibit to himself attitudes and feelings systematically repressed—or "selectively ignored"—becomes in the process a new and trusted significant other.

12. "Indeed . . . when the whole Sullivanian conception of the effect of significant others upon the origin and stability of self-conceptions is pushed

farther, really revolutionary vistas of guided personality emerge. If the maintenance of certain characteristic patterns of interpersonal behavior depends upon their support by significant others, then to alter the composition of any person's community of significant others is the most direct and drastic way of altering his 'personality.' This can be done. Indeed, it is being done, with impressive results, by the many types of therapeutic groups, or quasi-families of significant new others, which have come up in the past few years." Patrick Mullahy (ed.), *The Contributions of Harry Stack Sullivan* (New York: Hermitage House, 1952), p. 193.

13. It should be noted that there were certain important exceptions. . . .

14. An outstanding instance of authorities who are exponents of both is of that of H. H. Gerth and C. Wright Mills, whose study *Character and Social Structure* ranges very widely in both interpersonal theory and role psychology and uses them interchangeably.

15. Conceptually, the purest illustration of this notion might be seen in such an analogy as the following. Sarah Bernhardt, playing in *Phèdre*, enacted a role which had not altered since it was set down by Racine two centuries before her time, and she was neither the first woman who spoke those lines, nor was she the last. Nor, indeed, was *Phèdre* her only triumph. Such was Bernhardt's genius, such was her infinite plasticity, that she moved from immutable role to immutable role in the classic drama, making of each, as critic and theatergoer alike agreed, a masterpiece. Now Bernhardt herself is gone, yet the lines remain, waiting to be transfigured by some new genius.

16. In the resources of dramatic literature a variety of insights may await the "social scientist" equipped with both the imagination and the conceptual tools for exploiting them, and the emergence of role-psychology may represent the most promising step yet taken in this direction. A previous area of contact has been in the realm of Freudian psychology, but this has never been a very natural or comfortable meeting ground for either the analyst or the literary critic. For example, in Shakespeare's *Hamlet* there is the problem, both psychological and dramatic, of Hamlet's inability to kill his uncle. Dr. Ernest Jones (in *Hamlet and Oedipus*) reduces all the play's tensions to a single Freudian complex. It should be at once more "scientific" and more "literary," however, to consider the problem in terms of role-conflict (Hamlet as prince, son, nephew, lover, etc., has multiple roles which keep getting in the way of one another). Francis Fergusson, though he uses other terminology, in effect does this in his *Ideal of a Theater*.

17. In this paragraph I duplicate and paraphrase material from Eugene and Ruth Hartley, *Fundamentals of Social Psychology* (New York: Knopf, 1952), chap. xvi. See also David C. McClelland, *Personality* (New York: Sloane, 1951), pp. 289-332. Both these books are, strictly speaking, "texts," but this point could be misleading, inasmuch as the whole subject is one not normally studied at an "elementary" level anywhere. At the same time a highly successful effort has been made in each of these works to formulate the role concept with clarity and simplicity, and this makes their formulations peculiarly relevant to the empirical facts of the present problem. It may be that the very simplicity of the roles in both the plantation and concentration-camp settings accounts for this coincidence. Another reason why I am inclined to put a special premium on simplicity here is my conviction that the role concept has a range of "literary" overtones, potentially exploitable in realms other than psychology.

For a recent general statement, see Theodore R. Sarbin, "Role Theory," *Handbook of Social Psychology*, I, 223-58.

18. Hartley, *Fundamentals of Social Psychology*, p. 485.

19. "Personality development is not exclusively a matter of socialization. Rather, it represents the organism's more or less integrated way of adapting to *all* the influences that come its way—both inner and outer influences, both social and nonsocial ones. Social influences, however, are essential to human personality, and socialization accounts for a very great deal of personality development.

"From this point of view it would not be surprising to find that many personality disturbances represent some sort of breakdown or reversal of the socialization process." Theodore M. Newcomb, *Social Psychology* (New York: Dryden Press, 1950), p. 475.

20. Quoted in Leon Szalet, *Experiment "E"* (New York: Didier, 1945), p. 138.

21. Cohen, *Human Behavior*, pp. 173-74.

22. Theodore Newcomb is the only non-Freudian coming to my attention who has considered the concentration camp in the terms of social psychology. He draws analogies between the ex-inmates' problems of readjustment and those of returning prisoners of war. "With the return of large numbers of British prisoners of war . . . from German and Japanese camps, toward the end of World War II, it soon became apparent that thousands of them were having serious difficulties of readjustment. It was first assumed that they were victims of war neuroses. But this assumption had to be abandoned when it was discovered that their symptoms were in most cases not those of the commonly recognized neuroses. Most of the men having difficulty, moreover, did not have the kinds of personalities which would have predisposed them to neurotic disorders. Psychiatrists then began to wonder whether their disturbances represented only a temporary phase of the men's return to civilian life. But the difficulties were neither temporary nor 'self-correcting.' 'Even when men had been back for 18 months or even longer, serious and persistent difficulties were reported in something like one-third of the men.' . . . All in all . . . the authors were led to the conclusion that the returning war prisoner's troubles did not lie entirely within himself. They represented the strains and stresses of becoming *resocialized* in a culture which was not only different from what it had been but was radically different from that to which the men had become accustomed during their years of capture." "When a deliberate attempt is made to change the personality, as in psychotherapy, success brings with it changes in role patterns. When the role perscriptions are changed—as for . . . concentration-camp inmates—personality changes also occur. When forcible changes in role prescriptions are removed, the degree to which the previous personality is 'resumed' depends upon the degree to which the individual finds it possible to resume his earlier role patterns." Newcomb, *Social Psychology*, pp. 476-77, 482.

Social workers faced with the task of rehabilitating former concentration-camp prisoners rapidly discovered that sympathy and understanding were not enough. The normal superego values of many of the prisoners had been so thoroughly smashed that adult standards of behavior for them were quite out of the question. Their behavior, indeed, was often most childlike. They made extreme demands, based not on actual physical needs but rather on the fear that they might be left out, or that others might receive more than they. Those who regained their equilibrium most quickly were the ones who were able to begin new lives in social environments that provided clear limits, precise standards, steady goals, and specific roles to play. Adjustment was not easy, however, even for the most fortunate. On the collective farms of Israel, for example, it was understood that former concentration-camp inmates would be "unable to control their greed for food" for a number of months. During that time, concern for their neighbors' sensibilities was more than one could expect. Paul Friedman, "The Road Back for the DP's" *Commentary*, VI (December, 1948), 502-10; Eva Rosenfeld, "Institutional Change in Israeli Collectives" (Ph.D. diss., Columbia University, 1952), p. 278.

23. The experience of American prisoners taken by the Chinese during the Korean War seems to indicate that profound changes in behavior and values, if not in basic personality itself, can be effected without the use of physical torture or extreme deprivation. The Chinese were able to get large numbers of Americans to act as informers and to co-operate in numerous ways in the effort to indoctrinate all the prisoners with Communist propaganda. The technique contained two key elements. One was that all formal and informal authority structures within the group were systematically destroyed; this was done by isolating officers, non-commissioned officers, and any enlisted men who gave indications of leadership capacities. The other element involved the continual emphasizing of the captors' power and influence by judicious manipulation of petty rewards and punishments and by subtle hints of the greater rewards and more severe punishments (repatriation or non-repatriation) that rested with the pleasure of those in authority. See Edgar H. Schein, "Some Observations on Chinese Methods of Handling Prisoners of War," *Public Opinion Quarterly*, XX (Spring, 1956), 321-27.

24. In a system as tightly closed as the plantation or the concentration camp, the slave's or prisoner's position of absolute dependency virtually compels him to see the authority-figure as somehow really "good." Indeed, all the evil in his life may flow from this man—but then so also must everything of any value. Here is the seat of the only "good" he knows, and to maintain his psychic balance he must persuade himself that the good is in some way dominant. A threat to this illusion is thus in a real sense a threat to his very existence. It is a common experience among social workers dealing with neglected and maltreated children to have a child desperately insist on his love for a cruel and brutal parent and beg that he be allowed to remain with that parent. The most dramatic feature of this situation is the cruelty which it involves, but the mechanism which inspires the devotion is not the cruelty of the parent but rather the abnormal dependency of the child. A classic example of this mechanism in operation may be seen in the case of Varvara Petrovna, mother of Ivan Turgenev. Mme Turgenev "ruled over her serfs with a rod of iron." She demanded utter obedience and total submission. The slightest infraction of her rules brought the most severe punishment: "A maid who did not offer her a cup of tea in the proper manner was sent off to some remote village and perhaps separated from her family forever; gardeners who failed to prevent the plucking of a tulip in one of the flower beds before the house were ordered to be flogged; a servant whom she suspected of a mutinous disposition was sent off to Siberia." Her family and her most devoted servants were treated in much the same manner. "Indeed," wrote Varvara Zhitova, the

adopted daughter of Mme Turgenev, "those who loved her and were most devoted to her suffered most of all." Yet in spite of her brutality she was adored by the very people she tyrannized. David Magarshack describes how once when thrashing her eldest son she nearly fainted with sadistic excitement, whereupon "little Nicholas, forgetting his punishment, bawled at the top of his voice: 'Water! Water for mummy!'" Mme Zhitova, who knew Mme Turgenev's cruelty intimately and was herself the constant victim of her tyranny, wrote: "In spite of this, I loved her passionately, and when I was, though rarely, separated from her, I felt lonely and unhappy." Even Mme Turgenev's maid Agatha, whose children were sent to another village, when still infants so that Agatha might devote all her time to her mistress, could say years later, "Yes, she caused me much grief. I suffered much from her, but all the same I loved her! She was a real lady!" V. Zhitova, *The Turgenev Family*, trans. A. S. Mills (London: Havill Press, 1954), p. 25; David Magarshack, *Turgenev: A Life* (New York: Grove, 1954), pp. 14, 16, 22.

25. Bruno Bettelheim tells us of the fantastic efforts of the old prisoners to believe in the benevolence of the officers of the SS. "They insisted that these officers [hid] behind their rough surface a feeling of justice and propriety; he, or they, were supposed to be genuinely interested in the prisoners and even trying, in a small way, to help them. Since nothing of these supposed feelings and efforts ever became apparent, it was explained that he hid them so effectively because otherwise he would not be able to help the prisoners. The eagerness of these prisoners to find reasons for their claims was pitiful. A whole legend was woven around the fact that of two officers inspecting a barrack one had cleaned his shoes from mud before entering. He probably did it automatically, but it was interpreted as a rebuff of the other officer and a clear demonstration of how he felt about the concentration camp." Bettelheim, "Individual and Mass Behavior," p. 451.

26. Professor Stampp, in a chapter called "To Make Them Stand in Fear," describes the planter's resources for dealing with a recalcitrant slave. *Peculiar Institution*, pp. 141-91.

27. Edward A. Pollard, *Black Diamonds Gathered in the Darkey Homes of the South* (New York: Pudney & Russel, 1859), p. 58.

28. *Ibid.*, p. viii.

29. John Pendleton Kennedy, *Swallow Barn* (Philadelphia: Carey & Lea, 1832).

30. John Dollard, *Caste and Class in a Southern Town* (2nd ed.; New York: Harper, 1949), p. 255. The lore of "accommodation," taken just in itself, is very rich and is, needless to say, morally very complex. It suggests a delicate psychological balance. On the one hand, as the Dollard citation above implies, accommodation is fraught with dangers for the personalities of those who engage in it. On the other hand, as Bruno Bettelheim has reminded me, this involves a principle that goes well beyond American Negro society and is to be found deeply imbedded in European traditions: the principle of how the powerless can manipuate the powerful through aggressive stupidity, literal-mindedness, servile fawning, and irresponsibility. In this sense the immovably stupid "Good Soldier Schweik" and the fawning Negro in Richard Wright's *Black Boy* who allowed the white man to kick him for a quarter partake of the same tradition. Each has a technique whereby he can in a real sense exploit his powerful superiors, feel contempt for them, and suffer in the process no

great damage to his own pride. Jewish lore, as is well known, teems with this sort of thing. There was much of it also in the traditional relationships between peasants and nobles in central Europe.

Still, all this required the existence of some sort of alternative forces for moral and psychological orientation. The problem of the Negro in slavery times involved the virtual absence of such forces. It was with the end of slavery, presumably, that they would first begin to present themselves in generally usable form—a man's neighbors, the Loyal Leagues, white politicians, and so on. It would be in these circumstances that the essentially intermediate technique of accommodation could be used as a protective device beneath which a more independent personality might develop.

31. Even Negro officeholders during Reconstruction, according to Francis B. Simkins, "were known to observe carefully the etiquette of the Southern caste system." "New Viewpoints of Southern Reconstruction," *Journal of Southern History*, V (February, 1939), 52.

32. Virtually all the ex-prisoners whose writing I have made use of were men and women who had certain privileges (as clerks, physicians, and the like) in the camps. Many of the same persons were also active in the "underground" and could offer some measure of leadership and support for others. That is to say, both the objectivity necessary for making useful observations and the latitude enabling one to exercise some leadership were made possible by a certain degree of protection not available to the rank and file.

I should add, however, that a notable exception was the case of Bruno Bettelheim, who throughout the period of his detention had no privileged position of any kind which could afford him what I am calling an "alternative role" to play. And yet I do not think that it would be stretching the point too far to insist that he did in fact have such a role, one which was literally self-created: that of the scientific observer. In him, the scientist's objectivity, his feeling for clinical detail and sense of personal detachment, amounted virtually to a passion. It would not be fair, however, to expect such a degree of personal autonomy as this in other cases, except for a very few. I am told, for instance, that the behavior of many members of this "underground" toward their fellow prisoners was itself by no means above moral reproach. The depths to which the system could corrupt a man, it must be remembered, were profound.

33. See Tannenbaum, *Slave and Citizen*, pp. 64-65.

34. *Ibid.*, pp. 4 ff., 56-57, 90-93; see also Johnston, *Negro in the New World*, p. 90.

35. Compared with the countless uprisings of the Brazilian Negroes, the slave revolts in our own country appear rather desperate and futile. Only three emerge as worthy of any note, and their seriousness—even when described by a sympathetic historian like Herbert Aptheker—depends largely on the supposed plans of the rebels rather than on the things they actually did. The best organized of such "revolts," those of Vesey and Gabriel, were easily suppressed, while the most dramatic of them—the Nat Turner Rebellion—was characterized by little more than aimless butchery. The Brazilian revolts, on the other hand, were marked by imagination and a sense of direction, and they often involved large-scale military operations. One is impressed both by their scope and their variety. They range from the legendary Palmares Republic of the seventeenth century (a Negro state organized by escaped slaves and successfully defended for over fifty years), to the bloody revolts of the Moslem Negroes of Bahia

which, between 1807 and 1835, five times paralyzed a substantial portion of Brazil. Many such wars were launched from the *quilombos* (fortified villages built deep in the jungles by escaped slaves to defend themselves from recapture); there were also the popular rebellions in which th Negroes of an entire area would take part. One is immediately struck by the heroic stature of the Negro leaders: no allowances of any sort need be made for them; they are impressive from any point of view. Arthur Ramos has described a number of them, including Zambi, a fabulous figure of the Palmares Republic; Luiza Mahin, mother of the Negro poet Luiz Gama and "one of the most outstanding leaders of the 1835 insurrection"; and Manoel Francisco dos Anjos Fereira, whose followers in the *Balaiada* (a movement which drew its name from "Baliao," his own nickname) held the *entire province of* Maranhão for three years. Their brilliance, gallantry, and warlike accomplishments give to their histories an almost legendary quality. On the other hand, one could not begin to think of Nat Turner in such a connection. See Ramos, *The Negro in Brazil*, pp. 24-53; Herbert Aptheker, *American Negro Slave Revolts* (New York: Columbia University, 1943, *passim*.

36. See William R. Hogan and Edwin A. Davis (eds.), *William Johnson's Natchez: The Ante-Bellum Diary of a Free Negro* (Baton Rouge: Louisiana State University Press, 1951), esp. pp. 1-64.

37. Aptheker, *American Negro Slave Revolts*, pp. 220, 268-69, 295-96, and *passim*.

38. Vernon L. Wharton, *The Negro in Mississippi, 1865–1890* (Chapel Hill: University of North Carolina Press, 1942), p. 164.

• Elkins argues that those slaves who fit his "Sambo" model, crippled by the oppressive psychological and social constraints of ante-bellum slavery, failed to display any significant pattern of "resistance" to the system. There were few actual slave revolts in the United States and, according to Elkins, little of that persistent degree of unrest and dissension among Southern bondsmen that could be observed in most other New World slave societies. By and large, most North American blacks, he believes, remained docile and accommodating to the daily coercions of their enslavement, coercions that (excepting the Nazi concentration camps) Elkins feels were uniquely harsh among systems of enslavement. Scholars have quarreled with Elkins's theoretical view of slavery in the United States as distinctively "infantalizing" in its operation and also with his assertion that evidence of widespread resistance among slaves was absent. The writings of sociologist Ervin Goffman on the nature of "total institutions" has proved particularly helpful to Elkins's critics. "Total institutions," Goffman wrote, are places where "a large number of like-situated individuals" worked and lived, "cut off from the wider society for an appreciable period of time, [and] together lead an enclosed, formally administered round of life." George M. Frederickson and Christopher Lasch draw on Goffman's analysis to suggest an alternative to Elkins's concentration camp analogy as a tool in helping to explain slave behavior in ante-bellum America. A more useful analogy, the two authors argue, would be the prison experience. The latter analogy helps us understand, according to Frederickson and Lasch, the manner in which countless slaves escaped "infantalization."

Resistance to Slavery

GEORGE M. FREDERICKSON AND CHRISTOPHER LASCH

The issues involved in the study of "resistance" to slavery are badly in need of clarification. The problem, one would suppose, is not whether the plantation slave was happy with his lot but whether he actively resisted it. But even this initial clarification does not come easily. Too many writers have assumed that the problem of resistance consists mainly of deciding whether slaves were docile or discontented and whether their masters were cruel or kind. In this respect and in others, as Stanley Elkins noted several years ago, the discussion of slavery has locked itself into the terms of an old debate.[1] The proslavery stereotype of the contented slave, which was taken over without much conceptual refinement by U. B. Phillips and others, has been attacked by recent historians in language much the same as that employed by the abolitionists more than a hundred years ago, according to which slaves hated bondage and longed to be free. "That they had no understanding of freedom," Kenneth Stampp argues, ". . . is hard to believe." A few pages later, and without any intervening evidence, Stampp progresses from this cautious thought to a fullblown statement of the case for "resistance." "Slave resistance, whether bold and persistent or mild and sporadic, created for all slaveholders a serious problem of discipline." He concludes, in a burst of rhetoric, that "the record of slave resistance forms a chapter in the story of the endless struggle to give dignity to human life."[2]

It should be apparent that the traditional terms of reference, on either side of the dispute, are not sufficiently precise to serve as instruments of analysis. One of the faults of Phillips' work is his consistent failure to distinguish between cruelty and coercion. By compiling instances of the kindness and benevolence of masters, Phillips proved to his own satisfaction that slavery was a mild and permissive institution, the primary function of which was not so much to pro-

From George M. Frederickson and Christopher Lasch, "Resistance to Slavery," *Civil War History*, Vol. 13, No. 4 (December 1967), pp. 315-29. Reprinted by permission of The Kent State University Press and the editor of *Civil War History*.

duce a marketable surplus as to ease the accommodation of the lower race into the culture of the higher. The critics of Phillips have tried to meet him on his own ground. Where he compiled lists of indulgences and benefactions, they have assembled lists of atrocities. Both methods suffer from the same defect: they attempt to solve a conceptual problem—what did slavery do to the slave—by accumulating quantitative evidence. Both methods assert that plantations conformed to one of two patterns, terror or indulgence, and then seek to prove these assertions by accumulating evidence from plantation diaries, manuals of discipline, letters and other traditional sources for the study of slavery. But for every instance of physical cruelty on the one side an enterprising historian can find an instance of indulgence on the other. The only conclusion that one can legitimately draw from this debate is that great variations in treatment existed from plantation to plantation. (But as we shall see, this conclusion, barren in itself, can be made to yield important results if one knows how to use it.)

Even if we could make valid generalizations about the severity of the regime, these statements would not automatically answer the question of whether or not widespread resistance took place. If we are to accept the testimony of Frederick Douglass, resistance was more likely to result from indulgence and rising expectations than from brutalizing severity.[3] A recent study of the geographical distribution of authentic slave revolts shows that most of them occurred in cities and in areas of slavebreeding and diversified agriculture, where, according to all accounts, the regime was more indulgent than in the productive plantation districts of the Cotton Kingdom.[4] Open resistance cannot be inferred from the extreme physical cruelty of the slave system, even if the system's cruelty could be demonstrated statistically.

II

There is the further question of what constitutes resistance. When Kenneth Stampp uses the term he means much more than open and flagrant defiance of the system. To him resistance is all noncooperation on the part of the slaves. And it cannot be denied that the annals of slavery abound in examples of this kind of behavior. Slaves avoided work by pretending to be sick or by inventing a hundred other plausible pretexts. They worked so inefficiently as to give rise to the suspicion that they were deliberately sabotaging the crop. They stole from their masters without compunction, a fact which gave rise to the complaint that slaves had no moral sense, but which is better interpreted as evidence of a double standard—cheating the master while dealing honorably with other slaves. Nor was this all. Their grievances or frustrations led at times to the willful destruction of the master's property by destroying tools, mistreating animals, and setting fire to plantation buildings. Less frequently, they took the ultimate step of violent attack on the master himself. Perhaps the most common form of obvious noncooperation was running away; every large plantation had its share of fugitives.[5]

The question which inevitably arises, as Stampp piles up incident after incident in order to show that slaves were "a troublesome property," is whether this pattern of noncooperation constitutes resistance. [Resistance is a political concept. Political activity, in the strictest sense, is organized collective action which aims at affecting the distribution of power in a community; more broadly, it might be said to consist of any activity, either of individuals or of groups, which is designed to create a consciousness of collective interest, such consciousness being the prerequisite for effective action in the realm of power. Organized resistance is of course only one form of political action. Others include interest-group politics; coalitions of interest groups organized as factions or parties; reform movements; or, at an international level, diplomacy and war. In total institutions, however, conventional politics are necessarily nonexistent.[6] Politics, if they exist at all, must take the form of resistance: collective action designed to subvert the system, to facilitate and regularize escape from it; or, at the very least, to force important changes in it]

Among despised and downtrodden people in general, the most rudimentary form of political action is violence; sporadic and usually short-lived outbursts of destruction, based on a common sense of outrage and sometimes inspired by a millennialistic ideology. Peasant revolts, all over the world, have usually conformed to this type.[7] In total institutions, prison riots are perhaps the nearest equivalent. In American slavery, the few documented slave rebellions fall into the same pattern.[8] What makes these upheavals political at all is that they rest on some sense, however primitive, of collective victimization. They require, moreover, at least a minimum of organization and planning. What makes them rudimentary is that they do not aim so much at changing the balance of power as at giving expression on the one hand to apocalyptic visions of retribution, and on the other to an immediate thirst for vengeance directed more at particular individuals than at larger systems of authority. In the one case, the sense of grievance finds an outlet in indiscriminate violence (as against Jews); in the other, it attaches itself to a particular embodiment of authority (as in prisons, where a specific departure from established routine may set off a strike or riot demanding the authority's dismissal and a return to the previous regime). But in neither case does collective. action rest on a realistic perception of the institutional structure as a whole and the collective interest of its victims in subverting it. That explains why such outbreaks of violence tend to subside very quickly, leaving the exploitive structure intact. Underground resistance to the Nazis in western Europe, on the other hand, precisely because it expressed itself in an organized underground instead of in futile outbreaks of indiscriminate violence, had a continuous existence which testifies to the highly political character of its objectives.

[It is easy to show that Negro slaves did not always cooperate with the system of slavery. It is another matter to prove that noncooperation amounted to political resistance] Malingering may have reflected no more than a disinclination to work, especially when the rewards were so meager. Likewise, what is taken for sabotage may have originated in apathy and indifference. Acts of violence are subject to varying interpretations. If there is something undeniably political about an organized, premeditated rebellion, an isolated act of violence could arise from a purely personal grievance. Even the motive of flight is obscure: was it an impulse, prompted by some special and immediate affront, or was it desertion, a sort of separate peace? These acts in themselves tell us very little. We begin to understand them only when we understand the conceptual distinction between resistance and noncooperation; and even then, we still feel the need of a more general set of conceptions, derived from recorded experience, to which slavery—an unrecorded experience, except from the masters' point of view—can be compared; some general model which will enable us to grasp imaginatively the system as a whole.

III

Only the testimony of the slaves could tell us, once and for all, whether slaves resisted slavery. In the absence of their testimony, it is tempting to resort to analogies. Indeed it is almost impossible to avoid them. Those who condemn analogies, pretending to argue from the documentary evidence alone, delude themselves. Resistance to slavery cannot be established (any more than any other general conception of the institution can be established) without making an implicit analogy between Negro slavery and the struggles of free men, in our own time, "to give dignity to human life" by resisting oppression. The question, in the case of slavery, is not whether historians should argue from analogy but whether they are willing to make their analogies explicit.

Stanley Elkins compares slavery to the Nazi concentration camps and concludes that the effect of slavery was to break down the slave's adult personality and to reduce him to a state of infantile dependence, comparable to the condition observed by survivors of the concentration camps. In evaluating this particular analogy, we are entitled to ask how well it explains what we actually know about slavery. In one respect, it explains too much. It explains the fact that there were no slave rebellions in the United States comparable to those which took place in Latin America, but it also rules out the possibility of non-cooperation. [Elkins' analogy suggests a state of internalized dependency that does not fit the facts of widespread intransigence, insubordination, and mischief-making. Stampp may not adequately explain this pattern of behavior, but he convinces us that it existed. Elkins is open to criticism on empirical grounds for failing to take into account a vast amount of evidence that does not fit his theory of slave behavior.] Many of Elkins' critics, however, have not concerned themselves with the substance of his analogy. Raising neither empirical nor theoretical objections against it, they have seized on its mere existence as a means of discrediting Elkins' work. He should rather be congratulated for having made the analogy explicit, thereby introducing into the study of slavery the kinds of questions that modern studies of total institutions have dealt with far more systematically than conventional studies of slavery.

Elkins was careful to emphasize the limits of the comparison. He did not argue that the plantation resembled a concentration camp with respect to intentions or motives; "even 'cruelty,'" he added, "was not indispensable as an item in my equation." His "essentially limited purpose" in bringing the two institutions together was to show the psychological effects of closed systems of control; and the objections to the analogy may after all derive not from the analogy itself but from a tendency, among Elkins' critics, to take it too literally. As Elkins observes, the "very vividness and particularity [of analogies] are coercive: they are almost too concrete. One's impulse is thus to reach for extremes. The thing is either taken whole hog . . .; or it

is rejected out of hand on the ground that not all of the parts fit."
It is precisely because all the parts don't fit that an analogy is an
analogy rather than a literal correspondence, and it ought to be
enough, therefore, if just one of the parts demonstrably fits.[9]

[The real objection to Elkins' analogy is not that analogies in themselves are pernicious but that there is no compelling theoretical reason, in this case, to stop with one. The concentration camp is only one
of many total institutions with which slavery might have been compared; a total institution being defined, in Erving Goffman's words,
as "a place of residence and work where a large number of like-situated
individuals, cut off from the wider society for an appreciable period
of time, together lead an enclosed, formally administered round of
life."[10] An excellent example—the one, indeed, that springs immediately to mind—is the prison, "providing," Goffman says, that "we
appreciate that what is prison-like about prisons is found in institutions whose members have broken no laws."[11] [In several respects,
prisons, especially penitentiaries, are more analogous to plantation
slavery than concentration camps. Prisons are not, like the concentration camps, designed as experiments in deliberate dehumanization,
although they often have dehumanizing effects; in this respect the
motive behind the system more nearly approximates that of slavery
than of the concentration camp. More important, the problem of control is more nearly analogous. The disproportion between the authority of the guards and the impotence of the inmates is not absolute, as
it was at Dachau and Buchenwald, but subject, as it seems to have
been under slavery, to a number of variables—the temperament of
the guard or master, the composition of the prisoners or slaves, the
immediate history of the institutions involved]

Prison officials, like slaveowners and overseers, face a constant problem of noncooperation. "Far from being omnipotent rulers who have
crushed all signs of rebellion against their regime, the custodians are
engaged in a continuous struggle to maintain order—and it is a struggle in which the custodians frequently fail."[12] This situation occurs,
according to the sociologist Gresham Sykes, because although the
custodians enjoy an absolute monopoly of the means of violence, their
enormous power does not rest on authority; that is, on "a rightful or
legitimate effort to exercise control," which inspires in the governed
an internalized sense of obligation to obey. In the absence of a sense
of duty among the prisoners, the guards have to rely on a system of
rewards, incentives, punishments, and coercion. But none of these

methods can be carried too far without reaching dangerous extremes of laxity or demoralization. As in most total institutions—the concentration camp being a conspicuous exception—rigid standards of discipline tend to give way before the need to keep things running smoothly without undue effort on the part of the custodians. An absolute monopoly of violence can be used to achieve a state of total terror, but it cannot persuade men to work at their jobs or move "more than 1,200 inmates through the mess hall in a routine and orderly fashion."[13] The result, in the maximum-security prison, is a system of compromises, an uneasy give-and-take which gives prisoners a limited leverage within the system. To the extent that this adjustment limits the power of the guards, a corruption of authority takes place.[14]

Plantation literature produces numerous parallels. We can read the masters' incessant and heartfelt complaints about the laziness, the inefficiency, and the intractibility of slaves; the difficulty of getting them to work; the difficulty of enlisting their cooperation in any activity that had to be sustained over a period of time. We can read about the system of rewards and punishments, spelled out by the master in such detail, the significance of which, we can now see, was that it had had to be resorted to precisely in the degree to which a sense of internalized obedience had failed. We see the same limitation on terror and physical coercion as has been observed in the prison; for even less than the prison authorities could the planter tolerate the demoralization resulting from an excess of violence. We can even see the same "corruption of authority" in the fact that illicit slave behavior, especially minor theft, was often tolerated by the masters in order to avoid unnecessary friction.

One of the most curious features of the "society of captives," as described by Sykes is this: that while most of the prisoners recognize the legitimacy of their imprisonment and the controls to which they are subjected, they lack any internalized sense of obligation to obey them. "The bond between recognition of the legitimacy of control and the sense of duty has been torn apart."[15] This fact about prisons makes it possible to understand a puzzling feature of the contemporary literature on slavery, which neither the model of submission nor that of resistance explains—the curious contradiction between the difficulty of discipline and the slaves' professed devotion to their masters. Those who argue that the slaves resisted slavery have to explain away their devotion as pure hypocrisy. But it is possible to accept it as sincere without endorsing the opposite view—even in the sophisticated form in which it has been cast by Stanley Elkins—that slaves were children. The sociology of total institutions provides a theory with which to reconcile the contradiction. "The custodial institution," Sykes argues, "is valuable for a theory of human behavior because it makes us realize that men need not be motivated to conform to a regime which they define as rightful."[16] It is theoretically possible, in short, that slaves could have accepted the legitimacy of their masters' authority without feeling any sense of obligation to obey it. The evidence of the masters themselves makes this conclusion seem not only possible but highly probable. Logic, moreover, supports this view. For how could a system that rigorously defined the Negro slave not merely as an inferior but as an alien, a separate order of being, inspire him with the sense of belonging on which internalized obedience necessarily has to rest?

IV

It might be argued, however, that slaves developed a sense of obedience by default, having had no taste of life outside slavery which would have made them dissatisfied, by contrast, with their treatment as slaves. It might be argued that the convict's dissatisfaction with prison conditions and the insubordination that results derives from his sense of the outside world and the satisfactions it normally provides; and that such a perspective must have been lacking on the plantation. Elkins, in denying the possibility of any sort of accommodation to slavery short of the complete assimilation of the master's authority by the slave, contends that a consciously defensive posture could not exist, given the total authority of the master and the lack of "alternative forces for moral and psychological orientation."[17] This objection loses its force, however, if it can be shown that the slave did in fact have chances to develop independent standards of personal satisfaction and fair treatment within the system of slavery itself. Such standards would have made possible a hedonistic strategy of accommodation, and in cases where such a strategy failed, strong feelings of personal grievance.

It is true that the plantation sealed itself off from the world, depriving the slave of nearly every influence that would have lifted him out of himself into a larger awareness of slavery as an oppressive social system which, by its very nature, denied him normal satisfaction. In order to understand why slaves did not, as Elkins suggests, become totally submissive and ready to accept any form of cruelty and humiliation, it is necessary to focus on an aspect of slavery which has been almost totally ignored in discussion of slave personality. The typical slave, although born in slavery, was not likely to spend his entire life, or indeed any considerable part of it, under a single regime. The slave child could anticipate many changes of situation. It would appear likely, from what we know of the extent of the slave trade, that most slaves changed hands at least once in their lives; slave narratives and recollections suggest that it was not at all uncommon for a single slave to belong to several masters in the course of his lifetime of servitude. In addition, the prevalence of slave-hiring, especially in the upper South, meant that many slaves experienced a temporary change of regime. Even if a slave remained on the same plantation, things could change drastically, as the result of death and the accession of an heir, or from a change of overseer (especially significant in cases of absentee ownership).[18] Given the wide variation in standards of treatment and management techniques—a variation which, we suggested earlier, seems the one inescapable conclusion to be drawn from the traditional scholarship on the management of slaves—we are left with a situation that must have had important psychological implications. An individual slave might—like Harriet Beecher Stowe's Uncle Tom—experience slavery both at its mildest and at its harshest. He might be sold from an indulgent master to a cruel one or vice versa. He might go from a farm where he maintained a close and intimate relationship with his master to a huge impersonal "factory in the fields," where his actual master would be only a dim presence. These changes in situation led many slaves to develop standards of their own about how they ought to be treated and even to diffuse these standards among the stationary slave population. By comparing his less onerous lot under a previous master to his present hard one, a slave could develop a real sense of grievance and communicate it to others.[19] Similarly, slaves were quick to take advantage of any new leniency or laxity in control.[20] Hence it is quite possible to account for widespread noncooperation among slaves as resulting from a rudimentary sense of justice acquired entirely within the system of slavery itself. These standards would have served the same function as the standards convicts bring from the outside world into the prison. At the same time it is necessary to insist once again that they give rise to a pattern of intransigence which is hedonistic rather than political, accommodationist rather than revolutionary.

If this picture of slave motivation is less morally sublime than contemporary liberals and radicals would like, it should not be construed as constituting, in any sense, a moral judgment on the Negro slave.

[Sporadic noncooperation within a broad framework of accommodation was the natural and inevitable response to plantation slavery.] It should go without saying that white men born into the same system would have acted in the same way. Indeed, this is the way they have been observed to act in modern situations analogous to slavery. In total institutions, the conditions for sustained resistance are generally wanting—a fact that is insufficiently appreciated by those armchair moralists who like to make judgments at a safe distance about the possibilities of resistance to totalitarianism. Rebellions and mutinies "seem to be the exception," Erving Goffman observes, "not the rule." Group loyalty is very tenuous, even though "the expectation that group loyalty should prevail forms part of the inmate culture and underlies the hostility accorded to those who break inmate solidarity."[21]

Instead of banding together, inmates of total institutions typically pursue various personal strategies of accommodation. Goffman describes four lines of adaptation, but it is important to note that although these are analytically distinguishable, "the same inmate will employ different personal lines of adaptation at different phases in his moral career and may even alternate among different tacks at the same time." "Situational withdrawal," a fatalistic apathy, is the condition into which many inmates of concentration camps rapidly descended, with disastrous psychic consequences to themselves; it undoubtedly took its toll among slaves newly arrived from Africa during the colonial period. "Colonization," which in some cases can be regarded as another type of institutional neurosis, rests on a conscious decision that life in the institution is preferable to life in the outside world. Colonization, in turn, must be distinguished from "conversion," the inmate's internalization of the view of himself held by those in power. In Negro slavery, this is the "Sambo" role and is accompanied, as in the concentration camp, by an infantile sense of dependence. Colonization, on the other hand, would apply to the very small number of slaves who agreed to reenslavement after a period as free Negroes.[22]

The fourth type of accommodation is "intransigence," which should not be confused with resistance. The latter presupposes a sense of solidarity and an underground organization of inmates. Intransigence is a personal strategy of survival, and although it can sometimes help to sustain a high morale, it can just as easily lead to futile and even self-destructive acts of defiance. In slavery, there was a substantial minority who were written off by their masters as chronic troublemakers, "bad niggers," and an even larger group who indulged in occasional insubordination. It is precisely the pervasiveness of "intransigence" that made slaves, like convicts, so difficult to manage, leading to the corruption of authority analyzed above. But as we have already tried to show, there is nothing about intransigence that precludes a partial acceptance of the values of the institution. In fact, Goffman observes that the most defiant of inmates are paradoxically those who are most completely caught up in the daily round of institutional life. "Sustained rejection of a total institution often requires sustained orientation to its formal organization, and hence, paradoxically, a deep kind of involvement in the establishment."[23] The same immersion in the institutional routine that makes some inmates so easy to manage makes others peculiarly sensitive to disruptions of the routine, jealous of their "rights" under the system. Indeed, periods of intransigence can alternate, in the same person, with colonization, conversion, and even with periods of withdrawal.

The concentration camp was unique among total institutions in confronting the typical prisoner with a choice between situational withdrawal, which meant death, and conversion, which, in the absence of alternatives, came to dominate the personality as a fully internalized role. In other total institutions, however, all four roles can be played to some extent, and "few inmates seem to pursue any one of them very far. In most total institutions most inmates take the tack of what some of them call 'playing it cool.' This involves a somewhat opportunistic combination of secondary adjustments, conversion, colonization, and loyalty to the inmate group, so that the inmate will have a maximum chance, in the particular circumstances, of eventually getting out physically and psychologically undamaged."[24] The slave had no real prospect of "getting out," but unless he was infantilized—a hypothesis that now seems quite untenable—he had a powerful stake in psychic survival. He had every reason to play it cool; and what is more, slavery gave him plenty of opportunities.

But the most compelling consideration in favor of this interpretation of slavery is that the very ways in which slavery differed from other total institutions would have actually reinforced and stabilized the pattern of opportunistic response that we have described. The most obvious objection to an analogy between slavery and the prison, the mental hospital, or any other institution of this kind is that slaves for the most part were born into slavery rather than coming in from the outside as adults; nor did most of them have any hope of getting out.

We have answered these objections in various ways, but before leaving the matter we should point out that there is, in fact, a class of people in modern asylums—a minority, to be sure—who spend the better part of their lives in institutions of one kind or another. "Lower class mental hospital patients," for instance, "who have lived all their previous lives in orphanages, reformatories, and jails," are people whose experience in this respect approximates the slave's, especially the slave who served a series of masters. As a result of their continuous confinement, such patients have developed a kind of institutional personality. But they are not, as one might expect, Sambos—genuine converts to the institutional view of themselves. Quite the contrary; these people are the master-opportunists, for whom "no particular scheme of adaptation need be carried very far."[25] They have "perfected their adaptive techniques," experience having taught them a supreme versatility; and they are therefore likely to play it cool with more success than those brought in from the outside and incarcerated for the first time. These are the virtuosos of the system, neither docile nor rebellious, who spend their lives in skillful and somewhat cynical attempts to beat the system at its own game.

v

There is a passage in Frederick Douglass' *Narrative* that suggests how difficult it was even for an ex-slave—an unusually perceptive observer, in this case—to understand his former victimization without resorting to categories derived from experiences quite alien to slavery, categories that reflected the consciousness not of the slaves themselves but, in one way or another, the consciousness of the master-class. Douglass described how eagerly the slaves on Colonel Lloyd's Maryland plantations vied for the privilege of running errands to the Great House Farm, the master's residence and home plantation. The slaves "regarded it as evidence of great confidence reposed in them by the overseers; and it was on this account, as well as a constant desire to be out of the field from under the driver's lash, that they esteemed it a high privilege, one worth careful living for. He was called the smartest and most trusty fellow, who had this honor conferred upon him the most frequently."

Then follows a passage of unusual vividness and poignancy:

> The slaves selected to go to the Great House Farm, for the monthly allowance for themselves and their fellow-slaves, were

peculiarly enthusiastic. While on their way, they would make the dense old woods, for miles around, reverberate with their wild songs, revealing at once the highest joy and the deepest sadness. . . . They would sometimes sing the most pathetic sentiment in the most rapturous tone, and the most rapturous sentiment in the most pathetic tone. Into all of their songs they would manage to weave something of the Great House Farm. Especially would they do this, when leaving home. They would then sing most exultingly the following words:—

"I am going away to the Great House Farm!
O, yea! O, yea! O!"

This they would sing, as a chorus, to words which to many would seem unmeaning jargon, but which, nevertheless, were full of meaning to themselves. I have sometimes thought that the mere hearing of those songs would do more to impress some minds with the horrible character of slavery, than the reading of whole volumes of philosophy on the subject could do.

But as these passages so clearly show, the "horrible character of slavery" did not lie, as the abolitionists tended to think, in the deprivations to which the slaves were forcibly subjected—deprivations which, resenting, they resisted with whatever means came to hand—but in the degree to which the slaves (even in their "intransigence") inevitably identified themselves with the system that bound and confined them, lending themselves to their own degradation. In vying for favors they "sought as diligently to please their overseers," Douglass says, "as the office-seekers in the political parties seek to please and deceive the people."[26]

Even more revealing are the reflections that follow. "I did not, when a slave, understand the deep meaning of those rude and apparently incoherent songs. I was myself within the circle; so that I neither saw nor heard as those without might see and hear." It was only from without that the slave songs revealed themselves as "the prayer and complaint of souls boiling over with the bitterest anguish"—anguish, it should be noted, which expressed itself disjointedly, "the most pathetic sentiment" being set to "the most rapturous tone." It was only from without that the "dehumanizing character of slavery" showed itself precisely in the slave's incapacity to resist; but this perception, once gained, immediately distorted the reality to which it was applied. Douglass slides imperceptibly from these unforgettable evocations of slavery to an abolitionist polemic. It is a great mistake, he argued, to listen to slaves' songs "as evidence of their contentment and happiness." On the contrary, "slaves sing most when they are most unhappy." Yet the slaves whose "wild songs" he has just described were those who were "peculiarly enthusiastic," by his own account, to be sent to the Great House Farm, and who sang "exultingly" along the way. The ambiguity of the reality begins to fade when seen through the filter of liberal humanitarianism, and whereas the songs revealed "at once the highest joy and the deepest sadness," in Douglass' own words, as an abolitionist he feels it necessary to insist that "crying for joy, and singing for joy, were alike uncommon to me while in the jaws of slavery."[27]

If the abolitionist lens distorted the "horrible character" of slavery, the picture of the docile and apparently contented bondsman was no more faithful to the reality it purported to depict. But this should not surprise us. It is not often that men understand, or even truly see, those whom in charity they would uplift. How much less often do they understand those they exploit?

NOTES

1. Stanley Elkins, *Slavery: A Problem in American Institutional and Intellectual Life* (Chicago, 1959), Ch. I.

2. Kenneth Stampp, *The Peculiar Institution* (New York, 1956), pp. 88, 91.

3. Frederick Douglass, *The Narrative of the Life of Frederick Douglass, An American Slave* (Cambridge, 1960), pp. 132-133.

4. Martin D. de B. Kilson, "Towards Freedom: An Analysis of Slave Revolts in the United States," *Phylon*, XXV (1964), 179-183.

5. Stampp, *Peculiar Institution*, Ch. III.

6. Total institutions are distinguished not by the absolute power of the authorities—a definition which, as will become clear, prejudges an important issue—but by the fact that they are self-contained, so that every detail of life is regulated in accordance with the dominant purpose of the institution. Whether that purpose is defined as healing, punishment, forced labor, or (in the case of the concentration camps) terror, all total institutions are set up in such a way as to preclude any form of politics based on consent.

7. See E. J. Hobsbawm, *Primitive Rebels: Studies in Archaic Forms of Social Movement in the 19th and 20th Centuries* (Manchester, 1959); Norman Cohn, *The Pursuit of the Millennium* (New York, 1957).

8. Nat Turner's rebellion in 1831, the only significant slave uprising in the period 1820–1860 that got beyond the plotting stage, would seem to be comparable to a millennialist peasants' revolt. Turner was a preacher who, according to his own testimony, received the visitation of a spirit commanding him to "fight against the serpent, for the time was fast approaching when the first should be last and the last should be first." Quoted in Herbert Aptheker, *American Negro Slave Revolts* (New York, 1943), p. 296. See also Aptheker, *Nat Turner's Slave Rebellion* (New York, 1966).

9. Elkins, *Slavery*, pp. 104, 226.

10. Erving Goffman, *Asylums: Essays on the Social Situation of Mental Patients and Other Inmates* (Garden City, 1961; Chicago, 1962), p. xiii.

11. *Ibid.*

12. Gresham M. Sykes, *The Society of Captives: A Study of a Maximum Security Prison* (Princeton, 1958), p. 42.

13. *Ibid.*, p. 49.

14. *Ibid.*, pp. 52-58.

15. *Ibid.*, p. 46.

16. *Ibid.*, p. 48.

17. Elkins, *Slavery*, p. 133n.

18. Frederic Bancroft, in *Slave Trading in the Old South* (New York, 1959), concludes (pp. 382-406) that more than 700,000 slaves were transported from the upper South to the cotton kingdom in the years 1830–1860, and that most went by way of the slave trade. He also estimates (p. 405) that in the decade 1850–1860 an annual average of approximately 140,000 slaves were sold, interstate or *intra-state*, or hired out by their masters. This meant that one slave in twenty-five changed his *de facto* master in a given year. When we add to these regular exchanges the informal transfers that went on within families, we get some idea of the instability which characterized the slave's situation in an expansive and dynamic agricultural economy. The way slaves were sometimes shuttled about is reflected in several of the slave narratives, especially Frederick Douglass, *Narrative*; Solomon Northrop, *Twelve Years a Slave* (Auburn, Buffalo, and London, 1853); and [Charles Ball] *Fifty Years in Chains: Or the Life of an American Slave* (New York, 1858).

19. Positive evidence of this development of internal standards and of the vacillation between contentment and dissatisfaction to which it gave rise is as difficult to find as evidence on any other aspect of slave psychology. As we have indicated, adequate records of personal slave response simply do not exist. There is, however, some indication of this process in the slave narratives and recollections. One of the most revealing of the slave narratives is Charles Ball, *Fifty Years in Chains*. Ball's account seems truer than most to the reality of slavery because, unlike most fugitives, he escaped from servitude at an age when it was difficult for him to acquire new habits of thought from his free status and association with abolitionists. Ball recounts the common experience of being sold from the upper South with its relatively mild and permissive regime into the more rigorous plantation slavery farther south. Upon his arrival on a large South Carolina cotton plantation, Ball, who was from Maryland, makes the acquaintance of a slave from northern Virginia who tells him what he can now expect. "He gave me such an account of the suffering of the slaves, on the cotton and indigo plantations—of whom I now regarded myself as one—that I was unable to sleep this night." (pp. 103-104.) Later, he describes himself as "far from the place of my nativity, in a land of strangers, with no one to care for me beyond the care that a master bestows upon his ox . . ." (p. 115). The regime is indeed a harsh one, and he feels very dissatisfied, except on Sunday when he is taken up by the general hilarity that prevails in the slave quarters on the holiday. Eventually, however, he experiences a temporary improvement in his situation when he is given to his master's new son-in-law, who seems kindly and permissive. In a remarkable description of slave hedonism, Ball recalls his state of mind.

"I now felt assured that all my troubles in this world were ended, and that, in future, I might look forward to a life of happiness and ease, for I did not consider labor any hardship, if I was well provided with good food and clothes, and my other wants properly regarded." (p. 266.) This is too good to last, however; and Ball's new master dies, leaving him in the hands of another man, "of whom, when I considered the part of the country from whence he came, which had always been represented to me as distinguished for the cruelty with which slaves were treated, I had no reason to expect much that was good." (pp. 271-272.) His new master turns out to be much less harsh than anticipated, but the master's wife, a woman with sadistic tendencies, takes a positive dislike to Ball and resents her husband's paternal attitude toward him. When the master dies, Ball recognizes his situation as intolerable and resolves upon flight. (p. 307.) Ball's narrative reveals the way in which a slave could evaluate his changes of conditions by standards of comfort and accommodation derived from experience within the system itself. In desperate situations, this evaluation could lead to extreme forms of non-cooperation.

Despite the fact that he was recalling his experience after having escaped from slavery and, presumably, after coming under the influence of northern antislavery sentiment, Ball's general attitude remained remarkably accommodationist, at least in respect to slavery at its best. In a revealing passage, he notes that the typical slave lacks a real sense of identity of interest with his master, is jealous of his prerogatives, and steals from him without qualms. Yet, Ball concludes, there "is in fact, a mutual dependence between the master and his slave. The former could not acquire anything without the labor of the latter, and the latter would always remain in poverty without the judgment of the former in directing labor to a definite and profitable result." (p. 219.)

20. See Stampp, *Peculiar Institution*, pp. 104-108.

21. Goffman, *Asylums*, pp. 18-19. Cf. Donald Clemmer, *The Prison Community* (New York, 1958), pp. 297-298: "The prisoner's world is an atomized world. . . . There are no definite communal objectives. There is no consensus for a common goal. The inmates' conflict with officialdom and opposition toward society is only slightly greater in degree than conflict and opposition among themselves. Trickery and dishonesty overshadow sympathy and cooperation. . . . It is a world of 'I,' 'me,' and 'mine,' rather than 'ours,' 'theirs,' and 'his.'" Clemmer adds, p. 293: "Such collective action of protest as does arise, comes out of an immediate situation in which they themselves are involved, and not as protest to an idea."

22. Colonization, while uncommon among slaves, is frequently encountered in prisons and particularly in mental institutions. The high rate of recidivism among convicts and the frequency with which mental patients are sent back to asylums reflect not simply a relapse into a former sickness which the institution did not cure, but in many cases, a sickness which the institution itself created—an institutional neurosis which has its own peculiar characteristics, the most outstanding of which is the inability to function outside systems of total control.

23. Goffman, *Asylums*, p. 62.

24. *Ibid.*, pp. 64-65.

25. *Ibid.*, pp. 65-66.

26. Douglass, *Narrative*, pp. 35-37.

27. *Ibid.*, pp. 37-38.

• Because written records do not often bring us accurately into the world of the slave cabins, historians have begun to exploit a variety of nonliterary sources that do. Such tools according to Orlando Patterson are "material remains, Afro-American Creole languages and oral traditions, including transcribed folk tales, folksongs, and the like." The two articles that follow use such materials to dispute Stanley Elkins's "Sambo" thesis. They are significant, however, not merely because they effectively undermine the assertion that antebellum slavery rendered black bondsmen and bondswomen pliant or childlike. Their importance stems also from the contribution made by Sterling Stuckey and Lawrence W. Levine to our growing knowledge of the beliefs and culture of Negro slaves. In Stuckey's words, the articles sketch out the "ethos" of slave culture, that "life style and set of values" that allowed blacks to escape "from being imprisoned altogether by the definitions which the larger society sought to impose."

Through the Prism of Folklore:
The Black Ethos in Slavery

STERLING STUCKEY

It is not excessive to advance the view that some historians, because they have been so preoccupied with demonstrating the absence of significant slave revolts, conspiracies, and "day to day" resistance among slaves, have presented information on slave behavior and thought which is incomplete indeed. They have, in short, devoted very little attention to trying to get "inside" slaves to discover what bondsmen thought about their condition. Small wonder we have been saddled

From Sterling Stuckey, "Through the Prism of Folklore: The Black Ethos in Slavery," *The Massachusetts Review*, Vol. IX, No. 3 (Summer 1968), pp. 417-37. Reprinted from *The Massachusetts Review*. Copyright © 1968 by The Massachusetts Review, Inc.

with so many stereotypical treatments of slave thought and behavior.[1]

Though we do not know enough about the institution of slavery or the slave experience to state with great precision how slaves felt about their condition, it is reasonably clear that slavery, however draconic and well supervised, was not the hermetically sealed monolith—destructive to the majority of slave personalities—that some historians would have us believe. The works of Herbert Aptheker, Kenneth Stampp, Richard Wade, and the Bauers, allowing for differences in approach and purpose, indicate that slavery, despite its brutality, was not so "closed" that it robbed most of the slaves of their humanity.[2]

It should, nevertheless, be asserted at the outset that blacks could not have survived the grim experience of slavery unscathed. Those historians who, for example, point to the dependency complex which slavery engendered in many Afro-Americans, offer us an important insight into one of the most harmful effects of that institution upon its victims. That slavery caused not a few bondsmen to question their worth as human beings—this much, I believe, we can posit with certitude. We can also safely assume that such self-doubt would rend one's sense of humanity, establishing an uneasy balance between affirming and negating aspects of one's being. What is at issue is not whether American slavery was harmful to slaves but whether, in their struggle to control self-lacerating tendencies, the scales were tipped toward a despair so consuming that most slaves, in time, became reduced to the level of "Sambos."[3]

My thesis, which rests on an examination of folk songs and tales, is that slaves were able to fashion a life style and set of values—an ethos —which prevented them from being imprisoned altogether by the definitions which the larger society sought to impose. This ethos was an amalgam of Africanisms and New World elements which helped slaves, in Guy Johnson's words, "feel their way along the course of American slavery, enabling them to endure. . . ."[4] As Sterling Brown, that wise student of Afro-American culture, has remarked, the values expressed in folklore acted as a "wellspring to which slaves" trapped in the wasteland of American slavery "could return in times of doubt to be refreshed."[5] In short, I shall contend that the process of dehumanization was not nearly as pervasive as Stanley Elkins would have us believe; that a very large number of slaves, guided by this ethos, were able to maintain their essential humanity. I make this contention because folklore, in its natural setting, is of, by, and for those who create and respond to it, depending for its survival upon the accuracy with which it speaks to needs and reflects sentiments. I therefore consider it safe to assume that the attitudes of a very large number of slaves are represented by the themes of folklore.[6]

II

Frederick Douglass, commenting on slave songs, remarked his utter astonishment, on coming to the North, "to find persons who could speak of the singing among slaves as evidence of their contentment and happiness."[7] The young DuBois, among the first knowledgeable critics of the spirituals, found white Americans as late as 1903 still telling Afro-Americans that "life was joyous to the black slave, careless and happy." "I can easily believe this of some," he wrote, "of many. But not all the past South, though it rose from the dead, can gainsay the heart-touching witness of these songs."

> They are the music of an unhappy people, of the children of disappointment; they tell of death and suffering and unvoiced longing toward a truer world, of misty wanderings and hidden ways.[8]

Though few historians have been interested in such wanderings and ways, Frederick Douglass, probably referring to the spirituals, said the songs of slaves represented the sorrows of the slave's heart, serving to relieve the slave "only as an aching heart is relieved by its tears." "I have often sung," he continued, "to drown my sorrow, but seldom to express my happiness. Crying for joy, and singing for joy, were alike uncommon to me while in the jaws of slavery."[9]

Sterling Brown, who has much to tell us about the poetry and meaning of these songs, has observed: "As the best expression of the slave's deepest thoughts and yearnings, they (the spirituals) speak with convincing finality against the legend of contented slavery."[10] Rejecting the formulation that the spirituals are mainly otherworldly, Brown states that though the creators of the spirituals looked toward heaven and "found their triumphs there, they did not blink their eyes to trouble here." The spirituals, in his view, "never tell of joy in the 'good old days'. . . . The only joy in the spirituals is in dreams of escape."[11]

Rather than being essentially otherworldly, these songs, in Brown's opinion, "tell of this life, of 'rollin' through an unfriendly world!" To substantiate this view, he points to numerous lines from spirituals: "Oh, bye and bye, bye and bye, I'm going to lay down this heavy load"; "My way is cloudy"; "Oh, stand the storm, it won't be long, we'll anchor by and by"; "Lord help me from sinking down"; and "Don't know what my mother wants to stay here fuh, Dis ole world ain't been no friend to huh."[12] To those scholars who "would have us believe that when the Negro sang of freedom, he meant only what the whites meant, namely freedom from sin," Brown rejoins:

> Free individualistic whites on the make in a prospering civilization, nursing the American dream, could well have felt their only bondage to be that of sin, and freedom to be religious salvation. But with the drudgery, the hardships, the auction block, the slave-mart, the shackles, and the lash so literally present in the Negro's experience, it is hard to imagine why for the Negro they would remain figurative. The scholars certainly did not make this clear, but rather take refuge in such dicta as: "the slave never contemplated his low condition."[13]

"Are we to believe," asks Brown, "that the slave singing 'I been rebuked, I been scorned, done had a hard time sho's you bawn,' referred to his being outside the true religion?" A reading of additional spirituals indicates that they contained distinctions in meaning which placed them outside the confines of the "true religion." Sometimes, in these songs, we hear slaves relating to divinities on terms more West African than American. The easy intimacy and argumentation, which come out of a West African frame of reference, can be heard in "Hold the Wind."[14]

> When I get heaven, gwine be at ease,
> Me and my God *gonna do as we please.*

> Gonna chatter with the Father, argue with the Son,
> *Tell um 'bout the world I just come from.*[15] (Italics added.)

If there is a tie with heaven in those lines from "Hold the Wind," there is also a clear indication of dislike for the restrictions imposed by slavery. And at least one high heavenly authority might have a few questions to answer. *Tell um 'bout the world I just come from* makes it abundantly clear that some slaves—even when released from the burdens of the world—would keep alive painful memories of their oppression.

If slaves could argue with the son of God, then surely, when on their knees in prayer, they would not hesitate to speak to God of the treatment being received at the hands of their oppressors.

> Talk about me much as you please, (2)
> Chillun, talk about me much as you please,
> Gonna talk about you when I get on my knees.[16]

That slaves could spend time complaining about treatment received from other slaves is conceivable, but that this was their only complaint, or even the principal one, is hardly conceivable. To be sure, there is a certain ambiguity in the use of the word "chillun" in this context. The reference appears to apply to slaveholders.

The spiritual, *Samson*, as Vincent Harding has pointed out, probably contained much more (for some slaves) than mere Biblical implications. Some who sang these lines from *Samson*, Harding suggests, might well have meant tearing down the edifice of slavery. If so, it was the ante-bellum equivalent of today's "burn baby burn."

> He said, "An' if I had-'n my way,"
> He said, "An' if I had-'n my way,"
> He said, "An' if I had-'n my way,
> I'd tear the build-in' down!"
>
> He said, "And now I got my way, (3)
> And I'll tear this buildin' down."[17]

Both Harriet Tubman and Frederick Douglass have reported that some of the spirituals carried double meanings. Whether most of the slaves who sang those spirituals could decode them is another matter. Harold Courlander has made a persuasive case against widespread understanding of any given "loaded" song,[18] but it seems to me that he fails to recognize sufficiently a further aspect of the subject: [slaves, as their folktales make eminently clear, used irony repeatedly, especially with animal stories. Their symbolic world was rich. Indeed, the various masks which many put on were not unrelated to this symbolic process. It seems logical to infer that it would occur to more than a few to seize upon some songs, even though created originally for religious purposes, assign another meaning to certain words, and use these songs for a variety of purposes and situations.]

At times slave bards created great poetry as well as great music. One genius among the slaves couched his (and their) desire for freedom in a magnificent line of verse. After God's powerful voice had "Rung through Heaven and down in Hell," he sang, "My dungeon shook and my chains, they fell."[19]

In some spirituals, Alan Lomax has written, Afro-Americans turned sharp irony and "healing laughter" toward heaven, again like their West African ancestors, relating on terms of intimacy with God. In one, the slaves have God engaged in a dialogue with Adam:

> "Stole my apples, I believe."
> "No, marse Lord, I spec it was Eve."
> Of this tale there is no mo'
> Eve et the apple and Adam de co'.[20]

Douglass informs us that slaves also sang ironic seculars about the institution of slavery. He reports having heard them sing: "We raise de wheat, dey gib us de corn; We sift de meal, dey gib us de huss; We peel de meat, dey gib us de skin; An dat's de way dey take us in."[21] Slaves would often stand back and see the tragicomic aspects of their situation, sometimes admiring the swiftness of blacks:

> Run, nigger, run, de patrollers will ketch you,
> Run, nigger run, it's almost day.
> Dat nigger run, dat nigger flew;
> Dat nigger tore his shirt in two.[22]

And there is:

> My ole mistiss promise me
> W'en she died, she'd set me free,
> She lived so long dat 'er head got bal'
> An' she give out'n de notion a-dyin' at all.[23]

In the ante-bellum days, work songs were of crucial import to slaves. As they cleared and cultivated land, piled levees along rivers, piled loads on steamboats, screwed cotton bales into the holds of ships, and cut roads and railroads through forest, mountain, and flat, slaves sang while the white man, armed and standing in the shade, shouted his orders.[24] Through the sense of timing and coordination which characterized work songs well sung, especially by the leaders, slaves sometimes literally created works of art. These songs not only militated against injuries but enabled the bondsmen to get difficult jobs done more easily by not having to concentrate on the dead level of their work. "In a very real sense the chants of Negro labor," writes Alan Lomax, "may be considered the most profoundly American of all our folk songs, for they were created by our people as they tore at American rock and earth and reshaped it with their bare hands, while rivers of sweat ran down and darkened the dust."

> Long summer day makes a white man lazy,
>   Long summer day.
> Long summer day makes a nigger run away, sir,
>   Long summer day.[25]

Other slaves sang lines indicating their distaste for slave labor:

> Ol' massa an' ol' missis,
> Sittin' in the parlour,
> Jus' fig'in' an' a-plannin'
> How to work a nigger harder.[26]

And there are these bitter lines, the meaning of which is clear:

> Missus in the big house,
> Mammy in the yard,
> Missus holdin' her white hands,
> Mammy workin' hard (3)
> Missus holdin' her white hands,
> Mammy workin' hard.
>
> Old Marse ridin' all time,
> Niggers workin' round,
> Marse sleepin' day time,
> Niggers diggin' in the ground, (3)
> Marse sleepin' day time,
> Niggers diggin' in the ground.[27]

Courlander tells us that the substance of the work songs "ranges from the humorous to the sad, from the gentle to the biting, and from the tolerant to the unforgiving." The statement in a given song can be metaphoric, tangent or direct, the meaning personal or impersonal. "As throughout Negro singing generally, there is an incidence of social criticism, ridicule, gossip, and protest."[28] Pride in their strength rang with the downward thrust of axe—

> When I was young and in my prime, (hah!)
> Sunk my axe deep every time, (hah!)

Blacks later found their greatest symbol of manhood in John Henry, descendant of Trickster John of slave folk tales:

> A man ain't nothing but a man,
> But before I'll let that steam driver beat me down
> I'll die with my hammer in my hand.[29]

Though Frances Kemble, an appreciative and sensitive listener to work songs, felt that "one or two barbaric chants would make the fortune of an opera," she was on one occasion "displeased not a little" by a self-deprecating song, one which "embodied the opinion that 'twenty-six black girls not make mulatto yellow girl,' and as I told them I did not like it, they have since omitted it."[30] [What is pivotal here is not the presence of self-laceration in folklore, but its extent and meaning. While folklore contained some self-hatred, on balance it gives no indication whatever that blacks, as a group, liked or were indifferent to slavery, which is the issue.[31]]

To be sure, only the most fugitive of songs sung by slaves contained direct attacks upon the system. Two of these were associated with slave rebellions. The first, possibly written by ex-slave Denmark Vesey himself, was sung by slaves on at least one island off the coast of Charleston, South Carolina, and at meetings convened by Vesey in Charleston. Though obviously not a folksong, it was sung by the folk.

> Hail! all hail! ye Afric clan,
> Hail! ye oppressed, ye Afric band,
> Who toil and sweat in slavery bound
> And when your health and strength are gone
> Are left to hunger and to mourn,
> Let independence be your aim,
> Ever mindful what 'tis worth.
> Pledge your bodies for the prize,
> Pile them even to the skies![32]

The second, a popular song derived from a concrete reality, bears the marks of a conscious authority:

> You mought be rich as cream
> And drive you coach and four-horse team,
> But you can't keep de world from moverin' round
> Nor Nat Turner from gainin' ground.
>
> And your name it mought be Caesar sure,
> And got you cannon can shoot a mile or more,
> But you can't keep de world from moverin' round
> Nor Nat Turner from gainin' ground.[33]

The introduction of Denmark Vesey, class leader in the A.M.E. Church, and Nat Turner, slave preacher, serves to remind us that some slaves and ex-slaves were violent as well as humble, impatient as well as patient.

It is also well to recall that the religious David Walker, who had lived close to slavery in North Carolina, and Henry Highland Garnett, ex-slave and Presbyterian minister, produced two of the most inflammatory, vitriolic, and doomed-bespeaking polemics America has yet seen.[34] [There was theological tension here, loudly proclaimed, a tension which emanated from and was perpetuated by American slavery and race prejudice. This dimension of ambiguity must be kept in mind, if for no other reason than to place in bolder relief the possibility that a great many slaves and free Afro-Americans could have interpreted Christianity in a way quite different from white Christians.]

Even those songs which seemed most otherworldly, those which expressed profound weariness of spirit and even faith in death, through their unmistakable sadness, were accusatory, and God was not their object. If one accepts as a given that some of these appear to be almost wholly escapist, the indictment is no less real. Thomas Wentworth Higginson came across one—". . . a flower of poetry in that dark soil," he called it.[35]

> I'll walk in de graveyard, I'll walk through de graveyard,
>   To lay dis body down.
> I'll lie in de grave and stretch out my arms,
>   Lay dis body down.

Reflecting on "I'll lie in de grave and stretch out my arms," Higginson said that "Never, it seems to me, since man first lived and suffered, was his infinite longing for peace uttered more plaintively than in that line."[36]

[There seems to be small doubt that Christianity contributed in large measure to a spirit of patience which militated against open rebellion among the bondsmen. Yet to overemphasize this point leads one to obscure a no less important reality: Christianity, after being reinterpreted and recast by slave bards, also contributed to that spirit of endurance which powered generations of bondsmen, bringing them to that decisive moment when for the first time a real choice was available to scores of thousands of them.]

When that moment came, some slaves who were in a position to decide for themselves did so. W. E. B. DuBois re-created their mood and the atmosphere in which they lived.

> There came the slow looming of emancipation. Crowds and armies of the unknown, inscrutable, unfathomable Yankees; cruelty behind and before; rumors of a new slave trade, but

slowly, continuously, the wild truth, the bitter truth, the magic truth, came surging through. There was to be a new freedom! And a black nation went tramping after the armies no matter what it suffered; no matter how it was treated, no matter how it died.[37]

The gifted bards, by creating songs with an unmistakable freedom ring, songs which would have been met with swift, brutal repression in the ante-bellum days, probably voiced the sentiments of all but the most degraded and dehumanized. Perhaps not even the incredulous slavemaster could deny the intent of the new lyrics. "In the wake of the Union Army and in the contraband camps," remarked Sterling Brown, "spirituals of freedom sprang up suddenly. . . . Some celebrated the days of Jubilo: 'O Freedom; O Freedom!' and 'Before I'll be a slave, I'll be buried in my grave!', and 'Go home to my lord and be free.' " And there was: " 'No more driver's lash for me. . . . Many thousand go.' "[38]

DuBois brought together the insights of the poet and historian to get inside the slaves:

> There was joy in the South. It rose like perfume—like a prayer. Men stood quivering. Slim dark girls, wild and beautiful with wrinkled hair, wept silently; young women, black, tawny, white, and golden, lifted shivering hands, and old and broken mothers, black and gray, raised great voices and shouted to God across the fields, and up to the rocks and the mountains.[39]

Some sang:

> Slavery chain done broke at last, broke at last, broke at last,
> Slavery chain done broke at last,
> Going to praise God till I die.

> I did tell him how I suffer,
> In de dungeon and de chain,
> *And de days I went with head bowed down,*
> And my broken flesh and pain,
> Slavery chain done broke at last, broke at last, broke at last.[40]

Whatever the nature of the shocks generated by the war, among those vibrations felt were some that had come from Afro-American singing ever since the first Africans were forcibly brought to these shores. DuBois was correct when he said that the new freedom song had not come from Africa, but that "the dark throb and beat of that

Ancient of Days was in and through it."[41] Thus, the psyches of those who gave rise to and provided widespread support for folk songs had not been reduced to *tabulae rasae* on which a slave-holding society could at pleasure sketch out its wish-fulfillment fantasies.

We have already seen the acute degree to which some slaves realized they were being exploited. Their sense of the injustice of slavery made it so much easier for them to act out their aggression against whites (by engaging in various forms of "day to day" resistance) without being overcome by a sense of guilt, or a feeling of being ill-mannered. To call this nihilistic thrashing about would be as erroneous as to refer to their use of folk lore as esthetic thrashing about.[42] For if they did not regard themselves as the equals of whites in many ways, their folklore indicates that the generality of slaves must have at least felt superior to whites morally. And that, in the context of oppression, could make the difference between a viable human spirit and one crippled by the belief that the interests of the master are those of the slave.

When it is borne in mind that slaves created a large number of extraordinary songs and greatly improved a considerable proportion of the songs of others, it is not at all difficult to believe that they were conscious of the fact that they were leaders in the vital area of art—giving protagonists rather than receiving pawns. And there is some evidence that slaves were aware of the special talent which they brought to music. Higginson has described how reluctantly they sang from hymnals—"even on Sunday"—and how "gladly" they yielded "to the more potent excitement of their own 'spirituals.' "[43] It is highly unlikely that the slaves' preference for their own music went unremarked among them, or that this preference did not affect their estimate of themselves. "They soon found," commented Alan Lomax, "that when they sang, the whites recognized their superiority as singers, and listened with respect."[44] He might have added that those antebellum whites who listened probably seldom understood.

What is of pivotal import, however, is that the esthetic realm was the one area in which slaves knew they were not inferior to whites. Small wonder that they borrowed many songs from the larger community, then quickly invested them with their own economy of statement and power of imagery rather than yield to the temptation of merely repeating what they had heard. Since they were essentially group rather than solo performances, the values inherent in and given affirmation by the music served to strengthen bondsmen in a way that solo music could not have done.[45] In a word, slave singing often provided a form of group therapy, a way in which a slave, in concert with others, could fend off some of the debilitating effects of slavery.

The field of inquiry would hardly be complete without some mention of slave tales. Rich in quantity and often subtle in conception, these tales further illumine the inner world of the bondsmen, disclosing moods and interests almost as various as those found in folksongs. That folk tales, like the songs, indicate an African presence, should not astonish; for the telling of tales, closely related to the African griot's vocation of providing oral histories of families and dynastics, was deeply rooted in West African tradition. Hughes and Bontemps have written that the slaves brought to America the "habit of storytelling as pastime, together with a rich bestiary." Moreover, they point out that the folk tales of slaves "were actually projections of personal experiences and hopes and defeats, in terms of symbols," and that this important dimension of the tales "appears to have gone unnoticed."[46]

Possessing a repertoire which ranged over a great many areas, perhaps the most memorable tales are those of Br'er Rabbit and John.[47] Br'er Rabbit, now trickster, ladies' man and braggart, now wit, joker and glutton, possessed the resourcefulness, despite his size and lack of strength, to outsmart stronger, larger animals. "To the slave in his condition,". according to Hughes and Bontemps, "the theme of weakness overcoming strength through cunning proved endlessly fascinating."[48] John, characterized by a spiritual resilience born of an ironic sense of life, was a secular high priest of mischief and guile who delighted in matching wits with Ole Marster, the "patterollers," Ole Missy, and the devil himself. He was clever enough to sense the absurdity of his predicament and that of white people, smart enough to know the limits of his powers and the boundaries of those of the master class. While not always victorious, even on the spacious plane of the imagination, he could hardly be described as a slave with an inferiority complex. And in this regard it is important to note that his varieties of triumphs, though they sometimes included winning freedom, often realistically cluster about ways of coping with everyday negatives of the system.[49]

Slaves were adept in the art of storytelling, as at home in this area as they were in the field of music. But further discussion of the scope of folklore would be uneconomical, for we have already seen a depth and variety of thought among bondsmen which embarrasses stereotypical theories of slave personality. Moreover, it should be clear by now that there are no secure grounds on which to erect the old, painfully constricted "Sambo" structure.[50] For the personalities which lay beneath the plastic exteriors which slaves turned on and off for white people were too manifold to be contained by cheerful, childlike images. When it is argued, then, that "too much of the Negro's own lore" has gone into the making of the Sambo picture "to entitle one in good conscience to condemn it as "conspiracy',"[51] one must rejoin: Only if you strip the masks from black faces while refusing to read the irony and ambiguity and cunning which called the masks into existence. Slave folklore, on balance, decisively repudiates the thesis that Negroes *as a group* had internalized "Sambo" traits, committing them, as it were, to psychological marriage.

III

It is one of the curiosities of American historiography that a people who were as productive esthetically as American slaves could be studied as if they had moved in a cultural cyclotron, continually bombarded by devasting, atomizing forces which denuded them of meaningful Africanisms while destroying any and all impulses toward creativity. One historian, for example, has been tempted to wonder how it was ever possible that "*all* this (West African) native resourcefulness and vitality have been brought to such a point of *utter* stultification in America."[52] (Italics added.) This sadly misguided view is, of course, not grounded in any recognition or understanding of the Afro-American dimension of American culture. In any event, there is a great need for students of American slavery to attempt what Gilberto Freyre tried to do for Brazilian civilization—an effort at discovering the contributions of slaves toward the shaping of the Brazilian national character.[53] When such a study has been made of the American slave we shall probably discover that, though he did not rival his Brazilian brother in staging bloody revolutions, the quality and place of art in his life compared favorably. Now this suggests that the humanity of people can be asserted through means other than open and widespread rebellion, a consideration that has not been appreciated in violence-prone America. We would do well to recall the words of F. S. C. Northrop who has observed:

> During the pre-Civil War period shipowners and southern landowners brought to the United States a considerable body of people with a color of skin and cultural values different from those of its other inhabitants. . . . Their values are more emotive, esthetic and intuitive . . . (These) characteristics can become

an asset for our culture. For these are values with respect to which Anglo-American culture is weak.[54]

These values were expressed on the highest level in the folklore of slaves. Through their folklore, black slaves affirmed their humanity and left a lasting imprint on American culture. No study of the institutional aspects of American slavery can be complete, nor can the larger dimensions of slave personality and style be adequately explored, as long as historians continue to avoid that realm in which, as DuBois has said, "the soul of the black slave spoke to man."[55]

In its nearly two and one half centuries of existence, the grim system of American slavery doubtless broke the spirits of uncounted numbers of slaves. Nevertheless, if we look through the prism of folklore, we can see others transcending their plight, appreciating the tragic irony of their condition, then seizing upon and putting to use those aspects of their experience which sustain in the present and renew in the future. We can see them opposing their own angle of vision to that of their oppressor, fashioning their own techniques of defense and aggression in accordance with their own reading of reality and doing those things well enough to avoid having their sense of humanity destroyed.

Slave folklore, then, affirms the existence of a large number of vital, tough-minded human beings who, though severely limited and abused by slavery, had found a way both to endure and preserve their humanity in the face of insuperable odds. What they learned about handling misfortune was not only a major factor in their survival as a people, but many of the lessons learned and esthetic standards established would be used by future generations of Afro-Americans in coping with a hostile world. What a splendid affirmation of the hopes and dreams of their slave ancestors that some of the songs being sung in antebellum days are the ones Afro-Americans are singing in the freedom movement today: "Michael, row the boat ashore"; "Just like a tree planted by the water, I shall not be moved."

NOTES

[IX, 3, Summer 1968]

1. Historians who have provided stereotypical treatments of slave thought and personality are Ulrich B. Phillips, *American Negro Slavery* (New York, 1918); Samuel Eliot Morison, and Henry Steele Commager, *The Growth of the American Republic* (New York, 1950); and Stanley Elkins, *Slavery: A Problem in American Institutional and Intellectual Life* (Chicago, 1959).

2. See Herbert Aptheker, *American Negro Slave Revolts*; Kenneth M.

Stampp, *The Peculiar Institution* (New York, 1956); Richard Wade, *Slavery in the Cities* (New York, 1964); and Alice and Raymond Bauer, "Day to Day Resistance to Slavery," *Journal of Negro History*, XXVII No. 4, October, 1942.

3. I am here concerned with the Stanley Elkins version of "Sambo," that is, the inference that the overwhelming majority of slaves, as a result of their struggle to survive under the brutal system of American slavery, became so callous and indifferent to their status that they gave survival primacy over all other considerations. See Chapters III through VI of *Slavery* for a discussion of the process by which blacks allegedly were reduced to the "good humor of everlasting childhood." (p. 132).

4. I am indebted to Guy Johnson of the University of North Carolina for suggesting the use of the term "ethos" in this piece, and for helpful commentary on the original paper which was read before the Association for the Study of Negro Life and History at Greensboro, North Carolina, on October 13, 1967.

5. Professor Brown made this remark in a paper delivered before The Amistad Society in Chicago, Spring, 1964. Distinguished poet, literary critic, folklorist, and teacher, Brown has long contended that an awareness of Negro folklore is essential to an understanding of slave personality and thought.

6. I subscribe to Alan Lomax's observation that folk songs "can be taken as the signposts of persistent patterns of community feeling and can throw light into many dark corners of our past and our present." His view that Afro-American music, despite its original peculiarities, "expresses the same feelings and speaks the same basic language everywhere" is also accepted as a working principle in this paper. For an extended treatment of these points of view, see Alan Lomax, *Folk Songs of North America* (New York, 1960), Introduction, p. xx.

7. Frederick Douglass, *Narrative of the Life of Frederick Douglass* (Cambridge, Massachusetts: The Belknap Press, 1960), p. 38. Originally published in 1845.

8. John Hope Franklin (ed.), *Souls of Black Folk* in *Three Negro Classics* (New York, 1965), p. 380. Originally published in 1903.

9. Douglass, *Narrative*, p. 38. Douglass's view adumbrated John and Alan Lomax's theory that the songs of the folk singer are deeply rooted "in his life and have functioned there as enzymes to assist in the digestion of hardship, solitude, violence (and) hunger." John A. and Alan Lomax, *Our Singing Country* (New York: The Macmillan Co., 1941), Preface, p. xiii.

10. Sterling Brown, "Negro Folk Expression," *Phylon*, October, 1953, p. 47.

11. Brown, "Folk Expression," p. 48.

12. *Ibid.*, p. 47.

13. *Ibid.*, p. 48.

14. Addressing himself to the slave's posture toward God, and the attitudes toward the gods which the slave's African ancestors had, Lomax has written: "The West African lives with his gods on terms of intimacy. He appeals to them, reviles them, tricks with them, laughs at their follies. In this spirit the Negro slave humanized the stern religion of his masters by adopting the figures of the Bible as his intimates." Lomax, *Folk Songs of North America*, p. 463.

15. Quoted from Lomax, *Folk Songs of North America*, p. 475.

16. Quoted from Brown, Sterling A., Davis, Arthur P., and Lee, Ulysses, *The Negro Caravan* (New York: The Dryden Press, 1941), p. 436.

17. Vincent Harding, *Black Radicalism in America.* An unpublished work which Dr. Harding recently completed.

18. See Harold Courlander, *Negro Folk Music, U.S.A.* (New York: Columbia University Press, 1963), pp. 42, 43. If a great many slaves did not consider Harriet Tubman the "Moses" of her people, it is unlikely that most failed to grasp the relationship between themselves and the Israelites, Egypt and the South, and Pharaoh and slavemasters in such lines as: "Didn't my Lord deliver Daniel / And why not every man"; "Oh Mary don't you weep, don't you moan / Pharaoh's army got drowned / Oh Mary don't you weep"; and "Go down Moses / Way down in Egypt-land / Tell old Pharaoh / To let my people go."

19. Quoted from Lomax, *Folk Songs of North America,* p. 471.

20. *Ibid.,* p. 476.

21. Frederick Douglass, *The Life and Times of Frederick Douglass* (New York: Collier Books, 1962), p. 146.

22. Brown, "Folk Expression," p. 51.

23. Brown, *Caravan,* p. 447.

24. Lomax, *Folk Songs of North America,* p. 514.

25. *Ibid.,* p. 515.

26. *Ibid.,* p. 527.

27. Courlander, *Negro Folk Music,* p. 117.

28. *Ibid.,* p. 89.

29. Brown, "Folk Expression," p. 54. Steel-driving John Henry is obviously in the tradition of the axe-wielding blacks of the ante-bellum period. The ballad of John Henry helped spawn John Henry work songs:

Dis ole hammer—hunh
Ring like silver—hunh (3)
Shine like gold, baby—hunh
Shine like gold—hunh
Dis ole hammer—hunh
Killt John Henry—hunh (3)
Twon't kill me baby, hunh
Twon't kill me. (Quoted from Brown, "Folk Expression," p. 57.)

30. Frances Anne Kemble, *Journal of a Residence on a Georgia Plantation, 1838–1839* (New York: Alfred Knopf), pp. 260-61. Miss Kemble heard slaves use the epithet "nigger": "And I assure you no contemptuous intonation ever equalled the prepotenza (arrogance) of the despotic insolence of this address of these poor wretches to each other." Kemble, *Journal,* p. 281. Here she is on solid ground, but the slaves also used the word with glowing affection, as seen in the "Run, Nigger, Run" secular. At other times they leaned toward self-laceration but refused to go the whole route: "My name's Ran, I wuks in de sand, I'd rather be a nigger dan a po' white man." Brown, "Folk Expression," p. 51. Some blacks also sang, "It takes a long, lean, blackskinned gal, to make a preacher lay his Bible down." Newman I. White, *American Negro Folk Songs* (Cambridge, 1928), p. 411.

31. Elkins, who believes Southern white lore on slavery should be taken seriously, does not subject it to serious scrutiny. For a penetrating—and devastating—analysis of "the richest layers of Southern lore" which, according to Elkins, resulted from "an exquisitely rounded collective creativity," see Sterling A.

Brown, "A Century of Negro Portraiture in American Literature," *The Massachusetts Review* (Winter, 1966).

32. Quoted from Archie Epps, "A Negro Separatist Movement," *The Harvard Review*, IV, No. 1 (Summer-Fall, 1956), 75.

33. Quoted in William Styron, "This Quiet Dust," *Harpers*, April 1965, p. 135.

34. For excerpts from David Walker's *Appeal* and Henry H. Garnett's *Call to Rebellion*, see Herbert Aptheker (ed.), *A Documentary History of the Negro People in the United States*. 2 vols. (New York: Citadel Press, 1965). Originally published in 1951.

35. Thomas Wentworth Higginson, *Army Life in a Black Regiment* (New York: Collier, 1962), p. 199.

36. *Ibid.*

37. W. E. B. DuBois, *Black Reconstruction* (Philadelphia: Albert Saifer), p. 122. Originally published in 1935 by Harcourt, Brace and Company.

38. Brown, "Folk Expression," p. 49.

39. DuBois, *Reconstruction*, p. 124.

40. Quoted in Brown, *Caravan*, pp. 440–41. One of the most tragic scenes of the Civil War period occurred when a group of Sea Island freedmen, told by a brigadier-general that they would not receive land from the government, sang, "Nobody knows the trouble I've seen." DuBois, *Souls*, p. 381.

41. DuBois, *Reconstruction*, p. 124.

42. If some slavemasters encouraged slaves to steal or simply winked at thefts, then slaves who obliged them were most assuredly *not acting against their own interests*, whatever the motivation of the masters. Had more fruitful options been available to them, then and only then could we say that slaves were playing into the hands of their masters. Whatever the masters thought of slaves who stole from them—and there is little reason to doubt that most slaves considered it almost obligatory to steal from white people—the slaves, it is reasonable to assume, were aware of the unparalleled looting in which masters themselves were engaged. To speak therefore of slaves undermining their sense of self-respect as a result of stealing from whites—and this argument has been advanced by Eugene Genovese—is wide of the mark. Indeed, it appears more likely that those who engaged in stealing were, in the context of an oppressor-oppressed situation, on the way to realizing a larger measure of self-respect. Moreover, Genovese, in charging that certain forms of "day to day" resistance, in the absence of general conditions of rebellion, "amounted to individual and essentially nihilistic thrashing about," fails to recognize that that which was possible, that which conditions permitted, was pursued by slaves in preference to the path which led to passivity or annihilation. Those engaging in "day to day" resistance were moving along meaningful rather than nihilistic lines, for their activities were designed to frustrate the demands of the authority-system. For a very suggestive discussion of the dependency complex engendered by slavery and highly provocative views on the significance of "day to day" resistance among slaves, see Eugene Genovese, "The Legacy of Slavery and the Roots of Black Nationalism," *Studies on the Left*, VI, No. 6 (Nov.–Dec. 1966), especially p. 8.

43. Higginson, *Black Regiment*, p. 212. Alan Lomax reminds us that the slaves sang "in leader-chorus style, with a more relaxed throat than the whites,

and in deeper-pitched, mellower voices, which blended richly." "A strong, surging beat underlay most of their American creations . . . words and tunes were intimately and playfully united, and 'sense' was often subordinated to the demands of rhythm and melody." Lomax, *Folk Songs of North America*, Introduction, p. xx.

44. Lomax, *Folk Songs*, p. 460.

45. Commenting on the group nature of much of slave singing, Alan Lomax points out that the majority of the bondsmen "came from West Africa, where music-making was largely a group activity, the creation of a many-voiced, dancing throng. . . . Community songs of labour and worship (in America) and dance songs far outnumbered narrative pieces, and the emotion of the songs was, on the whole, joyfully erotic, deeply tragic, allusive, playful, or ironic rather than nostalgic, withdrawn, factual, or aggressively comic—as among white folk singers." Lomax, *Folk Songs*, pp. xix and xx of Introduction. For treatments of the more technical aspects of Afro-American music, see Courlander, *Negro Folk Music*, especially Chapter II; and Richard A. Waterman, "African Influences on the Music of the Americas," in *Acculturation in the Americas*, edited by Sol Tax.

46. Arna Bontemps and Langston Hughes (ed.), *The Book of Negro Folklore* (New York: Dodd, Mead & Company, 1965), Introduction, p. viii. Of course if one regards each humorous thrust of the bondsmen as so much comic nonsense, then there is no basis for understanding, to use Sterling Brown's phrase, the slave's "laughter out of hell." Without understanding what humour meant to slaves themselves, one is not likely to rise above the superficiality of a Stephen Foster or a Joel Chandler Harris. But once an effort has been made to see the world from the slave's point of view, then perhaps one can understand Ralph Ellison's reference to Afro-Americans, in their folklore, "backing away from the chaos of experience and from ourselves," in order to "depict the humor as well as the horror of our living." Ralph Ellison, "A Very Stern Discipline," *Harpers* (March, 1967), p. 80.

47. For additional discussions of folk tales, see Zora Neale Hurston, *Mules and Men* (Philadelphia: J. B. Lippincott, 1935); Richard Dorson, *American Negro Folktales* (Greenwich, Connecticut: Fawcett, 1967); and B. A. Botkin, *Lay My Burden Down* (Chicago: University of Chicago Press, 1945).

48. Bontemps and Hughes, *Negro Folklore*, Introduction, p. ix.

49. The fact that slaveowners sometimes took pleasure in being outwitted by slaves in no way diminishes from the importance of the trickster tales, for what is essential here is how these tales affected the slave's attitude toward himself, not whether his thinking or behavior would impress a society which considered black people little better than animals. DuBois's words in this regard should never be forgotten: "Everything Negroes did was wrong. If they fought for freedom, they were beasts; if they did not fight, they were born slaves. If they cowered on the plantation, they loved slavery; if they ran away, they were lazy loafers. If they sang, they were silly; if they scowled, they were impudent. . . . And they were funny, funny—ridiculous baboons, aping men." DuBois, *Reconstruction*, p. 125.

50. Ralph Ellison offers illuminating insight into the group experience of the slave: "Any people who could endure all of that brutalization and keep together, who could undergo such dismemberment and resuscitate itself, and

endure until it could take the initiative in achieving its own freedom is obviously more than the sum of its brutalization. Seen in this perspective, theirs has been one of the great human experiences and one of the great triumphs of the human spirit in modern times, in fact, in the history of the world." Ellison, "A Very Stern Discipline," p. 84.

51. Elkins sets forth this argument in *Slavery*, p. 84.

52. *Ibid.*, p. 93.

53. Gilberto Freyre, *The Masters and the Slaves* (New York: Alfred A. Knopf, 1956). Originally published by Jose Olympio, Rio de Janeiro, Brazil.

54. F. S. C. Northrop, *The Meeting of East and West* (New York: The Macmillan Co., 1952), pp. 159-60.

55. DuBois, *Souls*, p. 378. Kenneth M. Stampp in his *The Peculiar Institution* (New York: Alfred A. Knopf, 1956), employs to a limited extent some of the materials of slave folklore. Willie Lee Rose, in *Rehearsal for Reconstruction* (New York: The Bobbs-Merrill Company, 1964), makes brief but highly informed use of folk material.

Slave Songs and Slave Consciousness

LAWRENCE W. LEVINE

161

Negroes in the United States, both during and after slavery, were anything but inarticulate. They sang songs, told stories, played verbal games, listened and responded to sermons, and expressed their aspirations, fears, and values through the medium of an oral tradition that had characterized the West African cultures from which their ancestors had come. By largely ignoring this tradition, much of which has been preserved, historians have rendered an articulate people historically inarticulate, and have allowed the record of their consciousness to go unexplored.

Having worked my way carefully through thousands of Negro songs, folktales, jokes, and games, I am painfully aware of the problems inherent in the use of such materials. They are difficult, often impossible, to date with any precision. Their geographical distribution is usually unclear. They were collected belatedly, most frequently by men and women who had little understanding of the culture from which they sprang, and little scruple about altering or suppressing them. Such major collectors as John Lomax, Howard Odum, and Newman White all admitted openly that many of the songs they collected were "unprintable" by the moral standards which guided them and presumably their readers. But historians have overcome imperfect records before. They have learned how to deal with altered documents, with consciously or unconsciously biased firsthand accounts, with manuscript collections that were deposited in archives only after being filtered through the overprotective hands of fearful relatives, and with the comparative lack of contemporary sources and the need to use their materials retrospectively. The challenge presented by the materials of folk and popular culture is neither totally unique nor insurmountable.

In this essay I want to illustrate the possible use of materials of this kind by discussing the contribution that an understanding of Negro songs can make to the recent debate over slave personality. In the process I will discuss several aspects of the literature and problems related to the use of slave songs.

The subject of Negro music in slavery has produced a large and varied literature, little of which has been devoted to questions of meaning and function. The one major exception is Miles Mark Fisher's 1953 study, *Negro Slave Songs in the United States*, which attempts to get at the essence of slave life through an analysis of slave songs. Unfortunately, Fisher's rich insights are too often marred by his rather loose scholarly standards, and despite its continuing value his study is in many respects an example of how *not* to use Negro songs. Asserting, correctly, that the words of slave songs "show both accidental and intentional errors of transmission," Fisher changes the words almost at will to fit his own image of their pristine form. Arguing persuasively that "transplanted Negroes continued to promote their own culture by music," Fisher makes their songs part of an "African cult" which he simply wills into existence. Maintaining (again, I think, correctly), that "slave songs preserved in joyful strains the adjustment which Negroes made to their living conditions within the United States," Fisher traces the major patterns of that adjustment by arbitrarily dating these songs, apparently unperturbed by the almost total lack of evidence pertaining to the origin and introduction of individual slave songs.[1]

Fisher aside, most other major studies of slave music have focused almost entirely upon musical structure and origin. This latter question especially has given rise to a long and heated debate.[2] The earliest collectors and students of slave music were impressed by how different that music was from anything familiar to them. Following a visit to the Sea Islands in 1862, Lucy McKim despaired of being able "to express the entire character of these negro ballads by mere musical notes and signs. The odd turns made in the throat; and that curious rhythmic effect produced by single voices chiming in at different irregular intervals, seem almost as impossible to place on score, as the singing of birds, or the tones of an Aeolian Harp."[3] Although some of these early collectors maintained, as did W. F. Allen in 1865, that much of the slave's music "might no doubt be traced to tunes which they have heard from the whites, and transformed to their own use, . . . their music . . . is rather European than African in its character,"[4] they more often stressed the distinctiveness of the Negro's music and attributed it to racial characteristics, African origins, and indigenous developments resulting from the slave's unique experience in the New World.

This tradition, which has had many influential twentieth-century adherents,[5] was increasingly challenged in the early decades of this century. Such scholars as Newman White, Guy Johnson, and George Pullen Jackson argued that the earlier school lacked a comparative grounding in Anglo-American folk song. Comparing Negro spirituals with Methodist and Baptist evangelical religious music of the late eighteenth and early nineteenth centuries, White, Johnson, and Jackson found similarities in words, subject matter, tunes, and musical structure.[6] Although they tended to exaggerate both qualitatively and quantitively the degrees of similarity, their comparisons were often a persuasive and important corrective to the work of their predecessors. But their studies were inevitably weakened by their ethnocentric assumption that similarities alone settled the argument over origins. Never could they contemplate the possibility that the direction of cultural diffusion might have been from black to white as well as the other way. In fact, insofar as white evangelical music departed from traditional Protestant hymnology and embodied or approached the complex rhythmic structure, the percussive qualities, the polymeter, the syncopation, the emphasis on overlapping call and response patterns that characterized Negro music both in West Africa and the New World, the possibility that it was influenced by slaves who attended and joined in the singing at religious meetings is quite high.

These scholars tended to use the similarities between black and white religious music to deny the significance of slave songs in still another way. Newman White, for example, argued that since white evangelical hymns also used such expressions as "freedom," the "Promised Land," and the "Egyptian Bondage," "without thought of other than spiritual meaning," these images when they occurred in Negro spirituals could not have been symbolic "of the Negro's longing for physical freedom."[7] The familiar process by which different cultural groups can derive varied meanings from identical images is enough to cast doubt on the logic of White's argument.[8] In the case of white and black religious music, however, the problem may be much less complex, since it is quite possible that the similar images in the songs of both groups in fact served similar purposes. Many of those whites who flocked to the camp meetings of the Methodists and Baptists were themselves on the social and economic margins of their society, and had psychic and emotional needs which, qualitatively, may not have been vastly different from those of black slaves. Interestingly, George Pullen Jackson, in his attempt to prove the white origin of Negro spirituals, makes exactly this point:

> "I may mention in closing the chief remaining argument of the die-hards for the Negro source of the Negro spirituals. . . . How could any, the argument runs, but a natively musical and sorely oppressed race create such beautiful things as 'Swing Low,' 'Steal Away,' and 'Deep River'? . . . But were not the whites of the mountains and the hard-scrabble hill country also 'musical and oppressed'? . . . Yes, these whites were musical, and oppressed too. If their condition was any more tolerable than that of the Negroes, one certainly does not get that impression from any of their songs of release and escape."[9]

If this is true, the presence of similar images in white music would merely heighten rather than detract from the significance of these images in Negro songs. Clearly, the function and meaning of white religious music during the late eighteenth and early nineteenth centuries demands far more attention than it has received. In the interim, we must be wary of allowing the mere fact of similarities to deter us from attempting to comprehend the cultural dynamics of slave music.

Contemporary scholars, tending to transcend the more simplistic lines of the old debate, have focused upon the process of syncretism to explain the development of Negro music in the United States. The rich West African musical tradition common to almost all of the specific cultures from which Negro slaves came, the comparative cultural isolation in which large numbers of slaves lived, the tolerance and even encouragement which their white masters accorded to their musical activities, and the fact that, for all its differences, nothing in the European musical tradition with which they came into contact in America was totally alien to their own traditions—all these were conducive to a situation which allowed the slaves to retain a good deal of the integrity of their own musical heritage while fusing to it compatible elements of Anglo-American music. Slaves often took over entire white hymns and folk songs, as White and Jackson maintained, but altered them significantly in terms of words, musical structure, and especially performance before making them their own. The result was a hybrid with a strong African base.[10]

One of the more interesting aspects of this debate over origins is that no one engaged in it, not even advocates of the white derivation theory, denied that the slaves possessed their own distinctive music. Newman White took particular pains to point out again and again that the notion that Negro song is purely an imitation of the white man's music "is fully as unjust and inaccurate, in the final analysis, as the

Negro's assumption that his folk-song is entirely original." He observed that in the slaves' separate religious meetings they were free to do as they would with the music they first learned from the whites, with the result that their spirituals became "the greatest single outlet for the expression of the Negro folk-mind."[11] Similarly, George Pullen Jackson, after admitting that he could find no white parallels for over two-thirds of the existing Negro spirituals, reasoned that these were produced by Negro singers in true folk fashion "by endless singing of heard tunes and by endless, inevitable and concomitant singing differentiation." Going even further, Jackson asserted that the lack of deep roots in Anglo-American culture left the black man "even freer than the white man to make songs over unconsciously as he sang . . . the free play has resulted in the very large number of songs which, though formed primarily in the white man's moulds, have lost all recognizable relationship to known individual white-sung melodic entities."[12] [This debate over origins indicates clearly that a belief in the direct continuity of African musical traditions or in the process of syncretism is not a necessary prerequisite to the conclusion that the Negro slaves' music was their own, regardless of where they received the components out of which it was fashioned; a conclusion which is crucial to any attempt to utilize these songs as an aid in reconstructing the slaves' consciousness.]

[Equally important is the process by which slave songs were created and transmitted.] When James McKim asked a freedman on the Sea Islands during the Civil War where the slaves got their songs, the answer was eloquently simple: "Dey make em, sah."[13] Precisely *how* they made them worried and fascinated Thomas Wentworth Higginson, who became familiar with slave music through the singing of the black Union soldiers in his Civil War regiment. Were their songs, he wondered, a "conscious and definite" product of "some leading mind," or did they grow "by gradual accretion, in an almost unconscious way"? A freedman rowing Higginson and some of his troops between the Sea Islands helped to resolve the problem when he described a spiritual which he had a hand in creating:

> Once we boys went for some rice and de nigger-driver he keep a-callin' on us; and I say, "O de ole nigger-driver!" Den anudder said, "Fust ting my mammy tole me was, notin' so bad as nigger-driver." Den I made a sing, just puttin' a word, and den anudder word.

He then began to sing his song:

> *O, de ole nigger-driver!*
>   *O, gwine away!*
> *Fust ting my mammy tell me,*
>   *O, gwine away!*
>
> *Tell me 'bout de nigger-driver,*
>   *O, gwine away!*
> *Nigger-driver second devil,*
>   *O, gwine away!*

Higginson's black soldiers, after a moment's hesitation, joined in the singing of a song they had never heard before as if they had long been familiar with it. "I saw," Higginson concluded, "how easily a new 'sing' took root among them."[14]

[This spontaneity, this sense of almost instantaneous community which so impressed Higginson, constitutes a central element in every account of slave singing.] The English musician Henry Russell, who lived in the United States in the 1830's, was forcibly struck by the ease with which a slave congregation in Vicksburg, Mississippi, took a "fine old psalm tune" and, by suddenly and spontaneously accelerating the tempo, transformed it "into a kind of negro melody."[15] "Us old heads," an ex-slave told Jeanette Robinson Murphy, "use ter make 'em up on de spurn of de moment. Notes is good enough for you people, but us likes a mixtery." Her account of the creation of a spiritual is typical and important:

> We'd all be at the "prayer house" de Lord's day, and de white preacher he'd splain de word and read whar Esekial done say—
>
> *Dry bones gwine ter lib ergin.*
>
> And, honey, de Lord would come a-shinin' thoo dem pages and revive dis ole nigger's heart, and I'd jump up dar and den and holler and shout and sing and pat, and dey would all cotch de words and I'd sing it to some ole shout song I'd heard 'em sing from Africa, and dey'd all take it up and keep at it, and keep a-addin' to it, and den it would be a spiritual.[16]

This "internal" account has been verified again and again by the descriptions of observers, many of whom were witnessing not slave services but religious meetings of rural southern Negroes long after emancipation. The essential continuity of the Negro folk process in the more isolated sections of the rural South through the early decades of the twentieth century makes these accounts relevant for the slave period as well. Natalie Curtis Burlin, whose collection of spirituals is musically the most accurate one we have, and who had a long and close acquaintance with Negro music, never lost her sense of awe at the process by which these songs were molded. On a hot July Sunday in rural Virginia, she sat in a Negro meeting house listening to the preacher deliver his prayer, interrupted now and then by an "O Lord!" or "Amen, Amen" from the congregation.

> Minutes passed, long minutes of strange intensity. The mutterings, the ejaculations, grew louder, more dramatic, till suddenly I felt the creative thrill dart through the people like an electric vibration, that same half-audible hum arose,—emotion was gathering atmospherically as clouds gather—and then, up from the depths of some "sinner's" remorse and imploring came a pitiful little plea, a real "moan," sobbed in musical cadence. From somewhere in that bowed gathering another voice improvised a response: the plea sounded again, louder this time and more impassioned; then other voices joined in the answer, shaping it into a musical phrase; and so, before our ears, as one might say, from this molten metal of music a new song was smithied out, composed then and there by no one in particular and by everyone in general.[17]

Clifton Furness has given us an even more graphic description. During a visit to an isolated South Carolina plantation in 1926, he attended a prayer meeting held in the old slave cabins. The preacher began his reading of the Scriptures slowly, then increased his tempo and emotional fervor, assuring his flock that "Gawd's lightnin' gwine strike! Gawd's thunder swaller de ert!"

> Gradually moaning became audible in the shadowy corners where the women sat. Some patted their bundled babies in time to the flow of the words, and began swaying backward and forward. Several men moved their feet alternately, in strange syncopation. A rhythm was born, almost without reference to the words that were being spoken by the preacher. It seemed to take shape almost visibly, and grow. I was gripped with the feeling of a mass-intelligence, a self-conscious entity, gradually informing the crowd and taking possession of every mind there, including my own.

In the midst of this increasing intensity, a black man sitting directly in front of Furness, his head bowed, his body swaying, his feet patting up and down, suddenly cried out: "Git right—sodger! Git right—sodger! Git right—wit Gawd!"

> Instantly the crowd took it up, moulding a melody out of half-formed familiar phrases based upon a spiritual tune, hummed here and there among the crowd. A distinct melodic outline became more and more prominent, shaping itself around the central theme of the words, "Git right, sodger!"
>
> Scraps of other words and tunes were flung into the medley of sound by individual singers from time to time, but the general trend was carried on by a deep undercurrent, which appeared to be stronger than the mind of any individual present, for it bore the mass of improvised harmony and rhythms into the most effective climax of incremental repetition that I have ever heard. I felt as if some conscious plan or purpose were carrying us along, call it mob-mind, communal composition, or what you will.[18]

Shortly after the Civil War, Elizabeth Kilham witnessed a similar scene among the freedmen, and described it in terms almost identical to those used by observers many years later. "A fog seemed to fill the church," she wrote, ". . . an invisible power seemed to hold us in its iron grasp; . . . A few moments more, and I think we should have shrieked in unison with the crowd."[19]

These accounts and others like them make it clear that spirituals both during and after slavery were the product of an improvisational communal consciousness. They were not, as some observers thought, totally new creations, but were forged out of many preexisting bits of old songs mixed together with snatches of new tunes and lyrics and fit into a fairly traditional but never wholly static metrical pattern. They were, to answer Higginson's question, *simultaneously* the result of individual and mass creativity. They were products of that folk process which has been called "communal re-creation," through which older songs are constantly recreated into essentially new entities.[20] Anyone who has read through large numbers of Negro songs is familiar with this process. Identical or slightly varied stanzas appear in song after song; identical tunes are made to accommodate completely different sets of lyrics; the same song appears in different collections in widely varied forms. In 1845 a traveler observed that the only permanent elements in Negro song were the music and the chorus. "The blacks themselves leave out old stanzas, and introduce new ones at pleasure. Travelling through the South, you may, in passing from Virginia to

Louisiana, hear the same tune a hundred times, but seldom the same words accompanying it."[21] Another observer noted in 1870 that during a single religious meeting the freedmen would often sing the words of one spiritual to several different tunes, and then take a tune that particularly pleased them and fit the words of several different songs to it.[22] Slave songs, then, were never static; at no time did Negroes create a "final" version of any spiritual. Always the community felt free to alter and recreate them.

[The two facts that I have attempted to establish thus far—that slave music, regardless of its origins, was a distinctive cultural form, and that it was created or constantly recreated through a communal process—are essential if one is to justify the use of these songs as keys to slave consciousness] But these facts in themselves say a good deal about the nature and quality of slave life and personality. That black slaves could create and continually recreate songs marked by the poetic beauty, the emotional intensity, the rich imagery which characterized the spirituals —songs which even one of the most devout proponents of the white man's origins school admits are "the most impressive religious folk songs in our language"[23]—should be enough to make us seriously question recent theories which conceive of slavery as a closed system which destroyed the vitality of the Negro and left him a dependent child. [For all of its horrors, slavery was never so complete a system of psychic assault that it prevented the slaves from carving out independent cultural forms.] It never pervaded all of the interstices of their minds and their culture, and in those gaps they were able to create an independent art form and a distinctive voice. If North American slavery eroded the African's linguistic and institutional life, if it prevented him from preserving and developing his rich heritage of graphic and plastic art, it nevertheless allowed him to continue and to develop the patterns of verbal art which were so central to his past culture. Historians have not yet come to terms with what the continuance of the oral tradition meant to blacks in slavery.

In Africa, songs, tales, proverbs, and verbal games served the dual function of not only preserving communal values and solidarity, but also of providing occasions for the individual to transcend, at least symbolically, the inevitable restrictions of his environment and his society by permitting him to express deeply held feelings which he ordinarily was not allowed to verbalize. Among the Ashanti and the Dahomeans, for example, periods were set aside when the inhabitants were encouraged to gather together and, through the medium of song, dance, and tales, to openly express their feelings about each other. The psychological release this afforded seems to have been well understood. "You know that everyone has a *sunsum* (soul) that may get hurt or knocked about or become sick, and so make the body ill," an Ashanti high priest explained to the English anthropologist R. S. Rattray:

> Very often . . . ill health is caused by the evil and the hate that another has in his head against you. Again, you too may have hatred in your head against another, because of something that person has done to you, and that, too, causes your *sunsum* to fret and become sick. Our forbears knew this to be the case, and so they ordained a time, once every year, when every man and woman, free man and slave, should have freedom to speak out just what was in their head, to tell their neighbours just what they thought of them, and of their actions, and not only their neighbours, but also the king or chief. When a man has spoken freely thus, he will feel his *sunsum* cool and quieted, and the *sunsum* of the other person against whom he has now openly spoken will be quieted also.

Utilization of verbal art for this purpose was widespread throughout Africa, and was not confined to those ceremonial occasions when one could directly state one's feelings. Through innuendo, metaphor, and circumlocution, Africans could utilize their songs as outlets for individual release without disturbing communal solidarity.[24]
There is abundant internal evidence that the verbal art of the slaves in the United States served many of these traditional functions. Just as the process by which the spirituals were created allowed for simultaneous individual and communal creativity, so their very structure provided simultaneous outlets for individual and communal expression. The overriding antiphonal structure of the spirituals—the call and response pattern which Negroes brought with them from Africa and which was reinforced by the relatively similar white practice of "lining out" hymns—placed the individual in continual dialogue with his community, allowing him at one and the same time to preserve his voice as a distinct entity and to blend it with those of his fellows. Here again slave music confronts us with evidence which indicates that however seriously the slave system may have diminished the strong sense of community that had bound Africans together, it never totally destroyed it or left the individual atomized and emotionally and psychically defenseless before his white masters. In fact, the form and structure of slave music presented the slave with a potential outlet for his

individual feelings even while it continually drew him back into the communal presence and permitted him the comfort of basking in the warmth of the shared assumptions of those around him.

Those "shared assumptions" can be further examined by an analysis of the content of slave songs. [Our preoccupation in recent years with the degree to which the slaves actually resembled the "Sambo" image held by their white masters has obscured the fact that the slaves developed images of their own which must be consulted and studied before any discussion of slave personality can be meaningful.] The image of the trickster, who through cunning and unscrupulousness prevails over his more powerful antagonists, pervades slave tales. The trickster figure is rarely encountered in the slave's religious songs, though its presence is sometimes felt in the slave's many allusions to his narrow escapes from the devil.

> *The Devil's mad and I'm glad,*
> *He lost the soul he thought he had.*[25]
>
> *Ole Satan toss a ball at me.*
> *O me no weary yet . . .*
>
> *Him tink de ball would hit my soul.*
> *O me no weary yet . . .*
>
> *De ball for hell and I for heaven.*
> *O me no weary yet . . .*[26]
>
> *Ole Satan thought he had a mighty aim;*
> *He missed my soul and caught my sins.*
> *Cry Amen, cry Amen, cry Amen to God!*
>
> *He took my sins upon his back;*
> *Went muttering and grumbling down to hell.*
> *Cry Amen, cry Amen, cry Amen to God!*[27]

[The single most persistent image the slave songs contain, however, is that of the chosen people.] The vast majority of the spirituals identify the singers as "de people dat is born of God," "We are the people of God," "we are de people of de Lord," "I really do believe I'm a child of God," "I'm a child ob God, wid my soul sot free," "I'm born of God, I know I am." Nor is there ever any doubt that "To the promised land I'm bound to go," "I walk de heavenly road," "Heav'n shall-a be my home," "I gwine to meet my Saviour," "I seek my Lord and I find Him," "I'll hear the trumpet sound/In that morning."[28]

The force of this image cannot be diminished by the observation that similar images were present in the religious singing of white evangelical churches during the first half of the nineteenth century. White Americans could be expected to sing of triumph and salvation, given their long-standing heritage of the idea of a chosen people which was reinforced in this era by the belief in inevitable progress and manifest destiny, the spread-eagle oratory, the bombastic folklore, and, paradoxically, the deep insecurities concomitant with the tasks of taming a continent and developing an identity. But for this same message to be expressed by Negro slaves who were told endlessly that they were members of the lowliest of races *is* significant. It offers an insight into the kinds of barriers the slaves had available to them against the internalization of the stereotyped images their masters held and attempted consciously and unconsciously to foist upon them.

The question of the chosen people image leads directly into the larger problem of what role religion played in the songs of the slave. Writing in 1862, James McKim noted that the songs of the Sea Island freedmen "are all religious, barcaroles and all. I speak without exception. So far as I heard or was told of their singing, it was all religious." Others who worked with recently emancipated slaves recorded the same experience, and Colonel Higginson reported that he rarely heard his troops sing a profane or vulgar song. With a few exceptions, "all had a religious motive."[29] In spite of this testimony, there can be little doubt that the slaves sang nonreligious songs. In 1774, an English visitor to the United States, after his first encounter with slave music, wrote in his journal: "In their songs they generally relate the usage they have received from their Masters or Mistresses in a very satirical stile and manner."[30] Songs fitting this description can be found in the nineteenth-century narratives of fugitive slaves. Harriet Jacobs recorded that during the Christmas season the slaves would ridicule stingy whites by singing:

> Poor Massa, so dey say;
> Down in de heel, so dey say;
> Got no money, so dey say;
> God A'mighty bress you, so dey say.[31]

"Once in a while among a mass of nonsense and wild frolic," Frederick Douglass noted, "a sharp hit was given to the meanness of slaveholders."

We raise de wheat,
Dey gib us de corn;
We bake de bread,
Dey gib us de crust;
We sif de meal,
Dey gib us de huss;
We peal de meat,
Dey gib us de skin;
And dat's de way
Dey take us in;
We skim de pot,
Dey gib us de liquor,
And say dat's good enough for nigger.[32]

Both of these songs are in the African tradition of utilizing song to by-pass both internal and external censors and give vent to feelings which could be expressed in no other form. Nonreligious songs were not limited to the slave's relations with his masters, however, as these rowing songs, collected by contemporary white observers, indicate:

We are going down to Georgia, boys,
Aye, aye.
To see the pretty girls, boys,
Yoe, yoe.
We'll give 'em a pint of brandy, boys,
Aye, aye.
And a hearty kiss, besides, boys,
Yoe, yoe.[33]
Jenny shake her toe at me,
Jenny gone away;
Jenny shake her toe at me,
Jenny gone away.
Hurrah! Miss Susy, oh!
Jenny gone away;
Hurrah! Miss Susy, oh!
Jenny gone away.[34]

The variety of nonreligious songs in the slave's repertory was wide. There were songs of in-group and out-group satire, songs of nostalgia, nonsense songs, songs of play and work and love. Nevertheless, our total stock of these songs is very small. It is possible to add to these by incorporating such post-bellum secular songs which have an authentic slavery ring to them as "De Blue-Tail Fly," with its ill-concealed satisfaction at the death of a master, or the ubiquitous

> My ole Mistiss promise me,
> W'en she died, she'd set me free,
> She lived so long dat 'er head got bal',
> An' she give out'n de notion a dyin' at all.[35]

The number can be further expanded by following Constance Rourke's suggestion that we attempt to disentangle elements of Negro origin from those of white creation in the "Ethiopian melodies" of the white minstrel shows, many of which were similar to the songs I have just quoted.[36] Either of these possibilities, however, forces the historian to work with sources far more potentially spurious than those with which he normally is comfortable.

Spirituals, on the other hand, for all the problems associated with their being filtered through white hands before they were published, and despite the many errors in transcription that inevitably occurred, constitute a much more satisfactory source. They were collected by the hundreds directly from slaves and freedmen during the Civil War and the decades immediately following, and although they came from widely different geographical areas they share a common structure and content, which seems to have been characteristic of Negro music wherever slavery existed in the United States. It is possible that we have a greater number of religious than nonreligious songs because slaves were more willing to sing these ostensibly innocent songs to white collectors who in turn were more anxious to record them, since they fit easily with their positive and negative images of the Negro. But I would argue that the vast preponderance of spirituals over any other sort of slave music, rather than being merely the result of accident or error, is instead an accurate reflection of slave culture during the ante-bellum period. Whatever songs the slaves may have sung before their wholesale conversion to Christianity in the late eighteenth and early nineteenth centuries, by the latter century spirituals were quantitatively and qualitatively their most significant musical creation. In this form of expression slaves found a medium which resembled in many important ways the world view they had brought with them from Africa, and afforded them the possibility of both adapting to and transcending their situation.

It is significant that the most common form of slave music we know of is sacred song. I use the term "sacred" not in its present usage as something antithetical to the secular world; neither the slaves nor their African forebears ever drew modernity's clear line between the sacred and the secular. The uses to which spirituals were put are an unmistakable indication of this. They were not sung solely or even primarily in churches or praise houses, but were used as rowing songs, field songs, work songs, and social songs. On the Sea Islands during the Civil War, Lucy McKim heard the spiritual "Poor Rosy" sung in a wide variety of contexts and tempos.

> On the water, the oars dip "Poor Rosy" to an even andante; a stout boy and girl at the hominy-mill will make the same "Poor Rosy" fly, to keep up with the whirling stone; and in the evening, after the day's work is done, "Heab'n shall-a be my home" [the final line of each stanza] peals up slowly and mournfully from the distant quarters.[37]

For the slaves, then, songs of God and the mythic heroes of their religion were not confined to any specific time or place, but were appropriate to almost every situation. It is in this sense that I use the concept sacred—not to signify a rejection of the present world but to describe the process of incorporating within this world all the elements of the divine. The religious historian Mircea Eliade, whose definition of sacred has shaped my own, has maintained that for men in traditional societies religion is a means of extending the world spatially upward so that communication with the other world becomes ritually possible, and extending it temporally backward so that the paradigmatic acts of the gods and mythical ancestors can be continually reenacted and indefinitely recoverable. By creating sacred time and space, man can perpetually live in the presence of his gods, can hold on to the certainty that within one's own lifetime "rebirth" is continually possible, and can impose order on the chaos of the universe. "Life," as Eliade puts it, "is lived on a twofold plane; it takes its course as human existence and, at the same time, shares in a transhuman life, that of the cosmos or the gods."[38]

This notion of sacredness gets at the essence of the spirituals, and through them at the essence of the slave's world view. Denied the possibility of achieving an adjustment to the external world of the antebellum South which involved meaningful forms of personal integration, attainment of status, and feelings of individual worth that all human beings crave and need, the slaves created a new world by transcending the narrow confines of the one in which they were forced to live. They extended the boundaries of their restrictive universe backward until it fused with the world of the Old Testament, and upward until it became one with the world beyond. The spirituals are the record of a people who found the status, the harmony, the values, the order they needed to survive by internally creating an expanded universe, by literally willing themselves reborn. In this respect I agree with the anthropologist Paul Radin that

> The ante-bellum Negro was not converted to God. He converted God to himself. In the Christian God he found a fixed point and he needed a fixed point, for both within and outside of himself, he could see only vacillation and endless shifting. . . . There was no other safety for people faced on all sides by doubt and the threat of personal disintegration, by the thwarting of instincts and the annihilation of values.[39]

The confinement of much of the slave's new world to dreams and fantasies does not free us from the historical obligation of examining its contours, weighing its implications for the development of the slave's psychic and emotional structure, and eschewing the kind of facile reasoning that leads Professor Elkins to imply that, since the slaves had no alternatives open to them, their fantasy life was "limited to catfish and watermelons."[40] Their spirituals indicate clearly that there *were* alternatives open to them—alternatives which they themselves fashioned out of the fusion of their African heritage and their new religion—and that their fantasy life was so rich and so important to them that it demands understanding if we are even to begin to comprehend their inner world.

The God the slaves sang of was neither remote nor abstract, but as intimate, personal, and immediate as the gods of Africa had been. "O when I talk I talk wid God," "Mass Jesus is my bosom friend," "I'm goin' to walk with [talk with, live with, see] King Jesus by myself, by myself," were refrains that echoed through the spirituals.[41]

> *In de mornin' when I rise,*
>   *Tell my Jesus huddy [howdy] oh,*
> *I wash my hands in de mornin' glory,*
>   *Tell my Jesus huddy oh.*[42]

> *Gwine to argue wid de Father and chatter wid de son,*
> *The last trumpet shall sound, I'll be there.*
> *Gwine talk 'bout de bright world dey des' come from.*
> *The last trumpet shall sound, I'll be there.*[43]

> *Gwine to write to Massa Jesus,*
> *To send some Valiant soldier*
> *To turn back Pharaoh's army, Hallelu!*[44]

The heroes of the Scriptures—"Sister Mary," "Brudder Jonah," "Brudder Moses," "Brudder Daniel"—were greeted with similar intimacy and immediacy. In the world of the spirituals, it was not the masters and mistresses but God and Jesus and the entire pantheon of Old Testament figures who set the standards, established the precedents, and defined the values; who, in short, constituted the "significant others." The world described by the slave songs was a black world in which no reference was ever made to any white contemporaries. The salve's positive reference group was composed entirely of his own peers: his mother, father, sister, brother, uncles, aunts, preacher, fellow "sinners" and "mourners" of whom he sang endlessly, to whom he sent messages via the dying, and with whom he was reunited joyfully in the next world.

The same sense of sacred time and space which shaped the slave's portraits of his gods and heroes also made his visions of the past and future immediate and compelling. Descriptions of the Crucifixion communicate a sense of the actual presence of the singers: "Dey pierced Him in the side . . . Dey nail Him to de cross . . . Dey rivet His feet . . . Dey hanged him high . . . Dey stretch Him wide. . . ."

> *Oh sometimes it causes me to tremble,–tremble,–tremble,*
> *Were you there when they crucified my Lord?*[45]

The Slave's "shout"—that counterclockwise, shuffling dance which frequently occurred after the religious service and lasted long into the night—often became a medium through which the ecstatic dancers were transformed into actual participants in historic actions: Joshua's army marching around the walls of Jericho, the children of Israel following Moses out of Egypt.[46]

The thin line between time dimensions is nowhere better illustrated than in the slave's visions of the future, which were, of course, a direct negation of his present. Among the most striking spirituals are those which pile detail upon detail in describing the Day of Judgment: "You'll see de world on fire . . . see de element a meltin', . . . see the stars a fallin' . . . see the moon a bleedin' . . . see the forked lightning, . . . Hear the rumblin' thunder . . . see the righteous marching, . . . see my Jesus coming . . . ," and the world to come where "Dere's no sun to burn you . . . no hard trials . . . no whips a crackin' . . . no stormy weather . . . no tribulation . . . no evildoers . . . All is gladness in de Kingdom."[47] This vividness was matched by the slave's certainty that he would partake of the triumph of judgment and the joys of the new world:

> *Dere's room enough, room enough, room enough in de heaven,*
> *my Lord*
> *Room enough, room enough, I can't stay behind.*[48]

Continually, the slaves sang of reaching out beyond the world that confined them, of seeing Jesus "in de wilderness," of praying "in de lonesome valley," of breathing in the freedom of the mountain peaks:

> *Did yo' ever*
> *Stan' on mountun,*
> *Wash yo' han's*
> *In a cloud?*[49]

Continually, they held out the possibility of imminent rebirth; "I look at de worl' an' de worl' look new, . . . I look at my hands an' they look so too . . . I looked at my feet, my feet was too."[50]

These possibilities, these certainties were not surprising. The religious revivals which swept large numbers of slaves into the Christian fold in the late eighteenth and early nineteenth centuries were based upon a *practical* (not necessarily theological) Armianism: God would save all who believed in Him; Salvation was there for all to take hold of if they would. The effects of this message upon the slaves who were exposed to and converted by it have been passed over too easily by historians. Those effects are illustrated graphically in the spirituals which were the products of these revivals and which continued to spread the evangelical word long after the revivals had passed into history. The religious music of the slaves is almost devoid of feelings of depravity or unworthiness, but is rather, as I have tried to show, pervaded by a sense of change, transcendence, ultimate justice, and personal worth. The spirituals have been referred to as "sorrow songs," and in some respects they were. The slaves sang of "rollin' thro' an unfriendly world," of being "a-trouble in de mind," of living in a world which was a "howling wilderness," "a hell to me," of feeling like a "motherless child," "a po' little orphan chile in de worl'," a "home-e-less child," of fearing that "Trouble will bury me down.' "[51]

But these feelings were rarely pervasive or permanent; almost always they were overshadowed by a triumphant note of affirmation. Even so despairing a wail as "Nobody Knows the Trouble I've Had" could suddenly have its mood transformed by lines like: "One morning I was a-walking down, . . . Saw some berries a-hanging down, . . . I pick de berry and I suck de juice, . . . Just as sweet as de honey in de comb."[52] Similarly, amid the deep sorrow of "Sometimes I feel like a Motherless chile," sudden release could come with the lines: "Sometimes I feel like/A eagle in de air. . . . Spread my wings an/Fly, fly, fly."[53] Slaves spent little time singing of the horrors of hell or damnation. Their songs of the Devil, quoted earlier, pictured a harsh but almost semicomic figure (often, one suspects, a surrogate for the white man), over whom they triumphed with reassuring regularity. For all their inevitable sadness, slave songs were characterized more by a feeling of confidence than of despair. There was confidence that contemporary power relationships were not immutable: "Did not old Pharaoh get lost, get lost, get lost, . . . get lost in the Red Sea?"; confidence in the possibilities of instantaneous change: "Jesus make de dumb to speak. . . . Jesus make de cripple walk. . . . Jesus give de blind his sight. . . . Jesus do most anything"; confidence in the rewards of persistence: "Keep a' inching along like a poor inch-worm,/ Jesus will come by'nd bye"; confidence that nothing could stand in the way of the justice they would receive: "You kin hender me here, but you can't do it dah," "O no man, no man, no man can hinder me"; confidence in the prospects of the future: "We'll walk de golden streets/Of de New Jerusalem." Religion, the slaves sang, "is good for anything, . . . Religion make you happy, . . . Religion gib me patience . . . O member, get Religion . . . Religion is so sweet."[54]

The slaves often pursued the "sweetness" of their religion in the face of many obstacles. Becky Ilsey, who was 16 when she was emancipated, recalled many years later:

> 'Fo' de war when we'd have a meetin' at night, wuz mos' always 'way in de woods or de bushes some whar so de white folks couldn't hear, an' when dey'd sing a spiritual an' de spirit 'gin to shout some de elders would go 'mongst de folks an' put dey han' over dey mouf an' some times put a clof in dey mouf an' say: "Spirit don talk so loud or de patterol break us up." You know dey had white patterols what went 'roun' at night to see de niggers didn't cut up no devilment, an' den de meetin' would break up an' some would go to one house an' some to er nudder an' dey would groan er w'ile, den go home.[55]

Elizabeth Ross Hite testified that although she and her fellow slaves on a Louisiana plantation were Catholics, "lots didn't like that 'ligion."

> We used to hide behind some bricks and hold church ourselves. You see the Catholic preachers from France wouldn't let us shout, and the Lawd done said you gotta shout if you want to be saved. That's in the Bible.
>
> Sometimes we held church all night long, 'til way in the mornin'. We burned some grease in a can for the preacher to see the Bible by. . . .
>
> See, our master didn't like us to have much 'ligion, said it made us lag in our work. He jest wanted us to be Catholicses on Sunday and go to mass and not study 'bout nothin' like that on week days. He didn't want us shoutin' and moanin' all day'-long, but you gotta shout and you gotta moan if you wants to be saved.[56]

The slaves clearly craved the affirmation and promise of their religion. It would be a mistake, however, to see this urge as exclusively otherworldly. When Thomas Wentworth Higginson observed that the spirituals exhibited "nothing but patience for this life,—nothing but triumph in the next," he, and later observers who elaborated upon this judgment, were indulging in hyperbole. [Although Jesus was ubiquitous in the spirituals, it was not invariably the Jesus of the New Testament of whom the slaves sang, but frequently a Jesus transformed into an Old Testament warrior: "Mass' Jesus" who engaged in personal combat with the Devil,] "King Jesus" seated on a milk-white horse with sword and shield in hand. "Ride on, King Jesus," "Ride on, conquering King," "The God I serve is a man of war," the slaves sang.[57] This transformation of Jesus is symptomatic of the slaves' selectivity in choosing those parts of the Bible which were to serve as the basis of their religious consciousness. Howard Thurman, a Negro minister who as a boy had the duty of reading the Bible to his grandmother, was perplexed by her refusal to allow him to read from the Epistles of Paul.

> When at length I asked the reason, she told me that during the days of slavery, the minister (white) on the plantation was always preaching from the Pauline letters—"Slaves, be obedient to your masters," etc. "I vowed to myself," she said, "that if freedom ever came and I learned to read, I would never read that part of the Bible!"[58]

Nor, apparently, did this part of the Scriptures ever constitute a vital element in slave songs or sermons. The emphasis of the spirituals, as Higginson himself noted, was upon the Old Testament and the exploits of the Hebrew children.[59] It is important that Daniel and David and Joshua and Jonah and Moses and Noah, all of whom fill the lines of the spirituals, were delivered in *this* world and delivered in ways which struck the imagination of the slaves. Over and over their songs dwelt upon the spectacle of the Red Sea opening to allow the Hebrew slaves past before inundating the mighty armies of the Pharaoh. They lingered delightedly upon the image of little David humbling the great Goliath with a stone—a pretechnological victory which post-bellum Negroes were to expand upon in their songs of John Henry. They retold in endless variation the stories of the blind and humbled Samson bringing down the mansions of his conquerors; of the ridiculed Noah patiently building the ark which would deliver him from the doom of a mocking world; of the timid Jonah attaining freedom from his confinement through faith. The similarity of these tales to the situation of the slave was too clear for him not to see it; too clear for us to believe that the songs had no worldly content for the black man in bondage. "O my Lord delivered Daniel," the slaves observed, and responded logically: "O why not deliver me, too?"

> He delivered Daniel from de lion's den,
>   Jonah from de belly ob de whale,
> And de Hebrew children from de fiery furnace,
>   And why not every man?[60]

[These lines state as clearly as anything can the manner in which the sacred world of the slaves was able to fuse the precedents of the past, the conditions of the present, and the promise of the future into one connected reality. In this respect there was always a latent and symbolic element of protest in the slave's religious songs which frequently became overt and explicit.] Frederick Douglass asserted that for him and many of his fellow slaves the song, "O Canaan, sweet Canaan,/I am bound for the land of Canaan," symbolized "something more than a hope of reaching heaven. We meant to reach the *North*, and the North was our Canaan," and he wrote that the lines of another spiritual, "Run to Jesus, shun the danger,/I don't expect to stay much longer here," had a double meaning which first suggested to him the thought of escaping from slavery.[61] Similarly, when the black troops in Higginson's regiment sang:

> We'll soon be free, [three times]
> When de Lord will call us home.

a young drummer boy explained to him, "Dey think *de Lord* mean for say *de Yankees*."[62] Nor is there any reason to doubt that slaves could have used their songs as a means of secret communication. An ex-slave told Lydia Parrish that when he and his fellow slaves "suspicioned" that one of their number was telling tales to the driver, they would sing lines like the following while working in the field:

> *O Judyas he wuz a 'ceitful man*
> *He went an' betray a mos' innocen' man.*
> *Fo' thirty pieces a silver dat it wuz done*
> *He went in de woods an' e' self he hung.*[63]

And it is possible, as many writers have argued, that such spirituals as the commonly heard "Steal away, steal away, steal away to Jesus!" were used as explicit calls to secret meetings.

But it is not necessary to invest the spirituals with a secular function only at the price of divesting them of their religious content, as Miles Mark Fisher has done.[64] While we may make such clear-cut distinctions, I have tried to show that the slaves did not. For them religion never constituted a simple escape from this world, because their conception of the world was more expansive than modern man's. Nowhere is this better illustrated than during the Civil War itself. While the war gave rise to such new spirituals as "Before I'd be a slave/I'd be buried in my grave,/And go home to my Lord and be saved!" or the popular "Many thousand Go," with its jubilant rejection of all the facets of slave life—"No more peck o' corn for me, . . . No more driver's lash for me, . . . No more pint o' salt for me, . . . No more hundred lash for me, . . . No more mistress' call for me"[65]—the important thing was not that large numbers of slaves now could create new songs which openly expressed their views of slavery; that was to be expected. More significant was the ease with which their old songs fit their new situation. With so much of their inspiration drawn from the events of the Old Testament and the Book of Revelation, the slaves had long sung of wars, of battles, of the Army of the Lord, of Soldiers of the Cross, of trumpets summoning the faithful, of vanquishing the hosts of evil. These songs especially were, as Higginson put it, "available for camp purposes with very little strain upon their symbolism." "We'll cross de mighty river," his troops sang while marching or rowing,

> *We'll cross de danger water, . . .*
> *O Pharaoh's army drownded!*
> *My army cross over.*

"O blow your trumpet, Gabriel," they sang,

> *Blow your trumpet louder;*
> *And I want dat trumpet to blow me home*
> *To my new Jerusalem.*

But they also found their less overtly militant songs quite as appropriate to warfare. Their most popular and effective marching song was:

> *Jesus call you, Go in de wilderness,*
> *Go in de wilderness, go in de wilderness,*
> *Jesus call you. Go in de wilderness*
> *To wait upon de Lord.*[66]

Black Union soldiers found it no more incongruous to accompany their fight for freedom with the sacred songs of their bondage than they had found it inappropriate as slaves to sing their spirituals while picking cotton or shucking corn. Their religious songs, like their religion itself, was of this world as well as the next.

Slave songs by themselves, of course, do not present us with a definitive key to the life and mind of the slave. They have to be seen within the context of the slave's situation and examined alongside such other cultural materials as folk tales. But slave songs do indicate the need to rethink a number of assumptions that have shaped recent interpretations of slavery, such as the assumption that because slavery eroded the linguistic and institutional side of African life it wiped out almost all the more fundamental aspects of African culture. Culture, certainly, is more than merely the sum total of institutions and language. It is also expressed by something less tangible, which the anthropologist Robert Redfield has called "style of life." Peoples as different as the Lapp and the Bedouin, Redfield has argued, with diverse languages, religions, customs, and institutions, may still share an emphasis on certain virtues and ideals, certain manners of independence and hospitality, general ways of looking upon the world, which give them a similar life style.[67] This argument applies to the West African cultures from which the slaves came. Though they varied widely in language, institutions, gods, and familial patterns, they shared a fundamental outlook toward the past, present, and future and common means of cultural expression which could well have constituted the basis of a sense of community and identity capable of surviving the impact of slavery.

Slave songs present us with abundant evidence that in the structure of their music and dance, in the uses to which music was put, in the survival of the oral tradition, in the retention of such practices as spirit possession which often accompanied the creation of spirituals, and in the ways in which the slaves expressed their new religion, important elements of their shared African heritage remained alive not just as quaint cultural vestiges but as vitally creative elements of slave culture. This could never have happened if slavery was, as Professor Elkins maintains, a system which so completely closed in around the slave, so totally penetrated his personality structure as to infantalize him and reduce him to a kind of *tabula rasa* upon which the white man could write what he chose.[68]

[Slave songs provide us with the beginnings of a very different kind of hypothesis: that the preliterate, premodern Africans, with their sacred world view, were so imperfectly acculturated into the secular American society into which they were thrust, were so completely denied access to the ideology and dreams which formed the core of the consciousness of other Americans, that they were forced to fall back upon the only cultural frames of reference that made any sense to them and gave them any feeling of security.] I use the word "forced" advisedly. Even if the slaves had had the opportunity to enter fully into the life of the larger society, they might still have chosen to retain and perpetuate certain elements of their African heritage. But the point is that they really had no choice. True acculturation was denied to most slaves. The alternatives were either to remain in a state of cultural limbo, divested of the old cultural patterns but not allowed to adopt those of their new homeland—which in the long run is no alternative at all—or to cling to as many as possible of the old ways of thinking and acting. The slaves' oral tradition, their music, and their religious outlook served this latter function and constituted a cultural refuge at least potentially capable of protecting their personalities from some of the worst ravages of the slave system.

The argument of Professors Tannenbaum and Elkins that the Protestant churches in the United States did not act as a buffer between the slave and his master is persuasive enough, but it betrays a modern preoccupation with purely institutional arrangements.[69] [Religion is more than an institution, and because Protestant churches failed to protect the slave's inner being from the incursions of the slave system, it does not follow that the spiritual message of Protestantism failed as well. Slave songs are a testament to the ways in which Christianity provided slaves with the precedents, heroes, and

future promise that allowed them to transcend the purely temporal ||
bonds of the Peculiar Institution.]

Historians have frequently failed to perceive the full importance of
this because they have not taken the slave's religiosity seriously enough.
A people cannot create a music as forceful and striking as slave music
out of a mere uninternalized anodyne. Those who have argued that
Negroes did not oppose slavery in any meaningful way are writing from
a modern, political context. What they really mean is that the slaves
found no *political* means to oppose slavery. But slaves, to borrow Professor Hobsbawm's term, were prepolitical beings in a prepolitical situation.[70] Within their frame of reference there were other—and from
the point of view of personality development, not necessarily less effective—means of escape and opposition. If mid-twentieth-century historians have difficulty perceiving the sacred universe created by slaves
as a serious alternative to the societal system created by southern
slaveholders, the problem may be the historians' and not the slaves'.

Above all, the study of slave songs forces the historian to move out
of his own culture, in which music plays a peripheral role, and offers
him the opportunity to understand the ways in which black slaves
were able to perpetuate much of the centrality and functional importance that music had for their African ancestors. In the concluding
lines of his perceptive study of primitive song, C. M. Bowra has written:

> Primitive song is indispensable to those who practice it. . . .
> they cannot do without song, which both formulates and an-
> swers their nagging questions, enables them to pursue action
> with zest and confidence, brings them into touch with gods and
> spirits, and makes them feel less strange in the natural world.
> . . . it gives to them a solid centre in what otherwise would be
> almost chaos, and a continuity in their being, which would too
> easily dissolve before the calls of the implacable present . . .
> through its words men, who might otherwise give in to the mal-
> ice of circumstances, find their old powers revived or new powers
> stirring in them, and through these life itself is sustained and
> renewed and fulfilled.[71]

This, I think, sums up concisely the function of song for the slave.
Without a general understanding of that function, without a specific
understanding of the content and meaning of slave song, there can be
no full comprehension of the effects of slavery upon the slave or the
meaning of the society from which slaves emerged at emancipation.

NOTES

An earlier version of this essay was presented as a paper at the American Historical Association meetings on December 28, 1969. I am indebted to the two commentators on that occasion, Professors J. Saunders Redding and Mike Thelwell, and to my colleagues Nathan I. Huggins, Robert Middlekauff, and Kenneth M. Stampp for their penetrating criticisms and suggestions.

1. Miles Mark Fisher, *Negro Slave Songs in the United States* (New York, 1963, orig. pub. 1953), 14, 39, 132, and *passim*.

2. The contours of this debate are judiciously outlined in D. K. Wilgus, *Anglo-American Folksong Scholarship Since 1898* (New Brunswick, 1959), App. One, "The Negro-White Spirituals."

3. Lucy McKim, "Songs of the Port Royal Contrabands," *Dwight's Journal of Music*, XXII (November 8, 1862), 255.

4. W. F. Allen, "The Negro Dialect," *The Nation*, I (December 14, 1865), 744-745.

5. See, for instance, Henry Edward Krehbiel, *Afro-American Folksongs* (New York, 1963, orig. pub. 1914); James Wesley Work, *Folk Song of the American Negro* (Nashville, 1915); James Weldon Johnson, *The Book of American Negro Spirituals* (New York, 1925), and *The Second Book of Negro Spirituals* (New York, 1926); Lydia Parrish, *Slave Songs of the Georgia Sea Islands* (Hatboro, Penna., 1965, orig. pub. 1942); LeRoi Jones, *Blues People* (New York, 1963).

6. Newman I. White, *American Negro Folk-Songs* (Hatboro, Penna., 1965, orig. pub. 1928); Guy B. Johnson, *Folk Culture on St. Helena Island, South Carolina* (Chapel Hill, 1930); George Pullen Jackson, *White and Negro Spirituals* (New York, 1943).

7. White, *American Negro Folk-Songs*, 11-13.

8. Professor John William Ward gives an excellent example of this process in his discussion of the different meanings which the newspapers of the United States, France, and India attributed to Charles Lindbergh's flight across the Atlantic in 1927. See "Lindbergh, Dos Passos, and History," in Ward, *Red, White, and Blue* (New York, 1969), 55.

9. George Pullen Jackson, "The Genesis of the Negro Spiritual," *The American Mercury*, XXVI (June 1932), 248.

10. Richard Alan Waterman, "African Influence on the Music of the Americas," in Sol Tax (ed.), *Acculturation in the Americas: Proceedings and Selected Papers of the XXIXth International Congress of Americanists* (Chicago, 1952), 207-218; Wilgus, *Anglo-American Folksong Scholarship Since 1898*, 363-364; Melville H. Herskovits, "Patterns of Negro Music" (pamphlet, no publisher, no date); Gilbert Chase, *America's Music* (New York, 1966), Chap. 12; Alan P. Merriam, "African Music," in William R. Bascom and Melville J. Herskovits (eds.), *Continuity and Change in African Cultures* (Chicago, 1959), 76-80.

11. White, *American Negro Folk-Songs*, 29, 55.

12. Jackson, *White and Negro Spirituals*, 266-267.

13. James Miller McKim, "Negro Songs," *Dwight's Journal of Music*, XXI (August 9, 1862), 149.

14. Thomas Wentworth Higginson, *Army Life in a Black Regiment* (Beacan Press edition, Boston, 1962, orig. pub. 1869), 218-219.

15. Henry Russell, *Cheer! Boys, Cheer!*, 84-85, quoted in Chase, *America's Music*, 235-236.

16. Jeanette Robinson Murphy, "The Survival of African Music in America," *Popular Science Monthly*, 55 (1899), 660-672, reprinted in Bruce Jackson (ed.), *The Negro and His Folklore in Nineteenth-Century Periodicals* (Austin, 1967), 328.

17. Natalie Curtis Burlin, "Negro Music at Birth," *Musical Quarterly*, V (January 1919), 88. For Mrs. Burlin's excellent reproductions of Negro folk songs and spirituals, see her *Negro Folk-Songs* (New York, 1918-1919), Vol. I-IV.

18. Clifton Joseph Furness, "Communal Music Among Arabians and Negroes," *Musical Quarterly*, XVI (January 1930), 49-51.

19. Elizabeth Kilham, "Sketches in Color: IV," *Putnam's Monthly*, XV (March 1870), 304-311, reprinted in Jackson, *The Negro and His Folklore in Nineteenth-Century Periodicals*, 127-128.

20. Bruno Nettl, *Folk and Traditional Music of the Western Continents* (Englewood Cliffs, 1965), 4-5; Chase, *America's Music*, 241-243.

21. J. K., Jr., "Who Are Our National Poets?," *Knickerbocker Magazine*, 26 (October 1845), 336, quoted in Dena J. Epstein, "Slave Music in the United States Before 1860: A Survey of Sources (Part I)," *Music Library Association Notes*, XX (Spring 1963), 208.

22. Elizabeth Kilham, "Sketches in Color: IV," *Putnam's Monthly*, XV (March 1870), 304-311, reprinted in Jackson, *The Negro and His Folklore in Nineteenth-Century Periodicals*, 129.

23. White, *American Negro Folk-Songs*, 57.

24. Alan P. Merriam, "Music and the Dance," in Robert Lystad (ed.), *The African World: A Survey of Social Research* (New York, 1965), 452-468; William Bascom "Folklore and Literature," in *Ibid.*, 469-488; R. S. Rattray, *Ashanti* (Oxford 1923), Chap. XV; Melville Herskovits, "Freudian Mechanisms in Primitive Negro Psychology, in E. E. Evans-Pritchard *et al.* (eds.), *Essays Presented to C. G. Seligman* (London, 1934), 75-84; Alan P. Merriam, "African Music," in Bascom and Herskovits, *Continuity and Change in African Cultures*, 49-86.

25. William Francis Allen, Charles Pickard Ware, and Lucy McKim Garrison, compilers, *Slave Songs of the United States* (New York, 1867, Oak Publications ed., 1965), 164-165.

26. *Ibid.*, 43.

27. Harriet Jacobs, *Incidents in the Life of a Slave Girl* (Boston, 1861), 109.

28. Lines like these could be quoted endlessly. For the specific ones cited, see the songs in the following collections: Higginson, *Army Life in a Black Regiment*, 206, 216-217; Allen *et al.*, *Slave Songs of the United States*, 33-34, 44, 106-108, 131, 160-161; Thomas P. Fenner, compiler, *Religious Folk Songs of the Negro as Sung on the Plantations* (Hampton, Virginia, 1909, orig. pub. 1874), 10-11, 48; J. B. T. Marsh, *The Story of the Jubilee Singers; With Their Songs* (Boston, 1880), 136, 167, 178.

29. McKim, "Negro Songs," 148; H. G. Spaulding, "Under the Palmetto," *Continental Monthly*, IV (1863), 188-203, reprinted in Jackson, *The Negro and His Folklore in Nineteenth-Century Periodicals*, 72; Allen, "The Negro Dialect," 744-745; Higginson, *Army Life in a Black Regiment*, 220-221.

30. *Journal of Nicholas Cresswell, 1774–1777* (New York, 1934), 17-19, quoted in Epstein, *Music Library Association Notes*, XX (Spring 1963), 201.

31. Jacobs, *Incidents in the Life of a Slave Girl*, 180.

32. *Life and Times of Frederick Douglass* (rev. ed., 1892, Collier Books Edition, 1962), 146-147.

33. John Lambert, *Travels Through Canada and the United States of North America in the Years, 1806–1807 and 1808* (London, 1814), II, 253-254, quoted in Dena J. Epstein, "Slave Music in the United States Before 1860: A Survey of Sources (Part 2)," *Music Library Association Notes*, XX (Summer 1963), 377.

34. Frances Anne Kemble, *Journal of a Residence on a Georgian Plantation in 1838–1839* (New York, 1863), 128.

35. For versions of these songs, see Dorothy Scarborough, *On the Trail of Negro Folk-Songs* (Cambridge, 1925), 194, 201-203, 223-225, and Thomas W. Talley, *Negro Folk Rhymes* (New York, 1922), 25-26. Talley claims that the majority of the songs in his large and valuable collection "were sung by Negro fathers and mothers in the dark days of American slavery to their children who listened with eyes as large as saucers and drank them down with mouths wide open," but offers no clue as to why he feels that songs collected for the most part in the twentieth century were slave songs.

36. Constance Rourke, *The Roots of American Culture and Other Essays* (New York, 1942), 262-274. Newman White, on the contrary, has argued that although the earliest minstrel songs were Negro derived, they soon went their own way and that less than ten per cent of them were genuinely Negro. Nevertheless, these white songs "got back to the plantation, largely spurious as they were and were undoubtedly among those which the plantation-owners encouraged the Negroes to sing. They persist, to-day in isolated stanzas and lines, among the songs handed down by plantation Negroes . . ." White, *American Negro Folk-Songs*, 7-10 and Appendix IV. There are probably valid elements in both theses. A similarly complex relationship between genuine Negro folk creations and their more commercialized partly white influenced imitations was to take place in the blues of the twentieth century.

37. McKim, "Songs of the Port Royal Contrabands," 255.

38. Mircea Eliade, *The Sacred and the Profane* (New York, 1961), Chaps. 2, 4, and *passim*. For the similarity of Eliade's concept to the world view of West Africa, see W. E. Abraham, *The Mind of Africa* (London, 1962), Chap. 2, and R. S. Rattray, *Religion and Art in Ashanti* (Oxford, 1927).

39. Paul Radin, "Status, Phantasy, and the Christian Dogma," in Social Science Institute, Fisk University, *God Struck Me Dead: Religious Conversion Experiences and Autobiographies of Negro Ex-Slaves* (Nashville, 1945, unpublished typescript).

40. Stanley Elkins, *Slavery* (Chicago, 1959), 136.

41. Allen *et al.*, *Slave Songs of the United States*, 33-34, 105; William E. Barton, *Old Plantation Hymns: A Collection of Hitherto Unpublished Melodies of the Slave and the Freedmen* (Boston, 1899), 30.

42. Allen *et al.*, *Slave Songs of the United States*, 47.

43. Barton, *Old Plantation Hymns*, 19.

44. Marsh, *The Story of the Jubilee Singers*, 132.

45. Fenner, *Religious Folk Songs of the Negro*, 162; E. A. McIlhenny, *Befo' De War Spirituals: Words and Melodies* (Boston, 1933), 39.

46. Barton, *Old Plantation Hymns*, 15; Howard W. Odum and Guy B. Johnson, *The Negro And His Songs* (Hatboro, Penn., 1964, orig. pub. 1925)), 33-34; for a vivid description of the "shout" see *The Nation*, May 30, 1867, 432-433; see also Parrish, *Slave Songs of the Georgia Sea Islands*, Chap. III.

47. For examples of songs of this nature, see Fenner, *Religious Folk Songs of the Negro*, 8, 63-65; Marsh, *The Story of the Jubilee Singers*, 240-241; Higginson, *Army Life in a Black Regiment*, 205; Allen *et al.*, *Slave Songs of the United States*, 91, 100; Burlin, *Negro Folk-Songs*, I, 37-42.

48. Allen *et al.*, *Slave Songs of the United States*, 32-33.

49. *Ibid.*, 30-31; Burlin, *Negro Folk-Songs*, II, 8-9; Fenner, *Religious Folk Songs of the Negro*, 12.

50. Allen *et al.*, *Slave Songs of the United States*, 128-129; Fenner, *Religious Folk Songs of the Negro*, 127; Barton, *Old Plantation Hymns*, 26.

51. Allen *et al.*, *Slave Songs of the United States*, 70, 102-103, 147; Barton, *Old Plantation Hymns*, 9, 17-18, 24; Marsh, *The Story of the Jubilee Singers*, 133, 167; Odum and Johnson, *The Negro And His Songs*, 35.

52. Allen *et al.*, *Slave Songs of the United States*, 102-103.

53. Mary Allen Grissom, compiler, *The Negro Sings A New Heaven* (Chapel Hill, 1930), 73.

54. Marsh, *The Story of the Jubilee Singers*, 179, 186; Allen *et al.*, *Slave Songs of the United States*, 40-41, 44, 146; Barton, *Old Plantation Hymns*, 30.

55. McIlhenny, *Befo' De War Spirituals*, 31.

56. *Gumbo Ya-Ya: A Collection of Louisiana Folk Tales*, compiled by Lyle Saxon, Edward Dreyer, and Robert Tallant from materials gathered by workers of the WPA, Louisiana Writer's Project (Boston, 1945), 242.

57. For examples, see Allen *et al.*, *Slave Songs of the United States*, 40-41, 82, 97, 106-108; Marsh, *The Story of the Jubilee Singers*, 168, 203; Burlin, *Negro Folk-Songs*, II, 8-9; Howard Thurman, *Deep River* (New York, 1945), 19-21.

58. Thurman, *Deep River*, 16-17.

59. Higginson, *Army Life in a Black Regiment*, 202-205. Many of those northerners who came to the South to "uplift" the freedmen were deeply disturbed at the Old Testament emphasis of their religion. H. G. Spaulding complained that the exslaves needed to be introduced to "the light and warmth of the Gospel," and reported that a Union army officer told him: "Those people had enough of the Old Testament thrown at their heads under slavery. Now give them the glorious utterances and practical teachings of the Great Master." Spaulding, "Under the Palmetto," reprinted in Jackson, *The Negro and His Folklore in Nineteenth-Century Periodicals*, 66.

60. Allen *et al.*, *Slave Songs of the United States*, 148; Fenner, *Religious Folk Songs of the Negro*, 21; Marsh, *The Story of the Jubilee Singers*, 134-135; McIlhenny, *Befo' De War Spirituals*, 248-249.

61. *Life and Times of Frederick Douglass*, 159-160; Marsh, *The Story of the Jubilee Singers*, 188.

62. Higginson, *Army Life in a Black Regiment,* 217.

63. Parrish, *Slave Songs of the Georgia Sea Islands,* 247.

64. "Actually, not one spiritual in its primary form reflected interest in anything other than a full life here and now." Fisher, *Negro Slave Songs in the United States,* 137.

65. Barton, *Old Plantation Hymns,* 25; Allen *et al., Slave Songs of the United States,* 94; McKim, "Negro Songs," 149.

66. Higginson, *Army Life in a Black Regiment,* 201-202, 211-212.

67. Robert Redfield, *The Primitive World and Its Transformations* (Ithaca, 1953), 51-53.

68. Elkins, *Slavery,* Chap. III.

69. *Ibid.,* Chap. II; Frank Tannenbaum, *Slave and Citizen* (New York, 1946).

70. E. J. Hobsbawm, *Primitive Rebels* (New York, 1959), Chap. I.

71. C. M. Bowra, *Primitive Song* (London, 1962), 285-286.

• *Eugene D. Genovese, a current historian of ante-bellum slavery and a lively polemicist, has written imaginatively on a variety of important topics in the field: the character of the Southern master class (see p. 262), the comparative analysis of New World slave societies, the merits of proslavery ideology, and the social history of American slaves. Genovese addresses himself in this essay to the need for what Orlando Patterson called interpreting "the social and cultural response of the Blacks to their enslavement." In his discussion of family life, patterns of resistance, and work roles among Southern bondsmen, he faults most previous historians for viewing slaves only as victims and not "as creative participants in a social process." Genovese joins scholars such as Patterson, Stuckey, Levine, and Vincent Harding in complaining about the lack of "a synthetic record of [the Negro's] incessant struggle to escape from the culture as well as the psychological domination of the master class." He asks in the following essay, "What did the slaves do for themselves and how did they do it?"*

American Slaves and Their History

EUGENE D. GENOVESE

The history of the lower classes has yet to be written. The ideological impact of the New Left, the intellectual exigencies of the black liberation movement, and the developing academic concern for the cultural dimension of politics and history have converged to produce the expectation that it will be. If one per cent of the hosannas heaped upon E. P. Thompson's *The Making of the English Working Class* could be translated into disciplined effort to extend its achievement, the future would be bright. And indeed, good work is finally being done, although precious little of it by those who regularly pontificate on the need to rewrite history "from the bottom up."

History written from the bottom up is neither more nor less than history written from the top down: It is not and cannot be good history. To write the story of a nation without taking into consideration the vicissitudes of a majority of its people is simply not a serious undertaking. And yet, it is preposterous to suggest that there could conceivably be anything wrong with writing a book about the ruling class alone, or about one or another elite, or about any segment of society no matter how small. No subject is too small to treat. But a good historian writes well on a small subject while taking account (if only implicitly and without a single direct reference) of the whole, whereas an inferior one confuses the need to isolate a small portion of the whole with the license to assume that that portion thought and acted in isolation. One may, for example, write Southern history by focusing on either blacks or whites, slaves or masters, tenant farmers or landlords; it will be good or bad history if, among other things, the author knows that the one cannot be discussed without a deep understanding of the other. The fate of master and slave was historically intertwined and formed part of a single social process; each in his own way struggled for autonomy—struggled to end his dependence upon the other—but neither could ever wholly succeed. The first problem in the writing of social history lies in this organic antagonism: We tend to see the masters in their own terms, without acknowledgment of their dependence upon the slaves; but we also tend to see the slaves in the masters' terms, without acknowledgment of the extent to which the slaves freed themselves from domination.

There cannot be, therefore, any such thing as "history from the bottom up." A good study of plantation architecture, apart from its contribution to aesthetics, would be one that grasped the social link between the culture of the Big House and that of both the slave quarters and small nonslaveholding farmhouses, for the Big House, whatever else it did, served to impress the humbler men in and out of its orbit. Such a study need never mention the quarters of the farmhouses, but if the essential insight fails or remains undeveloped and abstract, then the entire effort must remain limited. Should it succeed, then it must be ranked as a valuable contribution to the history of Southern society and its constituent races and classes. To consider such a study "elitist" because it concerns itself with upper-class life or eschews moralistic pronouncements is a modern form of absurdity.

There is much to be said for the current notion that blacks will have to write their own history: Black people in the United States have strong claims to separate nationality, and every people must interpret its own history in the light of its own traditions and experience. At the same time, the history of every people must be written from without, if only to provide a necessary corrective in perspective; sooner or later the history of every people must flow from the clash of viewpoints and sensibilities that accompanies both external and internal confrontation. But for the South there is a more compelling reason for black and white scholars to have to live with each other. There is simply no way of learning about either blacks or whites without learning about the other. If it is true, as I suspect, that the next generations of black scholars will bring a special viewpoint to Southern history, then their success or failure will rest, in part, on their willingness to teach us something new about the masters as well as the slaves. He who says the one, is condemned to say the other.

I should like to consider some debilitating assumptions often brought by social historians to the study of the lower classes, and to suggest a way of avoiding the twin elitist notions that the lower classes are generally passive or generally on the brink of insurrection. We have so many books on slavery in the Old South that specialists need to devote full time merely to keeping abreast of the literature. Yet, there is not a single book and only a few scattered articles on life in the quarters—except of course for such primary and undigested sources as the slave narratives and plantation memoirs. A good student might readily be able to answer questions about the economics of the plantation, the life of the planters, the politics of slavery expansionism, or a host of other matters, but he is not likely to know much about slave life, about the relationship of field to house slaves, or about the relationship between the slave driver or foreman and other slaves. To make matters worse, he may well think he knows a good deal, for the literature abounds in undocumented assertions and plausible legends.

The fact remains that there has not been a single study of the driver—the most important slave on the larger plantations—and only a few sketchy and misleading studies of house slaves. So far as the life of the quarters is concerned, it is enough to note that the notion persists, in the face of abundant evidence, that slaves had no family life to speak of. Historians and sociologists, both white and black, have been guilty of reasoning deductively from purely legal evidence—slave marriages were not recognized by law in the United States—and have done little actual research.

I do not propose to discuss the family in detail here, nor house slaves and drivers for that matter, but I should like to touch on all three in order to illustrate a larger point. We have made a great error in the way in which we have viewed slave life, and this error has been perpetuated by both whites and blacks, racists and antiracists. The traditional proslavery view and that of such later apologists for white supremacy as U. B. Phillips have treated the blacks as objects of white benevolence and fear—as people who needed both protection and control—and devoted attention to the ways in which black slaves adjusted to the demands of the master class. Abolitionist propaganda and the later, and now dominant, liberal viewpoint have insisted that the slave regime was so brutal and dehumanizing that blacks should be seen primarily as victims. Both these viewpoints treat black people almost wholly as objects, never as creative participants in a social process, never as half of a two-part subject.

True, abolitionist and liberal views have taken account of the ways in which slaves resisted their masters by shirking their work, breaking tools, or even rebelling, but the proslavery view generally noted that much too, even if within the context of a different interpretation. Neither has ever stopped to consider, for example, that the evidence might reflect less a deliberate attempt at sabotage or alleged Negro inferiority than a set of attitudes toward time, work, and leisure which black people developed partly in Africa and partly in the slave quarters—a set of attitudes which constituted a special case in a general pattern of behavior associated with preindustrial cultures. Preindustrial peoples knew all about hard work and discipline, but their standards were those of neither the factory nor the plantation and were embedded in a radically different culture. Yet, even such sympathetic historians as Kenneth Stampp who give some attention to slaves as subjects and actors, have merely tried to show that slaves exercised some degree of autonomy in their responses to the blows or cajoling of their masters. We have yet to receive a respectful treatment—apart from some brief but suggestive passages in the work of W. E. B. Du Bois, C. L. R. James and perhaps one or two others—of their attempts to achieve an autonomous life within the narrow limits of the slave plantation.[1] We have yet to have a synthetic record of their incessant struggle to escape from the culture as well as the psychological domination of the master class.

In commenting briefly on certain features of family life, house slaves, and drivers, I should like to suggest some of the rich possibilities inherent in an approach that asks much more than "What was done to the slaves?" and, in particular, asks, "What did the slaves do for themselves and how did they do it?" In a more leisurely presentation it would be possible and, indeed, necessary to discuss slave religion, entertainment, songs and dances, and many other things. But perhaps we may settle for a moment on one observation about slave religion.

We are told a great deal about the religious instruction of the slaves, by which it meant the attempt to inculcate a version of Protestant Christianity. Sometimes this instruction is interpreted as a good thing in itself and sometimes as a kind of brainwashing, but we may leave this question aside. Recently, Vincent Harding, following the suggestive probing in Du Bois's work, has offered a different perspective and suggested that the slaves had their own way of taking up Christianity and forging it into a weapon of active resistance.[2] Certainly, we must be struck by the appearance of one or another kind of messianic preacher in almost every slave revolt on record. Professor Harding therefore asks that we look at the slaves as active participants in their own religious experience and not merely as objects being worked on by slaveholding ideologues. This argument may be carried further to suggest that a distinctly black religion, at least in embryo, appeared in the quarters and played a role—the extent and precise content of which we have yet to evaluate—in shaping the daily lives of the slaves. In other words, quite apart from the problem of religion as a factor in overt resistance to slavery, we need to know how the slaves developed a religious life that enabled them to survive as autonomous human beings with a culture of their own within the white master's world.

One of the reasons we know so little about this side of the story—and about all lower-class life—is that it is undramatic. Historians, white and black, conservative, liberal and radical, have a tendency to look for the heroic moments, either to praise or to excoriate them, and to consider ordinary daily life as so much trivia. Yet, if a slave helped to keep himself psychologically intact by breaking his master's hoe, he might also have achieved the same result by a special effort to come to terms with his God, or by loving a woman who shared his burdens, or even by aspiring to be the best worker on the plantation. We normally think of someone who aspires to be a good slave as an Uncle Tom, and maybe we should. But human beings are not so simple. If a slave aspires to a certain excellence within the system, and if his implicit trust in the generous response of the master is betrayed—as often it must be in such a system—then he is likely to be transformed into a rebel. And if so, he is likely to become the most dangerous kind of rebel, first because of his smashed illusions and second because of the skills and self-control he taught himself while appearing on the scene as an Uncle Tom. The historical record of slavery is full of people who were model slaves right up until the moment they killed their overseer, ran away, burned down the Big House, or joined an insurrection.

So what can be said about the decidedly non-Christian element in the religion of the slave quarters? The planters tell us repeatedly that every plantation had its conjurer, its voodoo man, its witch doctor. To the planters this meant a residue of African superstition, and it is, of course, possible by the 1830s all that remained in the slave quarters were local superstitions rather than a continuation of the highly sophisticated religions originally brought from Africa. But the evidence suggests the emergence of an indigenous and unique combination of African and European religious notions, adapted to the specific conditions of slave life by talented and imaginative individuals, which represented an attempt to establish a spiritual life adequate to the task of linking the slaves with the powerful culture of the masters and yet providing them with a high degree of separation and autonomy.

When we know enough of this story we shall know a good deal about the way in which the culture of an oppressed people develops. We often hear the expression "defenseless slaves," but, although any individual at any given moment may be defenseless, a whole people rarely, if ever, is. It may be on the defensive and dangerously exposed, but it almost invariably finds its own ways to survive and fight back. The trouble is that we keep looking for overt rebellious actions—the strike, the revolt, the murder, the arson, the tool-breaking—and often fail to realize that, in given conditions and at particular times, the wisdom of a people and their experience in struggle dictates a different course and an emphasis on holding together both individually and collectively. From this point of view, the most ignorant of the field slaves who followed the conjurer on the plantation was saying no to the boss and seeking an autonomous existence. That the conjurer may, in any one case, have been a fraud and even a kind of extortionist and, in another case, a genuine popular religious leader is, from this point of view, of little importance.

Let us take the family as an illustration. Slave law refused to recognize slave marriages and family ties. In this respect United States slavery was far worse than Spanish American or Luso-Brazilian. In those Catholic cultures the Church demanded and tried to guarantee that slaves be permitted to marry and that the sanctity of the slave family be upheld. As a result, generations of American historians have concluded that American slaves had no family life and that Cuban and Brazilian slaves did. This judgment will not bear examination. The slave trade to the United States was closed early: no later than 1808, except for statistically insignificant smuggling, and, in fact, for most states it ended decades earlier. The rise of the Cotton Kingdom and the great period of slavery expansion followed the closing of the slave trade. Slavery, in the numbers we are accustomed to thinking of, was a product of the period following the end of African importations. The slave force that was liberated during and after the War for Southern Independence was overwhelmingly a slave force born and raised in this country. We have good statistics on the rate of increase of that slave population, and there can be no doubt that it compared roughly to that of the whites—apart from the fact of immigration—and that furthermore, it was unique among New World slave classes. An early end to the slave trade, followed by a boom in cotton and plantation slavery, dictated a policy of encouraging slave births. In contrast, the slave trade remained open to Cuba and to Brazil until the second half of the nineteenth century; as a result, there was little economic pressure to encourage family life and slave-breeding. In Brazil and Cuba, far more men than women were imported from Africa until late in the history of the respective slave regimes; in the Old South, a rough sexual parity was established fairly early. If, therefore, religion and law militated in favor of slave families in Cuba and Brazil and against them in the Old South, economic pressure worked in reverse. The result was a self-reproducing slave force in the United States and nowhere else, so far as the statistics reveal.

It may immediately be objected that the outcome could have reflected breeding rather than family stability. But selective breeding was tried in the Caribbean and elsewhere and never worked; there is no evidence that it was ever tried on a large scale in the South. Abolitionists charged that Virginia and Maryland deliberately raised slaves—not merely encouraged, but actually fostered slave-breeding. There is no evidence. If slave-raising farms existed and if the planters were not complete fools they would have concentrated on recruiting women of childbearing age and used a relatively small number of studs. Sample studies of major slave-exporting counties in Virginia and Maryland show no significant deviations from the parallel patterns in Mississippi or other slave-buying regions.

Now, it is clear that Virginia and Maryland—and other states as well —exported their natural increase for some decades before the war. But this was a process, not a policy; it reflected the economic pressures to supplement a waning income from agriculture by occasional slave sales; it was not incompatible with the encouragement of slave families and, in fact, reinforced it. Similarly, planters in the cotton states could not work their slaves to death and then buy fresh ones, for prices were too high. They had been too high from the very moment the Cotton Kingdom began its westward march, and therefore a tradition of slave-killing never did take root. As time went on, the pressures mounted to provide slaves with enough material and even psychological satisfaction to guarantee the minimum morale needed for reproduction. These standards of treatment—so much food, living space, time off, etc.—became part of the prevailing standard of decency, not easily violated by greedy slaveholders. In some respects the American slave system may have been the worst in the world, as so many writers insist. But in purely material terms, it was probably the best. American slaves were generally fed, clothed, housed, and worked better than those of Cuba, Jamaica, or Brazil.

But the important thing here is that the prevailing standard of decency was not easily violated because the slaves had come to understand their own position. If a master wished to keep his plantation going, he had to learn the limits of his slaves' endurance. If, for example, he decided to ignore the prevailing custom of giving Sunday off or of giving an extended Christmas holiday, his slaves would feel sorely tried and would certainly pay him back with one or another form of wrecking. The slaves remained in a weak position, but they were rarely completely helpless, and by guile, brute courage and a variety of other devices they taught every master just where the line was he dared not cross if he wanted a crop. In precisely this way, slaves took up the masters' interest in their family life and turned it to account. The typical plantation in the South was organized by family unit. Man and wife lived together with children, and within a considerable sphere the man was in fact the man in the house.

Whites violated black family life in several ways. Many families were disrupted by sales, especially in the upper South, where economic pressures were strong. White men on the plantations could and often did violate black women. Nothing can minimize these injustices.

The frequency of sales is extremely hard to measure. Many slaves were troublesome and sold many times over; this inflated the total number of sales but obscured the incidence of individual transfers. The crimes against these black people are a matter of record, and no qualifications can soften their impact. But it is not at all certain that most slaves did not live stable, married lives in the quarters despite the pressures of the market. I do not wish to get into the vexing question of the violation of black women here, but certainly there was enough of it to justify the anger of those who condemned the slave regime on this ground alone. The evidence, however, does not warrant the assumption that a large percentage of black plantation women were so violated. In other words, for a judgment on the moral quality of the regime, this subject is extremely important; for an assessment of the moral life of the slaves, it is much less so.

What the sources show—both the plantation books and letters of the masters, and also the reports of runaway slaves and ex-slaves—is that the average plantation slave lived in a family setting, developed strong family ties, and held the nuclear family as the proper social norm. Planters who often had to excuse others, or even themselves, for breaking up families by sale, would sometimes argue that blacks did not really form deep and lasting attachments, that they lacked strong family sense, that they were naturally promiscuous, and so forth. Abolitionists and ex-slaves would reinforce the prevalent notion by saying that slavery was so horrible, no real family tie could be maintained. Since planters, abolitionists, and ex-slaves all said the same thing, it has usually been taken as the truth. Only it was not.

In the first place, these various sources also say opposite things, which we rarely notice. Planters agonized over the breakup of families and repeatedly expressed regrets and dismay. Often, they went to great lengths to keep families together at considerable expense, for they knew how painful it was to enforce separations. Whether they were motivated by such material considerations as the maintenance of plantation morale or more lofty sentiment is neither here nor there. They often demonstrated that they knew very well how strong the family ties were in the quarters. Planters did everything possible to encourage the slaves to live together in stable units; they recognized that a man was easier to control if he had a wife and children to worry about. The slaves, on their side, behaved variously, of course. Many were, indeed, promiscuous although much of the charge of promiscuity stemmed not so much from actual promiscuity as from sequential polygamy. They did change partners more often than Victorian whites could stomach. (In this respect, they might be considered the great forerunners of the white, middle-class sexual morality of the 1960s.) I stress this side of things—the interest of the master in slave family stability and the effort of the slave to protect his stake in a home, however impoverished—because it is now fashionable to believe that black people came out of slavery with little or no sense of family life. But if so, then we need to know why, during early Reconstruction, so many thousands wandered over the South looking for their spouse or children. We do not know just how many slaves lived as a family or were willing and able to maintain a stable family life during slavery. But the number was certainly great, whatever the percentage, and as a result, the social norm that black people carried from slavery to freedom was that of the nuclear family. If it is true that the black family has disintegrated in the ghettos—and we have yet to see conclusive evidence—then the source will have to be found in the conditions of economic and social oppression imposed upon blacks during recent decades. The slave experience, for all its tragic disruptions, pointed toward a stable postslavery family life, and recent scholarship demonstrates conclusively that the Reconstruction and post-Reconstruction black experience carried forward the acceptance of the nuclear family norm.[3]

Let us consider the role of the male and the legend of the matriarchy. Almost all writers on slavery describe the slave man as "a guest in the house" who could have no role beyond the purely sexual. The slave narratives and the diaries and letters of white plantation owners tell us something else. His position was undeniably precarious and frustrating. If his wife was to be whipped, he had to stand by and watch; he could not fully control his own children; he was not a breadwinner in the usual sense; and, in a word, there were severe restrictions imposed upon the manifestations of what we somewhat erroneously call manliness. But, both masters and ex-slaves tell us about some plantations on which certain women were not easily or often punished because it was readily understood that, to punish the woman, it would be necessary to kill her man first. These cases were the exception, but they tell us at the start that the man felt a duty to protect his woman. If circumstances conspired to prevent his fulfilling that duty, those circumstances often included his woman's not expecting it and, indeed, consoling him about the futility of such a gesture. We cannot know what was said between a man and a woman when they lay down together at night after such outrages, but there are enough hints in the slave narratives to suggest that both knew what a man could do, as well as what he "should" do, especially when there were children to consider. Many scholars suggest that black women treated their men with contempt for not doing what circumstances made impossible. This is a deduction from tenuous assumptions; it is not a demonstrated fact.

Beyond that, the man of the house did do various things. He trapped and hunted animals to supplement the diet in the quarters, and in this small but important and symbolic way he was a breadwinner. He organized the garden plot and presided over the division of labor with his wife. He disciplined his children—or divided that function with his wife as people in other circumstances do—and generally was the source of authority in the cabin. This relationship within the family was not always idyllic. In many instances, his authority over both wife and children was imposed by force. Masters forbade men to hit their wives and children and whipped them for it; but they did it anyway and often. And there is not much evidence that women readily ran to the master to ask that her husband be whipped for striking her. The evidence on these matters is fragmentary, but it suggests that the men asserted their authority as best they could; the women expected to have to defer to their husbands in certain matters; and that both tried hard to keep the master out of their lives. The conditions were unfavorable, and perhaps many men did succumb and in one way or another became emasculated. But we might also reflect on the ways in which black men and women conspired to maintain their own sense of dignity and their own autonomy by settling things among themselves and thereby asserting their own personalities.

Black women have often been praised—and justly so—for their strength and determination in holding their families together during slavery, when the man was supposedly put aside or rendered irrelevant. It is time, I think, to praise them for another thing they seem to have been able to do in large numbers: to support a man they loved in ways deep enough and varied enough to help him resist the mighty forces for dehumanization and emasculation. Without the support of their women, not many black men could have survived; but with it—and there is plenty of testimony that they often had it—many could and did.

If our failure to see the plantation from the vantage point of the slave quarters has led us to substitute abstractions for research on the slave family, so has it saddled us with unsubstantiated and erroneous ideas on house slaves. According to the legend, house slaves were the Uncle Toms of the system—a privileged caste apart, contemptuous of the field hands, jealous of their place in the affection or at least eye of the white master and mistress, and generally speaking, finks, sellouts, and white man's niggers. Like most stereotypes, this one has its kernel of truth. There were, indeed, many house slaves who fit the description. But we might begin by considering a small fact. Half the slaves in the rural South lived on farms of twenty or fewer slaves; another twenty-five per cent lived on plantations with twenty to fifty slaves. Only twenty-five per cent, in other words, lived on plantations of fifty or more, and of those, the overwhelming majority lived on units of less than one hundred—that is, on units of less than twenty slave families. In short, the typical house slave serviced either a small farm or, at best, a moderate plantation. Only a few lived and worked on plantations large enough to permit the formation of a separate group of house slaves—of enough house slaves to form a caste unto themselves.

Our idea of the fancy-dressed, uppity, self-inflated house slave who despised the field blacks and identified with the whites is a product of the relatively small group who lived in the towns and cities like Charleston, New Orleans, and Richmond. These townhouse slaves and a tiny group of privileged house slaves on huge plantations could and sometimes did form a separate caste with the attributes described in the literature. Certainly, the great planters and their families, who left most of the white-family records that have been relied on as the major source, would most likely have remembered precisely these slaves. Even these blacks deserve a more careful look than they have received, for they were much more complicated people than we have been led to believe. But, the important point is that the typical house slave was far removed from this condition. He, or more likely she, worked with perhaps one to three or four others on an estate too small to permit any such caste formation.

If the typical house slave was an Uncle Tom and a spoiled child of the whites, then we need to be told just why so many of them turn up in the records of runaways. There is abundant evidence from the war years. We hear much about the faithful retainers who held the Yankees off from the Big House, or protected young missus, or hid the family silver. Such types existed and were not at all rare. But they do not appear to have been nearly so numerous as those house slaves who joined the field slaves in fleeing to the Yankee lines when the opportunity arose. The best source on this point is the planters themselves, who were shocked at the defection of their favorite slaves. They could readily understand the defection of the field hands, whom they considered stupid and easily led, but they were unable to account for the flight, sometimes with expressions of regret and sometimes with expressions of anger and hatred, of their house slaves. They had always thought they knew these blacks, loved them, were loved by them, and they considered them part of the family. One day they learned that they had been deceiving themselves and living intimately with people they did not know at all. The house slaves, when the opportunity presented itself, responded with the same range of behavior as did the field slaves. They proved themselves just as often rebellious and independent as they did docile and loyal.

This display of independence really was nothing new. If it is true that house slaves were often regarded as traitors to the black cause during slave rebellions, it is also true that their appearance in those rebellions was not as rare as we are led to believe. A black rebel leader told Denmark Vesey and his followers not to trust the house slaves because they were too tied to the whites, but we ought also note that some of the toughest and most devoted of those leaders in Charleston in 1822 were themselves house slaves. In particular, the great scandal of the event in Charleston was the role played by the most trusted slaves, of the governor of South Carolina. Certainly, the role of the house slave was always ambiguous and often treacherous. But if many house slaves betrayed their fellows, many others collected information in the Big House and passed it on to the quarters. We know how well-informed the field slaves were about movements of Yankee troops during the war; we know that these field slaves fled to the Yankee lines with uncanny accuracy in timing and direction. Probably no group was more influential in providing the necessary information than those very house slaves who are so often denigrated.

The decision of slaves, whether house slaves or not, to protect whites during slave insurrections or other catastrophes, hardly proves them to have been Toms. The master-slave relationship, especially when it occurred in the intimacies of the Big House, was always profoundly ambivalent. Many of the same slaves who protected their masters and mistresses from harm and thereby asserted their own humanity were anything but docile creatures of the whites.

Since most house slaves worked on estates too small for a separate existence, their social life was normally down in the quarters and not apart or with the whites. The sexes were rarely evenly matched in the house, where women predominated, and even when they were, the group was too small for natural pairing off. A large number of house slaves married field hands or, more likely, the more skilled artisans or workers. Under such circumstances, the line between house slaves and field hands was not sharp for most slaves. Except on the really large units, house slaves were expected to help out in the fields during picking season and during emergencies. The average house slave got periodic tastes of field work and had little opportunity to cultivate airs.

There are two general features to the question of house slaves that deserve comment: first, there is the ambiguity of their situation and its resultant ambivalence toward whites; the other is the significance of the house slave in the formation of a distinctly Afro-American culture. The one point I should insist upon in any analysis of the house slave is ambivalence. People, black and white, slave and master, thrown together in the intimacy of the Big House, had to emerge loving and hating each other. Life together meant sharing each other's pains and problems, confiding secrets, having company when no one else would do, being forced to help one another in a multitude of ways. It also meant jointly experiencing, but in tragically opposite ways, the full force of lordship and bondage: that is, the full force of petty tyranny imposed by one woman on another; of expecting someone to be at your beck and call regardless of her own feelings and wishes; of being able to take out one's frustrations and disappointments on an innocent bystander, who would no doubt be guilty enough of something since servants are always falling short of the expectations.

To illustrate the complexity of black slave behavior in the Big House, let us take a single illustration. It is typical in the one sense that it catches the condition of ambiguity and of entwined, yet hostile, lives. Beyond that, it is of course unique, as is all individual experiences. Eliza L. Magruder was the niece of a deceased planter and politician from the Natchez, Mississippi, region and went to live with her aunt Olivia, who managed the old plantation herself. Miss Eliza kept a diary for the years 1846 and 1847 and then again for 1854 and 1857.[4] Possibly, she kept a diary for the intermittent years which has been lost. In any case, she has a number of references to a slave girl, Annica, and a few to another, Lavinia. We have here four women, two white and two black, two mistresses and two servants, thrown together in a single house and forced on each other's company all year long, year after year.

On April 17, 1846, Miss Eliza wrote in her diary more or less in passing, "Aunt Olivia whipped Annica for obstinacy." This unladylike chastisement had followed incidents in which Annica had been "impudent." About a month later, on September 11, Annica took another whipping—for "obstinacy." Miss Eliza appears to have been a bit squeamish, for her tone, if we read it correctly, suggests that she was not accustomed to witnessing such unpleasantness. On January 24, 1847, she confided to her diary, "I feel badly. Got very angry and whipped Lavinia. O! for government over my temper." But the world progresses, and so did Miss Eliza's fortitude in the face of other people's adversity. When her diary resumed in 1854, she had changed slightly: the squeamishness had diminished. Annica had not changed: she had remained her old, saucy self. October 26, 1854: "Boxed Annica's ears for impertinence."

Punctuated by this war of wills, daily life went on. Annica's mother lived in Jackson, Mississippi, and mother and daughter kept in touch. Since Annica could neither read nor write, Miss Eliza served as her helpmate and confidant. December 5, 1854: "I wrote for Annica to her mother." Mamma wrote back in due time, no doubt to Annica's satisfaction, but also to her discomfiture. As Miss Eliza observed on January 25, 1855, "Annica got a letter from her mammy which detected her in a lie. O! that negroes generally were more truthful." So, we ought not to be surprised that Miss Eliza could not write without a trace of the old squeamishness on July 1, 1855, "I whipt Annica."

The impertinent Annica remained undaunted. November 29, 1855: "Aunt Olivia gave Annica a good scolding and made her ask my pardon and will punish her otherwise." Perhaps we should conclude that Annica's atrocious behavior had earned the undying enmity of the austere white ladies, but some doubts may be permitted. On July 24, 1856, several of their neighbors set out on a trip to Jackson, Mississippi, where, it will be recalled, Annica's mother lived. Aunt Olivia, with Miss Eliza's concurrence, sent Annica along for a two-week holiday and provided ten dollars for her expenses. On August 3, Annica returned home in time for breakfast. In the interim Miss Eliza had Lavinia as an object of wrath, for Lavinia had "very much provoked" her by lying and by being impertinent. "Aunt Olivia boxed her ears for it." Lavinia's day of glory did not last; it was not long before Annica reclaimed full possession of the title of the most impudent nigger in the Big House. On September 4, 1856, "Annica was very impertinent, and I boxed her ears." Three days later, wrote Miss Eliza, "I kept Annica in in the afternoon for impudence." The next day (September 8) Miss Eliza told Aunt Olivia about Annica's misconduct. "She reproved her for it and will I suppose punish her in some way." Life traveled on into November, when on the tenth day of the month, "Aunt Olivia whipt Annica for impertinence."

At this point, after a decade of impudence, impertinence, obstinacy, whipping, and ear-boxing, one might expect that Annica would have been dispatched to the cotton fields by women who could not abide her. But she remained in the Big House. And what shall we make of such incidents as that which occurred on the night of December 29, 1856, when poor Annica was ill and in pain? It is not so much that Miss Eliza sat up with her, doing what she could; it is rather that she seemed both concerned and conscious of performing a simple duty. On the assumption that the illness left Annica weak for a while, Miss Eliza of course still had Lavinia. January 30, 1857: "I boxed Lavinia's ears for coming up late when I told her not."

On April 23, 1857, Annica greatly pleased Miss Eliza by making her a white bonnet. But by April 26, Annica was once again making trouble: "Aunt Olivia punished Annica by keeping her in her room all afternoon." And the next day: "Aunt Olivia had had Annica locked up in the garret all day. I pray it may humble her and make further punishment unnecessary."

On August 18, 1857, "Aunt Olivia held a court of enquiry, but didn't find out who ripped my pattern." There is no proof that Annica did it; still one wonders. Two weeks later in Miss Eliza's Sunday school, "Annica was strongly tempted to misbehave. I brought her in however." The entries end there.

Let us suppose the ladies had carried their household into the war years: What then? It would take little imagination to see Annica's face and to hear her tone as she marched into the kitchen to announce her departure for the federal lines. It would not even take much imagination to see her burning the house down. Yet, she had never been violent, and we should not be too quick to assume that she would easily have left the only home she had known as an adult and the women who wrote letters to her mamma, exchanged confidences, and stayed up with her on feverish nights. The only thing we can be sure of is that she remained impudent to the day she died.

What I think this anecdote demonstrates above all is the ambivalence inherent in the Big House relationship and the stubborn struggle for individuality that house slaves, whip or no whip, were capable of. Yet it may also hint at another side and thereby help explain why so many black militants, like so many historians before them, are quick to condemn the whole house-slave legacy as one to be exorcized. The house slaves were, indeed, close to the whites, and of all the black groups they exhibited the most direct adherence to certain white cultural standards. In their religious practices, their dress, their manners, and their prejudices they were undoubtedly the black group most influenced by Euro-American culture. But this kind of cultural accommodation was by no means the same thing as docility or Uncle Tomism. Even a relatively assimilated house slave could and normally did strike back, assert independence, and resist arbitrariness and oppression. We are today accustomed to thinking of black nationalists as "militants" and civil rights integrationists as "moderates," "conservatives," or something worse. Yet, Dr. Martin Luther King, Jr., and his followers were and are militant integrationists, prepared to give up their lives for their people; on the other hand, there are plenty of black nationalists who are anything but militant. The tension between integration and separatism has always rent the black community, but now it has led to confuse questions of militancy with those of nationalism. In fact, the combinations vary; there is no straight identification of either integrationists or separatists with either militancy or accommodation. Field hands or house slaves could be either docile, "accommodating," or rebellious, and in all probability most were all at once.

If today the house slaves have a bad press, it is largely because of their cultural assimilationism, from which it is erroneously deduced that they were docile. The first point may be valid; the second is not. LeRoi Jones, for example, in his brilliant book, *Blues People*, argues convincingly that field slaves had forged the rudiments of a distinct Afro-American culture whereas the house slaves largely took over the culture of the whites. He writes primarily about black music, but he might easily extend his analysis to language and other fields. There are clearly two ways of looking at this side of the house-slave experience. On the one hand, the house slaves reinforced white culture in the slave quarters; they were one of the Americanizing elements in the black community. On the other hand, they wittingly or unwittingly served as agents of white repression of an indigenous Afro-American national culture. Of course, both these statements are really the same; it is merely that they differ in their implicit value judgments. But we ought to remember that this role did not reduce the house slave to Uncle Tomism. Rather, it was played out by house slaves who were in their own way often quite rebellious and independent in their behavior. And therefore, even these slaves, notwithstanding their assimilationist outlook and action, also contributed in no small degree to the tradition

of survival and resistance to oppression that today inspires the black
liberation movement.

If today we are inclined to accept uncritically the contemptuous attitude that some critics have toward the house slave, we might ponder
the reflections of the great black pianist, Cecil Taylor. Taylor was
speaking in the mid-1960s—a century after slavery—but he was speaking
of his own father in a way that I think applies to what might be said of
house slaves. Taylor was talking to A. B. Spellman, as reported in
Spellman's book, *Four Lives in the Bebop Business:*

> Music to me was in a way holding on to Negro culture, be-
> cause there wasn't much of it around. My father has a great store
> of knowledge about black folklore. He could talk about how it
> was with the slaves in the 1860s, about the field shouts and
> hollers, about myths of black people . . . . He worked out in
> Long Island for a State Senator. He was a house servant and a
> chef at the Senator's sanatorium for wealthy mental wrecks. And
> actually it was my father more than the Senator himself who
> raised the Senator's children . . . .
> And I really used to get dragged at my father for taking such
> shit off these people. I didn't dig his being a house servant. I
> really didn't understand my old man; well, you're my generation
> and you know the difference between us and our fathers. Like,
> they had to be strong men to take what they took. But of course
> we didn't see it that way. So that I feel now that I really didn't
> understand my father, who was a really lovely cat. He used to
> tell me to stay cool, not to get excited. He had a way of letting
> other people display their emotions while keeping control of his
> own. People used to say to me, "Cecil, you'll never be the
> gentleman your father was." That's true. My father was quite a
> gentleman . . . . I wish that I had taken down more about all
> that he knew about black folklore, because that's lost too; he
> died in 1961.[5]

We may end with another misunderstood group of slaves—the
drivers. These black slave foremen were chosen by the master to work
under his direction or that of an overseer and to keep the hands moving. They would rouse the field slaves in the morning and check their
cabins at night; would take responsibility for their performance; and
often, would be the ones to lay the whip across their backs. In the
literature the drivers appear as ogres, monsters, betrayers, and sadists.
Sometimes they were. Yet, Mrs. Willie Lee Rose, in her book, *Rehearsal for Reconstruction,* notes that it was the drivers in the Sea

Islands who kept the plantations together after the masters had fled the approach of the Yankees, who kept up discipline, and who led the blacks during those difficult days. Now, it is obvious that if the drivers were what they have been reported as having been, they would have had their throats cut as soon as their white protectors had left. In my own research for the war years I have found repeatedly, almost monotonously, that when the slaves fled the plantations or else took over plantations deserted by the whites, the drivers emerged as the leaders. Moreover, the runaway records from the North and from Canada reveal that a number of drivers were among those who successfully escaped the South.

One clue to the actual state of affairs may be found in the agricultural journals for which many planters and overseers wrote about plantation matters. Overseers often complained bitterly that masters trusted their drivers more than they trusted them. They charged that quite often overseers would be fired at the driver's instigation and that, in general, masters were too close to their drivers and too hostile and suspicious toward their white overseers. The planters did not deny the charges; rather, they admitted them and defended themselves by arguing that the drivers were slaves who had earned their trust and that they had to have some kind of check on their overseers. Overseers were changed every two or three years on most plantations whereas drivers remained in their jobs endlessly. The normal state of affairs was for any given driver to remain in his position while a parade of overseers came and went.

It had to be so. The slaves had to be controlled if production was to be on schedule, but only romantics could think that a whip alone could effect that result. The actual amount of work done and the quality of life on the plantation was the result of a compromise between masters and slaves. It was a grossly unfair and one-sided compromise, with the master holding a big edge, but the slaves did not simply lie down and take whatever came. They had their own ways of foot-dragging, dissembling, delaying, and sabotaging. The role of the driver was to minimize the friction by mediating between the Big House and the quarters. On the one hand he was the master's man: he obeyed orders, inflicted punishments, and stood for authority and discipline. On the other hand, he could and did tell the master that the overseer was too harsh, too irregular; that he was incapable of holding the respect of the hands; that he was a bungler. The slaves generally knew just how much they had to put up with under a barbarous labor system but they also knew what even that system regarded as going too far. The driver was their voice in the Big House as well as the master's voice in the quarters.

Former slaves tell us of drivers who were sadistic monsters, but they also tell us of drivers who did everything possible to soften punishments and to protect the slaves as best they could. It was an impossible situation, but there is little evidence that drivers were generally hated by the field hands. The selection of a driver was a difficult matter for a master. First, the driver had to be a strong man, capable of bullying rather than being bullied. Second, he had to be uncommonly intelligent and capable of understanding a good deal about plantation management. A driver had to command respect in the quarters. It would be possible to get along for a while with a brutal driver who could rule by fear, but generally, planters understood that respect and acquiescence were as important as fear, and that a driver had to do more than make others afraid of him. It was then necessary to pick a man who had leadership qualities in the eyes of the slaves.

The drivers commanded respect in various ways. Sometimes they became preachers among the slaves and got added prestige that way. Sometimes, possibly quite often, they acted as judge and jury in the quarters. Disputes among slaves arose often, generally about women and family matters. If there were fights or bitter quarrels, and if they were called to the attention of the overseer or the master, the end would be a whipping for one or more participants. Under such circumstances, the driver was the natural choice of the slaves themselves to arbitrate knotty problems. With such roles in and out of the quarters, it is no wonder that so many drivers remained leaders during and after the war when the blacks had the choice of discarding them and following others.

Every plantation had two kinds of so-called "bad niggers." The first kind were those so designated by the masters because they were recalcitrant. The second kind were those so designated by the slaves themselves. These were slaves who may or may not have troubled the master directly but who were a problem to their fellow slaves because they stole, or bullied, or abused other men's women. The drivers were in a position to know what was happening in the quarters and to intervene to protect weaker or more timid slaves against these bullies. In short, the drivers' position was highly ambiguous and on balance was probably more often than not positive from the slave point of view. Whatever the intentions of the master, even in the selection of his own foremen—his own men, as it were—the slaves generally were not passive, not objects, but active agents who helped shape events, even if within narrow limits and with great difficulty.

We know that there were not many slave revolts in the South, and that those that did occur were small and local affairs. There were good reasons for the low incidence of rebellion: In general, the balance of forces was such that revolt was suicide. Under such conditions, black slaves struggled to live and to make some kind of life for themselves. If their actions were less bombastic and heroic than romantic historians would like us to believe, they were nonetheless impressive in their assertion of resourcefulness, dignity, and a strong sense of self and community. Had they not been, the fate of black America after emancipation would have been even grimmer than it was. For the most part the best that the slaves could do was live, not merely physically but with as much inner autonomy as was humanly possible.

Every man has his own judgment of heroism, but we might reflect on the kind of heroism alluded to by Cecil Taylor in his moving tribute to his father. There are moments in the history of every people —and sometimes these historical moments are centuries—in which they cannot do more than succeed in keeping themselves together and maintaining themselves as human beings with a sense of individual dignity and collective identity. Slavery was such a moment for black people in America, and their performance during it bequeathed a legacy that combined many negative elements to be exorcised[6] and repudiated with decisive elements of community self-discipline. If one were to tax even the privileged house slaves or drivers with the question, "Where were you when your people were groaning under the lash," they could, if they chose, answer with a paraphrase of the Abbé Sieyès, but proudly and without his cynicism, "We were with our people, and together we survived."

NOTES

This essay was originally published in *New York Review of Books*, Dec. 3, 1970, pp. 34-43.

1. See, e.g., C. L. R. James, "The Atlantic Slave Trade and Slavery: Some Interpretations of Their Significance in the Development of the United States and the Western World," *Amistad*, #1 (Vintage Books, 1970). Du Bois's writings are full of important ideas and hypotheses. See especially *Black Reconstruction in America* and *Souls of Black Folk*.

2. Vincent Harding, "Religion and Resistance Among Ante-Bellum Negroes, 1800–1860," August Meier and Elliott Rudwick, eds., *The Making of Black America* 1 (New York, 1969), 179-197.

3. Herbert Gutman has presented several papers to scholarly meetings and is close to completing a major book on the historical development of the black family from slavery to World War I. I am indebted to him for allowing me to see the manuscript in progress and for discussing the data with me.

4. Ms. diary in Louisiana State University library, Baton Rouge, La.

5. A. B. Spellman, *Four Lives in the Bebop Business* (New York, 1966), pp. 49-50.

6. I have discussed some of these negative features in "The Legacy of Slavery and the Roots of Black Nationalism," *Studies on the Left*, 6 (Nov.-Dec., 1966), 3-26. I stand by much of what I wrote there, but the essay is doubtless greatly weakened by a failure to appreciate black slave culture and its political implications. As a result, the political story I tried to tell is dangerously distorted. Still, that legacy of slavishness remains an important part of the story, and I think I identified some of its features correctly. I am indebted to many colleagues and friends for their criticism, without which I could not have arrived at the reconsiderations on which the present essay is based; in particular, the criticism of George Rawick has been indispensable.

III: THE MASTER

• When the Revolutionary generation made its appearance, slavery was still a national institution. By the time the last major Revolutionary figures had passed from the political stage early in the nineteenth century, slavery had become sectionalized—restricted to the Southern and Border states. Most Northern states by 1800 were well along the road to abolition without any accompanying social upheaval. Even in the South, where many leaders in the American struggle for independence proposed eventual emancipation, men such as Jefferson denounced slavery and searched for methods of eliminating it gradually. Yet Southern critics of the institution could not stem the rising tide of support for maintaining Negro slavery within their region. Nor did they succeed in devising means of achieving its abolition that they felt comfortable enough advocating publicly, much less enacting into law. William W. Freehling examines the mixture of failure and achievement in the Founding Fathers' response to the problem and points out the quandary they confronted when trying to cope with the entire question of Negro bondage.

The Founding Fathers and Slavery

WILLIAM W. FREEHLING

Only a few years ago, in a historical age now grown as arcadian as Thomas Jefferson himself, no man needed to defend the Founding Fathers on slavery. However serious were their sins and however greedy seemed their pursuits, the men who made the American Revolution

From William W. Freehling, "The Founding Fathers and Slavery," *The American Historial Review*, Vol. 77 (February 1972), pp. 81-93. Reprinted from *The American Historical Review*, Vol. 77, pp. 81-93 by permission of William W. Freehling.

were deemed to have placed black slavery at bay. Patriots such as George Washington, historians used to point out, freed their slaves. If Jefferson emancipated few of his, the condemnation of Jeffersonian ideology and the curse of a declining economy were fast driving Virginia's slavery to smash. Only the fabulous profits made possible by Whitney's invention of the cotton gin and the reactionary abstractions perpetuated by Calhoun's repudiation of Jefferson breathed life into the system and waylaid the Fathers' thrust toward peaceful abolition.

This happy tale, once so important and so widely believed, now lies withered by a decade of attack. Scholars such as Robert McColley, Staughton Lynd, William Cohen, and Winthrop Jordan have assaulted every aspect of the old interpretation.[1] Some revisionists write to correct excesses in the former view. Others are driven by a New Leftist contempt for reformers who repudiate radicalism and a modern-day repugnance for liberals contaminated by racism. Whatever their separate reasons and however qualified their individual positions, these scholars, taken together, have hammered out a new image of the Founding Fathers. The image is not attractive. In an era of racial turmoil, the racist taints portrayed by Jordan seem even more grotesque than the grasping materialism described by Beard.

The Declaration of Independence, it is now argued, was a white man's document that its author rarely applied to his or to any slaves. The Constitution created aristocratic privilege while consolidating black bondage. Virginia shrank from abolition, for slave prices were too high and race fears too great. Jefferson himself suspected blacks were innately inferior. He bought and sold slaves. He advertised for fugitives. He ordered lashes well laid on. He lived in the grand manner, burying prayers for freedom under an avalanche of debt. In all these evasions and missed opportunities Jefferson spoke for his age. For whatever the virtues of the Founding Fathers, concludes the new view, they hardly put slavery on the road to ultimate extinction. It seems fitting, then, that when Southerners turned their backs on the Declaration and swung toward reaction in the wake of the Missouri crisis, the sage of Monticello himself helped point the way.

Many admirers of Jefferson, aware of a brighter side, scorn this judgment and yearn for a reassessment. The following essay, while in sympathy with their position, is not written for their reasons. More is at stake than Thomas Jefferson; indeed Jefferson's agonized positions on slavery are chiefly important as the supreme embodiment of a generation's travail. Moreover, the historian's task is not to judge but to explain; and the trouble with the new condemnatory view is not so much that it is a one-sided judgment of the Founding Fathers as that it distorts the process by which American slavery was abolished. The new charge that the Founding Fathers did next to nothing about bondage is as misleading as the older notion that they almost did everything. The abolitionist process proceeded slowly but inexorably from 1776 to 1860: slowly in part because of what Jefferson and his contemporaries did not do, inexorably in part because of what they did. The impact of the Founding Fathers on slavery, like the extent to which the American Revolution was revolutionary, must be seen in the long run, not in terms of what changed in the late eighteenth century but in terms of how the Revolutionary experience changed the whole of American antebellum history. Any such view must place Thomas Jefferson and his contemporaries, for all their ironies and missed opportunities, back into the creeping American antislavery process.

If men were evaluated in terms of dreams rather than deeds, everyone would concede the antislavery credentials of the Founding Fathers. No American Revolutionary could square the principles of the Declaration with the perpetuation of human bondage. Only a few men of 1776 considered the evil of slavery permanently necessary. None dared proclaim the evil a good. Most looked forward to the day when the curse could be forever erased from the land. "The love of justice and the love of country," Jefferson wrote Edward Coles in 1814, "plead equally the cause of these people, and it is a moral reproach to us that they should have pleaded it so long in vain."[2]

If the Founding Fathers unquestionably dreamed of universal American freedom, their ideological posture was weighed down equally unquestionably with conceptions of priorities, profits, and prejudices that would long make the dream utopian. The master passion of the age was not with extending liberty to blacks but with erecting republics for whites. Creative energies poured into designing a political City on the Hill; and the blueprints for utopia came to be the federal Constitution and American union. When the slavery issue threatened the Philadelphia Constitutional Convention, the Deep South's ultimatums were quickly met. When the Missouri crisis threatened the Union, Jefferson and fellow spirits beat a retreat. This pattern of valuing the Union more than abolition—of marrying the meaning of America to the continuation of a particular government—would persist, producing endless compromises and finally inspiring Lincoln's war.

The realization of the Founding Fathers' antislavery dream was blocked also by the concern for property rights articulated in their Declaration. Jefferson's document at once denounced slave chains as immoral and sanctioned slave property as legitimate. It made the slave's right to freedom no more "natural" than the master's right to property. Liberty for blacks became irrevocably tied to compensation for whites; and if some proposed paying masters for slaves, no one conceived of compensating South Carolina planters for the fabulous swamp estates emancipation would wreck.

The financial cost of abolition, heavy enough by itself, was made too staggering to bear by the Founding Fathers' racism, an ideological hindrance to antislavery no less important than their sense of priorities and their commitment to property. Here again Jefferson typified the age. As Winthrop Jordan has shown, Jefferson suspected that blacks had greater sexual appetites and lower intellectual faculties than did whites. This racism was never as hidebound as its twentieth-century varieties. Jefferson kept an open mind on the subject and always described innate differences as but his suspicion. Still it is significant, as Merrill Peterson points out, that Jefferson suspected blacks were inferior rather than suspecting blacks were equal.[3] These suspicions, together with Jefferson's painfully accurate prophecy that free blacks and free whites could not live harmoniously in America for centuries, made him and others tie American emancipation to African colonization. The alternative appeared to be race riot and sexual chaos. The consequence, heaping the cost of colonization on the cost of abolition, made the hurdles to emancipation seem unsurmountable.

Jefferson and the men of the Revolution, however, continually dreamed of leaping ahead when the time was ripe. In 1814, while lamenting his own failure, Jefferson urged others to take up the crusade. "I had always hoped," he wrote Edward Coles, "that the younger generation receiving their early impressions after the flame of liberty had been kindled in every breast . . . would have sympathized with oppression wherever found, and proved their love of liberty beyond their own share of it." As late as 1824, five years after his retreat in the Missouri crisis, Jefferson suggested a federally financed postnati abolition scheme that would have ended slavery faster than the plan proposed by his grandson, Thomas Jefferson Randolph, in the famed Virginia slavery debate of 1832.[4]

The ideological stance of Jefferson and other Founding Fathers on slavery, then, was profoundly ambivalent. On the one hand they were restrained by their overriding interest in creating the Union, by their concern for property rights, and by their visions of race war and miscegenation. On the other hand they embraced a revolutionary ideology that made emancipation inescapable. The question is, How was this theoretical ambivalence resolved in practical action?

The answer, not surprisingly, is also ambivalent. Whenever dangers to Union, property, or racial order seemed to them acute, the Founding Fathers did little. In the short run, especially in those Deep Southern states where the going was stickiest, they did almost nothing. But whenever abolition dangers seemed to them manageable, Jefferson and his contemporaries moved effectively, circumscribing and crippling the institution and thereby gutting its long-range capacity to endure.

The revisionist view of the Founding Fathers is at its best in emphasizing slavery's short-run strength in Jefferson's South. In Virginia both secure slave prices and frenzied race fears made emancipation a distant goal. Jefferson as legislator did no more than draft abolitionist resolutions, and his revisions of the Virginia slave code did little to ease the lot of slaves and something to intensify the plight of free blacks. Jefferson's proposed clause, requiring a white woman who had a black child to leave the state within a year or be placed "out of the protection of the laws," speaks volumes on why abolition came hard in Virginia. South of Virginia, where percentages of slaves and profits from staple crops ran higher, abolition was more remote. Planters who worked huge gangs of slaves in pestilential Georgia and South Carolina's lowlands never proposed peacefully accepting the end of their world.

The federal Constitution of 1787 also reflected slavery's short-run strength. Garrison's instinct to consign that document to the flames was exactly right, for the Constitution perpetually protected an institution the Fathers liked to call temporary. Safeguards included the three-fifths clause, destined to help make the minority South political masters of the nation for years, and the fugitive slave clause, destined to help return to thralldom men who had risked everything for freedom. Moreover, to lure Georgia and South Carolina into the Union, the Fathers agreed to allow any state to reopen the African slave trade for twenty years. When South Carolina seized the option from 1803 to 1807 the forty thousand imported blacks and their hundreds of thousands of slave descendants paid an awesome price for the creation of the white man's republic.

After the Constitution was ratified, slavery again showed its strength by expanding over the West. "The years of slavery's supposed decline,"

Robert McColley points out, "were in fact the years of its greatest expansion."[5] In the age of Jefferson black bondage spread across Kentucky and engulfed Alabama and Mississippi. Furthermore, Jefferson as president acquired slave Louisiana, and Jefferson as elder statesman gave his blessings to the resulting diffusion of the system. If in the 1780s Jefferson had believed, as he did in 1819, that diffusing slavery made it more humane, the antislavery clause in the Northwest Ordinance might have been scotched and this essay could not have been written.

Slavery showed its strength not only in Jefferson's Virginia legislature, Philadelphia's Constitutional Convention, and Louisiana's black deltas but also at Monticello itself. By freeing their slaves George Washington and John Randolph lived up to Revolutionary ideals. These men, however, were exceptions. Thomas Jefferson, who freed nine while blithely piling up debts that precluded freeing the rest, was the rule. The plantation life style, with its elegant manner and extravagant tastes, lessened the chance of reducing debts and allowing quick manumission on a massive scale. That life style, in Virginia and throughout the South, was as integral a part of slavery as was South Carolina's hunger for Africans and the Southwest's commitment to cotton.

The master of Monticello, finally, revealed the towering practical strength of slavery in the notorious case of Sally Hemings, his mulatto house servant. Those who enjoy guessing whether Jefferson sired Sally's many offspring can safely be left to their own speculations. The evidence is wildly circumstantial and the issue of dubious importance. Of greater significance is the way Jefferson and his contemporaries handled the ugly controversy. Alexander Hamilton could cheerfully confess to ellicit relations with a white woman and continue with his career. Jefferson's supporters had to ward off all talk of the embarrassing Sally, for interracial sex would ruin anyone's reputation. Nor could Jefferson handle the problem resolutely in the privacy of his own mansion. Firm action would, as Dumas Malone points out, "have looked like a confession that something was wrong on the mountain."[6] Better to look the other way as Sally's light-skinned children multiplied. Better to keep blacks enchained for a time than risk a nation polluted by allegedly lascivious Sallys. Better, in short, to live uneasily in a corrupted City on the Hill than blurt out the full horror of America's nightmare.[7]

The old view, then, that slavery was dying in Jefferson's South cannot withstand the revisionist onslaught. The system was strong and, in places, growing stronger; and the combination of economic interest, concern for the Union, life style, and race prejudice made emancipationists rare in Virginia and almost nonexistent in South Carolina. Jefferson, no immediate emancipationist, refused as president to endorse an antislavery poem that had been sent to him for his approval. He could not, he said, "interpose with decisive effect" to produce emancipation. To interpose at all was to toss away other reforms.[8] Here as always Jefferson reveals himself as the pragmatic statesman, practicing government as the art of the possible. An idealist might fault him for refusing to commit political suicide by practicing utopian politics. But all the evidence of Robert McColley shows that as a practical politician Jefferson accurately gauged impassable obstacles. The point is crucial: long before Garrison, when Jefferson ruled, peaceful abolition was not possible.

What could be done—what Jefferson and his contemporaries did—was to attack slavery where it was weakest, thereby driving the institution south and vitiating its capacity to survive. In a variety of ways the Founding Fathers took positive steps that demonstrated their antislavery instincts and that, taken together, drastically reduced the slavocracy's potential area, population, and capacity to endure.

The first key reform took place in the North. When the American Revolution began slavery was a national institution, thriving both north and south of the Mason-Dixon line. Slaves comprised 14 per cent of the New York population, with other figures ranging from 8 per cent in New Jersey to 6 per cent in Rhode Island and 3 per cent in Connecticut and Pennsylvania. In these states, unlike Virginia, percentages of slaves were low enough to permit an unconclusive variety of reform.

Still, prior to 1776, abolitionists such as John Woolman found the North barren soil for antislavery ideas. As John Jay recalled, "the great majority" of Northerners accepted slavery as a matter of course, and "very few among them even doubted the propriety and rectitude of it."[9] The movement of 1776 changed all this. The humanitarian zeal of the Revolutionary era, together with nonslaveholder hatred of slave competition and universal acknowledgment that the economy did not need slavery, doomed Northern slavery to extinction. In some states the doom was long delayed as Northern slaveholders fought to keep their bondsmen. Slavery was not altogether ended in New York until 1827 and in New Jersey until well into the 1840s. By 1830, however, less than one per cent of the 125,000 Northern blacks were slaves. Bondage had been made a *peculiar* institution, retained alone in the Southern states.[10]

No less important than abolition in old Northern states was the long and bitter fight to keep bondage from expanding. In 1784 Jefferson drafted a congressional ordinance declaring slavery illegal in all Western territories after 1800. The proposed law, keeping bondage out of Alabama and Mississippi no less than Illinois and Indiana, lost by a single vote, that of a New Jerseyite ill in his dwelling. Seldom has a lone legislator lost so good a chance to turn around the history of a nation. "The fate of millions unborn," Jefferson later cried, was "hanging on the tongue of one man, and heaven was silent in that awful moment."[11]

Three years later, in the famed Northwest Ordinance of 1787, Congress decreed slavery illegal immediately in the upper Western territories. The new law left bondage free to invade the Southwest. But without the Northwest Ordinance slavery might have crept into Illinois and Indiana as well, for even with it bondage found much support in the Midwest.

In the years before 1809 Indiana settlers, led by William Henry Harrison and the so-called Virginia aristocrats, petitioned Congress again and again to allow Midwestern slavery. Indiana's pro-Harrison and anti-Harrison parties were both proslavery; they disagreed only on the tactical question of how to force Congress to budge. When Congress refused to repeal the ordinance, the Indiana legislature in 1805 passed a black indentured servitude act, in effect legalizing slavery. Indiana census takers, more honest than the legislature, counted 237 slaves in the territory in 1810 and 190 in 1820.

In 1809, when the part of Indiana that was most in favor of slavery split off as the new territory of Illinois, the battleground but not the issue shifted. The climax to the territorial phase of the Midwestern quest for slavery came in the Illinois Constitutional Convention of 1818, when proslavery forces, after winning a bitterly contested election to the convention, settled for a renewal of the territorial indentured servitude law because they feared that an explicit slavery law might jeopardize statehood.

With statehood secured the battle over slavery in Illinois continued in the 1820s. The hero of the antislavery forces was Edward Coles, an enlightened Virginian deeply influenced by Madison and Jefferson. Coles, who came to Illinois to free his slaves and stayed to protect the

Northwest Ordinance, narrowly defeated his proslavery rival for governor in 1822. In 1824 he helped secure, by the close vote of 6,640–4,973, final victory in a referendum on a proslavery constitutional convention. With Coles's triumph, slavery had again been restricted to the South.[12]

The crusade for slavery in Illinois and Indiana, lasting over a quarter of a century and so often coming so close to victory, forms a dramatic example of the institution's expansive potential in the age of the Founding Fathers. The proslavery drive was turned back in part because of race phobias and economic desires that obsessed nonslaveholding Midwestern farmers. But in an area where victory came so hard no one can deny the importance of the Northwest Ordinance and Edward Coles's crusade in keeping slavery away.

A third antislavery victory of the Founding Fathers, more important than Northern abolition and the Northwest Ordinance, was the abolition of the African slave trade. This accomplishment, too often dismissed as a nonaccomplishment, shows more clearly than anything else the impact on antislavery of the Revolutionary generation. Furthermore, nowhere else does one see so clearly that Thomas Jefferson helped cripple the Southern slave establishment.

The drive to abolish the African slave trade began with the drafting of the Declaration of Independence. Jefferson, with the concurrence of Virginia and the upper South, sought to condemn King George for foisting Africans on his colonies. South Carolina and Georgia, less sure they had enough slaves, demanded the clause be killed. Jefferson acquiesced. Thus was prefigured, at the first moment of national history, the split between upper and lower South that less than a century later would contribute mightily to the disruption of the republic.

At the Constitutional Convention, as we have seen, lower South delegates again postponed a national decision on slave importations. This time a compromise was secured, allowing but not requiring Congress to abolish the trade after twenty years. A year before the deadline Jefferson, now presiding at the White House, urged Congress to seize its opportunity. "I congratulate you, fellow citizens," he wrote in his annual message of December 2, 1806, "on the approach of the period when you may interpose your authority constitutionally" to stop Americans "from all further participation in those violations of human rights which have been so long continued on the unoffending inhabitants of Africa, and which the morality, the reputation, and the best interests of our country have long been eager to proscribe."

Although the law could not take effect until January 1, 1808, noted Jefferson, the reform, if passed in 1807, could make certain that no extra African was dragged legally across the seas.[13] In 1807 Congress enacted Jefferson's proposal.

The new law, although one of the most important acts an American Congress ever passed, did not altogether end African importations. Americans illegally imported approximately one thousand blacks annually until 1860. This is, however, a tiny fraction of the number that could have been imported if the trade had been legal and considered legitimate. Brazil imported over a million and a half slaves from 1807 to 1860, and the Deep South's potential to absorb bondsmen was greater. South Carolina alone imported ten thousand blacks a year in the early nineteenth century, before the law of 1808 went into effect. Louisiana creole planters sought unsuccessfully to make Jefferson's administration grant them the same privilege.[14] The desire of Virginia slaveholders to keep slave prices high no doubt helped feed the abolition of the trade, just as the desire of Illinois nonslaveholders to keep out blacks helped give Edward Coles his triumph. In both cases, however, the Revolutionary generation's conception of slavery as a moral disaster was of undeniable significance.

The law that closed the trade and saved millions of Africans from servitude on new Southwestern plantations also aided slaves already on those plantations. The great Southwestern boom came after the close of the African trade. Slaves could not be "used up," no matter how fantastic yearly profits were, for the restricted supply kept slave prices high. By mid-nineteenth century, moreover, almost all blacks were assimilated to the Southern way, making possible a paternal relationship between master and slave that could ease exploitation. One does not have to romanticize slave life or exaggerate planter paternalism to recognize that bondage would have been crueler if millions of Africans had been available in Mississippi and Louisiana to escalate profits.

The contrast with nineteenth-century South America, where the trade remained open, makes the point with precision. Wherever Latin Americans imported so-called raw Africans by the boatload to open up virgin territories, work conditions reached a level of exploitation unparalleled in the New World. Easy access to fresh recruits led to using up laborers; and the fact that slaves were unassimilated foreigners precluded the development of the kind of ameliorating relationship that was possible between master and bondsman in North America.[15]

The law profoundly affected North American whites as well as blacks. Most notably, it shut off the South's importation of labor during the period when immigrants were pouring into the North and the two societies were locked in mortal combat. If the trade had remained open, the operation of the three-fifths clause would have given the South greater congressional representation, and a massive supply of Africans might well have helped Southerners to compete more successfully in the race to Kansas and the campaign to industrialize. As it was, with the trade closed, fresh immigration fed the Northern colossus by the hour while Southerners fell ever more desperately behind.

Perhaps the most important long-run impact of closing the trade was to help push bondage deeper into the South, thereby continuing the work the Fathers had begun with Northern abolition and the Northwest Ordinance. Now that African markets were closed the new Southwest had to procure its slaves from Northern slave states. By 1860 the resulting slave drain had significantly reduced percentages of slaves and commitments to slavery throughout the border area stretching from Delaware through Maryland and Kentucky into Missouri. Whereas in 1790 almost 20 per cent of American slaves lived in this most northern tier of border slave states, the figure was down to 10 per cent and falling by 1860. On the other hand, in 1790 the area that became the seven Deep South states had 20 per cent of American slaves and by 1860 the figure was up to 54 per cent and rising. During the cotton boom the shift was especially dramatic. From 1830 to 1860 the percentage of slaves in Delaware declined from 4 to 1 per cent; in Maryland from 23 to 13 per cent; in Kentucky from 24 to 19 per cent; in Missouri from 18 to 10 per cent; and in the counties to become West Virginia from 10 to 5 per cent.[16]

By both reducing the economic reliance on slavery and the psychic fear of blacks this great migration had political consequences. Antislavery politicians, echoing Hinton R. Helper's appeals to white racism, garnered thousands of votes and several elections, especially in Missouri, during the 1850s.[17] It was only a beginning, but it was similar to the early stages of the demise of slavery in New York.

While the end of the slave trade indirectly drained slaves from the border South another Revolutionary legacy, the tradition of individual manumissions, further weakened the institution in the Northern slave states. Although Jefferson did not live up to his dictum that antislavery planters should free their slaves, many upper South masters followed precept rather than example in the antebellum years. The Virginia law of 1806, forcing freed slaves to leave the state in a year, did not halt the process as absolutely as some have supposed. Virginia laws passed in 1819 and 1837 allowed county courts to grant exceptions. The ensuing trickle of manumissions was a festering sore to the Virginia slave establishment.[18]

Meanwhile, in two border states, manumission sabotaged the institution more insistently. Delaware, which had 9,000 slaves and 4,000 free blacks in 1790, had 1,800 slaves and 20,000 free blacks in 1860. Maryland, with 103,000 slaves and 8,000 free blacks in 1790, had 87,000 slaves and 84,000 free blacks in 1860. These two so-called slave states came close to being free Negro states on the eve of Lincoln's election. Indeed, the Maryland manumission rate compares favorably with those of Brazil and Cuba, countries that supposedly had a monopoly on Western Hemispheric voluntary emancipation.[19]

The manumission tradition was slowly but relentlessly changing the character of states such as Maryland in large part because of a final Jeffersonian legacy: the belief that slavery was an evil that must some day be ended. Particularly in the upper South, this argument remained alive. It informed the works of so-called proslavery propagandists such as Albert T. Bledsoe; it inspired Missouri antislavery activists such as Congressman Frank Blair and the mayor of St. Louis, John M. Wimer; and it gnawed at the consciences of thousands of slaveholders as they made up their wills.[20] Jefferson's condemnation of slavery had thrown the South forever on the defensive, and all the efforts of the George Fitzhughs could never produce a unanimously proslavery society.

In summary, then, the Revolutionary generation found slavery a national institution, with the slave trade open and Northern abolitionists almost unheard. When Jefferson and his contemporaries left the national stage they willed to posterity a crippled, restricted, peculiar institution. Attacking slavery successfully where it was weakest they swept it out of the North and kept it away from the Northwest. They left the antebellum South unable to secure more slaves when immigrants rushed to the North. Most important of all, their law closing the slave trade and their tradition concerning individual manumissions constituted a doubly sharp weapon superbly calculated to continue pushing slavery south. By 1860 Delaware, Maryland, Missouri, and the area to become West Virginia all had a lower percentage of slaves than New York possessed at the time of the Revolution, and Kentucky's percentage was not much higher. The goal of abolition had become almost as practicable in these border states as it had been in the North in 1776. As the Civil War began, slavery remained secure in only eleven of the fifteen slave states. Meanwhile black migration toward the tropics showed every capacity to continue eroding the institution in Virginia and driving slavery down to the Gulf.

If the Founding Fathers had done none of this—if slavery had continued in the North and expanded into the Northwest; if millions of Africans had been imported to strengthen slavery in the Deep South, to consolidate it in New York and Illinois, to spread it to Kansas, and to keep it in the border South; if no free black population had developed in Delaware and Maryland; if no apology for slavery had left Southerners on shaky moral grounds; if, in short, Jefferson and his contemporaries had lifted nary a finger—everything would have been different. Because all of this was done, slavery was more and more confined in the Deep South as the nineteenth century progressed.

No one spied these trends better than the men who made the Southern revolution of 1860–61. Secessionist newspaper editorials in the 1850s can almost be summed up as one long diatribe against Jeffersonian ideology and the policy to which it led. Committed lower South slaveholders knew the world was closing in on them at the very time the more Northern slave states could not be relied on. Seeing the need not only to fight off Republicans from without but also to halt erosion from within, radical Southerners applauded the movement to re-enslave free blacks in Maryland; many of them proposed reopening the slave trade so that the Gulf states' hunger for slavery could be fed by imported Africans instead of black Virginians; and they strove to gain Kansas in large part to keep Missouri.

When this and much else failed and Lincoln triumphed, lower South disunionists believed they had reached the moment of truth. They could remain in the Union and allow the noose to tighten inexorably around their necks. They would then watch slavery slowly ooze out of the border South and permit their own domain to shrink to a handful of Gulf and lower Atlantic states. Or they could strike for independence while the upper South retained some loyalty to bondage, thereby creating a confrontation and forcing wavering slave states to make their choice. This view of the options helped to inspire the lower South's secession, in part a final convulsive effort to halt the insidious process the Founding Fathers helped begin.[21]

When war came the lower South's confrontation strategy was half successful. Four of the eight upper South states seceded in the wake of Sumter. But four others remained loyal to the North. In the most Northern slave states, Delaware, Maryland, Kentucky, Missouri, and also in the area to become West Virginia, the slave drain and manumission processes had progressed too far. When the crunch came, loyalty to the Union outweighed loyalty to slavery. Abraham Lincoln is said to have remarked that while he hoped to have God on his side, he had to have Kentucky. The remark, however apocryphal, clothes an important truth. In such a long and bitter war border slave states were crucial. If they, too, had seceded, the Confederacy might have survived. The long-run impact of the Founding Fathers' reforms, then, not only helped lead lower South slavocrats to risk everything in war but also helped doom their desperate gamble to failure.

Any judgment of the Founding Fathers' record on slavery must rest on whether the long or the short run is emphasized. In their own day the Fathers left intact a strong Southern slave tradition. The American Revolution, however, did not end in 1790. Over several generations, antislavery reforms inspired by the Revolution helped lead to Southern division, desperation, and defeat in war. That was not the most desirable way to abolish slavery, but that was the way abolition came. And given the Deep South's aversion to committing suicide, both in Jefferson's day and in Lincoln's, perhaps abolition could not have come any other way.

This conclusion would have brought tears to the eyes of Thomas Jefferson. Jefferson wrote St. George Tucker in 1797 that "if something is not done, and soon done" about slavery, "we shall be the murderers of our own children."[22] In 1820 he saw with a prophet's eye how that murder would take place. The Missouri crisis, coming upon him like "a Firebell in the Night," almost caused him to shrink from even his own antislavery actions. The "momentous question," he knew, was the "knell of the Union," if not in his own time inevitably soon enough. "I regret that I am now to die in the belief," he wrote John Holmes,

> that the useless sacrifice of themselves by the generation of 1776, to acquire self-government and happiness in their country, is to be thrown away by the unwise and unworthy passions of their sons, and that my only consolation is to be, that I live not to weep over it.[23]

No sadder note survives in American literature than this scream of failure from one of the most successful of the Founding Fathers. The irony is that the ambiguous antislavery posture of Jefferson and his contemporaries helped place the nation, unintentionally but perhaps irrevocably, in lockstep toward the blowup. In the late eighteenth century a statesman had two ways to lessen the chance of a civil war over slavery. He could ease the racial, sexual, and materialistic fears that made the lower South consider emancipation anathema. Or he could scotch the antislavery idealism the slavocracy found disquieting. Jefferson, mirroring his generation and generations yet unborn, could do neither. Both his antislavery beliefs and his fear of the consequences of those beliefs went too deep. He was caught up too completely in America's most anguishing dilemma. The famed wolf he complained of holding by the ears was his own revolutionary tradition no less than blacks chained in violation of that tradition.

Like reluctant revolutionaries before and since, Jefferson sought to have it both ways. He succeeded, as such men will, in starting something destined to get out of hand. He helped protect slavery where it was explosive and helped demolish it where it was manageable. Meanwhile, he helped give informal sanction to the lower South's worst racial fears at the same time that he helped intensify those fears by unintentionally driving more blacks toward the tropics. Over a seventy-five year period the Founding Fathers' reforms helped add claustrophobia to a lower South psyche inflamed enough in 1787. When that happened the day of the soldier was at hand.

If in 1820 Jefferson pulled back shuddering from the horror he saw ahead, his imperfect accomplishments had taken on a life of their own. And less than a half century later, though hundreds of thousands lay slain by bullets and slaves were but half freed, mournful bells in the night would herald the realization of his most radical dream.

NOTES

Earlier versions of this article were read before the Johns Hopkins History Seminar and at the annual meeting of the American Historical Association, Dec. 30, 1970. Benjamin Quarles, James Banner, Jr., Cecelia Kenyon, and especially David Donald offered cogent criticisms on those occasions. Others made helpful suggestions after reading written drafts: Alison Freehling, the late Adrienne Koch, R. Nicholas Olsberg, C. Vann Woodward, Eric Foner, Arthur Zilversmit, William Cohen, Bernard Bailyn, Robert McColley, John Shy, Bradford Perkins, and especially Kenneth M. Stampp. My thanks to them all.

1. Robert McColley, *Slavery and Jeffersonian Virginia* (Urbana, 1964); Staughton Lynd, *Class Conflict, Slavery and the United States Constitution* (Indianapolis, 1968); William Cohen, "Thomas Jefferson and the Problem of Slavery," *Journal of American History*, 56 (1969): 503-26; Winthrop D. Jor-

dan, *White Over Black: American Attitudes Towards the Negro, 1550–1812* (Williamsburg, 1968). For the fullest summation of the position, see Donald L. Robinson, *Slavery in the Structure of American Politics* (New York, 1971).

2. Thomas Jefferson to Edward Coles, Aug. 25, 1814, in Paul Leicester Ford, ed., *The Works of Thomas Jefferson* (New York, 1904–05), 11: 416.

3. Jordan, *White Over Black*, 429-81; Merrill D. Peterson, *Thomas Jefferson and the New Nation: A Biography* (New York, 1970), 263.

4. Jefferson to Coles, Aug. 25, 1814, Jefferson to Jared Sparks, Feb. 4, 1824, in Ford, *Works of Jefferson*, 11: 416, 12: 335-36.

5. McColley, *Slavery in Jeffersonian Virginia*, 3.

6. Dumas Malone, *Jefferson the President: First Term, 1801–1805* (Boston, 1970), 498.

7. See the stimulating comments on the matter in Jordan, *White Over Black*, 468, and Eric McKitrick, "The View from Jefferson's Camp," *New York Review of Books*, Dec. 17, 1970, p. 37.

8. Jefferson to George Logan, May 11, 1805, in Ford, *Works of Jefferson*, 10: 141-42.

9. Jay to Granville Sharp [1788], in Henry P. Jackson, ed., *The Correspondence and Public Papers of John Jay* (New York, 1890–93), 3: 342.

10. Arthur Zilversmit, *The First Emancipation: The Abolition of Slavery in the North* (Chicago, 1967).

11. Quoted in Peterson, *Jefferson*, 283.

12. The Indiana-Illinois story can best be followed in Jacob P. Dunn, Jr., *Indiana: A Redemption from Slavery* (Boston, 1888); Theodore Calvin Pease, *The Story of Illinois* (Chicago, 1949), 72-78; and, Adrienne Koch, *Madison's "Advice to My Country"* (Princeton, 1966), 144-51.

13. James D. Richardson, ed., *A Compilation of the Messages and Papers of the Presidents* (Washington, 1910), 1: 396.

14. Philip D. Curtin, *The Atlantic Slave Trade: A Census* (Madison, 1969).

15. See the judicious remarks in C. Vann Woodward, *American Counterpoint: Slavery and Racism in the North-South Dialogue* (Boston, 1971), 97-106.

16. U.S. Census Bureau, *The Statistics of the Population of the United States: Ninth Census—Volume I* (Washington, 1872), 3-8.

17. Helper is too often treated as a lone voice crying in the wilderness when in fact he was the man who summed up in book form an argument heard constantly in the upper South. See, for example, the files of the St. Louis *Democrat*, Baltimore *Patriot*, and Wheeling *Intelligencer* during the 1850s.

18. See, for example, John C. Rutherfoord, *Speech of John C. Rutherfoord of Goochland, in the House of Delegates of Virginia, on the Removal from the Commonwealth of the Free Colored Population* (Richmond, 1853).

19. James M. Wright, *The Free Negro in Maryland, 1634–1860* (New York, 1921).

20. The Wimer-Blair position is best laid out in the St. Louis *Democrat*. See also Albert T. Bledsoe, *An Essay on Liberty and Slavery* (Philadelphia, 1856), and the ambiguities omnipresent in such upper South newspapers as the Baltimore *American* and Louisville *Courier* throughout the fifties.

21. I hope to demonstrate at length the positions outlined in the last two paragraphs in my forthcoming *History of the South, 1850–61*, to be published by Harper and Row. The best sources on fire-eater positions in the 1850s are the Charleston *Mercury*, New Orleans *Delta*, and *DeBow's Review*. The clearest statements of the connection between lower South secession and upper South wavering are in John Townsend, *The South Alone Should Govern the South* (Charleston, 1860), and Henry L. Benning, *Speech . . . November 6, 1860* (Milledgeville, Ga., 1860). For a preliminary estimate of how the same thinking affected the Virginia Secession Convention, see William W. Freehling, "The Editorial Revolution, Virginia, and the Coming of the Civil War: A Review Essay," *Civil War History*, 16 (1970): 64-72.

22. Jefferson to St. George Tucker, Aug. 28, 1797, in Ford, *Works of Jefferson*, 8: 335.

23. Jefferson to John Holmes, Apr. 22, 1820, in *ibid.*, 12: 158-60.

• By the 1830's, Southern support for the abolition of slavery had generally disappeared. The growing pressures of abolitionist sentiment in the North and fears of slave uprisings in their own states led many Southerners to begin constructing an elaborate and belligerent ideological defense of Negro slavery. There were two pivotal episodes in the development of Southern sectional consciousness during the 1830's: the Nat Turner revolt in 1831 and the subsequent South Carolina Nullification Crisis. The brief but gory slave insurrection in Southampton County, Virginia, reinforced Southern fears of black violence and was partly responsible for defeat of a movement in the state for gradual abolition in 1831-32. Although, on its face, the Nullification Crisis involved a dispute over the tariff question between South Carolina and the federal government, William W. Freehling has shown in his book on the crisis, Prelude to Civil War, that the controversy exposed the growing anxieties throughout the South over possible Northern interference with the institution of slavery itself. The South Carolinian leader John C. Calhoun expressed the proslavery convictions held by most important Southerners of his generation when he declared in 1837 that "where two races of different origin, and distinguished by color and other physical differences, as well as intellectual, are brought together, the relation now existing in the slaveholding states between the two is, instead of an evil, a good—a positive good." During the three decades preceding the Civil War, as George M. Frederickson shows in the following article, the South's leading thinkers went to enormous lengths to construct their "positive-good," proslavery ideology.

Slavery and Race: The Southern Dilemma

GEORGE M. FREDERICKSON

Prior to the 1830s, black subordination was the practice of white Americans, and the inferiority of the Negro was undoubtedly a common assumption, but open assertions of *permanent* inferiority were exceedingly rare. It took the assault of the abolitionists to unmask the cant about a theoretical human equality that coexisted with Negro slavery and racial discrimination and to force the practitioners of racial oppression to develop a theory that accorded with their behavior. Well before the rise of radical abolitionism, however, spokesmen for the lower South gave notice that they were prepared to defend slavery as an institution against any kind of attack that might develop. In the 1820s the leadership of the major cotton-producing states made it clear that a national colonizationists effort was unacceptable because in their view slavery was an essential and Constitutionally protected local institution which was of no concern of the Federal government or the non-slaveholding states. These apologists for black servitude characteristically answered the colonizations by agreeing with them that emancipation on the soil was unthinkable and then proceeding to point out not only that colonization was impractical as a program of Negro removal but also that its very agitation was a danger to the security of a slave society because the expectations it raised among blacks threatened to undermine the discipline of the plantation. A permanent and rigid slave system, it was argued, was both economically necessary in the rice- and cotton-growing areas and vital as a system of control for a potentially dangerous black population. Such a viewpoint soon triumphed in all the slaveholding states. In 1831 and 1832, the Virginia legislature debated a colonization proposal that might have opened the way to gradual emancipation, but its defeat marked the end of a

From Chaper 2, "Slavery and Race: The Southern Dilemma," pp. 43-70, *The Black Image In The White Mind* by George M. Frederickson. Copyright © 1971 by George M. Frederickson. Reprinted by permission of Harper & Row, Publishers, Inc.

serious search, even in the upper South, for some way to set slavery on the path to extinction.[1]

After the Virginia debate, Professor Thomas R. Dew of William and Mary College, speaking for the victorious proslavery faction, set forth the most thorough and comprehensive justification of the institution that the South had yet produced. Dew's effort should properly be seen as reflecting a transitional stage in the proslavery argument. Since he was refuting the proponents of gradual emancipation and colonization who still thrived in western Virginia and not the new and radical abolitionists of the North, his arguments stressed practicality and expediency and, in a sense, did little more than help bring Virginia in line with the kind of proslavery sentiment already triumphant farther South. Much of his lengthy essay was devoted to showing that colonization was an impossible scheme because the natural increase of the black population would outrun any number that could possibly be colonized. His justification of slavery rested first of all on the contention that servitude had been a necessary stage of human progress and hence could not be regarded as evil in itself. He then went on to argue that the concrete circumstances of Southern life required the institution and that no set of abstract principles should be invoked to obscure the basic fact that the Negro was not prepared for freedom. Although this was fundamentally an extension of the kind of argument that had previously been the basis of the defense of slavery as "a necessary evil," Dew implied that such a practical adjustment to reality had no evil in it, and he raised expediency to the level of conservative principle when he cited Edmund Burke's dictum that "circumstances give in reality to every political principle its distinguishing color and discriminating effect."[2]

In his discussion of Negro character and prospects, Dew did not deviate forthrightly and insistently from traditional quasi-environmentalist assumptions about the nature of most racial differences. Although at the beginning of his essay he described Negroes as "differing from us in color and habits and vastly inferior in the scale of civilization," he did not deal consistently with the question whether this inferiority resulted from innate character or from the "habits" engendered by a long exposure to inhibiting circumstances. In his discussion of "obstacles to emancipation," Dew at one point provided an analysis not incompatible with the conservative environmentalism of the colonizationists. "The blacks," he wrote, "have now all the habits and feelings of slaves, the whites have those of masters; the prejudices are formed, and mere legislation cannot improve them. . . . Declare the Negroes of the South free tomorrow, and vain will be your decree until you have prepared them for it. . . . The law would make them freemen, and custom or prejudice, we care not which you call it, would degrade them to the condition of slaves." Such a prediction, he indicated, was merely an application of the rule that "each one should remain in society in the condition in which he has been born and trained, and not [try] to mount too fast without preparation."[3]

This ultraconservative principle could presumably have been applied to slaves or serfs of any race; and, as if to substantiate this inference, Dew went on to give as an example of premature emancipation the attempt to liberate the Polish peasants in the 1790s. But Dew could also describe black behavior as if it were predetermined by innate racial traits; for he contradicted his suggestion that Negro characteristics were simply acquired habits of servility by arguing, somewhat obscurely, that the supposed indolence of free blacks resulted from "an inherent and intrinsic cause." And when he asserted that "the free black will work *nowhere* except by compulsion," he decisively parted company with the colonizationists.[4] If Dew was a transitional figure in the general defense of slavery because he combined arguments from expediency with hints of a conservative, proslavery theory of society, he was equally transitional as a racial theorist, because of his vacillation between arguments for black inferiority drawn from a perception of the force of "habits," "customs," and "prejudices" and those suggesting that a permanency of racial type justified enslavement.

By the middle of the 1830s the full impact of the abolitionist argument had been felt in the South, and Dew's ambiguous treatment of the racial factor and his contention that slavery was sometimes justified by circumstances no longer provided Southern apologists with what they regarded as a fully adequate defense of the institution. The abolitionists' charge that slavery was inherently sinful was now met increasingly by the unequivocal claim that slavery was "a positive good." Furthermore their practical assertion of racial equality as something to be achieved in the United States and not through colonization inspired proslavery spokesmen to clarify their racial views and to assert, as a major part of their case, the unambiguous concept of inherent Negro inferiority.

South Carolinians led the way. In 1835 Governor George McDuffie told the South Carolina General Assembly that the Negroes were "destined by providence" for slavery and that this was made evident not only by the color of their skin but also by "the intellectual inferiority and natural improvidence of this race." They were, he indicated, "unfit for self-government of any kind," and "in all respects, physical, moral, and political, inferior to millions of the human race." McDuffie professed astonishment that anyone should "suppose it possible to reclaim the African race from their destiny" as slaves or subjects of some other form of absolute despotism.[5] The Charleston lawyer William Drayton said much the same thing the following year in a pamphlet attacking the abolitionists: "Personal observation must convince every candid man, that the negro is constitutionally indolent, voluptuous, and prone to vice; that his mind is heavy, dull, and unambitious; and that the doom that has made the African in all ages and countries, a slave—is the natural consequence of the inferiority of his character."[6] In 1837 John C. Calhoun made his famous defense of slavery before the Senate of the United States and showed how important racial doctrines really were in the new and militant defense of servitude which developed in the 1830s. "I hold that in the present state of civilization, where two races of different origin, and distinguished by color, and other physical differences, as well as intellectual, are brought together, the relation now existing in the slaveholding states between the two, is, instead of an evil, a good—a positive good."[7]

It was thus in tandem with the concept of slavery as "a positive good" that the doctrine of permanent black inferiority began its career as a rationale, first for slavery itself and later for postemancipation forms of racial oppression. The attitudes that underlay the belief that the Negro was doomed by nature itself to perpetual slavishness and subordination to the whites were not new, nor was the doctrine itself if considered as a popular belief that lacked intellectual respectability; but when asserted dogmatically and with an aura of philosophical authority by leading Southern spokesmen and their Northern supporters in the 1830s, it became, for the first time, the basis of a world view, an explicit ideology around which the beneficiaries of white supremacy could organize themselves and their thoughts.

The emergence of racist ideology in the United States was comparable in some respects to the rise of European conservative ideology, as described by Karl Mannheim in his essay on "Conservative Thought." Mannheim made a distinction between "traditionalism"—the emotional and relatively inarticulate tendency to hold on to established and inherited patterns of life—and "conservatism," which he saw as "conscious and reflective from the first, since it arises as a coun-

ter movement in conscious opposition to the highly organized, coherent, and systematic 'progressive' movement." This distinction is
clearly analogous to one that can be drawn between racial prejudice as
an emotional response to an enslaved and physically distinct group and
the early form of ideological racism as a "conscious and reflective"
attempt to develop, in response to an insistent egalitarianism, a world
view based squarely and explicitly on the idea that whites are unalter-
ably superior to blacks. As long as the traditional order was not threatened by radicalism, it required no elaborate theoretical defense. Or, as
Gustave de Beaumont, Tocqueville's companion, put it in his novel,
Marie: "As long as philanthropy on behalf of the Negroes resulted in
nothing but useless declamation, the Americans tolerated it without
difficulty; it mattered little to them that the equality of the Negroes
should be proclaimed in theory, so long as in fact they remained inferior to the whites." But abolitionism, like Jacobinism, forced previously
unarticulated assumptions to the level of defensive ideological conscious.[8]

The colonizationists may have stimulated an indirect and pragmatic
defense of slavery as a regional necessity, but their occasional expressions of a theoretical racial egalitarianism had not forced their Southern opponents to proclaim vigorously that the Negro was inherently
inferior and slavish, for the reason that proponents of colonization had
not challenged the necessity or inevitability of black subservience as a
fact of life in the United States. The abolitionist contention that
Christianity and the Declaration of Independence not only affirmed
equality in theory but cried out for its immediate implementation
could not go similarly unanswered by the defenders of black subordination.

In their efforts to justify slavery as a necessary system of race relations the proslavery theorists of the 1830s and 1840s developed an
arsenal of arguments for Negro inferiority which they repeated *ad
nauseam.* Heavily emphasized was the historical case against the black
man based on his supposed failure to develop a civilized way of life in
Africa. As portrayed in proslavery writing, Africa was and always had
been the scene of unmitigated savagery, cannibalism, devil worship, and
licentiousness. Also advanced was an early form of the biological argument, based on real or imagined physiological and anatomical differences—especially in cranial characteristics and facial angles—which
allegedly explained mental and physical inferiority. Finally there was
the appeal to deep-seated white fears of widespread miscegenation, as

proslavery theorists sought to deepen white anxieties by claiming that the abolition of slavery would lead to intermarriage and the degeneracy of the race. Although all these arguments had appeared earlier in fugitive or embryonic form, there is something startling about the rapidity with which they were brought together and organized in a rigid polemical pattern, once the defenders of slavery found themselves in a propaganda war with the abolitionists.

The basic racist case against the abolitionist assertion of equality sprang full blown—but without the authoritative "scientific" underpinning that would later give it greater respectability—in a pamphlet published in New York in 1833, entitled *Evidence Against the Views of the Abolitionists, Consisting of Physical and Moral Proofs of the Natural Inferiority of the Negroes*. In this extraordinary document a writer named Richard Colfax set forth in rudimentary form all the basic elements of the racist theory of Negro character. Colfax emphasized in particular a whole range of physical differences between whites and blacks which supposedly demonstrated inherent Negro inferiority. The Negro's facial angle, he contended, was "almost to a level with that of the brute"; hence "the acknowledged meanness of the Negro's intellect only coincides with the shape of his head." The lesson to be drawn from such data was that the black man's *"want of capacity to receive a complicated education renders it improper and impolitic that he should be allowed the privileges of citizenship in an enlightened country."* Since "the Negroes, whether physically or morally considered, are so inferior as to resemble the brute creation as nearly as they do the white species, . . . *no alteration of their present social condition would be productive of the least benefit to them,* inasmuch as no change of their nature can be expected to result therefrom." This unchangeability of the black character had been demonstrated historically, according to Colfax, because over a period of three or four thousand years Africans had had many opportunities to benefit from personal liberty and "their proximity to refined nations," but they had "never even *attempted* to raise themselves above their present equivocal station in the great zoological chain."[9]

The only element lacking in Colfax's racist argument was a full scientific explanation of the underlying *causes* of inequality. In the century that followed, theorists of racial inferiority would offer new and ingenious proofs or explanations for Colfax's assertions, but they would add very little to his general thesis.

As part of their effort to gain widespread support for such views, proslavery polemicists turned their attention to the free Negroes of the North, whom they presented not so much as a population degraded by white prejudice and color consciousness as one demonstrating its natural unfitness for freedom. When the census of 1840, which later proved to be inaccurate, revealed a very high rate of insanity among free Negroes as compared with slaves, they seized upon these statistics as evidence of the Negro's constitutional inability to function in a free society. In 1844 Calhoun, then Secretary of State, concluded that "the census and other authentic documents show that, in all instances in which the states have changed the former relation between the two races the African, instead of being improved, has become worse. They have been invariably sunk into vice and pauperism, accompanied by bodily and mental afflictions incident thereto—deafness, insanity and idiocy—to a degree without example. . . ."[10]

II

As the debate progressed, it became evident that Northern opponents of slavery could, if they chose, easily deflect the increasingly vexed question of biological differences by arguing that constitutional Negro deficiencies, even if they existed, provided no justification for slavery. On the contrary, they would only make it more sinful; for what could be more unchristian than exploitation of the weak by the strong? Owen Lovejoy, an abolitionist Congressman from Illinois and brother of the martyred editor Elijah P. Lovejoy, eloquently presented this point of view in 1860: "We may concede it as a matter of fact that [the Negro race] is inferior; but does it follow, therefore, that it is right to enslave a man simply because he is inferior? This, to me, is a most abhorrent doctrine. It could place the weak everywhere at the mercy of the strong; it would place the poor at the mercy of the rich; it would place those who are deficient in intellect at the mercy of those that are gifted in mental endowment. . . ."[11]

Many Southerners were themselves too strongly influenced by Christian and humanitarian values to let such an indictment stand. Their answer was that the slave was not only unfit for freedom but was ideally suited to slavery; for the Negro found happiness and fulfillment only when he had a white master. As one writer put it, Negro slaves are "the most cheerful and merry people we have among us."[12] For from the blacks' being "degraded," Southern apologists maintained that they were much better off in slavery than they had been in Africa. According to the South Carolina novelist William Gilmore

Simms, the Negro came from a continent where he was "a cannibal, destined . . . to eat his fellow, or be eaten by him." Southern slavery "brought him to a land in which he suffers no risk of life or limb other than that to which his owner is equally subjected," and had increased "his health and strength," improved "his physical symmetry and animal organization," elevated "his mind and morals," and given "him better and more certain food, better clothing, and more kind and valuable attendance when he is sick." It was no wonder, then, that he had developed a happy disposition.[13]

In promulgating the stereotype of the happy and contented bondsman, Southerners were doing more than simply putting out propaganda to counter the abolitionist image of the wretched slave. They were also seeking to put to rest their own nagging fears of slave rebellion. It was no accident that proslavery spokesmen in the Virginia legislature made much of the alleged contentment of the slaves; for the debate took place in the wake of the Nat Turner uprising of 1831, and servitude had come under attack as leading inevitably to black resistance. One of the proslavery members made it clear that the recent rebellion was a bizarre exception to the general pattern of master-slave relationships: "Our slave population is not only a happy one, but it is a contented, peaceful and harmless . . . during all this time [the last sixty years] we have had one insurrection."[14]

The image of black violence and retribution, drawn not only from Nat Turner but from memories of what had occurred in Santo Domingo, continued to haunt the Southern imagination however. Insurrection panics were frequent after 1830, and for men who supposedly ruled over a docile population, Southern slaveowners were extraordinarily careful to maintain absolute control over their "people" and to quarantine them from any kind of outside influence that might inspire dissatisfaction with their condition. In moments of candor, Southerners admitted their suspicion that duplicity, opportunism, and potential rebelliousness lurked behind the mask of Negro affability.[15]

A concept of the duality or instability of Negro character was in fact one of the most important contributions made by Southern proslavery propagandists to the racist imagery that outlasted slavery. In its original protoracist form, this duality was the one set forth by Thomas R. Dew between the savage Negro of Africa and the "civilized" black slave. Dew maintained that no large-scale insurrections were likely "where the blacks are as much civilized as they are in the United States. Savages and Koromantyn slaves can commit such deeds, because their whole life and education have prepared them; but the Negro of the United States has imbibed the principles, sentiments, and the feelings of the whites; in one word, he is civilized. . . ."[16] But Dew's analysis implicitly conceded too much to environment; indeed it made the Negro character seem almost infinitely plastic. What, it might be asked, was to prevent blacks from soon becoming "civilized" up to the level of the whites and claiming equality with them? Later writers often qualified the notion that slavery "civilized" the Negro by asserting that innate racial traits limited his potential development to a more or less tenuous state of "semi-civilization," a conception which provided an unequivocal justification of permanent servitude.

According to this theory, the Negro was by nature a savage brute. Under slavery, however, he was "domesticated" or, to a limited degree, "civilized." Hence docility was not so much his natural character as an artificial creation of slavery. As long as the control of the master was firm and assured, the slave would be happy, loyal, and affectionate; but remove or weaken the authority of the master, and he would revert to type as a bloodthirsty savage. That many Southerners did not believe, even in theory, in Negro docility under *all* conditions came out most vividly in proslavery discussions of emancipation and its probable consequences. Servile war was often seen as the inevitable result of loosening the bonds of servitude. In the words of William Drayton, who drew on the example of Santo Domingo, "the madness which a sudden freedom from restraint begets—the overpowering burst of a long buried passion, the wild frenzy of revenge, and the savage lust for blood, all unite to give the warfare of liberated slaves, traits of cruelty and crime which nothing earthly can equal."[17] Drayton's suggestion that emancipation would bring a reversion to basic savage type was set forth more explicitly by a writer in *De Bow's Review*, who described as follows the consequences of liberating a large black population: ". . . the brutish propensities of the negro now unchecked, there remains no road for their full exercise . . . but in the slaughter of his white master, and through the slaughter, he strides (unless he himself be exterminated) to the full exercise of his *native barbarity and savageness*."[18] As proof of the Negro's inevitable "reversion to type" when freed, defenders of slavery pointed continually to the alleged "relapse into barbarism" which had taken place in Haiti, the British West Indies, and Liberia, once the domesticating influence of slavery had been removed.[19]

The notion that bestial savagery constituted the basic Negro character and that the loyal "Sambo" figure was a social product of slavery served to channel genuine fears and anxieties by suggesting a program of preventive action, while at the same time legitimizing a conditional "affection" for the Negro. As a slave he was lovable but as a freedman he would be a monster. This duality was expressed in its most extreme form by Dr. Samuel A. Cartwright of Louisiana, who wrote in 1861 that ". . . the negro must, from necessity, be the slave of man or the slave of Satan."[20]

There were, however, ambiguities in the concept of Negro "domestication" or "semi-civilization" under slavery. One involved the question of whether or not, in the far distant future, the slave's savage instincts might entirely disappear as the result of some quasi-Lamarckian process of evolution, a development which would presumably fit the Negro for a change of status. Many writers regarded this question as open and undecided; others fell into blatant self-contradiction when they confronted it. William Gilmore Simms, in setting forth a proslavery theory of human progress, described how the rise of peoples to civilized status had often involved the tutelage of slavery as a stage in their development. "It is possible that a time will come," he wrote, "when, taught by our schools, and made strong by our training, the negroes of the southern states may arrive at freedom." Later in the same paragraph, however, he rudely shut the door that he had tentatively opened: "I do not believe that [the Negro] will ever be other than a slave, or that he was made to be otherwise; but that he is designed as an implement in the hand of civilization always."[21] This view was given authoritative expression from the mid-1840s on by "ethnological" writers like Samuel Cartwright and Josiah Nott. From a narrowly proslavery perspective, however, the whole question was in effect academic, because even those apologists who accepted the possibility that blacks might someday be ready for freedom maintained that additional centuries of servitude would be required to transform the essential Negro character.[22]

A more significant ambiguity, one which led to an important cleavage, resulted from differences over exactly what Negro "domestication" meant in terms of the actual relationships between masters and slaves. One way of suggesting what was at issue is to ask whether the model for the ideal slave was taken from the realm of the subhuman, with the slave as a high type of domesticated animal to serve as the white man's tool like another beast of burden, or from the human family as a "domestic" and domesticating institution, with the slave in the role of a child, responding with human affection to a kindly master. This ambiguity was related to an ambiguity about the nature of the plantation: was it a commercial enterprise with the blacks as a subhuman labor force, or a small patriarchal society?

George Fitzhugh, writing in the 1850s, was the most eloquent spokesman of the familial or paternalist view of slavery. For him, the harsh, exploitative side of slavery disappeared almost entirely; the master became a "parent or guardian," and the slave a child who, on the basis of a "common humanity," was admitted to "the family circle"[23] and subjected to "family government." The view of Negro psychology that sustained such a view was set forth by the Reverend H. N. McTyeire in a typical example of the advice that clergymen of a certain type gave to slaveholders:

> The sympathies which have their range within the social system—the emotions which form the ordinary cement of social existence, are found in the negro, and they are to be taken into account, in dealing with him. The master who ignores them and proceeds on brute principles, will vex his own soul and render his servants worthless and wretched. Love and fear, a regard for public opinion, gratitude, shame, the conjugal, parental, and filial feelings, these must all be appealed to and cultivated."[24]

The very fact, however, that such advice had to be given suggests that there was a contrary point of view. Paternalists emphasized the reality of slave "gratitude" as a natural human emotion deriving from kindly treatment; men with a different orientation thought differently. This, for example, is how George S. Sawyer, a Louisiana slaveholder, described the Negro character: "The very many instances of remarkable fidelity and attachment to their masters, a characteristic quite common among them, are founded not so much upon any high intellectual and refined sentiment of gratitude, as upon instinctive impulse, possessed to an even higher degree by some of the canine species."[25]

It was a short step from such an analogy to the argument that it was more difficult to mistreat Negroes or to overwork them than would be the case with whites; and some Southerners even concluded that for most purposes a master could simply forget about the possibility that his charges had normal human sensibilities. Cartwright, a Louisiana physician who had many years of practice on the plantations of what was then the Southwest, maintained in 1843 that the Negro race "has a peculiar instinct protecting it against the abuses of arbitrary power"; for blacks could not be overworked and were comparatively insensitive to sufferings that would be unbearable to whites. But Cartwright did believe that there was such a thing as "mismanagement" of Negroes. In a later "medical" essay, he described various Negro "diseases" that resulted from it, including drapetomia (running away) and rascality. Since such afflictions stemmed from bad government or imperfect slavery, their source was not in the harshness of servitude but in the unnatural liberty permitted by ineffectual masters.[26] The comforting notion that slaves did not suffer, even from flagrant mistreatment, was given expression by a Southern lady novelist in 1860. She not only argued that Negroes could not be overworked but claimed that it was physically impossible for a master to knock a slave "senseless to the ground"—as he was so often knocked in abolitionist writings—because the Negro skull was so thick that such an effort would bruise or break a white man's fist.[27]

The supposed animal insensitivity of the Negro was also invoked as a basis for denying familial affection among slaves and thereby implicitly justifying the breakup of families. According to Thomas R. R. Cobb of Georgia, the Negro's "natural affections are not strong, and consequently he is cruel to his offspring, and suffers little by separation from them."[28] Sawyer went further and asserted that blacks are totally lacking in family feeling and that it is "lust and beastly cruelty" and not "emotions of parental and kindred attachment" that "glow in the negro's bosom."[29] Such opinions suggest that the kind of "hard" racism that manifest itself in the image of "the Negro as beast" did not originate in the era of segregation late in the nineteenth century but had its origins in the antebellum period, when it vied for supremacy in Southern propaganda with the "soft" image of the black slave as beloved child.

III

The South's fundamental conception of itself as a slaveholding society was unstable. In the intellectual context of the time, the notion of the slave as dependent or child implied one kind of social order; the view that he was essentially subhuman suggested another.

Seeing the Negro as basically human despite his inferiority was compatible in theory with his integration into a certain type of human society—one based on a frank and open recognition of a whole range of inequalities. One branch of proslavery thought took this tack —the theoretical defense of a social order in which slavery was part of a larger hierarchy maintained by a sense of mutual obligation between superiors and inferiors. This viewpoint was foreshadowed by Thomas R. Dew's dictum that everyone, white or black, should be content to remain in the social station "in which he has been born and bred," and that consequently it was as ill advised for planters to encourage white overseers to aspire to gentility by giving them access to the drawing room as it was to invite expectations of freedom from the slaves.[30] In a defense of slavery published in 1838, Chancellor William Harper of the University of South Carolina elaborated on this hierarchical concept when he answered the abolitionist charge that the slave was denied the possibility of intellectual improvement by attacking the very notion of a society based on equality of opportunity. "The slave receives," Harper wrote, "such instruction as qualifies him to discharge the duties of his particular station. The Creator did not intend that every human being should be highly cultivated, morally and intellectually." Then, hitting even more directly at the American egalitarian ideal, he added: ". . . if, as Providence has evidently decreed, there can be but a certain portion of intellectual excellence in any community, it is better that it should be *unequally* divided. It is better that a part should be fully and highly cultivated, and the rest utterly ignorant." As a matter of principle, the lower classes, regardless of race, should be subordinated and kept in ignorance. Following the logic of his argument, Harper contended that the misery and uncertainty of status which seemed endemic to the "laborious poor" of nonslaveholding societies could be readily relieved by the imposition of something like slavery.[31]

Out of this kind of reactionary thinking there evolved by the early 1850s the fully developed thesis that slavery was "a positive good," not only as a system of controlling an inferior race but, more basically, as a way of providing security to the laboring class of any society. George Fitzhugh carried this line of thought to its logical extreme when he attacked the fundamental assumptions of capitalism and democracy by arguing that the working class of advanced industrial countries like Great Britain would be better off under slavery. For Fitzhugh and other Southern defenders of a reactionary seigneurialism, the patriarchal plantation was the best model for society in general, because the cement of all enduring social relationships was the pattern of responsibility and dependence that existed in the family and on the idealized plantation. Their attack on "free society" was based on the claim that a lack of such relationships led inevitably to misery, anarchy, and revolution.[32]

Fitzhugh was aware that his whole reactionary social philosophy would be undermined if slavery were justified principally in terms of racial differences; hence in his writings of the mid-1850s, he was emphatic in his assertion that the South must be willing to defend slavery in general and not just for blacks. "The strongest argument against slavery, and all the prejudice against it," he wrote in 1857, "arise from the too great inferiority of race, which begets cruel and negligent treatment in the masters, who naturally feel little sympathy for ignorant, brutal savages. Inferiority of race is quite as good an argument against slavery as in its favor." "The whole history of the institution," he concluded, "shows that in giving up slavery in the abstract, we take the weakest position of defense that we could possibly select. We admit it to be wrong and then attempt to defend it in that peculiar form that has always been most odious to mankind."[33]

Fitzhugh's concern with this ideological problem suggested that many people in the South had not in fact taken his high ground and were trying to justify slavery on what he considered the narrow and treacherous basis of race alone. And he was right; for the view that slavery was rooted in the peculiar nature of the Negro rather than in ultraconservative concepts of society and government was a popular one. James D. B. De Bow, editor of *De Bow's Review*, a major source of proslavery doctrine, encouraged Fitzhugh's assault on a free society and liberal ideas, but he also opened his journal to the ethnological school and actively endorsed the views of men like Cartwright, Josiah C. Nott, and John H. Van Evrie who defended slavery almost exclusively on the basis of racist anthropology, arguing that the Negro was so radically inferior to the Caucasian that his destiny in America was either brute servitude or extermination. The Biblical curse of Ham could serve almost as well, and in the hands of writers like Matthew Estes and Josiah Priest, it became a judgment of God which placed the black man virtually beyond the pale of humanity.[34]

If Fitzhugh envisioned a seigneurial society based on the image of a patriarchal plantation, the militant racists implicitly or explicitly projected a democratic and egalitarian society for whites, denying that the blacks were, in any real sense at all, part of the human community. They were advocates of what the sociologist Pierre L. van den Berghe has called "*Herrenvolk* democracy." In his comparative study

of racism, van den Berghe has contrasted *"Herrenvolk* democracies"—
"regimes like those of the United States or South Africa that are democratic for the master race but tyrannical for the subordinate groups"
—with genuinely aristocratic multiracial societies like those of colonial
Latin America.[35] The conflict between a developing *Herrenvolk* ideology and an aristocratic or seigneurial philosophy theoretically incompatible with democracy served to divide the mind of the Old South.
To understand this conflict, one must recognize that Southerners
could mean two different things when they questioned the applica-
bility of the Declaration of Independence. They could reject the idea
of equality in general, like Chancellor Harper and Fitzhugh, or they
could reject simply the interpretation of it which included the Negro
as a man created equal to the whites. Those who embraced the second
option saw themselves as preserving the egalitarian philosophy as a
white racial prerogative. This latter view was stated succinctly by the
Alabama fire-eater William L. Yancey before a Northern audience in
1860: "Your fathers and my fathers built this government on two
ideas: the first is that the white race is the citizen, and the master race,
and the white man is the equal of every other white man. The second
idea is that the Negro is the inferior race."[36] In the same year, a writer
in the *Southern Literary Messenger* made a similar point in an historical analysis of slavery. Unlike the paternalists, he condemned ancient
slavery and medieval serfdom in principle, because under such systems "races richly endowed by nature, and designed for high and lofty
purposes, were kept from rising to their natural level." But all forms of
white servitude and subordination had fallen before "the progress of
truth, justice, and Christianity." Negro slavery, on the other hand, had
persisted because it was not really incompatible with the growth of liberty and equality.[37]

Southerners often went further and contended that Negro slavery
was not only compatible with white equality but was the very foundation of it. Governor Henry A. Wise of Virginia contended that true
equality could exist among whites only where black servitude existed.
"Break down slavery," he argued, "and you would with the same blow
destroy the great democratic principle of equality among men."[38] The
claim was frequently made that the white South had no recognized
social classes; that far from establishing an aristocracy of slaveholders,
as the abolitionists claimed, it put all white men, whether they owned
slaves or not, on a dead level. Thomas R. R. Cobb described the
lower-class whites of the South as having the sense of belonging "to

an elevated class": "It matters not that he is no slaveholder; he is not of the inferior race; he is a freeborn citizen. . . . The poorest meets the richest as an equal; sits at the table with him; salutes him as a neighbor; meets him at a public assembly, and stands on the same social platform."[39]

Such observations obviously reflected a social ideal radically at variance with the image of the South as a seigneurial or quasi-feudal society. The proponents of this view made racial consciousness the foundation and cement of Southern society and not an incidental aspect. It was carried to its logical extreme in the writings of Dr. John H. Van Evrie, a proslavery New York physician and editor whose views were widely hailed in the South. In the 1853 pamphlet version of his *Negroes and Negro "Slavery,"* which carried on the cover the enthusiastic endorsements of Jefferson Davis, J. D. B. De Bow, and other prominent Southern spokesmen, Van Evrie combined arguments for the biological inequality of the blacks with a vigorous attack on all past or present forms of class privilege and social hierarchy within homogeneous white societies. He denounced with particular emphasis the oppression of British peasants and laborers by an "aristocracy" that was not naturally superior to those it governed. Having condemned all forms of subordination of whites to other whites as "artificial" and unjust, Van Evrie then relegated the blacks to abject and perpetual servitude for one reason alone—because they constituted a permanently inferior biological species. He even attacked those proslavery writers who attempted "to defend Southern institutions by comparing the condition of the Negro with the condition of the British laborer," because "no comparison is allowable or possible":

> The Negro is governed by those *naturally* superior, and is in the *best* condition of any portion or branch of his race, while the British laborer, governed by those *naturally* his equals, and even sometimes his inferiors, is in the *worst* condition of any portion of *his* race. The first is secure in all the rights that nature gives him, the latter is *practically* denied all or nearly all of his—the first is protected and provided for by those the Creator has designed should govern him, the latter is kept in ignorance, brutalized, over worked and plundered by those who it is designed should only *govern themselves—one is a normal condition*, the other an *infamous usurpation*.[40]

The most famous and authoritative statement of the principle that hierarchical subordination should always be strictly reserved for inferior races appeared in Alexander H. Stephens's famous "Cornerstone Speech" of 1861, heralding the foundation of the Confederacy. "Many governments," said the newly elected Vice President of the Confederate States of America, "have been founded on the principles of subordination and serfdom of certain classes of the same race; *such were, and are in violation of the laws of nature.* Our system commits no such violation of nature's laws. With us, all the white race, however high or low, rich or poor, are equal in the eyes of the law. Not so with the Negro. Subordination is his place. He, by nature, or by the curse against Canaan, is fitted for that condition which he occupies in our system." As for the basis of the new Confederate government: "Its foundations are laid, its cornerstone rests upon the great truth that the Negro is not equal to the white man, that slavery—subordination to the superior race—is his natural or normal condition."[41]

IV

Empirically speaking, Southern slavery was *both* an example of slavery in general *and* a form of servitude strictly limited to a single and supposedly inferior race. Two qualities about his laborers were thus bound to impress themselves upon the slaveholder's consciousness—that they were slaves and that they were black. On an unreflective attitudinal level these two aspects of the situation could coexist, reinforcing each other by creating a disposition to defend slavery because it was simultaneously the basis of concrete economic and social privilege for a class of Southerners and the institutional underpinning for a psychologically satisfying sense of racial superiority. But, as we have seen, the attempt to develop a consistent philosophical defense of the institution led inevitably to efforts to derive the argument principally from one facet or the other. Emphasis on slavery per se as an organizing principle of society led to a genuinely reactionary and paternalistic theory of society; but if racial differentiation was seen as the heart of the matter, then the result, in the larger American ideological context, was "*Herrenvolk* democracy" or "egalitarian" racism.

The elaborate intellectual efforts of writers like Fitzhugh and Henry Hughes (the Mississippi "sociologist") to prove that the "ethnical qualification" in the South's system of labor was "accidental,"[42] can perhaps best be seen as an attempt to articulate the genuinely antidemocratic aspirations of an elite of large planters by legitimizing in the abstract the self-serving principle of aristocratic domination. There is undoubtedly some truth in Eugene Genovese's assertion that the master-slave relationship and the plantation environment tended by their very nature to produce a class with "an aristocratic, antibourgeois spirit with values and mores emphasizing family and status, a strong code of honor, and aspirations to luxury, ease, and accomplishment."[43] Fitzhugh, Hughes, and other aristocratic paternalists with similar if less highly developed views—men like Edmund Ruffin, William J. Grayson, and George Frederick Holmes—probably did express, in some sense, the deeper impulses of the South's upper class, "the logical outcome" of its social thinking.[44]

It is doubtful, however, that these aristocratic proslavery theorists produced a coherent world view that placed the South as a whole on the road to accepting a reactionary class ideology as opposed to a modern type of race ideology. First of all, these thinkers betrayed their own ambivalence by giving greater attention to racial inferiority as a justification of Southern slavery than their general theory actually required. Although Hughes had described the racial factor as an "accidental" element in the Southern labor system, he went on to argue at some length that subordination of the blacks in the South was essential to prevent amalgamation and preserve the purity of the white race; Edmund Ruffin combined universalist arguments for slavery with a full rendition of the historical thesis that blacks as a race had demonstrated a peculiar intellectual inferiority and incapacity for freedom; even Fitzhugh maintained that the inherent "childlike" character of the Negro was in itself a persuasive argument for his enslavement.[45]

Moreover, it is questionable that even an "ethnically qualified" argument for aristocracy and slavery as being good in themselves won very many adherents outside a circle of slaveholding intellectuals who seemed alienated to some extent from their society and were without a determining influence on Southern politics or the formation of public opinion. Some of these theorists severely limited their own influence by openly manifesting aristocratic revulsion to the values and practices that resulted from the extension of democratic procedures and attitudes during the Jacksonian period. Among the older paternalistic theorists, Ruffin and Grayson belonged to the group that William R. Taylor describes as "Southern mugwumps," men who had retreated from politics in the 1820s and 1830s, partly because of their temperamental and ideological opposition to the changing character of public life. It also is noteworthy that most of the paternalist ideologues were from Virginia and South Carolina, the most conservative Southern states. Their point of view was not so commonly expressed by the proslavery apologists of the newer and increasingly dominant Southwestern states, where a quasi-democratic ethos and a forthright emphasis on *"Herrenvolk"* solidarity were made evident.[46]

The overwhelming majority of antebellum Southerners, it should be recalled, either owned no slaves or were farmers who owned only a few. Although many undoubtedly aspired to become planters, there is little indication that they accepted a reactionary social philosophy or even understood it. On the contrary, most signs would suggest that for intraracial purposes they were fiercely democratic in their political and social thinking, strongly opposed to any formal recognition of the principle of aristocracy among whites. The reactionary elements of the planter class could not readily force their values on such a population, because political democracy in the Old South, and particularly in the Southwest, was no sham: universal white manhood suffrage existed in most states during the late antebellum period, and candidates closely identified with a "black belt" or planter interest were sometimes defeated in bitterly contested elections which revealed a vigorous two-party system and a high level of popular interest and participation. The "plain folk," mostly stiff-necked back-country farmers with their own frontier-type traditions, were not, despite their relative poverty, economically or socially dependent, in any full sense, on the planter elite; and with the extension of the suffrage in the 1830s this element acquired a political leverage that required some upper-class accommodation.[47]

In the end, therefore, the planter class, whatever its own inner feelings, endeavored to maintain its *de facto* hegemony by making a "democratic" appeal, one which took into account the beliefs, desires, and phobias of an enfranchised nonslaveholding majority. No successful Southern politician, whatever his ties to the "aristocracy," was able to talk like Fitzhugh and give theoretical sanction to the enslavement or subordination of whites. When politicians justified slavery, they almost invariably did so largely in terms of race; the nonslaveholders feared blacks as potential competitors and opposed emancipation as a threat to their own "equal" status as whites. Because of inherent limitations on their ability to rule as they saw fit, the dominant class had to be content with a public defense of slavery that contradicted any consistently aristocratic pretensions they may have had; for they recognized that efforts to sanction white servitude in the abstract might endanger black servitude as a concrete reality. The fundamental insecurity that made such an adjustment mandatory was revealed by the hysterical reaction of Southern conservatives to the publication in 1857 of Hinton Rowan Helper's *The Impending Crisis of the South*, an attack on the slave system from a lower-class white point of view.[48] Not at all sure of the adherence of nonslaveholding whites to slavery itself, much less to a reactionary view of its implications, spokesmen for the planter class were generally willing to gain the necessary support for their concrete interests on any platform that would sanction them, even if it sacrificed their full ideological ambitions. In the last analysis, therefore, *Herrenvolk* egalitarianism was the dominant public ideology of the South, because it was the only one likely to ensure a consensus.

Spokesmen for the class of large planters were able to endorse such a doctrine without blatant hypocrisy because they themselves had never denied that inferiority of race was *one* justification of slavery. It has already been noted that Fitzhugh, who had tried harder than anyone to confine racial differences within an ultraconservative social perspective—as only one example of the manifold inequalities which ought to be reflected in paternalistic institutions—had nevertheless always argued that the inherent characteristics of the Negro race made its enslavement both natural and necessary. And at the very end of the antebellum period, when the sectional conflict was approaching its climax, Fitzhugh himself put an increasing stress on the racial factor and consented to an enlargement of the theoretical gap between the races. Indeed, one of the most dramatic indications that the effort to develop and promulgate a genuinely paternalistic world view was aborted by concessions to racism and Negrophobia can be found in the shifting emphasis in Ftzhugh's writings between 1857 and 1861. In 1857 Fitzhugh had warned against a defense of slavery that relied on "too great inferiority of race." But in his 1859 article "Free Negroes in Hayti," he revealed his own growing interest in racial doctrines. Paying tribute to "ethnology, a study almost neglected fifty years since," which had now "been elevated to the dignity of a science," he went on to describe how Haitian blacks were "relapsing into their former savage state." In support of the view that Haitian "degeneration" revealed basic Negro traits, he cited Count Joseph Arthur de Gobineau, the father of modern European racism, whose book *The Moral and Intellectual Diversity of Races* was published in the United States in 1856. But Fitzhugh still held back from an unequivocal endorsement of Gobineau's assertion that Negroes had an absolutely fixed and unchangeable set of undesirable traits. He acknowledged that the Haitian experience demonstrated the current inability of the Negro to make progress under freedom but intimated that it was still an open question what might eventually be made of him under slavery.[49] In 1861, however, Fitzhugh announced his capitulation to extreme racism. In a review of Van Evrie's *Negroes and Negro "Slavery,"* in book form, Fitzhugh concluded that Van Evrie had provided

> demonstrative reasoning, demonstrative proof, that the negro is of a different species, physically, from the white man. He then shows that the habitudes, instincts, moral and intellectual qualities and capabilities of all animals are the universal and necessary concomitants (if not the consequences) of their physical conformation. . . . We maintain then, that without descending to moral reasoning or speculation, he has *demonstrated* that the negro is physically, morally, and intellectually a different being (from necessity) from the white man, and must ever so remain. . . .

Fitzhugh concluded that Van Evrie had "a new idea, a new and fruitful idea."[50]

When he yielded to the pressure of Negrophobic opinion and to a materialist racism that by his own earlier admission was incompatible with a paternalist concept of slavery, Fitzhugh demonstrated that the aristocratic slaveholder's philosophy had failed to capture the Southern mind. His new racial emphasis reflected his inability to convert the South to reactionary seigneurialism as an alternative to the extreme racist doctrines that were growing in popularity as the basis of the proslavery argument during the 1850s. As his own heightened interest in "ethnology" suggests, one of the factors behind this rise in the significance of anti-Negro thought was the growth, outside the South as well as within it, of a body of "scientific" opinion which seemed to give the racial emphasis such intellectual authority that there was an almost irresistible temptation to make it a principal weapon against proponents of emancipation and racial equality.

NOTES

1. On proslavery attitudes in the lower South in the 1820s, see William W. Freehling, *Prelude to Civil War: The Nullification Controversy in South Carolina, 1816–1836* (New York, 1966), Chapter III and pp. 122-128; and William Sumner Jenkins, *Pro-Slavery Thought in the Old South* (Chapel Hill, N. C., 1935), pp. 65-79. The best account of the Virginia debate is Joseph Clarke Robert, *The Road from Monticello: A Study of the Virginia Slavery Debate of 1832* (Durham, N. C., 1941).

2. "Professor Dew on Slavery," *The Pro-Slavery Argument* (Charleston, 1852), p. 355, and *passim*. Dew's essay was originally published as *Review of the Debate of the Virginia Legislature of 1813 and 1832* (Richmond, 1832).

3. *Ibid.*, pp. 287, 435-456.

4. *Ibid.*, pp. 437, 429-430. (The italics are mine.)

5. Speech before the General Assembly of South Carolina, as reprinted in *The Source Book of American History*, ed. Albert Bushnell Hart (New York, 1905), p. 245.

6. William Drayton, *The South Vindicated from the Treason and Fanaticism of the Northern Abolitionists* (Philadelphia, 1836), p. 232.

7. John C. Calhoun, *Works*, ed. Richard K. Crallé (New York, 1853–1857), II, 631.

8. Karl Mannheim, *Essays on Sociology and Social Psychology* (London, 1953), pp. 99 and 74-164, *passim*; Gustave de Beaumont, *Marie, or Slavery in the United States* (Stanford, Cal., 1958), p. 11. (First published in 1835.)

9. Richard H. Colfax, *Evidence Against the Views of the Abolitionists* . . . (New York, 1833), pp. 25-26, 30, and *passim*. In the late 1840s and 1850s, these arguments would be placed in a framework of respectable scientific theory by the "American School of ethnology" (see Chapter Three below). Subsequent to the publication of Colfax's *Evidence Against the Views of the Abolitionists*, the same historical and biological case against the Negro was presented, for example, in Drayton's *The South Vindicated* (1836); James Kirke Paulding's *Slavery in the United States* (New York, 1836); J. H. Guenebault's *Natural History of the Negro Race* (Charleston, 1837); The Reverend Josiah Priest's *Slavery, As It Relates to the Negro or African Race* (Albany, N. Y., 1843); Samuel A. Cartwright's *Essays, Being Inductions Drawn from the Baconian Philosophy* . . . (Vidalia, La., 1843); and Matthew Estes, *A Defense of Negro Slavery, As It Exists in the United States* (Montgomery, Ala., 1846).

10. John C. Calhoun, *Works*, V, 337. There are excellent discussions of the controversy over the census of 1840 in Leon F. Litwack, *North of Slavery: The Negro in the Free States, 1790–1860* (Chicago, 1961), pp. 40-46, and Norman Dain, *Concepts of Insanity in the United States, 1789–1865* (New Brunswick, N. J., 1964), pp. 104-108.

11. "The principle upon which slaveholding was sought to be justified in this country would, if carried out in the affairs of the universe," Lovejoy added, "transform Jehovah, the supreme, into an infinite juggernaut, rolling the huge wheels of his omnipotence, ankle deep, amid the crushed, and mangled, and bleeding bodies of human beings on the ground that he was infinitely superior, and that they were an inferior race." (Cited in the *Liberator*, April 26, 1860.)

12. William A. Smith, *Lectures on the Philosophy and Practice of Slavery* . . . (Nashville, 1856), pp. 223-224.

13. William Gilmore Simms, "The Morals of Slavery," *The Pro-Slavery Argument*, p. 273. (Originally published in *The Southern Literary Messenger* III [November, 1837], 641-657.)

14. From a speech of James Gholson of Brunswick County, in Robert, *Road from Monticello*, p. 67.

15. See Mary Boykin Chesnut, *A Diary from Dixie*, ed. Ben Ames Williams (Boston, 1949), p. 141, for a classic expression of Southern doubts about slave contentment and docility.

16. *Pre-Slavery Argument*, p. 463.

17. Drayton, *The South Vindicated*, p. 246.

18. "L. S. M.," review of John Campbell's *Negromania*, in *The Industrial Resources of the Southern and Western States*, ed. J. D. B. De Bow (New Orleans, 1852), II, 203. (The italics are mine.)

19. See for example, Thomas R. R. Cobb, *An Inquiry into the Law of Negro Slavery in the United States of America* (Philadelphia, 1858), pp. cxcvii, ccxxvii.

20. Dr. Samuel Cartwright, "Negro Freedom: An Impossibility under Nature's Laws," *De Bow's Review*, XXX (May–June, 1861), 651.

21. *Pro-Slavery Argument*, pp. 266-268.

22. For an example of the thesis that blacks would be ready "at some distant day" for "the privileges of civil liberty," see W. A. Smith, *Lectures on . . . Slavery* (1856), p. 246 and *passim*. By the time Smith wrote, however, this was clearly not the dominant view among proslavery apologists.

23. George Fitzhugh, *Sociology for the South; or, the Failure of Free Society* (Richmond, 1854), pp. 82-83, 105-107; *Cannibals All! or, Slaves Without Masters*, ed. C. Vann Woodward (Cambridge, Mass., 1960), p. 205. (First published in 1857.)

24. H. N. McTyeire, "Plantation Life—Duties and Responsibilities," *De Bow's Review*, XXIX (September, 1860), 361.

25. George S. Sawyer, *Southern Institutes; or, an Inquiry into the Origin and Early Prevalence of Slavery and the Slave Trade* (Philadelphia, 1858), p. 197.

26. Samuel A. Cartwright, *Essays*, p. 3, and "Diseases and Peculiarities of the Negro," in De Bow, ed., *Industrial Resources*, II, 318-324. For another expression of the view that the Negro, like the mule, could not be overworked, see Estes, *Defense of Negro Slavery*, pp. 78-80.

27. Mrs. Henry Schoolcraft, *The Black Gauntlet: A Tale of Plantation Life in South Carolina* (Philadelphia, 1860), pp. 49, 61.

28. Cobb, *Inquiry*, p. 39.

29. Sawyer, *Institutes*, p. 222.

30. *Pro-Slavery Argument*, p. 436.

31. "Harper on Slavery," *ibid.*, pp. 35-36, 49-50 (originally published as *Memoir on Slavery* [Charleston, 1838]).

32. Fitzhugh, *Sociology for the South* and *Cannibals All!*, *passim*. See also Henry Hughes, *Treatise on Sociology: Theoretical and Practical* (Philadelphia, 1854), for a different formulation of the same basic argument.

33. George Fitzhugh, "Southern Thought Again," *De Bow's Review*, XXIII (November, 1857), 451.

34. For more on De Bow and the ethnological school see Chapter Three, below. The virulently racist use of the curse of Ham was most strikingly manifested in Josiah Priest's *Slavery, As It Relates to the Negro* (1843), reissued as *Bible Defense of Slavery* . . . (Glasgow, Ky., 1852). See also Estes, *Defense of Negro Slavery*.

35. Pierre L. van den Berghe, *Race and Racism: A Comparative Perspective* (New York, 1967), pp. 17-18.

36. Extracts from a speech of Yancey in Boston, October 12, 1860, in the *Liberator*, October 26, 1860.

37. "The Negro Races," the *Southern Literary Messenger*, XXXI (July, 1860), 9-10.

38. Quoted in Jenkins, *Pro-Slavery Thought*, p. 190.

39. Cobb, *Inquiry*, p. 213. This statement of Cobb and those of several other prominent Southern spokesmen who made the same points are quoted in Jenkins, *Pro-Slavery Thought*, pp. 190-194.

40. John H. Van Evrie, pamphlet *Negroes and Negro "Slavery": The First an Inferior Race: The Latter Its Normal Condition* (Baltimore, 1853), pp. 30-31 and *passim*. Van Evrie's doctrines as elaborated in the later book of the same title will be discussed more extensively in Chapter Three as applications of the "scientific" racism that burgeoned in the North as well as in the South during the 1850s.

41. Henry Cleveland, *Alexander H. Stephens, In Public and Private; With Letters and Speeches, Before, During, and Since the War* (Philadelphia, 1866), pp. 722-723, 721. (The italics are mine.)

42. Hughes, *Treatise*, p. 42.

43. Eugene D. Genovese, *The Political Economy of Slavery: Studies in the Economy and Society of the Slave South* (New York, 1965), p. 28.

44. See Edmund Ruffin, *The Political Economy of Slavery* (1859); William J. Grayson, *The Hireling and the Slave* . . . (Charleston, 1856); and Robert L. Dabney, *A Defense of Virginia* . . . (New York, 1867). For a provocative discussion of Fitzhugh's thought as the natural outgrowth of the slaveholder's situation, see Part Two of Eugene Genovese's *The World the Slaveholders Made: Two Essays in Interpretation* (New York, 1969). For reasons that will become clear, however, I dissent from Genovese's thesis that the reactionary, consistently antidemocratic slaveholder's philosophy was the dominant world view that emerged from the antebellum South.

45. Hughes, *Treatise*, pp. 238-243; Ruffin, *Political Economy*, pp. 10-19; Fitzhugh, *Sociology for the South*, pp. 82-83, and *Cannibals All!*, p. 20.

46. William R. Taylor, *Cavalier and Yankee: The Old South and American National Character* (New York, 1961), pp. 55-65. Edmund Ruffin's eschewal of a public career in the face of "democratic" tendencies that he refused to accept is further documented in Avery O. Craven's *Edmund Ruffin, Southerner* (New York and London, 1932), pp. 39-43.

47. That the Old South experienced a "democratic revolution" (for whites only) during the Jacksonian period has been argued most effectively by Fletcher M. Green and Charles S. Sydnor (see Green, *Democracy in the Old South and Other Essays*, ed. J. Isaac Copeland [Nashville, 1969], pp. 65-86; and Sydnor, *The Development of Southern Sectionalism 1819–1848* [Baton Rouge, La., 1948], Chapter XII), and has been reiterated in Clement Eaton's *The Growth of Southern Civilization, 1790–1860* (New York, 1961), pp. 172-175, 308-309. These historians recognize that this "democratization" was largely political and did not in the end undermine the social and economic dominance of the planter class, but contend that it did force the elite to ad-

just to the new order because it impelled them to profess a "democratic" ideology and to work through democratic electoral processes. Green and Sydnor have probably overstated their thesis because they have paid too little attention to persistently conservative and aristocratic facets of Southern life. But recent historians of basically Marxist orientation, such as Eugene Genovese and Barrington Moore, Jr. (see Moore's *Social Origins of Dictatorship and Democracy: Lord and Peasant in the Making in the Modern World* [Boston, 1966], Chapter Three), have gone to the other extreme by overlooking almost entirely the fact that the Old South had even a limited democratic aspect. They seem to imply that the planters ruled pretty much like the hereditary aristocracy of a typical premodern and hierarchical agrarian society. It admittedly strains credulity to describe the Old South as having been in any profound sense democratic or egalitarian. There were immense inequalities not only between masters and slaves but also between rich planters and much of the nonslaveholding population. But it seems clear that the late antebellum Southern oligarchy lacked the aura of unquestioned legitimacy that surrounds an established seigneurial class with a privileged status recognized and accepted by the community as a whole.

48. This reaction is discussed in the introduction to Hinton Rowan Helper, *The Impending Crisis of the South: How to Meet It*, ed. George M. Fredrickson (Cambridge, Mass., 1968), pp. xv-xix.

49. George Fitzhugh, "Free Negroes in Hayti," *De Bow's Review*, XXVII (November, 1859), 527-549.

50. George Fitzhugh, "The Black and White Races of Men," *De Bow's Review*, XXX (April, 1861), 447.

• As fears of slave revolts and of abolitionist intrigues grew during the Jacksonian period, Southerners became increasingly concerned with protecting the security of their slave system. Local militia units and patrols were not characteristic only of the South during the ante-bellum period, of course, and the tradition of vigilante-administered justice had become well established in this country even before the end of the colonial period. Responding to the growing political crisis over slavery in nineteenth-century America, however, the South mobilized its white citizens through slave patrols and constant militia duty in order to guard against the internal and external threats which it detected. John Hope Franklin describes the climate of Southern militancy.

The Militant South

JOHN HOPE FRANKLIN

"A MILITANT GENTRY"

. . . Despite the fact that the plantation sought to be self-sufficient and that it succeeded in many respects, the maintenance of a stable institution of slavery was so important that owners early sought the cooperation of the entire community. This cooperation took the form of the patrol, which became an established institution in most areas of the South at an early date. There were many variations in its size and organization. The South Carolina law of 1690 provided that each patrol detachment should be composed of ten men under the captain of a militia company. The number was reduced to five in 1721. All white men were eligible for patrol service when the system was established. Between 1737 and 1819, however, patrol service was limited to men of some affluence, presumably slaveholders. In the latter year all white males over eighteen were made liable for patrol duty; non-slaveholders, however, were excused from duty after reaching the age of forty-five.[1] In Alabama the law of 1819 required not less than three nor more than five owners of slaves for each patrol detachment, while the Mississippi law called for four men, slaveholders or non-slaveholders, for each detachment.[2]

The duties of the patrols were similar in all places. The detachment was to ride its "beat" at night for the purpose of apprehending any and all Negroes who were not in their proper places. Alabama empowered its patrols to enter, in a peaceable manner, upon any plantation; "to enter by force, if necessary, all Negro cabins or quarters, kitchens and outhouses, and to apprehend all slaves who may there be found, not belonging to the plantation or household, without a pass from their owner or overseer or strolling from place to place, without authority." [3] There were variations in the disposition of offenders taken up by patrols. If the violators were free Negroes or runaways, they were to be taken before a justice of the peace. If they were slaves, temporarily away from their master's plantation, they were to be summarily punished by a whipping, not to exceed thirty-nine lashes.[4] There were, of course, abuses. On occasion, for example, members of the patrol whipped slaves who were legally away from their masters' premises or who were even "peaceably at home." [5]

The patrol system tended to strengthen the position of the military in the Southern community. In most instances there was a substantial connection between the patrol and the militia, either through the control of one by the other or through identity of personnel. In South Carolina the patrol system was early merged into the militia, "making it a part of the military system, and devolving upon the military authority its arrangement and maintenance." There the "Beat Company" was composed of a captain and four others of the regular militia, all of whom were to be excused from any other military service.[6] Sydnor has observed that in Mississippi the structure of the patrol was "but an adaptation of the militia to the control of slaves." In Alabama the infantry captains of the state militia completely dominated the selection of personnel for patrol duty and designated the officers.[7] Under such circumstances the patrol system was simply an arm of the military. . . .

The South's greatest nightmare was the fear of slave uprisings; and one of the most vigorous agitations of her martial spirit was evidenced whenever this fear was activated by even the slightest rumor of revolt. Fear easily and frequently mounted to uncontrollable alarm in which the conduct of some citizens could hardly be described as sober or responsible. "We regard our Negroes as JACOBINS" of the country, Edwin Clifford Holland declared. The whites should always be on their guard against them, and although there was no reason to fear any permanent effects from insurrectionary activities, the Negroes "should be watched with an eye of steady and unremitted observation . . . Let it never be forgotten, that our Negroes are freely the JACOBINS of the country; that they are the ANARCHISTS and the DOMESTIC ENEMY: the COMMON ENEMY OF CIVILIZED SOCIETY, and the BARBARIANS WHO WOULD, IF THEY COULD, BECOME THE DESTROYERS OF OUR RACE." [8]

A farmer's account of how the fear of revolts completely terrified some Alabama whites suggested to Olmsted both the extent of fear and the impact of fear upon the mind. The farmer said that when he was a boy "folks was dreadful frightened about the niggers. I remember they built pens in the woods," he continued, "where they could hide, and Christmas time they went and got into the pens, 'fraid the niggers was risin' . . . I remember the same thing where we was in South Carolina . . . we had all our things put up in bags, so we could tote 'em, if we heerd they was comin' our way." [9]

This was hardly the usual reaction to threats of slave insurrections. To be sure, such grave eventualities threw them into a veritable paroxysm of fear; but they moved swiftly to put up a defense against the foe. Committees of safety sprang into existence with little prior notice, and all available military resources were mobilized for immediate action. These were not the times to entrust the lives of the citizens to the ordinary protective agencies of civil government. If a community or a state had any effective military force, this was the time for its deployment. Military patrols and guards were alerted, and volunteer troops and the regular militia were called into service. It was a tense martial air that these groups created. For all practical purposes, moreover, even the civil law of the community tended to break down in the face of the emergency. Something akin to martial law, with its arbitrary searches and seizures and its summary trials and executions, prevailed until the danger had passed.

Instances when fears of uprisings were not followed by immediate militarization of a wide area of the Southern countryside are practically non-existent. When Gabriel attempted the revolt in Richmond in 1800, the Light Infantry Blues were called into immediate service, the public guard was organized and drilled to help avert the calamity, and Governor Monroe instructed every militia commander in the state to be ready to answer the call to duty.[10] In 1822, when Charleston was thrown into a panic by rumors of Vesey's plot, all kinds of military groups were called into service. A person unfamiliar with the problem doubtless would have thought that such extensive mobilization was for the purpose of meeting some powerful foreign foe. The Neck Rangers, the Charleston Riflemen, the Light Infantry, and the Corps of Hussars were some of the established military organizations called up. A special city guard of one hundred and fifty troops was provided for Charleston. The cry for reinforcement by federal troops was answered before the danger had completely subsided.[11] The attempted revolt of Nat Turner in 1831 brought military assistance, not only from the governor of the state, "acting with his characteristic energy," but from neighboring North Carolina counties, and from the federal government.[12] Indeed, more troops reached Southampton County than were needed or could be accommodated.[13] With artillery companies and a field piece from Fort Monroe, detachments of men from two warships, and hundreds of volunteers and militia men converging on the place, there was every suggestion of a large-scale impending battle.[14]

There was a strong show of military force not only when large-scale plots like those of Gabriel, Vesey, and Turner were uncovered, but also whenever there was any intimation of insurrection, however slight. Even a cursory glance at the accounts of insurrections and threats or rumors of insurrections reveals the role of the military.[15] The rumor of revolt in Louisiana in January 1811, caused Governor Claiborne to call out the militia: a contingent of four hundred militiamen and sixty federal troops left Baton Rouge for the reported scene of action.[16] Two years later the Virginia militia was ordered out to quell a suspected revolt in Lancaster.[17] In 1816 the South Carolina militia took summary action against a group of Negroes suspected of subversive activities.[18] The militia of Onslow County, North Carolina, was so tense during a "Negro hunt" in 1821 that its two detachments mistook each other for the Negro incendiaries and their exchange of fire caused several casualties.[19] Alabama pressed its militia into service in 1841 to search for slave outlaws and to put down rumored uprisings.[20]

Few ante-bellum years were completely free of at least rumors of slave revolts. Agitation for stronger defenses against slave depredations was almost constant, with some leaders advocating a state of continuous preparation for the dreaded day of insurrection. Governor Robert Hayne of South Carolina told the state legislature, "A state of military preparation must always be with us a state of perfect domestic security. A period of profound peace and consequent apathy may expose us to the danger of domestic insurrection." [21] A New Orleans editor called for armed vigilance, adding that "The times are at least urgent for the exercise of the most watchful vigilance over the conduct of slaves and free colored persons." [22] . . .

"DEFENDING THE CORNERSTONE"

Slavery strengthened the military tradition in the South because owners found it desirable, even necessary, to build up a fighting force to keep the slaves under control. They also felt compelled to oppose outside attacks with a militant defense. They regarded the abolitionist attack as a war on their institutions. Calhoun called it "a war of religious and political fanaticism, mingled, on the part of the leaders, with ambition and the love of notoriety." The object being "to humble and debase us in our own estimation, and that of the world in general; to blast our reputation, while they overthrow our domestic institutions." [23] As they read antislavery literature, observed the establishment of organizations dedicated to the destruction of slavery, and felt the sting of "subversive" activities like the Underground Railroad, Southerners reasoned that they were the targets of an all-out offensive war. . . .

As Garrison and his fellows forced the North to consider the danger of the ever increasing slave power, the Southern leaders asserted themselves. From dozens of pens came ardent defenses of a social structure by which they would live or die. . . . They evolved a defense of slavery that was as full of fight as a state militia called out to quell a slave uprising. Chancellor Harper, Professor Dew, Governor Hammond, Fitzhugh, and others seemed aware of the fact that, however sound or logical their proslavery arguments might be, they must infuse in them a fighting spirit. The successful defense of slavery, whether by argument or by force, depended on the development of a powerful justification based on race superiority that would bring to its support all—or almost all—white elements in the South. Thus they redefined the "facts" of history, the "teachings" of the Bible, the "principles" of economics.[24] Convinced that thought could not be free, they believed that there should be some positive modifications of the democratic principles enunciated by the founding fathers. They rejected the equalitarian teachings of Jefferson and asserted that the inequality of man was fundamental to all social organization. There were no rights that were natural or inalienable, they insisted. In his *Disquisition on Government*, Calhoun asserted that liberty was not the right of every man equally. Instead of being born free and equal, men "are born subject not only to parental authority, but to laws and institutions of the country where born, and under whose protection they draw their first breath." [25] Fiery Thomas Cooper stopped working on the South Carolina statutes long enough to observe wryly, "we talk a great deal of nonsense about the rights of man. We say that man is born free, and equal to every other man. Nothing can be more untrue: no human being ever was, now is, or ever will be born free." [26]

In the rejection of the principles of liberty and equality, political democracy was also rejected. "An unmixed democracy," said one Mississippian, "is capricious and unstable, and unless arrested by the hand of despotism, leads to anarchy . . ." There was too much talk about democracy and too little about the aristocratic tradition. "Too much liberty and equality beget a dissolute licentiousness and a contempt for law and order." Virginians and South Carolinians led the demand for a recognition of Southern honor because they were true to their ancient sentiments and "with constant pride they guard their unstained escutcheons." [27] Life, liberty, and the pursuit of happiness were not inalienable rights. Every government, South Carolina's Chancellor William Harper explained, deprives men of life and liberty for offenses against society, while "all the laws of society are intended for nothing else but to restrain men from the pursuit of happiness . . ." It followed, accordingly, that if the possession of a black skin was dangerous to society, then that society had the right to "protect itself by disfranchising the possessor of civil privileges and to continue the disability to his posterity . . ." [28]

It was left to George Fitzhugh, that shrewd professional Southerner, to crystallize and summarize Southern thinking on social organization. Free society was an abject failure, he said; and its frantic, but serious consideration of radical movements like socialism, communism, and anarchism was a clear admission of its failure. If slavery was more widely accepted, man would not need to resort to the "unnatural remedies of woman's rights, limited marriages, voluntary divorces, and free love, as proposed by the abolitionists." [29] Only in a slave society were there proper safeguards against unemployment and all the evils that follow as a country becomes densely settled and the supply of labor exceeds its demand. Fitzhugh, with a sneer at the North, observed that the "invention and use of the word Sociology in a free society and the science of which it treats, and the absence of such word and science in slave society shows that the former is afflicted with disease, the latter healthy." It was bad enough that free communities were failures, but it was intolerable that they should try to impose their impossible practices on the South. "For thirty years," he argued, "the South has been a field on which abolitionists, foreign and domestic, have carried on offensive warfare. Let us now, in turn, act on the offensive, transfer the seat of war, and invade the enemy's territory." [30]

The South's society was to rest on the inequality of men in law and economics. Social efficiency and economic success demanded organization; and organization inevitably meant the enslavement of the ignorant and unfortunate. *Slavery was a positive good.* It was regarded by James H. Hammond as "the greatest of all the great blessings which a kind providence has bestowed." It made possible the transformation of the South from a wilderness into a garden, and gave the owners the leisure in which to cultivate their minds and create a civilization rich in culture and gentility. More than that, it gave to the white man the only basis on which he could do something for a group of "hopelessly and permanently inferior" human beings.[31]

The idea of the inferiority of the Negro enjoyed wide acceptance among Southerners of all classes and was an important ingredient in the theory of society promulgated by Southern leaders. It was organized into a body of systematic thought by the scientists and social scientists of the South, out of which emerged a doctrine of racial superiority to justify any kind of control maintained over the slave. In 1826, Dr. Thomas Cooper had said that he had not the slightest doubt that Negroes were of an "inferior variety of the human species; and not capable of the same improvement as the whites"; [32] but, while a mere chemist was apparently unable to elaborate the theory, the leading physicians of the South were. Dr. S. C. Cartwright of the University of Louisiana was only one of a number of physicians who set themselves up as authorities on the ethnological inferiority of the Negro. In his view, the capacities of the Negro adult for learning were equal to those of a white infant; and the Negro could properly perform certain physiological functions only when under the control of white men. For example, Negroes "under the compulsive power of the white man . . . are made to labor or exercise, which makes the lungs perform a duty of vitalizing the blood more perfectly than is done when they are left free to indulge in idleness. It is the red, vital blood sent to the brain that liberates their mind when under the white man's control; and it is the want of a sufficiency of red, vital blood that chains their mind to ignorance and barbarism when in freedom." Because of his inferiority, liberty and republican institutions were not only unsuited to the Negro, but actually poisonous to his happiness.[33] Variations on this theme were still being played by many Southern "men of science" when Sumter was bombarded. Like racists in other parts of the world, Southerners sought support for their militant racist ideology by developing a common bond with the less privileged. The obvious basis was race, and outside the white race there was to be found no favor from God, no honor or respect from man. Indeed, those beyond the pale were the objects of scorn from the multitudes of the elect.[34] By the time that Europeans were reading Gobineau's *Inequality of Races,* Southerners were reading Cartwright's *Slavery in the Light of Ethnology.* In both cases the authors conceded "good race" to some, and withheld it from others. In admitting all whites into the pseudo-nobility of race, Cartwright won their enthusiastic support in the struggle to preserve the integrity and honor of *the* race.

While uniting the various economically divergent groups of whites, the concept of race also strengthened the ardor of most Southerners to fight for the preservation of slavery. All slaves belonged to a degraded, "inferior" race; and, by the same token, all whites, however wretched some of them might be, were superior. In a race-conscious society whites at the lowest rung could identify themselves with the most privileged and affluent of the community. Thomas R. Dew, Professor of Political Law at the College of William and Mary, made this point clear when he said that in the South "no white man feels such inferiority of rank as to be unworthy of association with those around him. Color alone is here the badge of distinction, the true mark of aristocracy, and all who are white are equal in spite of the variety of occupation." [35] De Bow asserted this even more vigorously in a widely circulated pamphlet published in 1860. At one point, he said that the non-slaveholding class was more deeply interested than any other in the maintenance of Southern institutions. He said that non-slaveholders were made up of two groups: those who desired slaves but were unable to purchase them; and those who were able but preferred to hire cheap white labor. He insisted that there was no group of whites in the South opposed to slavery. One of his principal arguments was that the non-slaveholder preserves the status of the white man "and is not regarded as an inferior or a dependent. . . . No white man at the South serves another as a body servant, to clean his boots, wait on his table, and perform the menial services of his household. His blood revolts against this, and his necessities never drive him to it. He is a companion and an equal." [36]

Southern planters paid considerable attention to the non-slaveholding element whenever its support was needed in the intersectional struggle. Their common origins, at times involving actual kinship of planters and yeomen, gave them a basis for working together in a common cause. The opportunities for social mobility, however rare, provided the dreams of yeomen. These dreams strengthened their attachment to the planter class; while the fear of competition with a large group of freed men was a nightmare. But *race*—the common membership in a superior order of beings of both planters and poorer whites—was apparently the strongest point in the argument that the enslavement of the Negro was as good for small farmers as it was for large planters. The passion of the Southern planter and politician for oratory found ample release in the program to persuade Southern whites that theirs was a glorious civilization to be defended at all costs. In the absence of active and bitter class antagonisms, it was possible for the various white groups to cooperate especially against outside attacks and in behalf of slavery.[37]

Most Southerners were not satisfied merely to have their leaders restate the theory of Southern society and argue with abolitionists in Congress and other respectable places; they wanted to give effective and tangible support to their cause. Chancellor Harper had told them that, in the South as in Athens, "every citizen should be a soldier, and qualified to discharge efficiently the duties of a soldier." [38] In *De Bow's Review* "a Virginian" advised his fellows that *"without ceasing to be free citizens, they must cultivate the virtues, the sentiments, nay, the habits and manners of soldiers."* [39] They should be ready for vigorous, militant action to protect and defend the South's institutions. James Buckingham believed that they were determined to do exactly that. In 1839, he remarked, "Here in Georgia . . . as everywhere throughout the South, slavery is a topic upon which no man, and, above all, a foreigner, can open his lips without imminent personal danger, unless it is to defend and uphold the system." He stated further that the violence of the measures taken against the few who ventured to speak in favor of abolition was such as to strike terror in others.[40]

There was no strong antislavery sentiment in the Southern states after 1830. Moreover, Northern antislavery organizations were doing little to incite the slaves to revolt or, except for sporadic underground railroad activities, to engage in other subversive activities. It was enough, however, for Southerners to believe either that abolitionists were active or that there was a possibility of their becoming active. This belief, running very strong at times, placed under suspicion everything Northern, including persons and ideas. . . .

After 1830, the South increased its vigilance over outside subversion, and pursued the elusive, at times wholly imaginary, abolitionist with an ardor born of desperation. When they could not lay hands on him they seized the incendiary publications that were the products of his "fiendish" mind. In the summer of 1835, overpowering the city guard, they stormed the post office in Charleston and burned a bag of abolitionist literature. According to the postmaster, this act was not perpetrated by any "ignorant or infuriated rabble." [41] In the same year, citizens of Fairfax County, Virginia, formed local vigilance committees in each militia district "to detect and bring to speedy punishment all persons circulating abolitionist literature." A correspondence committee of twenty was to keep in touch with developments in other parts of the South. [42] . . .

All over the South mob action began to replace orderly judicial procedure, as the feeling against abolitionists mounted and as Southern views on race became crystallized. Even in North Carolina, where one citizen felt that there should be some distinction between that "civilized state and Mississippi and some other Western states," the fear of abolitionists caused many of its citizens to resort to drastic measures. [43] In 1850, two missionaries, Adam Crooks and Jesse Mc Bride, came into the state from Ohio, ostensibly to preach to these North Carolina Methodists who had not joined the newly organized Methodist Episcopal Church, South. [44] Soon they were suspected of abolitionist activities, and McBride was convicted of distributing incendiary publications. According to one source they were "mobed and drove out of Gulford." Ten years later a vigilance committee threatened to deal violently with one John Stafford whose crime had been to give food and shelter to Crooks and McBride during their sojourn in the state. [45] This was the kind of activity that Professor Benjamin S. Hedrick, dismissed from the University of North Carolina for his free-soil views, deprecated. Safe in New York City he asked Thomas Ruffin, Chief Justice of the North Carolina Supreme Court, to use his influence "to arrest the terrorism and fanaticism" that was rampant in the South. "If the same spirit of terror, mobs, arrests and violence continue," he declared, "it will not be long before civil war will rage at the South." [46]

NOTES

1. Howell M. Henry, *The Police Control of the Slave in South Carolina* (Emory, Virginia, 1914), pp. 31ff.
2. Charles S. Davis, *The Cotton Kingdom in Alabama* (Montgomery, 1939), p. 97; and Charles S. Sydnor, *Slavery in Mississippi* (New York, 1933), p. 78.
3. *The Code of Alabama* (Montgomery, 1852), p. 235.

4. *Ibid.*, p. 235 and John B. Miller, *A Collection of the Militia Laws of the United States and South Carolina* (Columbia, 1817), pp. 71ff.

5. Henry, *Police Control*, p. 40.

6. *Ibid.*, p. 32.

7. Sydnor, *Slavery in Mississippi*, p. 78; and Davis, *Cotton Kingdom in Alabama*, p. 97.

8. Edwin Clifford Holland, *A Refutation of the Calumnies Circulated Against the Southern and Western States Respecting the Institution and Existence of Slavery Among Them* (Charleston, 1822), pp. 61, 82.

9. Olmsted, *Back Country*, p. 203.

10. William Asbury Christian, *Richmond, Her Past and Present* (Richmond, 1912), p. 53; Herbert Aptheker, *American Negro Slave Revolts* (New York, 1943), pp. 218ff; and George Morgan, *The Life of James Monroe* (Boston, 1921), p. 228.

11. Theodore D. Jervey, *Robert Y. Hayne and His Times* (New York, 1909), pp. 131-132; Aptheker, *Slave Revolts*, pp. 273ff; and Henry, *Police Control*, pp. 152-153.

12. *Nashville Republican*, September 10, 1831.

13. *Norfolk Herald*, August 21, 1831, reprinted in *Nashville Republican*, September 10, 1831.

14. Frederick T. Wilson, *Federal Aid in Domestic Disturbances, 1787–1903* (Washington, 1903), pp. 56, 261-263.

15. In *American Negro Slave Revolts*, Aptheker calls attention to many instances in which military forces were used in connection with slave uprisings.

16. Charles Gayarré, *History of Louisiana* (New Orleans, 1903), IV, 267-268.

17. Aptheker, *Slave Revolts*, p. 255.

18. Harvey T. Cook, *The Life and Legacy of David Rogerson Williams* (New York, 1916), p. 130.

19. Guion G. Johnson, *Ante-Bellum North Carolina* (Chapel Hill, 1937), pp. 514-515.

20. Aptheker, *Slave Revolts*, p. 335.

21. *Journal of the Legislature of South Carolina for the Year 1833*, p. 6.

22. *Daily Picayune*, December 24, 1856.

23. John C. Calhoun, *The Works of John C. Calhoun* (New York, 1854), I, 483-484.

24. *Southern Literary Messenger*, XXIII (October 1856), 247.

25. Calhoun, *Works*, II, 58-59.

26. Jenkins, *Pro-slavery Thought*, p. 125.

27. Quoted in Edward Ingle, *Southern Sidelights* (New York, 1896), p. 31.

28. William Harper, *The Pro-slavery Argument* (Philadelphia, 1853), p. 11.

29. George Fitzhugh, *Cannibals All! or Slaves Without Masters* (Richmond, 1857), pp. 97-98.

30. George Fitzhugh, *Sociology for the South; or The Failure of Free Society* (Richmond, 1854), p. 222.

31. *Selections From the Letters and Speeches of the Hon. James H. Hammond of South Carolina* (New York, 1866), p. 34.

32. Thomas Cooper to Mahlon Dickerson, March 16, 1826, in "Letters of Dr. Thomas Cooper, 1825-1832," *American Historical Review*, VI (July, 1901), 729. The idea of Negro inferiority was believed by some Northerners,

but it neither was as widespread in that section nor did it constitute a whole body of thought as it did in the South.

33. S. C. Cartwright, "Diseases and Peculiarities of the Negro," *The Industrial Resources, etc., of the Southern and Western States* (New Orleans, 1853), II, 316.

34. See Alfred Vagts, *A History of Militarism* (New York, 1937), pp. 165, 479.

35. Thomas R. Dew, *Review of the Debate in the Virginia Legislature of 1831 and 1832* (Richmond, 1832), pp. 112-113.

36. J. D. B. De Bow, *The Interest in Slavery of the Southern Non-Slaveholder* (Charleston, 1860), pp. 3, 5, 8-10.

37. For discussions of inter-class harmony in the South see Frank L. Owsley, *Plain Folk of the Old South* (Baton Rouge, 1949), pp. 133-134; and Paul H. Buck, "Poor Whites of the Ante-Bellum South," *American Historical Review*, XXXI (October 1925), 41, 51-52.

38. Harper, *Pro-slavery Argument*, p. 80.

39. "The Black Race in North America," *De Bow's Review*, XX (February 1856), 209. (Italics in original.)

40. Buckingham, *Slave States*, I, 183.

41. Alfred Huger to Amos Kendall, July 30, 1855, in Theodore D. Jervey, *Robert Y. Hayne*, pp. 379-380.

42. Eaton, "Mob Violence," p. 358.

43. David W. Stone to Thomas Ruffin, May 3, 1842, in J. G. de Roulhac Hamilton, editor, *The Papers of Thomas Ruffin* (Raleigh, 1918), II, 206.

44. For a detailed account of the experiences of Crooks and McBride, see Eaton, *Freedom of Thought*, pp. 138-139.

45. John Stafford to Thomas Ruffin, January 24, 1860, in Hamilton, *Papers of Thomas Ruffin*, II, 65-67.

46. Benjamin S. Hedrick to Thomas Ruffin, January 16, 1860, in *Papers of Thomas Ruffin*, III, 64-65.

• The twain have met. The socialist and the paternalist have joined in evincing a fondness for social cohesion and in an antipathy for the fragmented and individualistic liberty of bourgeois capitalism. It is striking but not surprising, therefore, that the most forceful reassertion of Ulrich Phillips's view of the South as a distinct semifeudal subculture within ante-bellum America should come from a Marxist historian. Eugene D. Genovese's essays on "the political economy of slavery" combine Phillips's notion of an anticapitalistic, patriarchal slave civilization with Charles Beard's view that because of this uniqueness, the Civil War represented an inevitable clash of cultures moving daily further apart. As Genovese restates the Beardian argument, "slave civilization could not forever coexist with an increasingly hostile, powerful, and aggressive Northern capitalism," Genovese's article develops these perspectives on the slave South.

The Slave South: An Interpretation

EUGENE D. GENOVESE

THE PROBLEM

Two interpretations of antebellum Southern society have, for some years, contended in a perplexing and unreal battle. The first considers the Old South an agrarian society fighting against the enroachments of industrial capitalism; the second considers the slave plantation merely a form of capitalist enterprise and suggests that the differences between Northern and Southern capitalism were more apparent than real. These two views, which one would think contradictory, are sometimes combined in the thesis that the agrarian nature of planter capitalism, for some reason, made coexistence with industrial capitalism difficult. None of these interpretations is convincing. Slavery and the rule of a

From Eugene D. Genovese, "The Slave South: An Interpretation," *Science & Society*, XXV (December 1961), 320-37. Reprinted by permission.

special type of agrarians, the planters, characterized Southern society, which despite superficial resemblances to Northern was anti-bourgeois in structure and outlook.[1]

The first view cannot explain why some agrarian societies give rise to industrialization and some do not. A prosperous agricultural hinterland has generally served as a basis for industrial development by providing a home market for manufacturers and a source of capital accumulation; and the prosperity of farmers has largely depended on the rise of industrial centers as markets for foodstuffs. In a capitalist society, agriculture is one industry among many, and its conflict with manufacturing is one of many competitive rivalries. There must have been something unusual about an agriculture that generated violent opposition to the agrarian West as well as to the industrial Northeast.

The second view, which is the more widely held, stresses that the plantation system produced for a distant market, responded to supply and demand, invested capital in land and slaves, and operated with funds borrowed from banks and factors. This, the more serious of the two interpretations, cannot begin to explain the origins of the conflict with the North and is intrinsically unsatisfactory. The reply to it will be the burden of this article.

SLAVERY AND THE EXPANSION OF CAPITALISM

The proponents of the idea of "planter capitalism" draw heavily, wittingly or not, on Lewis C. Gray's theory of the genesis of the plantation system. Gray defines the plantation as a "capitalistic type of agricultural organization in which a considerable number of unfree laborers were employed under a unified direction and control in the production of a staple corp." [2] The plantation system is here considered inseparably linked with the international development of capitalism. Gray notes the plantation's need for large outlays of capital, its strong tendency toward specialization in a single crop, and its commercialism; and he argues that these are features that appeared with the industrial revolution.

In modern times the plantation often arose under bourgeois auspices to provide industry with cheap raw materials, but the consequences were not always harmonious with bourgeois society. Colonial expansion produced three diverse patterns: (1) the capitalists of the advanced country simply invested in colonial land—as illustrated by the recent practice of the United Fruit Company in the Caribbean; (2) the colonial planters were largely subservient to the advanced country—as illustrated by the British West Indies early in the nineteenth century; and

(3) the planters were able to win independence and build a society under their own direction—as illustrated by the Southern United States.

In alliance with the North, the planter-dominated South broke away from England, and political conditions in the new republic allowed it considerable freedom for self-development. The plantation society that had begun as an appendage of British capitalism ended as a powerful, largely autonomous, aristocratic civilization, although it was tied to the capitalistic world by bonds of commodity production. The essential element in this distinct civilization was the planter domination made possible by the command of slave labor. Slavery provided the basis for a special Southern economic and social life, special problems and tensions, and special laws of development.

THE RATIONALITY AND IRRATIONALITY OF SLAVE SOCIETY

Slave economies manifest irrational tendencies that inhibit economic development and endanger social stability. Max Weber, for one, has noted four important irrational features.[3] First, the master cannot adjust the size of his labor force in accordance with business fluctuations. In particular, efficiency cannot readily be achieved through the manipulation of the labor force if sentiment, custom, or community pressure makes separation of families difficult. Secondly, the capital outlay is much greater and riskier for slave labor than for free.[4] Thirdly, the domination of a planter class increases the risk of political influence in the market. Fourthly, the sources of cheap slave labor are usually exhausted rather quickly, and beyond a certain point, costs become excessively burdensome. Weber's remarks could be extended. For example, planters have little opportunity to select specifically trained workers for special tasks as they arise.

There are other telling aspects of this economic irrationality. Under capitalism the pressure of the competitive struggle and the bourgeois spirit of accumulation direct the greater part of profits back into production. The competitive side of Southern slavery produced a similar result but one that was modified by the pronounced tendency to heavy consumption. Economic historians and sociologists have long noted the high propensity to consume among landed aristocracies. No doubt this difference is one of degree, and the greater part of slavery's profits also find their way back into production; but the method of reinvestment in the two systems is substantially different. Under capitalism profits are largely directed into an expansion of plant and equipment, not labor; in a word, economic progress is qualitative. In slave societies, for economic reasons as well as for those of social prestige, reinvestment of funds takes place along the same lines as the original investment—in land and slaves; that is, economic progress is quantitative.

In the South this weakness was fatal for the slaveholding planters. They found themselves engaged in a growing conflict with Northern farmers and businessmen over tariffs, homesteads, internal improvements, and the decisive question of the balance of political power in the Union. The slow pace of their economic progress, in contrast to the long strides of the North, threatened to undermine their political parity and result in a Southern defeat on all major issues of the day. The qualitative leaps in the Northern economy were manifested in a rapidly increasing population, an expanding productive plant, and growing political, ideological, and social boldness. The South's voice grew shriller and harsher as it contemplated the impending disaster and sought solace in complaints of Northern aggression and exploitation.

Just as Southern slavery directed reinvestment along a path that led to economic stagnation, so too did it limit the volume of capital accumulated for investment of any kind. We need not reopen the tedious argument about which came first the plantation, the one-crop system, or slavery. It should be clear that while slavery existed, the South had to be bound to a plantation system and an agricultural economy based on a few crops. The resultant dependence on Northern and British markets and on outside credit facilities and the inevitably mounting middleman's charges are well known. Perhaps less obvious was the capital drain occasioned by the importation of industrial goods. While the home market was retarded, Southern manufacturers had a difficult time producing in sufficient quantities to keep costs and prices at levels competitive with Northerners. The attendant dependence on Northern and British imports intensified the outward flow of badly needed funds.

Yet, many of the elements of irrationality were irrational only from a bourgeois standpoint. The high propensity to consume luxuries, for example, has always been functional (i.e., socially if not economically rational) in aristocratic societies, for it has provided the ruling class with the façade necessary to overawe the middle and lower classes. We may speak of the slave system's irrationality only in a strictly economic sense and then only to indicate the inability of the South to compete with Northern capitalism on the latter's grounds. The planters, fighting for political power in an essentially capitalist Union, had to do just that.

BOURGEOIS AND PSEUDO-BOURGEOIS FEATURES OF THE SLAVE ECONOMY

The slave economy had close relations with, and was in a sense exploited by, the capitalist world market; consequently, slavery developed many ostensibly capitalist features, such as banking, commerce, and credit. These features were not *per se* capitalist and played a different role in the South than in the North. Capitalism has absorbed and even encouraged many kinds of precapitalist social systems serfdom, slavery, oriental state enterprises, and others. It has introduced credit, finance, banking, and similar institutions where they did not previously exist. It is pointless to suggest that therefore nineteenth-century India or twentieth-century Saudi Arabia are to be classified as capitalist countries. Our task is to analyze a few of the more important bourgeois and pseudo-bourgeois features and, in particular, to review the barriers to industrialization, for only by so doing can we appreciate the peculiar qualities of the slave economy.[5]

The defenders of the "planter capitalism" thesis have noted the extensive commercial links between the plantation and the world market and the modest commercial bourgeoisie in the South and have concluded that there is no good reason to predicate an antagonism between cotton producers and cotton merchants. However valid as a reply to the naïve arguments of the proponents of the agrarianism-versus-industrialism thesis, this criticism has unjustifiably been twisted to suggest that the presence of commercial activity proves the presence of capitalism.[6] Many precapitalist economic systems had well developed commercial relations, but if every commercial society is to be considered "capitalist," the word loses all meaning. In general, commercial classes have supported the existing system of production. As Maurice Dobb observes, their fortunes are bound up with those of the dominant producers, and merchants are more likely to seek an extension of their middlemen's profit than to try to reshape the economic order.[7]

In the Old South extensive and complicated commercial relations with the world market permitted the growth of a small commercial bourgeoisie. The resulting fortunes flowed into slaveholding, which offered prestige and was economically and politically secure in a planter-dominated society. Independent merchants found their business dependent on the patronage of the slaveholders. The merchants either became planters themselves or assumed a servile attitude toward the planters. The commercial bourgeoisie, such as it was, was tied to the slaveholding interest, had little desire or opportunity to invest capital in industrial expansion, and adopted the prevailing aristocratic attitudes.

The Southern industrialists were in an analogous situation, although one that was potentially subversive of the political power and ideological unity of the planters. Since the Southern countryside was dominated by large planters and slaves, the home market was retarded. The Southern yeomanry, unlike the Western, lacked the purchasing power to sustain rapid industrial development.[8] The planters spent much of their money abroad for luxuries. The plantation market consisted primarily of the demand for cheap slave clothing and cheap agricultural implements for use or misuse by the slaves. Southern industrialism needed a sweeping agrarian revolution to provide it with cheap labor and a substantial rural market, but the Southern industrialists were dependent on the existing, limited, plantation market. Leading industrialists like William Gregg and Daniel Pratt were plantation-oriented and proslavery. They could hardly have been otherwise.

The banking system of the South serves as an excellent illustration of an ostensibly capitalist institution that worked to augment the power of the planters and retard the development of the bourgeoisie. Southern banks functioned much as did those which the British introduced into Latin America, India, and Egypt during the nineteenth century. Although the British banks fostered dependence on British capital, they did not directly and willingly generate internal capitalist development. They were not sources of industrial capital but "large-scale clearing houses of mercantile finance vying in their interest charges with the local usurers." [9]

The difference between the banking practices of the South and those of the West reflects the difference between slavery and agrarian capitalism. In the West, as in the Northeast, banks and credit facilities promoted a vigorous economic expansion. During the period of irresponsible Western banking (1830–1844) credit was extended liberally for industrial development as well as for land purchases and internal improvements. Manufacturers and merchants dominated the boards of directors of Western banks, and landowners played a minor role. Undoubtedly, many urban businessmen speculated in land and were particularly interested in underwriting agricultural exports; but they gave attention to building up agricultural processing industries and urban enterprises, which guaranteed the region a many-sided economy.[10]

The slave states paid considerable attention to the development of a conservative, stable banking system, which could guarantee the movement of staple crops and the extension of credit to the planters. Southern banks were primarily designed to lend the planters money for outlays that were economically feasible and socially acceptable in a slave society: the movement of crops, the purchase of land and slaves, and little else.

Whenever easy credit policies were pursued in the South, the damage done outweighed the advantages of increased production. This imbalance probably did not occur in the West, for easy credit made possible agricultural and industrial expansion of a diverse nature and, despite acute crises, established a firm basis for long-range prosperity. Easy credit in the South led to expansion of cotton production with concomitant overproduction and low prices simultaneously, it increased the price of slaves.

Planters wanted their banks only to facilitate cotton shipments and maintain sound money. They purchased large quantities of foodstuffs from the West and, since they shipped little in return, had to pay in bank notes. For five years following the New Orleans bank failures of 1837, the city's bank notes were at a discount of from ten to twenty-five per cent. This condition could not be allowed to recur. Sound banking and sound money became the cries of the planters as a class.

Southern banking tied the planters to the banks but, more important, tied the bankers to the plantations. The banks often found it necessary to add prominent planters to their boards of directors and were, in any case, closely supervised by the planter-dominated state legislatures. In this relationship the bankers could not emerge as a middle-class counterweight to the planters but could only serve as their auxiliaries.[11]

The proponents of the "planter capitalism" thesis describe the planters and their society as bourgeois. Although this description is confusing and can serve no useful purpose, let us grant it for the moment. We are then confronted with a bourgeois society that impedes the development of every normal feature of capitalism; but when we realize that the planters were not bourgeois and that their society represented the antithesis of capitalism, these difficulties disappear. The fact of slaveownership is central to our problem. The seemingly formal question of whether the owners of the means of production command labor or purchase the labor power of free workers contains in itself the entire content of Southern life. All the essential features of Southern particularity and of Southern backwardness can be traced to the relationship of master to slave.

THE BARRIERS TO INDUSTRIALIZATION

If the planters were losing their economic and political cold war with the Northern bourgeoisie, the failure of the South to develop sufficient industry was the most striking immediate cause. Its inability to develop adequate manufactures is usually attributed to the inefficiency of the labor force. No doubt, slaves did not easily adjust to industrial employment, and the indirect effects of the slave system impeded the employment of whites. Slaves were used effectively in hemp, tobacco, iron, and cotton factories but only under socially dangerous conditions. They were given a wide variety of privileges and elevated to an elite status. Planters generally appreciated the potentially subversive quality of these arrangements and were hostile to their extension.

There were other, and perhaps more important, impediments to industrialization. Slavery concentrated economic and political power in the hands of a slaveholding class hostile to industrialism. The planters feared a strong urban bourgeoisie, which might make common cause with its Northern counterpart. They feared a white urban working class of unpredictable social tendencies. In general, they distrusted the city and saw in it something incongruous with their local power and status arrangements. The planters were unwilling to assume a heavy tax burden to assist manufacturers, and as the South fell further and further behind the North in industrial development, increasing state aid was required to help industry offset the Northerners' advantages of scale, efficiency, credit relations, and business reputation.

Slavery led to the rapid concentration of land and wealth and prevented the expansion of a Southern home market. Instead of providing a basis for industrial growth, the Southern countryside, economically dominated by a few large estates, provided only a limited market for industry. Data on the cotton textile factories almost always reveal that Southern producers aimed at supplying slaves with the cheapest and coarsest kind of cotton goods. Even so, local industry had to compete with Northern firms, which sometimes shipped direct and sometimes established Southern branches.

William Gregg, the South's foremost industrialist, was aware of the modest proportions of the Southern market and warned manufacturers against trying to produce exclusively for their local areas. His own company at Graniteville, South Carolina, produced fine cotton goods that sold much better in the North than in the South. Gregg was an unusually able man, and his success in selling to the North was a personal triumph. When he had to evaluate the general situation confronting Southern manufacturers, he asserted that he was willing to stake his reputation on their ability to compete with Northerners in the production of *"coarse cotton fabrics."* [13]

Some Southern businessmen, especially those in the border states, did good business in the North. Louisville tobacco and hemp manufacturers sold much of their output in Ohio. Some producers of iron and agricultural implements sold in nearby Northern cities. This kind of business was precarious. As Northern competitors arose and the market shrank, Southern producers had to rely on the narrow and undependable Southern market.[14] Well before 1840 iron manufacturing establishments in the Northwest provided local farmers with excellent markets for grain, vegetables, molasses, and work animals. During the ante-bellum period, and after, the grain growers of America found their market at home. America's rapid industrial development offered farmers a magnificently expanding urban market, and not until much later did they come to depend to any important extent on exports.

To a small degree the South benefited in this way. By 1840 the tobacco manufacturing industry began to absorb more tobacco than was being exported, and the South's few industrial centers provided markets for local grain and vegetable growers. Since the South could not undertake a general industrialization, few urban centers arose to provide substantial markets for farmers and planters. Apart from Baltimore and New Orleans, the slave states had no large cities, and few reached the size of 15,000. Southern grain growers, except for those close to the cities of the free states, had to be content with the market offered by planters who preferred to specialize in cotton or sugar and buy foodstuffs. This market was limited by the restricted rations of the slaves and was further narrowed by limited transportation. It did not pay the planters to appropriate state funds to build a transportation system into the back country, and any measure to increase the economic strength of the back-country farmers was politically dangerous to the aristocracy of the Black Belt. The farmers of the back country remained isolated, self-sufficient, and politically, economically, and socially backward. Those grain-growing farmers who could compete with producers in the Upper South and Northwest for the plantation market were in the Black belt itself. Since the planters did not have to buy from these local producers, the economic relationship greatly strengthened the political hand of the planters.

THE GENERAL FEATURES OF SOUTHERN AGRICULTURE

The South's greatest economic weakness was the low productivity of its labor force.[15] The slaves worked indifferently. They could be made to work reasonably well under close supervision in the cotton fields, but the cost of supervising them in more than one or two operations at a time was prohibitive. Without significant technological progress productivity could not be raised substantially, and slavery prevented such progress. Of greatest relevance, the impediments to technological progress damaged Southern agriculture, for improved implements and machines were largely responsible for the dramatic increases in crop yields per acre in Northern states during the nineteenth century.

Although slavery and the plantation system led to agricultural methods that depleted the soil, the frontier methods of the free states yielded similar results; but slavery forced the South into continued dependence upon exploitative methods after the frontier had been pushed further west and prevented reclamation of wornout lands. The plantations were much too large to be fertilized easily. Lack of markets and poor care of animals by slaves made it impossible to accumulate sufficient manure. The low level of capital accumulation made the purchase of adequate quantities of commercial fertilizer unthinkable. Proper crop rotation could not be practiced, for the pressure of the credit system kept most available land in cotton, and the labor force could not easily be assigned to the required tasks without prohibitive costs of supervision. The general inefficiency of labor thwarted most attempts at improvement of agricultural methods.[16]

The South, unable to feed itself, was caught in a series of dilemmas in its attempts to increase production of nonstaple crops and to improve its livestock. An inefficient labor force and the backward business practices of its ruling planter aristocracy were among the greatest difficulties. When planters did succeed in raising their own food, they also succeeded in depriving local livestock raisers and grain growers of whatever market they had. The stock raisers of the back country could not market their produce in the North because of the high costs of transportation.

The planters had little capital with which to buy improved breeds and could not guarantee the care necessary to make such investments worthwhile. Stock raisers too lacked the capital, and if they could get it, the investments would have been foolhardy without adequate urban markets.

Thoughtful Southerners, deeply distressed by the condition of their agriculture, made a determined effort to remedy it. In Maryland and Virginia significant progress was made in crop diversification and livestock improvement, but this progress was contingent on the sale of surplus slaves to the Black Belt. These sales provided an income that offset agricultural losses and made possible investments in fertilizers, equipment, and livestock. The concomitant reduction in the size of the slave force facilitated the problem of supervision and increased labor productivity and versatility. Even, so, the income from slave sales remained an important part of the gross income of the planters of the Upper South. In other words, the reform was incomplete and could not free agriculture from the destructive effects of the continued reliance on slave labor.

The reform process had several contradictions, the most important of which was the dependence on slave sales. Surplus slaves could be sold only while gang-labor methods continued to be used in other areas. By the 1850's the deficiencies of slavery that had forced innovations in the Upper South were felt in the Lower South. Increasingly, planters in the Lower South were exploring the possibilities of reform. If the deterioration of agriculture in the Cotton Belt had proceeded much further, the planters would have had to stop buying the slaves of Maryland and Virginia. They would have had to look for markets for their own surplus slaves. Without the acquisition of fresh cotton lands there could be no general reform of Southern agriculture. The entire Southern economy was moving steadily into an insoluble crisis.

THE IDEOLOGY OF THE MASTER CLASS

The planters commanded Southern politics and set the tone of social life. Theirs was an aristocratic, antibourgeois spirit with values and mores that emphasized family and status, had its code of honor, aspired to luxury, leisure and accomplishment. In the planters' community paternalism was the standard of human relationships, and politics and statecraft were the duties and responsibilities of gentlemen. The gentleman was expected to live for politics and not, like the bourgeois politician, off politics.

The planter typically recoiled at the notions that profit is the goal of life; that the approach to production and exchange should be internally rational and uncomplicated by social values; that thrift and hard work are the great virtues; and that the test of the wholesomeness of a community is the vigor with which its citizens expand the economy.

The planter was certainly no less acquisitive than the bourgeois, but an acquisitive spirit is compatible with values antithetical to capitalism. The aristocratic spirit of the planters absorbed acquisitiveness and directed it into channels that were socially desirable to a slave society: the accumulation of land and slaves and the achievement of military and political honors. Whereas in the North people were impelled by the lure of business and money for their own sake, in the South specific forms of property carried with them the badges of honor, prestige, and power. Even the rough parvenu planters of the Southwestern frontier—the "southern Yankees"—strove to accumulate wealth in the modes acceptable to plantation society. Only in their crudeness and naked avarice did they differ from the Virginia gentlemen. That is, they were a generation removed from the refinement that follows successful primitive accumulation.

The basis of the planter's position and power was his slaveownership. It measured his affluence, marked his status, and supplied leisure for social graces and aristocratic duties. The older New England bourgeoisie, in its own way, struck an aristocratic pose, but its wealth was rooted in commercial and industrial enterprises that were being pushed into the background by the newer heavy industries arising in the West, where bourgeois upstarts took advantage of the newer, more lucrative ventures like the iron industry. In the South few such opportunities were opening. The parvenu differed from the established planter only in being cruder and perhaps sharper in his business dealings. The road to power was via the plantation. The older aristocracy kept its leadership or made room for men in the same enterprises.

Many travelers commented on the difference in material conditions from one side of the Ohio River to the other, but the difference in sentiment was seen most clearly by de Tocqueville. Writing before the slavery issue had inflamed the nation, he remarked that slavery was attacking the Union "indirectly in its manners." The Ohioan "was tormented by the desire of wealth," and would turn to any kind of enterprise or endeavor to make a fortune. The Kentuckian coveted wealth "much less than pleasure or excitement," and money had "lost a portion of its value in his eyes." [17]

Achille Murat joined de Tocqueville in admiration for Southern ways. Compared with Northerners, Southerners were found to be more impulsive, frank, clever, charming, generous, and liberal.[18] The planters paid a price for these advantages. As one Southerner put it, the North led the South in almost everything because the Yankees had quiet perseverance over the long haul, whereas the Southerners had talent and brilliance but no taste for sustained labor. Southern projects came with a flash and died just as suddenly.[19] Despite such criticisms from within the ranks, the leaders of the Old South clung to their ideals, their faults, and their conviction of superiority. Farmers, said Edmund Ruffin, could not expect to achieve a cultural level above that of the "boors who reap rich harvests from the fat soil of Belgium." In the Northern states, he added with some justification, a farmer could rarely achieve the ease, culture, intellect, and refinement that slavery made possible.[20] The prevailing attitude of the aristocratic South toward itself and its Northern rival was ably summed up by William Henry Holcombe of Natchez: "The Northerner loves to make money, the Southerner to spend it." [21]

At their best Southern ideals constituted a rejection of the crass, vulgar, inhumane elements of capitalist society. The planter simply could not accept the idea that the cash nexus was a permissible basis for human relations. Even the vulgar parvenu of the Southwest embraced the plantation myth and refused to make a virtue of necessity by glorifying the competitive side of slavery as civilization's highest achievement. The planters did identify their own ideals with the essence of civilization, and given their sense of honor, were prepared to defend them at any cost.

This civilization and its ideals were profoundly antinational in a double sense. The plantation was virtually the only market for the small nonstaple-producing farmers and was the center of necessary services for the small cotton growers; thus, the paternalism of the planters toward their slaves was reinforced by a semi-paternal relationship between the planters and their neighbors. The planters were, in truth, the closest thing to feudal lords imaginable in a nineteenth-century bourgeois republic. The planters' protestations of love for the Union were not so much a desire to use the Union to protect slave property as a strong commitment to localism as the highest form of liberty. They genuinely loved the Union so long as it alone among the great states of the world recognized that localism had a wide variety of rights. The Southerners' source of pride was not the Union as such, nor the nonexistent Southern nation; it was the plantation, which they raised to a political principle.[22]

THE GENERAL CRISIS OF THE SLAVE SOUTH

The South's slave civilization could not forever coexist with an increasingly hostile, powerful, and aggressive Northern capitalism. On the one hand, the special economic conditions arising from the dependence on slave labor bound the South, in the colonial manner, to the world capitalist market. The concentration of landholding and slaveholding prevented the rise of a prosperous yeomanry and of urban centers. The inability to build urban centers, in turn, restricted the market for agricultural produce, weakened the rural producers, and dimmed hopes for agricultural diversification. On the other hand, the same concentration of wealth, the isolated, rural nature of the plantation system, the special social psychology engendered the slaveownership, and the political opportunity presented by the separation from England, converged to give the South considerable political and social independence. This independence was primarily the contribution of the slaveholding class, and especially of the planters. Slavery, while it bound the South economically, granted it the privilege of developing an aristocratic tradition, a disciplined and cohesive ruling class, and a mythology of its own.

Aristocratic tradition and ideology intensified the South's attachment to economic backwardness. Paternalism and the habit of command made the slaveholders tough stock determined to defend their Southern heritage. The more economically debilitating their way of life, the more they clung to it. It was this side of things—the political hegemony and aristocratic ideology of the ruling class—rather than economic factors that prevented the South from relinquishing slavery voluntarily.

As the free states stepped up their industrialization and as the westward movement assumed its remarkable momentum, the South's economic and political allies in the North were steadily isolated. Years of abolitionist and free soil agitation bore fruit as the South's opposition to homestead legislation, tariffs and the like clashed more and more dangerously with Northern needs. To protect their institutions and to try to lessen their economic bondage the slaveholders slid into violent collision with Northern interests and sentiments. The economic deficiencies of slavery threatened to undermine the planters' wealth and power. Such relief measures as cheap labor and more land for slave states (reopening the slave trade and territorial expansion) conflicted with Northern material needs, aspirations, and morality.[23] The planters faced a steady deterioration of their political and social power. Even if the relative prosperity of the 1850's had continued indefinitely, the slave states would have been at the mercy of the free, for the South could not compete with the capitalist North in population growth, capital accumulation, and economic development. Any economic slump threatened to bring with it an internal political disaster, for the planters could not rely on their middle and lower classes to remain permanently loyal.[24]

When we understand that the slave South was neither a strange form of capitalism nor an indefinable agrarianism but a special civilization built on the relationship of master to slave, the root of its conflict with the North is exposed. The internal contradictions in the South and the external conflict with the North placed the slaveholders hopelessly on the defensive with little to look forward to except slow strangulation. The only hope was a bold stroke to complete their political independence and to use it to provide an expansionist solution for their economic and social problems. The ideology and social psychology of the proud planter class made surrender or resignation to gradual defeat unthinkable, for its entire civilization was at stake.

NOTES

1. For a succinct statement of the first view see Frank L. Owsley, "The Irrepressible Conflict." In Twelve Southerners, *I'll Take My Stand* (New York, 1930), p. 74. One of the clearest statements of the second position is that of Thomas P. Govan, "Was the Old South Different?" *Journal of Southern History*, XXI (Nov., 1955), p. 448.

2. *History of Agriculture in the Southern United States to 1860* (2 Vols.; Gloucester, 1958), I, p. 302.

3. *The Theory of Social and Economic Organization* (New York, 1947), pp. 276 ff. The term "rational" is used in its strictly economic sense to indicate that production is proceeding in accordance with the most advanced methods to maximize profits.

4. This simple observation has come under curious attack. Kenneth M. Stampp, for example, insists that the cost of purchasing a slave forms the equivalent of the free worker's wage bill. The *Peculiar Institution* (New York, 1956), pp. 403 ff. That equivalent, however, is to be found only in the cost of maintaining the slave through the year. The initial outlay is the equivalent of part of the capitalist's investment in fixed capital and constitutes what U. B. Phillips called the "over-capitalization" of labor under slavery. Surely, the cost of maintaining a slave is only a small part of the free worker's wage bill; but the difference in their productivity is probably much greater than the difference in their cost

5. This colonial dependence on the British and Northern markets was not ended when slavery ended. Share-cropping and tenantry produced similar results. Moreover, slavery at least offered the South a measure of political independence under planter hegemony. Since abolition occurred under Northern guns and under the program of a victorious, predatory, outside bourgeoise, instead of under internal bourgeois auspices, the colonial bondage of the economy was preserved, but the South political independence was lost.

6. Govan, *op. cit.*, p. 448.

7. *Studies in the Development of Capitalism* (New York, 1947), pp. 17 f; cf., Gunnar Myrdal, *Rich Lands and Poor* (New York, 1957), pp. 52 ff.

8. Twenty years ago an attempt was made by Frank L. Owsley and his students to prove that the Southern yeomanry was prosperous and strong. See *Plain folk of the Old South* (Baton Rouge, 1949). This view was convincingly refuted by Fabian Linden, "Economic Democracy in the Slave South: An Appraisal of some Recent Views," *Journal of Negro History*, XXI (Jan., 1946), pp. 140-89. Cf., Eugene D. Genovese, "The Limits of Agrarian Reform in the

Slave South," unpublished doctoral dissertation, Columbia University, 1959, pp. 117-21.

9. Paul A. Baran, *The Political Economy of Growth* (New York, 1957), p. 194.

10. The best introduction to this period of Western banking is the unpublished doctoral dissertation of Carter H. Golembe, "State Banks and the Economic Development of the West, 1830–1844." Columbia University, 1952, esp. pp. 10, 82-91. Cf. also Bray Hammond, "Long and Short Term Credit in Earl American Banking," *Quarterly Journal of Economics*, XLIX (Nov., 1934), esp. p. 87.

11. The bankers of the free states were also closely allied with the dominant producers, but society and economy took on a bourgeois quality provided by the rising industrialists, the urban middle classes, and the farmers who were increasingly dependent on urban markets. The expansion of credit, which in the West financed mining, manufacturing, transport, agricultural diversification, and the numerous branches of a capitalist economy, in the South bolstered the economic position of the planters, prevented the rise of alternative industries, and guaranteed the extension and consolidation of the plantation system.

12. Slavery impeded white immigration by presenting Europeans with an aristocratic, caste-ridden society that scarcely disguised its contempt for the working classes. The economic opportunities in the North were, in most respects, far greater. When white labor was used in Southern factories, it was not always superior to urban slave labor. The incentives offered by the Northern economic and social system were largely missing; opportunities for acquiring skills were fewer; and in general, productivity was much lower than in the North.

13. William Gregg, *Essays on Domestic Industry* (first published 1845; Graniteville, S. C., 1941), p. 4. Original emphasis.

14. Consider the experience of locomotive, paper, and cotton manufacturers as reported in: Carrol H. Quenzel, "The Manufacture of Locomotives and Cars in Alexandria in the 1850's," *Virginia Magazine of History and Biography*, LXII (April, 1954), pp. 182 ff.; Ernest M. Lander, Jr., "Paper Manufacturing in South Carolina Before the Civil War," *North Carolina Historical Review*, XXIX (April, 1952), pp. 225 ff.; Adelaide L. Fries, "One Hundred Years of Textiles in Salem," *North Carolina Historical Review*, XXVII (Jan., 1950), p. 13.

15. Contemporary evidence points overwhelmingly to the conclusion that the productivity of slave labor was low. For a discussion of the relevant problems see my "Limits of Agrarian Reform in the Slave South," *loc. cit.*, chapters I and II. Extract measurement of slave productivity is not possible, for the data necessary for the calculations are not available. Nevertheless, from time to time someone tries to measure it anyway. Algie Simons and Lewis C. Gray made unsuccessful attempts earlier in the century, and recently, two Harvard economists, Alfred H. Conrad and John R. Meyers, rediscovered their method (apparently without knowing it) and presented an elaborate and thoroughly useless paper: "The Economics of Slavery in the Ante-Bellum South," *Journal of Political Economy*, LXVI (April, 1958), pp. 95-130. This is not the place to subject their views to detailed criticism, but one or two observations may suffice. They measure productivity by dividing the cotton crop by the number of slaves within certain age limits. To begin with, I think they use the wrong

age and price data, but let that pass. There are two troubles right at the start. This method assumes that the proportion of the cotton crop raised by white farmers in 1830, 1840, 1850, etc., was constant. There is not a shred of evidence for this; it is doubtful, and it cannot be verified. Secondly, it is well known that when cotton prices fell, some slaves were diverted to nonstaple production. Thus, the assumption that in any two years the same proportion of slave force worked in the cotton fields is simply wrong. In addition, the authors use a great many statistical tricks, such as "rounding off" figures. In one key instance rounding off makes a 4 per cent increase look like a 20 per cent increase. But these matters must be pursued elsewhere and at another time.

16. For a more detailed treatment of the problem of soil exhaustion see Eugene D. Genovese, "Cotton, Slavery and Soil Exhaustion in the Old South," *Cotton History Review*, II (Jan., 1961), p. 3-17; for a more extensive treatment of the attempts of the South to improve its agriculture in general see my "Limits of Agrarian Reform in the Slave South," *loc. cit.*

17. *Democracy in America* (2 Vols.; New York, 1948), I, p. 395.

18. *America and the Americans* (Buffalo, 1851), pp. 19, 75.

19. J. W. D. in the *Southern Eclectic*, II (Sept., 1853), pp. 63-66.

20. *Address to the Virginia State Agricultural Society* (Richmond, 1853), p. 9.

21. Diary dated Aug. 25, 1855 but apparently written later. MS in the University of North Carolina Southern Historical Collection, Chapel Hill.

22. No genuine Southern nationalism was possible, for the bonds of commodity production did not link every part of the region with every other part. Each state's transportation system was designed to connect the Cotton Belt with the export centers. The back country was largely closed, and the typically capitalist road-railroad network was missing even in the Cotton Belt.

23. These measures were opposed by powerful sections of the planter class itself for reasons that cannot be discussed here. The independence of the South would only have brought the latent intra-class antagonisms to the surface.

24. The loyalty of these classes was real enough but unstable. For our present purposes let us merely note that Lincoln's election and federal patronage would—if Southern fears were justified—have led to the formation of an anti-planter party in the South.

IV: THE SYSTEM

• Modern scholarship on the comparative analysis of New World slave systems began essentially with publication in 1947 of Frank Tannenbaum's book, Slave and Citizen, which analyzed the differences between North American and Latin American slavery. Since the time Tannenbaum's influential book first appeared, "comparatists" have converged on the question of slavery from several disciplines, with many of their works fusing insights and techniques from several distinct fields. Works by comparative historians, only a few of which could be reprinted in this collection, are listed in the bibliography. In the following article, David Brion Davis ranges across Latin American, North American, and ancient slave systems, offering a brief distillation of the inherent potential of a comparative approach to the study of ante-bellum slavery.

Slavery: A Comparative Approach

DAVID BRION DAVIS

Of all American institutions, Negro slavery has probably been the one most frequently compared with historical antecedents and foreign counterparts, and with the least benefit to systematic knowledge. Quite understandably, modern scholars have been so impressed by the long submission and degradation of southern Negroes, as well as by the extraordinary prevalence of racial prejudice in the United States, that they have often pictured American slavery as a system of unique and unmitigated severity that stands in marked contrast to other forms of servitude. Yet Thomas Jefferson could confidently assert that in Augustan Rome the condition of slaves was "much more deplorable than that of the blacks on the continent of America," and list bar-

From Chapter 9, "Slavery," by David Brion Davis, from A Comparative Approach to American History, C. Vann Woodward, ed. Copyright © 1968 by C. Vann Woodward, Basic Books, Inc., Publishers, New York.

barities and cruelties which were commonplace in Rome but presumably unknown in Virginia. Apologists for American slavery were always fond of comparing the mildness of their own institution, supposedly evidenced by a rapidly increasing Negro population, with the harshness of slavery in the West Indies or ancient Rome, where a constant supply of fresh captives made up for an appalling mortality. Yet abolitionists were always inclined to argue that the slave system of their own country or empire was the worst in history. Foreign travelers were not only subject to nationalistic prejudice but tended to rank various slave systems on the basis of fortuitous impressions or the biased accounts of hospitable planters. When we recognize how often comparisons have been influenced by ulterior motives and have been directed to the fruitless question "Which nation's slavery was the worst?" we might conclude that the subject can most profitably be studied in geographical isolation.

Yet American slavery was a product of the African slave trade, which was itself an integral part of both European commercial expansion and New World colonization. Most of the components of the slave-trading and plantation systems were developed in the thirteenth and fourteenth centuries by Italian merchants who purchased Circassians, Tartars, and Georgians at commercial bases on the Black Sea and then transported them to markets in Egypt, Italy, and Spain. As early as 1300 the enterprising Italians were even working Negro slaves on sugar plantations in Cyprus. In the fifteenth century, when the Portuguese adopted similar practices in trading with West Africa, Negro slaves displaced the Moors and Russians as the lowest element in the labor force of Spain. Negroes were shipped to Hispaniola as early as 1502; and as the Spanish colonists gradually turned to the cultivation of sugar, the rising demand for labor became an enormous stimulus to the Portuguese African trade. By the seventeenth century the Atlantic slave trade had become a vast international enterprise as the Dutch, British, French, Danes, Swedes, and even Brandenburgers established forts and markets along the West African coast. On both sides of the Atlantic there was close contact between merchants, seamen, and planters of various nationalities. In addition to competing and fighting with one another, they borrowed techniques and customs, cooperated in smuggling, and gathered to buy slaves at such entrepôts as Curação. If the British planters of Barbados looked to Brazil as a model, Barbados itself provided the impulse for settling Carolina. There was, then, a high degree of institutional continuity which linked the European maritime powers in a common venture. A trade which involved six major nations and lasted for three centuries, which transported some 10 to 15 million Africans to the New World, and which became a central part of international rivalry and the struggle for empire, cannot be considered as a mere chapter in the history of North America.

The unpleasant truth is that there could hardly have been successful colonization of the New World without Negro slaves, since there was no alternative source of labor to meet the needs required by the cultivation of sugar, rice, tobacco, and cotton, and since even the more diversified colonies were long dependent economically on the markets and earnings of the staple-producing regions. It must be emphasized that this common dependence on Negro slavery was never universally recognized or welcomed. From the first Spanish in Hispaniola to the British in Barbados and Virginia, colonists were slow and hesitant in committing themselves to a labor force of foreign captives. Among the frequent dreams of New World Utopias and second Edens, no one envisioned a model society of several thousand free Europeans overseeing the life and labor of several hundred thousand Negro slaves. From the beginning, racial antipathy was reinforced by the much stronger emotion of fear; and the dread of insurrection and racial war would always balance the desire for quick wealth through a reckless increase in slaves.

Nonetheless, from sixteenth-century Mexico to eighteenth-century Jamaica and South Carolina, colonial administrators were unable to maintain a reassuring ratio between white immigrants and Negro slaves. In regions where tropical or semitropical staples could be cultivated, it became clear that investment in slave labor was the key to expanded production and spectacular profit. The Negro slave played an indispensable role in the conquest and settlement of Latin America, and in the clearing and cultivation of virgin land from Trinidad to the lower Mississippi Valley and Texas. And as the possession of slaves became itself a symbol of affluence, prestige, and power, the demand for Negroes spread to urban and temperate zones. Important leaders in New England and French Canada seriously argued that only Negro slaves could meet the labor needs of their colonies. From 1732 to 1754 Negro slaves constituted more than 35 per cent of the immigrants entering New York City; by mid-century they were owned by about one-tenth of the householders of the province and accounted for 15 per cent of the total population. Meanwhile, the slave trade and American

Negro slavery were sanctioned by treaties and the law of nations, by the acts and edicts of kings and parliaments, by the Spanish Council of the Indies and the great trading companies of England, Holland, and France, by the Catholic Church and the major Protestant denominations. All the colonies of the New World legalized the institution, and many competed with one another for a supply of labor that was never equal to the demand. For more than three centuries the Negro slave was deeply involved in imperial wars, revolutions, and wars of independence. Insofar as the Western Hemisphere has a common history, it must center on a common experience with Negro slavery.

But did slavery mean the same thing to the various colonists of the New World? The fact that Dutch slave traders imitated the Portuguese and that a Dutch ship brought the first Negroes to Virginia did not mean that a Negro's status would be the same in Virginia as in Brazil. In England, unlike Italy and the Iberian Peninsula, true slavery disappeared by the thirteenth century. On the other hand, English jurists perpetuated the legal concept of unlimited servitude, and English judges recognized the validity of enslaving and selling infidels. We still have much to learn about the character of servitude in the sixteenth century and the later evolution of slave status in the British, Dutch, and French colonies. In making future comparative studies it would be well to keep in mind two points which should prevent hasty generalizations. First, in many societies the slave has only gradually been differentiated from other kinds of unfree workers, and his status, rights, and obligations have been defined in practice before receiving legal recognition. Second, although the actual condition of slaves has varied greatly even within a single society, there has been a remarkable persistence and uniformity in the legal concept of the slave. Since this last point has often been disregarded in comparative approaches to American slavery, we shall elaborate on it here.

The status of slavery has always been surrounded with certain ambiguities that seem related to the institution's origins. To be enslaved as a result of capture in war or punishment for crime implied total subordination to coercive authority. Yet bondage for debt or as the result of self-sale suggested merely a reciprocal exchange of labor and obedience for sustenance and protection. When a bondwoman's offspring were claimed by her owner on the same basis as the natural increase of livestock, the status was assimilated to that of movable property. In societies where slaves have largely been recruited from the native poor and have performed no specialized economic function, as in ancient

China, Egypt, and the Near East, the element of reciprocal rights and obligations has taken precedence over the elements of punishment and ownership. Nevertheless, the slave was legally defined as a thing not only in the Southern United States but in ancient Egypt, Babylonia, Greece, and Rome. And the Roman conception of the slave as at once a person and a piece of movable property prevailed in medieval France, Italy, and Spain; it was extended to Latin America and was incorporated in the Code Noir for the French colonies; and it reappeared in the laws and judicial decisions of British North America. A Virginia court merely affirmed the ancient Latin concept of chattel slavery when it ruled that "Slaves are not only property, but they are rational beings, and entitled to the humanity of the Court, when it can be exercised without invading the rights of property." And when an American master claimed the offspring of his female slaves or asserted his right to move, sell, trade, bequest, or give away his chattel property, he added nothing to a legal notion of slavery that had persisted in Europe for more than two thousand years.

The definition of the slave as chattel property implied a condition of rightlessness on the part of the slave. In neither Europe nor the Americas could a slave testify in court against a free person, institute a court action in his own behalf, make a legally binding will or contract, or own property. There were, to be sure, minor exceptions and variations. Slaves were sometimes allowed to testify in certain civil cases or give evidence against a master accused of treason. In North America at various times Negro bondsmen were permitted to plead benefit of clergy and to give evidence in capital cases involving other slaves. As in Rome and Latin America, they were accorded limited rights over personal property, including horses and cattle, and might act as a master's legal agent, though never with the freedom and complex prerogatives of the Roman slave. But what stands out above the exceptions and variations is the fact that from pre-Christian laws to the slave codes of the New World the bondsman had no civil capacities and was considered only as an extension of his master's legal personality. Even in Puritan Massachusetts slaves were, in the words of Cotton Mather, who was simply echoing Aristotle, "the *Animate, Separate, Active Instruments* of other men."

One of the few significant differences in the legal status of slaves was that bondsmen were denied legal marriage in ancient Rome and in Protestant America, whereas slave marriages were recognized in Carthage, Hellenistic Greece, and in Catholic Europe and America.

Largely to prevent the sin of fornication, Catholic theologians even ruled that a slave might marry against his master's will. Yet according to St. Thomas Aquinas, slavery was an "impediment" to marriage, comparable to impotence, and a slave's first obligation must be to his master, not his spouse. If a master had a moral duty to try to preserve the integrity of slave families, he still had a legal claim to all slave children, and might of necessity divide husband from wife or children from parents. Since there is evidence that Latin American masters often did little to encourage or respect slave marriages, and that North American masters often recognized such marriages and tried to keep families intact, one may suspect that actual differences were more the result of individual personality and economic pressure than of legal and moral rights. The main point is that in no society have slaves had a legal claim to their wives and children.

Religious conversion has always complicated the question of a slave's status. The Muslims and ancient Hebrews drew a sharp distinction between enslaving infidels and temporarily holding servants of their own faith who had been deprived of freedom by economic necessity. Although the first Church Fathers ruled unmistakably that baptism should have no effect on the temporal status of slaves, medieval Christians showed an increasing reluctance to enslave their fellow Christians and came to think of perpetual bondage as a punishment suitable only for infidels. But the authorities who condemned the sale of Christians and yet preached slaving crusades against the infidels were ultimately faced with the problem of the baptized infidel. In 1366 the priors of Florence explained that it was valid to buy or sell slaves who had been baptized so long as they had originally come "from the land and race of the infidels." This was, in effect, the same test later applied in Virginia and other North American colonies. Baptism was to have no effect on a slave's status unless he had been a Christian in his native country. And if the Catholic colonists felt a much greater obligation to have their slaves baptized, North American laws encouraged conversion and recognized that the Negro had a soul that might be redeemed. After a century of inaction, the Protestant churches slowly began their work of spreading religion among the slaves, and by the mid-nineteenth century the proportion of converted Negroes was probably as large in parts of the United States as in Brazil. It is doubtful, however, whether the mass of slaves in any country ever enjoyed a meaningful religious life.

There was little that was distinctive in the police regulations and penal laws restricting the lives of North American slaves. Throughout the ages, and in virtually all parts of the Western Hemisphere, slaves were prohibited from carrying arms, traveling at night or without permission, and acting with disrespect toward a freeman. Fairly typical was a law of 1785 for Spanish Santo Domingo which ordered one hundred lashes and two years in jail for any Negro who raised his hand against a white man. The penalties for such crimes as theft and assault were everywhere more severe for slaves than for others. During the eighteenth century there was a tendency in most New World colonies to abandon the most sanguinary punishments, such as mutilation, dismemberment, and burning at the stake. Harsh restrictions and terrifying punishments persisted longest in the West Indies, where the disproportion of Negroes to whites was the greatest. But even in the West Indies the long-term trend was toward more humane punishment and an extension of the slave's legal protections.

It is misleading to say that Anglo-American law never recognized the Negro slave as a human personality whose rights to life, food, and shelter were protected by law. There was ample precedent for the 1846 ruling of a Kentucky judge that "A slave is not in the condition of a horse. . . . He is made after the image of the Creator. He has mental capacities, and an immortal principle in his nature. . . . The law . . . cannot extinguish his high born nature, nor deprive him of many rights which are inherent in man." Although a master might kill his slave with impunity in the ancient Near East, the Roman Republic, Saxon England, and under certain circumstances in the Iberian Peninsula and Latin America, and although in much of British America the murder of a slave was thought to merit only a modest fine, by the early nineteenth century the slave states of North America had put the killing or maiming of a Negro bondsman on the same level of criminality as the killing or maiming of a white man. In both the British Caribbean and the Southern states, courts sometimes held that slaves were protected by common law against such crimes as manslaughter or unprovoked battery. Georgia and North Carolina both held that slaves had a right to trial by jury, and North Carolina went so far as to recognize a slave's right to resist unprovoked attack. Of course it was one thing for American states to threaten punishment for cruelty to slaves, and to make masters legally obligated to give their bondsmen adequate food and shelter and to provide for their care in sickness and old age, and it was another matter to enforce such laws when Negroes were barred from testifying against white men. Nevertheless, one can plausibly argue that in terms of legal protections and physical welfare American slaves by the 1850's were as favorably treated as any bondsmen in history.

Yet one of the paradoxes of American slavery was that the laws protecting the physical welfare of slaves were accompanied by the severest restrictions on manumission. This brings us to the most important distinction between the legal status of slaves in British and Latin America. It should be stressed that taxes and other restrictions on manumission were common in antiquity, particularly in Rome, and that freedom suffered from prejudice and legal disabilities even when the stigma of slavish origin was not associated with race. There were discriminatory freedmen's laws, for example, in medieval Spain and Italy, and in Latin America as well. But only in the Southern United States did legislators try to bar every route to emancipation and deprive masters of their traditional right to free individual slaves. It is true that thousands of American slaves were manumitted by their owners, many after buying their freedom in installments, as was far more common in Latin America. It is also true that in some areas of Latin America a slave had no more realistic chance of becoming free than did his brother in Mississippi. Nevertheless, one may conclude that slavery in North America was distinctive in its efforts to build ever higher barriers against manumission. And there is evidence that this had less to do with slavery as such than with social attitudes toward racial integration.

Although the questions are of compelling importance, we cannot begin to determine whether slavery was a source of racial prejudice or prejudice a source of slavery, nor can we explain why prejudice became more dominant in the United States than in other parts of the New World. One may briefly state the principal facts that are relevant to a comparative study of slavery. Without denying the significance of racial difference as an aggravation to American bondage, we may note that throughout history slaves have been said to be naturally inferior, lazy, cunning, thievish, lascivious, fawning, deceitful, and incapable of life's higher thoughts and emotions. When not differentiated by race, they have often been physically marked off by shaven heads, brands, tattoos, and collars. There is unmistakable evidence of racial prejudice in Italy and the Iberian Peninsula, where colored slaves generally suffered from various indignities and disabilities. In Latin America Negro bondsmen were long denied the privileges and protections of Indian workers. Nonetheless, while Latin America was by no means immune from racial prejudice, even against freemen of mixed blood, there was a gradual acceptance of racial intermixture and a willingness to accept each stage of dilution as a step toward whiteness. In the British colonies, although the first Negroes had an ill-defined status and worked side by side with white servants, there was never any tolerance of racial blending. White fathers seldom acknowledged their colored offspring, and a mulatto or quadroon was still legally classed as a Negro. These differences may have been related to religion, sexual mores, social stratification, or the proportion of white women in a colonial population. But whatever the reason, prejudice against Negroes seems to have grown in the United States with the advance of popular democracy. It can be argued that this had less to do with slavery than with the status of the free Negro in an unusually mobile and unstratified white society. In other words, differences in slave systems may not account for the fact that while the Negro in the United States today has far more economic and educational opportunities than the Negro in Latin America, he also suffers from more overt discrimination from whites who feel superior but are unsure of their own status.

By focusing thus far on the legal status of slaves, we have given an oversimplified picture of institutional homogeneity. In actuality, of course, American slavery took a great variety of forms that were largely the result of economic pressures and such derivative factors as the nature of employment, the number of slaves owned by a typical master, and the proportion of slaves in a given society. Thus we correctly categorize North American slavery as plantation and staple-crop slavery, but tend to forget that in 1820 Negro bondsmen constituted 20 per cent of the population of Southern cities and that in 1860 there were a half million slaves working in factories, on railroad construction, as stevedores, as lumberjacks, on steamboats, and in numerous other jobs unconnected with agriculture. As in ancient Athens and Rome, and as in Latin America, slaves in the Southern states were employed as valets, waiters, cooks, nurses, craftsmen, and prostitutes. In spite of these well-known facts, most comparisons of slavery in British and Latin America have assumed that the institutions were virtually monolithic. We still lack comparative studies of the domestic servant, the slave artisan, the rented worker, and the slave in manufacturing establishments.

It has been said that the latifundia of southern Italy and Sicily provided an ancient precedent for the gang labor, the rationalized system of production, and the absentee ownership of the Caribbean plantation. But one must be careful not to lump all plantation agriculture in an undifferentiated class. Since the production of sugar, for example, was a long and continuous process that could be ruined by a delay in cutting, milling, boiling, or curing, the rhythm of plantation life was probably much the same in parts of Brazil as in Jamaica and Louisiana. The cultivation of sugar and rice required heavy capital investment, and in the West Indies and South Carolina led to slave gangs of several hundred being divided for specialized tasks under constant surveillance. Slavery in colonial South Carolina, though less characterized by absentee ownership, had more in common with slavery in the West Indies than either had with the institution in Virginia and Maryland. By 1765 South Carolina's forty thousand whites were outnumbered by ninety thousand slaves; eight years later Jamaica's sixteen thousand whites kept uneasy watch over two hundred thousand slaves. In neither society could a field slave be in close or frequent contact with white men. In Virginia, on the other hand, the proportion of Negroes and whites was roughly equal, and the typical tobacco plantation employed less than twenty slaves. Unlike any of the previously mentioned staples, cotton did not require elaborate stages of preparation and processing, and could be profitably grown on small-scale farms. It was thus not uncommon for a cotton farmer to own less than ten slaves and even to work beside them in the field. Even by 1860, after a long period of rising slave prices, nearly one-half of the Southern slaveholders owned less than five Negroes apiece; 72 per cent owned less than ten apiece and held approximately one-quarter of the entire number of American slaves.

Compared with the plantation agriculture of the West Indies and Brazil, the striking features of the American South were the wide dispersal of slave ownership and the relatively small units of production scattered over immense areas. This may have led to a greater variation and flexibility in the relationship between master and slaves, although we still lack comparative research on such vital questions as labor management, the social roles and subculture of Negroes, and the relation of plantation life to social structure. It seems plausible that if American Negroes sometimes benefited by a close relationship with white families, they were also denied the sense of massive solidarity that was probably essential for revolt. In the West Indies slaves not only had the opportunity to plan and organize revolts, but they were seldom tied by the close bonds of loyalty that led so many North American slaves to divulge plots before they were hardly formed.

This is not to suggest that North American slaves were less oppressed than those of other times and regions, but only that there were different forms of oppression. As comparative studies move ahead toward finer distinctions and a typology of slave systems, it is likely that less attention will be paid to legal status than to stages of economic development. It would be absurd to claim that all slave economies must pass through a pre-set cycle of boom and depression. Nevertheless, regardless of cultural differences and other variables, there are striking examples throughout the Americas of a pattern which began with an unmitigated drive for quick profit, a rapid expansion in slaves and land under cultivation, and a subsequent overproduction of staples. Whenever slaves were worked under boom conditions, as in the West Indies in the mid-eighteenth century and the Brazilian coffee plantations in the nineteenth, the institution was one of grinding attrition. A more relaxed paternalism tended to appear when prices had fallen, when there was little incentive to maximize production, and when planters in longer-settled regions looked to social and cultural distinctions to differentiate themselves from new generations of hard-driving speculators. Thus in the mid-nineteenth century there is evidence that in such states as Virginia and Maryland a more easy-going, paternalistic pattern of slavery was emerging, not unlike that of the depleted sugar plantations of Brazil. In Maryland and Delaware there was even a rapid decline in the proportion of slaves to freedmen, though this was partly a result of interstate migration. At the same time there was a heavy drain of slaves toward the expanding cotton areas of the Southwest, where the price of labor kept rising and slaves became more concentrated in the hands of a relatively few planters.

The question of stages of economic development is related to the much larger question of the place of slavery in the evolution of industrial capitalism. And here, though historians have long acknowledged the dependence of the world's cotton textile industry on the slave systems of North and South America, there is an astonishing lack of systematic and comparative analysis. The whole complex relationship between capitalism and slavery is still in the realm of suggestive speculation. Scholars still debate whether slavery was profitable and whether the forms it took in America can be termed capitalistic. We do not yet fully understand why so many areas where slavery flourished were stultified by soil depletion and a lack of capital formation, by an absence of internal markets, of urbanization, and of technological innovation. And finally, if we are really to comprehend the significance of slavery and the burdens it has entailed, comparative history must explain the great challenge posed to the institution by an emerging urban, bureaucratic, and capitalistic civilization, which led to a bitter conflict between England and her Caribbean colonies, to a sharp struggle between the Brazilian coastal cities and the interior valleys, and to an epic contest between the North and South in the United States.

BIBLIOGRAPHY

The pioneering work in the comparative history of slavery is Frank Tannenbaum, *Slave and Citizen, The Negro in the Americas* (New York, 1947). Stanley M. Elkins, in *Slavery: A Problem in American Institutional and Intellectual Life* (Chicago, 1959), surveys much of the relevant literature and synthesizes the generalizations of Tannenbaum with concepts from the modern behavioral sciences. The Tannenbaum-Elkins thesis regarding the uniqueness of slavery in North America is challenged by Arnold A. Sio, "Interpretations of Slavery: The Slave Status in the Americas," in *Comparative Studies in Society and History*, VII (April 1965), 289-308; and by my own *The Problem of Slavery in Western Culture* (Ithaca, N. Y., 1966), which also analyzes attitudes toward slavery from antiquity to the early American abolitionists.

The most comprehensive study of North American slavery is still Ulrich B. Phillips, *American Negro Slavery* (New York, 1918), which needs to be supplemented by Kenneth M. Stampp, *The Peculiar Institution: Slavery in the Ante-Bellum South* (New York, 1956). John Hope Franklin, *From Slavery to Freedom* (2nd ed.; New York, 1956), offers a general survey of the Negro in America.

More specialized studies which shed light on important aspects of American slavery are Eugene D. Genovese, *The Political Economy of Slavery* (New York, 1965); Richard C. Wade, *Slavery in the Cities: The South, 1820–1860* (New York, 1964); Eric Williams, *Capitalism and Slavery* (New York, 1944); and Leon F. Litwack, *North of Slavery: The Negro in the Free States* (Chicago, 1961). The debate over the profitability of slave labor is summarized by Harold D. Woodman, "The Profitability of Slavery: A Historical Perennial," *Journal of Southern History*, XXIX (August 1963), 303-325.

Elsa V. Goveia, in *Slave Society in the British Leeward Islands at the End of the Eighteenth Century* (New Haven, 1965), presents a detailed study of West Indian slavery. Negro bondage in the French colonies is described by Gaston Martin, *Histoire de l'esclavage dans les colonies françaises* (Paris, 1948) and Lucien Peytraud, *L'Esclavage aux Antilles françaises avant 1789* (Paris, 1897). For other valuable material on slavery in the New World, the student should consult J. Harry Bennett, Jr., *Bondsmen and Bishops: Slavery and Apprenticeship on the Codrington Plantation of Barbados* (Berkeley, 1958); Frank Wesley Pitman, *The Development of the British West Indies, 1700–1763* (New Haven, 1917); Lowell Joseph Ragatz, *The Fall of the Planter Class in the British Caribbean, 1763–1833* (New York, 1928); Gilberto Freyre, *The Masters and the Slaves: A Study in the Development of Brazilian Civilization* (New York, 1946); Arthur Ramos, *The Negro in Brazil* (Washington, 1951); Stanley J. Stein, *Vassouras: A Brazilian Coffee County* (Cambridge, Mass., 1957); C. R. Boxer, *Race Relations in the Portuguese Colonial Empire, 1415–1825* (Oxford, 1963), and *The Golden Age of Brazil, 1695–1750* (Berkeley, 1962).

The best survey of the slave trade is Basil Davidson, *Black Mother: The Years of the African Slave Trade* (Boston, 1961). The monumental work on slavery in medieval Europe is Charles Verlinden, *L'Esclavage dans l'Europe médiévale* (Brugge, 1955). While one cannot begin to indicate the vast literature on slavery in various societies, three titles which should not go unmentioned are William L. Westermann, *The Slave Systems of Greek and Roman Antiquity* (Philadelphia, 1955); Isaac Mendelsohn, *Slavery in the Ancient Near East* (New York, 1949); and Moses I. Finley (ed.), *Slavery in Classical Antiquity: Views and Controversies* (Cambridge, England, 1960). Finally, one should note that the volumes of the *Journal of Negro History* contain a mine of information for anyone interested in slavery in the Western Hemisphere.

• Harold D. Woodman summarizes and assesses a century's historical literature on the still unresolved question of slavery's unprofitability. The student might keep in mind an underlying corollary of the argument. Some historians have assumed that since slavery had become unprofitable by the late antebellum period, means might have been found for its elimination short of armed sectional conflict. This viewpoint is identified particularly with historians who have defended Negro slavery as an institution of social control. On the other hand, if slavery continued to remain reasonably profitable throughout its existence, the South would have had no economic motive for abandoning it and, as David Brion Davis observed, "no country thought of abolishing the slave trade until its economic value had considerably declined." The argument over the profitability of slavery, therefore, is closely tied to another unresolved historical dispute over the Civil War's inevitability as a means of eliminating the institution.

The Profitability of Slavery

HAROLD D. WOODMAN

Abolitionists and their proslavery antagonists in the ante bellum period argued hotly over the profitability of slavery. Since the Civil War, historians and economists have continued the argument, less acrimoniously but no less vehemently. In part, solution of the problem of the profitability of slavery has been blocked by a lack of agreement as to how the problem is to be defined. Either implicitly or—as is more often the case—explicitly, contemporaries and modern scholars alike have begun their discussion of the profitability of slavery by posing the question: Profitable for whom? For the slave? For the slaveowner? For the South as a section? For the American economy as a whole? Answers to the general question, of course, depend upon how the question is posed. As a result, conflicting conclusions often reflect differing definitions of the problem as well as different solutions. What seem to be clashing opinions often do not clash at all but pass each other in the obscurity created by a lack of an agreed-upon definition of the problem.

When a writer answers the question, "Profitable for whom?" by limiting himself to the planter or slaveholder, he is dealing with the question of profitability in terms of a business or industry. He is concerned with such questions as: Did the planters make money? Did *all* planters make money? Did planters make as much on their investment in slaves as they would have made had they invested elsewhere? Staple production with slave labor is regarded as a business enterprise much as automobile manufacture is seen as a business enterprise today. Profitability relates only to the success or failure of slave production as a business and ignores the broader questions of the effect of this type of enterprise on the economy as a whole.

If, on the other hand, a writer answers the question, "Profitable for whom?" by discussing the effect of slavery on the South, he is treating slavery as an economic system rather than as a business enterprise. The issue of profits earned by individual planters is subordinated to the larger problems of economic growth, capital accumulation, and the effect of slavery on the general population.

Debate over the years has ranged on both aspects of the topic, with most writers emphasizing one or the other aspect and an occasional writer dealing with both. Despite the many contributions which have been made—and are still being made—historians and economists have not been able to reach a consensus on this vexing problem. The debate rages undiminished and, except for greater subtlety of method and sophistication of presentation, often rests today on substantially the same ground that it did a hundred years ago.

If we trace the development of this continuing controversy through the works of its most able participants, we can discern some reasons for the lack of substantial progress in solving the problem and suggest certain lines of approach which may lead to a more satisfactory solution.

Dispute on the profitability of slavery in the ante bellum period was confined almost solely to the question of slavery as a system rather than a business. This is not surprising. Proslavery writers could hardly be expected to defend the peculiar institution on the ground that it made the planters rich. In the face of obvious Southern economic backwardness and poverty, such a position would be tantamount to an argument for abolition in the eyes of anyone other than the favored planters. On the other hand, the antislavery or abolitionist group would have a weak argument indeed if they confined it to the contention that slaveowners made a profit. The right to make a profit was uniformly accepted in the United States, and to point out that planters made a profit by using slave labor was no indictment of them. The nature of the situation, then, led prewar commentators to deal with slavery primarily as an economic and social system rather than as a form of business enterprise and to argue its merits on the basis of its effects on the well-being of the whole population.

This did not mean, however, that the contenders clashed directly. Specific arguments seldom met with specific rebuttal. Rather, the antislavery group picked out those aspects of the question they felt most damaging and most to be condemned; defenders answered by pointing to what they considered to be the beneficial features of the peculiar institution. The antagonists, of course, were directly involved. Their aim was most often not to convince their opponents by scholarly argument but to attack or defend slavery within the larger context of the sectional controversy.

The essence of the antislavery economic argument was that the slave system caused Southern economic backwardness. The words of Hinton Rowan Helper, the North Carolina white farmer, summarize this position and at the same time show the intense feeling which the argument generated in the ante bellum South:

> . . . the causes which have impeded the progress and prosperity of the South, which have dwindled our commerce, and other similar pursuits, into the most contemptible insignificance; sunk a large majority of our people in galling poverty and ignorance, rendered a small minority conceited and tyrannical, and driven the rest away from their homes; entailed upon us a humiliating dependence on the Free States; disgraced us in the recesses of our own souls, and brought us under reproach in the eyes of all civilized and enlightened nations—may all be traced to one common source, and there find solution in the most hateful and horrible word, that was ever incorporated into the vocabulary of human economy—*Slavery!* [1]

The burden of Helper's argument was that even in the area of the South's touted superiority, agriculture, the North was far ahead. Using figures from the 1850 census, Helper argued that the value of agricultural products in the free states exceeded that of the slave states and that the value of real and personal property in the free states topped that of the slave states (when the value of slaves was excluded). Helper adduced figures for commercial and industrial development which told the same story. His contention that slavery was the cause of this economic inequality came from a process of elimination rather than from a direct analysis of the operation of the slave system. At the close of the eighteenth century the South stood in an equal or superior position to the North in all aspects of economic development. Since then the South had fallen further and further behind. Wherein lay the differences between North and South which could account for this? Slavery, obviously, was the culprit.[2]

The Kentucky editor, Cassius M. Clay, regularly condemned slavery in his newspaper, the Lexington *True American*. Slavery, he argued, was economically destructive. Because it degraded labor, whites refused to do physical work, thereby fostering idleness. Those who would work were faced by the competition of slave labor, and their wages never exceeded the subsistence level which was the pay accorded slaves. When whites did not work and slaves were kept ignorant, skill or excellence could not develop. In addition, slave labor was economically expensive for the South because capital was tied up or frozen in the form of labor:

> The twelve hundred millions of capital invested in slaves is a dead loss to the South; the North getting the same number of laborers, doing double the work, for the interest on the money; and sometimes by partnerships, or joint operations, or when men work on their own account, without any interest being expended for labor.[3]

Finally, slavery hindered the development of a home market for local industry and thereby retarded economic development:

> Lawyers, merchants, mechanics, laborers, who are your consumers; Robert Wickliffe's two hundred slaves? How many clients do you find, how many goods do you sell, how many hats, coats, saddles, and trunks, do you make for these two hundred slaves? Does Mr. Wickliffe lay out as much for himself and his two hundred slaves, as two hundred freemen do . . . ? Under the free system the towns would grow and furnish a home market to the farmers, which in turn would employ more labor; which would consume the manufactures of the towns; and we could then find our business continually increasing, so that our children might settle down among us and make industrious, honest citizens.[4]

Clay's arguments, written in the 1840's, attempted to *explain* the economic consequences of the slave system rather than to *describe* them as did Helper a decade later. Clay's three main points—slavery degrades labor and keeps it ignorant, thereby hindering the development of skills; slavery freezes capital in the form of labor, thereby making it unavailable for other enterprises; slavery limits the home market—were recurring themes in the economic attack on slavery. A pamphlet by Daniel Reaves Goodloe, written about the same time that Clay's articles appeared, raised the same arguments.[5] George Tucker, in a general economic treatise written a decade earlier, gave major stress to the problem of idleness which he felt was a result of the degradation of labor induced by slavery.[6]

The most detailed economic indictment of the slave system in the ante bellum period—published just after the outbreak of the war—was made by a British economist. J. E. Cairnes stressed the detrimental effects of slavery as a form of labor and as a form of capital. The weaknesses of slave labor, he maintained, stemmed from three characteristics: "It is given reluctantly; it is unskillful; it is wanting in versatility." Soil exhaustion necessarily followed from the use of such labor. Scientific agriculture was impossible; slaves who worked reluctantly and in ignorance were incapable of learning and applying new farming techniques. Only the best lands, therefore, were used and, losing their fertility, were left desolate.[7]

Slave labor also hindered industrial and commercial development, Cairnes continued. Slaves were kept in ignorance and were thus unable to cope with machinery. If educated and brought to the cities as industrial workers, the danger of their combining to better their conditions or of their engaging in insurrection was increased. Commerce likewise was impossible. The dangers of mutiny on the high seas or of desertion in free ports would deter slaveowners from using their property in this work.

Cairnes agreed with Clay and Goodloe that slave capital was economically expensive because it involved a larger capital outlay than free labor. Available capital was tied up in slaves and therefore unavailable for manufacturing and commerce. As manufacturing and commerce were important sources for the accumulation of capital, the lack of these enterprises hindered accumulation in the South. This completed a vicious circle, accentuating the shortage of capital and making non-agricultural pursuits even more difficult to begin.[8]

Ante bellum defenders of slavery, for the most part, did not meet these economic criticisms head on. Except for those who charged that

Helper manipulated his figures to produce the desired result,[9] upholders of slavery shifted the ground of controversy.

Slavery was defended as an economic good because it transformed ignorant and inferior African savages into productive workers. "There is nothing but slavery which can destroy those habits of indolence and sloth, and eradicate the character of improvidence and carelessness, which mark the independent savage," wrote Thomas R. Dew.[10] Another defender, Albert Taylor Bledsoe, after his sketch of the horrors of life in Africa, concluded that "No fact is plainer than that the blacks have been elevated and improved by their servitude in this country. We cannot possibly conceive, indeed, how Divine Providence could have placed them in a better school of correction." [11] William J. Grayson versified the same argument:

> Instructed thus, and in the only school
> Barbarians ever know—a master's rule,
> The Negro learns each civilising art
> That softens and subdues the savage heart,
> Assumes the tone of those with whom he lives,
> Acquires the habit that refinement gives,
> And slowly learns, but surely, while a slave,
> The lessons that his country never gave.
>
> . . . .
>
> No better mode can human wits discern,
> No happier system wealth or virtue find,
> To tame and elevate the Negro mind.[12]

Thus slavery was not only an economic good but a social and humanitarian blessing as well.

Slavery, according to its defenders, was economically beneficial in other ways. It was said to mitigate the class conflict which existed in every society.[13] "It is impossible to place labor and capital in harmonious or friendly relations, except by the means of slavery, which identifies their interests," George Fitzhugh wrote.[14] His *Cannibals All!* also stressed the well-being of the slave. Because capital and labor were united in the slave he was better cared for and suffered none of the privations visited upon the wage slave of the North for whom freedom was a condition of dubious value. Grayson employed his heroic couplets to make this point:

> It bound to daily labor while he lives,
> His is the daily bread that labor gives;
> Guarded from want, from beggary secure,

> He never feels what hireling crowds endure,
> Nor knows like them in hopeless want to crave,
> For wife and child, the comforts of the slave,
> Or the sad thought that, when about to die,
> He leaves them to the cold world's charity,
> And sees them slowly seek the poor-house door—
> The last, vile, hated refuge of the poor.[15]

Proslavery writers, virtually ignoring the view of slavery as economically debilitating to the South, argued instead that it strengthened the nation's economy.[16] They pointed to the products of slave labor, tracing their importance to the country as a whole. Upon slavery and slave labor, in fact, rested the economic well-being of the nation and the world. David Christy, writing that slavery was not "a self-sustaining system, independently remunerative," contended that "it attains its importance to the nation and to the world, by standing as an agency, intermediate, between the grain growing states and our foreign commerce." Taking the products of the North, slavery "metamorphoses them into cotton, that they may bear export." To the world it supplied cotton for manufacture into cloth and clothing, stimulating commerce and industry. For the United States it provided the largest cash exports (cotton and tobacco); it comprised a market for manufactured goods, supplied food and other groceries, and helped to pay for foreign imports.[17] Northern profits depended upon Southern wealth, argued Thomas Kettell in 1860; the North, therefore, should do everything in its power to keep the South, with its peculiar institution, in the Union.[18]

Whatever advantages did accrue to the South came, ironically, to those who did not own slaves, according to the editor J. D. B. De Bow. Not only did the nonslaveowning merchants benefit from slavery because they handled the goods produced by slave labor, but the white worker in the South also benefited. He had status by virtue of being a white man; he was not forced to work in unhealthy shops as was his white brother in the North; and most important of all, he had the opportunity of becoming a slaveholder and by so doing relieving himself and his wife of drudgery in the fields.[19]

Although ante bellum disputants thus came to opposite conclusions regarding the profitability of the slave system, not all of their arguments were mutually exclusive. This observation is most clearly illustrated by the manner in which Ulrich B. Phillips, reexamining the question in the twentieth century, was able to incorporate a large part of both ends of the argument into his economic analysis of the slave system. He accepted many of the conclusions of slavery's defenders while at the same time maintaining that the slave system was detrimental to the economic development of the South. He was able to unite the two points of view by clearly differentiating between the plantation system and slavery. At the same time he considered another factor in his discussion, that of slavery as a business enterprise.

While slavery existed, for the most part, within the plantation system, the two, Phillips maintained, were not inseparable. Indeed, the plantation regime "was less dependent upon slavery than slavery was upon it." The plantation system was a means of organizing labor; slavery, on the other hand, was a means of capitalizing labor.

The plantation system had definite advantages both economic and social. By routinizing labor, dividing different tasks rationally, and instituting strict supervision, while at the same time caring for the health of the workers (slaves), the plantation made for efficient methods of production.[20] Such methods were required because of the crude labor used. In effectively organizing ignorant and savage labor into efficient production it was economically advantageous; and "in giving industrial education to the laboring population, in promoting certain moral virtues, and in spreading the amenities" it was socially advantageous. The plantation was "a school constantly training and controlling pupils who were in a backward state of civilization." [21]

But the ante bellum plantation system hampered the economic development of the South. Its weakness stemmed less from its role as an organizer of labor and more from its close tie-in with slavery as an economic system. If the plantation was a school, the slave system prevented the apt students from ever being graduated. Laborers whose abilities transcended crude field work were yet harnessed to it and could not establish themselves as independent farmers. Unskilled labor was what was required and planters found it economically wasteful to train many skilled laborers despite any ability they might exhibit.[22]

Slavery, then, was harmful to the South because it prevented full utilization of the potential skills and abilities in the labor force. But the detrimental effects of slavery went deeper than this, according to Phillips. The central economic disadvantage of slavery was that it required that the entire life's labor of the worker be capitalized. Under a free labor system, wages are paid as work is done, and income from the sale of products can be used to pay future wage bills as they arise. The planter, however, was forced to buy his labor; that is, his wage bill became a long-term capital investment. Thus the slave system absorbed available capital. "Individual profits, as fast as made, went into the purchase of labor, and not into modern implements or land improvements." [23]

Because capital tended to be absorbed by the slave system, its availability was at a premium and planters were forced to look to outside sources for credit: "Circulating capital was at once converted into fixed capital; while for their annual supplies of food, implements, and luxuries the planters continued to rely upon their credit with the local merchants, and the local merchants to rely upon their credit with northern merchants and bankers." The result was a continuous economic loss as capital was drained from the South.[24]

The capital shortage stunted Southern economic development by hindering diversification in the economy, thereby keeping the South dependent upon the North. While Ohio benefited New York by becoming a market and a supplier of food and raw materials, Alabama had no such reciprocal relationship with Virginia or South Carolina. On the contrary, the Southwest competed with the Southeast to the detriment of the older regions because it could produce cotton more cheaply on the better lands and because increased production and labor needs drove the prices of slaves up. Economic benefits accrued to the North where manufactured goods and services had to be purchased; the Southeast was prevented from opening mills because all available capital was absorbed in slaves.[25]

Phillips introduced another dimension to this discussion of the economics of slavery—the question of the profitability of slavery to the individual slaveholder.[26] Matching the continual public loss as capital left the South was the private loss in the form of interest payments on borrowed capital. Profits were absorbed by the need to capitalize labor, a situation which was greatly aggravated in the 1850's when prices of slaves skyrocketed. As a result, Phillips declared, by the end of the 1850's only those plantations on the best lands, under the most efficient supervision, could make a profit for their owners.[27]

For Phillips, then, the plantation system was often economically beneficial to the South.[28] Its weakness stemmed from the fact that it was inextricably bound to slavery. It was slavery as an economic system which hindered and warped Southern development and kept the South backward in the prewar period. And it was slavery which made staple production in the ante bellum period an unprofitable enterprise for all but the most favorably situated planters. Phillips concluded that slavery was "an obstacle to all progress." He had to explain the continued existence of a personally and socially unprofitable system on noneconomic grounds. Slavery, he wrote, was initially introduced as a means of labor control and at first had proved to be profitable. As the number of slaves continued to rise, slavery became essential as an instrument of race control. It became the means to police an inferior race, to keep the Negroes' "savage instincts from breaking forth, and to utilize them in civilized industry." For the moment private gain and social gain were united. But as time went on the question of race control became most important—and an end to be attained only "at the expense of private and public wealth and of progress." [29]

Phillips' work was immensely influential. In the 1920's and 1930's a series of state studies were published which tended to support his conclusions. Perhaps because they were local studies and not concerned with overall Southern development, these monographs have major emphasis to slavery as a form of business enterprise rather than as an economic system. The question posed was simply whether the planters made money on their investment in slaves. Rosser Howard Taylor, basing his conclusions on the testimony of travelers and on extant plantation records, concluded that in North Carolina "slaveholding was not generally profitable." [30] Relph B. Flanders, in his study of Georgia slavery, found that although some planters were able to amass a fortune, many others made but a marginal living. He found much evidence showing that ante bellum Georgia planters bemoaned the unprofitability of the peculiar institution.[31] Slavery in Mississippi was investigated by Charles S. Sydnor. He found that free labor was much cheaper than slave and would have been more profitable for the planter to use. A thirty-slave plantation required a $40,000 investment, while if free labor had been used only $10,000 would have been needed. The greater the capital investment, he concluded, the greater the interest costs which had to be charged against profits. Furthermore, the large investment in labor the slaveowner was forced to make "added nothing to the productivity of the soil or to the betterment of the farm equipment," and it was doubtful whether the increased efficiency gained by slavery justified the "enlarged investment of capital." After calculating the costs of production on a typical fifty-slave Mississippi plantation, Sydnor concluded that profits were low. Only by spending the interest and other hidden charges (interest on capital invested in slaves, depreciation of slave property, land, and equipment) and by not calculating their own wages as supervisors of the business could planters seem to make a profit. A similar situation prevailed in Alabama, according to the historian of the cotton kingdom in that state, Charles S. Davis. Even with cotton selling at eight cents per pound, production by slave labor "was a fair business and nothing more." While some planters did make a great deal of money, "for the great majority the planting profession meant only a living." [32]

Further support for Phillips' views came from an influential article by Charles W. Ramsdell in 1929. Ramsdell maintained that slavery could be profitable only on the very best lands and since these lands, by the late 1850's, had been almost completely settled, slavery would have gradually become more and more decadent until, finally, economic causes would have required emancipation. He pointed out that high cotton prices of the 1850's could not last and, in fact, had already shown evidence of decline by 1860. As good lands were taken up and cotton prices declined, slave prices would drop also and Eastern states would no longer have the Western slave market in which to dispose profitably of excess slaves. In the meantime, with no new land available, more slaves would be on hand than could be used. Owners of large slave forces would find the expense of maintaining them too high to make cotton production by slave labor profitable. Slaves would become an economic handicap and slaveowners would look for a way to free their slaves and thereby relieve themselves of the burden of supporting them.[33]

While Phillips and his followers were amassing a formidable array of economic reasoning and statistical data to prove that slavery was unprofitable both as an economic system (because of its effects on the South) and as a business enterprise (because slaveowners made little profit), other historians were challenging this thesis on all levels. Some sought to show that Southern backwardness was not the fault of slavery; others stoutly maintained that planters on the whole made very substantial profits. The beginnings of this anti-Phillips or revisionist school can be traced back as far as the first decade of the twentieth century, but most of the revisionist work was done in the period beginning in the 1930's. It is this school which seems to be most active at the present time; nevertheless, there are still strong adherents to the traditional point of view.

The Mississippi planter and historian, Alfred Holt Stone, writing in the first decade of the century, relied heavily on Phillips but came to different conclusions. Stone's central argument was that it was the Negro and not slavery which retarded the ante bellum South. The Negro, according to Stone, was an inferior beging incapable of advancing whether free or slave: "The negro was a negro before he was a slave and he remained a negro after he became free. I recall no sound economic argument against slave negro labor per se . . . which is not today equally as sound against free negro labor per se." Had white free labor been used in Southern production, the foundation of Southern economic life would have been sounder. Some form of the plantation system would have undoubtedly developed, "but it would have been based upon free white labor, and would have served as a great training school for the production of small farmers." [34] The innate inferiority of Negroes prevented them from reaching this level.

But the most telling of the earlier blows struck in the revisionist cause were works of Robert R. Russel and Lewis C. Gray written in the 1930's. Neither sought to reverse completely Phillips' point of view, but both aimed at changing the emphasis of his analysis.

Russel made no effort to deny that the ante bellum Southern economy was backward; he did deny, however, that slavery was responsible. Rather, the South was hamstrung by its "climate, topography, natural resources, location with respect to the North and to Europe, means of transportation, and character of the white population." [35] The fact that population in the North was less dispersed led to more concentrated markets for Northern manufacturers and lessened the problems of transportation to and from these markets. Household manufacture was more firmly entrenched in the Northeast from the start, and, as Northwestern agricultural regions opened up, Easterners were forced to leave the countryside—they were no longer able to compete—and were thus available as operatives in industry. In the South, the profitability of staple agriculture and the fact that slaves "were certainly not as well adapted to mechanical employments as to agriculture" prevented the development of this same pattern. The central weakness in the South was not simply that slave labor was used but that it was primarily an area of commercial agriculture. Planters lived on further earnings and borrowed from Northern and British sources, thereby incurring an expense which limited the amount of capital accumulation in the region. Overproduction of the staples forced prices down and cut into profits and, therefore, into savings. But these were phenomena of agricultural production and had little to do with the use of slave labor. Furthermore, the argument that slavery absorbed Southern capital was incorrect: "Slavery did not absorb Southern capital in any direct sense; it affected the distribution of capital within the section. The mere capitalization of the anticipated labor of a particular class did not destroy or diminish any other kind of property." [36]

The central element in Lewis C. Gray's revisionist argument was that slavery was a highly profitable form of business enterprise. Slave labor, when used for staple production, would always supplant free labor because it was cheaper and more efficient. The employer of slave labor had a guaranteed labor supply; women as well as men could be used in the fields; child labor could be used extensively; labor troubles such as strikes and lockouts were unknown. The slaveowner could appropriate every bit of surplus created by the slave over and above bare subsistence. Thus, slaveowners had to give their slaves only just enough to keep them alive; wage laborers could not offer their services for less.[87] The high prices of slaves in the 1850's, Gray wrote, reflected accurately the profitability of such labor, and it was profitability that accounted for its continued use.[38]

Although Gray disputed the contention that all of the South's ills could be traced to slavery, he did argue that the "ultimate influence" of slavery "upon the economic well-being of the South was pernicious." Slavery was most profitable on the richest and most favorably situated lands; other lands were left to the free population which lived at a subsistence level. This free population provided a very small market and exerted little pressure for the construction of roads, canals, schools, and other necessary social improvements. Because slavery was profitable, all available capital that was accumulated went into expansion of staple production using slave labor and, hence, was unavailable to industry or trade. The South remained, therefore, "a predominantly agricultural country" and was "consequently subject to the disadvantages characteristic" of such an economy. The fundamental disadvantage was the slow accumulation of local capital which further intensified the problems of expansion, diversification, and economic growth. "Hence," he concluded, "we have the near-paradox of an economic institution competitively effective under certain conditions, but essentially regressive in its influence on the socio-economic evolution of the section where it prevailed."[39]

The work of Gray and Russel opened up a double-barreled assult on the Phillips point of view. Russel had questioned the allegation that slavery was the main cause of Southern backwardness, and Gray had disputed the contention that slaveowning was not a profitable business enterprise. Further revisionist work proceeded along these two lines, although most of the succeeding work gave major emphasis to the problem of slavery as a business rather than as an economic system.

Thomas P. Govan subjected the bookkeeping methods used by Phillips and his followers to critical scrutiny. The central problem in determining profitability, according to Govan, was simply to decide whether planters made money on their investment. He criticized the work of Phillips, Sydnor, Flanders, and others on two counts: They failed to consider all possible sources of profit in making their calculations, and they considered as an expense an item which should have been considered as part of the profit. Services received from household slaves, food and other provisions grown on the plantation and used by the owner, and the increase in the value of land and slaves must all be considered as part of profit; yet, Govan charged, these items were ignored in figuring income. Furthermore, interest on investment, which Sydnor and others listed as an expense, was, in reality, a profit item. According to the classical economists, profit is made up of interest on investment, payment for supervision, and payment for risk. Accountants usually do not separate the first and last of these, but they do include them in the profit column. When these adjustments in bookkeeping methods are made, Govan concluded, slaveownership emerges as a highly profitable business.[40]

The bookkeeping problem was approached somewhat differently by Robert Worthington Smith. It is a mistake, he insisted, to consider capital investment on the basis of current prices on slaves. While slave prices were extremely high in the 1850's, it would be incorrect to use the appreciated value of slaves owned from an earlier period (or those born and raised on the plantation) as the capital investment in figuring profit. If, Smith concluded, profit is calculated upon the "capital actually invested in slaves" rather than upon current prices, "a very good return seems to have been paid to the majority of owners." [41]

The most all-inclusive revisionist work on the question of American slavery is Kenneth M. Stampp's *The Peculiar Institution*, published in 1956. Disagreeing with Phillips about almost every aspect of slavery in the United States, Stampp differed with him, too, over the economics of slavery. But while Phillips gave major emphasis to the problem of slavery as an economic system, Stampp was mainly concerned with slavery as a business: ". . . allowing for the risks of a laissez-faire economy, did the average ante-bellum slaveholder, over the years, earn a reasonably satisfactory return from his investment?" [42] Stampp's answer was unequivocal: "On both large and small estates, none but the most hopelessly inefficient masters failed to profit from the ownership of slaves." Slave labor was cheaper and could be more fully exploited; this made up for any loss due to inefficiency. Capital invested in slaves was not an added expense but merely a payment in advance for work which would be performed over a period of years. Hidden sources of profit, such as food produced on the plantation, sale of excess slaves, natural increase of slaves, appreciation of land values because of improvements—all, when added to the income from the sale of the staple, served to increase profits.[43] Stampp concluded that there is no evidence that slavery was decadent, no evidence that it would soon have died had not the war brought it to an abrupt end.[44]

Two Harvard economists added their voices to the chorus of revisionist argument in a paper published in 1958. Their purpose, declared Alfred H. Conrad and John R. Meyer, was to take the argument over profitability out of the realm of accounting and instead, measure profitability according to economic concepts.[45] They constructed an economic model of a Southern cotton plantation for the years 1830 to 1860 and then computed the return on investment on the basis of a Keynesian capital-value formula.[46] Their calculations showed that returns on cotton production varied from 2.2 per cent on low-yield land to 13.0 per cent on very fertile land, with returns of 4½ to 8 per cent encompassing "the majority of ante bellum cotton operations." Profits on the raising and selling of slaves were considered separately. Their calculations for this part of the slave industry showed returns varying from 7.1 per cent to 8.1 per cent depending on the number of children produced. These figures, the authors maintained, showed not only that profits were made in slaveowning, but that this form of investment was as good as an investment elsewhere in the economy. This was true throughout the South and not only on the best lands. Where lands were good, profits came from the raising and selling of slaves.[47]

Up to this point Conrad and Meyer centered their argument on the question of slavery as a business. They then turned to the broader question of slavery and its effect on the South. Slavery, they concluded, did not hamper Southern economic growth. Available capital was not used for industrialization and diversification simply because it could be more profitably used in agricultural production. The economic problems of the South were the product of an agricultural community and not a result of the existence of slavery.[48]

Two recent works, in dealing with the question of profitability, show the influence of Conrad and Meyer's findings. Stanley M. Elkins in his study of slavery wrote that the economists, by dropping accounting methods and substituting "the economic . . . concept of profit" have made a "conceptual breakthrough" on the question of profitability. Paul W. Gates, in his discussion of slavery in *The Farmer's Age*, leaned heavily on Conrad and Meyer's analysis in concluding that slavery was profitable.[49] It is clear, however, that Conrad and Meyer's work will not find universal acceptance. It was almost immediately challenged, briefly but cogently, by Douglas F. Dowd.[50]

More recently another economist, Robert Evans, Jr., has published his findings on the question of profitability. Assuming a classical market, he calculated returns on investments in slave capital on the basis of profits earned through the hiring out of slaves during the three decades before the Civil War. He found that the rate of return on slaves varied from 9.5 per cent to 18.5 per cent, figures which were usually higher than those which could be earned in possible alternate areas of investment.[51]

Almost all the writers whose work has been discussed in these pages, whether economists or historians, have, to one degree or another, influenced the conclusions of writers of more general works, who show some of the same diversity of opinion as do the specialists.[52]

It would be folly to assume that this vexing question will ever be resolved to everyone's satisfaction. In part, the difficulty in arriving at a satisfactory solution stems from varying definitions of the problem. Contemporaries argued vociferously, but they were arguing about two very different things. They could agree that slavery had to be considered in its relation to the Southern economy, but there was no agreement as to the particular issues this consideration involved. Ulrich B. Phillips in his analysis gave major stress to slavery as an economic system, but he also introduced what to him apparently was a secondary question, the profitability of slavery as a business enterprise. It was this question which his followers, and the revisionists as well, have emphasized down to our own day.[53] Thus, a subtle shift in emphasis has taken place through the years in the discussion of slavery's profitability, a shift which is obvious if one compares not the conclusions but the central problem posed by Phillips early in the century with that considered by Conrad and Meyer several decades later.

Some light at least could be shed on the problem if there could be agreement as to what the pboblem is. In reality, two distinct topics have been discussed over the years, and they are not necessarily related. At least, their relationship has to be proved before they can be considered related. Even if every slaveowner were able to realize a twenty-five per cent return on his investment, it does not necessarily follow that slavery as a system was economically profitable. The real question is neither one of bookkeeping nor one of economic profit. It is a problem of economic history.

To deal with the question of slavery as an economic system, one must clearly distinguish those elements in the Southern economy which existed because of slavery and those which were unrelated to slavery. Those who argue that Southern backwardness arose, for the most part, because the South was primarily agricultural must first show that this would have been true whether or not the institution of slavery existed. Conversely, those who argue that slavery prevented diversification must prove (1) that economic diversification did take place in nonslave agricultural areas and (2) that it was slavery and not other factors which prevented diversified investment in the South. Furthermore, if slavery is to be called the cause of any given phenomenon in the Southern economy, the exact dynamics of the influence of slavery must be shown. It is not enough to juxtapose the results with the existence of slavery to establish a causal relationship. A final methodological question must be posed: Can the economics of slavery be discussed adequately in purely economic terms?

Some work has already been done along the lines suggested here. Two decades ago Fabien Linden considered the effect of slavery on the development of manufacturing in the prewar South. Treating slavery as a political and social as well as an economic institution, Linden traced the dynamics of the opposition to a move to establish widespread manufacturing establishments in the South in the 1840's.[54] More recently Eugene D. Genovese has, in a similar manner, investigated the problem of slavery in relation to the home market in the ante bellum South.[55]

A different line of approach has been taken by Douglas Dowd, who made a comparative analysis of economic development in the South and West. Further work in this direction, including comparisons with underdeveloped countries, might yield significant results. Dowd also suggested ways in which the economic question had to be broadened: "The nature and extent of resources are of course meaningless apart from the social context within which they exist." [56]

Certainly new lines of thought and research can be explored. If scholars are mindful of the complexities of the question of profitability, and cognizant of the nature of the work already accomplished, we can expect the writings of the future to increase our knowledge of the South and its peculiar institution. The prospect is of more than academic interest. Not only could further work in this field deepen our understanding of nineteenth-century American economic history. It might also give valuable insights into the dynamics of economic growth and development.

NOTES

1. Hinton Rowan Helper, *The Impending Crisis of the South* . . . (New York, 1859), 25.

2. *Ibid.*, 1-25, 33, 39, 66, 69, 72, 81, 283-86, esp.

3. Cassius Marcellus Clay, *Writings*, Horace Greely, ed. (New York, 1848), 204-205, 224.

4. *Ibid.*, 227, also 346-47.

5. [Daniel Reaves Goodloe], *Inquiry into the Causes Which Have Retarded the Accumulation of Wealth and Increase of Population in the Southern States: In Which the Question of Slavery Is Considered in a Politico-Economical Point of View* (Washington, 1846), *passim*. Goodloe added that the degradation of labor served to keep immigrants away from the South, thus depriving the section of the skills and capital which new arrivals brought to the North.

6. George Tucker, *The Laws of Wages, Profits, and Rent, Investigated* (Philadelphia, 1837), 46-48. Tucker argued that as the number of slaves increased, the cost of raising them would be greater than the gain from their use, and emancipation would result. *Ibid.*, 49.

7. J. E. Cairnes, *The Slave Power: Its Character, Career, and Probable Designs: Being an Attempt to Explain the Real Issues Involved in the American Contest* (2nd ed., London, 1863), 44, 54-56, 81.

8. *Ibid.*, 70-72, 74-75.

9. See Samuel M. Wolfe, *Helper's Impending Crisis Dissected* (Philadelphia, 1860); Elias Peissner, *The American Question in Its National Aspect, Being Also an Incidental Reply to Mr. H. R. Helper's "Compendium of the Impending Crisis of the South"* (New York, 1861). Obviously in response to Helper were two other works, Thomas Prentice Kettell, *Southern Wealth and Northern Profits* . . . (New York, 1860) and J. B. D. De Bow, *The Interest in Slavery of the Southern Non-Slaveholder* (Charleston, 1860). While Kettell presented figures which would dispute Helper, his main point was not to contend with Helper. De Bow was attempting to argue against Helper's contention that nonslaveholders were dupes of the planters. These two works will be discussed below.

10. Thomas R. Dew, *Review of the Debate in the Virginia Legislature, 1831-32*, as reprinted in *The Pro-Slavery Argument* . . . (Charleston, 1852), 328. Chancellor William Harper echoed these sentiments but in a more general way. Slavery, he wrote, is the only road to civilization. "If any thing can be predicated as universally true of uncultivated man, it is that he will not labor beyond what is absolutely necessary to maintain his existence . . . . The coercion of slavery alone is adequate to form man to habits of labor . . . . Since the existence of man upon the earth, with no exception whatever, either of ancient or modern times, every society which has attained civilization, had advanced to it through this process." Harper, "Slavery in the Light of Social Ethics," in E. N. Elliott (ed.), *Cotton Is King, and Pro-Slavery Arguments* (Augusta, Ga., 1860), 551-52.

11. Albert Taylor Bledsoe, "Liberty and Slavery; or, Slavery in the Light of Moral and Political Philosophy," *ibid.*, 413-16.

12. William J. Grayson, *The Hireling and the Slave* . . . (Charleston, 1856), 34-35. See also [Stephen Colwell], *The South: A Letter from a Friend in the North, with Special Reference to the Effects of Disunion upon Slavery* (Philadelphia, 1856), 14.

13. "It is the order of nature and of God, that the being of superior faculties and knowledge, and therefore of superior power, should control and dispose of those who are inferior. It is as much in the order of nature, that men should

enslave each other, as that other animals should prey upon each other." Harper, "Slavery in the Light of Social Ethics," 559-60.

14. George Fitzhugh, *Cannibals All! or, Slaves Without Masters* (Richmond, 1857), 48. Governor James Henry Hammond of South Carolina, while admitting that economically speaking "slavery presents some difficulties" and that it was more expensive than free labor, nevertheless concluded that it was economically beneficial. There was no overpopulation in the South, he argued, no group of men so hungry that they would work for next to nothing. He concluded self-righteously, "We must, therefore, content ourselves with our dear labor, under the consoling reflection that what is lost to us, is gained to humanity; and that, inasmuch as our slave costs use more than your free man costs you, by so much is he better off." Hammond, "Slavery in the Light of Political Science," in Elliott (ed.), *Cotton Is King*, 646-47.

15. Grayson, *The Hireling and the Slave*, 43-44.

16. Southern backwardness could not be ignored. The tariff, rather than slavery, was frequently pointed to as the cause. See Thomas Dew, *Review of the Debate*, 486. J. D. B. De Bow, in *De Bow's Review*, regularly called for the introduction of manufacturing in the South and the establishment of direct trade to Europe to solve the section's economic problems.

17. David Christy, *Cotton Is King* . . . (New York, 1856), 78-82, 163.

18. Kettell, *Southern Wealth and Northern Profits*, *passim*.

19. De Bow, *The Interest in Slavery of the Southern Non-Slaveholder*.

20. Ulrich B. Phillips, "The Decadence of the Plantation System," American Academy of Political and Social Science, *Annals*, XXXV (January 1910), 37-38, and "The Origin and Growth of the Southern Black Belts," *American Historical Review*, XI (July 1906), 803-804.

21. Phillips, "Decadence," 39; Ulrich B. Phillips, *American Negro Slavery* (New York, 1918), 291, 313-14, 342.

22. *Ibid.*, 343; Phillips, "Decadence," 40.

23. Ulrich B. Phillips, "The Economic Cost of Slaveholding in the Cotton Belt," *Political Science Quarterly*, XX (June 1905), 271-72; Phillips, *American Negro Slavery*, 395-96.

24. Phillips, "Economic Cost," 272; Phillips, *American Negro Slavery*, 397, 399.

25. Phillips, "Decadence," 39; Phillips, *American Negro Slavery*, 396.

26. This was not the first time this aspect of the problem was raised. Complaints by ante bellum planters that they made little money were common, and newspapers (especially during a crisis period) carried notices of sheriffs' sales of lands and slaves lost by planters. Slavery itself was seldom seen as the root cause of such difficulties. Low cotton prices, the closing of the slave trade, the tariff, the machinations of the middlemen, and other such factors were usually adduced as the reasons for poor return with slave labor. Antislavery disputants sometimes touched on the question also, but the emphasis was on the detrimental effects on the South in general. "Slavery *is* profitable to the few," Daniel Goodloe wrote to Frederick Law Olmsted, "because it is simply a privilege of robbing the many." Frederick Law Olmsted, *The Cotton Kingdom*, Arthur M. Schlesinger, ed. (New York, 1953), xxix.

27. Phillips, "Economic Cost," 271, 274; Phillips, *American Negro Slavery*, 391-92.

28. Writing soon after the turn of the century, Phillips concluded that the

continued backwardness of the South was due to the *absence* of the old planta-tion system. The problem of ignorant labor remained, Phillips argued, and its utilization is small-scale farming (through small landowning, tenantry, renting, or sharecropping) was inefficient. Restore the order, the discipline, the direc-tion, and the large-scale methods which characterized the ante bellum planta-tion, and the South, relieved of the burden of slavery, would prosper. All of the advantages of the ante bellum situation would be present with none of the disadvantages associated with slavery. Ulrich B. Phillips, "The Economics of the Plantation," *South Atlantic Quarterly*, II (July 1903), 231-36; Phillips, "Decadence," 40-41; Ulrich B. Phillips, "Conservatism and Progress in the Cotton Belt," *South Atlantic Quarterly*, III (January 1904), 1-10; Ulrich B. Phillips, "Plantations with Slave Labor and Free," *American Historical Review*, XXX (July 1925), 738-53.

29. Phillips, "Economic Cost," 259, 275. See also his "The Slave Labor Problem in the Charleston District," *Political Science Quarterly*, XXII (Sep-tember 1907), 416-39, and "The Central Theme of Southern History," *Amer-ican Historical Review*, XXXIV (October 1928), 30-43. In a more expansive mood, Phillips found the slave system socially useful for its benefits in building Southern character: ". . . In the large it was less a business than a life; it made fewer fortunes than it made men." *American Negro Slavery*, 401.

30. Rosser Howard Taylor, *Slaveholding in North Carolina, an Economic View* (Chapel Hill, 1926), 94-98.

31. Ralph Betts Flanders, *Plantation Slavery in Georgia* (Chapel Hill 1933), 221-30. As Phillips had done earlier, Flanders found the continued existence of a largely unprofitable business to be explained by noneconomic factors. The planters, he wrote, confused the plantation system, slavery, and the race question. "This confusion made it difficult for anti-slavery critics to understand the tenacity with which slave-owners clung to a social and economic system they despised, and which seemed to them unprofitable." *Ibid.* 231.

32. Charles Sackett Sydnor, *Slavery in Mississippi* (New York, 1933), 196-200; Charles S. Davis, *The Cotton Kingdom in Alabama* (Montgomery, 1939), 180. In a brief analysis of the economics of slavery during the last decade be-fore the Civil War, James D. Hill concluded that the business of production by slave labor was in general unprofitable. Many planters, he admitted, became rich, "but these cases were more than likely due to peculiar advantages in loca-tion, fertility of soil or individual administrative ability; on the whole, in spite of slavery rather than because of it." Hill, "Some Economic Aspects of Slavery, 1850–1860," *South Atlantic Quarterly*, XXVI (April 1927), 161-77.

33. Charles W. Ramsdell, "The Natural Limits of Slavery Expansion," *Mississippi Valley Historical Review*, XVI (September 1929), 151-71. Rams-dell's conclusion, of course, was that slavery would have disappeared within a generation, and therefore the Civil War had been unnecessary.

34. Alfred Holt Stone, "Some Problems of Southern Economic History," *American Historical Review*, XII (July 1908), 791; Alfred Holt Stone, "The Negro and Agricultural Development," American Academy of Political and Social Science, *Annals*, XXXV (January 1910), 13.

35. Robert R. Russel, "The General Effects of Slavery upon Southern Economic Progress," *Journal of Southern History*, IV (February 1938), 54.

36. *Ibid.*, 47-52. See also Robert R. Russel, "The Effects of Slavery upon Nonslaveholders in the Ante-Bellum South," *Agricultural History*, XV (April

1941), 112-26 and *Economic Aspects of Southern Sectionalism* 1861 (Urbana, 1924), 55-64.

37. Lewis Cecil Gray, *History of Agriculture in the Southern United States to 1860* (2 vols., Washington and New York, 1933–1941), I, 448, 462, 470-74. Gray disputed the contention that the planter's need to buy his labor supply was an added expense when figured in terms of the entire life of the slave: "When capitalization was accurately effected, the series of successive incomes as they became available actually were equivalent to interest and replacement; for interest and replacement would have been allowed for in the relatively low value that the owner paid for the services of the slave, capitalized on a terminable basis." In other words, Gray was arguing that the alleged extra cost in the form of interest and depreciation on the slave as a form of capital investment was not an extra cost at all but was a surplus which could be appropriated by the planter by virtue of his ownership of the slave over the entire period of his life. *Ibid.*, 473-74.

38. *Ibid.*, 488, 476-77; II, 933-34, 939.

39. *Ibid.*, 933-34, 940-42.

40. Thomas P. Govan, "Was Plantation Slavery Profitable?" *Journal of Southern History*, VIII (November 1942), 513-35.

41. Robert Worthington Smith, "Was Slavery Unprofitable in the Ante-Bellum South?" *Agricultural History*, XX (January 1946), 62-64.

42. Kenneth M. Stampp, *The Peculiar Institution* (New York, 1956), 390. Stampp denied that slavery kept the planters in debt. This problem arose from poor management and extravagance, a product, not of slavery, but of "the southern culture that required these etxravagances." *Ibid.*, 391. The charge that slavery absorbed capital and retarded industrialization was also false, according to Stampp: "It is doubtful . . . that slavery in any decisive way retarded the industrialization of the South. After the African slave trade was legally closed, the southern labor system absorbed little new capital that might have gone into commerce or industry . . . . The domestic slave trade involved no further investment; it merely involved thet transfer of a portion of the existing one between individuals and regions." *Ibid.*, 397. Another historian, George R. Woolfolk, in a study attacking what he called the Helper-Phillips thesis, argued that slavery did not freeze great wealth in slaves. On the contrary, he wrote, slave capital was easily converted into liquid capital because of the great facility with which slaves could be sold. Woolfolk, "Cotton Capitalism and Slave Labor in Texas," *Southwestern Social Science Quarterly*, XXXVII (June 1956), 43-52.

43. Stampp, *Peculiar Institution*, 400-11, 414. It is clear that Stampp relies heavily on Gray, Govan, and Smith. His footnotes give recognition of his debt to these earlier revisionist scholars.

44. ". . . If the slave-holder's economic self-interest alone were to be consulted, the institution should have been preserved. Nor is there any reason to assume that masters would have found it economically desirable to emancipate their slaves in the foreseeable future." *Ibid.*, 417-18.

45. Alfred H. Conrad and John R. Meyer, "The Economics of Slavery in the Ante Bellum South," *Journal of Political Economy*, LXVI (April 1958), 96.

46. "Investment returns are properly computed by using the capital-value formula $y = x_t/(1 + r)^t$, where y is the cost of the investment, x_t is realized

return t years hence, and r is the internal rate of return of what Keynes called the marginal efficiency of capital . . . . The criterion for a profitable investment is that the marginal efficiency exceeds the interest rate (in the Keynesian terminology)." *Ibid.*, 98. The authors calculated the longevity of slaves (assuming on the basis of available figures that a 20-year old field hand had a 30-year life expectancy), the cost of investment (average cost of slaves, land, equipment, and average annual maintenance costs over the period, 1830–1860), the annual average yield per hand, and the average annual price for cotton. Using 6 per cent as the rate of return slaveowners could earn in other investments outside of slavery, the authors applied these figures to the formula and solved for r. *Ibid.*, 99-107.

47. *Ibid.*, 106-107, 109-14, 120-22. Their explanation of how figures were calculated (and the assumptions they were forced to make in the absence of adequate figures) may be found on pp. 106 108.

48. *Ibid.*, 119-20. A brief article by John E. Moes suggested that the capitalization of labor "does of itself most probably have a detrimental effect on economic growth." But, Moes wrote, this is a problem only when a society "is dependent upon its own capital resources." Such was not the case in the South, for the section was able to import large amounts of capital, a situation which would tend to overcome the detrimental effects of slavery on economic growth. He concluded by questioning the generally accepted assertion that "investment (and development) in the Ante Bellum [South] lagged behind that of the North." John E. Moes, "The Absorption of Capital in Slave Labor in the Ante-Bellum South and Economic Growth," *American Journal of Economics and Sociology*, XX (October 1961), 535-41.

49. Stanley M. Elkins, *Slavery* (Chicago, 1959), 234; Paul W. Gates, *The Farmer's Age: Agriculture, 1815–1860* (New York, 1960), 154-55. Gates also cited as his sources the work of Gray and Stampp, but his argument parallels most closely that of Conrad and Meyer.

50. Douglas F. Dowd, "The Economics of Slavery in the Ante Bellum South: A Comment," *Journal of Political Economy*, LXVI (October 1958), 440-42.

51. Robert Evans, Jr., "The Economics of American Negro Slavery, 1830–1860," in National Bureau of Economic Research, *Aspects of Labor Economics* (Princeton, 1962), 185-243. Evans indicated that he used "the net rent received by owners of slaves when they rented them out as the estimate of the income earned by the capital good" (p. 191) and assumed "that the hired slave labor market was classical rather than Keynesian in character . . ." (p. 194n). Evans' method and his approach to the problem were immediately attacked by a historian (Thomas P. Govan) and an economist (John E. Moes). See "Comments" by these scholars, *ibid.*, 243-56. Govan wrote that he agreed with Evans' conclusion but added that the economist's evidence had "little relevance to this conclusion" (p. 243).

52. Avery Craven questioned whether slavery could be blamed for Southern backwardness. Southern values and ideals rather than slavery accounted for a lack of diversified economic life in the ante bellum South. "The South often deliberately chose rural backwardness." Avery Craven, *The Coming of the Civil War* (New York, 1942), 90-91. Allan Nevins came to exactly opposite colclusions. The South did not choose rural backwardness, according to Nevins; it was forced upon the section by the institution of slavery, which "discouraged

316 HAROLD D. WOODMAN

industrialism," kept immigrants from the region, discredited "the labor of the white artisan," and "tied the South to a slovenly and wasteful staple-crop system." Allan Nevins, *Ordeal of the Union* (2 vols., New York, 1947), I, 493-94. Two prominent Southern historians, Francis Butler Simkins and Clement Eaton, tend to straddle the fence in their textbooks. They recognize that the slave system was in many ways disadvantageous to the Southern economy, but they do not put the entire blame for Southern backwardness on the peculiar institution. Climate, improvidence, and, most important, the fact that the South was primarily agricultural must share the blame with slavery, according to these two. Simkins, *A History of the South* (New York, 1953), 129-32; Eaton, *A History of the Old South* (New York, 1949), 273-78. Economic historians seem to be more united in their opinions. Louis M. Hacker argued that only those few planters on the very best land could make money; most could not. Hacker, *The Triumph of American Capitalism* (New York, 1940), 317-21. The authors of current popular economic histories agree in general with this and also agree that slavery was responsible for retarding Southern economic development. Ernest L. Bogart and Donald L. Kemmerer, *Economic History of the American People* (New York, 1947), 386-410; Edward C. Kirkland, *A History of American Economic Life* (New York, 1951), 170-73; Herman E. Kroos, *American Economic Development* (Englewood Cliffs, N. J., 1956), 129-32; Gilbert C. Fite and Jim E. Reese, *An Economic History of the United States* (Boston, 1959), 164-65.

53. The works of Russel and, in part, Gray are the most noteworthy exceptions to this.

54. Fabien Linden, "Repercussions of Manufacturing in the Ante Bellum South," *North Carolina Historical Review*, XVII (October 1940), 313-31.

55. Eugene D. Genovese, "The Significance of the Slave Plantation for Southern Economic Development," *Journal of Southern History*, XXVIII (November 1962), 422-37.

56. Douglas F. Dowd, "A Comparative Analysis of Economic Development in the American West and South," *Journal of Economic History*, XVI (December 1956), 558-74.

• Robert Starobin examines the patterns of race relations among Negro and white industrial workers in the Old South. He finds a surprising amount of relaxed and amicable contact between the races, and he discusses the factors which encouraged this accommodation in industries using mixed labor forces.

Race Relations in Old South Industries

ROBERT STAROBIN

Of people, we've of every hue.
Some white, red, yaller, *black and blue*:
Others with dirt, so covered well,
What color they, I could not tell.

> Poet "Billy" describing Auraria, Georgia, gold miners in its *Western Herald*, April 9, 1833, quoted in E. M. Coulter, *Auraria* (Atkens, 1956).

Though the economy of the ante-bellum South was predominantly agricultural, it is also true that industrialization was beginning. As early as the 1790's, the processing of agricultural staples, the extraction of ores, turpentine, and timber, and the manufacture of tobacco, hemp, iron, and textiles were important Southern industries. By 1861, transportation facilities, such as turnpikes, canals, steamboats, and railroads, had already been built; and the slave states accounted for more thn 15 per cent of the capital invested in the nation's industry.[1]

Slavery was crucial to the industrialization of the South, since most industrial enterprises employed slave labor almost exclusively. In the 1850's, for example, about 200,000 bondsmen—or about 5 per cent of the total slave population—worked in industry. Most industrial slaves were young boys and prime males, but many were women and chil-

From Robert Starobin, "Race Relations in Old South Industries." Unpublished manuscript. Reprinted by permission. Robert Starobin, who was an associate professor at the State University of New York at Binghamton died in February 1971.

dren. About four-fifths of all industrial slaves were owned by industrial enterpreneurs; the rest were hired by the month or year.[2] Only about 20 per cent of the 70,000 urban slaves living in the Old South's leading cities were employed in industries. [The typical industrial slave therefore lived in a rural, plantation, or small-town setting, where most industry was located, not in a large city.[3] By the Civil War, the trend toward industrializing the South on the basis of slave labor was long underway]

Though most Old South industrial enterprises employed slave labor exclusively, a few of them successfully employed both whites and slaves at the same factory, mine, or transportation project. In short, some enterprises were "integrated." At such establishments, to a striking extent, whites often worked along side of, or in close physical proximity to, slaves who were working at similar tasks.

To be sure, even at integrated industrial enterprises, slaves were sometimes assigned to all-black work gangs, segregated into non-white areas of factories, or supervised by white overseers and artisans. Discrimination against slaves and unequal working conditions were common. Prejudice and the proslavery argument helped to make some white workers personally antagonistic toward bondsmen. Competition for jobs created racial hostility between native white craftsmen, immigrant laborers, and Negro slaves. Nevertheless, historians have exaggerated the extent of these antagonisms, for many white and black workers labored together harmoniously.[4]

[Moreover, the very nature of slavery necessitated some interracial association if white men were to oversee the lives of bondsmen closely for the maintenance of social order. Slavery thus created its own peculiar patterns of personal toleration and physical intimacy between the races]

[Integrated work forces were especially common in Southern extractive industries such as lumbering, salt boiling, and mining.[5] Integration at mines resulted partly from the employment of skilled British miners, but mainly because common laborers of both races frequently dug side by side. "A most motley appearance of whites, Indians, half-breeds and negroes, boys of fourteen and old men of seventy—and indeed their occupations appeared to be as various as their complexions, comprising diggers [and] sawyers," observed a visitor to Georgia's Chestatee gold mines in 1830. The most interesting integrated coal mine, however, was Virginia's Midlothian Company, which employed (and publicly advertised for) slaves, free Negroes, and "many white laborers." A visitor observing the Midlothian's two hundred miners, "made up of Americans, English, Scotch, free blacks, and slaves," concluded that, "though politically and naturally there is a difference in these operatives, yet every tub here stands on its own bottom." [6]

[Upper South transportation enterprises commonly utilized integrated work forces] Several black and several white chainmen and axemen surveyed a North Carolina railroad, while more than a dozen slaves, twenty free Negroes, and thirty whites together quarried rock for a nearby line. White and slave firemen and engineers together operated trains on several Virginia railroads, whose repair shops were also staffed by slave artisans working side by side with white mechanics.[7] Slave boatmen, quarriers, and carpenters labored together with white workmen on the James River Canal; both races jointly repaired Kentucky's public waterways, as well as at least one of its turnpikes. "A motley crew [of] Negro, Indian & white men" manned an Arkansas steamboat, according to one traveler; five whites and three Negroes together piloted a Baltimore harborboat.[8]

Deep South transportation enterprises sometimes employed integrated work forces. In South Carolina, for instance, sixteen slaves and five whites together quarried at the Blue Ridge Railroad's "18 Mile Creek Work," while twenty-five slaves and fourteen white's constructed a nearby line. The Greenville and Columbia Railroad's slave firemen assisted its white engineers, while brakemen—free and slave—together operated Mississippi Central equipment.[9] Negro deckhands complemented Irish firemen on one Mississippi steamer; however, a Mobile steamer employed Irish deckhands and Negro firemen. Four whites and seven slaves together manned a Savannah dredgeboat; six Louisiana pilotboats had sixteen slaves working with thirty-five whites.[10]

[Some tobacco factories, hemp factories, and brick works, as well as woodworking enterprises, used integrated work forces, even though such industries usually employed slave labor almost exclusively.[11]] According to one visitor, "a due admixture of whites and blacks assemble[d] together" to process tobacco in one room of a Louisville tobacco factory; "niggers and whites re-pick[ed] the fibres out more carefully" in another compartment; while "swarthy descendants of Ham" turned the screw press in still another room. Slave hirelings and whites, including several "Dutchmen," together worked a Louisville hemp factory; nine other Germans and six hired slaves jointly manufactured bricks in Texas. For twenty years, a dozen whites and slaves together built ships at a Gulf Coast yard; native whites, slaves, and "imported tutors" fabricated furniture in South Carolina.[12]

Slaves and whites were sometimes integrated at Southern iron works. Twenty free Pennsylvanians assisted forty local bondsmen at a Kentucky furnace; sixty-eight whites and fifty slaves worked a Virginia forge; and, in 1861, eighteen blacks and about fifteen whites chopped wood at a nearby furnace.[13] Slaves comprised almost half the work force at the famous Tredegar Iron Works in Richmond, but the greatest extent of integration occurred at Tennessee's Cumberland River iron works, where in the 1850's almost four thousand whites and slaves together operated nineteen furnaces, nine forges, and two rolling mills.[14]

About a dozen Southern textile mills successfully used integrated work forces. Some textile factories totally integrated the two races; others worked whites and blacks either in separate rooms or at different tasks. Half of a Tennessee textile factory's 120 hands were free and half were slaves; a North Carolina mill employed both white girls and slave girls. At a Georgia factory twenty-five whites worked with an equal number of slaves; at a South Carolina mill many slaves worked with five poor white apprentices.[15] A Kentucky woolen mill complemented one hundred whites with a score of slaves. In Camden, South Carolina, two-thirds of the famous DeKalb cotton mill's ninety-three hands were whites and one-third slaves. The same state's Vaucluse company combined thirty whites with twenty bondsmen, who reportedly were "equally apt and skilful in every department, except the weaving." An Alabama cotton mill added one slave family to its all-white labor force; by 1858, it was reported that "negro labor is much employed by them." [16]

Integrated textile factories so fascinated the British traveler James Silk Buckingham that he visited a Richmond, Virginia, factory, where one hundred whites and 150 slaves together were busily weaving and spinning. Buckingham also saw whites and blacks working "indiscriminately together" at another textile factory near Charlottesville, while near Athens, Georgia, he observed three cotton factories:

> In each of them there are employed from 80 to 100 persons, and about an equal number of white and black. In one of them, the blacks are the property of the mill-owners, but in the other two they are the slaves of planters, hired out at monthly wages to work in the factory. There is no difficulty among them on account of colour, the white girls working in the same room and at the same loom with the black girls; and boys of each colour,

as well as men and women, working together without apparent repugnance or objection. This is only one among the many proofs I had witnessed of the fact, that the prejudice of colour is not nearly so strong in the South as in the North. . . .[17]

[Integration was, of course, far from complete in ante-bellum Southern industries; racial antagonisms attested to that. Segregation of Negroes, for example, was common, but it resulted less from public legislation than from ingrained personal prejudices, the desire to avoid hostilities, or slaveowners' fears that whites would corrupt, harm, or agitate their Negroes.[18] Wagoners—black and white—often slept overnight at the same taverns on the National Road, for example, even though, according to one historian, "a separate table was invariably provided for the colored wagoners, a custom in thorough accord with the public sentiment of the time, and seemingly agreeable to the colored wagoners themselves." "So far as convenient they [the Negroes] were kept at work separately from the white hands; and they were also messed separately," observed a passenger on an Alabama steamer which hired slave and Irish crewmen at the same wage-rates. According to the foreman of a Louisville hemp factory that employed sixteen slaves and ten whites, "there were six two-story dwellings in a row for the slaves, [and] a large frame building, two-stories put up as a boarding house for the white people." A Georgia railroad publicly assured owners of slave hirelings that they would be "worked separately and at a distance from any white laborers who will be employed in the same line of work." [19]

Such segregation was partly an expression of underlying racial hostility which sometimes dramatically surfaced. At the Tredegar Iron Works, in 1847, skilled white "puddlers" refused to train slave apprentices. Similarly, the hiring of a few Negroes by the New Castle and Frenchtown Turnpike-Railroad (virtually all of whose workmen were whites from Delaware, Maryland, and Pennsylvania), created such "apprehensions" of racial conflict that the blacks were discharged. During the depression of 1837-43, the apprenticing of slave Frederick Douglass to learn caulking at a Baltimore shipyard, where white and Negro craftsmen previously had worked together without any serious friction, precipitated a near-fatal attack on Douglass by four Irish artisans.[20] In the 1830's, the Gosport Navy Yard's integration of about one hundred slave common laborers with 130 white day laborers so incensed some white stonecutters that they petitioned the Navy Department, the President, and the Congress of the United States to exclude slave hirelings from federal projects. Despite such protests, however, the yard's chief engineer continued to employ an integrated work force, convinced that blacks worked as well as whites and were physically better suited to the tasks.[21]

[Racial hostilities occurred, but they were much less significant than the striking extent of interracial harmony among workers at almost all integrated industries. Since whites were openly antagonistic to blacks only occasionally at integrated work places, the surprising fact is the depth of racial tolerance, considering the racist foundations upon which slavery rested.[22]] For instance, hardly any violence was reported where Irish dockworkers, deckhands, and diggers worked side by side with slaves. Racial antagonisms subsided once such enterprises as the Tredegar Iron Works had been successfully integrated. Textile millers —black and white—labored together "without apparent repugnance or objection," reported Buckingham. A Georgia poet penned the following verse, suggesting the absence of racial conflict at integrated Southern gold mines:

> Wend you to the Cherokee? . . .
> Where . . . "chuck-luck" boxes loud are rattling;
> Where gin by the barrel full is drank,—
> And whites and blacks are all the same;
> Where no respect is paid to rank,
> But every one's of equal fame.[23]

Moreover, newspapers,[24] travelers,[25] and Southern businessmen [26] almost never reported racial hostilities.

[A study of those racial antagonisms which did emerge suggests that they fall into several patterns. First, conflict between white workers and slaves was greatest when the Southern economy was most stagnant.] Irish artisans attacked Frederick Douglass during the depression of the late 1830's, for example.[Second, most racial friction seemed to occur in Maryland, Virginia, and Delaware, even though integrated work places were common in other Southern regions, including the Deep South. Third, most racial hostilities occurred when integration was first attempted—on the New Castle and Frenchtown line or at the Tredegar Iron Works, for instance. However, racial conflict failed to materialize at all when both races were working together under normal circumstances—as at Buckingham's textile mills and the Midlothian and Cherokee mines.]

[Racial antagonism at integrated work places was in part diminished because, during most of the ante-bellum period, Southern economic prosperity reduced competition for jobs between whites and slaves by creating work opportunities for both races. Racial tensions diminished further because slaves were after all a distinct caste, so firmly fixed in bondage that whites hardly felt threatened. Moreover, the proslavery argument convinced most nonslaveowners that economic advancement came through slaveownership, not through the abolition of slavery. So effective were the proslavery arguments that virulent racist ideologies, upon which those opposing integrated work forces could draw, were unneeded. Racism was, to be sure, common, but it hardened only after emancipation raised the specter of freedmen openly competing with whites. Neither legal proscription nor virulent racism was necessary, according to one authority,[27] so long as the status of Negroes was fixed by enslavement.

More important, since slaveowners so dominated the political economy of most Southern regions, they had the power to integrate work forces if they chose. Those opposing integration were powerless, and their objections went unheeded. In addition, since total segregation would have seriously obstructed the functioning of slavery, some physical association between whites and blacks was inevitable.[28]

Racial hostilities were more severe at integrated industrial establishments in the border slave states than in the Deep South, because slaveowners were often less powerful there. Moreover, the border states and New Orleans received large influxes of desperately poor European immigrants, who vigorously competed for jobs with Negroes and who sometimes precipitated racial violence. In any event, integration and racial harmony in ante-bellum Southern industries were more pronounced than might have been expected in a slave society.

It has long been understood that slavery was a means of "race adjustment" at the same time that it was always primarily a labor system. It is therefore not surprising that such post-bellum institutions as segregation partly originated in Old South industries and cities. However, the striking thing was the extent of racial harmony at integrated work places. Racial antagonisms certainly existed, but slave-employing industrialists and planters and sufficient economic and political power to use slave labor however they wished.

NOTES

1. See my manuscript, "Industrial Slavery in the Old South, 1790–1861," chap. 1. I would like to thank Professor Kenneth M. Stampp of the University of California, Berkeley, for his critical reading of this manuscript.
2. *Ibid.* chap. 1 and *passim*.

3. *Ibid.*; R. Wade, *Slavery in the Cities* (New York, 1964), chap. 1 and appendices.

4. C. V. Woodward, *The Strange Career of Jim Crow* (New York, 1955, 1967), 7, 11-13; J. Williamson, *After Slavery* (Chapel Hill, 1965), chap. 10; Wade, *Slavery in the Cities*, 266-78; L. Litwack, *North of Slavery* (Chicago, 1961); T. B. Wilson, *The Black Codes of the South* (University, Ala., 1965).

5. J. B. Smith Letterbooks and Papers (Duke Univ.); Silver Hill Mining Company Ledger, 1859–62 (Univ. of North Carolina, hereafter cited as UNC); F. Green, "Gold Mining in Ante-Bellum Virginia," *Virginia Magazine of History*, 45 (1937), 234, 363; Charleston *Courier*, July 18, 1845; *De Bow's Review*, 6 (1848), 295; Report of the Secretary of the Treasury, *House Exec. Doc.*, #6, 29 Cong., 1 sess., 1845, p. 660; M. Threlkel, "Mann's Lick," *Filson Club History Quarterly*, 1 (1927), 174; Letters and affidavits, 1815–22, Taliaferro Papers (Louisiana State Univ., hereafter cited as LSU); John Carter sawmill daybook, 1834–37 (Univ. of Georgia); D. Thomas and L. Beard sawmill book, 1838–39, vol. 7, Fisher Papers (UNC); Lumber Daybook of Plank Road Steam Mills, 1854–55, Jemison Papers (Univ. of Alabama); W. H. Fox to J. Fox, April 25, 1852, Fox Papers (Duke); sawmill account book, 1859–61, Affleck Papers (LSU).

6. P. Wager to A. Macomb, September 30, 1830, in J. W. Covington (ed.), "Letters from the Georgia Gold Regions," *Georgia Historical Quarterly*, 39 (1955), 407; *Harper's Monthly*, 15 (1857), 293; Gold Hill Mining Company Time Book, 1850–53 (UNC); Richmond *Whig*, January 2 and June 26, 1846; Richmond *Dispatch*, December 15 and 16, 1856.

7. Western North Carolina Railroad survey payroll, 1854, Treasurers Papers: Internal Improvements (North Carolina Archives); Raleigh and Gaston quarry time rolls, vols. 31 and 33, Hawkins Papers (UNC); reports of the Virginia Central, the Richmond and Petersburg, the Virginia and Tennessee, and the Richmond, Fredericksburg and Potomac railroads, Virginia *Board of Public Works Reports*, 1850–61.

8. Reports of the James River and Kanawha Canal, Virginia *Board of Public Works Reports*, 1820, 1854, and 1861; Report of Auditor of Public Accounts, pp. 20-43, Kentucky Legislature *Reports*, December 1849 session; Hardinsburg and Cloverport Turnpike Road Company Accounts, 1859–60 (Filson Club); B. L. C. Wailes Diary #16, Oct. 24, 1856 (Duke Univ.); New Orleans *Picayune*, November 27, 1845.

9. Statements and accounts, 1858 and July 13, 1860, and time and account books, vols. 42 and 43 (Hawkins Papers (UNC); statement, Aug. 11, 1855, Richardson Papers (Duke Univ.); Charleston *Mercury*, March 24, 1859; Jackson *Mississippian*, April 19, 1859.

10. F. L. Olmsted, *A Journey in the Seaboard Slave States* (New York, 1861), 607, 612; New Orleans *Picayune*, January 1, 1846; Report on Savannah River Improvement, *House Doc.*, #104, 21 Cong., 2 sess., 1831, p. 37; Report on Pilots' Association, Louisiana *Senate Journal*, 5 Legis., 1 sess., March, 1860, p. 91-2.

11. J. C. Robert, *Tobacco Kingdom* (Durham, 1938), tables; J. F. Hopkins, *A History of the Hemp Industry in Kentucky* (Lexington, 1951), *passim*.

12. H. A. Murray, *Lands of the Slave and the Free* (London, 1855), 168-9; Ford and Hawes Cash Book, 1844, Thruston Papers (Filson Club); H. T. Catterall (ed.), *Judicial Cases concerning American Slavery and the Negro*

(Washington, 1937), V, 290; Ebenezer Clark Ship Yard Account Books, 1838–41 and 1843–56 (Mississippi Archives); *De Bow's Review,* 14 (1853), 622-3.

13. J. Irwin to E. Irwin, May 20, 1839, Irwin Letters (Filson Club); G. M. Pennypacker to W. Weaver, November 4, 1831, W. W. Rex to D. Brady, September 6, 1860, and C. K. Gorgas to D. Brady, April 2, 1860, Weaver Papers (Duke Univ.); W. W. Rex to D. Brady, January 22, 1861, Weaver Papers (Univ. of Virginia).

14. C. Dew, Iron-Maker to the Confederacy, mss, chap. 2 and table 1; *Hunt's Magazine,* 28 (1853), 644-5, reported that 1045 whites and 1360 slaves worked the furnaces of Tennessee's Cumberland River iron region, while 260 whites and 410 slaves worked the forges, and 90 and 140 the rolling mills.

15. *Ibid.* 15 (1846), 598-9; R. W. Griffin and D. W. Standard, "The Textile Industry in Ante-Bellum North Carolina," *North Carolina Historical Review,* 34 (1957), 132-3; Jones, "Manufacturing in Richmond County, Georgia," *Georgia Historical Quarterly,* 78-9; D. Moore to T. Moore, November 5, 1817, Moore Papers (Duke Univ.).

16. Mill Ledger, 1856–70, pp. 86, 279, Wages Ledger, 1856–61, and letters dated June 2, 1861, March 13, 1862, and November 19, 1863, in Letterbook, 1859–64, Woolley Mill Papers (Univ. of Kentucky); *De Bow's Review,* 7 (1849), 372-3, 458; *Hunt's Magazine,* 22 (1850), 581-2; Charleston *Courier,* November 23, 1836; New Orleans *Picayune,* October 16, 1858; and *De Bow's Review,* 25 (1858), 717. Cf. Report of the Secretary of the Treasury, *House Exec. Doc. #6,* 29 Cong., 1 sess., 1845, p. 676; and B. Mitchell, *William Gregg* (Chapel Hill, 1928), 100.

17. J. S. Buckingham, *The Slave States of America* (London, 1842), II, 424, 411, and 112.

18. T. D. Jervey, *Robert Y. Hayne* (New York, 1909), 510-11, for example.

19. T. B. Searight, *The Old Pike* (Uuiontown, 1894), 109; Olmsted, *Seaboard Slave States,* 564; *Report of the Court of Claims, #81,* 34 Cong., 3 sess., 1857; R. B. Flanders, *Plantation Slavery in Georgia* (Chapel Hill, 1933), 198.

20. W. F. Holmes, "The New Castle and Frenchtown Turnpike and Railroad Company," *Delaware History,* 10 (1862–63), 172; Frederick Douglass, *Narrative* (Boston, 1845), 93-8. Douglass, a Negro slave hired to the shipyards by his owner to learn the caulker's trade, was apparently a victim of the competition for jobs between free Negro and white shipyard workers during the depression of 1837–43. When white workers struck to demand the discharge of the free Negroes, they did not object to Douglass's employment because he was a slave. According to Douglass, he was beaten up because he was a Negro. At the Tredegar Iron Works in Richmond, Virginia, in 1847, skilled white "puddlers" went out on strike when their employer, Joseph Reid Anderson, insisted that they train slaves as puddlers for a new rolling mill. Anderson dismissed the whites and employed slaves in their stead, insisting that he had the right to deploy his labor forces as he saw fit. This dramatic conversion from free labor to slave labor can be followed in the Richmond *Enquirer,* June 1, 11, and 15, 1847; Richmond *Whig,* May 28 and June 28, 1847. Cf. K. Bruce, *Virginia Iron Manufacture in the Slave Era* (New York, 1930), 224-37; C. Dew, "Iron-Maker to the Confederacy," mss, chap. 2.

21. "Memorandum of Work, February 1, 1831," and "Abstract from the Rolls of Labour on the Dry Dock in the Gosport Navy Yard," 1831–1832,

Baldwin Papers (Baker Library, Harvard Univ.); "Slaves on a Federal Project," Business Historical Society *Bulletin*, 8 (1934), 32-3.

22. For evidence of integration without antagonism at Old South ironworks, see: Cumberland Forge, Md., Daybook, 1802 (Library of Congress); Ridwell Furnace Book, and Shenandoah County, Va., Account Books vols. 3, 5, 6, 8 of "Pine Forge," 1804–1833 (UNC); payroll accounts with "Cesar a laborer," October 5, 1808, and March 25, 1809, Virginia Manufactory of Arms Papers, and letters of May 28, 1804, March 9, 1806, and January 29, 1808, and annual reports of December 25, 1804, and January 16, 1806, John Clarke Letterbook (Virginia State Library); Allatoona Iron Works Ledger, 1845 (Emory University); Report of the Secretary of the Treasury, *House Exec. Doc.*, #6, 29 Cong., 1 sess., (1845), 647-8; T. A. Moss account books, 1855–57, Fredericksburg, Va., Account Books (UNC); J. Bancroft, *Census of the City of Savannah* (Savannah, 1848), 36; Richmond *Dispatch*, January 14, 1858.

For mining: P. Ward to R. Leckie, October 25, 1818, Leckie Papers (Duke Univ.); J. G. Hamilton (ed.), *The Papers of William A. Graham* (Raleigh, 1957), I, 187; *Niles' Register*, 39 (1831), 334-5 and 40 (1831), 206; R. Smith Lead Mining Company Ledger, vol. 15, 1834–36 (Missouri Historical Society); *Mining Magazine*, 2 (1854), 304; F. Green, "Georgia's Forgotton Industry: Goldmining," *Georgia Historical Quarterly*, 19 (1935), 210-11.

For cotton mills: J. Stumpp and D. Ricketts Ledger, 1806–23 (New York Public Library); E. M. Coulter, "Scull Shoals," *Georgia Historical Quarterly*, 48 (1964), 41-3; Jones, "Manufacturing in Richmond County, Ga.," 81; I. Lippincott, *A History of Manufactures in the Ohio Valley* (New York, 1914), 169-70; W. Thomson, *A Tradesman's Travels* (Edinburgh, 1842), 112-15; Report of the Secretary of the Treasury, *House Exec. Doc.*, #6, 29 Cong., 1 sess., 1845, p. 649; Holt Diary, 1844–54 (UNC); *De Bow's Review*, 7 (1849), 458; R. S. Patterson to S. F. Patterson, January 7, 1855, Patterson Papers (Duke Univ.); vol. 38, Patterson Papers (UNC); Ivy Mills Ledger, 1858–63 (Georgia Archives); J. Webb Account Book, Vol. 8, 1852–63 (UNC).

For manufacturing and milling: Hopkins, *Hemp Industry*, 115; J. L. Mertens to W. W. Mertens, March 1, 1845, Mertens Papers (Duke Univ.); Olmsted, *Seaboard Slave States*, 346; Fogartie, Green & Co. Daybook, 1835 (Georgia Historical Society); J. H. Franklin, "Slaves Virtually Free in Ante-Bellum North Carolina," *Journal of Negro History*, 38 (1943), 299n.; account sheet, July 27, 1816, Kuntz Collection (Tulane Univ.); F. S. Klein, "Union Mills," *Maryland Historical Magazine*, 52 (1957), 293, 299; J. G. Taylor, *Negro Slavery in Louisiana* (Baton Rouge, 1963), 82.

For internal improvements projects: Expense Book of Saïd Plantation, November 12, 1806, McDonogh Papers (Tulane Univ.); G. R. Baldwin to J. F. Baldwin, February 5, 1837, vol. 25, Baldwin Papers (Baker Library, Harvard Univ.); *House Doc.* #201, 26 Cong., 1 sess., 1840, pp. 20ff; J. T. Hicks to S. S. Downey, March 25, 1838, Downey Papers (Duke Univ.); J. W. Livingood, "Chattanooga," *Tennessee Historical Quarterly*, 6 (1947), 245; W. H. Garland to wife, May 4, 1841, Garland Papers (UNC); reports of the Board of Internal Improvements, Kentucky *Legislative Reports*, 1841–42, pp. 265, 266; H. D. Dozier, *A History of the Atlantic Coast Line Railroad* (Boston, 1920), 45; *American Railroad Journal*, 21 (1848), 340-41, 361, and *American Railroad Journal*, 26 (1853), 622, 733; J. R. Kean, "The Development of the 'Valley Line' of the Baltimore and Ohio Railroad," *Virginia*

Magazine of History, 60 (1952), 541; V. McBee to V. A. McBee, November 9, 1851, McBee Papers (UNC); Charleston *Courier*, May 15, 1852; payrolls of surveys, October 29, 1853 and November 1, 1854, Treasurers Papers: Internal Improvements (North Carolina Archives); R. Bush to J. Buford, July 9, 1854, and T. W. Leftwich to J. Buford, December 4, 1854, Buford Papers (Duke Univ.); time rolls, vols. 31 and 38, Hawkins Papers (UNC); J. Stirling, *Letters from the Slave States* (London, 1857), 229; Report of the Little Rock and Napoleon Railroad, Arkansas *Journal of the Senate*, 11 sess., 1856–57, appendix, p. 129; Charleston *Mercury*, March 23, 1857; Treasurer's Report, table G, *Atlantic and North Carolina Railroad Report*, 1860; Western and Atlantic Railroad Payroll Books, 1852–64 (Georgia Archives); U. B. Phillips, *A History of Transportation in the Eastern Cotton Belt to 1860* (New York, 1908), 295; L. Armitage, "Louisa Railroad—1836–1850," Railroad and Locomotive Historical Society *Bulletin*, #65 (1944), 64; M. Chevalier, *Histoire et Description des Voies des Communications aux Etats-Unis* (Paris, 1841), II, 443; accounts, Cape Fear and Deep River Navigation Company Papers and London Papers (UNC and N.C. Archives).

23. Richmond *Whig*, June 26, 1846; Buckingham, *Slave States*, II, 112; a Milledgeville, Georgia, poet's verse in the Auraria, Ga., *Western Herald*, April 30, 1833, quoted in E. M. Coulter, *Auraria* (Athens, 1956), 58-9.

24. In 1858, the Petersburg *Express* reported that one tobacco manufacturer was employing forty white workers, whose department was kept very clean, "while all association with their 'odiferous' [black] co-laborers is entirely obviated."—quoted by E. A. Wyatt, "Rise of Industry in Ante-Bellum Petersburg," *William and Mary College Quarterly*, series 2, 17 (1937), 12-13. "A Southerner," writing to the Georgia *Citizen*, July 21, 1850, objected to the Atlanta *Intelligencer*'s advocacy of using slaves in cotton factories as follows: "*Negroes*, slaves, and *White* men, and *White Women*, cooperating in a cotton factory! What an association! Disgusting!"—quoted in Flanders, *Slavery in Georgia*, 205.

25. Olmsted, *Seaboard Slave States*, 48; F. L. Olmsted, *A Journey in the Back Country* (New York, 1907 edn.), II, 57; F. L. Olmsted, *A Journey Through Texas* (New York, 1857), 114-15; Taylor, *Slavery in Louisiana*, 83; R. B. Morris, "The Measure of Bondage in the Slave States," *Mississippi Valley Historical Review*, 41 (1954), 229; and F. Kemble, *Journal of a Residence* (New York, 1961 edn.), 104, 122-26, and 129, for protests by whites against slave competition or fear of racial hostility.

26. Negro Time Book, November 7 and 29, 1833, Graham Papers (Univ. of Virginia), for fight between "Capt. R." and "Bryce McC."; the objection by some Moravians to employing slaves, instead of whites, in textile mills, is recounted in A. L. Fries, "One Hundred Years of Textile in Salem," *North Carolina Historical Review*, 27 (1950), 13.

27. Woodward, *Strange Career of Jim Crow*, 13.

28. *Ibid.* 12.

• *Slavery was an urban as well as a rural phenomenon in the nineteenth-century South. Furthermore, the presence of large numbers of freed Negroes in the cities created a distinctly liberating atmosphere among the many slaves who worked in Southern industries and commerce. Richard C. Wade, one of the country's foremost urban historians, describes the institution's practices and customs in the urban South.*

Slavery in the Southern Cities

RICHARD C. WADE

By 1860 the institution of slavery was in great disarray in every Southern city. The number of Negroes had declined precipitously. Discipline over those remaining proved difficult to sustain. The network of restraint so essential to bondage no longer seemed to control the blacks nor wholly govern the whites. The distance between the races as well as separation of free colored from slave could not be maintained in the kinetic world of the city. In the most dynamic towns the whites overwhelmed the Negro population; even places with a larger proportion of slaves and less impressive growth tended to slough off at least their male blacks. In any case an institution which had been an integral part of urban life in Dixie in 1820 was languishing everywhere in 1860.

The census figures outlined the story. [Though the number of slaves rose throughout the South, the proportion living in cities declined. In addition, the Negroes lost their earlier share of the urban population.] In 1820, 37 per cent of all town dwellers were blacks; by 1860 that portion had dropped below 17 per cent. Urban slaves fell from 22 per cent to 10. The most dramatic shifts came, of course, in the border area, but everywhere the same pattern appeared. The New

328

Orleans statistics demonstrated the tendency most clearly. In 1820 one out of two residents was Negro; in 1860 only one in seven. To be sure, the black populations of smaller and newer cities, like Montgomery or the Texas towns, showed some vitality, but there is no reason to believe they would not have shared the same attrition as they expanded.

[This decline did not stem from any economic reasons.] There was plenty of work which whites had traditionally considered appropriate to blacks and particularly suited to slaves. Industrial employment, moreover, had proved feasible in a variety of enterprises. Hiring rates continued to rise throughout the last ante-bellum decades. And, perhaps most conclusively, the price of urban slaves on the market more than matched the general increase. In short, the usual indices suggested the continuing profitability of slavery as an economic institution. "In all departments of mechanical labor, the slaves of the South are profitably employed," the *Richmond Enquirer* asserted confidently in 1853. "As carpenters, as blacksmiths, as shoe-makers, as factory hands, they are far more valuable than field-laborers—indeed, intellectual expertness and manual dexterity are much more important elements in the price of a slave, than mere physical strength and power of endurance." [1] Or, as a visitor put it, "those whom good treatment has rendered most fit for freedom, are the most desired as slaves." [2]

[Slavery's compelling problem in the city was not finding work for bondsmen, but controlling them when they were off the job.] While busy, in the house or around the yard, on the docks or driving a dray, toiling in a factory or cotton press, they caused little trouble. When the task was finished or the supervision lifted, however, when the slaves became idle or contrived some free time, when dusk fell and the demand for service slackened, then the system weakened. And when the Negroes gathered by themselves, beyond the eye of masters and police, in homes, churches, or grog shops, the "peculiar institution" itself was jeopardized.

It was the total environment rather than industrial or commercial employment which eroded slavery in the cities. The problem was not what happened in the factory or shop but what happened in the back street, the church, the grocery store, the rented room, and the out-of-the-way house. It was not contact with machines or an industrial process which broke the discipline, it was contact with people of all kinds in numerous ways which generated the corrosive acids.

"The city, with its intelligence and enterprise, is a dangerous place for the slave," wrote a shrewd analyst. "He acquires knowledge of human rights, by working with others who receive wages when he receives none; who can come and go at their pleasure, when he from the cradle to the grave must obey a master's imperious will. . . . It is found expedient, almost necessary, to remove the slave from these influences, and send him back to the intellectual stagnation and gloom of the plantation." [3] Bondage "does not thrive with master or slave when transplanted to cities," a Louisiana planter observed, adding that in such surroundings "the slaves become dissipated, acquire the worst habits," and were generally "corrupted." [4] . . .

Slaves, on the other hand, found urban life to their liking. "The negroes are the most social of all human beings," De Bow asserted, "and after having hired in town, refuse to live again in the country." [5] Slavery's most famous refugee to attack the institution in all its aspects made the same point with elequent simplicity: "Life in Baltimore, when most oppressive, was a paradise" compared to "plantation existence," Frederick Douglass wrote.[6] When masters were forced to sell, their bondsmen pleaded to be kept in the city because—in the words of some Richmond blacks—"they had acquired town habits." [7] And often those sent into the country headed back at the first opportunity to run away. In short, how could you keep them down on the plantation once they had seen Mobile?

[The slave's preference was easily understood. Not only was urban life more congenial, but the alternative was especially grim.] Solomon Northup found that every Negro sharing his Washington pen "dreaded the thought of being put into the cane and cotton fields." [8] Douglass, too, remembered that it was "a source of deep consternation" to him and his friends in Maryland that "we should be hurried away to the cotton fields and rice swamps, of the sunny south." [9] A sympathetic Northern traveler caught both the white and Negro perspectives when he observed that "The atmosphere of the city is too life-giving, and creates thought. It is the doom of them all to be sent back to the gloom of the plantation cabin." [10]

[The cause of slavery's difficulty in the city was the nature of urban society itself. In the countryside physical isolation comprised one dimension of a successful discipline. Another was the simple division between master and slave, with virtually no other important element. The distinction between field hand and house servant, while important to the Negroes involved, constituted no significant fracture in the system.] Treatment and comforts might vary, privileges could be more extensive, and everyday tasks quite different, but no area of independence was thus created. Indeed, a house servant often fell more directly under the eye of his owner than the black in the field. Nor did the overseer create a new interest among the whites. Employed by the master, usually a short-term resident, living apart from the colored quarters, and only occasionally a confidant of the owner, the overseer had at most a marginal influence on the structure.

Between black and white the social distance was immense. Slaves were confined to primitive work at worst or acquired rudimentary skills at best. Their contacts with whites were few and seldom lasting. An occasional visitor sometimes broke the isolation; nearby white families were seen just often enough to be recognized; overseers came and went. Except for the infrequent trip to town or a neighboring farm, the possibilities of outside stimuli scarcely existed. Even on small plantations or farms, the contacts with the surrounding world were circumscribed. Indeed, without other slaves about he was deprived of even the most elementary association. Rural life had always involved some social remoteness; for the plantation slave, isolation, next to his servitude, was the most compelling fact of life.

The cities, on the other hand, developed more complex structures. Both white and Negro communities included many different parts, and in the larger places a highly sophisticated system evolved with almost endless groupings and distinctions. This fragmentation, which, of course, characterized urban life nearly everywhere, had a special significance for slavery. It meant that the great gap between owner and chattel would be filled with all kinds of diverse elements, inevitably disturbing the institution's ordinary relationships. The Louisiana planter who so feared town life saw this process clearly. "The distance is so vast between slave and master" under bondage, he argued, that in the city "the interval is filled up immediately by corrupting influences." And the slaveholder was helpless. He could perceive "the evil of his slave without being able to prevent it," since it sprang from the intractable nature of urban life itself.[11]

The most obvious added ingredient in the urban scene was the free Negro. He was, to be sure, also a rural resident, but the distance and detachment of the countryside greatly diluted his influence on slavery. Often living in a remote spot, sometimes as a yeoman, more often a hired hand, he was bound to have a modest role. His opportunity there moreover was limited. Without resources he found it hard to buy land; without many others of his own kind his social life was sparse. Hence he gravitated toward the metropolis.

Freedmen constituted the most highly urbanized group in Dixie.

By 1860 they outnumbered slaves ten to one in Baltimore and 9209 to 1774 in Washington. In the deep South, too, their numbers grew with each census. New Orleans always had a considerable contingent; on the eve of the Civil War it exceeded 10,000. Yet even the places which had tried hardest to limit their free colored population could not alter the trend. Charleston had 1475 in 1820 and over 3200 in 1860, while Mobile's figures in the same span were 183 and 817. Across the South nearly a third of the free blacks were found in the larger urban centers. The report of a visitor in 1836 that "the emancipated negroes generally leave the country, and congregate in the cities and larger towns" was a common observation.[12]

The free Negro's position in Southern towns was always precarious, occupying, as one Southerner put it, "a sort of uncertain and undefined position in our midst."[13] His color suggested servitude, but his status secured a portion of freedom. Hence he suffered many of the inhibitions of his slave brothers while enjoying some privileges denied them. His advantages over the slave were considerable. He could marry, have children, and enjoy something of a normal family life. He could own property, have the right to his earnings, and engage in a few trades forbidden the enslaved. Though the situation was never favorable to either domestic tranquillity or economic advancement, there was at least a measure of independence. And, most crucial of all, in the privacy of the home could be found a seclusion from the constant surveillance of the white world.

Free Negroes learned quickly not to count on much beyond this. "We know full well," the New Orleans *Picayune* wrote with candor, "that the pretence of any real freedom being designed or expected for these negroes is but a sham."[14] In the streets the distinction among colored people was not clear; in the courts the free were sometimes only fined while the slaves were whipped; and legislation increasingly covered all blacks with only nominal regard for status. City ordinances usually handled both categories in a single section. An 1832 Baltimore ordinance dealing with Negro discipline set forth the crucial identification: "such free negro or mulatto shall be subject to the same punishment, and be liable in every respect to the same treatment and penalty as slaves" and "be guilty of, and convicted of, any offense for which slaves are now punishable."[15]

Despite these obstacles, the free colored of every city struggled to establish a meaningful associational life. They formed congregations and erected churches, established schools and aid societies, and organized improvement projects aimed at bringing some of the better things of life to their members. . . .

To a few Southerners the presence of free Negroes created no great problem. . . .

But the common judgment went the other way. A Louisville editor in 1851 came close to the nearly universal view when he stated bluntly that "the free negro question is the most insoluble of all the social problems of the day, and stands as a practical sarcasm on all the theories of abolition and emancipation." [16] A Richmond memorial containing the signature of John Marshall elaborated the ordinary indictment. They numbered "not an eighth part of the inhabitants; yet it would be hazarding little to say that half the criminals tried in the City for the offense of larceny, are free persons of color." In addition, the petitioners said, "their idleness is proverbial; they live, few know in what way, and fewer still know where; their rate of increase far exceeds even that of the slaves, and in a higher degree that of the whites; and whatever energy can be spared from annoying both classes, appears to be expended in multiplying their own number." [17] And a New Orleans editor called the full roll when he spoke of "the absolute idleness, the thriftlessness, the laziness, the dishonesty, the drunkenness, the proneness to vagrancy and vice of the negro when free from all the restraints of servitude." [18]

The central complaint, however, had less to do with the wretchedness of free Negro life, or even with their high crime rate, than with their influence on slaves. Living amongst bondsmen, yet without masters, carrying by color the stigma of servitude, yet without its most humiliating features, shut off from white society, yet released from the confinements of slavery, the free blacks were always a disturbing factor. "They are a plague and pest in the community," the *New Orleans Daily Picayune* asserted, because they brought "the elements of mischief to the slave population." [19]

"The superior condition of the free persons of color," a memorial of Charleston citizens argued, "excites discontent among our slaves, who continually have before their eyes, persons of the same color, many of whom they have known in slavery, and with all of whom they associate on terms of equality." The slave saw these blacks "freed from the control of masters, working where they please, going whither they please, and spending money how they please." He thus became "dissatisfied" and "pants after liberty." [20] . . .

. . . Whatever the precise formulation of the argument, Southern town dwellers could agree that their free colored residents rendered control over their slaves increasingly difficult. . . .

[They could also agree that there were some whites who were almost as unsettling to the system as freed blacks. These people had found a place at the edge of slavery where their economic life was enmeshed in the irregular relationships bred by the system in its urban environment.] Some were grocers who sold to slaves; others ran shops which catered to a colored clientele; still others were ministers who organized Negro churches and sought to bring religion to the enslaved. Port merchants, too, could be included, since their trade brought ships with mixed crews into the harbor. Less easily identified, but also important, were whites sporadically connected with the informal life of town blacks. These interests were obviously quite different, but all developed a stake in the loose form of bondage which evolved in the cities. . . .

[In the metropolis the worlds of bondage and freedom overlapped. The line between free blacks and slaves became hopelessly blurred. Even whites and blacks found their lives entangled in some corners of the institution of slavery. No matter what the law said or the system required, this layer of life expanded.] Though much of it was subterranean, at points it could be easily seen. The mixed balls, the numberless grog and grocery shops, the frequent religious gatherings, and the casual acquaintances in the streets were scarcely private. Physical proximity bred a certain familiarity that most residents came to expect. . . .

What did bother townspeople, however, was the evidence that beyond these visible contacts lay a world of greater conviviality and equality. In this nether world blacks and whites mingled freely, the conventions of slavery were discarded, and the worst fears of Southerners became realized. Not only did the men find fellowship without regard to color in the tippling shops, back rooms, and secluded sheds, but the women of both races joined in. Such mixing engaged a good deal of the private conversation of white people in cities, but its public manifestations were usually found in only police reports and the major's court. . . .

[There can be no doubt of the wide extent of this miscegenation.] Visitors often commented on it; the newspapers complained about it; the court records teem with it. Even Governor Hammond, who defended the South in general against the charge of racial mixing, admitted its prominence in the cities. The clandestine nature of these attachments makes a more precise generalization risky, but the fear, if not the fact, of "amalgamation," "miscegenation," and "mixing," plainly increased in the decades before 1860. Few defenders, much less advocates, appeared. The public stigma and the hostility of the law made it clear why: those who practiced it did not preach it.

New Orleans, with its large population of free and enslaved blacks, had the most famous demi-world in Dixie. The celebrated masked balls and the casual acceptance of colored mistresses seemed to reflect its Spanish and French roots. Yet that explanation is too facile. The rural areas of Louisiana, some of which reflected similar origins, did not develop the same mores; and, more persuasively, other cities with quite different beginnings did. Actually what visitors noticed about New Orleans was true of urban life throughout the South.

Northern cities, too, had their disorganized elements who left a trail across police blotters, court records and poorhouse lists. There too community leaders, somewhat bewildered by the spread of undisciplined low life, sought some way to introduce a system and stability. But, important as this was to civic leaders elsewhere, in the South the problem was greatly complicated by the existence of slavery. On the one hand, the institution required a high degree of order, the careful regulation of Negro affairs, and a fixed status for bondsmen. On the other hand, the city demanded fluidity, a constant re-allocation of human resources, and a large measure of social mobility. Initially, it appeared as though slavery could provide the discipline town life seemed to need. In the long run, however, the force of urbanization loosened the restraints of bondage, smudged the distinctions of status among Negroes, and at points pierced the racial walls of Dixie's cities.

This antithesis was early felt by some municipal leaders. Since slavery was presumed to be an established part of Southern town life for any foreseeable future, none talked about incompatibility. Instead, the dominant race sought to solve it with ordinances, the orderly development of a legal hiring-out system, and a plentiful police force in case of trouble. Yet the acids of urbanization continually eroded the discipline on which bondage rested. Though the disintegration was often hard to gauge, those close to the problem knew it was happening.

To arrest the attrition and handle its consequences, Southern cities moved along three lines. One involved the sale of young male blacks into the countryside. This removed one of the most disturbing elements from the urban scene while meeting a constant demand for field hands in the cotton and cane regions. A second was the tightening of emancipation procedures to stop the accumulation of free Negroes in towns. A third was to develop racial arrangements which took into account the new situation and which embodied most of the features later identified as segregation. . . . By 1860 the percentage of free Negroes among the South's urban population had dropped considerably.

While Southern cities increasingly moved to reduce their colored population, both slave and free, they also developed a new system of racial deference more appropriate to urban life than slavery in its traditional form. As the institution of slavery encountered mounting difficulties and, as its control over the blacks weakened, another arrangement was devised which maintained great social distance within the physical proximity of town life. Increasingly public policy tried to separate the races whenever the surveillance of the master was likely to be missing. To do this, the distinction between slave and free Negro was erased; race became more important than legal status; and a pattern of segregation emerged inside the broader framework of the "peculiar institution."

In a sense this tendency was always present, though the reliance on traditional controls obscured its importance. The heart of the established system was, of course, the subordination of the slave to his owner. The wide discretion vested in the master made day-to-day discipline almost a private matter. But in the cities a public etiquette was needed to govern the relations of races when the blacks were beyond the supervision of their owners. Increasingly that etiquette required the separation of black and white without regard to legal status. Beginning in only a few areas, the arrangement spread to include the most important public aspects of life. . . .

Law and custom sanctioned the segregation of races in public places and accommodations as well as in churches and schools. To disentangle white and black in employment and housing was a different matter. Yet the significant fact is that such a separation took place increasingly often in the last few decades before the Civil War. Under the pressure of white craftsmen, Negroes were pushed out of one line of work after another. With the weakening of the reins of slavery, bondsmen found housing away from their owners and generally in areas of accumulating colored population. Both movements were far from complete, but the tendency was unmistakable.

In employment the clearest manifestation of segregation was the exclusion of blacks, slave and free, from the better jobs. A memorial of Charleston's City Council to the state legislature expressed both the difficulties and the objects of the policy. Noting that "slavery is so interwoven with the constitution of our Society that even if our interests permitted it would be impossible to eradicate it," the petitioners argued that it was "necessary to fix as far as possible the grade of employments" for slaves and "to exclude them by Legislative enactment from all others." [21] Charleston's own ordinances prohibited teaching slaves "in any mechanic or handicraft trade," though the wording was vague and its enforcement almost impossible.[22]

In Savannah the restrictions were more precise. No Negro could be apprenticed "to the trade of Carpenter, Mason, Bricklayer, Barber or any other Mechanical Art or Mystery." [23] Later, cabinetmaker, painter, blacksmith, tailor, cooper, and butcher were added to the list.[24] Georgia excluded blacks from "being mechanics or masons, from making contracts for the erection . . . or repair of buildings." [25] Though no two cities had the same categories, all tried to keep colored workers out of the higher skills. The fact that practice often belied the law simply underlined the significance of the intent.

If slaves and blacks were still found in many of the better crafts in 1860, they had been pushed out of many of the lesser-skilled jobs. In Baltimore whites took the carting and draying business from them by 1830.[26] A few years later, a visitor could report that "the Irish and other foreigners are, to a considerable extent, taking the place of colored laborers and of domestic servants." [27] In 1823 the City Council of New Orleans directed the mayor "to hire white labor for the city works, in preference to negroes." [28] Two decades later, some prominent citizens there described the extent of the attrition: "Ten years ago, say they, all the draymen of New Orleans, a numerous class, and the cabmen, were colored. Now they are nearly all white. The servants of the great hotels were formerly of the African, now they are of the European race." [29] Even in the home, the displacement occurred with the customary racial rationale. "We have all times spoken against the impropriety of having white and black servants in homes in the South," the *Richmond Enquirer* explained, "especially so in any capacity where slaves or negroes may be inclined to consider themselves on a par of equality with white servants." [30]

John S. C. Abbott, who toured the South in 1859, found this tendency pronounced everywhere. In Mobile, for instance, he was "surprised to see how effectually free labor seems to have driven slave labor from the wharves and streets." The Irish and Germans, he noted, did the outside work, while white girls moved into domestic service. When he saw New Orleans, he commented, though no doubt with exaggeration, that "hardly a colored face is to be seen on the levee, and the work is done by the Germans and the Irish. . . . Indeed, now, New Orleans and Mobile seem but little more like slave cities than do Philadelphia and New York." [31]

Though the process varied in Dixie's cities and Negroes hung on in many skills, "job busting" became a normal tactic for the growing white labor force faced with traditional colored employment practices. As the black population dropped, white newcomers moved in and took over craft after craft. Occasionally accompanied by violence and usually with official sanction, slave and free colored workers were shunted into the most menial and routine chores. In 1830 Negroes, both slave and free, had been used in a wide variety of employments; by 1860 the number of possibilities had shrunk markedly. The movement toward segregation, so noticeable in other aspects of urban life, was rapidly invading employment.

In housing the same trend was perceptible, though less advanced. The spread of the "living out" system, both in its legal and irregular form, gave slaves some choice of residence. Since the urge to leave the enclosure reflected the freedom from surveillance it entailed, slaves sought spots as removed from whites as possible. For most this meant a retreat to the outer edges of the city or beyond the municipal line altogether. There was seldom any escape from all whites, but there were parts of town with clusters of colored inhabitants. By the 'forties and 'fifties it was apparent in most places that Negroes were settling on the periphery of the cities. . . .

The movement to the periphery was increasingly common, though in some towns colored concentrations grew up more haphazardly in small enclaves or strips in out-of-the-way places. And the centers of Negro life, formal and informal, followed the people. Colored churches, especially those established after 1840, sought locations in these neighborhoods. Grocery stores and dram shops, too, settled there. Even the cemeteries were put near the living. In Savannah's case, for example, four Negro churches, three Baptist, and one Methodist, were on the west side, while another served the east side. The central city had none. Of 174 "grocers" 101 did business in the outer residential wards, West Broad alone accommodating 19.[32] In Charleston the convergence was on the northern border and the Neck beyond.

In no case did anything like full residential segregation emerge.

Few streets, much less blocks, were solidly black. Everywhere some whites occupied nearby dwellings. Still the inclination to cluster here, to concentrate there, was more marked by 1860 than in 1820. The separation apparent in other areas of life was slowly insinuated into housing.

Thus, even before slavery had been abolished, a system of segregation had grown up in the cities. Indeed, the whites thought some such arrangement was necessary if they were to sustain their traditional supremacy over the Negroes. The countryside provided enough room to give meaning to racial separation. The master could be physically quite removed from his blacks, though sharing the same plantation or farm. And together both were isolated from others. In cities these spatial relationships were quite different. Both races were thrown together; they encountered each other at every corner, they rubbed elbows at every turn; they divided up, however inequitably, the limited space of the town site. Segregation sorted people out by race, established a public etiquette for their conduct, and created social distance where there was proximity. Urban circumstances produced this system long before the destruction of slavery itself.

Of course, the complete separation of races was impossible in the city, and the practice differed from place to place. In some towns, public conveyances remained mixed; in others Negroes were not excluded from all public grounds; in still others housing continued scrambled. Yet every city developed its own arrangement expressed in the contrived separation of colored and white in countless ways. Though never total, the segregation was so extensive that Negroes were never permitted to forget their inferior position.

The rising incidence of segregation was another index of the increasing weakness of slavery in the cities. Rooted in the white's need for discipline and deference, it developed to take up the slack in the loosening system. It provided public control to replace dwindling private supervision of the master over his slave. To do this, the difference between free and enslaved Negroes had to be narrowed, depriving free blacks of part of their freedom even while permitting a wider latitude to bondsmen. To most whites, however, there seemed no alternative. The old system no longer really controlled; the walls no longer really confined; the chains no longer really held.

The decline of slavery in the cities was the central fact of race relations in the South's cities in the ante-bellum decades. It was also a fact that conditioned Negro life in subsequent generations, for it meant that, when emancipation finally did come, most of the colored population would be in the countryside rather than in cities. Accustomed only to routine tasks, imbruted by the severe limitations of plantation existence, and unused to managing their own affairs, they became free under the most difficult of circumstances.

If the Negro population in the cities had grown in the same proportion as the whites, there would have been present an invaluable pool of potential leadership, for there many blacks, even under slavery, had begun to develop the most important tools of citizenship. There they acquired some skills and learned the rudiments of reading and writing. There, too, many had commenced to manage their own affairs, and in churches they developed a capacity for organization. In short, the metropolis nourished the literacy and self-reliance needed in a free system. . . .

The full significance of the de-urbanization of the Negro under slavery was apparent only much later. Emancipation found him located primarily in the least dynamic area of American life. Capable of simple tasks, familiar only with rural routine, largely illiterate, and unused to managing his own affairs, he faced a long road to full freedom. Ultimately that road carried him to the city. Though confronted by both discrimination and segregation, he could find there the numbers and leadership which could one day spring him loose from the confinements of an earlier bondage.

NOTES

1. *Richmond Enquirer*, November 29, 1853.
2. Finch, *An Englishwoman's Experience in America*, 300.
3. Abbott, *South and North*, 112-13.
4. Walker, "Diary of a Louisiana Planter."
5. *De Bow's Review*, XXIX (1860), 615.
6. Douglass, *My Bondage*, 235.
7. Lyell, *Second Visit*, I, 209.
8. Solomon Northup, *Twelve Years a Slave; Narrative of Solomon Northup, A Citizen of New York, Etc.* (Auburn, 1853), 62.
9. Douglass, *My Bondage*, 176.
10. Abbott, *South and North*, 138-9.
11. Walker, "Diary of a Louisiana Planter."
12. Andrews, *Slavery*, 43.
13. Quoted in Everett, *Free Persons of Color in New Orleans*, 191.
14. Quoted in Everett, *Free Persons of Color in New Orleans*, 197.
15. Baltimore, Ordinances, March 14, 1832.
16. *Louisville Daily Democrat*, August 5, 1851.
17. Petition of the Colonization Society of Virginia to the Virginia State Legislature, Dec. 20, 1831, MSS., Virginia State Library, Richmond.

18. *New Orleans Bee*, April 16, 1858.

19. *New Orleans Daily Picayune*, March 8, 1856.

20. *A Documentary History of American Industrial Society*, II, 108-9.

21. Memorial of the City Council to the Legislature of South Carolina, 1826, MSS., South Carolina Archives Division.

22. Charleston, Ordinances, October 28, 1806.

23. Savannah, Minutes of the Council, October 15, 1822, MSS., City Hall, Savannah.

24. Savannah, Ordinances, November 11, 1831.

25. Quoted in Lyell, *Second Visit*, II, 81.

26. *Genius of Universal Emancipation*, January 12, 1828.

27. Andrews, *Slavery*, 73.

28. New Orleans, Proceedings, September 13, 1823.

29. Lyell, *Second Visit*, II, 125. John Milton Mackie found the same thing in Mobile; *From Cape Cod to Dixie and the Tropics* (N.Y., 1864), 158. Though the book bears a later date, this trip took place before the war.

30. *Richmond Enquirer*, August 27, 1857.

31. Abbott, *South and North*, 112, 113.

32. *Directory for the City of Savannah to Which is Added a Business Directory for 1860* (Savannah, 1860), 176-7.

• Both Frank Tannenbaum and Stanley Elkins have argued that slaves possessed legal, religious, and even economic status in Latin America not enjoyed by their United States counterparts. Carl N. Degler challenges a number of key features of the Tannenbaum-Elkins argument in the following comparative essay on the history of slavery in Brazil and the United States. "In Brazil the slave was feared, but the black man was not," Degler contends, "while in the United States the black man as well as the slave was feared." His article attempts to analyze, among other things, the reasons that white Brazilians never developed the degree of race phobia common among whites in this country throughout our history. In a careful comparative assessment of the two cultures, he concludes that "the differences between Brazilian and United States slavery, rather than being the sources of the different patterns of race relations in the two countries are, in fact, merely the consequences themselves of deeper divergences in the culture and history of the two peoples."

Slavery in Brazil and the United States: A Comparison

CARL N. DEGLER

Over twenty years ago Frank Tannenbaum made a comparison of slavery in the societies of the New World in which he argued that the differences in contemporary race relations between the United States and Latin America are to be traced to differences in the character of slavery in the two places. A decade later Stanley Elkins built a provocative book upon Tannenbaum's conclusions. More recently,

From Carl N. Degler, "Slavery in Brazil and the United States: An Essay in Comparative History," *The American Historical Review*, Vol. LXXV (April 1970), pp. 1004-28. Reprinted by permission of the author.

Arnold Sio and David Brion Davis entered strong demurrers to the Tannenbaum-Elkins conclusions by arguing that slavery as an institution was more similar than different throughout the societies of the New World.[1]

These and a number of other writings on the comparative history of slavery in the Western Hemisphere attest to a burgeoning scholarly interest. But throughout the debate one of the prominent difficulties has been the great breadth and diversity of the areas being compared. To make convincing comparisons among some two dozen societies presents obvious problems and is open to the dangers of superficiality. It is the intention here, therefore, to draw a much more restricted comparison, not because the large problem that Tannenbaum raised will finally be resolved by such a limited approach, but simply because two countries are more manageable as variables than two continents. It is also worth noting that Brazil and the United States have the advantage of being the two most important slave societies in the New World. Both had a long history of slavery—only Cuba and Brazil retained slavery longer than the United States—and in both societies slavery occupied an important, if not actually a central, place in the economy.[2]

Essentially this essay seeks to answer two quite limited questions: First, in what respects were the systems of slavery in Brazil and the United States alike during their mature years—that is, during the nineteenth century—and in what ways did they differ? Second, to what extent are these differences related to the laws and practices of the state and the Church in Brazil, as both Tannenbaum and Elkins have contended? Even if these questions can be answered with some degree of certainty, it should be said that the large question that Tannenbaum raised and sought to answer in his book will not be settled. But I hope that the ground will be cleared for a new attack upon the problem.

How were the two systems of slavery alike? Tannenbaum and Elkins stress the different legal conceptions of the slave in the United States and in Latin America. Tannenbaum, for example, contrasts the definition of a slave as a chattel in the United States with the more ambiguous definition in Latin America.

> In fact, *the element of human personality was not lost in the transition to slavery from Africa to the Spanish or Portuguese dominions.* He [the Negro] remained a person even while he was a slave. . . . He was never considered a mere chattel, never de-

fined as unanimated property, and never under the law treated as such. His master never enjoyed the powers of life and death over his body, even though abuses existed and cruelties were performed.[3]

Yet an examination of Brazilian and United States law reveals striking similarities in the definition of a slave.

The law in both the United States and Brazil, for example, recognized that a slave was both a human being and a piece of property. As a Tennessee court in 1846 put it,

> A slave is not in the condition of a horse, he is made after the image of the creator. He has mental capacities and an immortal principle in his nature, that constitute him equal to his owner but for the accidental position in which fortune has placed him . . . the laws . . . cannot extinguish his high born nature, nor deprive him of many rights which are inherent in man. . . .[4]

In 1818 a Mississippi court went so far as to observe that "Slavery is condemned by reason and the laws of nature. It exists and can only exist through municipal regulations, and in matters of doubt" the courts must lean in favor of freedom.[5] As late as 1861 an Alabama court concluded that because slaves "are rational beings, they are capable of committing crimes; and in reference to acts which are crimes, are regarded as persons. Because they are slaves, they are . . . incapable of performing civil acts, and, in reference to all such, they are things, not persons."[6]

That last statement is close, in phraseology as well as meaning, to that set forth in Brazilian slave law by its principal authority, Agostino Marques Perdigão Malheiro. "In regard to the penal code," he wrote, "the slave, as subject of the offense or agent of it, it not a *thing*, he is a *person* . . . he is a human entity." Hence he is held personally responsible for crimes. But when he is an "Object or sufferer of a crime" the matter is different. The slave is not indemnified for such injuries, though the master may be. "In the latter case the question is one of *property*, but in the other it is one of *personality*." Perdigão Malheiro makes clear, moreover, that the position of the slave in court was not much different from that of the slave in the United States. No slave in Brazil could enter a complaint himself; it had to be done by his master or by the public authority. Nor could a slave make an accusation against his master. In fact, a slave could not give sworn testimony, only information. Perdigão Malheiro writes that in only

three circumstances did a slave have standing in court: in regard to
spiritual matters, such as marriage; in regard to his liberty; and in
matters of obvious public concern. Only in regard to the first did the
legal position of the slave in the United States differ; slave marriages
had no legal basis in the United States.[7]

If there was little difference in the conception of the slave in Brazilian and United States law, there was also little difference in the
law's supposed protection of the slave's humanity. Despite the general statements of some scholars,[8] both societies had laws protecting
the slave against murder, mistreatment, or overwork by his master.[9]
The operative question is whether the law or the church in fact inter-
ceded between the master and the slave in behalf of the latter. Certainly for the United States the evidence is not convincing. And in
Brazil, too, the power of the state or the church to affect the life of
the slave seems to have been limited. As Henry Koster, an English
planter in Brazil, pointed out early in the nineteenth century, the
Brazilian government was a weak reed on which to lean for anything,
much less for control over members of the ruling slaveholding class.
He tells, for example, of an instance in which one of his own slaves
injured the slave of another man, but says that nothing was done
about the matter. The owner of the injured slave might have pressed
charges, if he so chose, "but the law of itself seldom does anything.
Even in the cases of murder the prosecutor . . . has it at his option
to bring the trial forward or not; if he can be bribed or otherwise
persuaded to give up the accusation, the matter drops to the ground."
It is not likely that the state, which was run by slaveholders, would
be more energetic in protecting the slave's humanity. Koster writes
that occasionally a cruel master was fined for maltreating his slaves,
"but," he adds, "I never heard of punishment having been carried
farther than this trifling manner of correction."[10] Later in the century
another traveler, the German painter John Rugendas, put the matter
even more directly. Although there were laws in Brazil limiting the
use of the whip and fixing the number of lashes at one time, he wrote
in 1835:

> these laws have no force and probably may be unknown to the
> majority of the slaves and masters; on the other hand, the au-
> thorities are so removed that in actuality the punishment of the
> slave for a true or imaginary infraction or the bad treatment
> resulting from the caprice and the cruelty of the master, only
> encounters limits in the fear of losing the slave by death, by

flight, or as a consequence of public opinion. But these considerations are never sufficient to impede the evil and it is inescapable that examples of cruelty are not lacking, which result in the mutilation and death of slaves.[11]

It is only toward the end of the era of slavery, when the abolitionists brought cases of mistreatment to court, that Brazilian laws in behalf of the slaves actually protected them.

Both Elkins and Tannenbaum emphasize the role of the Roman Catholic Church in giving the Negro slave in Latin America a higher "moral" position than in the United States.[12] If that means that the Church accepted Negro slaves as members, the churches of the United States did, too. If it means that the Church actively intervened between master and slave in behalf of the latter, then it must be said that in Brazil the interest of the Church in and its power to protect the slave's humanity were as limited as those of the state. For one thing, few plantations had resident priests; most plantations saw a priest only once a year when he came to legalize unions and to baptize. There were not, in fact, enough priests in the country to affect the daily life of the slave, even if they had the interest to do so. As Emilia Viotti da Costa points out, not until 1885 did the archbishop of Bahia rule that no master could prevent a slave from marrying or sell him away from his spouse. Yet even at that late date, a slave could marry against his master's will only if the slave could demonstrate that he knew Christian doctrine—the Lord's Prayer, the Ave Maria, the Creed, and the commandments—understood the obligations of holy matrimony, and was clear in his intention to remain married for life. Furthermore, as in the United States, religion in Brazil was used by churchmen to buttress slavery. One priest told a group of planters: "Confession is the antidote to insurrections, because the confessor makes the slave see that his master is in the place of his father to whom he owes love, respect, and obedience. . . ."[13]

In 1887, on the eve of abolition in Brazil, the abolitionist Anselmo Fonseca wrote a long book castigating the Brazilian Catholic clergy for its lack of interest in the then highly active abolitionist movement in his country. Caustically he observed that in 1871 when Rio Branco fought for the Law of the Free Womb of slave mothers, the Church was silent, for slavery "still had much vitality. . . . It was dangerous to take it on frontally. Why did not the Bishops then show the solidarity and courage and the energy with which in 1873–74 they combated Masonry and the government?" Fonseca draws the interesting contrast between the massive indifference to the plight of the slave on the part of the Brazilian Catholic Church throughout the history of slavery and the activities of Protestant clergymen like William Ellery Channing in behalf of the slave in the United States.[14]

Slave marriages were valid in the eyes of the Brazilian Church; marriages of slaves in Protestant churches in the United States also qualified as sacramental acts, though masters, it was understood, were not bound to honor such unions. Given the weakness of the Church's control over slave masters, it is not likely that marriages of slaves in Brazil were any more enduring or protected from disruption through sale than in the United States. In any event, in Brazil only a small proportion of slaves were married by the Church. Early in the nineteenth century the reformer José Bonifacio asked for laws to compel masters to permit slaves to marry freely and to require that at least two-thirds of a master's slaves be married. Yet, forty years later, travelers still reported that few Negroes were married and that "rarely were [marriages] confirmed by a religious act." A traveler in 1841 found only 10 slaves married out of 2,500 on the Isle of Santa Catherina in southern Brazil. In northeastern Brazil, in Rio Grande do Norte, a local document listed only about 5 per cent of the 13,000 slaves in the province in 1874 as married or widowed, though 30 per cent of free persons were married. Of the 660,000 slaves in all of Brazil in 1875, who were 14 years or older, only about 1 out of 6 was recorded as married or widowed.[15]

In the United States the lack of protection for the informal slave family is acknowledged as a fact of slave life. Tannenbaum has summarized it well: "Under the law of most of the Southern states there was no regard for the Negro family, no question of the right of the owner to sell his slaves separately, and no limitation upon separating husband and wife, or child from its mother."[16]

Yet, for most of the nineteenth century, the same generalization is quite accurate for Brazil. Prior to 1869 there was no legal protection for the slave family, though, as was the case in the United States, a vigorous internal slave trade was a powerful cause for the breaking up of many families, whether their ties had been solemnized by the Church or not. The internal slave trade in Brazil was especially active in the middle years of the nineteenth century when the coffee areas in the South were expanding and thousands of slaves were brought down from the economically declining Northeast. One estimate in 1862 put at five thousand per year the number arriving from the North at Rio de Janeiro by coastal shipping alone. A modern authority has cited thirty thousand a year as the number that went from the North of the state of São Paulo between 1850 and 1870.[17]

There is little doubt that the disruption of the slave family was common in Brazil at least prior to 1869. Indeed, to take an extreme example, one of the great Brazilian abolitionists, Luis Gama, was sold into slavery by his own white father. Stanley Stein reports that in the 1870's it was not unknown in Vassouras for a planter to sell his mulatto offspring to a passing slave trader.[18] A law passed in 1875, prohibiting the sale of one's own children, suggests that such a practice was known even at that late date.[19] Another sign that the slave family was disintegrating throughout the nineteenth century, at least, is that antislavery reformers like Bonifacio in the early nineteenth century and others as late as 1862 were demanding that ways be found to protect the slave family.[20] In 1854 Baron Cotegipe, who was later to oppose abolition, argued for limitations on the internal slave trade because it disrupted families. "It is a horror, gentlemen," he told the Senate, "to see children ripped from their mothers, husbands separated from wives, parents from children! Go to Law Street . . . and be outraged and touched by the spectacle of such sufferings. . . ." In 1866 Perdigão Malheiro was still asking that the law prevent the separation of married slave couples and children of less than seven years of age. Without such legal protection, he contended, there was little reason to expect the slave family to exist at all.[21]

The fact is that in Brazil prior to 1869 there was no law preventing the disruption of slave families. And even the law passed in 1869 required some nine years of agitation before it was enacted.[22] Most slave states in the US, as Tannenbaum has pointed out, never enacted such laws, but a few did. A law of 1829 in Louisiana prohibited the sale of children under ten; apparently it was adhered to by slave traders. Laws in Alabama and Georgia forbade the dissolution of inherited slave families, but not others. In practice, probably most planters in the United States tried to avoid breaking up slave families, though undoubtedly many were disrupted.[23]

Perhaps the most frequently stressed difference between slavery in Latin America and the United States concerns manumission. Yet, even here, as Davis has pointed out, manumission in Brazil was not unlimited, and in the US it was not absolutely denied.[24] The purchase of freedom by the slave himself, so much emphasized in discussions on Brazilian slavery, was, moreover, far from rare in the United States.

Sumner Matison, for example, found several hundred examples of self-purchase. Luther Jackson, studying self-purchase in three cities of Virginia, found twenty examples even at the height of the sectional conflict of the 1850's and despite a law requiring removal of manumitted slaves out of the state.[25]

On the Brazilian side of the comparison it must be said that prior to 1871, despite tradition and the assertions of Tannenbaum and Elkins,[26] there was no law requiring a master to permit a slave to buy his freedom. One American historian of Brazil made a search for such a law, but found none before 1871, when emancipationists insisted upon it; this suggests that the practice of self-purchase was not as firmly protected as has been alleged.[27] It is true that in Brazilian law there were none of the limitations that became increasingly common in the southern United States after 1830. Under Brazilian law emancipation was legal in almost any form: by letter, by will, or by explicit statement at baptism.[28] In Brazil, moreover, there were no statutes requiring the removal of emancipated slaves to other states, though such laws were characteristic of the southern United States. But Brazilian law contained a curious qualification to its otherwise liberal policy on emancipation: freedom might be revoked by the master for ingratitude on the part of the freedman, even if that ingratitude was expressed only orally and outside of the presence of the former master. Perdigão Malheiro, who reports this provision of the law, doubted that it was still valid in 1866. In 1871 the power to revoke freedom was explicitly withdrawn in an antislavery law, suggesting that the old provision was not such a dead letter that opponents of slavery were willing to let it remain on the statute books.[29] The provision also raises a question as to whether the law in Brazil was in fact helping to preserve the Negro's moral personality as some modern historians have argued. At the very least it encouraged masters to think of their Negroes as minors or wards rather than as persons on an equal footing. At worst, it perpetuated in the Negro that sense of subordination and inferiority derived from the degraded status of slavery, thereby counteracting whatever elevating effects might flow from the relative ease of manumission.

Some modern historians, like Tannenbaum and Elkins,[30] have emphasized the slave's right to hold property in Latin America and therefore to be in a position to buy his freedom, as contrasted with the lack of that right in the US. In Brazil, however, the law did not permit slaves to possess property, or a peculium, until near the end of the era of slavery. Perdigão Malheiro writes in his treatise on slave law that, as late as 1866, "Among us, no law guarantees to the slave his peculium; nor the disposition overall by the last will, nor the succession. . . ." However, he goes on, most masters tolerated the slave's holding property, generally permitting the slave to use it as he saw fit.[31] The same situation prevailed, by and large, in the United States, where slave property was neither recognized nor protected by law, but in practice was generally recognized by the master. Occasionally the courts would throw a protective arm around the peculium, as in a South Carolina case in 1792, when a slave was held capable of holding property separate from that of his master. On the basis of that case, a half century later, Judge J. B. O'Neall of South Carolina concluded that "by the law of this state a slave might acquire personal property."[32]

Yet, after all these qualifications have been made in the usually optimistic picture of manumission under Brazilian slavery, Brazil still appears to have been more liberal on manumission than was the US. And the principal reason for this conclusion is the higher proportion of free Negroes in Brazil than in the United States. Because of the paucity of adequate figures for both countries, a quantitative comparison can be made only for the nineteenth century. In 1817–1818 the number of slaves in Brazil was about three times that of free Negroes and mulattoes.[33] This ratio may be compared with that in the United States in 1860, when the number of free Negroes reached its maximum under slavery. At that date there were eight times as many slaves as free Negroes in the whole of the United States and sixteen times as many slaves if the comparison is made in the slave states only. As slavery came to an end in Brazil the number of free Negroes grew enormously, so that in 1872 the number of free Negroes and colored was more than double that of the slaves.[34]

Although it is not the intention of this essay to explain this difference in attitude toward manumission, if only because of the complexity of the issue, at least two suggestions are worth brief examination. One of these is that Brazilian masters were freeing the sick and the old in order to relieve themselves of responsibility and cost. Denunciations in newspapers and laws prohibiting such practices indicate that masters were indeed freeing their infirm, aged, and incurable slaves.[35] Yet it is difficult to believe that such practices, however widespread they appear to be, could have been the principal source of the relatively large free colored population. Infirm, aged, or sick slaves simply would not have been numerous enough or have been able to produce offspring in sufficient numbers to account for the great number of free colored.

Marvin Harris has advanced a more reasonable explanation, in which he emphasizes the differences in the processes of settlement and economic development in Brazil and the United States.[36] In Brazil a freed Negro or mulatto had a place in a society that was only sparsely populated and in a slave economy that was focused upon staple production. Free blacks and mulattoes were needed in the economy to produce food, to serve as slave catchers, militiamen, shopkeepers, craftsmen, artisans, and so forth. They filled the many petty jobs and performed the "interstitial" work of the economy that slave labor could not easily perform and that white labor was insufficient to man. Octavio Ianni, writing about slavery in southern Brazil, and Nelson de Senna, describing conditions in Minas Gerais, emphasize the great variety of occupations filled by free Negroes and mulattoes.[37]

In the southern United States many plantations also allocated their labor in this fashion, that is, by importing food rather than growing it. But the food was produced by a large number of nonslaveholding whites in the South and the Northwest. Virtually from the beginning of settlement in the South there had been more than enough whites to perform all the tasks of the society except that of compulsory labor. In fact, throughout the ante bellum years, as later, the South exported whites to the rest of the nation. Hence, in the US there was no compelling economic reason for emancipation; nor, more importantly, was there any economic place for those who were manumitted. But this demographic or materialist interpretation is not the complete explanation, suggestive as it is. As we shall see later, the relative ease of manumission in Brazil was part of a larger and deeper difference in attitudes between the two societies.

Comparisons between slavery in Brazil and the United States traditionally emphasize the greater rebelliousness of slaves in Brazil. But here, too, the distinction, when examined closely, is not as sharp as has frequently been alleged. The most often mentioned measure of the greater rebelliousness of Brazilian slaves is the large slave hideaway or *quilombo* of Palmares in northeastern Brazil, which, during the seventeenth century, resisted the attacks of government and other troops for more than fifty years. Examples of other *quilombos*, less spectacular or famous than Palmares, are also well documented.[38] It is questionable, however, whether such groups of runaways, no matter how long lived or large scale, ought to be classed as slave rebellions. Generally the *quilombos* neither attempted to overthrow the slave system nor made war on it, except when whites sought to destroy them. Even Palmares would have been content to remain as an African state separate from white society if the government and the *paulistas* had left it alone.[39] Thus, if one is counting armed uprisings against slaveholders, such as took place under Nat Turner in Virginia in 1831, then the total number in Brazil is considerably smaller if one excludes the *quilombos*. For in Brazil, as in the United States, the most common expression of slave unrest was the runaway, not the insurrectionist.

Rumors of revolts were common in both countries, but, except during the last years of slavery and with the exception of a series of revolts in Bahia in the early nineteenth century, slave revolts in Brazil were scattered, and in some areas almost nonexistent. Koster, the English planter, wrote in the early nineteenth century that "Pernambuco has never experienced any serious revolt among the slaves." Modern historians of the coffee region point out that neither slave revolts not *quilombos* were on anything but a small scale. Da Costa speaks of revolts as "rare in the coffee regions." F. H. Cardoso also found little opportunity for, or evidence of, slave revolts in Rio Grande do Sul. Girão writes that in Ceará Province in the early nineteenth century "fugitives were not common and rebellions very rare." Octavio Eduardo reports that "no series of revolts occurred in Maranhão as they did in Bahia, although the revolt of the Balaios from 1838 to 1841" attracted runaway slaves to the cause.[40]

On the other hand, general works on slave rebellions in Brazil as a whole emphasize their importance, and a recent study of the sugar areas in São Paulo Province refers to the large number of slave rebellions there.[41] In short, much work remains to be done on the extent and character of slave unrest in Brazil, and it seems safe to say that most of the writing on slave rebellions has not been careful to distinguish between military outbreaks and runaways or between those uprisings striking at the slave system directly and those simply fleeing from it, as, for example, has been done for American slave revolts by Marion Kilson.[42]

In the broadest sense, of course, both slave rebellions and runaways threatened the slave system, for they constituted avenues by which some slaves could escape from the system and raised the expectations of those who remained behind. In this regard, Brazilian slaves had somewhat greater opportunities for escape than had slaves in the United States. Actual revolts may not have been much more numerous in Brazil, but the numbers of slaves involved in those that did take place were greater, just as the size of the *quilombos* were larger than those in the United States. Stein described a revolt in Vassouras, for example, that mobilized three hundred slaves and required federal troops to suppress it. At least two revolts involving several hundred slaves were reported in 1820 in Minas Gerais. In the first half of the nineteenth century in the province of Espírito Santo, uprisings of two hundred and four hundred slaves occurred, though it is not clear whether these were revolts or collective runaways.[43]

The really striking examples of undoubted slave insurrections are the half dozen that erupted in and around the city of Bahia between 1807 and 1835, several of which involved pitched battles between armed slaves and government troops. It is significant that these rebellions occurred in the city, not in the plantation region. They are, moreover, among the few that can be confidently classified as violent attacks upon whites and the slave system rather than as flights to a *quilombo*.[44] But, in the history of Brazilian slavery, the Bahian revolts were unusual and, as we shall see, the consequence of special circumstances.

There were true slave revolts in the US, too, though they were fewer and generally much smaller in number of participants than in Brazil. Of the three biggest and best-known uprisings, those at Stono, South Carolina, in 1739, New Orleans in 1811, and Southampton, Virginia, in 1831, only the second involved more than one hundred slaves. The *quilombos* in the United States were considerably fewer and smaller in size than those in Brazil.[45] The climate in the US was largely responsible for the smaller number of maroons, or *quilombos*. In most of the United States the winter is simply too harsh for a *quilombo* to survive for very long, whereas the greater part of Brazil lies in the tropics. The frontier area in the United States was, moreover, too well settled and, accordingly, too well policed, especially after the seventeenth century, to provide many opportunities for colonies of runaways. The only example of a *quilombo* approaching the size and endurance of Palmares was the Second Seminole War, during which Indians and runaway blacks held out against the US Army for seven years.[46] It is significant that the struggle took place in the warmest part of the United States and in an area unsettled by whites.

Another difference between the two slave societies was the dependence of the Brazilians upon the African slave trade. Although the foreign slave trade in Brazil was supposedly ended in 1831 by treaty with Great Britain, all authorities agree that importations of slaves continued at high annual rates for another twenty years. Over 300,-000 slaves entered Brazil between 1842 and 1851 alone, bringing the total number of slaves in the country to 2,500,000 in 1850, probably the highest figure ever reached.[47] There is also general agreement that the importation of large numbers of slaves into the United States ceased in 1807, with the federal prohibition of the foreign trade. Actually, every one of the slave states themselves had prohibited importation prior to 1800. Only South Carolina reopened the trade before the federal government finally closed it. Thus even before 1807 the influx of native Africans had decreased considerably.

The larger number of recently imported Africans in Brazil all through the history of slavery probably accounts for the greater number of revolts there.[48] Revolts were hard enough to organize and carry out under any circumstances, but they were especially difficult under a slave system like that in the United States where the slaves were principally native and almost entirely shorn of their African culture or identity. In Brazil the presence of thousands of newly arrived Africans, alienated from their new masters and society while often united by their common African tribal culture, was undoubtedly a source of slave rebellion. Stein calls attention to a rash of attempted uprisings in Vassouras in the 1840's just as the number of imported Africans reached its peak. Particularly in the cities were the slaves able to retain their African languages, dances, religious rites, and other customs, even though the authorities, aware of the nucleus such African traits provided for discontent and revolt, attempted to suppress them.[49] It is certainly not accidental that the greatest revolts in Brazil were in the city of Bahia and that they were generally led by Hausa and Yoruba Negroes, who were Muslims. A common African tribal culture, language, and religion provided the necessary cement of organization and the incentives to resistance, which were almost wholly lacking among the slaves in the United States. It is significant that the documents captured from the Bahian rebels in 1835 were written in Arabic script, and, though there is some doubt as to the extent of the religious basis for the revolt, a number of the leaders were clearly Muslims.[50] In the nineteenth century, coffee planters in the southern part of Brazil were so conscious of the dangers of newly arrived slaves from the same African tribal background that they limited their purchases of such slaves to small numbers in order to minimize revolts. C. R. Boxer writes that the diversity of African nations among the slaves in eighteenth-century Minas Gerais was the chief safeguard against the outbreak of revolts.[51]

The connections between Brazil and Africa were so close in the nineteenth century that some slaves, after they earned their freedom or otherwise gained manumission, elected to return to Africa. One historian, for example, has reported on a number of leaders of nine-teenth-century Nigerian society who had been slaves in Brazil, but who after manumission returned to Africa to make a living in the slave trade. So intimate was the connection between Brazil and Africa that until 1905 at least—almost twenty years after abolition—ships plied between Bahia and Lagos, "repatriating nostalgic, emancipated Negroes and returning with West Coast products much prized by Africans and their descendants in Brazil."[52] In striking contrast is the well-known reluctance of Negroes in the United States during the ante bellum years to have anything to do with removal to Africa. That contrast emphasizes once again the overwhelmingly native character of slavery in the US and the dearth of African survivals.

The persistence, and even expansion, of the slave system of the United States without any substantial additions from importations is unique in history. Neither in antiquity nor in Latin America was a slave system sustained principally by reproduction. Even if one accepts the highest figure for smuggling into the United States—270,000 in the fifty years prior to 1860, or about 5,000 a year—the figure can hardly account for the steady and large increase in the slave popula-tion recorded by the decennial censuses. For example, in the 1790's, prior to the federal closing of the slave trade, the increase was 30 per cent; in the 1840's the increase was still 28 per cent, while the absolute average annual figures were 20,000 and 70,000, respectively. In short, it seems clear that reproduction was the principal source of slaves for the United States, at least since the first census.[53] One con-sequence was that the ratio between the sexes was virtually equal, a fact that was conducive to holding slaves in so-called family units as well as to breeding. (It was also conducive to greater control over the slaves.) Thus the ratio between the sexes in Mississippi counties ac-cording to the census of 1860 was about the same as among the whites. In 1860 in all of the southern slave states the numerical differ-ence between the sexes was 3 per cent or less of the total, except in Louisiana where the surplus of males was 3.6 per cent. This ratio among the slaves was closer to an absolute balance between the sexes than obtained among the whites themselves in five southern states, where the surplus of males ran between 4 and 8 per cent of the white population. Thus in both the so-called breeding and consuming regions of the South the sexes were remarkably well balanced.

Although Gilberto Freyre writes of the Brazilian master's interest in the "generative belly" of the female slave, other writers make clear that slave breeding was not important to Brazilian slaveholders. Stein, for example, found a genuine reluctance among slaveholders to breed and rear slaves; the very hours during which male and female slaves could be together were deliberately limited. Lynn Smith cites a number of sources to show that masters consciously restricted slave reproduction by locking up the sexes separately at night.[54]

Undoubtedly the availability of slaves from Africa accounts for some of the lack of interest in slave breeding in Brazil prior to 1851. For within five years after the closing of the slave trade, books began to appear in Brazil advising planters to follow the example of Virginians, who were alleged to be such efficient breeders of slaves that the infants were bought while still in the mother's womb.[55] These exhortations do not seem to have had much effect, however, for twenty years after the end of the African slave trade the slaveholder's customary rationale for not raising slaves was still being advanced:

> "One buys a Negro for 300 milreis, who harvests in the course of the year 100 arrobas of coffee, which produces a net profit at least equal to the cost of the slave; thereafter everything is profit. It is not worth the trouble to raise children, who, only after sixteen years, will give equal service. Furthermore, the pregnant Negroes and those nursing are not available to use the hoe; heavy fatigue prevents the regular development of the fetus in some; in others the diminution of the flow of milk, and in almost all, sloppiness in the treatment of the children occurs, from which sickness and death of the children result. So why raise them?"[56]

And apparently infant mortality among slaves was amazingly high, even after the foreign slave trade had ended. One authority on the coffee region has placed it as high as 88 per cent. The census of 1870 revealed that in the city of Rio de Janeiro the mortality of slave children exceeded births by 1.8 per cent; even this shocking figure must have been a minimum since most slaves in Rio were domestic and presumably better cared for than agricultural slaves. Rio Branco, the Brazilian statesman who gave his name to an important emancipationist law, calculated that on the basis of the excess of slave deaths over births alone slavery would die out within seventy-five years. And although the British minister at Rio, W. D. Christie, was highly incensed at Brazilian complacency over the persistence of slavery, he had to admit in 1863 in a report to his home government that

> the slave population is decreasing, though not considerably. . . . The mortality among the children of slaves is very great; and Brazilian proprietors do not appear to have given nearly so much attention as might have been expected, from obvious motives of self-interest, to marriages among slaves, or the care of mothers or children.[57]

One undoubted consequence of the continuance of the foreign slave trade was that Brazilian planters made no effort to balance the sexes among the slaves. Since male slaves were stronger and more serviceable, they apparently constituted the overwhelming majority of the importations throughout the history of Brazilian slavery. According to one authority, on some plantations there were no female slaves. For Brazil as a whole he estimates that one Negro woman was imported for each three or four males. The statistics compiled by Stein for Vassouras support that estimate, for he found that between 1820 and 1880 70 per cent or more of the African-born slaves were males. Robert Conrad, quoting from the records of captured slave ships in the 1830's and 1840's, found ratios of one to four and one to five in favor of males.[58] The heavy imbalance between the sexes meant that once the slave trade was stopped, Brazilian slavery began to decline, for the paucity of women, not to mention the masters' lack of interest in breeding, ensured that the reduction in the foreign supply of slaves would not be easily or quickly made up.

The imbalance between the sexes in Brazil may help also to explain the somewhat greater number of rebellions and runaways in that country as compared with the United States. In the US, with slaves more or less divided into family units, for a male slave to rebel or to run away meant serious personal loss, since he probably would have to leave women and children behind. Such a consequence was much less likely in Brazil. One indication that the pairing of the sexes in the United States reduced rebelliousness is provided by a report from São Paulo toward the last years of slavery when masters were quoted as saying about a restless or rebellious slave: "It is necessary to give that

Negro in marriage and give him a piece of land in order to calm him down and cultivate responsibility in him."[59]

Although it is often said or implied that slavery in Latin America in general was milder than in the United States,[60] there are several reasons for believing that in a comparison between Brazil and the US the relationship is just the reverse. Admittedly such comparisons are difficult to make since the evidence that might be mustered on either side is open to serious doubts as to its representativeness. But this problem can be circumvented in part, at least, if general classes of evidence are used. There are at least three general reasons, aside from any discrete examples of treatment of slaves, suggesting that slavery was harsher in Brazil than in the United States. First, the very fact that slavery in the US was able to endure and expand on the basis of reproduction alone is itself strong testimony to a better standard of physical care. It is true that the imbalance of the sexes in Brazil played a part in keeping down reproduction, but the high mortality of slave children and the care and expense involved probably account for the reluctance to rear slaves in the first place. Moreover, as we have seen, even after the slave trade was closed, the rearing of slave children was still resisted in Brazil. Masters said that it was easier to raise three or four white children than one black child, the difference being attributed to the "greater fragility of the black race." In 1862 a French visitor reported that "the most simple hygienic measures are almost always neglected by the owners of slaves, and the mortality of 'negrillons' is very considerable, especially on the plantations of the interior."[61] Brazilians, in short, simply did not take sufficient care of their slaves for them to reproduce.

Second, there are kinds of severe and cruel treatment of slaves in Brazil that rarely occurred in the United States. A number of Brazilian sources, both during the colonial period and under the Empire in the nineteenth century, speak of the use of female slaves as prostitutes.[62] So far as I know, this source of income from slaves was unknown or very rare in the United States. Brazilian sources also contain numerous references to the use of iron or tin masks on slaves, usually to prevent them from eating dirt or drinking liquor. Indeed, the practice of using masks was sufficiently common that pictures of slaves wearing them appear in books on slavery. I have yet to see such a picture in the literature of slavery in the US, and references to the use of the mask are rare, though not unknown.[63] As already noted, Brazilian sources call attention to another practice that also suggests severe treatment: the freeing of ill, old, or crippled slaves in order to escape the obligation of caring for them. The several efforts to legislate against this practice, much less to put a stop to it, were fruitless until just before the abolition of slavery.[64] Finally, because of the imbalance of the sexes, most slaves in Brazil had no sexual outlets at all.

Though making comparisons of physical treatment may have pitfalls, the effort has value because such comparisons give some insight into the nature of the slave systems in the two countries. Some authorities, like Elkins, for example,[65] argue that a comparative analysis of treatment is not germane to a comparison of the impact of slavery on the Negro, for "in one case [Latin America] we would be dealing with cruelty of man to men, and in the other [the United States], with the care, maintenance, and indulgence of men toward creatures who were legally and morally *not* men. . . ." But this argument collapses, as Davis has pointed out,[66] when it can be shown that the law in Brazil and the United States defined the slave as both a man and a thing. Under such circumstances, treatment can no longer be confidently separated from attitudes. Instead, the way a master treats a slave, particularly *when the slave is a member of a physically identifiable class,* becomes a part of the historian's evidence for ascertaining the attitude of white men toward black men who are slaves, and of the way in which blacks are conditioned to think of themselves. When a master muzzles a slave, for example, he is literally treating him like a dog. The master's behavior, at the very least, is evidence for concluding that he considered his slave on the level with a dog; at the most, his behavior suggests that its source was the belief that the slave was from the beginning no better than a dog. In either case, the master's treatment of the slave is part of the evidence to be evaluated in ascertaining white men's attitudes toward black slaves. Perhaps even more important is the real possibility that a slave who is muzzled or who sees other black men muzzled may well be led to think of himself as a dog, worthy of being muzzled. In short, the treatment accorded black slaves in both societies is relevant to the question of how white men think about black men.

A second reason for making a comparison of physical treatment is to call attention to the importance of the slave trade in accounting for some of the differences between slavery in Brazil and the United States. Brazilians simply did not have to treat their slaves with care or concern when new slaves were obtainable from outside the system. That the slave trade played this role was recognized by Perdigão

Malheiro in 1866, after the trade had been stopped for fifteen years. He asserted that since the closing of the traffic from abroad the treatment of slaves in Brazil had improved. No longer, he wrote, did one "meet in the streets, as in other not remote times, slaves with their faces covered by a wire mask or a great weight on the foot. . . ." Slaves were so well dressed and shod, he continued, "that no one would know who they are," that is, they could not be distinguished from free blacks. Two visiting Americans noticed the same change even earlier:

> Until 1850, when the slave-trade was effectually put down, it was considered cheaper, on the country plantations to use up a slave in five or seven years, and purchase another, than to take care of him. This I had, in the interior, from intelligent native Brazilians, and my own observation has confirmed it. But, since the inhuman traffic has ceased, the price of slaves has been enhanced, and the selfish motives for taking greater care of them have been increased.[67]

But it needs to be added that the closing of the foreign slave trade in Brazil had at least one worsening effect upon the lot of the slave. It undoubtedly increased the internal slave trade, thereby enhancing the likelihood of the dissolution of slave families. Prior to 1850 the foreign slave trade probably kept to a minimum the movement of established slaves from one part of the country to another. In the United States, on the other hand, slaves prior to 1850 probably experienced more disruption of families, simply because the foreign slave trade was closed and the opening of new areas in the Southwest provided a growing market for slaves, who had to be drawn from the older regions, especially the upper South.

One of the earliest signs of discrimination against Negroes in seventeenth-century Virginia, Maryland, and even New England was the legal denial of arms to blacks, free or slave, but not to white indentured servants.[68] This discrimination constitutes perhaps the sharpest difference between the slave systems of the US and Brazil. Almost from the beginning of settlement, the Portuguese and then the Brazilians permitted not only Negroes, but slaves themselves, to be armed. Arthur Ramos has even suggested that whites encouraged the slaves to arm themselves.[69] During the wars against the French and the Dutch invaders in the sixteenth and seventeenth centuries, large numbers of slaves and free Negroes fought on the side of the Brazilians. The Dutch occupation of northeastern Brazil, which entailed almost continuous warfare, lasted for a quarter of a century. Negroes, slave and free, also fought in the War of the Farrapos in southern Brazil against the Empire in the late 1830's. Indeed, as Roger Bastide has written, "the Negro appears in all the civil revolts, the war of the *paulistas* against the Emboabos, the wars of national independence, and one even sees them in the party struggles under the Empire, between royalists and republicans or in the rivalries of political leaders among themselves." Slaves served in the Paraguayan War of 1865–70, often being sent by masters to fight in their places or to win favor with the Emperor. Fugitive slaves also served in the Brazilian army in the nineteenth century. At the end of the Paraguayan War some twenty thousand slaves who had served in the army were given their freedom.[70]

When comparable occasions arose in the United States the results were quite different. During the American Revolution, for example, Henry and John Laurens, leading figures in South Carolina, proposed in 1779 that slaves be enlisted to help counter the military successes of the British in the southern colonies. It was understood that the survivors would be freed. Although the Laurenses were joined by a few other South Carolinians and the Continental Congress approved of the plan, the South Carolina legislature overwhelmingly rejected it. The Laurenses raised the issue again in 1781, but once more the proposal was rejected by both the South Carolina and Georgia legislatures. When the slave South was faced with a struggle for survival during the Civil War it again steadfastly refused to use slave soldiers until the very last month of the war; indeed, the Confederacy rejected even free Negroes when they offered their services at the beginning of the war.[71]

That slaves in Brazil were often armed and that they rarely were in the United States is obviously a significant difference between the practices of slavery in the two places. To arm Negro slaves surely affects how one feels about Negroes, whether slave or free. As Octavio Ianni has observed, concerning the use of Negro slaves in the Paraguayan War, Brazilian whites could not help but obtain a new and larger view of Negro capabilities when blacks served as defenders of the nation.[72] How can this difference in practice be explained?

A part of the explanation is undoubtedly related to the quite dissimilar colonial histories of the two countries. Sixteenth-century Brazil was a tiny, sparsely settled colony, desperately clinging to the coast, yet attractive to foreign powers because of its wealth, actual and potential. At different times during the sixteenth and seventeenth centuries the French and Dutch attempted to wrest the colony from Portugal by actual invasion. Since the mother country was too weak to offer much help, all the resources of the colony had to be mobilized for defense, which included every scrap of manpower, including slaves. The recourse to armed slaves, it is worth noticing, was undertaken reluctantly. For as Ramos writes, Negroes were first used only as a kind of advanced guard, being denied a place in the regular army during the sixteenth and seventeenth centuries. But as the need for soldiers continued and a new generation of Brazilian-born Negroes entered the scene, the whites came to demand that they serve in the armed forces. That the acceptance of Negro troops was the result of circumstances rather than ideology is shown by the fact that the Negroes were usually segregated until the years of the Empire, and even when they were no longer set apart, "whites tended to occupy the military posts of major responsibility."[73] Use of Negroes in the colonial period was, therefore, not the result of the prior acceptance of the colored man as an equal, but of the need of him as a fighter. Throughout the eighteenth century, as before, the law *denied* Negroes and mulattoes the right to carry arms.[74]

In striking contrast is the history of the Negro in the British colonies of North America, where conditions and circumstances of settlement and development differed. In the first fifty years of settlement, when the necessities of defense might have encouraged the arming of slaves, there were very few blacks available. As is well known, in the South white indentured servants made up the great preponderance of the unfree labor supply until the end of the seventeenth century. Even at that time, in both Maryland and Virginia, Negroes constituted considerably less than one-fifth of the population. Meanwhile, the white population, servant and free, had long been more than adequate for purposes of defense. Unlike the situation in Brazil, moreover, colonial Englishmen experienced no foreign invasions and only an occasional foreign threat. In short, neither at the beginning nor at the close of the formative seventeenth century were English colonists under any pressure to use Negroes or slaves as defensive troops. As a consequence they could indulge their acute awareness of their difference in appearance, religion, and culture from Africans by permitting their social institutions to reflect this awareness. Thus in both the southern and northern colonies Negroes were resolutely kept from bearing arms. At one time, in 1652, Massachusetts had enlisted Indians and Negroes in the militia, but in 1656 this policy was reversed by the statement that "henceforth no negroes or Indians, altho servants of the English, shalbe armed or permitted to trayne." In 1660 Connecticut also excluded Indians and "negar servants" from the militia.[75]

There is one exception to the English colonists' attitudes toward the arming of slaves, but it is an exception that proves the rule. Early in the eighteenth century, when South Carolina was weak and threatened by Spanish invasion, slaves were required to be trained in the use of arms and included in an auxiliary militia.[76] The policy, however, was only temporary, since the colony was soon able to protect itself by dependence upon whites alone and the feared invasions did not materialize.

Further differences in attitudes toward Negroes and slaves in the US and in Brazil are the responses that the two societies made to the threat of slave insurrections. In both societies, it should be said, fear of slave revolts was widespread. One of the several measures that whites in the southern United States took to forestall slave insurrections was to place restrictions upon free Negroes, who were widely believed to be fomenters of slave conspiracies and revolts. Thus the uncovering in 1820 of a plot allegedly organized by the free Negro Denmark Vesey moved South Carolina and other southern states to enact new and stricter limitations on the free movement of Negroes. Fear of the free Negro as a potential instigator of slave revolts was also the principal reason for the many restrictions placed upon manumission in the southern states during the nineteenth century. The most common limitation was the requirement that all newly manumitted Negroes must leave the state. At the end of the ante bellum era several southern states so feared the influence of the free Negro that they enacted laws prohibiting manumission; at least one state passed a law requiring the enslavement of all free Negroes found within the state after a certain date.[77] White society obviously saw a connection between the Negro slave and the free Negro; the important thing was not that one was free and the other a slave, but that both belonged to the same race.

In one sense, of course, Brazilian slavery was also racially based. Only Negroes, and, for a while, Indians, were slaves, though in Brazil, as in the US, there was an occasional slave who was fair-skinned and with blue eyes, so that he was a white in everything but status.[78] But in Brazil the connection between the inferior status of slavery and race did not persist into freedom to the same extent that it did in the United States. If slaveholders in the US viewed the free Negro as a potential threat to the slave system, their counterparts in Brazil saw him as a veritable prop to the system of slavery. Many, if not most of the *capitães de mato* (bush captains or slave catchers), for example, were mulattoes or Negroes. One nineteenth-century Brazilian asserted that two-thirds of the overseers, slave catchers, and slave dealers in Bahia were either mulattoes or blacks. Moreover, many free blacks and mulattoes showed little if any interest in abolition, and some, evidently, actively opposed the end of slavery.[79] In Brazil, in other words, more important than race in differentiating between men was legal status. The mere fact that a man was a Negro or a mulatto offered no presumption that he would identify with slaves.

The refusal of Brazilians to lump together free Negroes and slaves is reflected also in their failure to justify slavery on grounds of race. For, contrary to the prevailing situation in the southern United States, in Brazil there was no important proslavery argument based upon the biological inferiority of the Negro. It is true that a racist conception of the black man existed in nineteenth-century Brazil,[80] but defenders of slavery on clearly racist grounds were rare among public supporters of the institution. A Brazilian historian has written that in the debates in the Brazilian legislature concerning the treaty with Britain in 1827 that closed the international slave trade, only one member of that body clearly asserted the racial inferiority of Negroes, though other kinds of defenses of slavery were made.[81] A French commentator in 1862 noted that in Brazil slaveholders "do not believe themselves obliged, like their American colleagues, to invent for the Negro a new original sin, nor to erect a system of absolute distinction between the races, nor to place an insurmountable barrier between the offspring of descendants of slaves and of those of free men."[82] The most common defenses of the system were the argument in behalf of property and the assertion that the prosperity of the country depended on slave labor. Some defenders of the institution, even late in the nineteenth century, spoke of it as a "necessary evil," as North Americans had done in the early years of the century. In 1886, as slavery in Brazil was coming under increasing attack from abolitionists, a member of the Brazilian Congress from the coffee district asserted that the planters in his area would have no objection to emancipation if they could be assured of a new, adequate supply of labor, presumably immigrants.[83] Even more dramatic is the fact that some of the principal leaders of the abolition movement who held elective office came from the slave-holding provinces of Brazil. No such willingness to contemplate the wholesale increase in the number of free blacks was thinkable in the slaveholding regions of the United States. Even defenders of slavery in nineteenth-century Brazil spoke of the absence of color prejudice in their country and noted with apparent approval the high position achieved by some Negroes and mulattoes.[84] Leaving aside the assertion that there was no prejudice in Brazil, one would find it difficult indeed to point to a slaveholder in the US in the middle of the nineteenth century who would utter publicly a similar statement of praise for free Negroes as a class.

What may be concluded from this examination of slavery in Brazil and the United States? That there were in fact differences in the practices of slavery in the two countries there can be no doubt. The explanation for those differences, however, as I have tried to show, is to be sought neither in the laws of the Crown nor in the attitude and practices of the Roman Catholic Church in Brazil. The behavior of neither state nor Church displayed any deep concern about the humanity of the slave, and, in any event, neither used its authority to affect significantly the life of the slave. Certainly demographic, economic, and geographic factors account for some of the differences between the two slave systems that have been explored in this essay. But these materialist explanations do not help us to understand the more interesting and profound difference that emerges from the comparison.

This difference becomes evident only as one contemplates the various specific differences in conjunction with one another. In Brazil the slave was feared, but the black man was not, while in the United States the black man as well as the slave was feared. Once this difference in attitude is recognized, certain differences between the two systems are recognized as stemming from a common source. Thus the willingness of Brazilians to manumit slaves much more freely than North Americans is clearly a result of their not fearing free blacks in great numbers. (Indeed, in Brazil today, a common explanation for the obviously greater acceptance of blacks in northeastern Brazil than in the southern part of the country is that in the North there is a greater proportion of Negroes than in the South. Just the opposite explanation, of course, is current in the US, where it is said that when Negroes constitute a large proportion of the population they are more likely to be tightly controlled or restricted.) Brazilians, therefore, did not restrict manumission in anything like the degree practiced in the slave states of the United States. This same difference in attitude toward the Negro is also evident in the willingness of Brazilian slaveholders to use blacks as slave catchers and overseers, while in the US slaveholders in particular and white men in general could scarcely entertain the idea. Finally, this difference emerges when one asks why the slave trade remained open in Brazil to 1851, but was closed in most of the United States before the end of the eighteenth century. Even before the Revolution, in fact, Englishmen in North America had been seeking ways to limit the number of blacks in their midst, free or slave. In 1772, for example, the Virginia legislature asked the Crown to permit it to check the slave traffic since "The importation of slaves into the colonies from the coast of Africa hath long been considered as a trade of great inhumanity, and under its *present encouragement*, we have too much reason to fear, *will endanger the very* existence of your Majesty's American dominions. . . ." This fear that an unimpeded slave trade was dangerous ran through the history of all the English colonies, especially that of South Carolina. One of colonial South Carolina's several laws calling for limitation on the slave trade advocated encouragement to white immigration as "the best way to prevent the mischiefs that may be attended by the great importation of negroes into the province. . . ." In 1786 North Carolina placed a tax on slaves on the ground that "the importation of slaves into this state is productive of evil consequences, and highly impolitic."[85] The widespread fear of Negroes also explains why all but one of the states prohibited the importation of slaves years before the federal prohibition in 1808. Certainly there was a humanitarian motive behind the movement to stop the African slave trade, but also of great importance was the fear that if the importations were not limited or stopped white men would be overwhelmed by black. For as the founding and the work of the American Colonization Society in the nineteenth century reveal, even those people in the slave states who conscientiously opposed slavery did not want the Negro as a free man in the United States.

In Brazil, on the other hand, the slave trade came to an end principally because the pressures from *outside* the society. For a quarter of a century before 1851 the British government badgered the Brazilians to put an end to the trade. It is easy to believe that without the pressure from the British and the humiliating infringements of Brazilian sovereignty by ships of the Royal Navy the Brazilians would have kept the slave trade open even longer. Apparently Brazilians rarely worried, as did the North Americans, that they would be overwhelmed by blacks.

This article opened with the observation that Tannenbaum's work began a long and continuing scholarly debate over the role that slavery in North and South America had played in bringing about a different place for the Negro in the societies of the Western Hemisphere. If the evidence and argument of this essay are sound, then the explanations of the differences offered by Tannenbaum and Elkins, at least as far as Brazil is concerned, are not supported by the evidence. But if Tannenbaum's explanation has to be abandoned, his belief that there was a strikingly different attitude toward blacks in Brazil from that in the United States has not been challenged at all. Rather it has been reinforced. For if factors like demography, geography, and the continuance of the international slave trade in Brazil help to account for some of the differences in the practices of slavery in the two societies, those same factors do not really aid us in explaining why Brazilians feared slaves but not blacks, while North Americans feared both. What is now needed is a more searching and fundamental explanation than can be derived from these factors alone or found in the practices or laws of state and church regarding the slave. Clearly that explanation will have to be sought in more subtle and elusive places, such as among the inherited cultural patterns and social structures and values of the two countries. For it is the argument of this article that the differences between Brazilian and United States slavery, rather than being the sources of the different patterns of race relations in the two countries are, in fact, merely the consequence themselves of deeper divergences in the culture and history of the two peoples.

NOTES

1. The books and articles referred to are: Frank Tannenbaum, *Slave and Citizen: The Negro in the Americas* (New York, 1947); Stanley Elkins, *Slavery: A Problem in American Institutional and Intellectual Life* (2d ed., Chicago, 1969), the text of which is identical with the first edition of 1959 except for an added appendix; Arnold Sio, "Interpretations of Slavery: The Slave States in the Americas," *Comparative Studies in Society and History*, VII (Apr. 1965), 289-308; and David Brion Davis, *The Problem of Slavery in Western Culture* (Ithaca, N. Y., 1966).

2. It has sometimes been said that the diversity of the crops and topography of Brazil resulted in a diversity of slavery that makes it difficult if not impos-

sible to generalize about the institution in that country. It is true that slavery in the northeastern sugar regions was different in style from that practiced in Maranhão on the cotton and rice plantations. Writers on Brazilian history have noted, furthermore, that slavery was much harsher in a newly opened province like Maranhão than in the old and declining sugar areas in the northeast. (See Gilberto Freyre, *Nordeste* [Rio de Janeiro, 1937], 219; and Henry Koster, *Travels in Brazil* [2 vols., 2d ed., London, 1817], II, 292.) But the diversity of crops and terrain and the differences in "styles" of slavery that resulted are well recognized in the United States; the slavery on tobacco farms in Virginia, for example, is often contrasted with the kind of slavery on sugar or cotton plantations in Louisiana. In the United States, moreover, the threat to sell a slave "down the river" reflected a recognition that planters in the newer areas of the Deep South tended to work slaves harder than in the older regions where slavery was more firmly established. Despite their recognitions of regional diversity, however, historians of slavery in the United States have not been prevented from generalizing about the institution; hence, it would seem to be equally legitimate to ignore the regional differences in Brazilian slavery so long as an effort is made to draw evidence from most of the principal slave areas of the country. The regional differences are certainly there in both societies, but they are refinements rather than essentials. One further statement on the problems of comparison: although the literature on slavery in the United States is voluminous, there being a monograph for virtually every southern slave state, the literature on Brazilian slavery is uneven. For some important slave regions like Maranhão and Minas Gerais, for example, there are no monographic studies on slavery at all; scattered references in travel accounts and general histories must be relied upon. On the other hand, for other areas, like the coffee country to the south, two excellent, recently written monographs are available: Stanley Stein, *Vassouras: A Brazilian Coffee County, 1850–1900* (Cambridge, Mass., 1957); and Emília Viotti da Costa, *Da Senzala à Colônia* (São Paulo, 1966). Of immense importance for its historiographical impact, if nothing else, is the impressionistic, virtuoso performance of Gilberto Freyre, *The Masters and the Slaves* (New York, 1946), which deals primarily with domestic slavery in northeastern Brazil though it purports to speak of slavery in general.

3. Tannenbaum, *Slave and Citizen*, 97-98, 103.

4. *Judicial Cases concerning Slavery and the Negro*, ed. Helen T. Catterall (5 vols., Washington, D. C., 1926) II, 530.

5. Charles Sackett Sydnor, *Slavery in Mississippi* (New York, 1933), 239.

6. *Judicial Cases concerning Slavery and the Negro*, ed. Catterall, III, 247.

7. Agostino Marques Perdigão Malheiro, *A Escravidão no Brasil: Ensaio Historico-Juridico-Social* (reprint of 1867 ed., 2 vols., São Paulo, 1944), I, 39-40, 34-45, 67.

8. See, e.g., Tannenbaum, *Slave and Citizen*, 93.

9. Kenneth M. Stampp, *The Peculiar Institution: Slavery in the Ante-bellum South* (New York, 1956), 192, summarizes the situation in the United States as follows: "The law required that masters be humane to their slaves, furnish them adequate food and clothing, and provide care for them during sickness and old age. In short, the state endowed masters with obligations as well as

rights and assumed some responsibility for the welfare of the bondsmen." For elaboration of the obligations laid down by law, see *ibid.*, 218-24.

10. Koster, *Travels in Brazil*, I, 375-76; II, 237; Da Costa, *Da Senzala*, 295-96. Charles Expilly, a French traveler in Brazil in the 1860's, conceded that in the big cities like Rio a slave might occasionally be able to get to the police to complain of bad treatment, but, away from the cities, it was quite different. There, Expilly wrote, the power of the master was like that of "a feudal baron, who exercises in his dominion the highest and the lowest justice." There were no appeals from his sentences. "No guarantee is conceded to the slave." (Charles Expilly, *Mulheres e costumes do Brasil*, tr. Gastão Penalva [São Paulo, 1935], 361.)

11. João Mauricio Rugendas, *Viagem pitoresca através do Brasil*, tr. Sergio Milliet (3d ed., São Paulo, 1941.) 185.

12. Tannenbaum, *Slave and Citizen*, 62-64, 98; Elkins, *Slavery*, 73, 76-77.

13. Da Costa, *Da Senzala*, 250, 271, 249.

14. Luis Anselmo Fonseca, *A Escravidão, O clero e O abolicionismo* (Bahia, 1887), 440-41, 1-27. The references to Channing are on pages 12-15.

15. *Ibid.*, 268; Fernando Henrique Cardoso and Octávio Ianni, *Côr e mobilidade social em Florianopolis* (São Paulo, 1960), 128-29; Robert Edgar Conrad, "The Struggle for the Abolition of the Brazilian Slave Trade, 1808-1853," doctoral dissertation, Columbia University, 1967, 55-56.

16. Tannenbaum, *Slave and Citizen*, 77.

17. W. D. Christie, *Notes on Brazilian Questions* (London, 1865), 93; Pedro Calmon, *História social do Brasil* (São Paulo, 1937), 151. Roberto Simonsen, "As Consequências economica da abolição," *Revista do Arquivo Municipal de São Paulo*, XLVII (May, 1938), 261, says that in 1888 over two-thirds of the slaves in the Empire were in the provinces of Rio, Minas Gerais, São Paulo, and those to the south. I am indebted to Professor Richard Graham of the University of Utah for this reference.

18. Stein, *Vassouras*, 159.

19. Richard M. Morse, *From Community to Metropolis: A Biography of São Paulo, Brazil* (Gainesville, Fla., 1958), 146; Magnus Mörner, *Race Mixture in the History of Latin America* (Boston, 1967), 117.

20. Arthur Ramos, *The Negro in Brazil*, tr. Richard Pattee (Washington, D. C., 1939), 58-59.

21. Maurilio de Gouveia, *História da escravidão* (Rio de Janeiro, 1955), 134; Perdigão Malheiro, *A Escravidão no Brasil*, II, 223.

22. Da Costa, *Da Senzala*, 271, 385. The law prohibited selling children under fifteen away from their parents. The so-called Law of the Free Womb of 1871, however, lowered the age to twelve.

23. Joe Gray Taylor, *Negro Slavery in Louisiana* (Baton Rouge, La., 1963), 40-41; Stampp, *Peculiar Institution*, 252, 239-41; Edward W. Phifer, "Slavery in Microcosm: Burke County, North Carolina," *Journal of Southern History*, XXVIII (May 1962), 48.

24. Davis, *Problem of Slavery*, 262-64.

25. Sumner E. Matison, "Manumission by Purchase," *Journal of Negro History*, XXXIII (Apr. 1948), 165; Luther P. Jackson, "Manumission in Certain Virginia Cities," *ibid.*, XV (July 1930), 306.

26. Tannenbaum, *Slave and Citizen*, 54; Elkins, *Slavery*, 75.

27. Mary Wilhelmine Williams, "The Treatment of Negro Slaves in the Brazilian Empire: A Comparison with the United States of America," *Journal of Negro History*, XV (July 1930), 331.

28. Perdigão Malheiro, *A Escravidão no Brasil*, I, 95.

29. *Ibid.*, 167-68; Gouveia, *História da escravidão*, 396. The Code Noir of Louisiana, which also had liberal provisions for manumission, contained the following restrictions: "We command all manumitted slaves to show the profoundest respect to their former masters, to their widows and children, and any injury or insult offered by said manumitted slaves to their former master, their widows or children, shall be punished with more severity than if it had been offered by any other person." (Quoted in Taylor, *Negro Slavery in Louisiana*, 16.)

30. Tannenbaum, *Slave and Citizen*, 54; Elkins, *Slavery*, 246.

31. Perdigão Malheiro, *A Escravidão no Brasil*, I, 60.

32. *Judicial Cases concerning Slavery and the Negro*, ed. Catterall, II, 267, 275, n.

33. Agostinho Marques Perdigão Malheiro, *A Escravidão no Brasil: ensaio historico-juridico-social* (Rio de Janeiro, 1866), Pt. 3, 13-14.

34. Raymond Sayers, *Negro in Brazilian Literature* (New York, 1956), 7.

35. Da Costa, *Da Senzala*, 262-63; Stein, *Vassouras*, 79, n; see also the report of the British minister, August 1852, quoting the effort by the president of the province of Bahia to have the practice stopped by law. The report is given in Christie, *Notes on Brazilian Questions*, 218-19.

36. Marvin Harris, *Patterns of Race in the Americas* (New York, 1964), 84-89.

37. Octávio Ianni, *As Metamorfoses do escravo* (São Paulo, 1962), 175; Nelson de Senna, *Africanos no Brasil* (Bello Horizonte, Brazil, 1938), 62. Caio Prado Junior, *História economica do Brasil* (10th ed., n.p., n.d.), 45, asserts that cattle raising in the *sertão* of the northeast required free men rather than slaves.

38. The fullest and most recent account of Palmares in English is R. K. Kent, "Palmares: An African State in Brazil," *Journal of African History*, VI (No. 2, 1965), 161-75. As his title suggests, Kent argues (pp. 163-64) against depicting Palmares as merely a *quilombo*, but that issue is not important in this discussion. Clovis Moura, *Rebeliões da senzala* (São Paulo, 1959), contains a number of accounts of *quilombos* aside from Palmares.

39. See Edison Carneiro, *Ladinos e Crioulos* (*Estudos sôbre o negro no Brasil*) (Rio de Janeiro, 1964), 30-32, for a statement on this point by an authority on Palmares and *quilombos* in general.

40. Koster, *Travels in Brazil*, II, 258; *Relações raciais entre negros e brancos em São Paulo*, ed. Roger Bastide (São Paulo, 1955), 199; Da Costa, *Da Senzala*, 300-301, 315; Fernando Henrique Cardoso, *Capitalismo e escravidão no Brasil meridional* (São Paulo, 1962), 159-60; Raimundo Girão, *A Abolição no Ceará* (Forteleza, Brazil, 1956), 42; Aderbal Jurema, *Insurreições negras no Brasil* (Recife, Brazil, 1935), 53-55; Maura, *Rebeliões da senzala*, 65-66; Octavio da Costa Eduardo, *The Negro in Northern Brazil* (New York, 1948), 18.

41. See, e.g., Jurema, *Insurreições negras no Brasil;* Maura, *Rebeliões da senzala;* and Maria Thereza Schorer Petrone, *A Lavoura canavieira em São Paulo* (São Paulo, 1968), 121-25. Professor Graham brought the last reference to my attention.

42. Marion D. de B. Kilson, "Towards Freedom: An Analysis of Slave Revolts in the United States," *Phylon,* XXV (2d Quar., 1964), 175-87.

43. Da Costa, *Da Senzala,* 304; Maria Stella de Novaes, *A Escravidão e abolição no Espírito Santo* (Vitória, Brazil, 1963), 77.

44. Ramos, *Negro in Brazil,* 34-37. The basic source for the revolts in Bahia is Raymundo Nina Rodrigues, *Os Africanos no Brasil* (2d ed., São Paulo, 1935), Chap. II, but Raymond Kent will soon publish a thorough examination of the revolt of 1835, a copy of which he has kindly permitted me to read in typescript.

45. Herbert Aptheker, *American Negro Slave Revolts* (New York, 1943), *passim,* and Herbert Aptheker, "Maroons Within the Present Limits of the United States," *Journal of Negro History,* XXIV (April, 1939), 167-84.

46. See Kenneth W. Porter, "Negroes and the Seminole War, 1835-1842," *Journal of Southern History,* XXX (Nov., 1964), 427-40.

47. Mauricio Goulart, *Escravidão africana no Brasil* (2d ed., São Paulo, 1950), 249-63; the total figure for slaves is given in Stein, *Vassouras,* 294. Christie (*Notes on Brazilian Questions,* 69-70) insists that when he was writing, in 1865, slaves numbered three million. The lack of a census makes it impossible to arrive at anything more accurate than estimates.

48. Mörner (*Race Mixture in the History of Latin America,* 76) suggests that most slave revolts were led by African-born slaves.

49. Stein, *Vassouras,* 145; Da Costa, *Da Senzala,* 232; Cardoso and Ianni, *Côr e mobilidade,* 126-27.

50. Ramos, *Negro in Brazil,* 30-31, 36-37; Donald Pierson, *Negroes in Brazil* (Chicago, 1942), 39-40; E. Franklin Frazier, "Some Aspects of Race Relations in Brazil," *Phylon,* III (Third Quarter, 1942), 290. Kent, in the unpublished article referred to in note 44, above, strongly questions the religious basis for the 1835 revolt in Bahia, which heretofore has been the standard interpretation. (See, e.g., Roger Bastide, *Les religions africaines au Brésil* [Paris, 1960], 146.)

51. Da Costa, *Da Senzala,* 235, 252; Charles Ralph Boxer, *The Golden Age of Brazil, 1695–1750* (Berkeley, Calif., 1962), 176-77.

52. David A. Ross, "The Career of Domingo Martinez in the Bight of Benin," *Journal of African History,* VI (No. 1, 1965), 83. Freyre (*Nordeste,* 130-31) and Da Costa (*Da Senzala,* 56-57, n.) also report blacks returning to Africa and acting as slave traders. See also Donald Pierson, "The Educational Process and the Brazilian Negro," *American Journal of Sociology,* XLVIII (May 1943), 695, n.; and Gilberto Freyre, *Ordem e Progresso* (2d ed., Rio de Janeiro, 1962), 572, n. 33. The close connection between Africa and Brazil is forcefully demonstrated in José Honório Rodrigues, *Brazil and Africa* (Berkeley, Calif., 1965).

53. The above was written before the publication of Philip D. Curtin, *The Atlantic Slave Trade. A Census* (Madison, Wis., 1969). Curtin, p. 234, estimates that after 1808 the total number of slaves entering the United States directly from Africa was fewer than 55,000.

54. Stein, *Vassouras*, 155; T. Lynn Smith, *Brazil, People and Institutions* (Baton Rouge, La., 1963), 130.

55. Da Costa, *Da Senzala*, 130.

56. Quoted in Joaquim Nabuco, *O Abolicionismo*, in *Obras completas* (14 vols., São Paulo, 1944–49), VII, 89-90. The book from which Nabuco quoted was published in 1872.

57. Da Costa, *Da Senzala*, 256; Gouveia, *História da escravidão*, 208; Christie, *Notes on Brazilian Questions*, 102, n.

58. Rodrigues, *Brazil and Africa*, 159; Stein, *Vassouras*, 155; Conrad, "Struggle for Abolition of the Brazilian Slave Trade," 55.

59. *Relações raciais entre negros e brancos em São Paulo*, ed. Bastide, 81.

60. See, e.g., Elkins, *Slavery*, 77-78.

61. Da Costa, *Da Senzala*, 257-58; Élisée Reclus, "Le Brésil et la Colonisation. II," *Revue des deux mondes*, XL (July–Aug. 1862), 391.

62. Boxer, *Golden Age of Brazil*, 138, 165; Gilberto Freyre, *Masters and the Slaves*, 455.

63. See the picture, e.g., in Da Costa, *Da Senzala*, facing p. 240; Gilberto Freyre, *O Escravo nos anúncios de jornais brasilieros do seculo* XIX (Recife, Brazil, 1963), 100, discusses the use of the mask; Thomas Ewbank, *Life in Brazil* (New York, 1856), 437-38, describes the masks he saw worn on the street. Stampp (*Peculiar Institution*, 304) notes that masks were sometimes used in the United States to prevent eating clay. There is at least one reference to masks in that compendium of horrors by Theodore Weld, *American Slavery as It Is* (New York, 1839), 76.

64. References to the practice are common. See, e.g., Gouveia, *História, da escravidão*, 179; Perdigão Malheiro, *A Escravidão no Brasil*, II, 220, 348; Da Costa, *Da Senzala*, 263.

65. Elkins, *Slavery*, 78, n.

66. Davis, *Problem of Slavery in Western Culture*, 229, n.

67. Perdigão Malheiro, *A Escravidão no Brasil*, II, 114-15; D. P. Kidder and J. C. Fletcher, *Brazil and the Brazilians* (Philadelphia, 1857), 132.

68. Carl N. Degler, "Slavery and the Genesis of American Race Prejudice," *Comparative Studies in Society and History*, II (Oct. 1959), 57, 64; see also Winthrop D. Jordan, *White Over Black: American Attitudes toward the Negro, 1550–1812* (Chapel Hill, N. C., 1968), 71, 125-26. Jordan notes that free Negroes served in all the wars of colonial New England, but that few slaves served in any colonial militias.

69. Ramos, *Negro in Brazil*, 157.

70. Charles R. Boxer, *The Dutch in Brazil, 1624–1654* (Oxford, Eng., 1957), 166-69; Cardoso, *Capitalismo e escravidão*, 153-54, n; Bastide, *Religions africaines au Brésil*, 109; Da Costa, *Da Senzala*, 401. Ianni (*Metamorfoses*, 175-76) cites an example of a slave being sent by his master to serve in place of a white man; after service, he was freed. Rodrigues (*Brazil and Africa*, 45-52) is one of several sources for the figure of twenty thousand slaves freed after the Paraguayan War.

71. John Alden, *The First South* (Baton Rouge, La., 1961), 37-40; Benjamin Quarles, *The Negro in the American Revolution* (Chapel Hill, N. C., 1961), 60-67. Some slaves, however, were enlisted by their masters in the northern states, usually as substitutes. On the offer of blacks to support the

Confederacy, see D. E. Everett, "Ben Butler and the Louisiana Native Guards, 1861–1862," *Journal of Southern History*, XXIV (May 1958), 202-204.

72. Ianni, *Metamorfoses*, 217.

73. Ramos, *Negro in Brazil*, 151-54.

74. Mörner, *Race Mixture in the History of Latin America*, 52.

75. *Records of the Governor and Company of the Massachusetts Bay in New England*, ed. N. F. Shurteff (5 vols., Boston, 1853–54), III, 268, 397; *Public Records of the Colony of Connecticut* [1636–1776] (15 vols., Hartford, Conn., 1850–1890), I, 349. See Jordan, *White over Black*, 122-28, for a survey of legal discrimination against free blacks in the English colonies of North America.

76. Ulrich B. Phillips, *American Negro Slavery* (New York, 1928), 87.

77. Stampp, *Peculiar Institution*, 232-35; John Hope Franklin, *From Slavery to Freedom* (New York, 1947), 218-19.

78. Freyre (*O Escravo nos anúncios de jornais brasilieros do seculo* xix, 195) cites examples of light-colored slaves in the advertisements for runaways and refers to a royal order of 1773 in which it was said that, much to the shame of humanity and religion, there were slaves who were lighter than their owners, but who were called "Pretos e . . . negras." Freyre also cites an advertisement in a newspaper in 1865 in which the fugitive was described as having blond hair and blue eyes. Stampp (*Peculiar Institution*, 194) refers to blond, blue-eyed runaways in newspaper advertisements in the U. S.

79. Williams, "Treatment of Negro Slaves in the Brazilian Empire," 327; Da Costa, *Da Senzala*, 29; Pierson, *Negroes in Brazil*, 47, n.

80. See Stein, *Vassouras*, 133-34; Da Costa, *Da Senzala*, 354-55. Expilly provides probably the most explicit examples of racial arguments in defense of slavery. He quotes one slaveholder as saying that one could free slaves "today, and tomorrow, instead of using this freedom, they will rob and kill in order to satisfy their needs. Only by terror do they perform services. . . . I believe, gentlemen, Negroes would be baffled by freedom. God created them to be slaves." A little later, Expilly quotes the planter as saying: "The Africans represent an intermediate race between the gorilla and man. They are improved monkeys, not men." A priest is also cited as justifying slavery on the grounds that St. Thomas Aquinas claimed "that nature intended certain creatures for physical and moral reasons to be slaves." (Expilly, *Mulheres e costumes do Brasil*, 381-83.)

81. Rodrigues, *Brazil and Africa*, 151.

82. Reclus, "Brésil et la Colonisation," 386.

83. Da Costa, *Da Senzala*, 354-56; Cardoso, *Capitalismo e escravidão*, 280; Florestan Fernandes, *A Integração do negro no Sociedade de classes* (2 vols., São Paulo, 1965), I, 200, n.

84. Da Costa, *Da Senzala*, 358.

85. W. E. Burghardt Du Bois, *The Suppressions of the African Slave-Trade to the United States of America 1638–1870* (New York, 1896), 221, 215, 229. The appendix to this work contains a number of other excerpts from colonial statutes to the same effect. Don B. Kates, Jr., "Abolition, Deportation, Integration: Attitudes toward Slavery in the Early Republic," *Journal of Negro History*, LIII (Jan. 1968), 33-47, contains a number of expressions by white Americans of their opposition to freed Negroes remaining in the United States.

• "This seems incredible," the New York City diarist George Templeton Strong noted in 1864 in his Civil War journal, "but all the foundations of Southern society have been shaken or destroyed." Not the least of these changes, certainly the most paradoxical, came to the institution of slavery itself. Under the pressures of mobilizing to fight a "total war," the Confederates employed many thousands of slaves in non-combatant war work: driving wagons and ambulances, working in armament factories, serving as nurses in hospitals, and performing other vitally important tasks. "Wartime necessity forced white Southerners to 'use' and depend upon black Southerners," Emory M. Thomas points out in the following selection. "Yet in the very process of 'using,' the whites undermined their mastery, and the blacks shed a portion of their dependence." By the end of the war, in March 1865, the Confederate Congress had even authorized recruiting up to 300,000 slaves for the army, implicitly approving eventual freedom in return for their services. Lee's surrender at Appomattox the following month prevented the black companies then being formed from ever serving in the field. But the irony of this situation, Confederate military men drilling a legion of possible Spartacus-figures to help defend a rebellion committed to the fictitious image of "Sambo," was not lost upon Americans, not even on many white Southerners themselves.

Black Confederates: Slavery and Wartime

EMORY M. THOMAS

If the antebellum Southern way of life contained a *sine qua non*, that indispensable factor was racial slavery. As we have seen, Confederate

Southerners during the course of the war, consciously or unconsciously, willingly or grudgingly, abolished much of what they had gone to war to protect. The Confederacy abandoned a state rights polity, severely altered an agrarian economy, and experienced social upheaval—all for the sake of victory and independence. But what about slavery? If the Confederate experience did not affect the South's "peculiar institution," the other changes wrought by that experience lose a great deal of their significance. In fact the Confederate experience did affect slavery. Under the conditions of wartime the institution of slavery changed in vital ways. And ultimately the Confederacy was willing to give up her "peculiar institution," just as she had forsaken other cherished institutions, for the sake of independence.

The demands of total war led Confederates to "use" black people in ways and to degrees unknown in the antebellum period. When the planter master and his sons marched off to war, his slaves assumed greater responsibility for the work of the farm. Even if an overseer or an active and knowledgeable wife remained, the bondsmen labored under far less supervision than before. And statistically, very few overseers remained—only 201 for the entire state of Georgia in 1863, for example. Slaves were most often left in the charge of wives, old men, or young boys. In some communities one man oversaw the work of slaves on several farms and plantations. Black "drivers" took on added responsibility for directing the efforts of their fellow slaves.

Some masters took their body servants with them into the army. These slaves performed camp chores and in emergencies even fought the enemy to protect their masters. In New Orleans, a group of free blacks formed a military regiment and offered their services to the Confederacy. The Confederacy refused, and the "Native Guards" eventually fought for the Union after the capture of the city.

White Southerners depended upon black Southerners to do more than till the fields and tend the campfires. The Confederacy impressed large amounts of black labor to dig field fortifications and to throw up earthworks around cities and towns. Some of these laborers were impressed field hands levied from nearby farms and plantations. The War Department alone was authorized to impress up to 20,000 blacks. State governors also drew upon "private property" so that whites could fight more and dig less. In some instances military and local authorities herded free blacks into gangs, paid them a private's wage ($11 per month), and marched them off to the trenches. Those "free" blacks who resisted this fate had to hire substitutes or lawyers to escape.

The military also rented or impressed black men, slave and free, to cook and to drive wagons and ambulances. Both public and private hospitals employed black nurses and maintenance workers. In several large hospitals over one-half of the male nurses were black. Government and private manufacturers hired or rented black labor for skilled and unskilled work. In 1865, for example, 310 of 400 workers in the naval ordnance works at Selma, Alabama, were black. As the war wore on the trend toward black labor became more pronounced. Every black man employed meant one more available white soldier.

Black Confederates served the white man's "cause" in subtler ways, too. One August day in 1864 a group of white grave-diggers in Richmond walked off the job in an attempt to secure higher wages. The municipal government immediately hired free blacks to replace the striking whites. As the newly hired black gravediggers began their work, the whites returned, attacked the blacks, and drove them away. Then the whites went back to work. In the course of one day the blacks had served as both "scabs" and "whipping boys," having both broken a strike and absorbed the hostility of the unsuccessful strikers.

That black people should make such a great contribution to the "cause" which kept them enslaved was cruelly ironic. But there was more than irony here. At its core slavery depended upon a master-slave relationship. The Confederate experience served to break down or at least alter that vital personal relationship by removing the master. The master left his plantation to fight in the war. The impressed military laborer served a succession of strange and sometimes conflicting masters. The hired-out nurse, teamster, or factory worker rarely saw his master and often "lived out" beyond any white authority.

Slavery in the Confederate South became a paradoxical institution. Wartime necessity forced white Southerners to "use" and depend upon black Southerners. Yet in the very process of "using" the whites undermined their mastery, and the blacks shed a portion of their dependence. The Confederates strained their "peculiar institution" by demanding that chattel black men act more like slaves while white men acted less like masters. On the surface it would seem that the institution of slavery in the Confederate South met these demands. Black men did serve the Confederacy. They did not rise up en masse and throw off their bonds. But the strains imposed upon the institution of slavery did manifest themselves. Slavery in the wartime South was an institution in flux.

On plantations the bondsmen did not well serve an absent master. The decline in authoritative supervision usually coincided with a decline in productivity. A wife or teenage boy might threaten or cajole or even shorten rations in an attempt to make the slaves work. Generally, however, no extremes of kindness or cruelty could supplant the authority of an absent master. There were exceptions, but the myth that Southern blacks carried on with their work as though the war did not exist is indeed myth and little more. On numerous farms and plantations the slaves revolted—not actively, but passively by allowing chores to go undone and weeds to grow where none had grown before. Letters and diaries of the period are full of references to shiftlessness and insubordination among slaves.

After sifting available evidence on the subject, historian Bell I. Wiley concluded in 1938:

> That disorder and unfaithfulness on the part of Negroes were far more common than post-war commentators have usually admitted. A correspondent of Senator [Clement] Clay's wife in 1863 from Selma, Alabama . . . "the faithful slave is about played out. They are the most treacherous, brutal, and ungrateful race on the globe." This statement is doubtless extreme, but it is no farther from the truth than the encomiums of the slaves' loyalty and devotion which have been so universally circulated and accepted in the South.[1]

The experience of Mrs. W. H. Neblett, cited by Wiley, illustrates exactly how many things could and did go wrong on a masterless farm. Mrs. Neblett constantly wrote her husband that the slaves left in her care would not work. They destroyed tools and fences, abused or neglected the livestock, and paid no attention to her instructions. To remedy this condition, she hired a part-time overseer. But the overseer spent too much time with the black women in the slave quarters and neglected his duties in the fields, so Mrs. Neblett finally fired the wretch and hired another overseer. The new man offered little improvement. He beat his charges brutally and on occasion shot at them. The Neblett slaves would not work for this tyrant, and Mrs. Neblett's patience was all but exhausted. She wrote to her husband that she was overcome by the "thought of negroes to be clothed and fed, the crop yet to make, the oxen so poor, no corn, and to cap the climax, the black wretches trying all they can, it seems to me, to aggravate me, taking no interest, . . . neglecting their duty." A little later she informed her husband, "you may give your negroes away if you won't hire them, and I'll move into a white settlement and work with my hands." Still later Mrs. Neblett wrote: "The negroes care no more for me than if I was an old free darkey and I get so mad sometimes that I think I don't care sometimes if Myers [the overseer] beats the last one of them to death. I can't stay with them another year alone."[2]

Mrs. Neblett's exasperation was common among plantation women alone in kind if not degree. Her difficulties were symptomatic of strained slavery. The attitude of the Neblett slaves clearly manifested the destruction of master-slave bonds. They responded neither to weakness nor brutality in whites with whom they had no personal ties.

Many whites interpreted the increase in black restlessness as a portent of a general slave insurrection. Especially after Abraham Lincoln issued the Emancipation Proclamation, rural whites lived in fear of a domestic bloodbath. They heard rumors of plots, and they remembered Nat Turner. For the most part, however, the white fears were phantoms. Indeed the depth of concern over potential slave revolts in the Confederate hinterland was more of a comment on white guilt, than on realistic black aspirations. The restless tendency among black Confederates was a reaction to the loss or abdication of personal mastery on the part of white Confederates. When the white man shed his mastery, the black man of necessity abandoned much of his dependence. Had the Confederacy remained frozen in a wartime condition indefinitely, black assertions doubtless would have challenged the whole of white mastery. But this did not happen, and in the Confederate reality, the subservient nature of the slave experience and the isolation of rural slaves made mass revolt impossible. The black Confederates responded to their immediate personal circumstances; they asserted themselves with the means at hand, idleness, insolence, and occasionally violence; and they waited to see what would happen to the institution which bound them.

The story is often told of one slave likening the Civil War to two dogs (North and South) fighting over a bone (black people). The bone, he pointed out, has no business joining in the fray. Slaves accepted this piece of folk wisdom for the most part in the Confederate hinterland. Yet when Union armies approached, the "bone" regularly fled to them. More than one "old massa" watched his labor force melt away as the Yankees drew nearer his plantation. The blacks kept themselves apprised of the military situation by listening to whites and sharing whatever "grease" (war news) they were able to pick up.

When the Federal lines were near enough the slaves could "demonstrate with their feet" their desire for freedom. The proximity of the Union army had much the same unsettling effect on slavery as did the prolonged absence of the slave masters. Slavery in the Confederate South was threatened from without by the ideal of freedom and from within by the breakdown of the master-slave relationship. And the best reflection of these threats came in the response of the slaves themselves.

In the urban Confederacy, whites subjected blacks to more intense supervision than was possible in the countryside. This supervision, though, was largely institutional, and the absence of a personal master was perhaps even more common in the cities than on the plantations. Confederate municipalities could and did make and enforce laws forbidding black people to enter the marketplaces or even the cities themselves without a certificate of good behavior signed by a white man. A white man who appeared on the street in the company of black women was guilty of "conduct unbecoming a white man and a Christian." Slave codes forbade cursing, spitting, and congregating for free and bonded blacks alike. But a city's police power could not function as a surrogate master. Even though cities and towns were more vigilant and more repressive than rural areas, slave conduct in the cities reflected the unsettled condition of Confederate slavery.

Perhaps the best single example of unrest among urban slaves occurred in the household of the president of the Confederate States. Jefferson Davis experienced a veritable parade of runaway chattels, and before they decamped the Davis runaways usually stole some of the president's clothes or silver. In the month of January 1864 three of Davis' slaves escaped. The last of the three even attempted to burn down the Executive Mansion as a parting gesture. Nor were Davis' troubles unique in the capital. The Richmond *Enquirer* reported in early 1864, "hardly a day passes but that some darkey is not missing."

Many urban bondsmen who did not escape nevertheless found the Confederate experience a liberating one. By 1861 the custom of "hiring out" was well established in Southern cities. The master struck a rental bargain with someone in need of labor, and the slave served the renter for a prescribed period of time. Slavebrokers sometimes facilitated transactions in the "rent-a-slave" market. But quite often the slave was free to make his own bargain and pay his owner a specified amount. If he earned more than his owner demanded, he kept the excess. In addition to "hiring out" many slaves also "lived out." If the owner or renter had no quarters for his chattels, he allowed his slave to find his own lodging and paid him a few more dollars per week to cover the cost. During the Confederate period the hiring market for domestic servants remained firm through 1862 and then fell off a bit. Yet the need for black labor in hospitals, public works, and industries increased. And these nondomestic occupations were those most likely to permit "living out."[3]

If a black man "hired out" and if he "lived out," he might see his master once a week at most. He might work under supervision, but then so did most white workingmen. The slave in this circumstance had few reminders that he was enslaved. The white community might restrict his movements or regulate his conduct through the police and the courts, but he did not feel the absolute dependence of personal contact with his master. And to some extent he was able to achieve a greater sense of community with his fellow blacks.

The urban Confederacy acted harshly in matters of race. "Free" blacks often found themselves commandeered to dig earthworms, and many provisions of "slave codes" applied to all black people whether slave or free. Yet at the same time Confederate cities served to ameliorate slave conditions by removing the master's influence from the slave's daily life. Again, the paradox—at the same time the city fathers were most repressive in terms of race, the city, by the very nature of its economic and social life, made possible a heightened sense of independent black identity.

We cannot be sure in the matter of degree—how many slaves felt how much change in the slave system. Suffice it to say here that change did occur within the institution, substantive change which affected the slave himself whether he lived in an urban or rural setting.

WHITE CONFEDERATES AND THE "DYING INSTITUTION"

In the subtle breakdown of the master-slave relationship just described, white Confederates played a passive role. Some whites, however, actively sought to reform the institutions of slavery. A significant movement among churches and church leaders in the Confederacy began serious agitation in 1863 for liberalization in the slave system. Led by Mississippi Presbyterian James A. Lyon, the reformers proposed that no slaveholder be allowed to separate slave children from their mothers, and that absentee masters not be allowed to place their chattels in the charge of an overseer. They also asked that the testimony of slaves be-

admissible as evidence in courts of law and that slave assemblies of a religious nature be sanctioned in law. Such reforms, had they been enacted, would have ameliorated some of the worst features of the slave system. Black family structure would have no longer been destroyed. Slaves would have had a recourse in law against brutal masters, and the law would have prohibited the unrestrained cruelty of some overseers. The reform program might have signaled the beginning of the end for slavery itself. For even though the reformers were loud in their support of the institutions per se, their proposed reforms considered the bondsman more as a person and less as property. Such a consideration if carried to its logical extreme could only lead to the end of slavery.

As the war wore on, the reform impulse gathered strength. In 1863, Calvin H. Wiley, a North Carolina religious leader, published a book entitled *Scriptural Views of National Trials*, in which he suggested that the war was God's method for chastening Southerners for the ways in which they managed their "peculiar institution." He pointed to Saint Paul's strictures on the obligations of masters to servants and endorsed reform of the slave system as divinely inspired. Many churchmen throughout the South took up Wiley's cry and exhorted their flocks to appease the wrath of God by setting their domestic institutions aright.

The reform impulse bore some fruit. In April 1863 the Georgia legislature repealed a law which forbade issuing licenses to preach to black men. In Alabama in late 1864 the legislature enacted a law requiring masters to provide legal counsel and insure a fair trial when their slaves were indicted "for any offense."

The tangible effects of slavery reform in the Confederacy end here however. It may have been, as Bell I. Wiley suggests, that slavery in the Confederate South was a "dying institution," and that it is not altogether unlikely that ultimately it (slavery) would have been "reformed to death" by its friends.[4] The movement to reform the slave system, although it failed to produce the results it desired, did help prepare the Confederate mind to accept far more sweeping changes in the South's "social mores."

Beginning with its refusal in 1861 to accept the services of the black "Native Guards" regiment from New Orleans, the Confederacy during the first two years of its life resisted the possibility that black men would or could fight for the "cause." Very few Southerners advised using slaves as soldiers, but no one seemed to hear or heed such advice. By 1863, however, the Confederacy had begun to feel her relative shortage of manpower. In the fall of that year talk of enrolling slaves as soldiers began in earnest. Early in 1864 General Patrick Cleburne of the Army of Tennessee presented to his fellow officers a paper proposing that a large force of slaves be armed and freed if they served faithfully. No less an authority than Jefferson Davis suppressed Cleburne's paper; however, Davis could not silence debate on the subject. As the South's manpower drain became more acute during the campaigns of 1864, the question of arming the slaves increasingly attracted the attention of newspaper editors and public men.

In October 1864 a conference of the governors of North Carolina, South Carolina, Georgia, Alabama, and Mississippi passed a resolution urging the employment of black troops. The Confederate Congress took up the subject a short time later. Jefferson Davis again counseled against arming slaves. In early November, however, Davis did ask Congress for authority to purchase 40,000 black men for noncombatant military duty. He even suggested that these men be freed after the war if they performed faithfully. Finally he stated, "Should the alternative ever be presented of subjugation or of the employment of the slave as a soldier, there seems no reason to doubt what should then be our decision." In Congress there were many who believed the time had indeed come to choose between the alternatives described by the president. Within the administration Judah Benjamin carried on an active campaign to arm the slaves. Eventually Davis himself favored the move.

Robert E. Lee spoke the most decisive words. In January 1865 Lee wrote to a Virginia legislator in support of a proposal to recruit black soldiers authored by Virginia's Governor William Smith. Benjamin and Mississippi senator Ethelbert Barksdale requested Lee to express himself fully on the matter to the Congress. In a letter to Barksdale, Lee affirmed that black troops were indeed required, that black men would make good soldiers, and that slave soldiers ought to receive their freedom. The Richmond *Examiner* best spoke the reaction to Lee's blanket endorsement. The paper had opposed editorially the employment of slaves as soldiers but "the country will not deny to General Lee . . . *anything* he may ask for."

Congress changed its mind only a little slower than the *Examiner*. On March 13, 1865, the Southern solons authorized the president to recruit up to 300,000 slaves for the army. No more than 25 per cent of the male slaves between eighteen and forty-five years old could be drawn from any one state. And "nothing in this act shall be construed to authorize a charge in the relation which the said slaves shall bear toward their owners. . . ." The latter provision was understood as little more than verbiage. Those who stood highest in the Confederacy (Davis, Lee, Benjamin, and others) recognized that should the slave soldiers eventually be part of a victorious army, freedom would be their only just reward. The problem remained hypothetical. Black Confederates never officially served the Southern cause. They formed companies, drilled, and even paraded in Southern cities. Before the black units were incorporated into Confederate field armies, however, the Confederacy had ceased to exist.

It was left to Jefferson Davis to demonstrate just how far the Confederacy was willing to go in the matter of emancipation. Later in March of 1865 Davis played what he believed was his final diplomatic trump card. He realized that only immediate foreign intervention would save the Confederacy by that time. Accordingly Davis dispatched Louisianian Duncan F. Kenner to the Confederacy's unofficial embassies in Britain and France. Kenner's mission was no less than to offer in the name of the Confederacy to emancipate all the slaves in exchange for recognition. The offer was as desperate as it was vain. Neither European power was willing to recognize a moribund South. Emancipation would come with a Union victory, and this would cost Britain and France nothing.

The Confederacy was past saving by March of 1865. The Kenner mission did, however, carry to completion the internal revolution in the Confederate South. Having sacrificed other features of the "Southern way of life," the Confederacy ultimately placed slavery on the altar of independence. The Southern nation became an end in itself. Independence required the sacrifice. Faced with choosing between independence and the Southern way of life, the Confederacy chose independence.

Two editorials from Mississippi newspapers best illustrate the point. During the controversy over arming the slaves the Jackson *Mississippian* argued, "Let not slavery prove a barrier to our independence. If it is found in the way—if it proves an insurmountable object of the achievement of our liberty and separate nationality, away with it! Let it perish!" On the negative side the Jackson *News* fulminated, "We consider the position [of the *Mississippian*] as a total abandonment of the chief object of this war, and if the institution is already irretrievably undermined, the rights of the States are buried with it. When we admit this to be true beyond adventure, then our voice will be for peace; for why fight one moment longer, if the object and occasion of the fight is dying, dead, or damned?"

The fact was that the Confederacy was prepared to let slavery perish and to fight on! For what? The new nation and its war had achieved a dynamic of their own—a dynamic which overshadowed principles and poses. In four years the Southern nation had given up that which called it into being. Independence at the last was no longer means but end. Born in revolution the Confederacy herself became revolutionized. The Confederate experience had cut the heart out of the Southern way of life. Had the heavens opened, the waters parted, and the Confederacy achieved independence, the postwar South would have resembled the prewar South in little more than name. The Confederate revolution had consumed not only its authors, but their way of life as well.

NOTES

1. Bell I. Wiley, *Southern Negroes, 1861–1865* (New Haven, Conn.: Yale University Press, 1938), p. 83.

2. Ibid., p. 52n.

3. A full discussion of "hiring out" and "living out" in the antebellum South is found in Richard C. Wade, *Slavery in the Cities: The South 1820–1860* (New York: Oxford University Press, 1964).

4. Wiley, *Southern Negroes,* p. 172.

V. ASSESSMENTS

• The trio of reviews which follow presents a small cross-section of the current dialogue among historians on the problems of studying American slavery. Stanley M. Elkins (whose own book has already been criticized extensively elsewhere in this collection) assesses Eugene D. Genovese's concept of a paternalistic ante-bellum slave system. M. I. Finley evaluates David Brion Davis's attempt to treat comparatively the idea of slavery. Finally, J. H. Plumb examines Winthrop D. Jordan's study of white Americans' attitudes toward the Negro.

On Eugene D. Genovese's The Political Economy of Slavery: Studies in the Economy and Society of the Slave South

STANLEY M. ELKINS

There was a time when Charles Beard's "Second American Revolution" chapter in *The Rise of American Civilization* passed for a "Marxist" interpretation of the Civil War, even with Marxists who ought to have known better. Beard argued that the "so-called Civil War" was no mere clash over constitutional principles or the morality of holding slaves. It was a revolutionary upheaval

> ending in the unquestioned establishment of a new power in the government, making vast changes in the arrangement of classes, in the accumulation and distribution of wealth, in the course of industrial development, and in the Constitution inherited from the Fathers. . . . Viewed under the light of uni-

From Stanley M. Elkins, review of Genovese, *The Political Economy of Slavery* . . . , in *Commentary* (July 1966), pp. 73-75. Reprinted from *Commentary*, by permission; Copyright © 1966 by the American Jewish Committee.

387

versal history, the fighting was a fleeting incident; the social revolution was the essential portentous outcome.

But such language, which seemed to imply a line of interpretation suggested a half-century earlier by Marx and Engels themselves—that the American Civil War might best be understood as a struggle between an expanding, bourgeois North and a static, semi-feudal South—was misleading. For all his talk about underlying economic forces and social revolution, Beard found the classic Benthamite pleasure-pain calculus far more congenial to his own habits of mind than any Marxian dialectic. He could never grasp the subtle relationship between class interest, ideological conviction, and political action which Marx and Engels insisted upon. That a man living in a society wherein wealth, status, and self-esteem all rested on the possession of slaves might come to believe that slavery was a just and humane institution, and that such a man could be prepared on moral grounds to fight for its preservation, was a view of human psychology which Beard found incomprehensible. For Beard to see the connection between economic interest and political action, something more had to be at stake than "mere" ideological conviction, or even conviction rooted in the primary economic interests of a ruling class. He would finally conclude that the real key was not slavery at all (for all the bitter polemics, men never say what they really mean), but rather the tariffs, ship subsidies, bounties, and banking legislation (all "hard" things) that an industrializing North demanded and that an agrarian South, still in control of the federal government, could not afford to grant.

Eugene Genovese's *The Political Economy of Slavery* is an effort, by one far better versed in Marxist theory than Beard ever was, to put the argument back on the track and to reconsider the problem of meaningful connections between fundamental economic forces and the coming of the Civil War. Genovese is much too intelligent to pose the matter in terms of specific clashes of interest between North and South. Such clashes, in the light of the broader context, certainly created irritation but they were hardly central. What *was* central was the position of slave labor in the Southern economy. Bound up with this was, on the one hand, the slaveholder's power to impose himself and his values on Southern society, and, on the other, the inherent weakness of slavery as a labor system. "Slavery," according to Genovese, "gave the South a social system and a civilization with a distinct class structure, political community, economy, ideology, and set of psychological patterns [that set the South increasingly apart] from the rest of the nation and from the rapidly developing sections of the world." This happened because slavery was more than a system of labor. It was

> the foundation on which rose a powerful and remarkable social class: a class constituting only a tiny portion of the white population and yet so powerful and remarkable as to try, with more success than our neo-abolitionists care to see, to build a new, or rather to rebuild an old, civilization.

And yet that system upon which their economy, indeed their entire civilization, rested was woefully inefficient.

This fatal weakness, the full implication of which was the last thing the Southern elite was prepared to face, occupies most of the essays in Genovese's sharply and often brilliantly argued book. The slave was a careless and slovenly worker who needed constant supervision and could be trusted with only the most primitive of tools. He was especially hopeless at such work as animal husbandry, which required close attention and some sense of personal initiative. Southern agriculture had already completely adjusted to its labor force. It discouraged innovation, since the slave could barely cope with existing technology; it largely ignored crop rotation, which made economic sense only in conjunction with a thriving livestock industry; and it concentrated its energies on a few staples, mainly cotton, finding it cheaper to import food from the West. The result was a steady decline, which the planters were helpless to remedy, in the fertility of Southern soils.

Serious agricultural reform would have required skilled labor and commercial fertilizer, neither of which the South could afford; and a shift from cotton to truck would have required urban markets and proper transportation, neither of which the South had developed nor, with its existing economy, could hope to develop. The South's economic impasse, in short, was fundamental. It could only be remedied by measures which would have undermined the power and influence of the slaveholding elite. Such measures—emancipation, urban development, the systematic use of slaves in industry—would destroy the very thing the dominant class in the South had committed itself to building, an aristocratic, semi-feudal plantation society.

The one alternative that did not directly challenge the existing social arrangements was territorial expansion. If slave labor could be used on fresh lands in Cuba or Central America, or possibly in Western mines where it could be rigidly supervised and guarded, the South's most pressing problems might at least be postponed, if not solved. But when the Republican party moved to block even this distant hope, the stage was set for insurrection. The planters "could never agree to renounce the foundations of their power and moral sensibility and to undergo a metamorphosis into a class the nature and values of which were the inversion of their own." Given the choice of slipping into the bourgeoisie or fighting, they fought.

I am thoroughly persuaded by Genovese's analysis of the South's agricultural economy. He spells out the weakness of Southern farming in such specific terms as hogs that weighed from forty to fifty per cent less than those in the Midwest, a pitifully low production of butter and milk throughout the lower South, and a livestock industry so poorly managed that the South had to import substantial amounts of meat even though more than half of the country's cattle were located within its borders. He shows at every point the direct connection between such problems and slavery, and how the entire region was trapped by its commitment to a labor system both inefficient and economically stultifying—a dilemma doubly painful in view of the dynamic, expanding economies of the North and Midwest. Moreover, Genovese's discussion of the importance of territorial expansion in Southern thinking makes sense out of the South's seemingly irrational response to the free-soil movement and the Republican party.

Though his tone is frequently polemical, Genovese is always open-minded and flexible, and quite above squabbling with his many predecessors and contemporaries who have written on this same subject. His scholarship, indeed, is so thoroughly scrupulous that I believe it can be depended upon to reinforce conclusions quite different from his. He argues, in effect, that the plantation society of the ante-bellum South reflected a flawed form of latter-day feudalism, and that the flaw was slavery. A very slight change of definition would not in the least disturb the edifice of Genovese's scholarship, though I suppose it would threaten all his most basic theoretical convictions. Still, it seems to me just as plausible—indeed, more so—to say instead that the South reflected a flawed form of capitalism, and that the flaw was race.

Genovese's thesis that a dominant class can by an act of will "rebuild an old civilization" strikes me as gravely unhistorical. He argues that once a class becomes dominant in an economic order it is then in a position not only to impose its recently acquired values, standards, and beliefs on the entire society but also to shed its own past values with relatively little strain. The Southern planters had inherited a republican, bourgeois, contractual society many of whose intellectuals, such as Jefferson and Madison, continued to receive the deference of the ante-bellum South. To believe that these planters could in a single generation impose a set of quasi-feudal values and social arrangements on themselves and on the rest of society—that they could reverse the tide of history—is in itself almost an act of faith.

There were certainly Southerners who did think in such terms. George Fitzhugh was one, though I suspect Fitzhugh's relationship to the planter class was not unlike that between Barry Goldwater and today's business corporations—of a man who may be acceptable as a ceremonial spokesman but whose intellectual prescriptions are almost worthless as a basis for predicting actual behavior and polities. I am reluctant to take the Fitzhughs with a fully straight face, and in any case, I question the depth of the South's commitment to an organic, semi-feudal society in which both status and social responsibility would be fixed by law and custom.

Genovese is of the opinion that the South's basic values were "pre-capitalistic," and that even the aggressive "cotton snobs" of Alabama and Mississippi only needed a little time to wear down their rough edges before slipping naturally into the ranks of the aristocracy. But planting was a speculative business, and few planters were ever free from the shadow of crop failure and bankruptcy. What sort of aristocratic ethos is it possible to construct in a community where one or two bad crops can change a man from a rural magnate into just another farmer? How much mobility, in either direction or both, can a society absorb and still be described as semi-feudal?

Genovese explains the planters' desperate fear of emancipation by their determination to maintain the particular labor system on which depended their class position and their dreams of an organic feudal order. But the special quality of their desperation strikes me as very unfeudal. Their values were not those of a human organic community at all; they were far too bourgeois. Nobody could really see the Negro as an organic member, because every systematic effort had been made to define him as outside that community—as property. The underlying egalitarianism in Southern values was such, and the South's faith in barriers between classes was so limited, that once the Negro's bonds of chattel slavery were removed and once he was redefined as human, the first thing he was likely to do, for all anyone knew, was to marry somebody's daughter.

A true sense of stratified social hierarchy—as in Latin America, where the historical background was genuinely "feudal"—would have protected the Southerners from any such nightmare. They had no real faith in the justice of stability of their community, or any willingness to offer adequate human compensations for all of its members; no one could imagine the Negroes as a "loyal peasantry." An axiom of slave law was that if the master's power were relaxed in any way whatever, the whole system would collapse.

The Southern slaveholders, Genovese says, were a vital and dynamic class determined to create—or recreate—a society, and when it appeared that they were not to succeed, they fought rather than give up a cherished way of life. I should say they were a pathetic class, trapped by history, their minds frozen by the dilemma of race in a bourgeois culture. Their status, power, and pride, says Genovese, depended on their ownership of slaves, whose labor, as he shows so well, was under existing conditions very inefficient and less and less profitable. I should say that the irrational role of race in a contractual society, which defined the black slave as property, created such a narrow view of the Negro that the slaveholder could no longer be inventive. He could only develop a rigid and unimaginative system of labor and then try to justify it as a "way of life," even though it may be doubted whether in his heart he ever really believed it.

Otherwise, why the unwillingness to manipulate, to experiment? Why not some alternative arrangement short of full emancipation? A program of placing slaves and their families on individual plots of land? With some independence and adequate incentives, could they not have proven as efficient at growing cotton or caring for animals as they were in raising chickens or tending their gardens? Since this would in fact be done after emancipation, we know there was no inherent reason why it should not have worked. Indeed, all the precedents of feudalism pointed straight in that direction.

Instead, the South created for the slave the role of a helpless, pathetic dependent, insisted that he live up to it, and then justified the system to itself and to the world by claiming that the helpless Negro could survive under no other. But with slavery under attack from literally everywhere—destructive to retain, destructive to get rid of— it became an intolerable burden, and many a planter said so. This was the kind of tension that produced the Fitzhughs and the paranoia of the 1850's.

I agree with Genovese that the South's decision to fight represented the planters' final, superhuman effort in defense of slavery. I have followed his argument with admiration, and hold his skill and learning in the very highest respect. But I should think the test of the argument would be what happened after they lost their cherished institution. The reaction, if I read my postwar history right, was one of universal relief. For all the exasperating lost-cause sentimentalism of the New South, there was hardly a trace of an *ancien régime* mentality regarding slavery. "I am rejoiced," declared Robert E. Lee (along with many another aristocrat), "that slavery is abolished." George Fitzhugh was quickly forgotten. Slavery was gone; the South did not want to get it back; and no Southern leader, not the most passionate of the ante-bellum defenders, seriously proposed trying.

But they did set to work all over again, being just as implacably determined as they ever were, to avert what they had been convinced all along would be the real disaster, a mingling of two racial communities under a single set of standards. In this, as we know, they succeeded. Race was always the flaw in Southern capitalism, as it is still.

On David Brion Davis's *The Problem of Slavery in Western Culture*

M. I. FINLEY

In the year AD 61 the prefect of the city of Rome, Pedanius Secundus, was murdered by one of the slaves in his town house. Under the law, not only the culprit but all the other slaves in the household had to be executed, in this instance numbering four hundred. There was a popular outcry and the Senate debated the question. Some senators rose to plead clemency, but the day was carried by the distinguished jurist, Gaius Cassius Longinus, who argued that all change from ancestral law and customs is always for the worse. When a mob tried to prevent the sentence from being carried out, the emperor personally intervened on the side of the law, though he rejected another proposal that Pedanius ex-slaves should also be punished by banishment. That, he said, would be unnecessary cruelty.

The emperor was Nero and it has been suggested that one of the unsuccessful advocates of mercy may have been his closest adviser, the Stoic philosopher Seneca, in whose writings there are some powerful passages calling for the treatment of slaves as fellow-humans. Not once, however, did Seneca suggest that the institution itself was so immoral that it ought to be abolished. For that radical idea the western world still had to wait more than 1500 years, while philosophers, moralists, theologians, and jurists—save for an isolated voice here and there to whom no one listened—discovered and propagated a variety of formulas which satisfied them and society at large that a man could be both a thing and a man at the same time. This ambiguity or "dualism" is the "problem of slavery" to which Professor Davis has devoted a large, immensely learned, readable, exciting, disturbing, and sometimes frustrating volume, one of the most important to have been published on the subject of slavery in modern times.

From M. I. Finley, "The Idea of Slavery," a review of Davis, *The Problem of Slavery in Western Culture*, in *The New York Review of Books*, VIII (January 26, 1967), pp. 6-9. Reprinted by permission of *The New York Review of Books*. Copyright © 1967 The New York Review Inc.

The genesis of the book was a modest one. Professor Davis set out to make a comparative study of British and American antislavery movements. Gradually he began to appreciate that "the problem of slavery transcended national boundaries" in ways he "had not suspected." Slavery was brought to the New World at a time when it had disappeared from most of Europe; yet there were no hesitations, no gropings, because the heritage of the Bible, classical philosophy, and Roman law provided a ready-made set of regulations and a ready-made ideology. Differences within the New World, between the Anglo-Saxons in the north and the Latins in the south, between Protestant and Catholic colonies, appeared, on closer examination, to be tangential and far less significant than "their underlying patterns of unity." On this particular topic Professor Davis has now come forward with powerful support for a recent trend in scholarship running counter to the romantic idealized image of Latin American slavery, and in particular of race relationship in the southern hemisphere, which had long prevailed, a view perhaps best known from the works of the Brazilian Gilberto Freyre and from Frank Tannenbaum's seminal little book *Slave and Citizen*. In short, Professor Davis came to the conclusion that "there was more institutional continuity between ancient and modern slavery than has generally been supposed" and that "slavery has always raised certain fundamental problems that originated in the simple fact that the slave is a man."

From this conclusion a new and fundamental question followed. If the "legal and moral validity of slavery was a troublesome question in European thought from the time of Aristotle to the time of Locke," why was it that not until the 1770s were there "forces in motion that would lead to organized movement to abolish . . . the entire institutional framework which permitted human beings to be treated as things"? This development, he rightly says, "was something new to the world." Slavery had declined markedly in the later Roman Empire, not as a result of an abolitionist movement but in consequence of complex social and economic changes which replaced the chattel slave by a different kind of bondsman, the *colonus*, the *adscriptus glebi*, the serf. Modern slavery, in contrast, did not become slowly transformed. It was abolished by force and violence. Attempts to picture "anti-slavery and efforts to Christianize and ameliorate the condition of slaves as parts of a single swelling current of humanitarianism" falsify the historical record. "All such dreams and hopes ran aground on the simple and solid fact, which for centuries had been obscured by philosophy and law, that a slave was not a piece of property, nor a half-human instrument, but a man held down by force."

The book Professor Davis started to write was thus converted into a large project of which this is the first volume (though a self-contained one) carrying the story from antiquity to the early 1770s. The story, it must be stressed, is essentially one in the history of ideas. "A problem of moral perception" is how he himself phrases it.

> This book . . . makes no pretense of being a history of slavery as such, or even of opinion concerning slavery . . . I have been concerned with the different ways in which men have responded to slavery, on the assumption that this will help us to distinguish what was unique in the response of the abolitionist. I have also been concerned with traditions in thought and value from which both opponents and defenders of slavery could draw. I hope to demonstrate the slavery has always been a source of social and psychological tension, but that in Western culture it was associated with certain religious and philosophical doctrines that gave it the highest sanction.

As an essay in the history of ideas—more precisely, of ideology, a word which Professor Davis curiously shies away from—the book is brilliant, filled with detail yet never losing control of the main threads, subtle and sophisticated and penetrating. Even the relatively brief and derivative first part, on ancient and medieval thinking, has some fine insights. Then, with the discovery of America, Professor Davis comes into his own. No man, surely, has read so much or so deeply on the subject: the footnotes provide the most complete bibliography we have; too complete indeed, and one wishes he had been more discriminating in his selection of titles. It is impossible in a review to survey the ground covered or the multiplicity of fresh ideas and suggestions. But an example or two will indicate how complicated is the counterpoint that is woven throughout around the "dualism" concept. Early on the *leitmotif* emerges. The question is posed as to why in the later Roman Empire and the early Middle Ages, when "slavery all but disappeared from most parts of the Europe," we do not find "the Church turning away from its compromises with the Roman world and using its great moral power to hasten a seemingly beneficial change." Professor Davis answers:

> The most plausible explanation would seem to lie in the complex network of mental associations, derived from antiquity, which connnected slavery with ideas of sin, subordination, and the divine order of the world. To question the ethical basis of slavery, even when the institution was disappearing from view, would be to question fundamental conceptions of God's purpose

and man's history and destiny. If slavery were an evil and performed no divinely appointed function, then why had God authorized it in Scripture and permitted it to exist in nearly every nation? If slavery violated the natural law of equality and the divine law of human brotherhood, could not the same be said of the family, private property, social orders, and government?

The heretical sects were a threat all the time, for they seized on those ideas implicit in Christianity "that were potentially explosive when torn from their protective casings and ignited in the charged atmosphere of class rivalry and discontent." They had to be contained, and they were. Not until the middle of the eighteenth century did an English sect finally take a firm official stand against slavery (while the Church of England remained indifferent). The Quakers came to that after a long period of inner conflict on the subject, but by then society had been so transformed that the moral issues acquired new practical implications.

> In a period of intense soul-searching, of desire for self-purification and of concern over their image in the eyes of others, a decision to refrain from dealing in slaves was a means of reasserting the perfectionist content of their faith. It was a way of proscribing a form of selfish economic activity without repudiating the search for wealth; . . . a way of affirming the individual's moral will, and the historic mission of the church, without challenging the basic structure of the social order.

So bald a summary invites the charge of mere cynicism, but nothing would be more unjust. Behind the summaries lie meticulous accounts of the intense intellectual and moral struggles that went on in the search for a moral position. In all societies which are characterized by class or national conflicts and divergence of interests, ideology is necessarily ambivalent. No account is adequate which fails to reveal how ideology serves both to criticize and to preserve the social order at the same time, and the careless or blinkered observer automatically dismisses as cynicism any analysis which gives due weight to the second function. On the subject of slavery, the crowning paradox is that the rationalist attack on Christian theology in the eighteenth century brought the slave no nearer to freedom. Locke had already shown how a defense of slavery could be reconciled with natural rights. Now, "insofar as the Enlightenment divorced anthropology and comparative anatomy from theological assumptions, it opened the way for theories of racial inferiority."

And yet, at the point where this book ends, anti-slavery *had* become a program and eventually it was to become a successful major political issue. Slavery *was* finally abolished in the West. Why? It is on that decisive question that I find Professor Davis's account frustrating. "For some two thousand years men thought of sin as a kind of slavery. One day they would come to think of slavery as sin." Who are "they"? "By the early 1770s a large number of moralists, poets, intellectuals, and reformers had come to regard American slavery as an unmitigated evil." It is only a little unfair to remind Professor Davis of Jim Farley's remark, towards the close of Adlai Stevenson's first presidential campaign. Someone at a party was being jubilant over the fact that nearly all intellectuals were for Stevenson. "All sixty thousand of them," retorted Farley. Moralists, poets, intellectuals, and reformers did not destroy slavery. The Civil War did that, and Professor Davis himself has, as a by-product, delivered a crushing blow against the "unnecessary conflict" school of historians. I do not, of course, wish to deny the essential role of several generations of abolitionists. But nothing did or could happen until their moral fervor became translated into political and military action, and how that came about cannot be answered by the history of ideas. Nothing is more difficult perhaps than to explain how and why, or why not, a new moral perception becomes effective in action. Yet nothing is more urgent if an academic historical exercise is to become a significant investigation of human behavior with direct relevance to the world we now live in.

It would be gross injustice to call this book an academic historical exercise or to suggest that Professor Davis is unaware of the central question. Throughout the volume there are sharp comments very much to the point. In a brief note on the rather mechanical economic explanations in Eric Williams's *Capitalism and Slavery*, Davis joins the opposition but then adds that one cannot "get around the simple fact that no country thought of abolishing the slave trade until its economic value had considerably declined." He knows and uses the most recent discussions (down to Eugene Genovese's *Political Economy of Slavery*, published in 1965) of the profitability of slavery and its effects on economic growth. He agrees that it is "theoretically possible" that such divergences with respect to freed slaves as existed between North and South America "had less to do with the character of slavery in the two countries than with economic and social structures which defined the relations between colored freedmen and the dominant white society." He mentions the wars of the eighteenth century and the changes in the balance of power, which "brought a growing awareness of the instability and inefficiency of the old colonial system." And it may be that what I am looking for will find its proper place in the next volumes.

Yet the fact remains that the comments I have just quoted are really asides, often relegated to footnotes, and I do not think it is a sufficient defense that a man has a right to choose his own subject, in this case the history of ideas. Slavery is not an autonomous system; it is an institution embedded in a social structure. It is no longer the same institution when the structure is significantly altered, and ideas about slavery have to be examined structurally too. Only by remaining in the realm of abstractions can Professor Davis lay so much emphasis on the "institutional continuity" between ancient and modern slavery. He is in consequence led astray on several important aspects. His account of slavery among the Hebrews and other ancient Near Eastern societies suffers from precisely the weakness he has so effectively exposed in the case of Latin American slavery. He has allowed his authorities to mislead him into taking at face value pious hopes which he penetrates easily when they appear in Seneca or modern writers. And he has misjudged the social ambience by failing to appreciate sufficiently that for most of human history labor for others has been involuntary (quite apart from compulsions exercised by either family or wage-earning, which are of a different order from the kind of force that is the final sanction against slaves, serfs, peons, debt bondsmen, coolies, or untouchables). Slavery in that context must have different overtones from slavery in a context of free labor. The way slavery declined in the Roman Empire, to repeat an example I have already given, illustrates that. Neither moral values nor economic interests nor the social order were threatened by the transformation of slaves and free peasants together into tied serfs. They were—or at least many powerful elements in society thought they were —by proposals to convert slaves into free men.

What sets the slave apart from all other forms of involuntary labor is that, in the strictest sense, he is an outsider. He is brought into a new society violently and traumatically; he is cut off from all traditional human ties of kin and nation and even his own religion; he is prevented, insofar as that is possible, from creating new ties, except to his masters, and in consequence his descendants are as much outsiders, as unrooted, as he was. The final proof of non-status is the free sexual access to slaves which is a fundamental condition of all slavery (with complex exceptions in the rules regarding access of free females to slave males). When Professor Davis writes, "Bondwomen have always been the victims of sexual exploitation, which was perhaps the clearest recognition of their humanity," he has stood the situation on its head.

Sexual *exploitation* is a denial, not a recognition, of a woman's humanity, whether she is slave or free.

I have stated the slave-outsider formula schematically and therefore too rigidly. Structural differences emerge clearly when one considers how much societies have differed with respect to the freed slave. At one extreme stood Rome, which not only allowed almost unlimited rights to individual masters to free their slaves but which also automatically enrolled the freedmen as citizens if their owners were citizens. At the other extreme was the American South. Professor Davis produces evidence that by 1860 there were more free Negroes, even in the South, than is often realized. Nevertheless, the emancipation process was hemmed in by very stringent regulations. And the fate of the freed slave in the United States hardly needs spelling out. What does need a careful look is the question of color, which is too central to be evaded out of sentimentality and on which Professor Davis has an important chapter (as usual, in the realm of ideas). Dr. Williams holds that "slavery was not born of racism, rather, racism was the consequence of slavery." One wishes profoundly that one could believe that. However, the slave-outsider formula argues the other way, as does the fact that as early as the 1660s southern colonies decreed that henceforth all Negroes who were imported should be slaves, but whites should be indentured servants and not slaves. The connection between slavery and racism has been a dialectical one, in which each element reinforced the other.

Racism has already outlived slavery by a century. Why, we are entitled to ask, did the "revolutionary shift in attitudes towards sin, human nature, and progress," which we may concede to have been a necessary condition of antislavery, not extend to racism? Is slavery any more a sin than the denial of civil rights, concentration camps, Hiroshima, napalm, torture in Algeria, or apartheid in South Africa or Rhodesia? Why did the new moral perception succeed in wiping out one sin and not the others? It is that question which makes this book a profoundly disturbing one. There is cold comfort here for anyone who trusts to the slow ameliorative process of a growing humanitarianism, of the "progressive development of man's moral sense" which Thomas Jefferson found in history. In Professor Davis's lapidary phrase, "faith in progress smothered [Jefferson's] sense of urgency" when it came to slavery.

On Winthrop D. Jordan's *White Over Black:*
American Attitudes Toward the Negro, 1550–1812

J. H. PLUMB

Often social change is imperceptible to those living in its midst. It is like water oozing through a dam—at first a faint dampness, a trickle, a spurt, the cracks multiply and either the dam crumbles or the pushing waters are sufficiently eased to create a new, if unstable, equilibrium. To the Black Panthers and other groups of activists the change in social attitudes in America toward the Negro is derisory, and when not derisory a conscience-easing fake. To WASPS, conscious or unconscious, or to ethnic groups living near black ghettos or in competition with blacks for jobs, the rushing of the waters is so deafening that they are driven toward panic and hysteria. To the uneasy liberal, the situation borders on the grotesque. He wants to be fair, to make retribution, and yet he cannot easily accept the new black contempt toward the white, and he is also conscious, perhaps over-conscious, of a hatred of white democracy, a growing insistence on authoritarian, almost totalitarian, attitudes within the black community.

The situation of the historian is equally acute. What has been the role of the Nego in American history? What have been the long-term results of slavery and deprivation of civil rights? Indeed, what was the true nature of American slavery—was it the most evil type the world has known or no better and no worse than the rest of the New World experienced? These problems have never been easy to answer, but in the context of the present time they are much more difficult, for now the question has to be posed: how far was racism itself responsible for the wretchedness of the Negro slave? Did it give a peculiarly vicious twist to slavery? Indeed what are the connections between racism and slavery? Of course this raises the question of the nature of slavery—unbridled racism combined with absolute, or near absolute, authority of the racist master was unlikely to lead to anything but social brutality, to treating the slave more as a chattel than as a person.

At the present time the problem of racism and slavery is possibly the most insistent, for obvious reasons. For the professional historian there are other questions relating to slavery that are equally difficult but intellectually perhaps more exciting. There is Stanley M. Elkins's brilliant and disturbing investigation of slavery and the Negro personality, examining the reasons for the development of the "Sambo" response of the Negro slave to his environment which help to explain the paucity of slave revolts in America. (No amount of black protest or black re-writing of history can overcome that fact. The American Negro slave protested less in his society than the free peasant class of Europe, or of England for that matter, and this needs explanation.) Less original, but more deeply and professionally argued is Eugene Genovese's memorable book, *The Political Economy of Slavery* (1965), which attempts to relate all aspects of Southern life to its peculiar means of economic exploitation. Indeed, Genovese analyzes the social system based on slavery from its basic economic structure, through its institutionalization of power, to its self-justification and sense of pride in itself. Slave society, Genovese has shown, was far more complex than most historians have allowed.

Apart from Elkins and Genovese many historians have recently made contributions of great value to the study of slavery and the South. . . . Yet in all this wide range of work on slavery, as exciting and original as any going forward on any other aspect of American social history, there is one omission. There is no comparative study of slavery and poverty. By this I do not mean a study of the economic condition of slaves compared with free Negroes in the slums of Southern cities such as New Orleans, which in fact has been examined by Richard C. Wade, but of the attitude of slaveowners toward slaves, compared with the attitude, not only of industrial, but of pre-industrial owners of wealth toward the poor, especially in the period 1540–1750 in Europe —for in a sense America had very few poor in the early centuries.

New World slavery raises two very serious questions. Why was it so easily accepted by all Western European nations at a time when slavery had ceased to be socially important? And, secondly, why did abolitionists become socially and politically effective from the last third of the eighteenth century onward? The answers to these questions will obviously illuminate the whole notion of slavery, but it is my conviction that these answers can be found only within the non-servile context of the exploitation of labor, and the ideology that goes with it. This brings one to Winthrop D. Jordan's outstanding book, a volume to be placed alongside Stampp, Elkins, Davis, and Genovese. Jordan's thesis is straightforward. The Elizabeth Englishmen coming across primitive black men for the first time were repelled. To them black men were associated with beastliness; their inferiority made them the lowest link in the Great Chain of Being. Blackness stimulated the Englishman's sense of guilt and horror. His Devil was, after all, black, and he always put a high price upon fairness of skin. The primitive societies of West Africa, with their strange and divergent customs, strengthened the Elizabethan's belief in the eternal, God-given inferiority of the Negro—a little higher, maybe, than the apes, but infinitely lower than the white Englishman. Negroes naturally were "addicted unto Treason, Treacherie, Murther, Theft and Robberie" as well as idleness and lechery.

Hence the proper status of Negroes was slavery. Slavery fitted their natures whose outward sign was the blackness of their skin. And it was because they were black that it became easy to justify slavery and maintain it. This racism can be further illustrated by the treatment of free or freed Negroes, whose rights were subject to strict limitation; even the onus of proof that he was free rested with the Negro, for society expected, because of his color, that he would necessarily be a slave. From the earliest days of slavery this element of racism—for example the detestation of miscegenation—was dominant and it became more and more powerful as Negroes grew in number and slavery became the dominant social system of the South. This, in essence, is Jordan's argument and it is based on material which ranges from the sermons of sixteenth-century English bishops, obscure travelers' reports from Africa, Court session records of the slave states, newspaper files throughout the South, the meditations of philosophers in the eighteenth century, and the voluminous correspondences of the Founding Fathers and many other sources. Indeed, the range of Jordan's reading is prodigious.

That racism gave an added dimension to slavery cannot be doubted; but it is difficult to decide how extensive this dimension was. Jordan contends, with much quotation from Elizabethan literature and from African travelers' tales, that the sixteenth-century Englishman regarded the Negro as not only savage, heathen, biologically close to the ape, but also as theologically damned; for the Negro was descended from Ham, Noah's disinherited son, who was cursed by having black offspring.

What was more, the Englishman's Devil was always portrayed as black, so Negroes were associated with evil and linked ever more firmly to God's curse. Furthermore, they proved helpless against the "angel-like" English, whose whiteness proclaimed them to be beloved of God: so, rightly, good was triumphing over evil.

These attitudes toward the Negroes made the enslavement of them by the English both natural and ferocious. Unlike Catholic Europeans, the English had no interest in conversion, and so long as the black remained a heathen savage in a Christian society the Negro slave could have no rights. Hence the slave possessed fewer human rights in English slave-holding societies than in others ancient or modern. From start to finish American slavery had an extensive racial quality: indeed Jordan calls it racial slavery. In one essential Jordan is correct. Negroes were considered born inferiors, born slaves if you will, to a degree that was never applied to many other groups of slaves. The Roman slave was treated just as brutally, at times far more brutally, than the Southern Negro. He certainly possessed no more rights. But, once freed, the world was open to him. He and his family could rise or fall like any other man in the Roman state, so long as he had either ability or money or both. Not so the Negro. The freed Negro entered a caste which was excluded from most of the benefits and all of the power in the society to which it belonged. And the basis of this exclusion was racial. This far one can go with Jordan.

But it could also be argued that racism went far beyond slavery so that it cannot be viewed simply as the major cause of slavery. Racism was not, of course, confined to the Southern slave masters or to Southern slave society in the sixteenth and seventeenth centuries. It was just as rampant in the Portuguese Empire. Franciscans in the seventeenth century in Goa attempted to prevent Portuguese born of pure white parents from entering their order on the grounds that having been suckled by Indian wet-nurses, their blood was contaminated for life (ex. inf. Professor C. R. Boxer). This surely is racism as extravagant as any to be found in the Southern states.

Again, Jordan makes a great deal of the deliberate exclusion of the Negro from the Anglican Church, but Catholic slaveowners were no more eager for their blacks to be a part of their Church. As one Portuguese slaveowner exclaimed indignantly, "Should my Kaffirs receive communion? God forbid that I should ever allow them." Indeed the literature of the sixteenth and seventeenth centuries is full of savagely expressed racism directed not only to the Negro but to the Hindu, the Hottentot, the Welsh, Scots, Irish, French against English, English against the Dutch.

Nor was Negro slavery the only kind of slavery justified on racist grounds, nor was the Englishman's attitude unique, as Jordan implies. If one glances at the reaction of the mandarins of the T'ang dynasty to the primitive peoples of Nam Viet (the tropical South), the response is the same: a combination of curiosity, superiority, and utter loathing. "Both conscience and law permitted the enslavement of these subject peoples all the more readily because of two persistent views of them," writes Edward Schafer in *The Vermilion Bird*, his remarkable study of the T'ang mandarins' attitude to the South, "an older one, that they were not really human, and a younger one derived from the first, that they were not really civilized." These are arguments frequently used about the Negro; yet the enslavement of the primitive people of the Nam Viet never developed into the equivalent of Negro slavery, for the Chinese economy did not require slaves on such a scale.

Racism does not create slavery. It is an excuse for it. Racism was a rampant feature of the centuries when slavery was being established in America and it was, therefore, easy to make it one of the justifications for the institution. But racism could be intense and not lead to slavery—and racism does not explain why the European nations found so little difficulty in adopting slavery in their colonies long after the institution had become insignificant in Europe's economic structure.

Although the institution had no economic relevance in contemporary Europe, the idea of slavery was both potent and entirely acceptable to Englishmen on stronger grounds than those of race. The House of Commons did not even turn a hair at the suggestion that persistent English vagabonds should be enslaved by their countrymen, and they passed an Act in 1547 for this purpose, along, of course, with branding the victims with a large S. It failed and was repealed, not on humanitarian grounds. No one wanted slaves—there was enough cheap labor without them, requiring no more food and less supervision. But the idea of white slavery was in no way repellent to the Tudors, or limited by them to savages and heathens. Indeed the condition of slavery had been accepted by the Church and by society from time out of mind; a part of that great law of subordination without which the whole edifice of society might crash to the ground. Without slave status, what would happen to bonded servants, to children sold as apprentices, to the indigent poor who had no rights in society except to labor? Slavery was only the most extreme of all servile conditions. Servant and slave were more than semantically linked.

The type of abuse that was hurled at the slave was hurled at the poor: particularly in English society, from which many Southern slave masters were drawn. Take these remarks of William Perkins, the popular puritan preacher of the early seventeenth century:

> Rogues, beggars, vagabonds . . . commonly are of no civil society or corporation nor of any particular Church: and are as rotten legs and arms that drop from the body. . . . To wander up and down from year to year to this end, to seek and procure bodily maintenance is no calling, but the life of a beast.

or this, from his colleague Sibbes:

> They are the refuse of mankind: as they are in condition so they are in disposition.

These puritan divines were more charitable than many. The rogues and vagabonds were, of course, the wandering poor desperate for food. Their lot was bloody whippings, frequent branding, and enforced labor. The early slave codes were very similar to the legislation designed to control the Elizabethan unemployed poor. Again, the poor were, it is now thought, expected neither to go to Church nor to be welcomed there. As for cruelty, treatment of apprentices could be vicious, the floggings and brandings meted out to the "dregs of society" of Elizabethan and Stuart England almost as savage as anything the Negro knew; perhaps at times more so, for the poor were no man's property, hence valueless if sick, weak, or contumacious.

Again, miscegenation: the taboos against marrying the poor were formidable; for a woman it usually meant total ostracism. Yet, of course, the young servant women, like slave negresses, could be and were fair game for their masters. Even the Sambo mentality can be found in the deliberately stupid country yokel or the cockney clown of later centuries. So, too, the belief, as with Negroes, that they were abandoned sexually, given to both promiscuity and over-indulgence. Slave, servant, worker were the objects of exploitation, the sources of labor, therefore wealth. Hence we should not be surprised to find similar attitudes, similar social oppressions operating against the poor as against the slave. Slavery and poverty in these centuries are not different in kind but different in degree, and the disadvantage was not always the slave's, for, as property, he might be treated with greater consideration in sickness or in age than the wage-slave.

Because America did not know poverty, rural or urban, as Europe did in those early formative years, historians tend to attribute to slavery conditions that spring from the intensive exploitation of labor, whether "free" or servile. I do not doubt that racism gave an added intensity, a further degree of hopelessness and degradation to slavery and the slave's lot, and Jordan's book is of immense value in driving this home. But it is important to see the similarities in the treatment of slaves and the poor: otherwise one cannot realize how natural slavery was to the majority of men who practiced it or accepted it. To underline this, if underlining be needed, slavery was often—not always, but often—at its cruellest where intensive economic exploitation was at its highest, namely on the great plantations. The comparatively mild slavery of Cuba became far more vicious and disciplined with the rise of the large sugar plantations, as Michael Banton points out in his admirable *Race Relations,* a book which really deserves far more extensive treatment than can be given it here.

Just as a discussion of slavery without a consideration of the exploitation of other laborers tends to obscure fundamental issues, so too can racism and questions of civil rights obscure the deeper issues. No amount of civil rights can alleviate the Negro's lot, for much of the hatred of the blacks springs from the rich's fear of the poor and dispossessed. The basis of the problem is exploitation: the gross injustice which acquisitive society always inflicts on those who have nothing to offer but their body's labor. Hence an absence of an extended consideration of other laboring poor weakens to some extent the force of Jordan's book.

Once Jordan moves into the eighteenth century there is a greater sense of mastery and he is particularly skillful in tracing the evasions of the Founding Fathers and the reasons why they could not face the question of abolition. Jordan analyzes very subtly the conflict between the insistence on natural rights and the Lockeian concept of the holiness of property. The easiest escape was to defend natural rights negatively, and, after the first flush of idealism, Revolutionary America had little difficulty in pushing the question of slavery to the sidelines. But that was as far as it could be pushed; for by 1800 white America's dilemma became both clearer and more devastating to its conscience. How could they retain the purity of white America from black contamination? How could they preserve all that they thought was best in

American society, even the inviolability of family life, if they allowed Negroes to be emancipated?

Yet their Revolutionary cultural heritage, their growing sense that Destiny had placed the moral future of the world in their hands "prohibited extreme, overt manifestations of aggression against them." Here were the roots both of a crisis of conscience and of its solution. Slavery was destroyed, yet racism preserved. How this was achieved has been little understood. Presumably there will be a second volume which will deal with the complex issues of abolition, for only the early stages are touched on here.

The story of abolition, the reasons why the whole of Europe in the last third of the eighteenth century began to acquire a strong distaste first for the slave trade and then even for slavery itself is a vast question which none of the great historians of slavery—Davis, Jordan, Stampp, Genovese, Elkins—has attempted. It is a highly complex issue. The important factor is not the conversion of Quakers to anti-slavery attitudes, nor the convictions of a few intellectuals (voices, some weak, some powerful, had always been raised against slavery). The real question is why did abolition acquire a strong social basis, why did it become a passionate political issue? Again, I believe that this cannot be understood in isolation from the working class and the different attitude which was developing toward it. The most fertile ground for conversion to anti-slavery agitation, besides the Quakers, was in England among the entrepreneurs of the industrial revolution. The manufacturing districts (as against the commercial) were inclined to produce the subscribers, the speakers, and the supporters of the anti-slavery movement: not all, of course, but it was an area of marked sympathy.

From the middle of the eighteenth century, and indeed far earlier among the Quaker industrialists, one can find a changing attitude to the poor laboring man, the attitude that he turned into a better, more profitable tool if he were given incentives, that is, if he were encouraged to feel that his work possessed opportunities for self-advancement and better conditions, no matter how rudimentary. Furthermore, the new industrial methods required more self-disciplined, skillful, better educated, literate laborers. The more imaginative, speculative manufacturers, such as Josiah Wedgwood, Jedediah Strutt, and Robert Owen, experimented with bonus schemes, better housing, workers' canteens, schools, and the like. Instead of laboring men, exploiters now wanted tools, and far more tools than the old craftsman methods of industrial organizations permitted; also their new tools needed to be more specialized. Master craftsmen were not wanted. Tools or "hands" were wanted, and they could be created from the laboring masses. Moreover, a pool of laboring men, skilled, semi-skilled and unskilled, selling their labor on a free market, was invaluable for keeping down wages. In a world of violent business cycles, "free" labor obviously had great advantages over unfree. Manufacturers' attitudes were rarely as crudely materialistic as this, any more than were those of the slave-owners. Many were devoted to their workers, helped them in harsh times, and developed a patriarchal attitude, but this does not change the basic situation.

So the whole attitude toward exploitation began to change, very slowly but with gathering momentum, and the poor began to turn into the working class. But this working class, of course, was sharply differentiated internally and, needing a mass base of free wage-slaves, was treated often with a callousness which was no less evil than that of slavery, and which was often justified by the same bogus scientific arguments that were used to justify racism. Of course, racism did not die. Indeed, given the right conditions, as with the influx of East European Jews into London's East End in the late nineteenth century, it intensified. The same is true with Negroes in America.

The flourishing state of racism throughout the world, *post abolition,* should make us chary of explaining slavery in its terms. Still, slavery was abolished and the most powerful world leaders, for the first time in recorded history, deliberately set out to get both the slave trade and slavery abolished. It became politically and socially useful for them to pursue such a policy. Slavery began to appear as archaic and its personal brutalities and restrictions were anathematized. Slavery became the antithesis of modernity. It cannot be an accident that the leadership of the anti-slavery agitation on a world-wide scale was concluded by Great Britain, the most industrialized nation in the world. However, that is another and a longer story. The point that I wish to emphasize is that the study of slavery, disengaged from the general history of the exploitation of labor, has inherent dangers, leading to a false emphasis and to a too simplified causation. It is even more confusing to see it entirely in terms of racism.

It is good to see so many of the best American historians tackling one of the greatest historical problems of their society—the slave South and its complex repercussions. Among these Winthrop Jordan has won a deservedly high place with this magnificent book—scholarly, perceptive, and intellectually sophisticated. . . .

A Selected Modern Bibliography

GENERAL WORKS

John W. Blassingame, *The Slave Community: Plantation Life in the Ante-Bellum South* (New York, 1972).

Alfred H. Conrad and J. R. Meyers, *The Economics of Slavery and Other Studies in Economic History* (Chicago, 1964).

David Brion Davis, *The Problem of Slavery in Western Culture* (Ithaca, 1966).

Thomas E. Drake, *Quakers and Slavery in America* (New Haven, 1950).

Stanley M. Elkins, *Slavery, A Problem in American Institutional and Intellectual Life* (Chicago, 1959).

Eugene D. Genovese, *In Red and Black: Marxian Explorations in Southern and Afro-American History* (New York, 1971).

———, *The Political Economy of Slavery: Studies in the Economy and Society of the Slave South* (New York, 1965).

———, *The World the Slaveholders Made: Two Essays in Interpretation* (New York, 1969).

Barnett Hollander, *Slavery in America: Its Legal History* (New York, 1963).

Herbert S. Klein, *Slavery in The Americas: A Comparative Study of Cuba and Virginia* (Chicago, 1967).

Donald G. Mathews, *Slavery and Methodism: A Chapter in American Morality, 1780–1845* (Princeton, 1965).

Richard B. Morris, *Government and Labor in Early America* (New York, 1946).

Ulrich B. Phillips, *American Negro Slavery* (New York, 1918).

———, *Life and Labor in the Old South* (Boston, 1929).

Donald L. Robinson, *Slavery in the Structure of American Politics, 1765–1820* (New York, 1971).

Abbot Emerson Smith, *Colonists in Bondage: White Servitude and Convict Labor in America, 1607–1776* (Chapel Hill, 1947).

Kenneth M. Stampp, *The Peculiar Institution: Slavery in the Ante-Bellum South* (New York, 1956).

Frank Tannenbaum, *Slave and Citizen: The Negro in the Americas* (New York, 1946).

Eric Williams, *Capitalism and Slavery* (Chapel Hill, 1944).

C. Vann Woodward, *American Counterpoint: Slavery and Racism in the North-South Dialogue* (New York, 1971).

Arthur Zilversmit, *The First Emancipation: The Abolition of Negro Slavery in the North* (Chicago, 1967).

STATE AND LOCAL STUDIES OF SLAVERY

THE NORTH

Noel P. Conlon, "Rhode Island Negroes in the Revolution: A Bibliography," *Rhode Island History* (Winter-Spring 1970).

Lorenzo J. Greene, *The Negro in Colonial New England, 1620–1776* (New York, 1942).

Norman Dwight Harris, *The History of Negro Servitude in Illinois . . .* (Chicago, 1909).

David M. Katzman, "Black Slavery in Michigan," *Midcontinent American Studies Journal*, XI (Fall 1970).

Gwendolyn Evans Logan, "The Slave in Connecticut During the Revolution," *Connecticut Historical Society Bulletin*, XXX (July 1965).

Elaine MacEacheren, "Emancipation of Slavery in Massachusetts: A Reexamination, 1770–1790," *Journal of Negro History*, LV (October 1970).

Edgar J. McManus, *A History of Negro Slavery in New York* (Syracuse, 1966).

Richard C. Twombly and Robert H. Moore, "Black Puritan: The Negro in Seventeenth-Century Massachusetts," *William and Mary Quarterly*, 3rd series, XXIV (April 1967).

Donald D. Wax, "The Demand for Slave Labor in Colonial Pennsylvania," *Pennsylvania History*, XXXIV (October 1967).

Arthur Zilversmit, *The First Emancipation: The Abolition of Slavery in the North* (Chicago, 1967).

———, "Liberty and Property: New Jersey and the Abolition of Slavery," *New Jersey History*, LXXXVIII (Winter 1970).

———, "Quok Walker, Mumbet, and the Abolition of Slavery in Massachusetts," *William and Mary Quarterly*, XXV (October 1968).

THE SOUTH

Richard C. Wade, *Slavery in the Cities, The South, 1820–1860* (New York, 1964).

Charles S. Davis, *The Cotton Kingdom in Alabama* (Montgomery, 1939).

Weymouth T. Jordan, *Ante-Bellum Alabama, Town and Country* (Tallahassee, 1957).

James B. Sellers, *Slavery in Alabama* (Tuscaloosa, 1950).

Orville W. Taylor, *Negro Slavery in Arkansas* (Durham, 1958).

John A. Munroe, "The Negro in Delaware," *South Atlantic Quarterly*, LVI (1957).

Norman J. Cobb and Don McWalters, "Historical Report on Evelyn Plantation," *Georgia Historical Quarterly*, LV (Fall 1971).

William G. Proctor, Jr., "Slavery in Southwest Georgia," *Georgia Historical Quarterly*, XLIX (March 1965).

Donald D. Wax, "Georgia and the Negro Before the American Revolution," *Georgia Historical Quarterly*, LI (March 1967).

J. Winston Coleman, Jr., *Slavery Times in Kentucky* (Chapel Hill, 1940).

John S. Kendall, "New Orleans' 'Peculiar Institution,'" *Louisiana Historical Quarterly*, XXIII (July 1940).

Joseph Karl Menn, *The Large Slaveholders of Louisiana, 1860* (New Orleans, 1964).

V. A. Moody, "Slavery on Louisiana Sugar Plantations," *Louisiana Historical Quarterly*, VII (1924).

John Milton Price, "Slavery in Winn Parish," *Louisiana History*, VIII (Spring 1967).

Robert C. Reinders, "Slavery in New Orleans in the Decade Before the Civil War," *Mid-America*, XLIV (October 1962).

William L. Richter, "Slavery in Baton Rouge, 1820–1860," *Louisiana History*, X (Spring 1969).

Roger Shugg, *Origins of Class Struggle in Louisiana* . . . *1840–1875* (Baton Rouge, 1939).

Joe Gray Taylor, *Negro Slavery in Louisiana* (Baton Rouge, 1963).

——, "Slavery in Louisiana During the Civil War," *Louisiana History*, VIII (Winter 1967).

Jonathan L. Alpert, "The Origin of Slavery in the United States—The Maryland Precedent," *American Journal of Legal History*, XIV (July 1970).

Charles S. Sydnor, *Slavery in Mississippi* (New York, 1933).

Lester B. Baltimore, "The Fight for Slavery on the Missouri Border," *Missouri Historical Review*, LXII (October 1967).

Lyle W. Dorsett, "Slaveholding in Jackson County, Missouri," *Bulletin of the Missouri Historical Society*, XX (October 1963).

George R. Lee, "Slavery and Emancipation in Lewis County, Missouri," *Missouri Historical Review*, LXV (April 1971).

Arvarh E. Strickland, "Aspects of Slavery in Missouri," *Missouri Historical Review*, LXV (July 1971).

Guion G. Johnson, *Ante-Bellum North Carolina: A Social History* (Chapel Hill, 1937).

Edward W. Phifer, "Slavery in Microcosm: Burke County, North Carolina," *Journal of Southern History*, XXVII (May 1962).

Rosser H. Taylor, *Slaveholding in North Carolina: An Economic View* (Chapel Hill, 1926).

Frank Klingberg, *The Negro in Colonial South Carolina: A Study in Americanization* (Washington, 1941).

Robert E. Corlew, "Some Aspects of Slavery in Dickson County," *Tennessee Historical Quarterly*, X (September–December 1951).

Chase C. Mooney, *Slavery in Tennessee* (Bloomington, 1957).

Earl W. Fornell, "The Abduction of Free Negroes and Slaves in Texas," *Southwestern Historical Quarterly* (January 1957).

George R. Woolfolk, "Cotton Capitalism and Slave Labor in Texas," *Southern Social Science Quarterly* (June 1956).

——, "Sources of the History of the Negro in Texas, With Special Reference to Their Implications for Research in Slavery," *Journal of Negro History*, XLII (January 1957).

Dennis L. Lythgoe, "Negro Slavery in Utah," *Utah Historical Quarterly*, 39 (Winter 1971).

Susie M. Ames, *Studies of the Virginia Eastern Shore in the Seventeenth Century* (Richmond, 1940).

Richard R. Beeman, "Labor Forces and Race Relations: A Comparative View of the Colonization of Brazil and Virginia," *Political Science Quarterly*, LXXXVI (December 1971).

Wesley Frank Craven, *White, Red and Black: The Seventeenth-Century Virginian* (Charlottesville, 1971).

Robert McColley, *Slavery and Jeffersonian Virginia* (Urbana, Ill., 1964).

Joseph Clarke Robert, *The Road from Monticello: A Study of the Virginia Slavery Debate of 1832* (Durham, 1941).

Thad W. Tate, *The Negro in Eighteenth-Century Williamsburg* (Charlottesville, 1965).

Alden T. Vaughan, "Blacks in Virginia: A Note on the First Decade," *William and Mary Quarterly*, 3rd series, XXIX (July 1972).

Constance McLaughlin Green, *Washington, Village and Capitol, 1800–1878* (Princeton, 1962).

A number of older studies, many originally published as part of the Johns Hopkins University series of historical studies, are still useful to modern historians of the question. Among them are the following:

Bernard C. Steiner, *History of Slavery in Connecticut* (Baltimore, 1893).

Edward Ingle, *The Negro in the District of Columbia* (Baltimore, 1893).

N. Dwight Harris, *The History of Negro Servitude in Illinois, 1719–1864* (Chicago, 1904).

Ivan E. McDougle, *Slavery in Kentucky, 1792–1865* (Lancaster, Pa., 1918).

John H. T. McPherson, *History of Liberia* (Baltimore, 1891).

Jeffrey R. Brackett, *The Negro in Maryland: A Study of The Institution of Slavery* (Baltimore, 1904).

Eugene I. McCormac, *White Servitude in Maryland* (Baltimore, 1904).

Harrison A. Trexler, *Slavery in Missouri, 1804–1865* (Baltimore, 1914).

Henry S. Cooley, *Slavery in New Jersey* (Baltimore, 1896).

Edward Raymond Turner, *The Negro in Pennsylvania, 1639–1861* (American Historical Association, 1911).

John S. Bassett, *History of Slavery in North Carolina* (Baltimore, 1899).

R. H. Taylor, *Slaveholding in North Carolina: An Economic View* (Chapel Hill, 1926).

H. M. Henry, *Police Control of the Slave in South Carolina* (Emory, Va., 1914; Ph.D. thesis, Vanderbilt University).

Edson L. Whitney, *Government in the Colony of South Carolina* (Baltimore, 1895).

Caleb P. Patterson, *The Negro in Tennessee, 1790–1865* (Austin, Texas, 1922).

THE ANTEBELLUM NEGRO AND THE PROBLEM OF RACE

GENERAL STUDIES AND SLAVE NARRATIVES

Herbert Aptheker, *A Documentary History of the Negro People in the United States*, 2 vols. (New York, 1951).

———, *Essays in the History of the American Negro* (New York, 1964).

Richard Bardolph, *The Negro Vanguard* (New York, 1959).

John F. Bayliss (ed.), *Black Slave Narratives* (New York, 1970).

Arna Bontemps, *Five Slave Narratives: A Compendium* (New York, 1968).

——— (ed.), *Great Slave Narratives* (Boston, 1969).

Benjamin F. Botkin (ed.), *Lay My Burden Down: A Folk History of Slavery* (Chicago, 1945).

Helen T. Catterall (ed.), *Judicial Cases Concerning American Slavery and the Negro*, 5 vols. (Washington, 1926–37).

Daedalus, The Negro in America, 2 vols. (1966).

Basil Davidson, *The Lost Cities of Africa* (Boston, 1959).

Frederick Douglass, A Narrative of the Life of Frederick Douglass, an American Slave, Written by Himself (Boston, 1845). (Ten years later expanded into My Bondage and My Freedom [New York, 1855].)

Stanley Feldstein (ed.), Once a Slave: The Slaves' View of Slavery (New York, 1971).

Leslie Fishel and Benjamin Quarles (eds.), The Negro American: A Documentary History (Chicago, 1967).

Miles Mark Fisher, Negro Slave Songs in the United States (Ithaca, N. Y., 1953).

Fisk University, God Struck Me Dead, Religious Conversion Experiences and Autobiographies of Negro Ex-Slaves (Nashville, 1945). (Reprinted in paperback, Clifton Johnson [ed.], Philadelphia, 1969.)

Fisk University, Unwritten History of Slavery: Autobiographical Accounts of Negro Ex-Slaves (Nashville, 1945). (Reprinted Washington, D. C., 1968.)

John Hope Franklin, From Slavery to Freedom: A History of Negro Americans, 3rd ed. (New York, 1967).

E. Franklin Frazier, The Negro in the United States, 2nd ed. (New York, 1957).

George M. Fredrickson, The Black Image in the White Mind: The Debate on Afro-American Character and Destiny, 1817–1914 (New York, 1971).

J. C. Furnas, Goodbye to Uncle Tom (New York, 1956).

Oscar Handlin, Race and Nationality in American Life (Boston, 1957).

Marvin Harris, Patterns of Race in the Americas (New York, 1964).

Robert V. Haynes (ed.), Blacks in White America Before 1865 (New York, 1972).

Melville J. Herskovits, The Myth of the Negro Past (New York, 1941).

Nathan I. Huggins, Martin Kilson, and Daniel M. Fox (eds.), Key Issues in the Afro-American Experience, 2 vols. (New York, 1971).

James Weldon Johnson and J. Rosamund Johnson (eds.), The Book of American Negro Spirituals (New York, 1925).

J. W. Johnson and J. R. Johnson (eds.), The Second Book of Negro Spirituals (New York, 1926). (Both first and second books reprinted in one vol., The Books of American Negro Spirituals [New York, 1956].)

J. Ralph Jones, "Portraits of Georgia Slaves" (interviews with ex-slaves), Tom Landess (ed.), Georgia Review (Spring, Summer, Fall, and Winter 1967, Spring and Summer 1968).

Winthrop D. Jordan, White Over Black: The Development of American Attitudes Toward the Negro, 1550–1812 (Chapel Hill, 1968).

Abraham Kardiner and Lionel Ovesey, The Mark of Oppression: A Psycho-Social Study of the American Negro (New York, 1951).

Bernard Katz (ed.), The Social Implications of Early Negro Music in the United States (New York, 1969).

William Loren Katz (gen. ed.), The American Negro: His History and Literature (New York, 1969). (141 vols. reprinted.)

Julius Lester (ed.), To Be a Slave (New York, 1968).

Leon Litwack, North of Slavery: The Negro in the Free States, 1790–1860 (Chicago, 1961).

Joseph Logsdon, "Diary of a Slave: Recollection and Prophecy," in William G.

Shade and Roy C. Herrenkohl (eds.), *Seven on Black: Reflections on the Negro Experience in America: Selected Essays* (Austin, Tex., 1970).

August Meier (ed.), *Studies in American Negro Life Series* (New York, 1968–).

August Meier and Elliott Rudwick (eds.), *The Making of Black America*: Vol. 1, *The Origins of Black Americans* (New York, 1969).

———, *From Plantation to Ghetto*, rev. ed. (New York, 1970).

Gunnar Myrdal *et al.*, *An American Dilemma: The Negro Problem and Modern Democracy*, 2 vols. (New York, London, 1944).

Charles H. Nichols, *Many Thousand Gone: The Ex-Slaves' Account of Their Bondage and Freedom* (Leiden, 1963).

Gilbert Osofsky (ed.), *Puttin' on Ole Massa* (three slave narratives) (New York, 1969).

Talcott Parsons and Kenneth B. Clark (eds.), *The Negro American* (New York, 1967).

Jane H. and William H. Pease (eds.), *Austin Steward: Twenty-Two Years a Slave and Forty Years a Freeman* (Reading, Mass., 1969).

Newton M. Puckett, *Folk Beliefs of the Southern Negro* (Chapel Hill, 1926).

A Report of the Ninth Newberry Library Conference on American Studies, "The Question of 'Sambo,'" *The Newberry Library Bulletin*, V (December 1958).

George P. Rawick (ed.), *The American Slave: A Composite Autobiography* (Westport, Conn., 1972). (18 vols. of reprinted W. P. S. Federal Writers' Project slave narratives and interviews with ex-slaves.)

———, *From Sundown to Sunup: The Making of the Black Community* (Westport, Conn., 1972).

Peter I. Rose (ed.), *Americans from Africa: Slavery and its Aftermath* (New York, 1970).

Marion L. Starkey, *Striving to Make it My Home: The Story of Americans from Africa* (New York, 1964).

Maxwell Whiteman (ed.), *Afro-American History Series*, 10 vols. (Wilmington, Del., 1970).

Robin W. Winks, *The Blacks in Canada: A History* (New Haven, 1971).

Robin W. Winks (gen. ed.), *Four Fugitive Slave Narratives* (Reading, Mass., 1969).

Carter Woodson, *The Mind of the Negro as Reflected in Letters Written during the Crisis, 1800–1860* (Washington, D. C., 1926).

Carter F. Woodson and Charles H. Wesley, *The Negro in Our History*, 10th ed. (Washington, 1962).

Norman R. Yetman, "The Background of the Slave Narrative Collection" (of the Federal Writers' Project), *American Quarterly*, XIX (Fall 1967).

Norman R. Yetman (ed.), *Life Under the "Peculiar Institution": Selections from the Slave Narrative Collection* (New York, 1970).

PATTERNS OF SLAVE RESISTANCE

Wendell G. Addington, "Slave Insurrections in Texas," *Journal of Negro History*, XXXV (October 1950).

Jervis Anderson, "Styron and His Black Critics," *Dissent*, XVI (March-April 1969).

Herbert Aptheker, *American Negro Slave Revolts* (New York, 1943).

———, *Nat Turner's Slave Rebellion* . . . (New York, 1966).

———, "Slave Guerilla Warfare," in *To Be Free: Studies in American Negro History* (New York, 1948).

Herbert Aptheker and William Styron, "Truth and Nat Turner: An Exchange," *Nation*, CCVI (April 22, 1968).

Raymond A. Bauer and Alice H. Bauer, "Day to Day Resistance to Slavery," *Journal of Negro History*, XXVII (October 1942).

Elwood L. Bridner, Jr., "The Fugitive Slaves of Maryland," *Maryland Historical Magazine*, 66 (Spring 1971).

Joseph C. Carroll, *Slave Insurrections in the United States, 1800–1865* (Boston, 1938).

William F. Cheek (ed.), *Black Resistance Before the Civil War* (Beverly Hills, Calif., 1970).

John Hendrik Clarke (ed.), *William Styron's Nat Turner: Ten Black Writers Respond* (Boston, 1968).

T. Wood Clarke, "Negro Plot, 1741," *New York History*, XXV (April 1944).

Thomas J. Davis, "The New York Slave Conspiracy of 1741 as Black Protest," *Journal of Negro History*, LVI (January 1971).

John W. Dobbs, "Crispus Attucks, one of America's First and Noblest Heroes," *Negro History Bulletin*, 34 (February 1971).

William S. Drewry, *Slave Insurrections in the United States* (Washington, 1900).

John B. Duff and Peter M. Mitchell (eds.), *The Nat Turner Rebellion: The Historical Event and the Modern Controversy* (New York, 1971).

Robert F. Durden, "William Styron and His Black Critics," *South Atlantic Quarterly*, LXVIII (Spring 1969).

George M. Frederickson and Christopher Lasch, "Resistance to Slavery," *Civil War History*, XIII (December 1967).

Larry Gara, *The Liberty Line: The Legend of the Underground Railroad* (Lexington, Ky., 1961).

Eugene Genovese, "The Nat Turner Case," *New York Review of Books*, XI (September 12, 1968).

Eugene D. Genovese, "Rebelliousness and Docility in the Negro Slave: A Critique of the Elkins Thesis," *Civil War History*, XIII (December 1967).

Richard Gilman, "Nat Turner Revisited," *New Republic*, CLVIII (April 27, 1968).

Lorenzo J. Greene, "Mutiny on the Slave Ships," *Phylon*, V (4th quarter 1944).

Seymour L. Gross and Eileen Bender, "History, Politics and Literature: The Myth of Nat Turner," *American Quarterly*, XXIII (October 1971).

Nicholas Halasz, *The Rattling Chains: Slave Unrest and Revolt in the Ante-Bellum South* (New York, 1966).

Thomas Wentworth Higginson, *Black Rebellion*, James M. McPherson (ed.) (New York, 1969).

Donald M. Jacobs, "David Walker: Boston Race Leader, 1825–1830," *Essex Institute Collections*, CVII (January 1971).

——, "William Lloyd Garrison's *Liberator* and Boston's Blacks, 1830–1865," *New England Quarterly*, XLIV (June 1971).

F. Roy Johnson, *The Nat Turner Slave Insurrection* (Murfreesboro, N. C., 1966).

Sidney Kaplan, "Black Mutiny on the Amistad (1840)," *Massachusetts Review*, (Summer 1969).

John Oliver Killens (ed.), *The Trial Record of Denmark Vesey* (Boston, 1970).

Marion D. deB. Kilson, "Towards Freedom: An Analysis of Slave Revolts in the United States," *Phylon*, XXV, No. 2 (1964).

Ann J. Lane (ed.), *The Debate Over Slavery: Stanley Elkins and His Critics* (Urbana, 1971).

John Lofton, *Insurrection in South Carolina: The Turbulent World of Denmark Vesey* (Yellow Spring, Ohio, 1964).

Katherin Lumpkin, " 'The General Plan was Freedom': A Negro Secret Order on the Underground Railway," *Phylon* (Spring 1967).

Mary Agnes Lewis, "Slavery and Personality: A Further Comment," *American Quarterly* (Spring 1967).

David B. McKibber, "Negro Slave Insurrections in Mississippi, 1800–1865," *Journal of Negro History*, XXXIV (January 1949).

Christopher Martin, *The Amistad Affair* (New York, 1970).

Clarence L. Mohr, "Samboization: A Case Study," *Research Studies* (June 1970).

Edwin A. Miles, "The Mississippi Slave Insurrection Scare of 1835," *Journal of Negro History*, XLII (January 1957).

Gerald W. Mullin, *Flight and Rebellion: Slave Resistance in Eighteenth-Century Virginia* (New York, 1972).

——, "Gabriel's Insurrection," in Peter I. Rose (ed.), *Americans from Africa*, Vol. II: *Old Memories, New Moods* (New York, 1970).

William A. Owens, *Slave Mutiny: The Revolt on the Schooner Amistad* (New York, 1953). (Retitled in paperback *Black Mutiny*.)

Orlando Patterson, "Slavery and Slave Revolts," *Social and Economic Studies*, Vol. 19, No. 3 (1970).

George Rawick, "The Historical Roots of Black Liberation," *Radical America*, II (July–August 1968).

Marion J. Russell, "American Slave Discontent in Records of the High Courts," *Journal of Negro History*, XXXI (October 1946).

Kenneth Scott, "The Slave Insurrection in New York in 1712," *New York Historical Society Quarterly*, XLV (January 1961).

Kenneth M. Stampp, "Rebels and Sambos: The Search for the Negro's Personality in Slavery," *Journal of Southern History*, XXXVII (August 1971).

Robert S. Starobin (ed.), *Denmark Vesey: The Slave Conspiracy of 1822* (Englewood Cliffs, N. J., 1970).

Sterling Stuckey, "Remembering Denmark Vesey," *Negro Digest*, XV (February 1966).

William Styron, *The Confessions of Nat Turner* (New York, 1966).

Ferenc M. Szasz, "The New York Slave Revolt of 1741: A Re-Examination," *New York History*, XLVIII (July 1967).

William Styron, C. Vann Woodward, R. W. B. Lewis interviewed in *The Yale Alumni Magazine* (November 1967).

R. H. Taylor, "Slave Conspiracies in North Carolina," *North Carolina Historical Review* (January 1928).

Earle E. Thorpe, "Chattel Slavery and Concentration Camps," *Negro History Bulletin*, XXV (May 1962).

Henry Irving Tragle (ed.), *The Southampton Slave Revolt of 1831* (Amherst, Mass., 1971).

Richard C. Wade, "The Vesey Plot: A Reconsideration," *Journal of Southern History*, XXX (May 1964).

William W. White, "The Texas Slave Insurrection of 1860," *Southwestern Historical Quarterly*, LII (January 1949).

Harvey Wish, "American Slave Insurrections before 1861," *Journal of Negro History*, XXII (July 1937).

J. Leitch Wright, Jr., "A Note on the First Seminole War as Seen by the Indians, Negroes, and Their British Advisers," *Journal of Southern History*, XXXIV (November 1968).

RACE RELATIONS

Jonathan L. Alpert, "The Origin of Slavery in the United States—the Maryland Precedent," *American Journal of Legal History*, XIV (July 1970).

Michael Banton, *Race Relations* (New York, 1967).

Richard R. Beeman, "Labor Forces and Race Relations: A Comparative View of the Colonization of Brazil and Virginia," *Political Science Quarterly*, LXXXVI (December 1971).

Eugene H. Berwanger, *The Frontier Against Slavery: Western Anti-Negro Prejudice and the Slavery Extension Controversy* (Urbana, 1967).

Lee Calligaro, "The Negro's Legal Status in Pre-Civil War New Jersey," *New Jersey History*, LXXXV.

Alfred A. Cave, "The Case of Calvin Colton: White Racism in Northern Antislavery Thought," *New York Historical Society Quarterly*, LIII (July 1969).

Daedalus, Color and Race (A Symposium) (Spring 1967).

Carl Degler, *Neither Black Nor White: Slavery and Race Relations in Brazil and the United States* (New York, 1971).

Carl N. Degler, "Slavery and the Genesis of American Race Prejudice," *Comparative Studies in Society and History*, II (October 1959).

Roger A. Fischer, "Racial Segregation in Ante-Bellum New Orleans," *American Historical Review*, LXXIV (February 1969).

James A. Fisher, "The Struggle for Negro Testimony in California, 1851–1863," *Southern California Quarterly*, LI (December 1969).

Eric Foner, *Free Soil, Free Labor, Free Men: The Ideology of the Republican Party Before the Civil War* (New York, 1970).

George M. Fredrickson, *Toward a Social Interpretation of the Development of American Racism in Huggins, Kilson, Fox*, Vol. 1 (New York, 1971).

Thomas F. Gossett, *Race, the History of an Idea in America* (Dallas, 1963).

Constance McLaughlin Green, *The Secret City; A History of Race Relations in the Nation's Capitol* (Princeton, N. J., 1967).

John S. Haller, Jr., "Concepts of Race Inferiority in Nineteenth-Century Anthropology," *Journal of the History of Medicine and Allied Sciences*, XXV (January 1970).

John S. Haller, "Civil War Anthropometry: The Making of a Racial Ideology," *Civil War History* (December 1970).

Oscar and Mary Handlin, "Origins of the Southern Labor System," *William and Mary Quarterly*, 3rd series, XIX (April 1962).

James Hugo Johnston, *Race Relations in Virginia and Miscegenation in the South, 1776–1860* (Amherst, Mass., 1970).

Winthrop D. Jordan, "American Chiaroscuro: The Status and Definition of Mulattoes in the British Colonies," *William and Mary Quarterly*, 3rd series, XIX (April 1962).

Winthrop D. Jordan, "Modern Tensions and the Origins of American Slavery," *Journal of Southern History*, XXVIII (February 1962).

Linda K. Kerber, "Abolitionists and Amalgamation: The New York City Race Riots of 1834," *New York History*, XLVIII (January 1967).

Eileen S. Kraditor, *Means and Ends in American Abolitionism . . . 1834–1850* (New York, 1950).

Donald G. Mathews, "The Abolitionists on Slavery: The Critique Behind the Social Movement," *Journal of Southern History*, XXXIII (May 1967).

James M. McPherson, "A Brief for Equality: The Abolitionist Reply to the Racist Myth, 1860–1865," in Martin Duberman (ed.), *The Anti-Slavery Vanguard* (Princeton, 1965).

Richard B. Morris, "The Measure of Bondage in the Slave States," *Mississippi Valley Historical Review* (September 1954).

Phillips Moulton, "John Woolman's Approach to Social Action—As Exemplified in Relation to Slavery," *Church History*, XXXV (December 1966).

Gary B. Nash, "Red, White and Black: The Origins of Racism in Colonial America," in Gary B. Nash and Richard Weiss (eds.), *The Great Fear: Race in the Mind of America* (New York, 1970).

Gilbert Osofsky (ed.), *The Burden of Race: A Documentary History of Negro-White Relations* (New York, 1967).

Rembert W. Patrick, *Race Relations in the South* (Tallahasse, Fla., 1958).

Lorman Ratner, *Powder Keg: Northern Opposition to the Anti-Slavery Movement, 1831–1840* (New York, 1968).

Leonard L. Richards, *"Gentlemen of Property and Standing": Anti-Abolition Mobs in Jacksonian America* (New York, 1970).

Louis Ruchames, "The Sources of Racial Thought in Colonial America," *Journal of Negro History*, LII (October 1967).

William R. Stanton, *The Leopard's Spots: Scientific Attitudes Toward Race in America, 1815–1859* (Chicago, 1960).

Ronald Takaki, "The Black Child-Savage in Ante-Bellum America," in Gary B. Nash and Richard Weiss (eds.), *The Heat Fear: Race in the Mind of America* (New York, 1970).

V. J. Voegeli, *Free but not Equal: The Midwest and the Negro During the Civil War* (Chicago, 1967).

Donald D. Wax, "The Image of the Negro in the *Maryland Gazette*, 1745–75," *Journalism Quarterly*, 46 (Spring 1969).

Mary W. Williams, "The Treatment of Negro Slaves in the Brazilian Empire: A Comparison with the United States," *Journal of Negro History*, XV (1930).

Forrest G. Wood, *Black Scare: The Racist Response to Emancipation and Reconstruction* (Berkeley, 1968).

SPECIAL STUDIES

Slavery

S. Sydney Bradford, "The Negro Ironworker in Ante-Bellum Virginia," *Journal Southern History*, XXV (May 1959).

Kathleen Bruce, "Slave Labor in the Virginia Iron Industry," *William and Mary Quarterly*, series 2, VII (January 1927).

Mina Davis Caulfield, "Slavery and the Origins of Black Culture," in Peter I. Rose (ed.), *Americans from Africa*, Vol. I (New York, 1970).

M. Ray Della, Jr., "The Problems of Negro Labor in the 1850's," *Maryland Historical Magazine*, 66 (Spring 1971).

Clement Eaton, "Slave-Hiring in the Upper South: A Step Toward Freedom," *Mississippi Valley Historical Review*, XLVI (March 1960).

Walter Fisher, "Physicians and Slavery in the Antebellum Southern Medical Journal," *Journal of History of Medicine* (January 1968).

Edward A. Freeman, "Negro Baptist History," *Baptist History and Heritage*, 4 (July 1969).

Romeo B. Garrett, "African Survivals in American Culture," *Journal of Negro History*, LI (October 1966).

Eugene D. Genovese, "American Slaves and Their History," *New York Review of Books* (December 3, 1970).

———, "The Legacy of Slavery and the Roots of Black Nationalism," Commentary by Aptheker and C. Vann Woodward, *Studies on the Left*, 6 (November-December 1966).

———, "Materialism and Idealism in the History of Negro Slavery in the Americas," *Journal of Social History*, 1 (Summer 1968).

Lyle Glazier, "The Uncle Remus Stories: Two Portraits of American Negroes," *Hacettepe Bulletin of Social Sciences and Humanities*, 1 (June 1969).

Lorenzo J. Greene, *The Negro in Colonial New England, 1620–1776* (New York, 1942).

Harold B. Hancock (ed.), "William Yates's Letter of 1837: Slavery and Colored People in Delaware," *Delaware History*, XIV (April 1971).

Chadmich Hansen, "Jenny's Tow: Negro Shaking Dances in America," *American Quarterly*, XIX (Fall 1967).

Vincent Harding, "Religion and Resistance Among Antebellum Negroes, 1800–1860," in August Meier and Elliott Rudwick (eds.), *The Making of Black America*, 2 vols. (New York, 1969), Vol. I.

G. B. Johnson, *Folk Culture on St. Helena Island, South Carolina* (Chapel Hill, 1930).

G. B. Johnson, A *Social History of the Sea Islands* (Chapel Hill, 1930).

Leonard Kriegel, "Uncle Tom and Tiny Tim: Some Reflections on the Cripple as Negro," *American Scholar*, 38 (Summer 1969).

Lawrence W. Levine, "Slave Songs and Slave Consciousness: An Exploration in Neglected Sources," in Tamara Hareven (ed.), *Anonymous Americans* (Englewood Cliffs, N. J., 1971).

Jack M. Moore, "Images of the Negro in Early American Short Fiction," *Mississippi Quarterly*, XXII (Winter 1968–69).

John H. Moore, "Simon Gray, Riverman: A Slave Who was Almost Free," *Mississippi Valley Historical Review*, XLIX (December 1962).

LeRoy Moore, Jr., "The Spiritual: Soul of Black Religion," *American Quarterly*, XXIII (December 1971), also *Church History*, 40 (March 1971).

William Dostite Postell, *The Health of Slaves on Southern Plantations* (Baton Rouge, La., 1951).

Walter Rodney, "Upper Guinea and the Significance of the Origins of Africans Enslaved in the New World," *Journal of Negro History*, LIV (October 1969).

Lewight Sikes, "Medical Care for Slaves. A Review of the Welfare State," *Georgia Historical Quarterly*, LII (December 1968).

M. Eugene Sirmans, "The Legal Status of the Slave in South Carolina, 1670–1740," *Journal of Southern History*, XXVIII (November 1962).

Kenneth Stampp, "The Daily Life of the Southern Slave," in Nathan I. Huggins, Martin Kilson, and Daniel M. Fox (eds.), *Key Issues in the Afro-American Experience*, 2 vols. (New York, 1971), Vol. I.

Robert Starobin, "Disciplining Industrial Slaves in the Old South," *Journal of Negro History*, LIII (April 1968).

———, *Industrial Slavery in the Old South* (New York, 1970).

Sterling Stuckey, "Through the Prism of Folklore: The Black Ethos in Slavery," *Massachusetts Review*, IX (Summer 1968).

William C. Suttles, Jr., "African Religious Survivals as Factors in American Slave Revolts," *Journal of Negro History*, LVI (April 1971).

Robert Farris Thompson, "African Influence on the Art of the United States," in Armstead L. Robinson *et al.* (ed.), *Black Studies in the University* (New Haven, 1969).

Howard Thurman, *Deep River: Reflections on the Religious Insight of Certain of the Negro Spirituals*, rev. ed. (New York, 1955).

William Toll, "The Crisis of Freedom: Toward an Interpretation of Negro Life," *Journal of American Studies*, 3 (December 1969).

Lorenzo D. Turner, "African Survivals in the New World with Special Emphasis on the Arts," in John A. Davis, *Africa Seen by American Negro Scholars* (New York, 1963).

Mary A. Twining, "An Anthropological Look at Afro-American Folk Narrative," *CLA Journal* (September 1970).

David O. Whitten, "Slave Buying in 1835: Virginia as Revealed by Letters of a Louisiana Negro Sugar Planter," *Louisiana History*, XI (Summer 1970).

Bell I. Wiley, *Southern Negroes, 1861–1865* (New Haven, 1938).

Free Negroes, North and South

Richard H. Abbott, "Massachusetts and the Recruitment of Southern Negroes, 1863–1865," *Civil War History*, IV (September 1963).

Warren B. Armstrong, "Union Chaplains and the Education of the Freedmen," *Journal of Negro History*, LII (April 1967).

George R. Bentley, *A History of the Freedmen's Bureau* (Philadelphia, 1955).

Mary F. Berry, "Negro Troops in Blue and Gray: The Louisiana Native Guards, 1861–1863," *Louisiana History*, VIII (Spring 1967).

John W. Blassingame, "The Recruitment of Colored Troops in Kentucky, Maryland, and Missouri, 1863–1865," *Historian*, XXIX (August 1967).

Letitia Woods Brown, *Free Negroes in the District of Columbia, 1790–1846* (New York, 1972).

J. W. Cook, "Freedom in the Thoughts of Frederick Douglass, 1845–1860," *Negro History Bulletin*, 32 (February 1969).

Alfred E. Cowdrey, "Slave into Soldier," *History Today* (October 1970).

Dudley T. Cornish, *The Sable Arm: Negro Troops in the Union Army, 1861–1865* (New York, 1956).

Edwin A. Davis, "William Johnson: Free Negro Citizen of Ante-Bellum Mississippi," *Journal of Mississippi History*, XV (1953).

Edwin A. Davis and William R. Hogan, *The Barber of Natchez* (Baton Rouge, La., 1954).

C. Ashley Ellefson, "Free Jupiter and the Rest of the World: The Problems of a Free Negro in Colonial Maryland," *Maryland Historical Magazine*, 66 (Spring 1971).

J. Merton England, "The Free Negro in Ante-Bellum Tennessee," *Journal of Southern History*, IX (February 1943).

Horace Fitchett, "The Origin and Growth of the Free Negro Population of Charleston, South Carolina," *Journal of Negro History*, XXVI (October 1941).

Ralph B. Flanders, "The Free Negro in Ante-Bellum Georgia," *North Carolina Historical Review*, IX (July 1932).

Philip S. Foner, "The First Negro Meeting in Maryland," *Maryland Historical Magazine*, 66 (Spring 1971).

———, *Frederick Douglass* (New York, 1964).

Jack D. Forbes, "Black Pioneers: The Spanish-Speaking Afro-Americans of the Southwest," *Phylon* (Fall 1966).

John Hope Franklin, *The Free Negro in North Carolina, 1790–1860* (Chapel Hill, 1943).

———, "James Boon, Free Negro Artisan," *Journal of Negro History*, XXX (April 1945).

E. Franklin Frazier, *The Free Negro Family* (Nashville, 1932).

Russell Garvin, "The Free Negro in Florida Before the Civil War," *Florida Historical Quarterly*, XLVI (July 1967).

Carl E. Hatch, "Negro Migration and New Jersey—1863," *New Jersey History*, LXXXVII (Winter 1969).

William R. Hogan and Edwin A. Davis (eds.), *William Johnson's Natchez* (Baton Rouge, La., 1951).

James C. Jackson, "The Religious Education of the Negro in South Carolina Prior to 1850," *Historical Magazine of the Protestant Episcopal Church* (March 1967).

Luther Porter Jackson, *Free Negro Labor and Property Holding in Virginia, 1830–1860* (New York, 1942).

Partrena L. James, "Reconstruction in the Chickasaw Nation: The Freedmen Problem," *Chronicles of Oklahoma*, LXV (Spring 1967).

Harold D. Langley, "The Negro in the Navy and Merchant Service 1789–1860," *Journal of Negro History*, LII (October 1967).

Hollis R. Lynch, "Pan-Negro Nationalism in the New World Before 1862," *Boston University Papers on Africa*, Vol. II, *African History*, Jeffrey Butler (ed.) (Boston, 1966).

William McFeely, *Yankee Stepfather: General O. O. Howard and the Freedmen's Bureau* (New Haven, 1968).

Tom McLaughlin, "Sectional Responses of Free Negroes to the Idea of Colonization," *Washington State University Research Studies* (September 1966).

Richard K. MacMaster, "Henry Highland Garnet and the African Civilization Society," *Journal of Presbyterian History*, 48 (Summer 1970).

James M. McPherson, *The Negro's Civil War; How American Negroes Felt and Acted During the War for the Union* (New York, 1965).

———, *The Struggle for Equality; Abolitionists and the Negro in the Civil War and Reconstruction* (Princeton, 1964).

August Meier, "Negroes in the First and Second Reconstructions of the South," *Civil War History*, XIII (June 1967).

John L. Meyers, "American Antislavery Society Agents and the Free Negro, 1833–1838," *Journal of Negro History*, LII (July 1967).

Alice D. Nelson, "People of Color in Louisiana," *Journal of Negro History*, I (October 1916); and II (January 1917).

Daniel Perlman, "Organizations of the Free Negro in New York City, 1800–1860," *Journal of Negro History*, LVI (July 1971).

Richard W. Pih, "Negro Self-Improvement Efforts in Ante-Bellum Cincinnati, 1836–1850," *Ohio History*, 78 (Summer 1969).

William A. Poe, "Lott Cary [of American Colonization Society]: Man of Purchased Freedom," *Church History*, 39 (March 1970).

Kenneth W. Porter, "Florida Slaves and Free Negroes in the Seminole War, 1835–1842," *Journal of Negro History*, XXVIII (October 1943).

———, "Negroes and the Seminole War, 1835–1842," *Journal of Southern History*, XXX (November 1964).

C. Daniel Potts and Annette Potts, "The Negro and the Australian Gold Rushes, 1852–1857," *Pacific Historical Review*, XXXVII (November 1968).

Benjamin Quarles, *Black Abolitionists* (New York, 1969).
———, *Frederick Douglass* (Washington, D. C., 1948).
———, *Lincoln and the Negro* (New York, 1962).
———, *The Negro in the American Revolution* (Williamsburg, Va., 1961).
———, *The Negro in the Civil War* (Boston, 1953).
Joe M. Richardson, "Christian Abolitionism: The American Missionary Association and the Florida Negro," *Journal of Negro Education*, XXXX (Winter 1971).
Henry S. Robinson, "Some Aspects of the Free Negro Population of Washington, D. C., 1800–1862," *Maryland Historical Magazine*, 64 (Spring 1969).
Willie Lee Rose, *Rehearsal for Reconstruction: The Port Royal Experiment* (Indianapolis, 1964).
Judith P. Ruchkin, "The Abolition of 'Colored Schools' in Rochester, New York, 1832–1856," *New York History*, LI (July 1970).
John H. Russell, *The Free Negro in Virginia 1617–1865* (Baltimore, 1913).
Harold Schoen, "The Free Negro in the Republic of Texas," *Southwestern Historical Quarterly*, XXXIX (April 1936); XL (July 1936); (October 1936); (January 1937); (April 1937); XLI (July 1937).
Terry L. Seip, "Slaves and Free Negroes in Alexandria, 1850–1860," *Louisiana History*, X (Spring 1969).
James B. Sellers, "Free Negroes of Tuscaloosa County Before the Thirteenth Amendment," *Alabama Review*, XXIII (April 1970).
Donald J. Senese, "The Free Negro and the South Carolina Courts, 1790–1860," *South Carolina Historical Magazine*, 68 (July 1967).
Roger W. Shugg, "Negro Voting in the Ante-Bellum South," *Journal of Negro History*, XXI (October 1936).
Robert M. Spector, "The Quack Walker Cases (1781–83): The Abolition of Slavery and Negro Citizenship in Early Massachusetts," *Journal of Negro History* (January 1968).
Annie L. W. Stahl, "The Free Negro in Ante-Bellum Louisiana," *Louisiana Historical Quarterly*, XXV (April 1942).
John L. Stanley, "Majority Tyranny in Tocqueville: America: The Failure of Negro Suffrage in 1846," *Political Science Quarterly*, LXXXIV (September 1969).
Philip J. Staudenraus, *The African Colonization Movement* (New York, 1961).
Aaron Stopak, "The Maryland State Colonization Society: Independent State Action in the Colonization Movement," *Maryland Historical Magazine*, 63 (September 1968).
Charles S. Sydnor, "The Free Negro in Mississippi before the Civil War," *American Historical Review*, XXXII (July 1927).
David Y. Thomas, "The Free Negro in Florida before 1965," *South Atlantic Quarterly*, X (October 1911).
Emma L. Thornbrough, *The Negro in Indiana: A Study of a Minority* (Indianapolis, 1957).
Miriam L. Ustey, "Charles Lenox Remond, Garrison's Ebony Echo: World

Anti-Slavery Convention, 1840," *Essex Institute History Colloquium* (April 1970).

Arthur O. White, "The Black Movement Against Jim Crow Education in Lockport, New York, 1835–1876," *New York History*, L (July 1969).

James E. Winston, "The Free Negro in New Orleans, 1803–1861," *Louisiana Historical Quarterly*, XXI (October 1938).

Carter G. Woodson, *Free Negro Heads of Families in the United States in 1830* (Washington, D. C., 1925).

———, *Free Negro Owners of Slaves in the United States in 1830* (Washington, D. C., 1925; reprinted, 1968).

James M. Wright, *The Free Negro in Maryland, 1634–1860* (New York, 1921; reprinted New York, 1969).

Wilbur Zelinsky, "The Population Geography of the Free Negro in Ante-Bellum America," *Population Studies*, III (March 1950).

THE OLD SOUTH

GENERAL STUDIES

David Bertelson, *The Lazy South* (New York, 1967).

Carl Bridenbaugh, *Myths and Realities: Societies of the Colonial South* (Baton Rouge, La., 1952).

Jesse T. Carpenter, *The South as a Conscious Minority, 1789–1861; A Study in Political Thought* (New York, 1930).

Wilbur J. Cash, *The Mind of the South* (New York, 1941).

William E. Dodd, *The Cotton Kingdom* (New Haven, 1919).

Clement Eaton, *The Growth of Southern Civilization, 1790–1860* (New York, 1961).

———, *A History of the Old South*, 2nd ed. rev. (New York, 1966).

John Hope Franklin, *The Militant South, 1800–1861* (Cambridge, Mass., 1956).

Lewis C. Gray, *History of Agriculture in the Southern United States in 1860*, 2 vols. (Washington, D. C., 1933).

William Sumner Jenkins, *Pro-Slavery Thought in the Old South* (Chapel Hill, 1935). (Reprinted Gloucester, Mass., 1960.)

Fabian Linden, "Economic Democracy in the Slave South: An Appraisal of Some Recent Views," *The Journal of Negro History*, XXXI (April 1946).

Arthur Young Lloyd, *The Slavery Controversy, 1831–1860* (Chapel Hill, 1939).

Frank L. Owsley, *Plain Folk of the Old South* (Baton Rouge, La., 1949).

David M. Potter, *The South and the Sectional Conflict* (Baton Rouge, La., 1968).

Francis B. Simkins, *A History of the South*, 2nd ed. rev. (New York, 1953).

Wendell H. Stephenson, *A Basic History of the Old South* (Princeton, 1959).

———, *The South Lives in History* (Baton Rouge, La., 1955).

C. Vann Woodward, *The Burden of Southern History* (Baton Rouge, La., 1960).

THE SLAVE TRADE

Frederic Bancroft, *Slave-Trading in the Old South* (Baltimore, 1931).

Thomas D. Clark, "The Slave Trade between Kentucky and the Cotton Kingdom," *Mississippi Valley Historical Review*, XXI (December 1934).

Reginald Coupland, *The British Anti-Slavery Movement* (London, England, 1933).

———, *East Africa and its Invaders* . . . (Oxford, England, 1956).

Phillip D. Curtin, "Epidemiology and the Slave Trade," *Political Science Quarterly*, LXXXIII (June 1968).

Basil Davidson, *Black Mother: The Years of the African Slave Trade* (Boston, 1961).

Kenneth G. Davies, *The Royal African Company* (London, England, 1957).

Robert R. Davis, Jr. (ed.), "Buchanian Espionage: A Report on Illegal Slave Trading in the South in 1859," *Journal of Southern History* XXXVII (May 1971).

Elizabeth Donnan (ed.), *Documents Illustrative of the History of the Slave Trade to America*, 4 vols. (Washington, D. C., 1930–35).

W. E. B. DuBois, *The Suppression of the African Slave Trade to the United States of America, 1638–1870* (New York, 1896).

Peter Duignan and C. Clendenen, *The United States and the African Slave Trade, 1619–1862* (Stanford, 1963).

J. D. Fage, "Slavery and the Slave Trade in the Context of West African History," *Journal of African History*, 10 (1969).

James Paisley Hendrix, Jr., "The Effort to Reopen the African Slave Trade in Louisiana," *Louisiana History*, X (Spring 1969).

Melville J. Herskovitz, *Dahomey: An Ancient West African Kingdom* (New York, 1938).

James High, "The African Gentleman: A Chapter in the Slave Trade," *Journal of Negro History*, XLIV (October 1959).

Warren S. Howard, *American Slavers and the Federal Law, 1837–1862* (Berkeley, 1963).

James F. King, "The Evolution of the Free Slave Trade Principle in Spanish Colonial Administration," *Hispanic American Historical Review* (February 1942).

Kenneth F. Kipte, "The Case Against a Nineteenth-Century Cuba-Florida Slave Trade," *Florida Historical Quarterly*, XLIX (April 1971).

Herbert S. Klein, "North American Competition and the Characteristics of the African Slave Trade to Cuba, 1790 to 1794," *William and Mary Quarterly*, 3rd series, XXVIII (January 1971).

William T. Laprade, "The Domestic Slave Trade in the District of Columbia," *Journal of Negro History*, XI (January 1926).

Averil Mackenzie-Grieve, *The Last Years of the English Slave Trade: Liverpool, 1750–1807* (London, England, 1941).

Daniel Mannix, *Black Cargoes: A History of the Atlantic Slave Trade, 1619–1862* (Stanford, 1963).

William L. Miller, "A Note on the Importance of the Interstate Slave Trade of the Ante-Bellum South," *Journal of Political Economy*, LXXIII (April 1965).

Karl Polanyi, *Dahomey and the Slave Trade* . . . (Seattle, 1966).

James Pope-Hennessey, *Sins of the Fathers: A Study of the Atlantic Slave Traders, 1441–1807* (New York, 1968).

Simon Rottenberg, "The Business of Slave Trading," *South Atlantic Quarterly*, LXVI (Summer 1967).

R. B. Sheriden, "Commercial and Financial Organization of the British Slave Trade, 1750–1807," *Economic History Revue*, 2nd series, XV (December 1958).

Francis T. Stafford, "Illegal Importations Enforcement of the Slave Trade Laws Along the Florida Coast, 1810–1828," *Florida Historical Quarterly* (October 1967).

Wendell H. Stephenson, *Isaac Franklin, Slave Trader and Planter of the Old South* (Baton Rouge, La., 1938).

Ronald T. Takaki, *A Pro-Slavery Crusade: The Agitation to Reopen the African Slave Trade* (New York, 1971).

W. E. F. Ward, *The Royal Navy and the Slavers: The Suppression of the Atlantic Slave Trade* (New York, 1969).

Howard S. Warren, *American Slavers and the Federal Law, 1837–1862* (Berkeley, 1963).

E. Richmond Ware, "Health Hazards of the West African Trader 1840–1870," *American Neptune*, XXVII (April 1967).

Darold D. Wax, "A Philadelphia Surgeon on a Slaving Voyage to Africa [1749–51]," *Pennsylvania Magazine of History and Biography* (October 1968).

———, "Quaker Merchants and the Slave Trade in Colonial Pennsylvania," *Pennsylvania Magazine of History*, LXXXVI (April 1962).

Charles H. Westey, "Manifests of Slave Shipments Along the Waterways, 1808–1864," *Journal of Negro History*, XXVII (April 1942).

H. A. Wyndham, *The Atlantic and Slavery* (London, England, 1935).

SPECIAL STUDIES

Chronological

Wesley Frank Craven, *The Southern Colonies in the Seventeenth Century, 1607–1689* (Baton Rouge, La., 1949).

John R. Alden, *The South in the Revolution, 1763–1789* (Baton Rouge, La., 1957).

Thomas P. Abernethy, *The South in the New Nation, 1789–1819* (Baton Rouge, La., 1961).

Glover B. Moore, *The Missouri Controversy, 1819–1821* (Lexington, Ky., 1953).

William W. Freehling, *Prelude to Civil War: The Nullification Controversy in South Carolina, 1816–1836* (New York, 1966).

Charles S. Sydnor, *The Development of Southern Sectionalism, 1819–1848* (Baton Rouge, La., 1948).

Avery D. Craven, *The Growth of Southern Nationalism, 1848–1861* (Baton Rouge, La., 1953).

Steven A. Channing, *Crisis of Fear: Secession in South Carolina* (New York, 1970).

Emory M. Thomas, *The Confederacy as a Revolutionary Experience* (Englewood Cliffs, N. J., 1971).

The Southern Economy

Agricultural History, XLIV (January 1970) issue devoted to Ante-Bellum Cotton Economy and Slavery.

Hugh G. J. Aitken (ed.), *Did Slavery Pay? Readings in the Economies of Black Slavery in the United States* (Boston, 1971).

Kathleen Bruce, *Virginia Iron Manufacturer in the Slave Era* (New York, 1931).

Stuart Bruchey (ed.), *Cotton and the Growth of the American Economy, 1790–1860* (New York, 1967).

Alfred H. Conrad, "Econometrics and Southern History," *Explorations in Entrepreneurial History,* 2nd series, VI (Fall 1968). (Comments by Fogel, Bruchey, and Chandler.)

A. Conrad, D. Dowd, S. Engerman, E. Ginzberg, C. Icelso, John R. Meyer, H. N. Scheiber and R. Sutch, "Slavery as an Obstacle to Economic Growth in the United States. A Panel Discussion," *Journal of Economic History,* XXVII (December 1967).

Alfred H. Conrad and John R. Meyer, *The Economics of Slavery* (Chicago, 1964).

Charles B. Dew, *Ironmaker to the Confederacy: Joseph R. Anderson and the Tredegar Iron Works* (New Haven, 1966).

Douglas F. Dowd, "A Comparative Analysis of Economic Development in the American South and West," *Journal of Economic History,* XVII (December 1956).

Stanley L. Engerman, "The Effects of Slavery upon the Southern Economy. A Review of the Recent Debate," *Explorations in Entrepreneurial History,* 2nd series, 4 (Winter 1967).

Marvin Fischbaum and Julius Rubin, "Slavery and the Economic Development of the American South," *Explorations in Entrepreneurial History,* 6 (Fall 1968).

Robert W. Fogel and Stanley L. Engerman (eds.), *The Reinterpretation of American Economic History* (New York, 1968). Part VII, "The Economics of Slavery."

Robert W. Fogel and Stanley L. Engerman, "The Relative Efficiency of Slavery. A Comparison of Northern and Southern Agriculture in 1860," *Explorations in Economic History,* 8 (Spring 1971).

James D. Foust and Dale E. Swan, "Productivity and Profitability of Antebellum Slave Labor: A Micro-Approach," *Agricultural History,* XLIV (January 1970).

Charles D. Hart, "The Natural Limits of Slavery Expansion: The Mexican Territories a Test Case," *Mid-America,* 52 (April 1970).

———, "The Natural Limits of Slavery Expansion: Kansas-Nebraska, 1854," *Kansas Historical Quarterly,* XXXIV (Spring 1968).

Sam Hilliard, "Hog Meat and Cornpone: Food Habits in the Ante-Bellum

South," *Proceedings of the American Philosophical Society*, 113 (February 20, 1969).

———, "Pork in the Ante-Bellum South: The Geography of Self-Sufficiency," *Annals of the Association of American Geographers*, 59 (September 1969).

Wm. K. Hutchinson and S. H. Williamson, "The Self-Sufficiency of the Ante-Bellum South: Estimates of the Food Supply," *Journal of Economic History*, XXXI (September 1971).

Aubrey C. Land, *The Dulanys of Maryland* (Baltimore, 1955).

Ernest M. Lander, Jr., "Slave Labor in South Carolina Cotton Mills," *Journal of Negro History*, XXXVIII (April 1953).

Arthur Pierce Middleton, *Tobacco Coast: A Maritime History of Chesapeake Bay in the Colonial Era* (Newport News, Va., 1953).

Warren L. Miller, "Slavery and the Population of the South," *Southern Economic Journal*, XXVIII (July 1961).

Louis Morton, *Robert Carter of Nomini Hall: A Virginia Planter of the Eighteenth Century* (Williamsburg, Va., 1941).

John H. Moore, *Agriculture in Ante-Bellum Mississippi* (New York, 1958).

William N. Parker, "Slavery and Southern Economic Development: An Hypothesis and some Evidence," *Agricultural History*, XLIV (January 1970).

William N. Parker (ed.), *The Structure of the Cotton Economy of the Antebellum South* (Washington, D. C., 1970).

U. B. Phillips, *The Slave Economy of the Old South: Selected Essays in Economic and Social History*, Eugene Genovese (ed.) (Baton Rouge, La., 1968).

Norris W. Preyer, "The Historian, the Slave, and the Ante-Bellum Textile Industry," *Journal of Negro History*, XLVI (April 1961).

Joseph Clarke Robert, *The Tobacco Kingdom: Plantation, Market, and Factory in Virginia and North Carolina, 1800–1860* (Durham, N. C., 1938).

Morton Rothstein, "The Antebellum South as a Dual Economy: A Tentative Hypothesis," *Agricultural History*, XLI (October 1967).

William K. Scarborough, *The Overseer: Plantation Management in the Old South* (Baton Rouge, La., 1966).

Joseph C. Sitterson, *Sugar Country: The Cane Sugar Industry in the South, 1753–1950* (Lexington, Ky., 1953).

Robert S. Starobin, "The Economics of Industrial Slavery in the Old South," *Business History Review*, XLIV (Summer 1970).

———, *Industrial Slavery in the Old South* (New York, 1970).

Richard Stutch, "The Profitability of Ante-Bellum Slavery—Revisited," *Southern Economic Journal* (April, 1965).

Edgar T. Thompson, "The Natural History of Agricultural Labor in the South," in David K. Jackson (ed.), *American Studies in Honor of William Kenneth Boyd* (Durham, N. C., 1940).

Harold D. Woodman, "The Profitability of Slavery: A Historical Perennial," *Journal of Southern History*, XXIX (August 1963).

Harold D. Woodman, *Slavery and the Southern Economy* (New York, 1966).

Yasukichi Yasuba, "The Profitability and Viability of Plantation Slavery in the United States," *The Economic Studies Quarterly*, 12 (September 1961).

Slavery and Ideology

Kenneth M. Bailor, "John Taylor of Caroline: Continuity, Change, and Discontinuity in Virginia's Sentiments toward Slavery," *Virginia Magazine of History and Biography* (July 1967).

Leland J. Bellot, "Evangelicals and the Defense of Slavery in Britain's Old Colonial Empire," *Journal of Southern History*, XXXVII (February 1971).

Paul F. Boller, Jr., "Washington, The Quakers and Slavery," *Journal of Negro History*, 46 (January 1961).

Guy A. Cardwell, "Jefferson Renounced: Natural Rights in the South," *Yale Review*, LVIII (March 1969).

Jack J. Cardoso, "Southern Reaction to *The Impending Crisis*," *Civil War History*, XVI (March 1970).

William Cohen, "Thomas Jefferson and the Problem of Slavery," *Journal of American History*, LVI (December 1969).

W. Harrison Daniel, "Virginia Baptists and the Negro in the Antebellum Era," *Journal of Negro History*, LVI (January 1971).

David Brion Davis, *The Slave Power Conspiracy and the Paranoid Style* (Baton Rouge, La., 1969).

David Brion Davis, *Was Thomas Jefferson an Authentic Enemy of Slavery?* (Oxford, England, 1970).

Donald J. D'Ella, "Dr. Benjamin Rush and the Negro," *Journal of the History of Ideas* (July–September 1969).

David Donald, "The Proslavery Argument Reconsidered," *Journal of Southern History*, XXXVII (February 1971).

John L. Eighmy, "The Baptists and Slavery. An Examination of the Origins and Benefits of Segregation," *Social Science Quarterly* (December 1968).

Gordon E. Finnie, "The Antislavery Movement in the Upper South Before 1840," *Journal of Southern History*, XXXV (August 1969).

William W. Freehling, "The Founding Fathers and Slavery," *American Review*, 77 (February 1972).

Eugene D. Genovese, "The Logical Outcome of the Slaveholders' Philosophy . . . The Social Thought of George Fitzhugh," in Genovese, *The World the Slaveholders' Made* (New York, 1969).

John C. Greene, "The American Debate on the Negro's Place in Nature, 1780–1815," *Journal of the History of Ideas*, XV (June 1954).

James D. Guillory, "The Pro-Slavery Arguments of Dr. Samuel A. Cartwright," *Louisiana History*, IX (Summer 1968).

David C. Harell, Jr., "Sin and Sectionalism: A Study of Morality in the Nineteenth-Century South," *Mississippi Quarterly*, XIX (Fall 1966).

Don B. Kates, Jr., "Abolition, Deportation, Integration: Attitudes Toward Slavery in the Early Republic," *Journal of Negro History*, LIII (January 1968).

David S. Lovejoy, "Samuel Hopkins, Religion, Slavery, and the Revolution," *New England Quarterly*, XL (June 1967).

Dennis L. Lythgoe, "Negro Slavery and Mormon Doctrine," *Western Humanities Review*, XXI (Autumn 1967).

Edmund S. Morgan, "Slavery and Freedom: The American Paradox," *Journal of American History*, LIX (June 1972).

Howard A. Ohline, "Republicanism and Slavery: Origins of the Three-Fifths Clause in the United States Constitution," *William and Mary Quarterly*, 28 (October 1971).

Ulrich B. Philips, "The Central Theme of Southern History," *American Historical Review*, XXXIV (October 1928).

Valerie Quinney, "Decisions on Slavery . . . in the Early French Revolution," *Journal of Negro History*, LV (April 1970).

Tommy W. Rogers, "Dr. Frederick A. Ross and the Presbyterian Defense of Slavery," *Journal of Presbyterian History*, 45 (June 1967).

Charles Grier Sellers, Jr., "The Travail of Slavery," from Sellers (ed.), *The Southerner as American* (Chapel Hill, 1960).

Lynda Worley Skelton, "The States Rights Movement in Georgia, 1825–1850," *Georgia Historical Quarterly*, 6 (December 1966).

Douglas C. Stange, " 'A Compassionate Mother to Her Poor Negro Slaves': The Lutheran Church and Negro Slavery in Early America," *Phylon* (Fall 1968).

————, "Our Duty to Preach the Gospel to Negroes: Southern Lutherans and American Slavery," *Concordia Historical Institute Quarterly* XLII (November 1969).

Gaston H. Wamble, "Negroes and Missouri Protestant Churches Before and After the Civil War," *Missouri Historical Review*, LXI (April 1967).

Henry Warnoch, "Southern Methodists, the Negro, and Unification: The First Phase," *Journal of Negro History*, LII (October 1967).

Harvey Wish, *George Fitzhugh: Propagandist of the Old South* (Baton Rouge, La., 1943).

C. Vann Woodward, "George Fitzhugh, Sui Generis," introduction to Woodward (ed.), Fitzhugh's *Cannibals All!*

Miscellaneous

Florence R. Beatty-Brown, "Legal Status of Arkansas Negroes Before Emancipation," *Arkansas Historical Quarterly*, XXVIII (Spring 1969).

Joseph C. Burke, "The Proslavery Argument and the First Congress," *Duquesne Review*, XIV (1969).

Penelope Campbell, "Some Notes on Frederick County's Participation in the Maryland Colonization Scheme," *Maryland Historical Magazine*, 66 (Spring 1971).

Stanley W. Campbell, *The Slave Catchers: Enforcement of the Fugitive Slave Law, 1850–1860* (Chapel Hill, 1970).

Evsy D. Domar, "The Causes of Slavery or Serfdom: A Hypothesis," *Journal of Economic History*, XXX (March 1970).

Walter Ehrlich, "Was the Dred Scott Case Valid?" *Journal of American History*, LV, No. 2 (September 1968).

Larry Gara, "Slavery and the Slave Power: A Crucial Distinction," *Civil War History*, XV (March 1969).

E. D. Genovese, "A Georgia Slaveholder [1859] Looks at Africa," *Georgia Historical Quarterly* (June 1967).

Adele Hast, "The Legal Status of the Negro in Virginia, 1705–1765," *Journal of Negro History*, LIV (July 1969).

Vincent C. Hopkins, *Dred Scott's Case* (New York, 1951).

Bertram W. Korn, "Jews and Negro Slavery in the Old South, 1789–1865," *Publication of the Jewish Historical Society*, L (March 1961).

Harold D. Moser, "Reaction in North Carolina to the Emancipation Proclamation," *North Carolina Historical Review*, XLIV (January 1967).

A. E. Keir Nash, "A More Equitable Past? Southern Supreme Courts and the Protection of the Antebellum Negro," *North Carolina Law Review*, XLVIII (February 1970).

———, "Fairness and Formalism in the Trials of Blacks in the State Supreme Courts of the Old South," *Virginia Law Review*, LVI (February 1970.)

———, "The Texas Supreme Court and Trial Rights of Blacks, 1845–1860," *Journal of American History*, LVIII (December 1971).

Jane H. Pease, "A Note on Patterns of Conspicuous Consumption Among Seaboard Planters, 1820–1860," *Journal of Southern History*, XXXV (August 1969).

Walter F. Peterson, "Slavery in the 1850's: The Recollections of an Alabama Unionist [Wade Hampton Richardson]," *Alabama Historical Quarterly* (Fall–Winter 1968).

Arthur G. Pettit, "Mark Twain, Unreconstructed Southerner, and His View of the Negro, 1835–1860," *Rocky Mountain Social Science Journal*, VII (April 1970).

Tommy W. Rogers, "D. R. Hundley: A Multi-Class Thesis of Social Stratification in the Ante-Bellum South," *Mississippi Quarterly*, XXIII (Spring 1970).

Donald M. Roper, "In Quest of Judicial Objectivity: the Marshall Court and the Legitimation of Slavery," *Stanford Law Review*, XXI (February 1969).

Sudie Duncan Sides, "Southern Women and Slavery," *History Today*, XX (January and February 1970).

Albert F. Simpson, "The Political Significance of Slave Representation, 1787–1821," *Journal of Southern History*, VII (August 1941).

Patrick Sowle, "The Abolition of Slavery [in Georgia]," *Georgia Historical Quarterly*, LII (September 1968).

John C. Staley III, "The Responsibilities and Liabilities of the Barter of Slave Labor in Virginia," *American Journal of Legal History*, 12 (October 1968).

Carl Brent Swisher, "Dred Scott One Hundred Years After," *Journal of Politics*, XIX (May 1957).

Martin Torodash, "Constitutional Aspects of Slavery," *Georgia Historical Quarterly*, LV (Summer 1971).

COLLECTIONS AND EDITED VOLUMES

Richard D. Brown (ed.), *Slavery in American Society* (Lexington, Mass., 1969).
Thomas D. Clark, *Travels in the Old South: A Bibliography,* 3 vols. (Norman, Okla., 1956–59).
Katherine M. Jones (ed.), *The Plantation South* (Indianapolis, 1951).
Eric McKitrick (ed.), *Slavery Defended: The Views of the Old South* (Englewood Cliffs, N. J., 1963).
Frederick Law Olmsted, *The Cotton Kingdom,* Arthur M. Schlesinger (ed.) (New York, 1953).
Willard Thorp (ed.), *A Southern Reader* (New York, 1955).
Irwin Unger and David Reimars (eds.), *The Slavery Experience in the United States* (New York, 1970).
Ian W. Van Noppen, *The South, A Documentary History* (Princeton, 1958).
Harvey Wish (ed.), *Slavery in the South: A Collection of Contemporary Accounts . . .* (New York, 1964).
Harold D. Woodman (ed.), *Slavery and the Southern Economy* (New York, 1966).
C. Vann Woodward (ed.), George Fitzhugh, *Cannibals All! or Slaves Without Masters* (Cambridge, Mass., 1960).

GUIDES TO FURTHER READING

HISTORIOGRAPHY

James C. Bonner, "Plantation and Farm: The Agricultural South," in Arthur S. Link and Rembert W. Patrick (eds.), *Writing Southern History: Essays in Historiography in Honor of Fletcher M. Green* (Baton Rouge, La., 1965).
Eugene D. Genovese, "Marxian Interpretations of the Slave South," in Barton J. Bernstein (ed.), *Towards a New Past: Dissenting Essays in American History* (New York, 1968).
———, Race and Class in Southern History: An Appraisal of the Work of Ulrich Bonnel Phillips," *Agricultural History,* XLI (October 1967).
———, "Recent Contributions to the Economic Historiography of the Slave South," *Science and Society,* XXIV (Winter 1960).
Louis R. Harlan, "The Negro in American History," *Service Center for Teachers of History,* Publication No. 61 (Washington, D. C., 1965).
Richard Hofstadter, "U. B. Phillips and the Plantation Legend," *Journal of Negro History,* XXIX (April 1944).
Ruben F. Kugler, "U. B. Phillips' Use of Sources," *Journal of Negro History,* XLVII (July 1962).
Staughton Lynd, "On Turner, Beard and Slavery," *Journal of Negro History,* XLVIII (October 1963).
Chase C. Mooney, "The Literature of Slavery: A Re-evaluation," *Indiana Magazine of History,* VII (April 1965).
Orlando Patterson, "Rethinking Black History," *Harvard Educational Review,* Vol. 41 (August 1971).

David M. Potter, "The Work of Ulrich B. Phillips: A Comment," *Agricultural History* (October 1967).

Arnold A. Sio, "Interpretations of Slavery," *Comparative Studies in Society and History*, VII (April 1965).

Kenneth M. Stampp, "The Historian and Southern Negro Slavery," *American Historical Review*, LVII (April 1952).

Robert Starobin, "The Negro: A Central Theme in American History," *Journal of Contemporary History*, 111 (April 1968).

Robert S. Starobin and Dale Tomich, "Black Liberation Historiography," *Radical America*, II (September–October 1968).

Bennett H. Wall, "African Slavery" in Arthur S. Link and Rembert W. Patrick (eds.), *Writing Southern History: Essays in Historiography in Honor of Fletcher M. Green* (Baton Rouge, 1965).

C. S. Wesley, *Neglected History: Essays in Negro-American History by a College President* (Wilberforce, Ohio, 1965).

Harold D. Woodman, "The Profitability of Slavery: A Historical Perennial," *Journal of Southern History*, XXIX (August 1963).

C. Vann Woodward, "Clio With Soul," *Journal of American History*, LVI (June 1969).

BIBLIOGRAPHIC AIDS

Rita M. Cassidy, "Black History: Some Basic Reading," *History Teacher*, 2 (May 1964).

W. E. B. DuBois *et al.*, *Encyclopedia of the Negro: Preparatory Volume with Reference Lists and Reports* (New York, 1946).

The Journal of Negro History (1916–present).

James McPherson *et al.*, *Blacks in America: Bibliographic Essays* (New York, 1971). This book is the best one-volume annotated bibliography in the general field of black studies and is highly recommended.

Elizabeth W. Miller (compiler), *The Negro in America: A Bibliography* (Cambridge, Mass., 1966).

Monroe N. Work, *A Bibliography of the Negro in Africa and America* (New York, 1928).

Excellent bibliographies of American slavery can be found in the footnotes of two previously cited works; Stanley M. Elkins, *Slavery* . . . , and David Brion Davis, *The Problem of Slavery in Western Culture*. All of the historiographic articles listed also contain good bibliographies.

AMERICAN SLAVERY IN WORLD PERSPECTIVE

GREECE AND ROME

Victoria Cuffel, "The Classical Greek Concept of Slavery," *Journal of Historical Ideas* (July–September 1966).

David Brion Davis, *The Problem of Slavery in Western Culture* (Ithaca, 1966).

A. M. Duff, *Freedmen in the Early Roman Empire*, 2nd ed. (Cambridge, England, 1958).

Moses I. Finley (ed.), *Slavery in Classical Antiquity: Views and Controversies* (Cambridge, England, 1960).

Moses I. Finley, *The World of Odysseus* (Meridian Paperback edition, New York, 1959).

C. A. Forbes, "The Education and Training of Slaves in Antiquity," *Transactions of the American Philological Association*, 86 (1955).

F. M. Snowden, *Blacks in Antiquity* (Cambridge, Mass., 1970).

William Linn Westerman, *The Slave Systems of Greek and Roman Antiquity* (Philadelphia, 1955).

LATIN AMERICA AND THE WEST INDIES

Richard R. Beeman, "Labor Forces and Race Relations: A Comparative View of the Colonization of Brazil and Virginia," *Political Science Quarterly*, LXXXVI (December 1971).

Gonzalo Aguirre Beltran, "The Slave Trade in Mexico," *Hispanic American Historical Review*, XXIV (1944).

J. Harry Bennett, Jr., *Bondsmen and Bishops: Slavery and Apprenticeship . . . Barbados, 1710–1838* (Berkeley, 1958).

Leslic Bethell, *The Abolition of the Brazilian Slave Trade: Britain, Brazil and the Slave Trade Question 1807–1869* (New York, 1970).

C. R. Boxer, *The Golden Age of Brazil, 1690–1750: Growing Pains of a Colonial Society* (Berkeley, 1962).

——, *Race Relations in the Portuguese Empire, 1415–1825* (Oxford, England, 1963).

Peter Boyd-Bowman, "Negro Slaves in Early Colonial Mexico," *The Americas,* XXVI (October 1969).

George Breathitt, "Religious Protection and Haitian Slaves," *Catholic Historical Review*, LV (April 1969).

W. L. Burn, *Emancipation and Apprenticeship in the British West Indies* (London, England, 1937).

David W. Cohen and Jack P. Greene (eds.), *Neither Slave Nor Free: The Freedman of African Descent in the Slave Societies of the New World* (Baltimore, 1972).

Robert Conrad, "The Contraband Slavery Trade to Brazil, 1831–1845," *Hispanic American Historical Review*, XLIX (November 1969).

David Brion Davis, "Slavery" in C. Vann Woodward (ed.), *The Comparative Approach to American History* (New York, 1968).

Arthur F. Corwin, *Spain and the Abolition of Slavery in Cuba* (Austin, Texas, 1967).

David M. Davidson, "Negro Slave Control and Resistance in Colonial Mexico," *Hispanic American Historical Review*, XLVI (1966).

Carl N. Degler, *Neither Black nor White: Slavery and Race Relations in Brazil and the United States* (New York, 1971).

——, "Slavery in Brazil and the United States: An Essay in Comparative History," *American Historical Review* (April 1970).

Laura Foner and Eugene D. Genovese (eds.), *Slavery in the New World: A Reader in Comparative History* (Englewood Cliffs, N. J., 1969).

438 A Selected Modern Bibliography

Gilberto Freyre, *The Masters and the Slaves: A Study in the Development of Brazilian Civilization* (New York, 1946).

Eugene D. Genovese, *The World the Slaveholders Made: Two Essays in Interpretation* (New York, 1969).

Elsa V. Goveia, *Slave Society in the British Leeward Islands . . .* (New Haven, 1965).

Richard Graham, "Brazilian Slavery Re-Examined: A Review Article," *Journal of Social History*, 3 (Summer 1970).

———, "Causes for the Abolition of Negro Slavery in Brazil," *Hispanic American Historical Review*, XLIV (May 1966).

Ramiro Guerra y Sánchez, *Sugar and Society in the Caribbean* (New Haven, 1964).

Gwendolyn Midlo Hall, *Social Control in Slave Plantation Societies: A Comparison of St. Domingue and Cuba* (Baltimore, 1972).

Lewis Hanke, *Aristotle and the American Indians* (Chicago, 1959).

Marvin Harris, *Patterns of Race in the Americas* (New York, 1964).

Harry Hoetink, *The Two Variants in Caribbean Race Relations* (London, England, 1967).

Norman Holub, "The Brazilian Sabinada (1837–38) Revolt of the Negro Masses [Bahia]," *Journal of Negro History* (July 1969).

C. L. R. James, *The Black Jacobins' Toussaint L'Ouverture and the San Domingo Revolution*, rev. ed. (New York, 1968).

Winthrop D. Jordan, *White Over Black: American Attitudes Toward the Negro, 1550–1812* (Chapel Hill, 1968).

———, "The Influence of the West Indies on the Origins of New England Slavery," *William and Mary Quarterly*, XVIII (April 1961).

James F. King, "The Negro in Continental Spanish America: A Select Bibliography," *Hispanic American Historical Review*, XXIV (August 1944).

James Ferguson King, "Negro Slavery in New Granada," in *Greater America: Essays in Honor of Herbert Eugene Colton* (Berkeley, 1945).

Herbert S. Klein, *Slavery in the Americas: A Comparative Study of Cuba and Virginia* (Chicago, 1967).

Franklin W. Knight, *Slave Society in Cuba During the Nineteenth Century* (Madison, 1970).

Claude Levy, "Slavery and the Emancipation Movement in Barbados, 1650–1833," *Journal of Negro History*, LV (January 1970).

John V. Lombardi, *The Decline and Abolition of Negro Slavery in Venezuela, 1820–1854* (Westport, Conn., 1970).

Edgar F. Love, "Legal Restrictions on Afro-Indian Relations in Colonial Mexico," *Journal of Negro History*, LV (April 1970).

Alexander Marchant, *From Barter to Slavery: The Economic Relations of Portuguese and Indians in the Settlement of Brazil, 1500–1580* (Baltimore, 1942).

Sidney W. Mintz, "Slavery and the Afro-American World," in John F. Szwed (ed.), *Black America* (New York, 1970).

Vienna Moog, *Bandeirantes and Pioneers* (New York, 1964).

Magnus Morner, "The History of Race Relations in Latin America," *Latin American Research Review*, I (1966).

———, *Race Mixture in the History of Latin America* (Boston, 1967).

Richard Pares, *Merchants and Planters*, (Cambridge, England, 1960).

Orlando Patterson, *The Sociology of Slavery: An Analysis of the Origins, Development and Structure of Negro Slave Society in Jamaica* (London, England, 1967).

Oriol Pi-Sunyer, "Historical Background to the Negro in Mexico," *Journal of Negro History*, XLII (October 1957).

Caio Prado, Jr., *The Colonial Background of Modern Brazil* (Berkeley, 1967).

Mary Reckord, "The Jamaica Slave Rebellion of 1831," *Past and Present*, No. 40 (July 1968).

J. H. Rodrigues, *Brazil and Africa* (Berkeley, 1965).

Monica Schuler, "Ethnic Slave Rebellions in the Caribbean and the Guianas," *Journal of Social History*, 3 (Summer 1970).

Stanley J. Stein, *Vassouras: A Brazilian Coffee County, 1850–1900* (Cambridge, Mass., 1957).

Frank Tannenbaum, *Slave and Citizen: The Negro in the Americas* (New York, 1946).

D. W. Thoms, "Slavery in the Leeward Islands in the Mid-Eighteenth Century: A Reappraisal," *Bulletin Institute Historical Research* (May 1969).

Ralph H. Vigil, "Negro Slaves and Rebels in the Spanish Possessions, 1503–1558," *Historian*, XXXIII (August 1971).

Eric Williams, *Capitalism and Slavery* (Chapel Hill, 1944).

C. Vann Woodward, "Protestant Slavery in a Catholic World," in C. Vann Woodward, *American Counterpoint: Slavery and Race in the North-South Dialogue* (Boston, 1971).

OTHER CULTURES

Abdel-Moshen Bakir, *Slavery in Pharaonic Egypt* (Cairo, 1952).

Dev Raj Chanana, *Slavery in Ancient India, As Depicted in Pali and Sanskrit Texts* (New Delhi, 1960).

Hannah S. Goldman, "American Slavery and Russian Serfdom: A Study in Fictional Parallels" (unpublished Ph.D. thesis, Columbia University, 1955, University Microfilms No. 11, 453).

Melville Herskovits, *Dahomey: An Ancient West African Kingdom* (New York, 1938).

Isaac Mendelsohn, *Slavery in the Ancient Near East: A Comparative Study of Slavery in Babylonia, Assyria, Syria, and Palestine, from the Middle of the Third Millennium to the End of the First Millennium* (New York, 1949).

Virginia S. Platt, "The East India Company and the Madagascar Slave Trade," *William and Mary Quarterly*, XXVI (October 1969).

E. G. Pulleyblank, "The Origins and Nature of Chattel Slavery in China," *Journal of the Economic and Social History of the Orient*, I, pt. 2 (1958).

Lowell J. Ragatz, *The Fall of the Planter Class in the British Caribbean, 1763–1833* (New York, 1928).

C. Martin Wilbur, *Slavery in China During the Former Han Dynasty, 206 B.C.–A.D. 25* (Chicago, 1945).